$24.99

iPhone
The Missing Manual

Eleventh Edition

iPhone: The Missing Manual, Eleventh Edition BY DAVID POGUE

Printed in Canada.

Published by O'Reilly Media, Inc., 1005 Gravenstein Highway North, Sebastopol, CA 95472.

O'Reilly books may be purchased for educational, business, or sales promotional use. Online editions are also available for most titles *(safari.oreilly.com)*. For more information, contact our corporate/institutional sales department: 800.998.9938 or *corporate@oreilly.com.*

Copy Editor: Julie Van Keuren

Indexers: David Pogue, Julie Van Keuren

Cover Designers: Monica Kamsvaag and Phil Simpson

Interior Designer: Phil Simpson (based on a design by Ron Bilodeau)

Print History:

January 2018. First Printing.

ISBN: 978-1-491-99950-9

[TI] [2018-01-12]

Contents

Part Three: The iPhone Online

Part Four: Connections

Part Five: Appendixes

The Missing Credits

David Pogue (author, illustrator) is the tech columnist for Yahoo Finance (*yahoofinance.com*), the world's biggest business publication. He was groomed for that job by 13 years of writing the weekly tech column for *The New York Times*. He's also a monthly columnist for *Scientific American*, a four-time Emmy-winning correspondent for *CBS News Sunday Morning*, the host of 20 *NOVA* specials on PBS, and the creator of the Missing Manual series.

David has written or cowritten more than 100 books, including dozens in the Missing Manual series, six in the *For Dummies* line (including *Macs, Magic, Opera,* and *Classical Music*), two novels (one for middle-schoolers called *Abby Carnelia's One and Only Magical Power*), *The World According to Twitter,* and three books of essential tips and shortcuts: *Pogue's Basics: Tech*, *Pogue's Basics: Life*, and *Pogue's Basics: Money*.

In his other life, David is a former Broadway show conductor, a magician, and a funny public speaker. He lives in Connecticut with his wife, Nicki, and three awesome children.

Links to his columns and videos await at *www.davidpogue.com*. He welcomes feedback about his books by email at *david@pogueman.com*, and you can sign up to get his columns by email at *authory.com/davidpogue*.

Julie Van Keuren (editor, indexer, layout) spent 14 years in print journalism before deciding to upend her life, move to Montana, and live the freelancing dream. She now works for a variety of terrific clients who understand that skilled editing, writing, book layout, and indexing don't have to come from inside a cubicle. She and her husband, sci-fi writer M.H. Van Keuren, have two teenage sons. Email: *little_media@yahoo.com*.

Rich Koster (technical reviewer) bought his first iPhone on the first evening it was available. He began corresponding with David Pogue, sharing tips, tricks, and observations; eventually, David asked him to be the beta reader for the first edition of *iPhone: The Missing Manual*—and hired him as the tech editor of subsequent editions. For this edition of the book, all the work involved was accomplished on the iPhone X. Rich is a husband, father, graphic artist, writer, and Disney fan (@DisneyEcho on Twitter).

Phil Simpson (book design) runs his graphic design business from Southbury, Connecticut. His work includes corporate branding, publication design, communications support, and advertising. He lives with his wife and several great felines. Email: *phil.simpson@pmsgraphics.com*.

Acknowledgments

The Missing Manual series is a joint venture between the dream team introduced on these pages and O'Reilly Media. I'm grateful to all of them, especially to the core of the iPhone Missing Manual team.

The work done on previous editions lives on in this one; for that, I'm grateful to Jude Biersdorfer, Matt Gibstein, Teresa Brewer, Brian Jepson, Apple's Trudy Muller, Philip Michaels, O'Reilly's Nan Barber, and my incredible assistant Jan Carpenter, who keeps me from falling apart like wet Kleenex. Thanks to David Rogelberg and Tim O'Reilly for believing in the idea; to Apple's Jacqueline Roy for chasing down dozens of technical answers; to Kellee Katagi for her sharp-eyed proofreading; to Judy Le for assisting with cross-references and illustrating the iPhone's many icons; and above all, to Nicki, Kell, Tia, and Jeffrey. They make these books—and everything else—possible.

—David Pogue

Also by David Pogue

- *macOS High Sierra: The Missing Manual*

- *Windows 10: The Missing Manual*

- *David Pogue's Digital Photography: The Missing Manual*

- *The World According to Twitter*

- *Pogue's Basics: Tech*

- *Pogue's Basics: Life*

- *Pogue's Basics: Money*

Introduction

How do you make the point that the iPhone has changed the world? The easy answer is "use statistics"—1 billion sold, 2.2 million apps on the App Store, 200 billion downloads.... Trouble is, those statistics get stale almost before you've finished typing them.

Maybe it's better to talk about the aftermath. How the invention of the iPhone changed society, business, and culture forever. With the iPhone (and Google's imitator, Android), we became, for the first time, a society of people who are online continuously, wherever we go. Our communications blossomed from text messages to video calls, WhatsApp, FaceTime, and Skype. Billion-dollar businesses like Uber, Snapchat, and Instagram sprang into existence. Distracted driving, distracted walking, distracted eating, distracted dating, and even distracted sex all became "things."

Apple introduces a new iPhone model every fall. In September 2017, for example, it introduced the 11th and 12th iPhone models, the iPhone 8, iPhone 8 Plus, and—to celebrate the iPhone's 10th birthday—the state-of-the-art, $1,000 iPhone X.

There's also a new, free version of the iPhone's software, called iOS 11.

You can run iOS 11 on *older* iPhone models without having to buy a new phone. This book covers all the phones that can run iOS 11, from the iPhone 5s through the iPhone X.

About the iPhone

So what is the iPhone? Really, the better question is what *isn't* the iPhone?

It's a cellphone, obviously. But it's also a full-blown multimedia player, complete with a dazzling screen for watching videos. And it's a sensational pocket Internet viewer. It shows fully formatted email (with attachments, thank you) and displays entire web pages with fonts and design intact. It's tricked out with a tilt sensor, a proximity sensor, a light sensor, Wi-Fi, Bluetooth, GPS, a gyroscope, a barometer, and that amazing multitouch screen.

The iPhone is also the most used *camera* in the world. Furthermore, it's a calendar, address book, calculator, alarm clock, stopwatch, stock tracker, traffic reporter, and weather forecaster. It even stands in for a flashlight and, with the screen off, a pocket mirror.

TIP: If you want a *really* good pocket mirror, you can also use the front camera. It's a brighter view (and you don't have to actually take a selfie).

And don't forget the App Store. Thanks to the 2.2 million add-on programs that await there, the iPhone can also be a medical reference, a musical keyboard, a time tracker, a remote control, a sleep monitor, a tip calculator, an ebook reader, and more. Plus, the App Store is a portal to thousands of games, with smooth 3D graphics and tilt control.

All of this sends the iPhone's utility and power through the roof. Calling it a phone is practically an insult. (Apple probably should have called it an "iPod," but that name was taken.)

About This Book

You don't get a printed manual when you buy an iPhone. Online, you can find an electronic PDF manual, but it's largely free of details, hacks, workarounds, tutorials, humor, and any acknowledgment of the iPhone's flaws. You can't easily mark your place, underline, or read it in the bathroom.

The purpose of this book, then, is to serve as the manual that should have accompanied the iPhone. (If you have an iPhone 5 or an earlier model, then you really need one of this book's earlier editions. And if you do have an iPhone 5s or later model, this book assumes that you've installed iOS 11.2 or later; see Appendix A.)

Writing a book about the iPhone is a study in exasperation, because the darned thing is a moving target. Apple updates the iPhone's software fairly often, piping in new features, bug fixes, speed-ups, and so on.

About the Outline

iPhone: The Missing Manual is divided into five parts, each containing several chapters:

- Part One, **The iPhone as Phone**, covers everything related to phone calls: dialing, answering, voice control, voicemail, conference calling, text messaging, iMessages, MMS, and the Contacts (address book) program. It's also where you can read about FaceTime, the iPhone's video-calling feature; Siri, the voice-operated "virtual assistant"; and the surprisingly rich array of features for people with disabilities— some of which are useful even for people without them.

- Part Two, **Pix, Flix & Apps**, is dedicated to the iPhone's built-in software, with a special emphasis on its multimedia abilities: playing music, podcasts, movies, and TV shows; taking and displaying photos; capturing photos and videos; using the Maps app; reading ebooks; and so on. These chapters also cover some of the standard techniques that most apps share: installing, organizing, and quitting them; switching among them; and sharing material from within them.

- Part Three, **The iPhone Online**, is a detailed exploration of the iPhone's ability to get you onto the Internet, either over a Wi-Fi hotspot connection or via the cellular network. It's all here: email, web browsing, and Personal Hotspot (letting your phone serve as a sort of Internet antenna for your laptop).

- Part Four, **Connections**, describes the world beyond the iPhone itself—like the copy of iTunes on your Mac or PC that can fill up the iPhone with music, videos, and photos; and syncing the calendar, address book, and mail settings. These chapters also cover Apple's iCloud service, Continuity (the wireless integration of iPhones and Macs), and the Settings app.

- Part Five, **Appendixes**, contains two reference chapters. Appendix A walks you through the setup process; Appendix B is a master compendium of troubleshooting, maintenance, and battery information.

About→These→Arrows

Throughout this book, and throughout the Missing Manual series, you'll find sentences like this one: Tap **Settings→General→Keyboard**. That's shorthand for a much longer instruction that directs you to open three nested screens in sequence, like this: "Tap the **Settings** icon. On the next screen, tap **General**. On the screen after that, tap **Keyboard**." (In this book, tappable things on the screen are printed in **orange** to make them stand out.)

About MissingManuals.com

Missing Manuals are witty, well-written guides to computer products that don't come with printed manuals (which is just about all of them). Each book features a handcrafted index; cross-references to specific page numbers; and an ironclad promise never to put an apostrophe in the possessive pronoun *its*.

To get the most out of this book, visit *www.missingmanuals.com*. Click the **Missing CDs** link, and then click this book's title to reveal a neat, organized list of the shareware, freeware, and bonus articles mentioned in this book.

The website also offers corrections and updates to the book; to see them, click the book's title, and then click **View/Submit Errata**. In fact, please submit corrections yourself! Each time we print more copies of this book, we'll make any confirmed corrections you've suggested. We'll also note such changes on the website, so you can mark important corrections into your own copy of the book, if you like. And we'll keep the book current as Apple releases more iPhone updates.

iPhone 8 and 8 Plus: What's New

Apple's usual routine is to introduce a new iPhone shape every other year (iPhone 3G, iPhone 4, iPhone 5, iPhone 6)—and then release a follow-up, upgraded "s" model in alternate years (iPhone 3GS, iPhone 4s, iPhone 5s, iPhone 6s). The 2017 models, though, broke the pattern. There was an iPhone 7, but no iPhone 7s. Instead, Apple named its new phone the iPhone 8.

It looks exactly like the 7 but has a few enhancements:

- **Magnetic "wireless" charging.** The back of the iPhone 8 and 8 Plus is made of glass, but not for cosmetic reasons. Apple uses glass so that it can offer magnetic *inductive charging*.

  Apple and Samsung call it wireless charging, but what they actually mean is "laying your phone on a special charging pad." True, you're no longer plugging in a cord to the phone, but the pad itself still has to be plugged into a power outlet.

- **Better guts.** What else is new? A faster processor, of course. Opening apps is faster. Pulling up web pages is faster. Opening attachments is faster.

- **True Tone.** The screen now adapts to the color of the ambient light, adjusting its own white balance as necessary to make colors look right.

- **Better cameras.** The 12-megapixel camera has what Apple calls a "larger, faster sensor; a new color filter; deeper pixels."

  On the larger iPhone 8 Plus, there's some fancy stuff going on with its dual-lens setup. When in Portrait mode (which uses the camera's dual lenses to create a softly blurred background), the quality of the blurriness is improved. And then, after taking a Portrait shot, you can tap **Edit** and then fiddle with the lighting, experimenting with different studio-light setups. The feature is in beta, so not quite finished, but already, the results can be pretty amazing. One of them, Stage Light, even cuts out the background entirely (see page 293).

Just between us, that's not a lot of upgrades. Apple saved most of its innovation juice for a radically rethought, $1,000, 10th-anniversary phone: the iPhone X (you pronounce it "ten").

iPhone X: What's New

Everybody talks about the iPhone X's face-recognition feature, but the *best* thing about the iPhone X is its size.

It's a standard-sized phone, only a hair bigger than an iPhone 7 or 8, and therefore easy to wrap your fingers around without growing extra knuckles. Yet the X has the screen size of the iPhone Plus models. By lopping off all the margins that usually surround an iPhone's screen, Apple has found a much sweeter spot on the screen/body trade-off spectrum. It's all screen, much like recent Samsung smartphones.

And what a screen it is. It's Apple's first OLED screen, meaning that it's got much darker darks and brighter brights than what's come before.

As a bonus, Apple maintains that the iPhone X gets two hours more life per battery charge than the iPhone 7 or 8.

Facial Recognition

OK, so Apple made this phone all screen. In that case, where's the home button?

It's gone. On the iPhone X, **there is no home button**.

Wait, what? On the iPhone, we use it to open the Home screen, trigger Siri, switch apps, pay with Apple Pay, take screenshots, turn on the screen magnifier, force-quit an app, force-restart the whole phone when it gets locked up, and so on. Without a home button, what happens to all of that?

You have to learn new techniques. Apple has come up with replacement gestures for all of the above.

To return to the Home screen, you swipe up from the bottom of the screen. This can be a tiny swipe, even a quarter of an inch upward; it quickly becomes quick and instinctive. (Until, that is, you try to do it on someone's iPad and feel like an idiot.)

To open the app switcher, you make the same swipe up, but then stop with your finger in the center. The app "cards" now appear.

You trigger Siri using the button on the right side. OK, fine. But what about the fingerprint reader?

It's gone, too. Instead, Apple says it's come up with something better: Face ID.

When you get your phone, you train it to recognize your face in Settings. Now the iPhone knows the exact contours of your face.

After that, just looking at the phone unlocks it—so fast that you may not even realize what's happened. There are only two clues that the phone is unlocked: a tiny padlock icon opens, and any notification banners ("Message from: Robin") expand to reveal their potentially embarrassing contents.

Unlocking the phone doesn't take you all the way to the Home screen, which would be cool. You still have to do a little up-swipe after unlocking.

In any case, you can't fool Face ID with a photo, a mask, or even a 3D model of your head. It's also not thrown off by a wig, fake mustache, hats, glasses, scarves, or makeup. Since it uses infrared light, Face ID works even in the dark.

Face ID continues to fine-tune its mathematical model of your face every time you use it, so things like hair growth (and wrinkle growth) won't fool it. If you *do* do something radical (like shaving off your beard), you just retrain it.

You'll use Face ID wherever you used to use your fingerprint: triggering Apple Pay, for example, or logging into apps. Any app that was ever unlocked by your fingerprint automatically works with Face ID, without needing to be rewritten.

TrueDepth Camera

Face ID relies on a mass of sensors Apple calls TrueDepth. It involves an infrared lamp, a tiny infrared projector, and a camera that read the distortion of their spacing and shape to find the contours of your face.

That depth camera does more than just recognize your face. Because it can tell the difference between the foreground and the background, the iPhone X can take *front*-facing Portrait-mode photos, which means beautifully blurry backgrounds.

It can also create what Apple calls Animoji—a choice of 12 animated cartoon faces whose expressions follow and mimic your expressions in real time, by tracking the motion of 50 different muscles in your face. Happy, sad, wink, frown, laugh, mouth open, eyebrows up, whatever—your little cartoon-animal avatar does the same. You can record yourself saying something and then send the resulting animation via the Messages app. Suddenly, you're Warner Bros.

Software companies can write apps that exploit the depth camera, too. Snapchat's fun superimposed-face filters (masks, glasses, and so on) now use real-time lighting information for realistic reflections and shadows. And Apple has built a new Scenes feature into its free Clips video-recording app that replaces your background, green-screen style, in real time. You can shoot yourself with a new background of your choosing, like an artsy linescape, the bridge of the Millennium Falcon, and so on.

The Rest of the Package

Like the iPhone 8, the iPhone X is waterproof—it can tolerate 30 minutes of being 3 feet underwater. The glass front and back are, Apple says, 50 percent stronger. The speakers are louder. You can charge "wirelessly" on a pad, just as on the iPhone 8.

And the iPhone X runs iOS 11, of course—with a few special tweaks just for Xers. For example, the flashlight on/off switch is now right there on the Lock screen, not even hiding in the Control Center anymore. And you can now move among open apps just by dragging your finger along the bottom edge of the screen, without even opening the app switcher first. It's pretty great.

What's New in iOS 11

The design for iOS 11 doesn't look much different from iOS 10 before it (or iOS 9, or iOS 8, or iOS 7); the improvements are focused on features and flexibility.

You'd have to write an entire book to document everything that's new or changed in iOS 11; it's a *huge* upgrade. But here's a quick rundown.

The New Control Center

The Control Center has blossomed into the magnificence of adulthood. Now *you* decide which controls should appear on it. And you no longer have to hunt among multiple pages to find the one you want; the Control

Center is once again a single screen. If you're a true Control freak, it even scrolls.

The Control Center can include new buttons it's never had before, like these:

- **Notes.** This is a great addition. The idea is to give you immediate access to notes, so you can jump in, no matter what you were doing, to write down something quickly: a phone number someone's giving you, dosage instructions your doctor's rattling off, or a brainstorm you've just had for a million-dollar product.

- **Screen Recording.** Here's a Control Center button for a feature you can't trigger in any other way (there's no app, no Settings page). The idea, of course, is to let you record videos of what's happening on the iPhone screen—with narration, if you like. It's fantastic as a teaching tool, if you want to capture some anomaly to send to tech support, or to demo a new app you wrote. And it's a first in the history of phones! The finished video winds up in your Photos app with all your other videos.

- **Apple TV Remote.** In case you've lost the physical one.

- **Do Not Disturb While Driving.** This important new iOS feature prevents notifications, calls, or texts from lighting up your phone or making it ring whenever you're behind the wheel and in motion. Usually, you'll want it to turn on automatically when you're driving; this button is primarily useful for turning DNDWD *off*—when you're in the passenger seat.

- **Voice Memos.** The Voice Memos app is handy for recording speeches, interviews, song ideas, and so on. Tap this button to open the Voice Memos app, where another tap begins the recording. Better yet, a hard-press on this Control Center button produces a menu that lists your three most recent recordings (for instant playback)—and a New Recording button.

Storage Help

Another category of new features is designed to assist with the chronic problem of running out of room on the iPhone:

- **Camera formats.** iOS 11 invites you to adopt new file formats for photos (HEIF) and videos (HEVC, or H265), which look the same as they did before but consume only half the space. (When you export them to someone else, they convert to standard formats.)

- **Storage optimization.** As your phone begins to run out of space, your oldest files and least-used apps can be quietly and automatically stored online, leaving Download icons in their places on your phone, so that you can retrieve them if you ever need them.

- **Siri updates.** Apple's done some work on its voice assistant, too. There are new male and female voices that sound more like actual people.

  Siri can now translate phrases from English into Chinese, French, German, Italian, or Spanish. For example, you can say, "How do you say, 'Where's the bathroom?' in French?" It works surprisingly well— she nails the accents. Siri also does better at understanding follow-up questions. ("Who directed Disney's *Zootopia*? Who starred in it?")

A Lot of Misc.

The rest of iOS 11 falls into the category called "Everything else." Little nips and tucks like these:

- **A file manager.** A new app called Files lets you work with (and search) files and folders, just as you do on the Mac or PC. You can tag them, search them, sort them, and view them as a list or as icons. The Files app shows the contents of your iCloud Drive, as well as your Box and Dropbox files (!!). You can select files (but, alas, not folders) to share with other people.

- **Redesigned apps drawer in Messages.** All the stuff Apple added to Messages last year (stickers, apps, live drawing) cluttered up the design. The new look is cleaner, with only two icons eating up your text-typing space instead of three.

- **Person-to-person payments.** Now, you can send payments directly to your friends—your share of the pizza bill, for example—right from within the Messages app, much as people do with Venmo, PayPal, and their ilk. (Of course, this works only if your friends have iPhones, too.) When money comes to you, it accrues to a new, virtual Apple Pay Cash Card; from there you can send it to your bank, buy things with it, or send it on to other people.

- **App Store.** The App Store has gotten a big redesign. One chief fix is breaking out Games into its own tab, so that game and non-game bestseller lists are kept separate.

- **One-handed typing.** With a tap on the little globe key, you can opt for a narrower keyboard huddled against one side, for easier one-handed typing when you're carrying a cup of coffee.

- **Improvements to Photos.** The Photos app offers smarter auto-slideshows (called Memories). Among other improvements, they now work even when you're holding the phone upright.

- **Improvements to Live Photos.** Live Photos are weird, three-second video clips, which Apple introduced in iOS 9. In iOS 11, you can shorten one, mute its audio, or extract a single frame from its clip to use as a still photo. The phone can also suggest a "boomerang" effect (bounces the motion back and forth) or a loop (repeats it over and over). And it has a new Slow Shutter filter, which (for example) blurs a babbling brook or stars moving across the sky, as though the photo was taken with a long exposure.

- **Swipe the Lock screen back down.** You used to see your notifications on two slightly different screens. There was your Lock screen, and there was the Notifications screen (swipe down from the top of the screen). Now it's all the same screen. Swiping down from the top brings back the identical list of missed notifications—and even the wallpaper and time—that you'd see on your Lock screen. Makes a ton of sense.

- **Smarter typing suggestions.** When you're typing, the auto-suggestions above the keyboard now offer movie names, song names, or place names that you've recently viewed in other apps. Auto-suggestions in Siri, too, include terms you've recently read. And if you book a flight or buy a ticket online, iOS offers to add it to your calendar.

- **AirPlay 2.** If you buy certain speakers from Bose, Marantz, and a few other manufacturers (unfortunately not Sonos), you can use your phone to control multiroom audio. You can start the same song playing everywhere, or play different songs in different rooms.

- **Lane guidance.** When you're driving, Maps now lets you know which lane to be in for your next turn, just as Google Maps does.

- **Indoor Maps.** The Maps app can now show you floor plans for a few malls and 30 airports.

- **Messages in iCloud.** Your entire text-message history can now be auto-synced to all your new Apple devices. (In the old days, when you bought a new iPhone and opened Messages, it was empty.) This feature also means that huge, multigigabyte hunk of Messages won't have to sit on your phone, eating up space. (This feature isn't part of iOS 11.2; it's coming in an update in early 2018, Apple says.)

There are also dozens of improvements to the features for overseas iPhones (China, Russia, India, for example). And there are many, many enhancements to features for the disabled (like spoken captions for videos and pictures).

What It All Means

Let's be honest: Apple is finding it harder to say "no" to new features these days. iOS has become a very dense operating system, with more features than you could master in years.

Then again, the public may not care about simplicity the way it once did. People who got their first smartphones as teenagers grew up along with iOS and Android—and evolved along with them—so the sheer complexity doesn't bother them much. It's usually only their parents who complain.

But never mind. iOS 11 is better, smarter, faster, clearer, and more refined than what came before. It takes hundreds of steps forward, and only a couple of tiny steps back.

That's a lot of tweaks, polishing, and finesse—and a lot to learn. Fortunately, 650 pages of instructions now await you.

PART ONE

The iPhone as Phone

1

The Guided Tour

You can't believe how much is hidden inside this sleek, thin slab. Microphone, speaker, cameras, battery. Processor, memory, power processing. Sensors for brightness, tilt, and proximity. Twenty wireless radio antennas. A gyroscope, accelerometer, and barometer. On the iPhone X, the face-recognition system includes an infrared lamp, infrared camera, and a tiny projector.

For the rest of this book, and for the rest of your life with the iPhone, you'll be expected to know what's meant by, for example, "the side button" and "the Lock screen." A guided tour, therefore, is in order.

Side Button (On/Off)

You could argue that knowing how to turn on your phone might be a useful skill.

—Side button

For that, you use what Apple calls the side button. (It used to be called the "sleep switch," but it now has more responsibilities.) On the iPhone 6 and later, it's on the right edge; on the 5s and SE, it's on the top. (That's right—on those phones, the *side* button is on the *top*. Keep up.)

The side button has several functions:

- **Sleep/wake.** Tapping it once puts the iPhone into Sleep mode, ready for incoming calls but consuming very little power. Tapping it again turns on the screen so it's ready for action.

- **On/off.** The same switch can also turn the iPhone off completely so it consumes no power at all; incoming calls get dumped into voicemail. You might turn the iPhone off whenever you're not going to use it for a few days.

  To turn the iPhone off, hold down the side button for three seconds. The screen changes to say **slide to power off**.

  Confirm your decision by placing a fingertip on the ⏻ and sliding to the right. The device shuts off completely.

  iPHONE X: Hold down the side button and the volume-up button that's across from it. (Apple had to redefine this button press, since holding the side button by itself triggers Siri.)

  If you change your mind about turning the iPhone off, then tap the **Cancel** button or do nothing; after a moment, the iPhone backs out of the **slide to power off** screen automatically.

  To turn the iPhone back on, press the side button again for one second. The Apple logo appears as the phone boots up.

- **Answer call/Dump to voicemail.** When a call comes in, you can tap the side button *once* to silence the ringing or vibrating. After four rings, the call goes to voicemail.

  You can also tap it *twice* to dump the call to voicemail immediately. (Of course, because they didn't hear four rings, iPhone veterans will know you've blown them off. Bruised egos may result. Welcome to the world of iPhone etiquette.)

In combination with other buttons, the side button is also involved in turning off fingerprint or face recognition (page 64) and restarting a frozen, locked-up phone (page 626).

iPhone X Functions

The iPhone X has no home button, so its button assignments have gotten rejiggered a bit. OK, rejiggered a *lot*. For example, here are some of the side button's duties on the iPhone X:

- **Talk to Siri** by holding in the side button (see page 159).

- **Shut down the phone** by holding in the side button and the volume-up button together.

- **Take a screenshot** by *briefly* pressing the side button and the volume-up button together (page 340).

- **Pay with Apple Pay** by double-clicking the side button (page 542).

- **Open the Magnifier or another accessibility feature** by triple-clicking the side button (page 242).

Sleep Mode

When you don't touch the screen for one minute (or another interval you choose), or when you press the side button, the phone goes to sleep. The screen is dark and doesn't respond to touch.

If you're on a call, the call continues; if music is playing, it keeps going; if you're recording audio, the recording proceeds. But when the phone is asleep, you don't have to worry about accidental button pushes. You wouldn't want to discover that your iPhone has been sending texts or taking photos from the depths of your pocket or purse. Nor would you want it to dial a random number from your back pocket, a phenomenon that's earned the unfortunate name *butt dialing*.

The Lock Screen

In iOS 11, the iPhone has a state of being that's somewhere between Sleep and on. It's the Lock screen. You can actually get a lot done here, without ever unlocking the phone and advancing to its Home screens.

You can wake the phone by pressing the home button or the side button. Or you can just lift the phone to a vertical position.

iPHONE X: You can also wake the phone by tapping anywhere on the screen, if **Tap to Wake** is turned on in **Settings→ Accessibility→Tap to Wake**.

The screen lights up, and you're looking at the Lock screen. Here—even before you've entered your password or used fingerprint or face recognition—you can check the time, read your missed messages, consult your calendar, take a photo, and more.

NOTE: You can turn off the "wake when I lift you" feature. It's in **Settings→Display & Brightness**; turn off **Raise to Wake**. Now you have to press the side or home buttons to wake the phone, as before.

This Lock screen is a complex, rich, busy universe; see Chapter 2.

Now then: If you want to proceed to the Home screen—to finish turning on the phone—then *click the home button* at this point.

iPHONE X: Swipe up from the bottom of the screen. It can be a very short, light, quick swipe.

The Auto-Home Screen Option

iOS 11 offers a buried but powerful option: **Rest Finger to Open**. (It's in **Settings→General→Accessibility→Home Button**.) When you turn this on, the second click—the one to get past the Lock screen—is no longer necessary.

If your phone is asleep, then just lifting it (with your finger touching the home button) wakes it and unlocks it; you never even see the Lock screen. Or, if the phone is asleep, you can click the home button and just leave your finger on it. In each case, you save at least one home-button press.

So what if you *do* want to visit the Lock screen? Just raise the phone, or click the side button, without touching the home button.

iPHONE X: Unfortunately, there's no equivalent option on the iPhone X. Once you've unlocked the phone (with your face, for example), you *must* do a quick swipe up from the bottom to proceed to the Home screen.

Home Button

Here it is: the single button on the front of every iPhone ever made (until the iPhone X). Push it to summon the Home screen, your gateway to everything the iPhone can do.

Home button

The home button is a wonderful thing. It means you can never get lost. No matter how deeply you burrow into the iPhone software, no matter how far off-track you find yourself, one push of the home button takes you back to the beginning. (On the iPhone 7 and 8, this "button" doesn't actually move, but it feels like it does; see page 573.)

---

iPHONE X: A swipe up from the bottom the of screen—it can be short and quick—performs the home-button function. (A black or white bar, technically called the ***home indicator***, appears there to remind you.)

Of course, the home button is also a fingerprint scanner.

But Apple has saddled the home button with tons of other functions, too. In iPhone Land, you can press the home button one, two, or three times for different features—or even hold it down or touch it lightly for others. Here's the rundown—with plenty of parentheticals to address the new way of doing things on the iPhone X.

Quick Press: Wake Up

Pressing the home button once wakes the phone if it's asleep. That's sometimes easier than finding the side button. It opens the Lock screen, where you can check notifications or the time, hop into the camera, check your calendar, and more. See Chapter 2.

> **iPHONE X:** Press the side button to wake the phone, or just tap the screen. (That's an option you can turn off in Settings→General→Accessibility→Tap to Wake.)

Momentary Touch: Unlock

Whenever you're looking at the Enter Passcode screen, just resting your finger on the home button is enough to unlock the phone. (Teaching the iPhone to recognize your fingerprint is described on page 61.) You proceed to the Home screen. That convenience is brought to you by the Touch ID fingerprint reader that's built into the home button.

> **iPHONE X:** *Look* at the screen, so that Face ID unlocks it instead (page 64).

Long Press: Siri

If you hold down the home button for about three seconds, you wake up Siri, your virtual voice-controlled assistant. Details are in Chapter 5.

> **iPHONE X:** You summon Siri by holding in the side button.

Two Quick Presses: App Switcher

If, once the phone is awake, you press the home button *twice quickly*, the current image fades away—to reveal the app-switcher screen, the key to the iPhone's multitasking feature (facing page).

> **iPHONE X:** Swipe up the screen from the bottom—but pause when your finger has traveled at least an inch up the screen. The multitasking "cards" appear after about a second.

What you see here are **currently open screens** of the apps you've used most recently (older ones are to the left). Swipe horizontally to bring more apps into view; the Home screen is always at the far right.

With a single tap on a screen's "card," you jump right back into an app you had open. See page 358 for more on the app switcher; for now, just remember that it gives you a way to jump *directly* to another app, without a layover at the Home screen first.

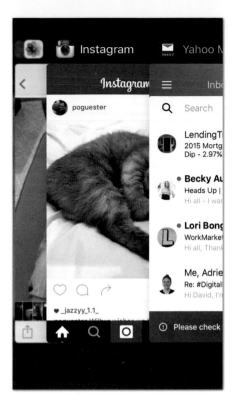

Two Touches: Reachability

Starting with the iPhone 6, the standard iPhone got bigger than previous models—and the Plus models are even *biggerer*. Their screens are so big, in fact, that your dinky human thumb may be too short to reach the top portion of the screen (if you're gripping the phone near the bottom).

For that reason, Apple has built a feature called Reachability into the iPhone 6 and later models.

When you tap the home button twice (don't click it—just *touch* it), the entire screen image slides halfway down the glass, so that you can reach the upper parts of it with your thumb!

iPHONE X: Tug downward at the bottom edge of the screen—for example, on the home indicator bar. (This works only if you've turned on Reachability in **Settings→General→ Accessibility**.)

As soon as you touch anything on the screen—a link, a button, an empty area, anything—the screen snaps back to its usual, full-height position.

TIP: Here's a related note: On larger iPhones, the Home screen turns 90 degrees when you rotate it. The Dock jumps to the right edge, vertically. Try it!

Three Presses: Magnifier, VoiceOver, Zoom...

In **Settings→General→Accessibility**, you can set up a triple-press of the home button to turn one of several accessibility features on or off.

iPHONE X: Triple-press the side button instead.

There's the **Magnifier** (turns the iPhone into a giant electronic illuminated magnifying glass); **VoiceOver** (the phone speaks whatever you touch), **Invert Colors** (now in Classic and Smart varieties), **Color Filters** (screen modes to assist people with color-blindness), **Reduce White Point** (which makes all colors less intense), **Zoom** (magnifies the screen), **Switch Control** (accommodates external gadgets like sip-and-puff straws), and **AssistiveTouch** (help for people who have trouble with physical switches).

These features are all described in Chapter 7.

Silencer Switch, Volume Keys

Praise be to the gods of technology—this phone has a silencer switch! This tiny flipper, on the left edge near the top, means that no ringer or alert sound will humiliate you in a meeting, at a movie, or in church. To turn off the ringer, push the flipper toward the back of the phone.

NOTE: Even when silenced, the iPhone still makes noise in certain circumstances: when an alarm goes off; when you're playing music; when you're using Find My iPhone (page 536); when you're using VoiceOver; or, sometimes, when a game is playing. Also, the phone still vibrates when the silencer is engaged, although you can turn that off in **Settings→Sounds & Haptics**.

Silencer switch

Volume keys

On the left edge are the volume controls. They work in five ways:

- On a call, these buttons adjust the speaker or earbud volume.

- When you're listening to music, they adjust the playback volume—even when the phone is locked and dark.

- When you're taking a photo or video, either one serves as a shutter button or as a camcorder start/stop button.

- At all other times, they adjust the volume of sound effects like the ringer, alarms, and Siri.

- When a call comes in, they silence the ringing or vibrating.

In each case, if the screen is on, a volume graphic appears to show you where you are on the volume scale.

Screen

The touchscreen is your mouse, keyboard, dialing pad, and notepad. You might expect it to get fingerprinty and streaky.

But the modern iPhone has an **oleophobic** screen. That may sound like an irrational fear of yodeling, but it's actually a coating that repels grease. A single light wipe on your clothes restores the screen to its right-out-of-the-box crystal sheen.

You can also use the screen as a mirror when the iPhone is off.

The iPhone's Retina screen has crazy=high resolution (the number of tiny pixels per inch). It's really, really sharp, as you'll discover when you try to read text or make out the details of a map or a photo. The iPhone 5s and SE manage 1136×640 pixels; the iPhone 6/6s/7 packs in 1334×750; the Plus models have 1920×1080 (the same number of dots as a high-definition TV); and the iPhone X packs an awe-inspiring 2436×1125 pixels.

The front of the iPhone is a special formulation made by Corning, to Apple's specifications—even better than the Gorilla Glass used on previous models, Apple says. It's unbelievably resistant to scratching. (You can still shatter it if you drop it just the wrong way, though.)

If you're nervous about protecting your iPhone, you can always get a case for it (or a "bumper"—a silicone band that wraps the edges). But if you're worried about scratching the glass, you're probably worrying too much. Even many Apple employees carry the iPhone in their pockets without cases.

Status-Bar Icons

Here's a roundup of the icons you may see in the status bar at the top of the standard iPhone screen, from left to right.

iPHONE X: The iPhone X's status bar is quite different; see page 27.

- **Cell signal (▮▮▮).** As on any cellphone, the number of bars indicates the strength of your cell signal, and thus the quality of your call audio and the likelihood of losing the connection. If there are no bars, then the dreaded words "No service" appear here.

- **Network name and type.** These days, different parts of the country—and even your street—are blanketed by cellular Internet signals of different speeds, types, and ages. Your status bar shows you the kind of network signal it has.

From slowest to fastest:

E or **o** means your iPhone is connected to your carrier's slowest, oldest Internet system. You might be able to check email, but you'll lose your mind waiting for a web page to load.

If you see **3G**, you're in a city where your cell company has installed a 3G network—still slow compared to **4G**, which offers speed in between 3G and LTE.

And if you see **LTE** up there—well, get psyched. You have an iPhone 5 or later model, and you're in a city with a 4G LTE cellular network. And that means *very* fast Internet.

You may also see a notation like "T-Mobile Wi-Fi" or "VZW Wi-Fi." The iPhone 6 and later models, it turns out, can make free phone calls over a Wi-Fi network—if your cellphone carrier has permitted it, and if you've turned the feature on (page 152). It's a great way to make calls indoors where the cell signal is terrible.

- **Airplane mode (✈).** If you see the airplane instead of signal and Wi-Fi bars, then the iPhone is in airplane mode (page 456).

- **Do Not Disturb (☾).** When the phone is in Do Not Disturb mode, nothing can make it ring, buzz, or light up except calls from the most important people. Details are on page 138.

- **Wi-Fi signal (◗).** When you're connected to a wireless Internet hotspot, this indicator appears. The more "sound waves," the stronger the signal.

- **9:41 PM.** When the iPhone is unlocked, a digital clock appears on the status bar.

- **Alarm (◐).** You've got an alarm set. This reminder can be valuable, especially when you intend to sleep late and don't want an alarm to go off.

- **Bluetooth (✲).** The iPhone is connected wirelessly to a Bluetooth earpiece, speaker, or car system. (If this symbol is gray, then it means Bluetooth is turned on but not connected to any other gear—and not sucking down battery power.)

- **TTY (☷).** You've turned on Teletype mode, meaning that the iPhone can communicate with a Teletype machine. (That's a machine that lets deaf people make phone calls by typing and reading text. It hooks up to the iPhone with a special cable that Apple sells from its website.)

- **Call forwarding (↪).** You've told your iPhone to auto-forward any incoming calls to a different number. This icon is awfully handy— it explains at a glance why your iPhone never seems to get calls anymore.

- **VPN (▬).** You corporate stud, you! You've managed to connect to your corporate network over a secure Internet connection, proba- bly with the assistance of a systems administrator—or by consulting page 576.

- **Syncing (✳).** The iPhone is currently syncing with some Internet ser- vice—iCloud, for example (Chapter 16).

- **Battery meter (▬▸⚡).** When the iPhone is charging, the lightning bolt appears. Otherwise, the battery logo "empties out" from right to left to indicate how much charge remains. (You can even add a "% full" indicator to this gauge; see page 584.)

- **Navigation active (➤).** You're running a GPS navigation app, or some other app that's tracking your location, in the background (yay, multi- tasking!). Why is a special icon necessary? Because those GPS apps slurp down battery power like a thirsty golden retriever. Apple wants to make sure you don't forget you're running it.

- **Rotation lock (🔒).** This icon reminds you that you've deliberately turned off the screen-rotation feature, where the screen image turns 90 degrees when you rotate the phone. Why would you want to? And how do you turn the rotation lock on or off? See page 52.

From time to time, you'll see the entire status bar change color. That's its way of saying, "Hey, watch what you're saying or doing, because an app in the background is observing you!" For example, the whole bar turns:

- **Red** when you're recording in the background—either using the Voice Memos app to record audio, or using the screen-recording feature described on page 341.

- **Green** when you're on a phone call or FaceTime call in the back- ground. They can still hearrrrrr youuuuuu!

- **Blue** when an app is actively tracking your *location* in the background. If you're using GPS or something, well, that's fine. But if it's some evil app that's tracking you, now you'll know.

TIP: In each case, you can tap that colored status bar (or iPhone X "ear"—see below) to jump into the app responsible.

iPhone X: The Notch

Most people adore the iPhone X—enough, in fact, to pay that handsome $1,000 for it. If anyone grumbles at all, it's about the Notch.

That's the dark area at the top center that contains the front-facing camera, the earpiece, and the phone's Face ID sensors (page 64). Apple decided that, to keep the phone as small as possible, this Notch would interrupt the standard status bar, splitting it into two "ears."

You can't see the Notch when the status bar is black—on a black Home screen, for example. You don't see it when you're looking at photos or videos, either, unless you zoom into them.

You do see the Notch when the status bar is white or another color, and it's also noticeable when you're using an app that hasn't been updated for the iPhone X. Sometimes those apps try to display information right where the Notch sits!

In any case, on those ears, there's very little room for the usual array of status icons. The left ear shows the time and, sometimes, the location services logo (✈); and the right ear shows icons for your cellular bars, Wi-Fi strength, and battery level. (Only the left ear turns red, green, or blue to provide privacy warnings from background apps, as described already.)

To see the full range of icons described on these pages, swipe down from the right ear to open the Control Center (page 49). Everything, including the cell network name, appears on this screen—although if you're having a bad day, you'll see the words "No Service" here instead.

Cameras and Flash

At the top of the phone, above the screen, there's a horizontal slot. That's the earpiece. Just above it or beside it, the tiny pinhole is the front-facing camera. It's more visible on the white-faced iPhones than on the black ones.

iPHONE X:	Your earpiece and front-facing camera are inside the Notch.

This camera's primary purpose is to let you take selfies and conduct videochats using the FaceTime feature, but it's also handy for checking for spinach in your teeth.

It's not nearly as good a camera as the one on the back, though. The front camera is worse in low light and takes much lower-resolution shots.

A tiny LED lamp appears next to this back lens—actually, it's two lamps on the 5s, 6, and 6s iPhones, and **four** on the 7, 8, and X families. That's the flash for the camera, the video light when you're shooting movies, and a darned good flash-light for reading restaurant menus and theater programs in low light. (Swipe up from the bottom of the screen and tap the ▼ icon to turn the light on and off.)

iPHONE X:	Swipe down from the **top right** of the screen for the Control Center, where you'll find the flashlight control.

The tiny pinhole between the flash and the lens is a microphone. It's used for recording clearer sound with video, for better noise cancellation on phone calls, and for better directional sound pickup.

The iPhone Plus and X models actually have two lenses on the back—one wide-angle, one zoomed in. Details on this feature and everything else on the iPhone's cameras are in Chapter 9.

Sensors

Behind the glass, above or beside the earpiece (and in the iPhone X Notch), are two sensors. (On the black iPhones, you can't see them except with a flashlight.) First, there's an ambient-light sensor that brightens the display when you're in sunlight and dims it in darker places.

Second, there's a proximity sensor. When something (like your head) is close to the sensor, it shuts off the screen and touch sensitivity. It works only in the Phone app. With the screen off, you save power and avoid dialing with your cheekbone when you're on a call.

SIM Card Slot

On the right edge of the iPhone, there's a pinhole next to what looks like a very thin slot cover. If you push an unfolded paper clip straight into the hole, the **SIM card** tray pops out.

So what's a SIM card?

It turns out that there are two major cellphone network types: **CDMA**, used by Verizon and Sprint, and **GSM**, used by AT&T, T-Mobile, and most other countries around the world.

Every GSM phone stores your phone account info—things like your phone number and calling-plan details—on a tiny memory card known as a SIM (subscriber identity module) card.

What's cool is that, by removing the card and putting it into **another** GSM phone, you can transplant a GSM phone's brain. The other phone now knows your number and account details, which can be handy when your iPhone goes in for repair or battery replacement. For example, you can turn a Verizon iPhone 8 into a T-Mobile iPhone 8 just by swapping in a T-Mobile SIM card.

The World Phone

AT&T is a GSM network, so AT&T iPhones have always had SIM cards. But, intriguingly enough, every iPhone has a SIM card, too—even the Verizon and Sprint models. That's odd, because most CDMA cellphones don't have SIM cards.

These iPhones contain antennas for **both** GSM and CDMA. It's the same phone, no matter which cell company you buy it from. Only the SIM card teaches it which one it "belongs" to.

Even then, however, you can still use any company's phone in any country. (That's why the latest iPhones are said to be "world phones.") When you use the Verizon or Sprint iPhone in the United States, it uses only the CDMA network. But if you travel to Europe or another GSM part of the world, you can still use your Verizon or Sprint phone; it just hooks into that country's GSM network.

If you decide to try that, you have two ways to go. First, you can contact your phone carrier and ask to have international roaming turned on. You'll keep your same phone number overseas, but you'll pay through the nose for calls and, especially, Internet use. (One exception: On T-Mobile, international texting and Internet use are free.)

Second, you can rent a temporary SIM card when you get to the destination country. That's less expensive, but you'll have a different phone number while you're there.

Apple thinks SIM cards are geeky and intimidating and that they should be invisible. That's why, unlike most GSM phones, your iPhone came with the card preinstalled and ready to go. Most people never have any reason to open this tray.

If you were curious enough to open it up, you can close the tray simply by pushing it back into the phone until it clicks.

NOTE: Many countries offer LTE high-speed cellular Internet on all different radio frequencies. The iPhone 6 and later models can hop onto more of these networks than any other cellphones, but they still don't work in *every* country. Ask your carrier which countries your model works with.

Headphone Jack

Until the iPhone 7 came along, iPhones contained a standard jack for plugging in the white earbuds that came with it—or any other earbuds or headphones.

Headphones
(models before
iPhone 7) Microphone Charge/sync
(Lightning connector) Speakerphone

It's more than an ordinary 3.5-millimeter audio jack, however. It contains a secret fourth pin that conducts sound *into* the phone from the microphone on the earbuds' cord. You, too, can be one of those executives who walk down the street barking orders, apparently to nobody.

The iPhone can stay in your pocket. You hear the other person through your earbuds, and the mike on the cord picks up your voice.

NOTE: Next to the headphone jack, inside a perforated grille, a tiny second microphone lurks. It's the key to the iPhone's noise-cancellation feature. It listens to the sound of the world around you and pumps in the opposite sound waves to cancel out all that ambient noise. It doesn't do anything for *you*—the noise cancellation affects what the *other* person on the phone hears.

That's why there's also a third microphone at the top back (between the camera and flash); it's designed to supply noise cancellation for you so that the other person sounds better when you're in a noisy place.

iPhone 7, 8, X: No Headphone Jack

We, the people, may complain about how exhausting it is to keep up with the annual flood of new smartphones. But at least we don't have to *think up* a new set of features every year. That's *their* problem.

Not just because it's increasingly difficult to think of new features, but also because the phone makers have pretty much run out of room for new components inside.

That, says Apple, is why it removed the headphone jack from the iPhone 7 and later models. The headphone jack may not seem very big—but on the *inside* of the phone, the corresponding receptacle occupies an unnerving amount of nonnegotiable space.

So how are you supposed to listen to music without a headphone jack? Apple offers three ways:

- **Using the adapter.** In the iPhone box, Apple includes a 2-inch adapter cord that connects any headphones to the phone's Lightning (charging) jack.

- **Use the earbuds.** The phone also comes with new white earbuds that connect to the Lightning jack.

TIP: Of course, if your headphones are plugged into the Lightning jack, you can't charge your phone while listening over them. Fortunately, Amazon is full of cheap adapters that let you charge and plug in headphones simultaneously.

- **Use wireless headphones.** You can also use any Bluetooth wireless earbuds—from $17 plastic disposable ones to Apple's own, super-impressive AirPods. Page 153 has more on Bluetooth headsets.

In theory, those three approaches should pretty much cover you whenever you want to listen.

In practice, though, you'll still get zapped by the occasional inconvenience. You'll be on a flight, for example, listening to your laptop with headphones—and when you want to switch to the phone, you'll realize that your adapter cord is in the overhead bin. (Based on a true story.)

But this kind of hassle is the new reality. Motorola, Google, and LeEco (in China) have already ditched the headphone jack on their phones, and other phone makers will follow suit.

Microphone, Speakerphone

On the bottom of the iPhone, Apple has parked two important audio components: the speaker and the microphone.

On the iPhone 7/8/X, actually, there are two speakers, on the top and bottom of the phone. Stereo sound has finally come to the iPhone.

The Lightning Connector

On the bottom edge of the phone, right in the center, you'll find the connector that charges and syncs the iPhone with your computer.

30-pin connector (iPhone 4S)

Lightning connector (iPhone 5 and later)

For nearly 10 years, the charge/sync connector was identical on every iPhone, iPod, and iPad—the famous 30-pin connector. But starting on the iPhone 5, Apple replaced that inch-wide connector with a new, far-smaller one it calls Lightning. The Lightning connector is a great design: It clicks nicely into place (you can even dangle the iPhone from it), yet you can yank it right out. You can insert the Lightning into the phone either way—there's no "right-side up" anymore. It's much sturdier than the old connector. And it's tiny, which was Apple's primary goal—only 0.3 inches wide (the old one was almost 0.9 inches wide).

Unfortunately, you may still occasionally encounter a car adapter or hotel-room alarm clock with the old kind of connector. (For $30, you can buy an adapter.)

Little by little, a new ecosystem of accessories based on the Lightning connector is arising. We'll enjoy a new era of standardization—until Apple changes jacks again.

Antenna Band

Radio signals can't pass through metal. That's why there are strips or panels of plastic or glass on every iPhone.

And there are a *lot* of radio signals in this phone. All told, there are *20* different radio transceivers inside the modern iPhone. They tune in to the LTE and 3G (high-speed Internet) signals used in various countries around the world, plus the three CDMA signals used in the U.S.; and one each for Wi-Fi, Bluetooth, American GPS, and Russian GPS.

In the Box

Inside the minimalist box, you get the iPhone and these items:

- **A Lightning cable.** When you connect your iPhone to your computer using this white USB cable, it simultaneously syncs and charges. See Chapter 15.

- **The AC adapter.** When you're traveling without a computer, you can plug the dock's USB cable into the included two-prong outlet adapter, so you can charge the iPhone directly from a wall socket.

- **The earbuds.** Every iPhone comes with a pair of the iconic white earbuds that announce to the world, "I have an iPhone!" These days, they're what Apple calls EarPods. They sound great, although their bulbous shape may get uncomfortable in smaller ears. A volume control/ clicker is right there on the cord, so you can answer phone calls and pause the music without even taking the phone out of your pocket. (The EarPods that come with the iPhone 7/8/X, of course, plug into the Lightning jack, since there's no headphone jack. These phones also come with that 2-inch adapter cable for existing earbuds.)

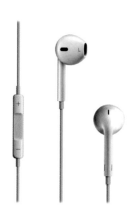

- **Decals and info card.** iPhone essentials.

Seven Basic Finger Techniques

On the iPhone, you do everything on the touchscreen instead of with physical buttons.

Tap

The iPhone's onscreen buttons are big, giving your fingertip a fat target.

You can't use a fingernail or a pen tip; only skin contact works. (You can also buy an iPhone stylus. But a fingertip is cheaper and harder to misplace.)

Double-Tap

Double-tapping is generally reserved for two functions:

- In the Safari, Photos, and Maps apps, double-tapping zooms in on whatever you tap, magnifying it. (At that point, double-tapping means "Restore to original size.") Double-tapping also zooms in to formatted email messages, PDF files, Microsoft Office files, and other things.

- When you're watching a video (or recording one), double-tapping switches the aspect ratio (video screen shape).

Swipe

In some situations, you're asked to confirm an action by *swiping* your finger across the screen. That's how you confirm that you want to shut off the phone, for example. Swiping is also a great shortcut for deleting an email or a text message.

Pinch and Spread

In apps like Photos, Mail, Safari, and Maps, you can zoom in on a photo, message, web page, or map by *spreading*.

That's when you place two fingers (usually thumb and forefinger) on the glass and spread them. The image magically grows, as though it's printed on a sheet of rubber.

Once you've zoomed in like this, you can zoom out again by putting two fingers on the glass and pinching them together.

Drag

When you're zoomed into a map, web page, email, or photo, you scroll around by sliding your finger across the glass in any direction—like a flick (described next), but slower and more controlled. It's a huge improvement over scroll bars, especially when you want to scroll diagonally.

Flick

A *flick* is a faster, less-controlled *drag*. You flick vertically to scroll lists on the iPhone. The faster you flick, the faster the list spins downward or upward. But lists have a real-world sort of momentum; they slow down after a second or two, so you can see where you wound up.

At any point during the scrolling of a list, you can flick again (if you didn't go far enough) or tap to stop the scrolling (if you see the item you want).

Edge Swipes

Swiping your finger inward from *outside* the screen has a few variations:

- **From the top edge.** Opens the Notification Center, which lists all your missed calls and texts, shows your appointments, and so on.

IPHONE X: Swipe down from either the left ear or the Notch.

- **From the bottom edge.** Opens the Control Center, a unified miniature control panel for brightness, volume, Wi-Fi, and so on.

IPHONE X: Swipe down from the right ear to open the Control Center.

- **From the left edge.** In many apps, this means "Go back to the previous screen." It works in Mail, Settings, Notes, Messages, Safari, Facebook, and some other apps. At the Home screen, it opens the Today screen (page 75).

It sometimes makes a difference whether you begin your swipe **within** the screen or **outside** it. At the Home screen, for example, starting your downward swipe within the screen area doesn't open the Notification Center—it opens the iPhone's search function.

3D Touch

The screen on the iPhone 6s and later models doesn't just detect a finger touch. It also knows how **hard** your finger is pressing, thanks to a technology Apple calls 3D Touch. This feature requires that you learn two more finger techniques.

Quick Actions

iOS interprets the pressure of your touch in various ways. On the Home screens, you can make a shortcut menu of useful commands pop out of various app icons, like this:

Apple calls these commands **quick actions**, and each is designed to save you a couple of steps. Some examples:

- **The Camera app** icon offers shortcut menus like **Take Selfie**, **Record Video**, **Record Slo-mo**, and **Take Portrait**.

- **The Clock app** gives you direct access to its **Create Alarm**, **Start Timer**, and **Start Stopwatch** functions.

- **Notes** gives you **New Note**, **New Checklist**, **New Photo**, and **New Sketch** commands (a reference to the finger-drawing features). At the

top, you see the last note you added or edited—not, for some reason, the note you've pinned to the top of the list (page 428).

- **Maps** offers **Directions Home** (a great one), **Mark My Location**, **Send My Location**, and **Search Nearby** (for restaurants, bars, shops, and so on). (When you already *are* home, you may see your travel time to work and the current traffic situation.)

- **The Phone app** sprouts icons for people you've called recently, as well as commands like **Create New Contact** and **View Most Recent Voicemail** (handy!).

- **Calendar** shows your next appointment, plus an **Add Event** command.

- **Reminders** displays whatever To Do deadline is coming up next. It also lists your reminder categories, so you can create a new To Do directly inside one of them (for example, **New in Family**).

- **Mail and Messages** offer **New Message** commands. Mail also offers **Search**, **Inbox** (with a new-message counter), and **VIPs** (also with a counter); Messages lists the three people with whom you text the most.

- **Home-screen folders** sprout a **Rename** command at your fingertip.

- **The Notification Center** (the list that appears when you swipe down from the top of the screen) offers a ⊗ button. Hard-press it to reveal the **Clear All Notifications** command.

- **The Control Center icons** offer some very important, but very hidden options. See page 49.

Similar quick actions also sprout from these Apple apps' icons: Photos, Video, Wallet, iTunes Store, App Store, iBooks, News, Safari, Music, FaceTime, Podcasts, Voice Memos, Contacts, and Find My Friends.

And, of course, you can use hard presses to respond to notifications: Reply to a text message, accept a Calendar invitation, or see where your Uber is on a map.

Other software companies have added shortcut menus to their app icons, too—Facebook, Fitbit, Google Maps, and so on.

If you force-press an app that ***doesn't*** have quick actions, you just feel a buzz and nothing else happens.

> **NOTE:** At the outset, this force-pressing business can really throw you when you're trying to rearrange icons on your Home screens. As described on page 348, that usually involves *long*-pressing an icon, which for most people is too similar to *hard*-pressing one. The trick is to long-press *very lightly*. You'll get used to it.

Peek and Pop

Hard to explain, but very cool: You hard-press something in a list—your email Inbox, for example (below, left). Or a link in a text message, or a photo thumbnail. You get a pop-up bubble showing you what's inside (middle):

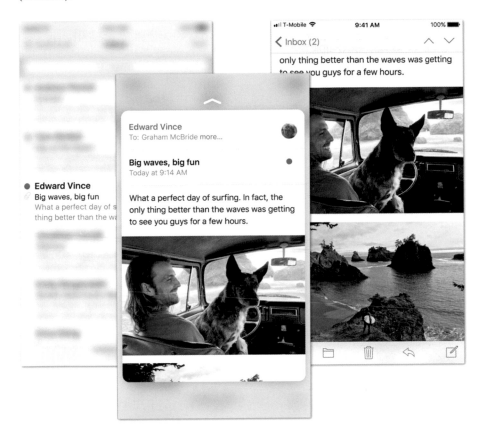

When you release your finger, the bubble disappears, and you're right back where you started. Peeking, in other words, is exactly like the Quick Look feature on the Mac. It lets you see what's inside a link, icon, or list item without losing your place or changing apps.

Email is the killer app here. You can whip through your Inbox, hard-pressing one new message after another—"What's this one?" "Do I care?"—simply inspecting the first paragraph of each but not actually opening any message.

Then, if you find one that you do want to read fully, you can press harder *yet* to open the message normally (above, right). Apple calls that "popping."

Here are some places where you can peek in the basic iPhone apps: **Mail** (preview a message in a list), **Messages** (see recent exchanges with someone in the list of people), **Maps** (preview information about a push-pin), **Calendar** (see details of an event), **Photos** (preview a photo in a screenful of thumbnails), **Safari** (preview the page hiding behind a link), **Weather** (see weather details for a name in the list of cities), **Music** (see information about a song or album in a list), **Video** (read details about a video in a list), **Notes** (see the contents of a note's name in a list), **iBooks** (view a book-cover thumbnail larger), **News** (preview the body of an article in a list), and **Find My Friends** (see the map identifying the location of someone in your list).

If you do nothing else, at least get to know peek and pop in Mail and Messages. It's really kind of awesome.

And, again, app makers can add this feature to their own apps.

Charging the iPhone

The iPhone has a built-in, rechargeable battery that fills up most of its interior. How long a charge lasts depends on what you're doing—music playback saps the battery the least; games and GPS navigation sap it the most. But one thing is for sure: You'll have to recharge the iPhone regularly. For most people, it's every night.

NOTE: The iPhone's battery isn't user-replaceable. It's *rechargeable*, but after 400 or 500 charges, it starts to hold less juice. Eventually, you'll have to pay Apple to install a new battery. (Apple says the added bulk of a protective plastic battery compartment, a removable door and latch, and battery-retaining springs would have meant a much smaller battery—or a much thicker iPhone.)

Charging with the Cable

You recharge the iPhone by connecting the white USB cable that came with it. You can plug the far end into either of two places to supply power:

- **Your computer's USB jack.** In general, the iPhone charges even if your computer is asleep. (If it's a laptop that itself is not plugged in, though, the phone charges only if the laptop is awake. Otherwise, you could come home to a depleted laptop.)

- **The AC adapter.** The little white two-prong cube that came with the iPhone connects to the end of the cradle's USB cable.

Unless the charge is *really* low, you can use the iPhone while it charges. The battery icon in the upper-right corner displays a lightning bolt to let you know it's charging.

TIP: If you have an iPhone 6 or later, it'll charge much faster if you charge it with the 2.1-amp wall adapter that comes with an iPad, instead of the 1-amp adapter that comes with the phone. How's a 90 percent charge in two hours sound?

Better yet: If you have an iPhone 8 or X, you can get *really* fast charging—along the lines of 50 percent charge in 30 minutes—but only if you connect it to a USB-C power brick plugged into the wall. Apple sells one for $50—but the cable you need (USB-C to Lightning) isn't included. That's another $25. Fast charging is cool, but it ain't cheap.

Charging on a Pad (iPhone 8 and X)

iPhone fans can stop looking over at Samsung owners with envy: Now you, too, can recharge your phone just by setting it down on a Qi charging pad.

NOTE: Qi, pronounced "chee," is the Chinese word for the life force in everyone and everything. It's also an extraordinarily useful word to know if you're playing Scrabble.

You can buy one of these tabletop charging pads from any company; they cost about $12 on Amazon. (Surprisingly, at the dawn of the iPhone 8, Apple didn't even offer one. The company is working on a super-wide one for release in 2018, called the AirPower pad, that can charge an iPhone, an Apple Watch, and a special AirPods case simultaneously.)

You have to plug the pad into a power outlet, of course—wireless charging isn't really wireless at all. But at least you're spared the hassle of plugging and unplugging a cable every night. You just place the iPhone's back onto the pad, and boom: The little lightning-bolt icon appears, and the little "now charging" chime sounds.

Some fun facts about speed:

- Charging a dead iPhone for two hours brings it to about 80 percent charge if you use the Lightning cable; to about 50 percent if you use "fast charging" (on a compatible 7.5-watt pad); and about 40 percent with regular charging (5-watt pads).

- If you plug in the Lightning cable **and** put the phone on the charging pad, you don't cut the time in half. In that situation, the cable wins. The pad does nothing.

- If you want **really** fast charging—a 50 percent charge in 30 minutes—buy a USB-C power brick ($50 and up) and a USB-C to Lightning cable (Apple's is $25).

Battery Life Tips

For most people, the battery life of the iPhone is about a day. But if you can't even make it to bedtime, then knowing how to scale back your iPhone's power appetite should come in extremely handy.

These are the biggest wolfers of electricity: the screen and background activity (especially Internet activity). Therefore, when you're nervous about your battery making it through an important day, here are your options:

- **Low Power mode** can squeeze another three hours of life out of a charge.

  In Low Power mode, your iPhone quits doing a lot of stuff in the background, like fetching new mail and updating apps. It also stops playing most of iOS's cute animations and stops listening for you to say "Hey Siri" (page 160). The processor slows down, too; it takes longer to switch between apps, for example. And the battery indicator turns yellow, to remind you why things have suddenly slowed down.

Unless you've fiddled with the settings, you get an invitation to turn on Low Power mode when your battery sinks to 20 percent remaining, and then again at 10 percent. You can also turn on this mode manually, using the Control Center (page 49) or the switch in **Settings→Battery** (below, top right).

If your phone is plugged in, it exits Low Power mode automatically once it has enough juice (below, lower right).

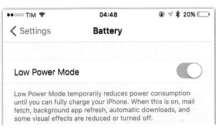
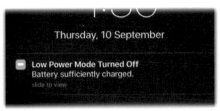

At any time, you can also shut down juice-guzzling features manually. Here they are, roughly in order of power appetite:

- **Dim the screen.** Turning down your screen saves a lot of battery power. The quickest way is to open the Control Center (page 49), and then drag the brightness slider.

  On a new iPhone, Auto-Brightness is turned on, too. In bright light, the screen brightens automatically; in dim light, it darkens. That's because when you unlock the phone after waking it, it samples the ambient light and adjusts the brightness.

NOTE: This works because of the ambient-light sensor near the earpiece. Apple says it experimented with having the light sensor active all the time, but it was weird to have the screen constantly dimming and brightening as you used it.

(You can turn this auto-brightness feature off in **Settings→Display & Brightness**.)

TIP: You can set things up so that a triple-click on the home button or side button instantly dims your screen, for use in the bedroom, movie theaters, or planetariums—without having to fuss with settings or sliders. See page 241 for this awesome trick.

- **Turn off "push" data.** This is a big one. If your email, calendar, and address book are kept constantly synced with your Macs or PCs, then you've probably gotten yourself involved with Yahoo Mail, iCloud (Chapter 16), or Microsoft Exchange. It's pretty amazing to know that your iPhone is constantly kept current with the mother ship.

  Unfortunately, all that continual sniffing of the airwaves, looking for updates, costs you battery life. If you can do without the immediacy, visit **Settings→Accounts & Passwords→Fetch New Data**. If you turn off the Push feature for each email account and set it to **Manually** instead, then your iPhone checks for email and new appointments only when you actually *open* the Mail or Calendar apps. Your battery goes a lot further.

- **Beware GPS.** GPS navigation, in Maps or Google Maps, drains your battery power like a hole in a water bucket. So as you drive, once your guidance app has led you to a place you recognize, by all means shut it off.

  But there's more. In **Settings→Privacy→Location Services**, there's a list of all the apps on your phone that are using its location feature to know where you are. (It's a combination of GPS, cell-tower triangulation, and Wi-Fi hotspot triangulation.) And it uses battery power.

  Some apps, like Maps, Find My Friends, and Yelp, don't do you much good unless they know your location. But plenty of others don't really need to know where you are. Facebook and Twitter, for example, want that information only so that they can location-stamp your posts. In any case, the point is to turn off Location Services for each app that doesn't really need to know where you are.

TIP: In the list of apps under Location Services, tiny ➤ icons show you which apps are using GPS right now and which have used it in the past 24 hours. These icons can guide you in shutting off the GPS use of various apps.

- **Turn off background updating.** Non-Apple apps check for frequent updates, too: Facebook, Twitter, stock-reporting apps, and so on. Not all of them need to be busily toiling in the background. Your best bet for battery life, then, involves visiting **Settings→General→Background App Refresh** and turning the switch off for each app whose background activity isn't strictly necessary.

- **Turn off automatic app updates.** As you'll soon discover, app companies update their wares far more often than PC or Mac apps. Some get updated many times a year. Your phone comes set to download them automatically when they become available. But that constant checking and downloading costs you battery life.

  To shut that feature down, open **Settings→iTunes & App Store**. In the **Automatic Downloads** section, turn off **Updates**. (The other switches—**Music**, **Apps**, **Books**—are responsible for auto-downloading things that you or your brood have downloaded on other iOS gadgets. You might want to make sure they're off, too, if battery life is a concern.)

- **Turn off Wi-Fi.** If you're not in a wireless hotspot, you may as well stop the thing from using its radio. Open the Control Center and tap the 📶 icon to turn it off.

  Or at the very least tell the iPhone to stop *searching* for Wi-Fi networks it can connect to. Page 454 has the details.

- **Turn off Bluetooth.** If you're not using a Bluetooth gadget (headset, fitness band, or whatever), then for heaven's sake shut down that Bluetooth radio. Open the Control Center and tap the ✳ icon to turn it off.

- **Turn off Cellular Data.** This option (in **Settings→Cellular**, but there's also a Control Center button for it) turns off the cellular Internet features of your phone. You can still make calls, and you can still get online in a Wi-Fi hotspot.

  This feature is designed for people who have a capped data plan—a limited amount of Internet use per month—which is a lot of people. If you discover that you've used up almost all your data allotment for the month, and you don't want to go over your limit (and thereby trigger an overage charge), you can use this option to shut off all data. Now your phone is just a phone—and it uses less power.

- **Consider airplane mode.** In airplane mode, you shut off *all* the iPhone's power-hungry radios. Even a nearly dead iPhone can hobble on for a few hours in airplane mode—something to remember when you're desperate. To enter airplane mode, tap the ✈ icon in the Control Center (page 49).

> **TIP:** For sure turn on airplane mode if you'll be someplace where you *know* an Internet signal won't be present—like on a plane, a ship at sea, or Montana. Your iPhone never burns through a battery charge faster than when it's hunting for a signal it can't find; your battery will be dead within a couple of hours.

- **Turn off the screen.** With a press of the side button, you can turn off the screen, rendering it black and saving huge amounts of power. That won't interrupt audio playback, like music or podcasts, or Maps navigation.

  Of course, if you want to actually *interact* with the phone while the screen is off, you'll have to learn the VoiceOver talking-buttons technology; see page 216.

By the way, beware of 3D games and other graphically intensive apps, which can be serious power hogs. And turn off EQ when playing your music (see page 263).

If your battery still seems to be draining too fast, check out the table at right, which shows you exactly which apps are using the most power:

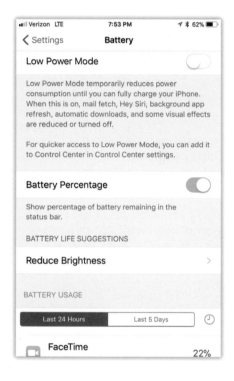

To see it, open **Settings→Battery**. You can switch between battery readouts for the past 24 hours, or for the past seven days.

Keep special watch for labels like these:

- **Low Signal.** A phone uses the most power of all when it's hunting for a cellular signal, because the phone amplifies its radios in hopes of finding one. If your battery seems to be running down faster than usual, the "Low Signal" notation is a great clue—and a suggestion that maybe you should use airplane mode when you're on the fringes of cellular coverage.

- **Background activity.** As hinted on the previous pages, background Internet connections are especially insidious. These are apps that do online work invisibly, without your awareness—and drain the battery in the process. Now, for the first time, you can clearly see which apps are doing it.

  Once you know the culprit app, it's easy to shut its background work down. Open **Settings→General→Background App Refresh** and switch off each app whose background activity isn't strictly necessary.

TIP: If you tap the little ⊘ in **Settings→Battery** (previous page, right), the screen shows you how much time each app has spent running— both in the foreground and in the background. It's an incredibly informative display if you've been wondering where all your battery power has been going.

The Home Screen

The Home screen is the launching pad for every iPhone activity. It's what appears when you press the home button or swipe up on the screen (iPhone X). It's the immortal grid of colorful icons.

It's such an essential software landmark, in fact, that a quick tour might be helpful:

- **Icons.** Each icon represents one of your iPhone apps (programs)— Mail, Maps, Camera, and so on—or a folder that you've made to *contain* some apps. Tap one to open that app or folder.

  Your iPhone comes with a couple of dozen apps preinstalled by Apple; you can't remove them. The real fun, of course, comes when you download *more* apps from the App Store (Chapter 10).

- **Badges.** Every now and then, you'll see a tiny red number "badge" (like ❷) on one of your app icons. It's telling you that something new awaits: new email, new text messages, new chat entries, new updates for the apps on your iPhone. It's saying, "Hey, you! Tap me!"

- **Home page dots.** The standard Home screen can't hold more than 20 or 24 icons. As you install more and more programs on your iPhone, you'll need more and more room for their icons. Fortunately, the iPhone makes room for them by creating *additional* Home screens automatically. You can spread your new programs' icons across 11 such launch screens.

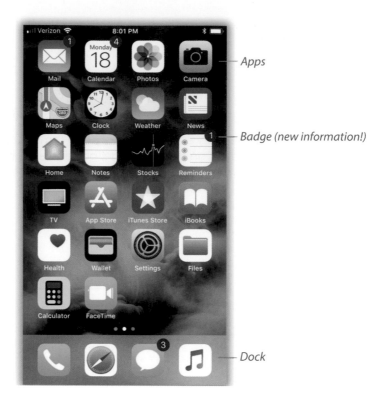

Apps

Badge (new information!)

Dock

The little white dots are your map. Each represents one Home screen. If the third one is "lit up," then you're on the third Home screen.

To move among the screens, swipe horizontally—or tap to the right or left of the little dots to change screens.

And if you ever scroll too far from the *first* Home screen, here's a handy shortcut: Press the home button (yes, even though you're technically already home). That takes you back to the first Home screen.

iPHONE X: Swipe a finger up from the bottom of the screen instead.

- **The Dock.** At the bottom of the Home screen, four exalted icons sit in a row on a light-colored panel. This is the Dock—a place to park the most important icons on your iPhone. These, presumably, are the ones you use most often. Apple starts you off with the Phone, Mail, Safari, and Music icons there.

  What's so special about this row? As you flip among Home screens, the Dock never changes. You can never lose one of your four most cherished icons by straying from the first page; they're always handy.

- **The background.** You can replace the background image (behind your app icons) with a photo. A complicated, busy picture won't do you any favors—it will just make the icon names harder to read—so Apple provides a selection of handsome, relatively subdued wallpaper photos. But you can also choose one of your own photos.

  For instructions on changing the wallpaper, see page 580.

It's easy (and fun!) to rearrange the icons on your Home screens. Put the most frequently used icons on the first page, put similar apps into folders, and reorganize your Dock. Full details are on page 348.

 TIP: You can set up a nearly empty first Home screen by moving all of its app icons onto other home pages, if you want. That's a weird but fun arrangement for anyone with a really great wallpaper photo.

Control Center

For such a tiny device, there are an awful lot of settings you can change—**hundreds** of them. Trouble is, some of them (volume, brightness) need changing a lot more often than others (language preference, voicemail greeting).

That's why Apple invented the Control Center: a panel that offers quick access to the controls you need the most.

In iOS 11, the Control Center is no longer a stunted toddler; it has blossomed into the magnificence of adulthood. Now **you** decide which controls should appear on it. And you no longer have to hunt among multiple pages to find the one you want; the Control Center is once again a single screen. If you're a true Control freak, it even scrolls.

To open the Control Center, no matter what app you're using, swipe upward from beneath the screen. You can even open it from the Lock screen (unless you've turned off that feature in **Settings→Control Center→Access on Lock Screen**).

iPHONE X: Swipe **down** from the upper-right ear. In iOS 11.2, a small horizontal bar appears there to remind you, as shown on page 27.

Now, it's worth pointing out that many of the Control Center's settings are even faster to change using Siri, as described in Chapter 5. When it's not socially awkward to speak to your phone (like at the symphony or during a golf game), you can use spoken commands to adjust settings without even touching the screen.

The Starter Set

Yes, you can customize what appears on the Control Center. But the following controls are nonnegotiable. They're your starter set, and you can't remove most of them.

TIP: In many cases, you can **hard-press** or **long-press** one of these buttons to open a sub-panel that offers even more controls (next page, right). Apple greatly expanded this feature in iOS 11, so the following writeup dives into those hard-press options in detail.

- **Airplane mode (✈).** Tap to turn the icon orange. Now you're in airplane mode; the phone's wireless features are all turned off. You're saving the battery and obeying flight attendant instructions. Tap again to turn off airplane mode.

  Sample Siri command: "Turn airplane mode on." (Siri warns you that if you turn airplane mode on, Siri herself will stop working. Say "OK.")

- **Cellular data (📶).** This icon is new in iOS 11. It's the on/off switch for your iPhone's connection to the Internet over the cellular airwaves (rather than Wi-Fi). Cellular data, after all, costs you money—especially when you're roaming (page 569)—and you may have a monthly limit. So it's good to be able to control when you're using it up.

  Sample Siri command: "Turn off cellular data."

- **Wi-Fi (📶).** Tap to turn your phone's Wi-Fi off (gray) or on (blue).

  Sample Siri commands: "Turn off Wi-Fi." "Turn Wi-Fi back on."

- **Bluetooth (❊).** Tap to turn your Bluetooth transmitter off (gray) or on (blue). That feature alone is a godsend to anyone who uses the iPhone with a car's Bluetooth audio system. Bluetooth isn't the battery drain it once was, but it's still nice to be able to flick it on so easily when you get into the car.

  Sample Siri commands: "Turn Bluetooth on." "Turn off Bluetooth."

  Hard-press options: If you hard-press or long-press anywhere in this cluster of four wireless buttons, you pop open a new panel. It offers the same buttons—**Airplane Mode, Cellular Data, WiFi, Bluetooth**—with labels, this time, along with two more.

  First, there's **AirDrop (◉).** This feature gives you a quick, effortless way to shoot photos, maps, web pages, and other stuff to nearby iPhones, iPads, iPod Touches, and even Macs. (See page 364 for details.) It used to be on the Control Center itself but has now been

Airplane mode, Cellular data,
Wi-Fi, Bluetooth

What you get when you
hard-press the Brightness slider

Notes

buried on this sub-panel. Tap it to see the AirDrop controls described on page 364.

Second, there's **Personal Hotspot**, which lets your phone act as a Wi-Fi hotspot for your laptop or other gadgets (page 457). It makes its first Control Center appearance in iOS 11.

- **Music.** Praise the software gods: The music playback controls are no longer hiding on a separate page of the Control Center. Right here on this little tile, you see information about the current song, plus play-back controls (◀◀, ▶, ▶▶).

These controls govern playback in whatever app is playing music or podcasts in the background: the Music app, Pandora, Spotify, what-ever it is. You can skip a horrible song quickly and efficiently without having to interrupt what you're doing, or pause the music to chat with a colleague.

Sample Siri commands: "Pause the music." "Skip to the next song." "Play some Billy Joel."

Hard-press options: The sub-panel offers a scrubber bar that shows where you are in the song, the album art, and a little button (⊚) that lets you choose what speaker you want to use. It always lists iPhone (the built-in speakers), but it may also list things like a Bluetooth speaker, earbuds, or AirPlay, which sends music or video to a wireless speaker system or TV (see page 273).

There's also a volume slider. It lets you make big volume jumps faster than you can by pressing the volume buttons on the side of the phone.

- **Rotation lock (⊕).** When rotation lock is turned on (red), the screen no longer rotates when you turn the phone 90 degrees. The idea is that sometimes, like when you're reading an ebook on your side in bed, you don't want the screen picture to turn; you want it to stay upright relative to your eyes. (A little ⊕ icon appears at the top of the screen to remind you why the usual rotating isn't happening. On the iPhone X, open the Control Center to see that icon.)

The whole thing isn't quite as earth-shattering as it sounds—first, because it locks the image in only one way: upright, in portrait orientation. You can't make it lock into widescreen mode. Furthermore, many apps don't rotate with the phone to begin with. But when that day comes when you want to read in bed on your side with your head on the pillow, your iPhone will be ready. (Tap the button again to turn rotating back on.)

There are no Siri or hard-press options for this control.

- **Do Not Disturb (☾).** Do Not Disturb mode, described on page 138, means that the phone won't ring or buzz when people call—except a few handpicked people whose communiqués are allowed to ring through. Perfect for sleeping hours; in fact, you can set up an automated schedule for Do Not Disturb (midnight to 7 a.m., say).

But what if you wake up early or want to stay up late? You can tap to turn Do Not Disturb on (blue) or off (gray).

There are no hard-press options for this control.

Sample Siri commands: "Turn on Do Not Disturb." "Turn Do Not Disturb off."

- **Brightness (☀).** Hallelujah! Here's a screen-brightness slider—now in the form of a big, fat vertical bar that's very easy to operate. Drag anywhere within it, up or down, to change the brightness.

Sample Siri commands: "Make the screen brighter." "Dim the screen."

Hard-press options: The sub-panel presents on/off buttons for Night Shift, which makes the screen yellower before bedtime to prevent sleep disturbance (page 578), and True Tone, a feature of the iPhone 8 and X that tweaks the screen colors to make them look consistent in whatever ambient light you're in (page 578).

- **Volume (◀))).** Here it is, next to brightness: an equally big, fat volume slider. Slide your finger up or down to adjust the audio volume.

  Hard-press options: Hard-pressing doesn't gain you any **new** controls. It does, however, open up a much bigger version of the volume slider. It's now easier to make finer adjustments.

- **AirPlay Mirroring (▱).** The AirPlay button lets you send your iPhone's video and audio to a wireless speaker system or TV—if you have an AirPlay receiver, of which the most famous is the Apple TV. Details are on page 273.

  Hard-press options: A sub-panel appears, listing any available wireless receivers, like an Apple TV or a wireless projector.

The bottom row of the starter icons, described next, are removable. If they're not floating your boat, see the next section for instructions on how to get rid of them.

- **Flashlight (▯).** Tap to turn on the iPhone's "flashlight"—actually the LED lamp on the back that usually serves as the camera flash. Knowing that a source of good, clean light is a few touches away makes a huge difference if you're trying to read in the dark, find your way along a path at night, or fiddle with wires behind your desk.

IPHONE X: There's also a flashlight button right on the Lock screen. Press it hard to turn it on.

  Hard-press options: You get a four-segment "slider" that controls the flashlight's brightness. The top segment means full brightness; the bottom one means Off. That's super cool, especially on the iPhone 7/8/X, whose LED flashlight is enough to light up a high-school football game at night.

- **Camera (◎).** Tap to jump directly into the Camera app. Because photo ops don't wait around.

  Hard-press options: Handy! Here are the **Take Selfie**, **Record Video**, **Record Slo-mo**, and (on Plus and X models) **Take Portrait** commands. Each saves you a little fiddling in the Camera app.

  Sample Siri commands: "Take a picture." "Open the camera."

- **Calculator (▦).** Tap to open the Calculator app—a handy shortcut if it's your turn to figure out how to divide up the restaurant bill.

  Hard-press options: A Copy Last Result button appears, so you can snag whatever.

  Sample Siri commands: "Open the calculator." Or, better yet, without opening any app: "What's a 106 divided by 5?"

- **Timer (◐).** Tap to open the Clock app—specifically, the Timer mode, which counts down to zero. Apple figures you might appreciate having direct access to it when you're cooking, for example, or waiting for your hair color to set.

  There are no hard-press options for this icon.

  Sample Siri commands: "Open the Timer." Or, better yet, bypass the Clock and Timer apps altogether: "Start the timer for three minutes." "Count down from six minutes." (Siri counts down right there on the Siri screen.)

Customizing the Control Center

This is one of the biggest chunks of good news in iOS 11: You can make Control Center your own. You can add all kinds of new buttons to it, including some (like recording a video of the screen) that have never been possible on the iPhone before.

The Center for Control Center Customization, as it turns out, is **Settings→Control Center→Customize Controls**. Here's a giant list of the buttons you're allowed to add or remove. It's very simple: Tap ● to remove a button that's already installed. Tap ⊕ to install a button that's not yet on the Control Center.

And drag the little ☰ handles up or down to choose an *order* for your icons on the Control Center.

Here are your options (except as noted, none of them offer further options when you hard-press):

- **Flashlight, Camera, Calculator, Stopwatch.** As described previously.

- **Stopwatch.** Tap to open the Clock app, already tuned to the Stopwatch mode (page 384). You're all ready to time that 50-yard dash or teenage room-cleaning.

- **Accessibility Shortcuts.** Opens the same list of accessibility shortcuts (**Zoom, VoiceOver, AssistiveTouch**, and so on) that you've chosen to list for quick access when you triple-click the home button. These options, and the triple-clicking business, are described on page 242.

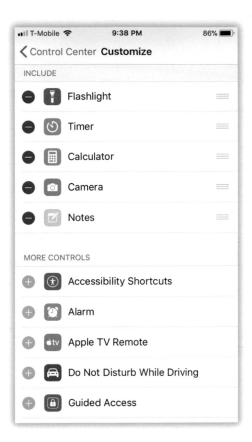

- **Alarm.** Tap to open the Clock app, this time set to Alarm mode (page 380), where you can set (or turn off) an upcoming alarm.

- **Apple TV Remote.** Pops open an onscreen version of your Apple TV remote control, complete with Menu, Play, and Siri buttons—plus a large trackpad area for scrolling around. This item is fantastic when you can't seem to dig your actual Apple TV remote from under the couch cushions.

- **Do Not Disturb While Driving.** Apple is very proud of this new iOS 11 feature, which prevents notifications, calls, or texts from lighting up your phone or making it ring whenever you're behind the wheel and in motion.

    You can read all about this feature on page 140. There you'll learn that you can (and probably should) set it to turn on *automatically* when you're driving. In other words, this button is primarily useful for turning DNDWD *off*—when you're in the passenger seat.

- **Guided Access.** Opens the on/off switch for Guided Access, otherwise known as "kiosk mode." It locks the phone into one particular app, so that (for example) your toddler can play with it without wreaking any real havoc on your phone. See page 239.

- **Low Power Mode.** Here's a one-touch way to manually switch on the battery-saving feature known as Low Power Mode (page 42).

- **Magnifier.** Turns the entire phone into a powerful illuminated magnifying glass, as described on page 223.

- **Notes.** This is a big, big deal. The idea is to give you immediate access to Notes, so you can jump in, no matter what you were doing, to write down something quickly: a phone number someone's giving you, dosage instructions your doctor's rattling off, or a brainstorm you've just had for a million-dollar product.

TIP: One tap opens directly into the Notes app. But if you hard-press instead, you get a list of commands like **New Note**, **New Checklist**, **New Photo**, and **New Sketch**.

Now then. If you make Notes part of the Control Center, it will be available even when the phone is locked. Clearly, that could be a privacy disaster if your phone falls into the hands of some passing evildoer.

Apple has given that scenario a lot of thought. First of all, if you open Notes from the Lock screen, there's no way to see any *existing* notes. You're stuck on a single page.

But that's not the end of the privacy control—oh, heavens, no. Open **Settings→Notes→Access Notes from Lock Screen**.

At the top, you have three choices. **Off** means forget it—you can't open Notes from the Lock screen at all. (So why bother putting the Notes button on the Control Center? Because you can still use it when the phone *isn't* locked.)

Always Create New Note means that every time you open Notes from the Lock screen, you wind up at another fresh, empty Notes page.

And **Resume Last Note**...well, if you choose this option, Settings has a whole bunch more questions for you.

For example, if you open Notes from the Lock screen, do you want it to reopen the last note you viewed in the app? Or just the last note you opened *from the Lock screen*? That second option is another security precaution, keeping your Lock-screen doodlings separate from your other stuff.

You also get a bunch of time settings, like **After 5 Minutes**, **After 15 Minutes**, and so on. What Apple is saying here: "Even though you've selected **Resume Last Note**, you're still going to get a new, *empty* note if it's been at least five minutes since the last time you looked at it. Just in case you wander off during a meeting and some idiot picks up your phone six minutes later to see what you were writing."

Once Daily here means that you'll get a new, fresh note the first time you open Notes from the Lock screen *each day*—handy for a journal or a daily log.

Finally, **Never** ignores all these options. It means that *every* time you open Notes from the Lock screen, you'll return to whatever Note page you've been working on.

And if all of these options make sense to you, there are fine career opportunities awaiting you at the Internal Revenue Service.

- **Screen Recording.** Here's a freak of iOS nature: a Control Center button for a feature you can't trigger in any other way. The idea, of course, is to let you record videos of what's happening on the iPhone screen—with narration, if you like. See page 341 for details.

- **Text Size.** There are all kinds of ways to make text bigger and more readable on the iPhone's screen (see page 228). But this new Control Center option gives you a more immediate way of making adjustments—say, when you find yourself on some web page in 3-point type. Tap to see a vertical slider, whose segments indicate increasingly larger type sizes. Slide your finger accordingly.

- **Voice Memos.** The Voice Memos app has always been handy for recording speeches, interviews, song ideas, and so on. What *hasn't* been handy is the long slog to get into the app and start recording.

  No more! Tap this button to open the Voice Memos app, where another tap begins the recording. Better yet, a hard-press on this Control Center button produces a menu that lists your three most recent recordings (for instant playback)—and a **New Recording** button. In other words, you can now get the audio capture going with only one tap-and-slide in the Control Center.

- **Wallet.** Here's another way to jump into your Apple Wallet—usually because you want to use Apple Pay (page 542). Tap this button to open the Apple Pay screen with your preferred card selected; at this point, you will use your fingerprint—or on the iPhone X, your face—to complete the transaction.

  If you hard-press, though, you get a list of your credit cards—handy if you want to choose one that's not your primary card.

Closing the Control Center

The Control Center closes when any of these things happen:

- You tap one of the buttons that opens an app (Timer, Calculator, Camera, Notes, and so on).

- You tap anywhere on the gray background of the Control Center.

- You swipe downward anywhere on the Control Center (except on the brightness or volume sliders).

iPHONE X: Swipe *upward*.

- You press the home button (or, on the iPhone X, swipe upward from the bottom edge).

NOTE: In some apps, swiping up doesn't open the Control Center on the first try, much to your probable bafflement. Instead, swiping just makes a tiny ⌃ appear at the edge of the screen. (You'll see this behavior whenever the status bar—where the time and battery gauge appear—is hidden, as in the full-screen modes of iBooks, Maps, Videos, and so on. It also happens in the Camera app.)

In those situations, Apple is trying to protect you from opening the Control Center accidentally—for example, when what you really wanted to do was scroll up. No big deal; once the ⌃ appears, swipe up *again* to open the Control Center panel.

If you find yourself opening the Control Center accidentally—when playing games, for example—you can turn it off. Open **Settings→Control Center**. Turn off **Access Within Apps**. Now swiping opens the Control Center only at the Home screen. (You can also turn off **Access on Lock Screen** here, to make sure the Control Center never appears when the phone is asleep.)

Passcode Protection

Like any smartphone, the iPhone offers a first line of defense for a phone that winds up in the wrong hands. It's designed to keep your stuff private from other people in the house or the office, or to protect your information in case you lose the iPhone.

Plenty of iPhone owners don't bother setting up a passcode. Maybe they never set the thing down, so they don't worry about thieves. Or maybe there's just not that much personal information on the phone—and meanwhile, having to enter a passcode every time you wake the phone can get to be a hassle.

TIP: If you ever do lose your phone, you can put a passcode on it by remote control; see page 537.

The other half of people reason that the inconvenience of entering a passcode many times a day is a small price to pay for the knowledge that nobody can get into your stuff if you lose your phone.

Of course, you can also protect your phone with a fingerprint or (on the iPhone X) face recognition. But both of those require that you **first** create a passcode, which will always be the fallback.

Even if you **usually** unlock the phone with your finger or your face, you'll still be required to use that passcode, for added security, after any of these things occur:

- You've restarted or shut down the phone.
- You've made several failed attempts to log in with a finger or face.
- It's been two days since you unlocked the phone.
- It's been six days since you last entered your passcode, and you haven't used your finger or face in eight hours.

None of that will be on the test. The point is that sometimes, even with finger or face recognition, you'll need your passcode.

Setting Up a Passcode

Now, you probably created a phone passcode the first time you turned your iPhone on (see page 58); the iPhone practically insists on it.

But if you skipped that step, here's how to do it now.

Open **Settings→Touch ID & Passcode**. (On the 5c, it's just called **Passcode Lock**; on the iPhone X, it's called **Face ID & Passcode**.)

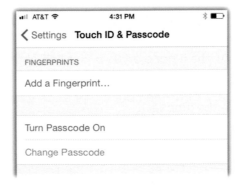

Tap **Turn Passcode On**. iOS proposes that you make up a six-digit passcode. But if you tap **Passcode Options**, you can choose instead a **Custom Alphanumeric Code** (any password, any length), **Custom Numeric Code** (an all-number code, any length), or **4-Digit Numeric Code** (you know—ATM style).

You're asked to type the passcode you want twice, to make sure you didn't make a typo.

> **NOTE:** Don't kid around with this passcode. If you forget the iPhone code, you'll have to *restore* your iPhone (page 627), which wipes out everything on it. You've probably still got most of the data on your computer or backed up on iCloud, of course (music, video, contacts, calendar), but you may lose text messages, mail, and so on.

Once you confirm your passcode, you return to the **Passcode Lock** screen. Here you have a few more options.

The **Require Passcode** option lets you specify how quickly the passcode is requested before locking somebody out: immediately after the iPhone wakes or 1, 15, 30, 60, or 240 minutes later. (Those options are a convenience to you, so you can quickly check your calendar or missed messages without having to enter the passcode—while still protecting your data from, for example, criminals who pick up your iPhone while you're out getting coffee.)

Certain features are accessible on the Lock screen even before you've entered your passcode: the **Today** and **Notifications** tabs of the Notification Center; the **Control Center**; **Siri**, **Wallet**, **Home Control**, **Reply with Message** (the ability to reply to text messages right from their notification bubble on the Lock screen), and **Return Missed Calls** (the option to return a missed call from *its* bubble, without unlocking the phone; that's new in iOS 11).

These are huge conveniences, but also, technically, a security risk. Somebody who finds your phone on your desk could, for example, blindly voice-dial your colleagues or use Siri to send a text. If you turn these switches off, then nobody can use these features until after unlocking the phone with your passcode, fingerprint, or face.

Finally, here is **Erase Data**—an option that's scary and reassuring at the same time. When this option is on, if someone makes 10 incorrect guesses at your passcode, your iPhone erases itself. It's assuming that some lowlife burglar is trying to crack into it to have a look at all your personal data.

This option, a pertinent one for professional people, provides potent protection from patient password prospectors.

And that is all. From now on, each time you wake your iPhone (if it's not within the window of repeat visits you established), you're asked for your passcode.

Fingerprint Security (Touch ID)

Most iOS 11 phones offer the option of using a more secure and convenient kind of "passcode": your fingertip. (The exceptions are the iPhone 5c, which has no biometric features, and the iPhone X, which uses face recognition instead.)

The lens built right into the home button (clever!) reads your finger at any angle. It can't be faked out by a plastic finger or even a chopped-off finger. You can teach it to recognize up to five fingerprints; they can all be yours, or some can belong to other people you trust.

Before you can use your fingertip as a passcode, though, you have to teach the phone to recognize it. Here's how that goes:

1. **Create a passcode.** You can't use a fingerprint *instead* of a passcode, only in addition to one. You'll still need a passcode from time to time to keep the phone's security tight. For example, you need to enter your passcode if you can't make your fingerprint work (maybe it got encased in acrylic in a hideous crafts accident), or if you restart the phone, or if you haven't used the phone in 48 hours or more.

   So open **Settings→Touch ID & Passcode** and create a password, as already described.

2. **Teach a fingerprint.** At the top of the Touch ID & Passcode screen, you see the on/off switches for the three things your fingerprint can do: unlock the phone (**iPhone Unlock**), pay for things (**Apple Pay**), and serve as your password when you buy books, music, apps, and videos from Apple's online stores (**iTunes & App Store**).

   But what you really want to tap here, of course, is **Add a Fingerprint**.

   Now comes the cool part. Place the finger you want to train onto the home button—your thumb or index finger are the most logical candidates. You're asked to touch it to the home button over and over, maybe six times. Each time, the gray lines of the onscreen fingerprint darken a little more.

   Once you've filled in the fingerprint, you see the Adjust Your Grip screen. Tap **Continue**. Now, the iPhone wants you to touch the home

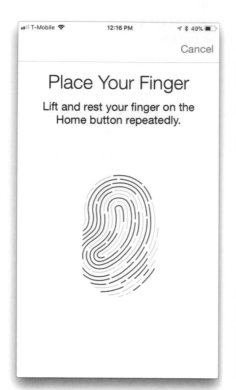

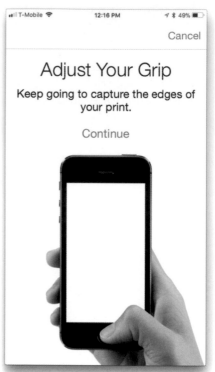

button another few times, this time tipping the finger a little each time so the sensor gets a better view of your finger's *edges*.

Once that's done, the screen says "Success!"

You're now ready to start using the fingerprint. Try it: Put the phone to sleep. Then wake it by pressing the home button, and leave your finger on the button for about a second. The phone reads your fingerprint and instantly unlocks itself.

And now, a few notes about using your fingerprint as a password:

- Yes, you can touch your finger to the home button at the Lock screen. But you can also touch it at any Enter Passcode screen.

  Suppose, for example, that your Lock screen shows that you missed a text message. And you want to reply. Well, you can swipe across that notification to open it in its native habitat—the Messages app—but first you're shown the Enter Passcode screen. Ignore that. Just touch the home button with the finger whose print you recorded.

- Apple says the image of your fingerprint is encrypted and stored in the iPhone's processor chip. It's never transmitted anywhere, it never goes online, and it's never collected by Apple.

- If you return to the Touch ID & Passcode screens, you can tap **Add a Fingerprint** again to teach your phone to recognize a second finger. And a third, fourth, and fifth.

- On the other hand, it makes a lot of sense to register the *same* finger *several* times. You'll be amazed at how much faster and more reliably your thumb (for example) is recognized if you've trained it as several different "fingerprints."

- To rename a fingerprint, tap its current name ("Finger 1" or whatever). To delete one, tap its name and then tap **Delete Fingerprint**. (You can figure out which finger label is which by touching the home button; the corresponding label blinks. Sweet!)

- You can register your toes instead of fingers, if that's helpful. Or even patches of your wrist or arm, if you're patient (and weird).

- The Touch ID scanner may have trouble recognizing your touch if your finger is wet, greasy, or scarred.

- The iPhone's finger reader isn't just a camera; it doesn't just look for the image of your fingerprint. It's actually measuring the tiny differences in electrical conductivity between the raised parts of your fingerprint (which aren't conductive) and the skin just beneath the surface (which is). That's why a plastic finger won't work—and even your own finger won't work if it's been chopped off (or if you've died).

Fingerprints for Apps, Websites, and Apple Pay

So if your fingerprint is such a great solution to password overload, how come it works only to unlock the phone and to buy stuff from Apple's online stores? Wouldn't it be great if your fingerprint could also log you into secure websites? Or serve as your ID when you buy stuff online?

That dream is finally becoming a reality. Software companies can now use your Touch ID fingerprint to log into their apps. Mint (for checking your personal finances), Evernote (for storing notes, pictures, and to-do lists), Amazon (for buying stuff), and other apps now permit you to substitute a fingerprint touch for typing a password.

What's really wild is that password-storing apps like 1Password and LastPass have been updated, too. Those apps are designed to memorize your passwords for all sites on the web, of every type—and now you can use your fingerprint to unlock them.

Moreover, your fingerprint is now the key to the magical door of Apple Pay, the wireless pay-with-your-iPhone technology described on page 542.

All of this is great news. Most of us would be happy if we never, ever had to type in another password.

Face ID (iPhone X)

When Apple decided to cover the entire face of the iPhone X with screen, there was an obvious problem: the home button. Were they really going to interrupt that gorgeous ocean of OLED screen with a cutout for the home button?

Nope. The home button went away. In place of its functions, Apple came up with the various swipes and side-button presses described in this book. And in place of the fingerprint reader, the iPhone X has a *facial recognition* system. Basically, you unlock the phone by looking at it.

You can't fool Face ID with a photo, a mask, or even a 3D model of your head. It works in the dark. It works if you change hairstyles, glasses, makeup, or facial hair. It works through most sunglasses. It works if you're wearing a hat and scarf (it just has to see your eyes, nose, and mouth).

If you grow fat, or skinny, or old, it will still work, because it gradually updates its model of your face as you use it. (And if you have radical plastic surgery, well, you'll have to retrain it. Takes about a minute.)

It can't be forced on you when you're sleeping, because you have to be *looking* at the phone. It can't be forced on you by a police officer, because you can disable it with a quick, secret button press (page 80).

Whereas one in 50,000 people might be able to get into your phone with a fingerprint, Face ID's miss rate is one in *a million*. (The exception: Your identical twin might be able to fool Face ID. You've been warned.)

You'll use Face ID wherever you used to use your fingerprint: triggering Apple Pay, for example, or logging into apps like Mint, 1Password, and E-Trade.

TrueDepth

So how does the phone recognize your face? Using a mass of sensors Apple calls TrueDepth. They're hiding in the Notch at the top of the iPhone X.

When you wake the phone, an infrared lamp (called the *flood illuminator*—but you knew that) blasts invisible light forward to see if a face is in range. If so, a tiny *dot projector* blasts 30,000 pinpoints of infrared light onto your face, and an infrared camera reads the distortion of their spacing and shape to find its contours. (That's why Face ID works in the dark—it relies on infrared light.)

If the infrared camera confirms that you're you—if the mathematical model of your facial contours matches what it captured when you trained it—then the phone unlocks. Only the tiny opening of a padlock on the Lock screen signifies that facial recognition has done its thing.

Training Face ID

In most ways, Face ID works exactly like Touch ID, described earlier. For example, you must create a passcode as a backup before you can turn on Face ID.

You'll need that passcode from time to time, for added security—after you've restarted the phone, after five failed attempts to log in with facial recognition, and so on (see page 58).

After creating your passcode in **Settings→Face ID & Passcode**, tap **Set Up Face ID**. Center your face in the circle, and then trace a circle in the air with your nose, so that the frame of your face circle fills in. You're asked to do this a second time—and that's all it needs to create its model of your face.

(Apple stresses that the scan of your face is never transmitted, not even to Apple, and not part of any backup. It's stored in a protected piece of memory called the Secure Enclave.)

Using Face ID

From now on, you can unlock your iPhone X like this:

- **Wake the phone** by tapping the screen, pressing the side button, or tipping the phone upright.

- **Look at the phone.** A white padlock at the top of the screen opens to show you that Face ID has recognized you and unlocked the phone.

  If all you wanted to do was check your notifications or something, that's all there is to it. In fact, what's especially cool is that when you wake the phone, message and mail notifications don't reveal their contents (below, left)—but once the phone recognizes you, they expand in place (right)!

If you actually want to *proceed*—to go to the Home screen, for example—then there's one more step:

- **Swipe up from beneath the screen.** It can be a short, quick swipe. The Home screen (or whatever app you were using) appears. You're in.

Every now and then, Face ID doesn't unlock when you look at it, and asks that you enter your passcode. Do so! Each time, Face ID learns from its mistake and is more likely to recognize you the next time.

TIP: There are some useful options to change in Face ID: See page 583.

2

The Lock Screen & Notifications

The Lock screen—the first thing you see when you wake the iPhone—is more than just a big Do Not Disturb sign. It's a lively bulletin board for up-to-date information about your life. It's possible to have complete work sessions right at the Lock screen, without even fully unlocking the iPhone.

For starters, you can use the iPhone as a watch—millions of people do. Just lift the sleeping phone, or press the side button, to consult the Lock screen's time and date display, and then shove the phone right back into your pocket. The iPhone goes back to sleep after a few seconds.

Better yet, the Lock screen is a handy status screen. Here you see a record of everything that happened while you weren't paying attention. It's a list of missed calls, text messages received, notifications from your apps, and other essential information.

Three Swipes, You're In

The Lock screen is the centerpiece of three *other* important screens. You can swipe up, left, or right to bring them into view.

- **Swipe left** to open the Camera app (page 275).

- **Swipe right** to reveal the Today (Widgets) screen (page 75).

- **Swipe up** from the bottom of the screen to open the Control Center shortcuts screen (page 49).

IPHONE X: Swipe down from the upper-right corner for the Control Center.

Keep this map in your head every time you wake your phone:

Today view Lock screen Camera

Control Center

Notifications

A notification is an update from an app trying to get your attention. You get one every time a text message comes in, an alarm goes off, a calendar appointment is imminent, your battery is running low, and so on. Almost every app can display a notification, if you let it.

In iOS 11, Apple gave notifications a thorough makeover. The old system was pretty complicated—three places to find them, two kinds to deal with. Now things are simpler (mostly). Notifications now appear in only two different places. Maybe 2½:

- **On your screen, while you're working.** They pop up to get your attention, as shown on the following pages.

- **On the Lock screen,** in a scrolling list of alerts that came in while you were away (below, left). (Unlocking the phone wipes them away. The *next* time you unlock the phone, that batch will be gone.)

- **On the pull-down Lock screen.** Weirdly enough, if you swipe down from the top of the screen, iOS 11 presents you with—the Lock screen!

Lock screen

*Pull-down Lock screen
(or swipe up on real Lock screen)*

Again! Yes, it's exactly the same thing you see when you unlock your phone, complete with wallpaper, day, and date. You can even swipe left for the Camera, or swipe right for the Today screen!

There's only one difference: On the pull-down Lock screen (above, right), you see *all* the notifications that have come in recently, even ones you've previously dismissed, even if they're several days old. (On the actual Lock screen, you have to swipe up to see these older ones.)

To close this screen, just swipe any empty area up and away, or press the home button.

The following pages tackle these 2½ notification situations one by one.

Dealing with Notifications

These days, there's a lot more you can do with a notification than just read it and nod. Apple has tried to make notifications as productive, customizable, and un-interrupty as possible.

For example, you can deal with one in any of these ways, even if they're on the Lock screen:

- **Flick it away.** If a notification banner appears while the phone is on, flick it upward to make it disappear.

- **Answer it in place.** You can take direct action on many kinds of notifications—incoming text messages, emails, or calendar invitations, for example. Without leaving the notification banner, you can reply to a text message, delete an email, accept a calendar invitation, see where your Uber car is, mark a Reminder as done, and so on.

  If you have an iPhone 6s or later model, you have 3D Touch (page 37). Just *hard-press* on the banner to expand it and see your action options—to reply to a text message, for example (facing page, right).

  If you have an earlier model, swipe to the left on the banner to reveal your option buttons. For a text message, they might be **View** and **Clear** (facing page, top left); if it's an email, they say **Trash** and **Mark as Read**; and so on.

- **Open it.** Finally, here's the obvious one: You can tap a notification to open the app it came from. (If the phone is locked, you'll be asked to unlock it first.) Tap an email notification to open the message in Mail; tap a text-message notification to open it in Messages; and so on. That's handy when you want to dig in and see the full context of the notification.

(If you've broken your tapping finger, there are two other ways to go about it: Swipe to the right to reveal the **Open** button shown below at bottom left. Either *continue* swiping, all the way to the edge of the screen, or stop and tap **Open**. Either way, you open the message in the corresponding app.)

- **Clear it.** Once you've tapped a banner to open it, that notification no longer appears on either Lock screen. It's gone.

  You can also dismiss a banner without opening it by swiping all the way to the left (or swiping slightly leftward and tapping **Clear**).

Dismissing Clumps of Notifications

There's no way to clear out notifications in a bunch when you're on the actual Lock screen. On the *pull-down* Lock screen, though, you can clear all the notifications for an entire listed day by tapping the ⊗ next to a day's name and then tapping **Clear**.

If you have an iPhone 6s or later, you can also erase your *entire* list of notifications, like this: Hard-press the ⊗ next to a day's name; tap **Clear All Notifications**. (There's no Clear All function on older iPhone models.)

Customizing Notifications

You can (and should) specify *which* apps are allowed to junk up your notification screens. Open **Settings→Notifications** to see the master list, with one entry for every app that might ever want your attention. (Or just tell Siri, "Open notification settings.")

You'll quickly discover that *every* app thinks it's important; *every* app wants its notifications to blast into your face when you're working.

You, however, may not agree. You may not consider it essential to know when your kid's Plants vs. Zombies score has changed, for example.

So: Tap an app's name to open its individual Notifications screen (below—the News app, in this example). Here you'll find settings that vary by app, but they generally run along these lines:

- **Allow Notifications.** If you don't want this app to make any notifications pop up at all, turn this off.

- **Sounds.** Some apps try to get your attention with a sound effect when a notification appears. Turn this off if you think your phone makes too many beeps and burbles as it is. (Some apps also let

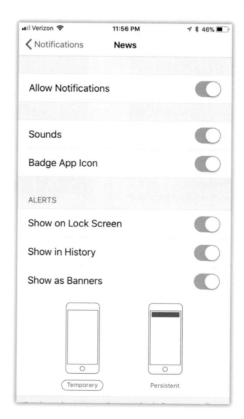

you choose *which* sound effect plays to get your attention. You can change the sound or choose **None**.)

- **Badge App Icon.** A badge is a little red circled number (**2**, for example). It appears right on an app's icon to indicate how many updates are waiting for you. Turn it off if you really don't need that reminder.

- **Show on Lock Screen.** Here you control whether this app's banners appear on the actual Lock screen at all. This switch has no effect on the *pull-down* Lock screen. This app's banners still show up there, which means that you can set up different sets of banners on each one.

  Maybe you want the real Lock screen to show only missed calls, new text messages, and new email—but you'd like the pull-down Lock screen to be fully stocked with Twitter and Facebook updates, for example. Or maybe you'd rather not permit passing evildoers to pick up your phone and see your notifications without even having to unlock it.

  That's why you have this switch. It governs your ability to see this app's updates on the Lock screen.

- **Show in History.** The History is a list of notifications that in theory you've already seen. (On the Lock screen, you swipe up to see them. On the pull-down Lock screen, they're always visible.)

  Once you've unlocked your phone, any notifications on its Lock screen get moved into the History list. That is, the next time you look at the Lock screen, you'll have to swipe up to see them.

  Unless, of course, you turn off **Show in History** for this app. Now, this app's notifications disappear completely after you unlock the phone.

- **Show as Banners.** In iOS 11, there's no more choice of banners versus alerts. All notifications look and work alike. The only choice you have to make, for each app, is whether they linger on your screen—or disappear after a moment.

  If you turn off **Show as Banners**, then *nothing* appears on the screen when an app wants your attention. (You can still direct these alerts to appear on your Lock screen, as described already.)

  A **Temporary** banner appears at the top of the screen, holds still long enough for you to read it, and then goes away after a few seconds. Facebook and Twitter updates and incoming email messages do well as temporary banners.

A **Persistent** banner stays on your screen until you tap or swipe it. You might use this option for apps whose messages are too important to miss, like alarms, flight updates, or texts.

- **Show Preview.** This is a privacy thing. When someone sends you a text, do you want the notification banner to include ***the message itself***? (That's the Preview.) Or do you want the banner to indicate only that a person has sent ***some*** message, which you then have to tap to read?

  And it's not just texts. Do you want the Uber information to appear in the banner? How about the Facebook status? The name of your alarm or reminder?

  You have three choices here: **Always** (always show the message in the notification banner), **When Unlocked** (show it only if I'm using the phone—not when it's locked), and **Never**.

As you poke around in the Notifications settings, you'll discover that certain oddball apps offer some options that don't match up with the settings you see for most apps. Don't freak out. It's all part of Apple's master plan to put controls where it hopes you'll find them.

Locking Down the Lock Screen

Now, remember: You can enjoy any of these activities, and see any of this information, even ***before*** you've entered your password or used fingerprint or face recognition. The bad guys don't need a password to view your Lock screen.

For privacy purposes, therefore, you can turn those features off individually in **Settings→Touch ID & Passcode** (or **Face ID & Passcode**). Here you'll find on/off switches for a whole raft of Lock screen features: the **Today View**, **Recent Notifications**, **Control Center**, **Siri**, **Reply with Message** (to text messages), **Home Control** (of your app-controllable home-automation devices), **Wallet** (for Apple Pay), and **Return Missed Calls** (right from the "missed call" notification banner).

> **NOTE:** If you turn off **Recent Notifications**, you eliminate the sole difference between the actual Lock screen and the pull-down Lock screen: the listing of older notifications. Notifications will appear on the Lock screen as they come in, but you'll have no way to swipe to see earlier ones you've already seen.

There's no way to block access to the Camera from the Lock screen. (Well, you can open **Settings→General→Restrictions** and turn off **Camera**. That step, however, hides the Camera ***completely***—it even disappears from the Home screen.)

The Today Screen (Widgets)

To the left of the Lock screen, you'll find a motley assortment of panels that Apple calls widgets. Some are quick-access buttons that launch related apps, like quick-dial (or quick-text) buttons for your favorite contacts; others are info-bits that you might want to check throughout the day, like your calendar, news, sports, and weather.

This entire wonderland is available before you've even unlocked the phone—quickly. Just swipe right from the Lock screen. Great when you want to check your calendar for your next thing.

It's also available when you've opened the pull-down Lock screen (swipe right, above or below the notification banners), and even when you're at the Home screen (swipe right).

Truth is, many people don't even know the Today screen is there; even if they do, most people don't use it. And sure enough, this feature doesn't really become useful until you customize it: Rearrange the widgets, remove the ones you'd never touch, and install more useful ones.

The very first time you open the Widgets screen, you see things like the search bar (page 108), Up Next, Siri App Suggestions, and News. (They're described on these pages.) But the key to the real magic is the **Edit** button, which is hiding below all the widgets, several scrolls down.

The list you find here has two parts: the widgets that are currently installed and the ones that aren't. Delete a widget by tapping its ●; add one by tapping its ⊕. Rearrange the installed ones by dragging their ☰ handles. When you're finished, tap **Done**.

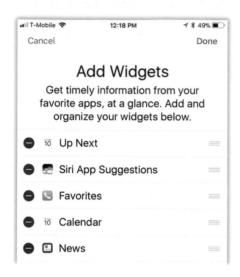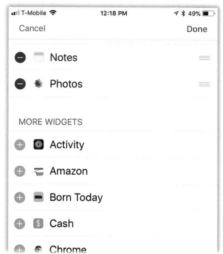

So what widgets are available? Here's a rundown:

- **Up Next.** The next couple of things on your calendar. Tap to log in and open the Calendar app, which shows you details of the event.

- **Siri App Suggestions.** This little row of app icons actually have nothing to do with Siri, the voice-controlled assistant. Instead, these are the iPhone's suggestions of apps you may want to use right now, based on your location, the time of day, and your typical routine. For example, if you open the Music app every evening during your 6:30 p.m. gym workout, then the Music app appears at that time, ready to open. If you check your Fitbit app every morning when you wake, then this screen offers its icon at that time of day. The idea is to save you from having to hunt for these apps when you need them again.

  If you find these icons unhelpful, you can turn off this widget (above). You can also prevent *certain* apps' icons from appearing here. Open **Settings→Siri & Search**. Here, if you scroll down, you'll find the names of all apps that might be inclined to appear as a Siri Suggestion; you can tap them to turn them off, one at a time.

- **Suggestions in Look Up** means, "When I highlight text and tap Look Up, I want to see only its definition or web results—not app suggestions."

- **News.** Headlines from the News app (page 417).

- **Weather.** You guessed it.

- **Batteries.** Hey, it's your phone's current battery charge!

- **Maps Destinations.** If you use Apple's Maps app, and routinely enter the addresses of your appointments on the Calendar, here's the pay-off: a list of upcoming and predicted destinations, including your next calendar appointment and where you parked your car (page 414).

- **Calendar.** Today's agenda. Tap an appointment to unlock your phone and see its details screen.

- **Reminders.** Your unfinished to-dos. You can mark one as done here, without having to unlock the phone and open the app. That's a big deal.

- **Favorites.** This is your speed-dial list. The first four people you've designated as favorites appear here, for quick speed-dialing.

  But it's not just about phone calls (who does *that* anymore?). You can also designate a texting or email address, Skype handle, or other communication address as a favorite (page 114). Which means that, using this widget, you can insta-text your spouse or your kid without having to open the app, access the address book, choose the person's name, and so on. Shortcuts, baby!

- **Files.** Here are the most recent files you've moved to or from your iCloud Drive (page 387).

- **Find Friends.** This widget shows a map that pinpoints the location of any loved ones you're tracking (page 553).

- **Mail.** A speed-dial list of the people you've designated as VIPs (page 495), for quick emailing.

- **Maps Nearby.** These icons are shortcuts for time-appropriate searches, like coffee in the morning, or nightlife after dark.

- **Maps Transit.** If you use Maps' public-transportation feature, this widget lets you know about delays and service interruptions.

- **Music.** Playback controls for whatever you were playing last.

- **Notes.** You see the first couple of lines of the Notes page you most recently edited.

- **Photos.** Thumbnails that, after you unlock the phone, open recent Memories (automated slideshows of recent time periods).

- **Reminders.** Here's where you see to-do items you've set up in the Reminders app with a time and date.

- **Files.** This widget shows the icons of any files you've recently added to your iCloud Drive (page 387).

- **TV.** Shows any shows you've been watching in the TV app (page 268).

- **Stocks.** The latest on whatever stocks you follow (page 438).

- **Tips.** This is the closest Apple comes to offering a manual for iOS 11.

You probably have many other widgets, too, installed by your apps. Waze, Yelp, The New York Times, NPR, Google Maps, Kindle, Evernote, Dropbox, Chrome, Amazon, and many other apps put widgets here for your quick-glancing pleasure.

TIP: Many widgets are expandable. If you see a **Show More** button on a widget, it means that a larger area, showing more information, is available to you. For example, expanding the Favorites widget shows icons for *eight* speed-dial people instead of four; expanding the Notes widget shows the *three* notes you've most recently viewed instead of one; and so on.

Widgets on the Home Screen

You don't have to swipe onto the Today screen to view a widget you need right now. On the recent models, you can hard-press (page 37) an app's *home-screen icon* to view not just its shortcut menu but also its widget, for quick consultation. (This pop-up panel also includes an **Add Widget** button, should you decide to install it on the Widgets *screen*.)

In Case of Emergency

In iOS 11, Apple has turned the iPhone into an ingenious, smart emergency beacon. When you're in trouble—you're being followed, you're being attacked, you've fallen and you can't get up—the phone can automatically dial both 911 *and* send text messages to specified loved ones, letting them know you have an emergency and including your location. (If you move, they get additional texts letting them know where.)

When you need help, trigger the automatic emergency call like this:

- **iPhone SE, 5s, 6, 6s, 7.** Click the side button five times fast.

- **iPhone 8, X.** Hold in the side button and either volume button simultaneously for two seconds.

  (Alternatively, press those buttons for a full second and then drag the **Emergency SOS** slider on the Shut Down screen. But there's an advantage to doing it the other way: You can do it without looking at the phone, or even taking it out of your pocket.)

TIP: In **Settings→Emergency SOS**, you'll find a fascinating option called **Also Works with 5 Clicks**. If you turn it on, then pressing the side button five times rapidly *also* works to trigger the emergency dialing, just as it does on older iPhones. In times of danger, this method may be faster than pressing and waiting.

In all cases, a whooping alarm begins, and a big red 3-second countdown starts. At zero, the phone dials 911. (The countdowns are designed to give you a chance to change your mind.) Then, after a 10-second countdown, it sends texts to your designated contacts, accompanied by a little map. "Emergency SOS," it says. "[Your name] has made an emergency call from this approximate location. You are receiving this message because [your name] has listed you as an emergency contact."

To set this up, open **Settings→Emergency SOS**. Here you can turn off the countdown; you can choose who gets notified (tap **Set Up Emergency**

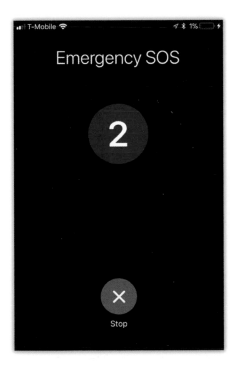
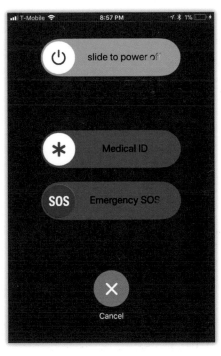

Contacts in Health, and then tap Edit); and you can turn off Auto Call. In that case, there's no countdown or alarm or auto-dialing. You must swipe your finger across an Emergency SOS slider to place the call, and the call goes to the nearest police office line (not 911).

Help from the Shutdown Screen

To turn your phone fully off, you're supposed to hold in the side button for a few seconds (page 15). But if you hold in the side button *and* either of the volume buttons simultaneously, you get new additional sliders:

- **Medical ID.** Swipe to open a screenful of essential medical information about you. And where does the Medical ID screen get this information? You've filled it out in the Health app (page 391).

- **Emergency SOS.** This is the same auto-dialing process described already.

Note that both of these features are available even if the phone is locked. Anyone can hold in those buttons for a couple of seconds and get help on the way.

The "Forcible Unlock" Situation

When the public first heard about Face ID on the iPhone X, there was panic. "Oh, *great*," they said. "So now a mugger can force me to unlock the phone by holding it up to my face!" (There were also variants: "So now a *cop* can force me to unlock the phone by holding it up to my face!")

Apple has you covered. If anyone demands your phone under threat, bring up the shutdown screen described above. What your antagonist probably doesn't realize is that once that screen appears, *Touch ID and Face ID are turned off*. Neither your face nor your fingerprint will unlock the phone at this point—only the passcode will work.

Of course, the mugger or rogue officer could still try to force you to enter your passcode—but now you've got bigger problems.

3

Typing, Editing & Searching

As a pocket computer, the iPhone faces a fundamental limitation: It has no real keyboard or mouse. Which might be considered a drawback on a gadget that's capable of running millions of programs.

Fortunately, where there's a problem, there's software that can fix it. The modern iPhone's virtual keyboard is smart in all kinds of ways—automatically predicting words and correcting typos, for example. And besides: If you don't like the iPhone's onscreen keyboard, you can just choose one designed by a different company.

This chapter covers every aspect of working with text on the iPhone: entering it, dictating it, fixing it, and searching for it.

The Keyboard

It's true, boys and girls: The iPhone has no physical keys. A virtual keyboard, therefore, is the only possible built-in system for typing text. Like it or not, you'll be doing a lot of tapping on glass.

The keyboard appears automatically whenever you tap in a place where typing is possible: in an outgoing email or text message, in the Notes program, in the address bar of the web browser, and so on.

Just tap the key you want. As your finger taps the glass, a "speech balloon" appears above your finger, showing an enlarged version of the key you actually hit (since your finger is now blocking your view of the keyboard).

TIP: If you worry about spies nearby figuring out what you're typing by watching those bubbles pop up over your fingertips, you can turn them off. Open **Settings→General→Keyboard**, and turn off **Character Preview**.

In darker gray, surrounding the letters, you'll find these special keys:

- **Shift (⇧).** When you tap this key, the arrow turns dark to indicate that it's in effect. The next letter you type appears as a capital. Then the ⇧ key returns to normal, meaning that the next letter will be lowercase.

> **TIP:** It used to be that the color of the Shift key was your only clue that you were about to type a capital letter; the actual letters on the onscreen keyboard's keys always appeared AS CAPITALS. But these days, the key letters appear in lowercase until you press Shift. (If you prefer that old system, though, open **Settings→General→Accessibility→Keyboard**. Turn off **Show Lowercase Keys**.

- **Caps Lock (⇪).** The iPhone has a Caps Lock "key," but it's hidden. To engage it, **double-tap** the ⇧ key; it changes to ⇪. You're now in Caps Lock mode, and you'll type in ALL CAPITALS until you tap the ⇪ key again (or the 123 or ☺ keys). If you can't seem to make Caps Lock work, try double-tapping the ⇧ key **fast**. Or see if maybe Caps Lock got turned off in **Settings→General→Keyboard**.

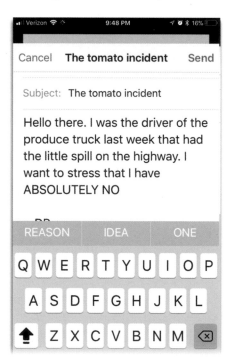

- **Backspace (⌫).** This key actually has three speeds:

  Tap it once to delete the letter just before the blinking insertion point.

Hold it down to "walk" backward, deleting as you go.

If you hold down the key long enough, it starts deleting **words** rather than letters, one whole chunk at a time.

- ∧. Tap this button when you want to type numbers or punctuation. The keyboard changes to offer a palette of numbers and symbols. Tap the same key—which now says ABC—to return to the letters keyboard.

  Once you're on the numbers/symbols pad, a new dark-gray button appears, labeled #+=. Tapping it summons a **third** keyboard layout, containing the less frequently used symbols, like brackets, the # and % symbols, bullets, and math symbols.

- **return.** Tapping this key moves to the next line, just as on a real keyboard. (There's no Tab key or Enter key in iPhone Land.)

Making the Keyboard Work

Some people have no problem tapping those tiny virtual keys; others struggle for days. Either way, here are some tips:

- As you type, use the whole pad of your finger or thumb. Don't try to tap with only a skinny part of your finger to match the skinny keys. You'll be surprised at how fast and accurate this method is. (Tap, don't mash.)

- This may sound like New Age hooey, but **trust** the keyboard. Don't pause to check the result after each letter. Just plow on.

NOTE: Although you don't see it, the sizes of the keys on the iPhone keyboard are changing all the time. That is, the software enlarges the "landing area" of certain keys, based on probability.

For example, suppose you type **tim**. The iPhone knows that no word in the language begins with **timw** or **timr**—and so, invisibly, it enlarges the "landing area" of the E key, which greatly diminishes your chances of making a typo on that last letter.

- Without a mouse, how are you supposed to correct an error you made a few sentences ago? Easy—use the **loupe**.

  Hold your fingertip down anywhere in the text until the magnified circle appears. Without lifting your finger, drag anywhere in the text; the insertion point moves along with it. Release when the cursor line is where you want to delete or add text, just as though you'd clicked there with a mouse.

TIP: If you have an iPhone 6s or later, you may prefer to use the invisible trackpad to correct an error instead; see page 97.

- Don't bother using the Shift key to capitalize a new sentence. The iPhone does that capitalizing automatically. (To turn this feature on or off, use **Settings→General→Keyboard→Auto-Capitalization**.)

- Don't type a period at the end of each sentence, either. Because the period is such a frequently used symbol, there's an awesome short-cut that doesn't require switching to the punctuation keyboard: At the end of a sentence, **tap the space bar twice**. You get a period, a space, **and** a capitalized letter at the beginning of the next word. (This, too, can be turned off—in **Settings→General→Keyboard→"." Shortcut**—although it's hard to imagine why you'd want to.)

- You can save time by leaving out the apostrophe in contractions. Type **im**, **dont**, or **cant**. The iPhone proposes **I'm**, **don't**, or **can't**, so you can just tap the space bar to fix the word and continue.

- Many beginners hold the phone with one hand and tap keys with the index finger of the other. As you become more proficient, though, you may prefer two-thumb typing—or, faster yet, type with your left thumb (so that your left hand can grip the phone) and right index finger (which is more agile).

Autocorrect: Your Typing Assistant from Hell

The iPhone, like all smartphones, offers a feature called autocorrect. Whenever the software thinks you've made a spelling error, it **auto-matically** substitutes the "correct" word or spelling. For example, if you type **imsame**, the iPhone realizes that you meant **insane** and replaces it automatically.

Most of the time, that's helpful; autocorrect even finishes long words for you sometimes. But you have to be vigilant; many times, autocorrect substitutes the **wrong** word! And sometimes you don't notice it, and you wind up texting gibberish to your correspondent. The Internet is filled with hilarious examples of autocorrect gone wrong. (Pay a visit someday to *damnyouautocorrect.com* to read some choice ones.)

So here's the important thing: The iPhone always shows you the replacement it intends to make before making it, either as one of the QuickType suggestions (below, top left) or as a blue-type bubble (lower left). To accept its suggestion, tap the space bar or any punctuation. To **prevent** the replacement, tap the first QuickType word (the one in quotes) or the blue-type bubble.

> **TIP:** If you turn on Speak Auto-text (in **Settings→General→Accessibility→ Speech →Typing Feedback**), the iPhone even speaks the suggested word out loud. That way, you can keep your focus on the keyboard.

And by the way: If you **accidentally** accept an autocorrect suggestion, tap the Backspace key. A word bubble appears, which you can tap to reinstate what you'd originally typed (shown above at right).

> **TIP:** If you think autocorrect is doing you more harm than good, you can turn it off in **Settings→General→Keyboard**. Turn off **Auto-Correction**.

QuickType

What Apple calls its QuickType keyboard can save you a **lot** of time, tapping, and errors.

The idea is simple: As you type a sentence, the software **predicts** which word you might type next—which are the three most likely words, actually—and displays them as three buttons above the keyboard.

If you begin the sentence by typing, "I really," then the three suggestions might be **want**, **don't**, and **like**.

But what if you intended to say, "I really **hope**..."? In that case, type the first letter of "hope." Instantly, the three suggestions change to **"h"**, **hope**, and **hate**. (The first button always shows, in quotes, whatever non-word you've typed so far, just in case that's what you intend. To place it into your text, you can tap that button **or** tap the space bar or some punctuation.)

In other words, QuickType is autocomplete on steroids. (In fact, one of the three suggestions is always the same one you would have seen in the little autocomplete bubble.) Frankly, it's a rush when QuickType correctly proposes finishing a long word for you.

With QuickType, you can produce a sentence like "I'll gladly pay you Tuesday for a hamburger today" with 26 taps on the screen. (If you had to type out the whole thing, you'd have tapped 50 keys.) QuickType also adds spaces for you.

QuickType is smart in several ways:

- QuickType's suggestions are **different** in Messages (where language tends to be casual) than in Mail (where people write more formally).

- Similarly, QuickType modifies its suggestions based on whom you're writing to. It **learns**.

- Sometimes, QuickType offers you several words on a single button, to save you even more time (for example **up to** or **in the**).

- When you're in the Messages app, QuickType suggests an emoji (a tiny cartoon drawing) when you've typed a corresponding word. Page 198 has the details.

- QuickType automatically adds a space after each word you select, so you don't have to mess with the space bar.

- When someone texts you a question that ends with a choice ("Coffee, tea, or me?"), the QuickType buttons cleverly offer those choices on the buttons. Before you've even typed a single letter, the choices say *coffee*, *tea*, and *you*.

- New in iOS 11: QuickType's suggestions may offer movie names, song names, or place names that you've recently viewed in other apps.

- If you forget to capitalize a word, double-tap to select it. Now tap Shift once (To Initial Cap The Word) or twice (FOR ALL CAPS). Lo and behold, the QuickType suggestions are now capitalized renditions of the word, ready to replace it!

- You can hide the QuickType bar if it's getting on your nerves, but it's not as easy as it used to be. Hold down the button next to the 123 key (it usually looks like 😊 or 🌐); from the shortcut menu, tap **Keyboard Settings** (below, left). You wind up in **Settings→General→Keyboard**, where you'll find the **Predictive** on/off switch (right).

 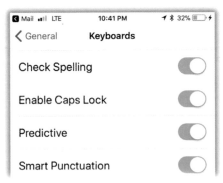

QuickType does mean that you have to split your focus. You have to pay attention to both the keys you're tapping and the ever-changing word choices above the keyboard. With practice, though, you'll find that QuickType offers impressive speed and accuracy. You won't miss the little autocorrect bubbles of old.

The Spelling Dictionary

If you start typing a word the iPhone doesn't recognize, the first of the three suggestion buttons displays your word in quotation marks. If you really do intend to type that nonstandard word, tap its button. You've just allowed the "mistake" to stand—and you've added it to the iPhone's dictionary. The phone assumes that you've just typed some name, bit of slang, or terminology that wasn't in its dictionary originally.

From now on, it will accept that bizarre new word as legitimate—and, in fact, will even *suggest* it the next time you start typing it.

The Spelling Checker

Here's the world's friendliest typo-fixer. Apple calls it a spelling checker, but maybe that's stretching it.

Anytime the iPhone doesn't recognize something you've typed, it draws a dotted red underline beneath it. Tap the word to see a pop-up balloon with one, two, or three alternate spellings. Often, one of them is what you wanted, and you can tap it to fix the mistake. (Equally often, none of them is, and it's time to break out the loupe and the keyboard.)

TO DO TODAY

Buy a tube of caulk at
hadware store

TO DO TODAY

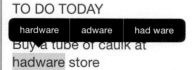
Buy a tube of caulk at
hadware store

Punctuation with One Touch

On the iPhone, the punctuation and alphabet keys appear on two differ-ent keyboard layouts. That's a hassle, because each time you want, say, a comma, it's an awkward, three-step dance: (1) Tap the ∧ key to get the punctuation layout. (2) Tap the comma. (3) Tap the ABC key or the space bar to return to the alphabet layout.

Imagine how excruciating it is to type, for example, "a P.O. box in the U.S.A." That's 34 finger taps and 10 mode changes!

Fortunately, there's a secret way to get a punctuation mark with only a *single* finger gesture. The iPhone doesn't register most key presses until you *lift* your finger. But the Shift and punctuation keys register their taps on the press *down* instead.

So here's what you can do, all in one motion:

1. **Touch the** 123 **key, but don't lift your finger.** The punctuation layout appears.

2. **Slide your finger onto the period or comma key, and release.** The ABC layout returns automatically. You've typed a period or a comma with one finger touch instead of three.

TIP: If you're a two-thumbed typist, you can also hit the 123 key with your left thumb and then tap the punctuation key with your right. It even works on the #+= sub-punctuation layout, although you'll probably visit that screen less often.

In fact, you can type any of the punctuation symbols the same way. This technique makes a *huge* difference in the usability of the keyboard.

TIP: This same trick saves you a finger-press when capitalizing words. You can put your finger down on the ⇧ key and slide directly onto the letter you want to type in its uppercase version. Or, if you're a two-handed typist, you can work the Shift key just like the one on your computer: Hold it down with your left thumb, type a letter with your right, and then release both.

Accented Characters

To produce an accented character (like é, ë, è, ê, and so on), keep your finger pressed on that key for one second. A palette of diacritical marks appears; slide onto the one you want.

Not all keys sprout this pop-up palette. Here's a list of the keys that do:

Key	Alternates
A	à á â ä Æ ã å ā
C	ç ć č
E	è é ê ë ę ė ē
I	ī į í ì ï î
L	ł
N	ń ñ
O	ō ø œ õ ó ò ö ô
S	ß ś š
U	ū ú ù ü û
Y	ÿ
Z	ź ž ż
?	¿
'	' ' '
"	" " " " "
-	—
$	€ £ ¥ ₩
&	§
0 (zero)	°
.	…
%	‰

Typing Shortcuts (Abbreviation Expanders)

Here's a feature that hardly anyone ever talks about—probably because nobody knows it exists. But it can be a huge time- and sanity-saver.

You can program the phone to expand abbreviations that you type. Set up *addr* to type your entire mailing address, or *eml* to type out your email address. Create two-letter abbreviations for big legal or technical words you have to type a lot. Set up *goaway* to type out a polite rejection paragraph for use in email. And so on.

This feature has been in Microsoft Office forever (called AutoCorrect). And it's always been available in add-on apps. But since it's now built right into the operating system, it works anywhere you can type.

You can start building your list of abbreviations in **Settings→General→Keyboard→Text Replacement**. Tap the + button. On the resulting screen, type the expanded text into the **Phrase** box. (It can be very long, but it has to be one continuous blob of text; it can't contain returns.) In the **Shortcut** box, type the abbreviation you want to trigger the phrase.

That's it! Now, whenever you type one of the abbreviations you've set up, the iPhone proposes replacing it with your substituted text.

The One-Handed Keyboard

iOS 11 may go down in history as the first software version that acknowledged morning coffee.

For the first time, you can carry a cup in one hand while typing on your iPhone with the other. That's because there's a new, optional keyboard layout on larger iPhones (but not the iPhone 5s or SE): an extra-skinny one that huddles against one side, within reach of a single thumb.

To make it so, hold down the button next to the 123 key (it usually looks like 😊 or 🌐); from the shortcut menu, choose one of the outer two keyboard icons, as shown here. (They represent the left- and right-huddling keyboard, respectively.)

Swype, SwiftKey, and Other Keyboards

You're not stuck with Apple's onscreen keyboard. You can, if you like, install virtual keyboards from other companies. (Hey—just like on Android phones!)

Many people swear that these rival keyboard systems are superior to the standard iOS keyboard in speed and accuracy. In particular, people like the Swype and SwiftKey keyboards; in these systems, you don't have to **tap** each key to spell out a word. Instead, you rapidly and sloppily drag your finger **across** the glass, hitting the letters you want and lifting your finger at the end of a word. The software figures out which word you were going for.

Sounds bizarre, but it's fast and very satisfying. And pretty—your finger leaves a sort of fire trail as it slides across the glass.

These keyboards generally incorporate their own versions of QuickType— that is, they offer three predictions about the word you're going to type next.

Most don't vary their predictions depending on the person you're writing to or which app you're using, as iOS's predictions do. But they do offer other impressive features; for example, SwiftKey can sync what it's learned to your other gadgets (iOS doesn't do that; it learns, but its education is locked on your iPhone). The Minuum keyboard is weird-looking but very compact, leaving a lot more room for your writing.

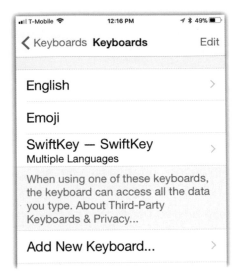

Then there's Fleksy, TouchPal, Kuaiboard, and a raft of others.

Note, however, that none of them offer a 🎤 button. Apple doesn't allow them access to Siri, so you can't use voice dictation when one of these keyboards is on the screen. And, sometimes, you can't use these alternate keyboards for typing into password boxes.

Otherwise, these alternate keyboard systems are fascinating and, often, faster than Apple's. Many are free, so they're well worth exploring.

To install an alternate keyboard, download it from the App Store (page 343).

Then go to **Settings→General→Keyboard→Keyboards** (above, left). When you tap **Add New Keyboard**, you'll see your newly down-loaded keyboard's name. Turn it on by tapping it and then turning on **Full Access**.

Now, when you arrive at any writing area in any app, you'll discover that a new icon has appeared on the keyboard: a tiny globe (🌐) next to the space bar. Tap it. The keyboard changes to the new one you installed. (Each tap on the 🌐 button summons the next keyboard you've installed—or you can hold your finger down on it for a pop-up list.)

NOTE: Until iOS 11 came along, turning the iPhone 90 degrees (to landscape orientation) gave you a wider, expanded keyboard with some extra keys on each side, like Copy, Paste, punctuation, and cursor keys. It's not your imagination: For some reason known only to Apple, the keyboard no longer changes when you rotate the phone. Those useful extra keys are gone, replaced by empty gray space.

International Typing

Because the iPhone is sold around the world, it has to be equipped for non-English languages—and even non-Roman alphabets. Fortunately, it's ready.

To prepare the iPhone for language switching, go to **Settings→General→Language & Region**. Tap **iPhone Language** to set the iPhone's primary language (for menus, button labels, and so on).

To make other *keyboards* available, go to **Settings→General→Keyboard→Keyboards**, tap **Add New Keyboard**, and then turn on the keyboard layouts you'll want available: Russian, Italian, whatever.

If you choose Japanese or Chinese, you're offered the chance to specify which *kind* of character input you want. For Japanese, you can choose a QWERTY layout (Romaji) or a Kana keypad. For Simplified or Traditional Chinese, your choices include the Pinyin input method (which uses a QWERTY layout) or handwriting recognition, where you draw your symbols onto the screen with your fingertip; a palette of potential interpretations appears to the right. (That's handy, since there are thousands of

characters in Chinese, and you'd need a 65-inch iPhone to fit the keyboard on it.) Or hey—it's a free tic-tac-toe game!

As described in the previous section, a new key now appears on the keyboard: 🌐 next to the space bar. (It replaces the 😊 emoji key, if you had it.) Each time you tap it, you rotate to the next keyboard you requested earlier. The new language's name appears briefly on the space bar to identify it.

Thanks to that 🌐 button, you can freely mix languages and alphabets within the same document without having to duck back to some control panel to make the change. And thanks to the iPhone's virtual keyboard, the actual letters on the "keys" change in real time.

The 🌐 button works in three ways:

- Tap it once to restore the most recent keyboard. Great if you're frequently flipping back and forth between two languages.

- Tap it rapidly to cycle among all the keyboards you've selected. (The name of the language appears briefly on the space bar to help you out.)

- If you, some United Nations translator, like to write in a lot of different languages, you don't have to tap that 🌐 key over and over again to cycle through the keyboard layouts. Instead, hold your finger down on the 🌐 key. You get a convenient pop-up menu of the languages you've turned on, so you can jump directly to the one you want.

The Emoji Keyboard

Even if you speak only one language, don't miss the emoji keyboard. It gives you a palette of smileys and fun symbols, also known as emoticons, to use in your correspondence.

When you tap the ☺ button, you're offered hundreds and hundreds of little symbols. They're spread across eight categories (plus a Frequently Used category), each represented by a small icon below the keyboard.

Emoji are even smarter in the Messages app; see page 198.

TIP: To return to a category's first page, you don't have to swipe; just tap the category's icon.

The bottom line is clear: Smileys are only the beginning.

NOTE: These symbols show up identically on Apple machinery (phones, tablets, Macs) but may look slightly different on other kinds of phones.

Connecting a Real Keyboard

This iPhone feature barely merits an asterisk in Apple's marketing materials. But if you're any kind of wandering journalist, blogger, or writer, you might flip your lid over this: You can type on a real, full-sized, physical keyboard, and watch the text magically appear on your iPhone's screen—wirelessly.

That's because you can use a Bluetooth keyboard (the Apple Wireless Keyboard, for example) to type into your iPhone.

To set this up, from the Home screen, tap **Settings→Bluetooth**. Turn Bluetooth on, if it's not already.

Now turn on the wireless keyboard. After a moment, its name shows up on the iPhone screen in the Devices list; tap it. You'll know the pairing was successful, because when you tap in a spot where the onscreen keyboard would usually appear—well, it doesn't.

Typing is a lot easier and faster with a real keyboard. As a bonus, the Apple keyboard's brightness, volume, and playback controls actually work to control the iPhone's brightness, volume, and playback.

TIP: The Apple keyboard's ⏏ key even works: It makes the iPhone's onscreen keyboard appear or disappear. And to switch languages, press ⌘-space bar on the wireless keyboard. You'll see the list of languages. Tap the space bar again to choose a different language.

When you're finished using the keyboard, turn it off. The iPhone goes back to normal.

3D Touch: The Secret Trackpad

You may remember hearing about the 3D Touch screen on your iPhone (or reading about it, on page 37). But you can also use pressure on the screen to create a trackpad for editing text!

Whenever text is on the screen and the keyboard is open, press firmly anywhere on the keyboard. All the keys go blank, as shown below.

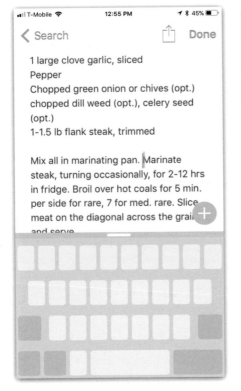 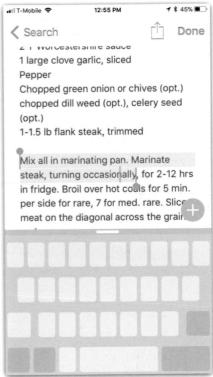

You can ease up on the pressure, but **don't lift your finger** from the glass. You can now move the insertion-point cursor through the text just by dragging your finger across the keys. If it hits the edge of the window, it scrolls automatically.

Still keep your finger down. At this point, **hard** presses also let you select (highlight) text:

- **Hard-press twice** to select an entire sentence.
- **Hard-press three times** to select an entire paragraph.

Or use this trick: Move the insertion point to a word; if you now press hard, you highlight that word.

At this point, you can expand the selection by doing any of these things:

- **Drag up or down.** (Again, you don't have to keep pressing hard, but you do have to keep your finger on the glass.)

- **Hard-press twice** to extend the selection to the entire sentence.

- **Hard-press three times** to extend the selection to the entire paragraph.

Once you've selected text in this way, the usual command bar (Cut, Copy, Paste, and so on) appears, for your text-manipulation pleasure.

Little by little, the iPhone is revealing its secret ambition to be a laptop.

Dictation

The iPhone's speech-recognition feature, sometimes called Siri (even though Siri is also the voice *command* feature), lets you enter text anywhere, into any program, just by *speaking*. (Behind the scenes, it's using the same Nuance recognition technology that powers the Dragon line of dictation programs.)

It's extremely fast and, usually, remarkably accurate. Suddenly you don't have to fuss with the tiny keyboard. The experience of "typing" is no longer claustrophobic. You can blather away into an email, fire off a text message, or draft a memo without ever looking at the screen.

Now, before you get all excited, here are the necessary footnotes:

- Voice typing works best if there's not a lot of background noise.

- Voice typing isn't always practical, since everybody around you can hear what you're saying.

- Voice typing isn't always accurate. Often you'll have to correct an error or two.

All right—expectations set? Then here's how to type by speaking.

First, fire up someplace where you can call up the keyboard: Messages, Notes, Mail, Safari, whatever. Tap, if necessary, so that the onscreen keyboard appears.

Tap the 🎙 next to the space bar.

When you hear the xylophone note, say what you have to say (below, left). If there's background noise, hold the phone up to your head; if it's relatively quiet, a couple of feet away is fine. You don't have to speak slowly, loudly, or weirdly; speak normally.

As you speak, the words fly onto the screen.

 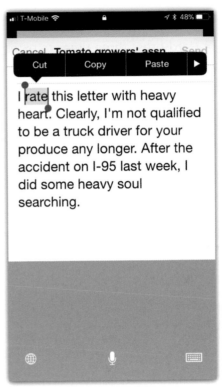

You have to speak your own punctuation, like this: "Dear Dad (colon): Send money (dash)—as much as you can (comma), please (period)." The table at the end of this section describes all the different punctuation symbols you can dictate.

After you finish speaking, tap anywhere in the big gray sound waves area. Another xylophone note plays—higher, this time—and you may see some of the words *change* right before your eyes, as though Siri is changing her mind. In fact, she is; she's using the context of *all* the words you said to revise what she *originally* thought you said, as you said it. See?

In iOS 11, Apple believes that you'll love dictating so much that you won't often even need the keyboard. So tapping in the gray area to stop dictating no longer brings up the keyboard so you can make corrections.

Instead, after you've stopped transcribing with a tap, it takes another tap—on the little ⌨ icon—to bring back the keyboard. Now you can tap with your finger in the text to edit any mistakes, exactly as you would fix an error in something you typed. (Make the effort; you're simultaneously teaching your iPhone to do better the next time.)

TIP: Here's a thought: If you notice an error while you're dictating, tap the ⌨ button to stop the dictation (instead of tapping in the gray area). That way, you stop dictating *and* summon the keyboard, saving yourself a tap.

Or, if the whole thing is a mess, you can **shake** your iPhone, the universal gesture for Undo (as long as **Shake to Undo** is turned on in **Settings→General→Accessibility**).

NOTE: Often, the iPhone knows perfectly well when it might have gotten a word wrong—it draws a dashed underline beneath words or phrases it's insecure about. You can tap that word or phrase to see the iPhone's alternative interpretation, which is often correct.

Usually, you'll find the accuracy pretty darned good, considering you didn't have to train the software to recognize your voice, and considering that your computer is a **cellphone**, for crying out loud. You'll also find that the accuracy is better when you dictate complete sentences, and that long words fare better than short ones.

Punctuation

Here's a handy table that shows what punctuation you can say and how to say it.

NOTE: If you've ever used Dragon NaturallySpeaking (for Windows) or Dragon Dictation (for the Mac), then you already know these commands; they're the standard Nuance dictation-software shortcuts, because that's what the iPhone uses behind the scenes.

Say this:	To get this:	For example, saying this:	Types this:
"period" or "full stop"	. [space and capital letter follow]	"Best (period) date (period) ever (period)"	Best. Date. Ever.
"dot" or "point"	. [no space follows]	"My email is frank (dot) smith (at sign) gmail (dot) com"	My email is frank.smith@ gmail.com
"comma," "semicolon," "colon"	, ; :	"Mom (comma) hear me (colon) I'm dizzy (semi-colon) tired"	Mom, hear me: I'm dizzy; tired
"question mark," "exclamation point"	? ! [space and capital letter afterward]	"Ellen (question mark) Hi (exclamation point)"	Ellen? Hi!
"inverted question mark," "inverted exclamation point"	¿ ¡	"(inverted question mark) Que paso (question mark)"	¿Que paso?
"ellipsis" or "dot dot dot"	…	"Just one (ellipsis) more (ellipsis) step (ellipsis)"	Just one… more…step…
"space bar"	[a space, especially when a hyphen would normally appear]	"He rode the merry (space bar) go (space bar) round"	He rode the merry go round
"open paren" then "close paren" (or "open bracket/ close bracket," or "open brace/ close brace")	( ) or [ ] or { }	"Then she (open paren) the doctor (close paren) gasped"	Then she (the doctor) gasped
"new line"	[a press of the Return key]	"milk (new line) bread (new line) quinoa"	Milk Bread Quinoa

Say this:	To get this:	For example, saying this:	Types this:
"new paragraph"	[two presses of the Return key]	"autumn leaves (new paragraph) softly falling"	autumn leaves softly falling
"quote," then "unquote"	" "	Her perfume screamed (quote) available (unquote)	Her perfume screamed "available"
"numeral"	[writes the following number as a digit instead of spelling it out]	"Next week she turns (numeral) eight"	Next week she turns 8
"asterisk," "plus sign," "minus sign," "equals sign"	*, +, −, =	"eight (asterisk) two (plus sign) one (minus sign) three (equals sign) fourteen"	8*2+1−3=14
"ampersand," "dash"	&, —	"Logan (ampersand) Dexter (dash) the best (exclamation point)"	Logan & Dexter—the best!
"hyphen"	- [without spaces]	"Don't give me that holier (hyphen) than (hyphen) thou attitude"	Don't give me that holier-than-thou attitude
"backquote"	'	"Back in (backquote) (numeral) fifty-two"	back in '52
"smiley," "frowny," "winky" (or "smiley face," "frowny face," "winky face")	:-) :-(;-)	"I think you know where I'm going with this (winky face)"	I think you know where I'm going with this ;-)

You can also say "percent sign" (%), "at sign" (@), "dollar sign" ($), "cent sign" (¢), "euro sign" (€), "yen sign" (¥), "pounds sterling sign" (£), "section sign" (§), "copyright sign" (©), "registered sign" (®), "trademark sign" (™), "greater-than sign" or "less-than sign" (> or <), "degree sign" (°), "caret" (^), "tilde" (~), "vertical bar" (|), and "pound sign" (#).

The software automatically capitalizes the first new word after a period, question mark, or exclamation point. But you can also force it to capitalize words you're dictating by saying "cap" right before the word, like this: "Dear (cap) Mom (comma), I've run away to join (cap) The (cap) Circus (comma), a nonprofit cooperative for runaway jugglers."

Here's another table—this one shows the other commands for capitalization, plus spacing and spelling commands.

TIP: Speak each of the on/off commands as a separate utterance, with a small pause before and after.

Say this:	To get this:	For example, saying this:	Types this:
"cap" or "capital"	Capitalize the next word	"Give me the (cap) works"	Give me the Works
"caps on," then "caps off"	Capitalize the first letter of every word	"Next week, (caps on) the new england chicken cooperative (caps off) will hire me"	Next week, The New England Chicken Cooperative will hire me
"all caps on," then "all caps off"	Capitalize everything	"So (all caps on) please please (all caps off) don't tell anyone"	So PLEASE PLEASE don't tell anyone
"all caps"	Type just the next word in all caps	"We (all caps) really don't belong here"	We REALLY don't belong here
"no caps"	Type the next word in lowercase	"See you in (no caps) Texas"	See you in texas
"no caps on," then "no caps off"	Prevents any capital letters	"I'll ask (no caps on) Santa Claus (no caps off)"	I'll ask santa claus

Say this:	To get this:	For example, saying this:	Types this:
"no space"	Runs the two words together	"Try our new mega (no space) berry flavor"	Try our new megaberry flavor
"no space on," then "no space off"	Eliminates all spaces	"(No space on) I can't believe you ate all that (no space off) (comma) she said excitedly"	Ican'tbelieveyou ateallthat, she said excitedly
[alphabet letters]	Types the letters out (usually not very accurately)	"The stock symbol is A P P L"	The stock symbol is APPL

You don't always have to dictate these formatting commands, by the way. The iPhone automatically inserts hyphens into phone numbers (you say, "2125561000," and get "212-556-1000"); formats two-line street addresses without your having to say, "New line" before the city); handles prices automatically ("6 dollars and 32 cents" becomes "$6.32").

It formats dates and web addresses well, too; you can even use the nerdy shortcut "dub-dub-dub" when you want the "www" part of a web address.

The phone recognizes email addresses, too, as long as you remember to say "at sign" at the right spot. You'd say, "harold (underscore) beanfield (at sign) gmail (dot) com" to get harold_beanfield@gmail.com.

TIP: You can combine these formatting commands. Many iPhone owners have wondered: "How do I voice-type the *word* "comma," since saying "comma" types out only the symbol?"

The solution: Say, "No space on, no caps on, C, O, M, M, A, no space off, no caps off." That gives you the *word* "comma."

Then again, it might just be easier to type that one with your finger.

Cut, Copy, Paste

Copy and Paste do just what you'd expect. They let you grab some text off a web page and paste it into an email message, copy directions from email into Notes, paste a phone number from your address book into a text message, and so on.

So how do you select text and use Cut, Copy, and Paste on a machine with no mouse or menus? As on the Mac or PC, it takes three steps.

Step 1: Select the Text

Start by highlighting the text you want to cut or copy.

- **To select some.** Double-tap the first word (or last word) that you want in the selection. That word is now highlighted, with blue dots at diagonal corners. Drag these handles to expand the selection. The magnifying loupe helps you release the dot at just the right spot.

TIP: On a web page, you can't very well double-tap to select a word, because double-tapping means "zoom in." Instead, **hold your finger down** on a word to produce the blue handles; the loupe helps you. (If you highlight the wrong word, keep your finger down and slide to the correct one; the highlighting goes with you.)

However, if you're zoomed out to see the whole page, holding down your finger highlights the **entire block** of text (a paragraph or even a whole article) instead of one word. Now you can expand the selection to include a photo, if you like; that way, you can copy and paste the whole enchilada into an outgoing email message.

Double-tap...

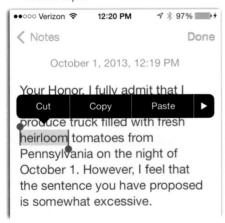 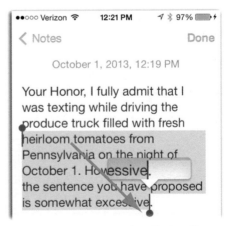

...drag the handle.

- **To select all.** Suppose you intend to cut or copy *everything* in the text box or message. Tap anywhere in the text to place the insertion point. Then tap the insertion point itself to summon the selection buttons—one of which is **Select All**.

TIP: Selecting text is much easier on an iPhone 6s or later, because you have a built-in trackpad; see page 97.

Step 2: Cut or Copy

At this point, you've highlighted the material you want, and the Cut and Copy buttons are staring you in the face. They're word buttons above your text.

Tap **Cut** (to remove the selected text) or **Copy** (to leave it but place a duplicate on your invisible Clipboard). If you want to get rid of the text *without* copying it to the Clipboard—because you want to preserve something else you copied there, for example—just tap the key.

TIP: And what if you want to copy text without the formatting (bold, italics, underlining) that it might have? After selecting the text, tap **Share** and then tap **Copy** in the Share sheet.

Step 3: Paste

Finally, switch to a different spot in the text, even if it's in a different window (for example, a new email message) or a different app (for example, Calendar or Notes). Tap in any spot where you're allowed to type. Tap the **Paste** button to paste what you cut or copied. Ta-da!

(Possible Step 4: Undo)

Everyone makes mistakes, right? Fortunately, there's a secret Undo command, which can come in handy when you cut, copy, or paste something by mistake.

The trick is to *shake* the iPhone. It then offers you an Undo button, which you can tap to confirm the backtracking. One finger touch instead

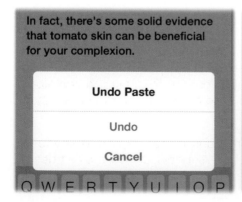

of three. (This feature has to be turned on in **Settings→General→ Accessibility**.)

In fact, you can even undo the Undo. Just shake the phone again; now the screen offers you a **Redo** button. Fun! (Except when you shake the phone by accident and get the **Nothing to Undo** message. But still.)

The "Look Up" Dictionary

On page 87, you can read about the spelling dictionary that's built into iOS—but that's just a dumb list of words. Your iPhone also has a *real* dictionary, one that shows you definitions.

In many apps, you can look up any word that appears on the screen. Double-tap it to get the editing bar shown below at left; then tap **Look Up**. (You may have to tap ▶ to bring that button into view.)

> **TIP:** You can also double-tap the blinking insertion point that's just before a word. On the editing bar, tap ▼ to see the **Look Up** button.

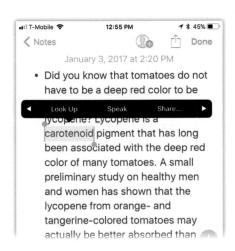 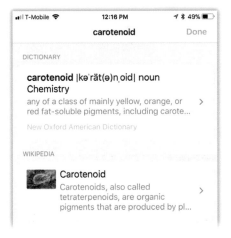

(If you discover that there are "No definitions found," then tap **Manage** at the bottom of this screen for a list of dictionaries that you can download: English, French, Simplified Chinese, and so on. Tap ⬇ to download the ones you think you'll use.)

But there's more to Look Up than definitions. Depending on what you're looking up, you may also see listings for Wikipedia entries, movie titles, sports scores, App Store apps, Twitter tweets, songs from Apple Music, web videos, and the web at large. It's all meant to put the power of iOS search—including the entire Internet—behind any word you see on any page of any app.

> **TIP:** If you'd prefer just to look up definitions, open **Settings→Siri & Search**, and turn off **Suggestions in Look Up**. Now, tapping **Look Up** means only "check the dictionary." (Then again, it still offers a **Search Web** button in case you change your mind).

Speak!

The iPhone can read to you, too. Visit **Settings→General→Accessibility→ Speech** and turn on **Speak Selection** and/or **Speak Screen**. Choose a language (or accent), a voice, and a speaking rate. (The more realistic voices, like Ava and her brother Alex, require you to download audio files from Apple. Just tap the ⬇ to begin the download.)

It's fun to turn on **Highlight Content**, too. (Each word will light up in color as the phone speaks it. Great for kids learning to read!)

From now on, among the other buttons that pop up when you select text, a **Speak** button appears. Or, if you swipe down the screen with two fingers (and you've turned on **Speak Screen**), your iPhone reads the entire screen.

You can use these features whenever you want to double-check the pronunciation of a word, whenever you want to have a web article or email read to you while you're getting dressed for the day, or whenever you lose your voice and just want to communicate with the rest of the world.

> **NOTE:** Once you tap **Speak**, the button changes to say **Pause**. You're in charge.

Searching Your iPhone

The iPhone's global search feature, formerly called Spotlight, can find information on your phone within any app—but it's also something like a typed version of Siri, in that it can call up information about movies, restaurants, news, and so on.

How to Use Search

Apple has rejiggered the search bar in iOS 11; you can no longer access it from within any app. You must start at the Home screen. From there, you have two options:

- **Swipe downward on the middle of the screen.** Don't swipe down from the top of the screen, which brings up the pull-down Lock screen (page 69). Instead, drag down on the middle of a Home screen.

- **Swipe to the right** from the first Home screen. Lurking to its left is the Today screen (page 75)—with, once again, a search box at the top.

When you tap into the search box, the keyboard opens automatically. Begin typing to identify what you want to find and open. For example, if you were trying to find a file called *Pokémon Fantasy League*, typing just *pok* or *leag* would probably suffice. (Spotlight doesn't find text in the **middles** of words; it searches from the beginnings of words.)

In iOS 11, there are two stages of results: what you see **before** you tap the **Search** button on the keyboard, and what you see **after**.

- **Before you tap Search** (while you're typing), you get, just below the typing box, a list of autocomplete suggestions. It's composed of data bits that are actually on your phone: app names, people's names, calendar appointment names, and so on. For example, if you've typed **app** so far, the suggestions may include **apple**, **appearance schedule**, and so on. The idea is to save you some typing.

 TIP: If you tap an app's name in this list, you get to see what **folder** contains that app. (We're talking about the text list just under the search box—not the rows of app names that display their icons.)

Below that, iOS makes additional guesses at what you're seeking, grouped by category: Applications, Voice Memos, Mail, Contacts, Notes, News, Safari, Reminders, Dictionary, and so on (next page, left). In iOS 11, in fact, these suggestions may even come from within non-Apple apps.

All of this is part of what Apple calls Siri Suggestions. You can turn them off, either globally or one app at a time; see page 111.

At the very bottom, you get buttons for **Search Web**, **Search App Store**, and **Search Maps**, for the sake of completeness.

TIP: If you drag your finger to scroll the list, the keyboard helpfully vanishes so you can see more results.

- **After you tap Search,** you get a list of results that contain *exactly* what you typed as your search term (above, right). If you've typed *app* so far, the suggestions may include **App Store**, **Train App**, and so on. (If the search can't find many exact matches, it may show you some autocompleted suggestions as well, of the *apple*, *appearance schedule* sort.)

Either way, you wind up with a list of tappable search results, each showing a few lines of a preview, and all organized by category or app. This list may reveal matching terms from these categories:

- **Apple's apps.** Music, Podcasts, Videos, Audiobooks (song, performer, and album names, plus the names of podcasts, videos, and audiobooks); Notes, Messages, Reminders, Voice Memos (actual text of your notes, texts, and to-do items; names and descriptions of voice memos); calendar events (including meeting invitees and locations); Mail (To, From, and Subject fields of all accounts; body text in some accounts).

- **Other companies' apps.** Search can also find recent destinations you've used in Google Maps, Uber, or Lyft; photo album names in Flickr; and so on. (Not all apps are searchable—only those updated since iOS 11 came along.)

- **Applications.** For frequent downloaders, this may be the juiciest function. If you have dozens of apps installed, this is a much more efficient way to find one than trying to page through all the Home screens, eyeballing the icons as you go. The search results even identify which *folder* an app is in.

- **Siri Suggestions.** The Search feature can find movies, music, apps, and other stuff from the web. It works beautifully. The hard part is just remembering that it's available.

  You can get results from Wikipedia (when you search for, say, "rhubarb" or "Thomas Edison"); news (search for "SF Giants" or "Middle East negotiations"); restaurants, shops, and businesses ("Olive Garden" or "Apple Store"); the App Store ("Instagram" or "Angry Birds"); the iTunes Store ("Gravity" or "Beatles"); and the iBooks Store ("Grisham" or "Little Women").

  The results list identifies which category each hit comes from. Tapping a result does what you'd expect: for a web article, opens the article; for a business, opens its Maps page so you can call it or get instant directions; for something from an Apple store, opens the appropriate store.

  Really, don't miss this. When you hear about a cool app, don't open the App Store to look for it. When you want to know a sports score, don't start with Safari. When you need the phone number of a restaurant, don't call 411. Instead, use Spotlight for all those things.

- **Google Web Results.** You can tap **Search Web** at the bottom of the results list to hand off to Safari for a search. Handy to have it built right into the Search screen.

> **TIP:** Many apps, like Contacts, Mail, Calendar, Music, and Notes, have their *own* search boxes (usually hidden until you scroll to the top of their lists). Those individual search functions are great when you're already *in* the program where you want to search. The Spotlight difference is that it searches all these apps at once.

If you see the name and icon of whatever you were hoping to dig up, tap to open it. The corresponding app opens automatically.

Controlling What Shows Up

Fortunately, Apple has seen fit to let you limit which apps' data shows up in the Search results. If you don't ever think you'll search your email from this screen (and maybe, for privacy reasons, you'd rather not see email snippets show up in the results), you can turn it off, thus hiding it from Spotlight's tentacles.

In **Settings→Siri & Search**, you'll find a master list of apps that Spotlight can "see into." Tap one and turn off its switch to exclude it from search results. (You can still find that app's icon by typing its name—you just won't see any information from *inside* that app.)

4

Phone Calls & FaceTime

With each successive iPhone model, Apple improves the iPhone's antennas, circuitry, speakers, microphone, and software. And features like Siri, auto-reply, and Do Not Disturb have turned Apple's phone from an also-ran into one of the most useful gadgets ever to hop onto a cellular network.

Dialing from the Phone App

Suppose you're in luck. Suppose the bars at the top of the iPhone's screen tell you that you've got cellular reception. You're ready to start a conversation. To make a phone call, open the Phone app like this:

1. **Go Home, if you're not already there.** Press the home button (or, on the iPhone X, swipe up from the bottom).

2. **Tap the Phone icon.** It's usually at the bottom of the Home screen. (The tiny circled number in the corner of the Phone icon tells you how many missed calls and voicemail messages you have.)

TIP: Using Siri is often faster. You get good results saying things like, "Call Casey Robin's cell" or "Dial 866-2331."

Now you've arrived in the Phone app. A new row of icons appears at the bottom, representing your voicemail (page 130) and the four ways of dialing from here:

- **Favorites.** Here's the iPhone's version of speed dial: It lists up to 50 people you think you call most frequently. Tap a name to make the call. (Details on building and editing this list begin on page 114.)

- **Recents.** Every call you've recently made, answered, missed, or even just dialed appears in this list. Missed callers' names appear in red lettering, which makes it easy to spot them—and to call them back.

Tap a name or a number to dial. Or tap the ⓘ button to view the details of a call—when, where, how long—and, if you like, to add this number to your Contacts list.

- **Contacts.** This program also has an icon of its own on the Home screen; you don't have to drill down to it through the Phone button. It's your phone book; tap somebody's name or number to dial it.

- **Keypad.** This dialing pad's big, fat buttons are easy to hit even with big, fat fingers. You can punch in any number and then tap to place the call.

Once you've dialed, no matter which method you used, either hold the iPhone up to your head, put in the earbuds, turn on the speakerphone, or put on your Bluetooth earpiece—and start talking!

This, however, is only the Quick Start Guide. Here's a more detailed look at each of the Phone-app modules.

The Favorites List

You may not wind up dialing much from Contacts. That's the master list, all right, but it's too unwieldy when you just want to call your spouse, your boss, or your lawyer. Dialing by voice (Chapter 5) is almost always faster. But when silence is golden, at the very least use the Favorites list—a short, easy-to-scan list of the people you call most often (facing page, left).

Actually, *calling* is only the beginning. A favorite can be any kind of "address": for triggering an email, a text message, a video call, or even an Internet voice call in an app like WhatsApp, Skype, or Cisco Spark. In other words, you can set things up so that one tap on a favorite opens an outgoing text to your beloved, and a different tap triggers a Skype call to your boss.

TIP: Once you've set up these favorites, you can add them to the Today screen (page 75), so that placing one of these calls or text communications is only a swipe and a tap away.

You can add names to this list in any of three ways:

- **From the Favorites list itself.** Tap + to view your Contacts list. Tap the person you want. If there's more than one phone number or email address on the info screen, then tap the one you want to add to Favorites.

TIP: Each favorite doesn't represent a *person*; it represents a *number or address*. So if your best friend Chris has both a home number and a cell number, then add two items to the Favorites list. Gray lettering in the list lets you know whether each number or address is mobile, home, Skype, Messages, FaceTime, or whatever.

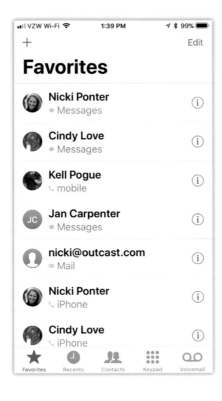
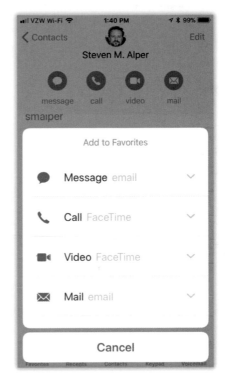

- **From the Contacts list.** Tap a name to open the info screen, where you'll find a button called **Add to Favorites**. It opens the Add to Favorites panel shown above at right. For each of its four communication methods—Message, Call, Video, Mail—you get a pop-up menu that lists your available apps for performing that sort of human contact.

  Tap the one you want to add to Favorites.

- **From the Recents list.** Tap ⓘ next to any name or number in the Recents list. If it's somebody who's already in your Contacts list, then you arrive at the Call Details screen, where one tap on **Add to Favorites** does what it says.

  If it's somebody who's not in Contacts yet, then you'll have to *put* her there first. Tap **Create New Contact**, and then proceed as described on page 121. After you hit **Save**, you return to the Call Details screen so you can tap **Add to Favorites**.

TIP: To help you remember that a certain phone number or email address is already in your Favorites list, a gray star appears next to it in certain spots, like the Call Details screen and the Contact Info screen.

The Favorites list holds 50 numbers. Once you've added 50, the **Add to Favorites** and + buttons disappear.

NOTE: The face of each favorite peeks out of a round frame next to the name, and if your Contact card for that person doesn't have a photo, the circle shows the person's initials instead.

Reordering Favorites

Tapping that **Edit** button at the top of the Favorites list offers another handy feature, too: It lets you drag names up and down, so the most important people appear at the top of the list. Just use the grip strip (≡) as a handle to move entire names up or down the list.

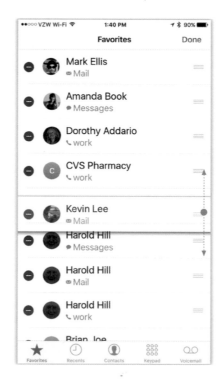

Deleting from Favorites

To delete somebody from your Favorites—the morning after a nasty political argument, for example—use the iPhone's standard swipe-to-delete shortcut: Swipe leftward across the undesired name. Tap the **Delete** button that appears.

(If you're paid by the hour, you can use the slow method, too. Tap **Edit**. Now tap the ⊖ button next to the unwanted entry and tap **Delete** to confirm.)

The Recents List

Like any self-respecting cellphone, the iPhone maintains a list of everybody you've called or who's called you recently. The idea, of course, is to provide you with a quick way to call someone you've been talking to lately.

To see the list, tap **Recents** at the bottom of the Phone app. You see a list of the last 75 calls that you've received or placed, along with each person's name or number (depending on whether that name is in Contacts or not), city of the caller's home area code (for callers not in your Contacts), time or date of the call, and what kind of call it was—mobile, home, work, FaceTime, FaceTime Audio, Skype, or whatever.

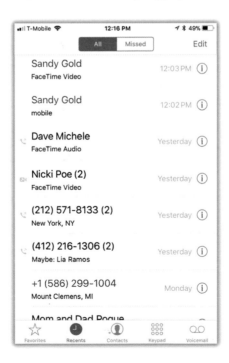

Here's what you need to know about the Recents list:

- Calls that you missed (or sent to voicemail) appear in red type. If you tap **Missed** at the top of the screen, you see *only* your missed calls. The color-coding and separate listings are designed to make it easy for you to return calls you missed, or to try again to reach someone who didn't answer when you called.

- A tiny ↪ icon lets you know which calls you *made* (to differentiate them from calls you *received*).

- To call someone back—regardless of whether you answered or dialed the call—tap that name or number in the list.

- Tap ⓘ next to any call to open the info screen. At the top of the screen, you can see whether this was an outgoing call, an incoming call, a missed call, or a canceled call (in which you chickened out and hung up before your callee answered).

What else you see here depends on whether the other person is in your Contacts list.

If so, the info screen displays the person's whole information card (below, left). A little table displays all the incoming and outgoing calls to or from this person that day. A small gray star denotes a phone number that's also in your Favorites list, and a Recent label indicates a recent call from that number.

If the call *isn't* from someone in your Contacts, then you get to see a handy notation at the top of the info screen: the city and state where the calling phone is registered (below, right).

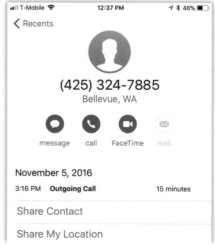

If someone who isn't in Contacts has called you, iOS takes a guess at that person's name—by looking for a matching phone number in the signature portion of your email! For example, if Frank Smythe has called you from 213-292-3344, and there's also an email from him with his phone number as part of his signature, then the Recents list will say: *Maybe: Frank Smythe*. Clever!

- To save you scrolling, the Recents list thoughtfully combines consecutive calls to or from the same person. If some obsessed ex-lover has been calling you every 10 minutes for four hours, you'll see "Chris Meyerson (24)" in the Recents list. (Tap ⓘ to see the exact times of the calls.)

- You can erase one call from this list exactly the same way you'd delete a favorite: Swipe leftward across the undesired name. Tap the **Delete** button that appears. (Once again, there's also a long way: Tap **Edit**, tap ⊖ next to the unwanted entry, and then tap **Delete**.)

  You can also erase the *entire* list, thus preventing a coworker or significant other from discovering your illicit activities: Tap **Edit**, and then tap **Clear** at the top of the screen. You're asked to confirm your decision.

Contacts

The Phone app may offer four ways to dial—Favorites, Recents, Contacts, and Keypad—but the Contacts list is the source from which all other lists spring. That's probably why it's listed three times: once with its own icon on the Home screen, again at the bottom of the Phone app, and also in the FaceTime app.

Contacts is your address book—your master phone book.

Your iPhone's own phone number appears at the top of the Contacts list. That's a much better place for it than deep at the end of a menu labyrinth, where it is on most phones.

If your social circle is longer than one screenful, you can navigate this list in any of three ways:

- **First,** you can savor the distinct pleasure of flicking through it.

- **Second,** if you're in a hurry to get to the T's, use the A-to-Z index down the right edge of the screen. Just tap the first letter of the last name you're looking for. Or slide your finger up or down the index. The list scrolls with it.

- **Third,** you can use the search box at the very top of the list, above the A's.

  Tap to make the keyboard appear. As you type, Contacts pares down the list, hiding everyone whose first, last, or company name doesn't match what you've typed so far. It's a really fast way to pluck one name out of a haystack.

  (You can clear the search box by tapping the ⊗ at its right end or restore the full list by tapping **Cancel**.)

In any case, when you see the name you want, tap it to open its information card. Tap the number you want to dial.

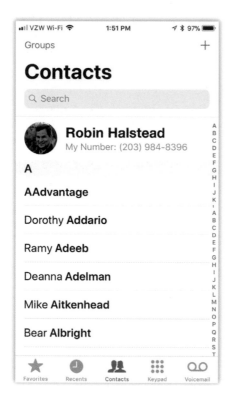 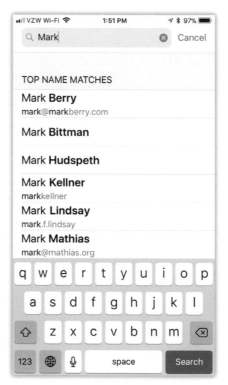

Groups

Many computer address book programs, including the Mac's Contacts app, let you place your contacts into *groups*—subsets like Book Club or Fantasy League Guys. You can't create or delete groups on the iPhone without a special app, but at least the groups from your Mac, PC, Exchange server, or iCloud account get synced over to it. To see them, and to switch them all on or off at once, tap **Groups** at the top of the Contacts list.

Here's where groups come into play:

- If you can't seem to find someone in the list, you may be looking in the wrong list. Tap **Groups** at the top-left corner to return to the list of accounts. Tap **All Contacts** to view a single, unified list of everyone your phone knows about.

- If you've allowed your iPhone to display your contacts from Facebook or Twitter, then each of those lists is a group, too. (If your Contacts list seems hideously bloated with hundreds of people you never actually call, it's probably your Facebook list. Pop into Groups and touch **All Facebook**, removing the checkmark, to hide them all at once.)

- If you do use the Groups feature, remember to tap the group name you want *before* you create a new contact. That's how you put someone into an existing group. (If not, tap **All Contacts** instead.)

Adding to the Contacts List

Every cellphone has a Contacts list, of course, but the beauty of the iPhone is that you don't have to type in the phone numbers one at a time. Instead, the iPhone sucks in the entire phone book from your Mac or PC, iCloud, and/or an Exchange server at work.

It's infinitely easier to edit your address book on the computer, where you have an actual keyboard and mouse. The iPhone also makes it easy to add someone's contact information when she calls, emails, or text messages you, thanks to a prominent **Add to Contacts** button.

But if, in a pinch, on the road, at gunpoint, you have to add, edit, or remove a contact manually, here's how to do it:

Make sure you've selected the right group or account, as described already. Now, on the Contacts screen, tap +. You arrive at the New Contact screen, which teems with empty boxes.

It shouldn't take you long to figure out how to fill in this form: You tap in a box and type. But here are a few tips and tricks for data entry:

- **The keyboard opens automatically** when you tap in a box. And the iPhone capitalizes the first letter of each word for you.

- **Phone numbers are special.** When you enter a phone number, the iPhone adds parentheses and hyphens for you. (You can even enter text phone numbers, like 1-800-GO-BROWNS; the iPhone converts the letters to digits when it dials.)

  If you need to insert a pause—for dialing access numbers, extension numbers, or voicemail passwords—type **#**, which introduces a two-second pause in the dialing. You can type several of them to create longer pauses.

To change the label for a number ("mobile," "home," "work," and so on), tap the label that's there now. The Label screen shows you your choices. There's even a label called "iPhone," so you and your buddy can gloat together.

TIP: If you scroll down the Label screen, you'll see that you can also create **custom** labels. You might prefer someone's cellphone number to be identified as "cell" instead of "mobile," for example. Or you might want to create a label that says "Skype," "Google Voice," "Line 2," "Yacht Phone," or "Bat Phone." The secret: Tap **Add Custom Label**. (Once you've created a custom label, it's there in the list of options for your use later.)

The Custom option, by the way, is brought to you by iCloud. If your default group is any other mail account, the Custom option doesn't appear. To check, open **Settings→Contacts→Default Accounts**, and choose **iCloud**.

- **Expand-O-Fields mean you'll never run out of room.** Almost every field (empty box) on a Contacts card is infinitely expanding. That is, the instant you start filling in a field, another empty box (labeled ⊕ **add phone** or whatever) appears right below it, so you can immediately add **another** phone number, email address, URL, or street address. (The only nonexpanding fields are First name, Last name,

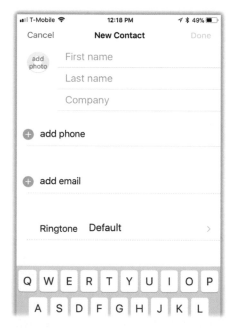 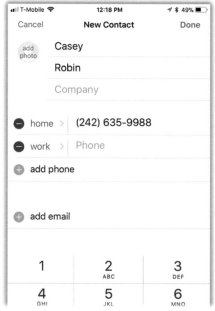

Company, Ringtone, Text Tone, Notes, and whatever oddball fields you add yourself.)

For example, when you first tap **add phone**, the phone-number box you get is labeled "home." (If that's not the right label, you can tap it to choose from one of nine others—or add a custom label.) A new **add phone** button appears so you'll have a place to enter a second phone number for this person. When you do that, a *third* **add phone** button appears. And so on.

In other words, you can never run out of places to add more phone numbers, addresses, URLs, and social media profiles.

NOTE: Tapping **add field** at the bottom of this screen lets you add a new miscellaneous field, like Nickname or Department.

- **Relatives are here.** In iCloud accounts, there's also the **social profile** field, where you can list somebody's Twitter, LinkedIn, Flickr, Facebook, and even Myspace addresses. There's an **instant message** field, too, where you can record addresses for chat networks like Yahoo Messenger.

  And there's **add related name**. Here's where you can list this person's mother, father, spouse, partner, child, manager, sibling, and so on—or even specify a different type of relationship (tap the existing label and then **Add Custom Label**).

NOTE: As you may discover in Chapter 5, Siri knows about your relationships. You can tell her to "Call my mom" or "Text my boss." Does the **add related name** feature mean that you can now ask Siri to "Call Chris Robin's manager"?

Alas, no. These fields are for your reference only.

- **You can add a photo of the person, if you like.** Tap **add photo**. If you have a photo of the person on your phone already, tap **Choose Photo**. You're taken to your photo collection, where you can find a good headshot (Chapter 9).

  Alternatively, tap **Take Photo** to activate the iPhone's built-in camera. Frame the person, and then tap the white camera button to snap the shot.

  In any case, you wind up at the **Move and Scale** screen. Here you can frame up the photo so the person's face is nicely sized and centered. Spread two fingers to enlarge the photo; drag your finger to move the image within the frame. Tap **Choose** to commit the photo to the address book's memory. (Back on the info screen where you started,

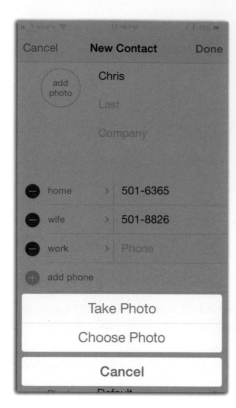

a miniature version of the photo now appears. Tap **edit** if you want to change the photo, take a new one, adjust the Move and Scale screen, or get rid of the photo altogether.)

From now on, this photo will pop up whenever the person calls. It also appears next to the person's name in your Favorites list.

- **You can import photos from Facebook.** Here's a wild guess: Most of the photo boxes in your Contacts list are empty. After all, who's going to go to the trouble of hunting down headshots of 500 acquaintances, just for a fully illustrated Contacts app?

  Fortunately, with one click, the iPhone can harvest headshots from the world's largest database of faces: Facebook.

  Visit **Settings→Facebook** to see the magical button: **Update All Contacts**. When you click it, the iPhone goes online for a massive research mission. Using your contacts' names and phone numbers as matching criteria, it ventures off to Facebook, finds the profile photos of everyone who's also in your Contacts list, and installs them into Contacts automatically. (If you already have a photo for somebody, don't worry; it doesn't get replaced.)

As a handy bonus, this operation also adds the @facebook.com email addresses for the people you already had in Contacts.

TIP: Actually, there's another side effect of this operation: It adds all your Facebook friends' names to your main Contacts list.

Now, you may not be crazy about this. Most of these Facebook folk you'll never call on the phone—yet here they are, cluttering up the Contacts list within the Phone app.

Fortunately, the **Update All Contacts** button doesn't *really* mix your Facebook friends in with your local Contacts list. It just subscribes to your Facebook address book—adds a new *group*, which you can turn off with one quick click; see page 120.

Even if you do choose to hide all their entries, you still get the benefit of the imported headshots and Facebook email addresses for the people you *do* want to see in Contacts.

- **You can import Twitter addresses.** In Settings→Twitter, the **Update Contacts** button awaits. Its purpose is to fill in the Twitter handles for everyone who's already in your Contacts, matching them by phone number or email address.

- **You can choose a ringtone.** You can choose a different ringtone for each person in your address book. The idea is that you'll know by the sound of the ring who's calling you.

NOTE: It's one tone per person, not per phone number. Of course, if you really want one ringtone for your buddy's cellphone and another for his home phone, you can always create a different Contacts card for each one.

To choose a ringtone, tap **Default**. On the next screen, tap any sound in the Ringtones or Alert Tones lists to sample them. (Despite the separate lists, in this context, these sounds are all being offered as ringtones.) When you've settled on a good one, tap **Done** to return to the info screen where you started.

TIP: Here, on the ringtone selection screen, you're offered an **Emergency Bypass** switch. Turn it on to say, "Whenever this person calls or texts, I want my phone to ring or vibrate *even* if I've turned on Do Not Disturb" (page 138).

- **You can specify a vibration pattern for incoming calls.** This unsung feature lets you assign a custom vibration pattern to each person in your Contacts, so you know by *feel* who's calling—without even removing the phone from your pocket, even if your ringer is off. It's a surprisingly useful option.

To set it up, start on the Ringtone screen described already; tap **Default** next to the word **Vibration**. You're offered a choice of canned patterns (Alert, Heartbeat, Quick, Rapid, and so on). But if you tap **Create New Vibration**, you can then tap the screen in whatever rhythm you like. It can be diddle diddle dee...or the opening notes to the Hallelujah Chorus...or the actual syllables of the person's name. ("Maryanna Beckleheimer." Can you feel it?)

The phone records your pattern, which you can prove to yourself by tapping **Play**. If you tap **Save** and name that pattern, then it becomes one of the choices when you choose a vibration pattern for someone in your Contacts. It's what you'll feel whenever this person calls you. Yes, it's tactile caller ID. Wild.

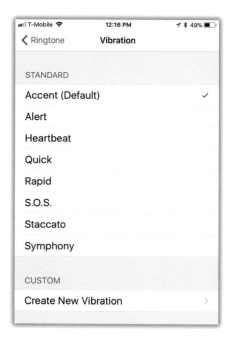 

- **You can also pick a text-message sound (and vibration).** Just as you can choose sounds and vibrations for incoming phone calls, you can tap **Text Tone** to choose sounds and vibrations for incoming text messages and FaceTime invitations.

- **You can add new fields of your own.** Very cool: If you tap **add field** at the bottom of the screen, then you go down the rabbit hole into Field Land, where you can add any of 13 additional info bits about the person whose card you're editing: a prefix (like Mr. or Mrs.), a suffix (like M.D. or Esq.), a nickname, a job title, a phonetic pronunciation for people with weird names, and so on.

When you tap one of these labels, you return to the info screen, where you'll see that the iPhone has inserted the new, empty field in the most intelligent spot. For example, if you add a phonetic first name, that box appears just below the First Name box. The keyboard opens so you can fill in the blank.

- **You can link and unlink Unified Contacts.** As noted earlier, your phone can sync up with different accounts. Your Contacts app might list four sets of names and numbers: one stored on your phone, one from an iCloud account, one from Facebook, and a fourth from your corporate Exchange server at work. In the old days, therefore, certain names might have shown up in the All Contacts list two or three times—not an optimal situation.

  Now, as a favor to you, the iPhone displays each person's name only once in that master All Contacts list. If you tap that name, you open up a unified information screen for that person. It includes *all* the details from *all* the underlying contact cards.

NOTE: The iPhone combines cards in the All Contacts list only if the first and last names are exactly the same. If there's a difference in name, suffix, prefix, or middle name, then no unifying takes place. Remember, too, that you see the unification only if you view the All Contacts list.

To see which cards the iPhone is combining for you, scroll to the bottom of the card. There the **Linked Contacts** section shows you which cards have been unified.

You can tap a listing to open the card in the corresponding account. For that matter, you can manually link a card, too; tap **Edit**, tap **link contacts**, and then choose a contact to link to this unified card—even if the name isn't a perfect match.

NOTE: It's OK to link Joe Carnelia's card with Joseph Carnelia's card—they're probably the same person. But don't link up *different* people's cards. Remember, the whole point is to make the iPhone combine all the phone numbers, email addresses, and so on onto a single card—and seeing two sets on one card could get confusing fast.

This stuff gets complex. But, in general, the iPhone tries to do the right thing. For example, if you edit the information on the unified card, you're changing that information only on the card in the corresponding account. (Unless you *add* information to the unified card. In that case, the new data tidbit is added to *all* the underlying source-account cards.)

NOTE: To delete any info bit from a Contacts card, tap the ⊖ next to it, and then tap the **Delete** button to confirm.

Adding a Contact on the Fly

There's actually another way to add someone to your Contacts list—a faster, on-the-fly method that's more typical of cellphones. Start by bringing the phone number up on the screen:

- In the Phone app, open the **Keypad**. Dial the number, and then tap ⊕.

- You can also add a number that's in your Recents (recent calls) list, storing it in Contacts for future use. Tap the ⓘ button next to the name.

In both cases, finish up by tapping **Create New Contact** (to enter this person's name for the first time) or **Add to Existing Contact** (to add a new phone number to the card of someone who's already in your list). Off you go to the Contacts editing screen shown on page 122.

Editing Someone

To make corrections or changes, tap the person's name in the Contacts list. In the upper-right corner of the info card, tap **Edit**.

You return to the screens already described, where you can make whatever changes you like. After you tap **Done** (or **Cancel**), you can return to the Contacts list by swiping to the right.

Deleting Someone

Truth is, you'll probably *add* people to your address book far more often than you'll *delete* them. After all, you meet new people all the time—but you delete them primarily when they die, move away, or dump you.

To zap someone, tap the name in the Contacts list and then tap **Edit**. Scroll down, tap **Delete Contact**, and confirm by tapping **Delete Contact** again. (Weirdly, the **Delete Contact** option doesn't appear if you open someone's info card from the Recents or Favorites lists—only from the main Contacts list.)

Sharing a Contact

There's a lot of work involved in entering someone's contact information. It's a nice touch, therefore, that you can spare the next guy all that effort—by sending a fully formed electronic business card to him. It can be yours or that of anyone in your Contacts list.

To do that, open the contact's card, scroll to the bottom, and tap **Share Contact**. On the Share sheet, you're offered a choice of **AirDrop**, **Message**, **Mail**, and **More**. ("Message" means an iMessage—page 186—if it's a fellow Apple fan, or a text message otherwise. AirDrop is described on page 364. And **More** is a place for new apps to install their sharing options.)

Tap your choice, address the message (to an email address or, for a message, a cellphone number), and send it. The recipient, assuming he has a half-decent smartphone or address-book program on the receiving end, can install that person's information with a single tap on the attachment.

The Keypad

The fourth way to place a call is to tap **Keypad** at the bottom of the screen. The standard iPhone dialing pad appears. It's just like the number pad on a normal cellphone, except that the "keys" are much bigger and you can't feel them.

To make a call, tap out (or paste) the phone number—use the ⊗ key to backspace if you make a mistake—and then tap the 📞 button.

You can also use the keypad to enter a phone number into your Contacts list, thanks to the ⊕ button, as described earlier.

Visual Voicemail

On the iPhone, you don't **dial in** to check for answering-machine messages people have left for you. You don't enter a password. You don't sit through some Ambien-addled recorded voice saying, "You have...17...messages. To hear your messages, press 1. When you have finished, you may hang up...."

Instead, whenever somebody leaves you a message, the phone wakes up, and a notification lets you know who it's from. You also hear a sound (unless you've turned on the silencer switch).

That's your cue to open **Phone→Voicemail**. There you see all your messages in a tidy chronological list. (The list shows the callers' names if they're in your Contacts list; otherwise it shows their numbers.) You can listen to them in any order—you're not forced to listen to three long-winded friends before discovering that there's an urgent message from your boss. It's a game-changer.

iOS even makes an attempt to **transcribe** your voicemails—to understand them and type out what they say. It's pretty crude, with lots of wrong and missing words. But it's usually enough to get the gist.

Setup

To access your voicemail, open the **Phone** app; tap **Voicemail**.

The very first time you visit this screen, the iPhone prompts you to make up a numeric password for your voicemail account—don't worry, you'll never have to enter it again, unless you plan to actually dial in for messages (page 134). Record a "Leave me a message" greeting.

You have two options for the outgoing greeting:

- **Default.** If you're microphone-shy, or if you're famous and don't want stalkers calling just to hear your famous voice, then use this option. It's a prerecorded, somewhat uptight female voice that says, "Your call has been forwarded to an automatic voice message system. 212-661-7837 is not available." **Beep!**

- **Custom.** This option lets you record your own voice saying, for example, "You've reached my iPhone X. You may begin drooling at the tone." Tap **Record**, hold the iPhone to your head, say your line, and then tap **Stop**.

Check how it sounds by tapping **Play**.

Then just wait for your fans to start leaving you messages!

Using Visual Voicemail

In the voicemail list, a blue dot (●) indicates a message you haven't yet played.

> **TIP:** You can work through your messages even when you're out of cellular range—on a plane, for example—because the recordings are stored on the iPhone itself.

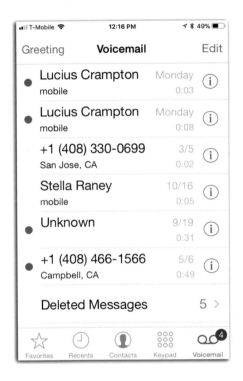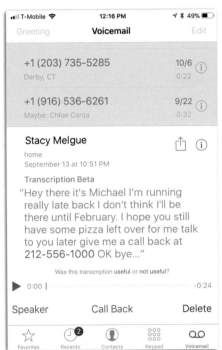

When you tap the name of a message, you instantly see the date and time it came in, the person's name (if it's in your Contacts) or the cell-phone's registered city and state (if not), and a rough transcription. The Play slider tells you how many seconds long the message is.

And all the controls you need are right there, surrounding the message you tapped:

- **Share (⬆).** Yes, you can send a voicemail recording to someone else— by email, text message, or whatever (page 363). That's a handy bit of record-keeping that could be very useful in, say, a criminal trial.

- **The transcript.** Yes, this is a crude transcript (Apple labels it *beta*, after all). There's no punctuation. There may be missing _____ and phrases. Some words might be completely wrong. But it's usually good enough that you can tell if a message is some robocall asking for money, or a message from the school nurse saying that your kid has a broken rib.

- ▶. Tap to listen to the message.

- **Speaker.** As the name "Visual Voicemail" suggests, you're *looking* at your voicemail list—which means you're *not* holding the phone up to your head. The first time people try using Visual Voicemail, therefore, they generally hear nothing!

  But if you hit **Speaker** before you tap ▶, you can hear the playback *and* continue looking over the list.

> **NOTE:** If you're listening through the earbuds, a Bluetooth earpiece, or a car kit, of course, then you hear the message playing back through *that*. If you really want to listen through the iPhone's speaker instead, tap **Audio** and then **Speaker**. (You switch back the same way.)

- **Call Back.** Tap **Call Back** to return the call. Very cool—you never even encounter the person's phone number.

- **Delete.** You might want to keep the list manageable by deleting old messages. To do that, tap a message's **Delete** button.

  If you have a lot of messages to delete, here's a faster way: Swipe across the first one's name right to left, and then tap **Delete**. The message disappears instantly. You can work down the list quickly this way.

  If you didn't know that trick, you could also do it the slow way: Tap **Edit** (upper right of the screen). Tap the ⊖ button next to a message's name and then tap **Delete** to confirm. Tap the next ⊖ button and continue.

> **TIP:** To listen to deleted messages that are still on the phone, scroll to the bottom of the list and then tap **Deleted Messages**.
>
> On the Deleted screen, you can undelete a message that you actually don't want to lose yet (that is, move it back to the Voicemail screen—tap it and then tap **Undelete**) or tap **Clear All** to erase these messages for good.

- **Rewind, Fast Forward.** Drag the little vertical line in the scrubber bar (beneath the message) to skip backward or forward in the message. It's a great way to replay something you didn't catch the first time.

To collapse the expanded message, tap another message in the list, if it's visible, or just tap the caller's name.

Even before you've expanded a message's row to view the **Play**, **Speaker**, **Call Back**, and **Delete** buttons, a few other Visual Voicemail buttons are awaiting your inspection:

- **Greeting.** Tap **Greeting** (upper-left corner) to record your voicemail greeting.
- **Call Details.** Tap ⓘ to open the info screen—the Contacts card—for the message that was left for you.

  If it was left by somebody who's in your Contacts list, you can see *which* of that person's phone numbers the call came from (indicated in blue type), plus a ★ if that number is in your Favorites list. Oh, and you can add this person to your Favorites list at this point by tapping **Add to Favorites** (at the bottom of the screen).

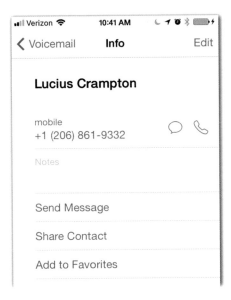

If the caller's number isn't in Contacts, then you're offered a **Create New Contact** button and an **Add to Existing Contact** button, so you can store it for future reference.

In both cases, you also have the option to return the call (right from the info screen), fire off a text message, or place a FaceTime audio or video call.

Dialing in for Messages

Gross and pre-iPhonish though it may sound, you can also dial in for your messages from another phone.

To do that, dial your iPhone's number. Wait for the voicemail system to answer. As your own voicemail greeting plays, dial * (or # if you have Verizon), your voicemail password, and then #.

You hear the Uptight Carrier Lady announce how many messages you have, and then she'll start playing them for you. After you hear each message, she'll offer you the following options (but you don't have to wait for her to announce them):

- To delete the message, press 7.

- To save it, press 9.

- To replay it, press 4. (On T-Mobile, it's 1.)

Conveniently enough, these keystrokes are the same on Verizon, Sprint, and AT&T.

> **TIP:** If this whole Visual Voicemail thing freaks you out, you can also dial in for messages right from the iPhone. Open the keypad and hold down the 1 key, just as though it were a speed-dial key on any normal phone.
>
> After a moment, the phone connects; you're asked for your password, and then the messages begin to play back, just as described already.

Answering Calls

When someone calls your iPhone, you'll know it; three out of your five senses are alerted. Depending on how you've set up your iPhone, you'll *hear* a ring, *feel* a vibration, and *see* the caller's name and photo fill the screen. (Smell and taste will have to wait until iOS 12.)

> **NOTE:** For details on Vibrate mode and on choosing a ringtone, see page 581.

How you answer depends on what's happening at the time:

- **If you're using the iPhone,** tap the green **Accept** button. Tap the red hang-up button when you've both said enough.

- **If the iPhone is asleep or locked,** the screen lights up and says **slide to answer**. If you slide your finger as indicated by the arrow, you simultaneously unlock the phone and answer the call.

- **If you're wearing earbuds,** the music fades out and then pauses; you hear the ring both through the phone's speaker and through your earbuds. Answer by squeezing the clicker on the earbud cord or by using either of the methods already described.

When the call is over, you can click again to hang up—or just wait until the other guy hangs up. Either way, the music fades in again and resumes from the spot where you were so rudely interrupted.

Same thing if you were watching a video or listening to a podcast; it pauses for the duration of the call and resumes when you hang up.

TIP: If the caller is not in your Contacts, iOS makes an educated *guess* as to the name. Instead of no name at all, you'll see something like "Maybe: Casey Robin."

How does the iPhone do it? When a call comes in, iOS searches your *email* in hopes of finding a matching phone number in somebody's email signature. If it finds one, it extracts that person's name and proposes it. Apple should call it "Likely Caller ID."

Online and on the Phone, Together

Don't forget that the iPhone is a multitasking master. Once you're on the phone, you can dive into any other program—to check your calendar, for example—without interrupting your call.

You may even be able to use the phone's Internet functions (web, email, apps, and so on) without interrupting the call. To be precise, you can be online and on the phone simultaneously if any of these things is true:

- You're in a Wi-Fi hotspot.

- You have AT&T or T-Mobile.

- You have an iPhone 6 or later, and you've turned on VoLTE calling (see page 452).

In other words, if you have Verizon (non-VoLTE) or Sprint, and if you're not in a Wi-Fi hotspot, then you can't get online until the call is complete.

Not Answering Calls

Maybe you're in a meeting. Maybe you're driving. Maybe the call is coming from someone you *really* don't want to deal with right now. Fortunately, you have all kinds of ways to slam the cellular door in somebody's face.

Silencing the Ring

You might need a moment before you can answer the call, or you need to exit a meeting or put in the earbuds. In those cases, you can stop the ringing and vibrating by pressing one of the physical buttons on the edges (the side button or either volume key). The caller still hears the phone ringing, and you can still answer it within the first four rings, but at least the sound won't be annoying those around you.

(This assumes, of course, that you haven't just flipped the silencer switch.)

Ignore It—or Dump It to Voicemail

If you wait long enough (four rings), the call goes to voicemail (even if you silence the ringing as described already).

Or you can dump it to voicemail *immediately* (instead of waiting for the four rings). How you do that depends on the setup:

- **If the iPhone is asleep or locked,** tap the side button twice fast.

- **If you're using the iPhone,** tap the **Decline** button on the screen.

- **If you're wearing the earbuds,** squeeze the microphone clicker for two seconds. You hear two low beeps, meaning: "OK, Master; dumped."

Of course, if your callers know you have an iPhone, they'll also know that you've deliberately dumped them into voicemail—because they won't hear all four rings.

Respond with a Text Message

Whenever your phone rings, the screen bears a small white **Message** button (shown on page 135). If you tap it, you get a choice of three canned text messages. Tapping one immediately dumps the caller to voicemail and sends the corresponding text message to the phone that's calling you. If you're driving or in a meeting, this feature is a lot more polite and responsive than just dumping the poor slob to voicemail.

> **TIP:** You can edit any of these three canned messages; they don't have to say, "Sorry, I can't talk right now," "I'm on my way," and "Can I call you later?" forever. To do that, open **Settings→Phone**, tap **Respond with Text**, and replace the text in the three placeholder boxes.

The fourth button, **Custom**, lets you type or dictate a new message on the spot. ("I'm in a meeting and, frankly, your call isn't worth getting fired for" comes to mind.)

Remind Me Later

The trouble with **Respond with Text**, of course, is that it sends a text message. What if the caller is using a landline that can't receive text messages? Fortunately, you have another option: **Remind Me**.

Tapping this button offers you one time-based option, **In 1 Hour** (which sets up a reminder to return the call an hour from now), and up to three location-based options (previous page, right): **When I leave**, **When I get home**, and **When I get to work**. (The home and work options appear only if the iPhone *knows* your home and work addresses—because you've entered them in your own card in Contacts.)

These options use the phone's GPS circuitry to detect when you've left your current inconvenient-to-take-the-call location, whether it's a job interview, a first date, or an outhouse.

Do Not Disturb

When you turn on Do Not Disturb, the phone is quiet and dark. It doesn't ring, chirp, vibrate, light up, or display messages. A ☾ appears on the status bar to remind you why it seems to be so uncharacteristically depressed.

Yes, airplane mode does the same thing, but there's a big difference: In Do Not Disturb, *the phone is still online*. Calls, texts, emails, and other communications continue to chug happily away; they just don't draw attention to themselves.

Do Not Disturb is what you want when you're in bed each night. You don't really want to be bothered with chirps for Facebook status updates and Twitter posts, but it's fine for the phone to collect them for the morning.

Bedtime is why Do Not Disturb comes with two fantastic additional settings: one that turns it on and off automatically on a schedule, so that the phone goes dark each night at the same time you do, and another that lets you designate important people whose calls and texts are allowed to get through. You know—for emergencies.

Turning on Do Not Disturb

To turn on Do Not Disturb manually, you have three options:

- Tell Siri, "Turn on Do Not Disturb."

- Swipe upward to open the Control Center (or on the iPhone X, swipe down from the right ear), and tap the ☾ icon so that it turns blue (facing page, right).

- Open Settings, tap **Do Not Disturb**, and turn on **Do Not Disturb** (facing page, left).

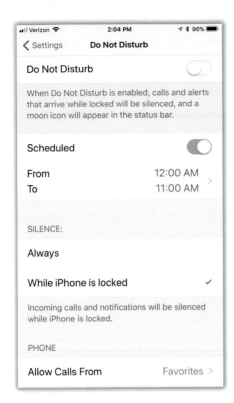

To set it up on a schedule, open **Settings→Do Not Disturb**. Turn on **Scheduled**, and then tap the **From/To** block to specify starting and ending hours. (There's no separate setting for weekends; Do Not Disturb will turn on and off for the same hours every day of the week.)

Locked or Unlocked

The Silence option on the settings screen works like this: If you choose **Always**, then Do Not Disturb works exactly as described.

But if you choose **Only while iPhone is locked**, then the phone *does* ring and vibrate *when you're using it*. Because, obviously, if the phone is awake, so are you. It's a great way to ensure that you don't miss important calls if you happened to have awakened early today and started working.

Allowing Special Callers Through

What if your child, your boss, or your elderly parent needs you urgently in the middle of the night? Turning the phone off completely, or putting it into airplane mode, would leave you unreachable in an emergency.

Fortunately, you can create wormholes through your Do Not Disturb blockade for specified callers and texters:

- **Allow Calls From.** When you open **Settings→Do Not Disturb** and then tap **Allow Calls From**, you're offered options like **Everyone** (all calls and texts come through), **No One** (the phone is still online, but totally silent), or **Favorites**, which may be the most useful option of all.

  That setting permits calls and texts from anybody you've designated as a favorite in the Phone app (page 114). Since those are the people you call most often, it's fairly likely that they're the most important people in your life.

  You can also create an arbitrary group of people—just your mom and sister, just your boss and nephew, whatever. You have to create these address-book groups on your computer (page 120)—for example, in Contacts on the Mac. Once you've done that, their names appear on the Allow Calls From screen under Groups. You can designate any one of them as the lucky exception to Do Not Disturb.

> **NOTE:** Actually, there are apps that let you create groups right on your iPhone. Groups by Qbix is a free one, for example.

- **Emergency Bypass.** This feature lets you designate any random person in your Contacts list as an "It's OK to Disturb" person. That person's calls and texts will always go through. See the Tip on page 125.

One More Safety Measure

The Do Not Disturb settings screen also offers something called **Repeated Calls**. If you turn this on, then if *anybody* tries to call you more than once within three minutes, he'll ring through.

The idea here is that nobody *would* call you multiple times unless he needed to reach you urgently. You certainly wouldn't want Do Not Disturb to block somebody who's trying to tell you that there's been an accident, that you've overslept, or that you've just won the lottery.

Do Not Disturb While Driving

According to the latest statistics, 100 percent of all car accidents are caused by *people*. Human beings are the *worst* drivers.

One of our chief idiocies is attempting to handle text messages and calls while we're driving. In iOS 11, Apple has tried to do something about it.

If you turn on the Do Not Disturb While Driving feature, then whenever you're driving, notifications from your apps don't show up to distract you. Your phone remains dark and silent. (Alarms and timers still ring, and you still see and hear Maps navigation instructions. Incoming phone calls follow whatever Do Not Disturb exceptions you've set up as described on the previous pages.)

You can set it up so that if someone texts you, they get an auto-response like, "I'm driving. I'll see your message when I get where I'm going."

A second text from you then says, "(I'm not receiving notifications. If this is urgent, reply "urgent" to send a notification through with your original message.)"

Isn't that smart? Now senders know that if this really is an emergency, they can send an "urgent" text. Now you'll see that and the original text, and you can pull over to see what the issue is.

How to Turn On Do Not Disturb While Driving

The first time you drive with your iOS 11 phone, an introductory screen appears. "Your iPhone can detect when you may be driving and automatically silence your incoming alerts and notifications." Tap the big fat **Turn On While Driving** button to make sure that this feature is always on when you're behind the wheel.

If you missed that opportunity (by tapping **Not Now**), then here's how you set up DND While Driving: Open **Settings→Do Not Disturb→ Activate**. Here you have three options:

- **Automatically.** This is by far the best option. Let Do Not Disturb turn itself on automatically, every time you're driving. The phone will use its motion sensors and its network sensors to figure out when it's in motion.

TIP: This setting engages DND even when you're on a bus or a train, or in the passenger seat of a car. In those situations, wake the phone. Hard-press the **DO NOT DISTURB** bubble on the Lock screen (or swipe left on it and then tap **View**) to view the **I'm Not Driving** button. Tap it to let messages through. This feature was intended to prevent you from being distracted behind the wheel, not to ruin your life.

- **When Connected to Car Bluetooth.** If your car has Bluetooth—if, for example, you make calls and play music wirelessly through its sound system—this is a better option. It means that the phone will know it's in your car by recognizing its Bluetooth. As a bonus, you'll still be able to make and receive phone calls through the car's audio, using the car's buttons.

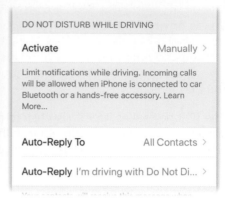

- **Manually.** This option means that you intend to turn DND While Driving on and off manually, using the Control Center. See page 54 for instructions on adding the DND While Driving button to the Control Center.

  But you know what? Don't use this option. It's much easier and safer to let DND While Driving switch on automatically. If you have to do it manually, you'll forget. You'll fall out of the habit. You won't enjoy its life-saving safeguards.

Auto-Reply Settings

Who should receive those "I'm driving; I'll get back to you later" text messages? That's up to you.

Open **Settings→Do Not Disturb→Auto-Reply To**. Here you can choose **No One** (nobody gets an auto-reply), **Recents**, **Favorites** (page 114), or **All Contacts**. In other words, total strangers (people not in your Contacts, people you've never communicated with before) never get the auto-reply, no matter what you choose here.

You can also tap **Auto-Reply** on this screen to edit the actual message. You can make it say, for example, "I'm sorry, my car can't talk right now." Or "Your text is very important to us…"

Note, however, that you can't edit the second text reply, the one that says "I'm not receiving notifications. If this is urgent, reply 'urgent' to send a notification through with your original message." That one always goes out as you see it here.

Making DND Mandatory

If you're the parent of a teenager, you might wish that DND While Driving weren't quite so optional. You might wish you could require that it's turned on when your newbie driver is behind the wheel.

You can. Do Not Disturb While Driving is now one of the options in **Settings→General→Restrictions**, which means your offspring won't be able to turn off DND without your special password (see page 619).

Fun with Phone Calls

The iPhone makes it pitifully easy to perform stunts like turning on the speakerphone, putting someone on hold, taking a second call, and so on. Here are the options you get when you're on a call.

Mute

Tap this button to mute your own microphone, so the other guy can't hear you. (You can still hear him, though.) Now you have a chance to yell upstairs, to clear the phlegm from your throat, or to do anything else you'd rather the other party not hear. Tap again to unmute.

Keypad

Sometimes you have to input touchtones, which used to be a perk only of phones with physical dialing keys. For example, that's usually how you operate home answering machines when you call in for messages, and it's often required by automated banking, reservations, and conference-call systems.

Tap this button to produce the traditional iPhone dialing pad. Each digit you touch generates the proper touchtone for the computer on the other end to hear.

When you're finished, tap **Hide** to return to the dialing-functions screen, or tap **End** if your conversation is complete.

Speaker

Tap this button to turn on the iPhone's built-in speakerphone—a great hands-free option when you're caught without your earbuds or Bluetooth headset (page 153). (In fact, the speakerphone doesn't work if the earbuds are plugged in or if a Bluetooth headset is connected.)

When you tap the button, it turns white to indicate that the speaker is activated. Now you can put the iPhone down on a table or a counter and have a conversation with both hands free. Tap **speaker** again to channel the sound back into the built-in earpiece.

 TIP: On iPhones before the 7, the speaker is on the bottom edge of the phone. If you're having trouble hearing it, and the volume is all the way up, consider pointing the speaker toward you, or even cupping one hand around the bottom to direct the sound. (That works on later models, too, although there's a second speaker in the earpiece.)

Add Call (Conference Calling)

The iPhone is all about software, baby, and that's nowhere more apparent than in its facility at handling multiple calls at once.

The simplicity and reliability of this feature put other cellphones to shame. Never again, in attempting to answer a second call, will you have to tell the first person, "If I lose you, I'll call you back."

As you'll read, however, this feature is much better on a GSM phone (AT&T or T-Mobile) than on a CDMA phone (Verizon or Sprint).

Suppose you're on a call. Here are some of the tricks you can do:

- **Make an outgoing call.** Tap **add call**. The iPhone puts the first person on hold—neither of you can hear the other—and returns you to the Phone app and its various phone-number lists. You can now make a second call in any way you want. The top of the screen makes clear that the first person is still on hold as you talk to the second.

- **Receive an incoming call.** What happens when a second call comes in while you're already on a call?

  To answer on a GSM phone, tap **End Call + Answer**. On a CDMA phone, tap **End Current Call**; the new call makes the phone ring again, at which point you can answer it normally. Weird but true.

You can also tap **End Current Call** (answer the incoming call, hang up on the first) or **Decline Incoming Call** (send it to voicemail).

When you're on two calls at once, the top of the screen identifies both other parties. Two new buttons appear, too:

- **Swap** (GSM phones only) lets you flip between the two calls. At the top of the screen, you see the names or numbers of your callers. One says **Hold** (the one who's on hold, of course) and the other bears a time counter, which lets you know whom you're actually speaking to.

  Think how many TV and movie comedies have relied on the old "Whoops, I hit the wrong button and now I'm bad-mouthing somebody directly instead of behind his back!" gag. That can't happen on the iPhone.

  You can swap calls by tapping **swap** or by tapping the **Hold** person's name or number.

- **Merge Calls** combines your two calls so all three of you can converse at once. Now the top of the screen announces the names of your callers. Note that on a CDMA phone, you can merge calls only if *you placed* the second call—not if it was incoming.

TIP: On a GSM phone, you can tap ⓘ next to someone's name; at this point, you can drop someone from the call by tapping **End**, or talk privately with someone by tapping **Private**. Tap **Merge Calls** to return to the group call.

This business of combining calls doesn't have to stop at two. At any time, you can tap **Add Call**, dial a third number, and then tap **Merge** to combine it with your first two. And then a fourth call, and a fifth. With you, that makes six people on the call.

Then your problem isn't technological; it's social, as you try to conduct a meaningful conversation without interrupting one another.

FaceTime

Tap this button to switch from your current phone call into a face-to-face video call, using the FaceTime app described starting on page 149.

(This feature requires that both you and the other guy have iPhones, iPads, iPod Touches, or Macs.)

Hold

The FaceTime button appears in place of what, on earlier iPhones, was the Hold button. But you can still trigger the Hold function—by holding down the **Mute** button for a couple of seconds. Now neither you nor the other guy can hear anything. Tap again to resume the conversation.

Contacts

This button opens the address book program so you can look up a number or place another call.

Call Waiting

Call waiting has been around for years. With a call-waiting feature, when you're on one phone call, you hear a beep indicating that someone else is calling. You can tap the Flash key on your phone to answer the second call while you put the first one on hold.

Some people don't use call waiting because it's rude to both callers. Others don't use it because they have no idea what the Flash key is.

On the iPhone, when a second call comes in, the phone rings (and/or vibrates) as usual, and the screen displays the name or number of the caller, just as it always does. Buttons on the screen offer you three choices:

- **End Current Call.** Hangs up on the first call and takes the second one.

- **Answer (Hold Current Call).** This is the traditional call-waiting effect. You say, "Can you hold on a sec? I've got another call," to the first caller. The iPhone puts her on hold, and you connect to the second caller.

  At this point, you can jump back and forth between the two calls, or you can merge them into a conference call.

- **Decline Incoming Call.** The incoming call goes straight to voicemail. Your first caller has no idea that anything has happened.

If call waiting seems a bit disruptive, you can turn it off, at least on the AT&T iPhone (the switch is in **Settings→Phone→Call Waiting**). When call waiting is turned off, incoming calls go straight to voicemail when you're on the phone.

If you have T-Mobile, Sprint, or Verizon, then you can turn off call waiting only one call at a time; just dial *70 before you dial the number. You won't be disturbed by call-waiting beeps while you're on that important call.

Call Forwarding

Here's a pretty cool feature you may not have known you had. It lets you route all calls made to your iPhone number to a *different* number. How is this useful? Let us count the ways:

- **When you're home.** You can have your cellphone's calls ring your home number so you can use any extension in the house, and so you don't miss any calls while the iPhone is turned off or charging.

- **When you send your iPhone to Apple for battery replacement.** You can forward the calls you would have missed to your home or work phone number.

- **When you're overseas.** You can forward the number to one of the web-based services that answers your voicemail and sends it to you as an email attachment (like Google Voice).

- **When you're going to be in a place with little or no cell coverage.** Let's say you're in Alaska. You can have your calls forwarded to your hotel or to a friend's cellphone. (Forwarded calls eat up your allotment of minutes, though.)

You have to turn on call forwarding while you're still in an area with cell coverage. Here's how:

- **AT&T.** Tap **Settings→Phone→Call Forwarding**, turn call forwarding on, and then tap in the new phone number. That's all there is to it—your iPhone will no longer ring. At least not until you turn the same switch off again.

- **Verizon, Sprint, T-Mobile.** On the dialing pad, dial *72, plus the number you're forwarding calls to. Then tap 📞. (To turn off call forwarding, dial *73, and then tap 📞.)

Caller ID

Caller ID is another classic cellphone feature. It's the one that displays the phone number of the incoming call (and sometimes the name of the caller).

The only thing worth noting about the iPhone's own implementation of caller ID is that you can prevent *your* number from appearing when you call *other* people's phones:

- **AT&T.** Tap **Settings→Phone→Show My Caller ID**, and then tap the on/off switch.

- **Verizon, Sprint, T-Mobile.** You can disable caller ID only for individual calls. For example, if you're calling your ex, you might not want your number to show up on his phone. Just dial *67 before you dial the number. (Caller ID turns on again for subsequent calls.)

Custom Ringtones

The iPhone comes with more than 50 creative and intriguing ringing sounds, from an old car horn to a peppy marimba lick. Page 581 shows you how to choose the one you want to hear when your phone rings. You can also buy ready-made pop-music ringtones from Apple for $1.29 each. (On your iPhone, open the iTunes Store app. Tap **More** and then **Tones**).

But where's the fun in that? Surely you don't want to walk around listening to the same ringtones as the millions of *other* iPhone owners.

Fortunately, you can also make up *custom* ring sounds, either to use as your main iPhone ring or to assign to individual callers in your Contacts list. All kinds of free or cheap apps are available for doing that, with names like Ringtone Designer Pro and Ringtones for iPhone; they let you make ringtones out of songs you already own, or even sounds you record yourself.

You can also use GarageBand, a free Apple program available for iOS or Mac. For instructions, see this chapter's free online appendix, "Making Custom Ringtones." It's a PDF available on this book's "Missing CD" page at *missingmanuals.com*.

Because apps aren't allowed to manipulate the iPhone's ringtones list directly, the process isn't altogether automatic; it involves syncing the ringtone to iTunes on your computer and then syncing it again to your phone. But the app's instructions will guide you. (iPhone ringtones must be in the .m4r file format.)

> **TIP:** One feature that's blatantly missing on the iPhone is a "vibrate, *then* ring" option for incoming calls. That's where the phone first vibrates silently to get your attention—and begins to ring only if you haven't responded after, say, 10 seconds.
>
> GarageBand offers the solution: Create a ringtone that's silent for the first 10 seconds and only *then* plays a sound. Then set your iPhone to vibrate and ring. When a call comes in, the phone plays the ringtone immediately as it vibrates—but you won't hear anything until after the silent portion of the ringtone has been "played."

Get Your Ringtones Back

If you used to have custom ringtones, but they no longer show up in iOS 11, you have two options:

- **If they came from the iTunes store, re-download them.** (On the phone, open **Settings→Sounds & Haptics**, and tap **Download All Purchased Tones**.)

- **If they're on your computer, reinstall them.** Connect your phone to your computer, open iTunes, and drag the ringtone files (which are in your computer's iTunes→iTunes→Media Tones folder) into the left-side sidebar, where your phone's name appears. Details are at *support.apple.com/en-us/HT201593*.

FaceTime Video Calls

Your iPhone, as you're probably aware, has two cameras—one on the back and one on the front. And that can mean only one thing: Video calling has arrived.

The picture and audio are generally rock-solid, with very little delay. Now Grandma can see the baby, or you can help someone shop from afar, or you can supervise brain surgery from thousands of miles away (some medical training recommended).

You can enjoy these *Jetsons* fantasies not just when calling other iPhones; you can also make video calls between iPhones and iPads, iPod Touches, and Macs. You can even place these calls when you're not in a Wi-Fi hotspot, over the cellular airwaves, when you're out and about.

FaceTime couldn't be easier to fire up—in many different ways:

- **From Siri.** The quickest way to start a video call may be simply to say, "FaceTime Mom," "FaceTime Chris Taylor," or whatever.

- **From Favorites.** Whenever you designate someone's FaceTime contact info as a favorite, a new entry appears in the Phone app's Favorites list (page 114).

- **When you're already on a phone call with someone.** This is a good technique when you want to ask first if the other guy *wants* to do video, or when you've been chatting and suddenly there's some *reason* to do video. In any case, there's nothing to it: Just tap the **FaceTime** button that's right on the screen when you pull the phone away from your face. (Your buddy can either accept or, if he just got out of the shower, decline.)

- **From the FaceTime app.** You can also start up a videochat without placing a phone call first. That's handy when you have Wi-Fi but no cell signal; FaceTime can make the call even when Verizon can't.

  Of course, if you're not already on a call, the iPhone doesn't yet know whom you want to call. So you have to tell it. Open the FaceTime app. It presents a list of your recent FaceTime calls. Tap a name to place a new call to that person, or tap ⓘ to view a history of your calls with that person (and buttons for placing new ones).

  Or, to find your callee from your own Contacts list, tap the + button. Find a name, tap it, and then tap ▢◁ to place the call.

If your future conversation partner *isn't* in Contacts yet, then tap where it says **Enter name, email, or number**, and do just that.

- **From Contacts.** In the Contacts app, if you tap a person's name, you'll find buttons that place FaceTime calls. Or, in the Phone app, call up your Favorites or Recents list. Tap ⓘ next to a name to open the contact's card; tap **FaceTime**.

- **From Messages.** If you're chatting away with somebody by text and you realize that typing is no longer appropriate for the conversation, tap ⓘ at the top of the screen. Tap ◼◀.

At this point, the other guy receives an audio and video message inviting him to a chat. If he taps **Accept**, you're on. You're on each other's screens, seeing and hearing each other in real time. (You appear on your own screen, too, in a little inset window. It's spinach-in-your-teeth protection.)

Once the chat has begun, here's some of the fun you can have:

- **Show what's in front of you.** Sometimes you'll want to show your friend what you're looking at. That is, you'll want to turn on the camera on the *back* of the iPhone, the one pointing away from you, to show off the baby, the artwork, or the broken engine part.

  Just tap 🔄. Now you and your callee can both see what you're seeing. Tap 🔄 again to return to the front camera.

- **Snap a commemorative photo.** You can immortalize a chat by using the screenshot keystroke (sleep + home on most iPhones; see page 340). You wind up with a still photo of your videochat in progress, safely nestled in the Camera Roll of your Photos app.

- **Rotate the screen.** FaceTime works in either portrait (upright) or landscape (widescreen) view; just turn your phone 90 degrees. Of course, if your calling partner doesn't *also* turn her gadget, she'll see your picture all squished and tiny, with big black areas filling the rest of the screen. (On the Mac, the picture rotates automatically when your partner's gadget rotates. You don't have to turn the monitor 90 degrees.)

> **TIP:** The ⊕ (rotation lock) button described on page 52 works in FaceTime, too. That is, you can stop the picture from rotating when you turn the phone—as long as you're happy with full-time upright (portrait) orientation.

- **Mute the audio.** Tap 🎤 to silence the audio you're sending. Great when you need to yell at the kids.

- **Mute the video.** When you leave the FaceTime app for any reason (open a different app), the other guy's screen goes black. He can't see what you're doing when you leave the FaceTime screen. He can still hear you, though.

  This feature was designed to let you check your calendar, look something up on the web, or whatever, while you're still chatting. But it's also a great trick when you need to adjust your clothing, pick at your teeth, or otherwise shield your activity from the person on the other end.

  In the meantime, the call is technically still in progress—and a green banner at the top of the Home screen reminds you of that. Tap there, on the green bar, to return to the video call.

When you and your buddy have had quite enough, tap the **End** button to terminate the call. (Although it's easy to jump from phone call to videochat, there's no way to go the other direction.)

And marvel that you were alive to see the day.

FaceTime Audio Calls

Video calling is neat and all, but be honest: Don't you find yourself making *phone* calls more often? Video calling forces us to be "on," neatly dressed and well behaved, because we're on camera. Most of the time, we're perfectly content (in fact, *more* content) with audio only.

And FaceTime audio calls don't eat into your cellphone minutes and aren't transmitted over your cell carrier's voice network; instead, these are *Internet* calls. (They use data, not minutes.)

When you're in a Wi-Fi hotspot, they're free. When you're not, your carrier's data network carries your voice.

You start out exactly as you would when making a video call, as described already. That is, you can start from the FaceTime app, the Contacts app, the Phone app, Messages, and so on.

In each spot where FaceTime is available, you get a choice of two types of calls: **Video** (▢◁) and **Audio** (✆). (In Messages, if you tap the ✆, you get a choice of two voice options: **Voice Call** and **FaceTime Audio**.)

When you place an audio FaceTime call, the other person's phone rings exactly as though you'd placed a regular call. All the usual buttons and options are available: **Remind Me**, **Message**, **Decline**, **Accept**, and so on.

Once you accept the call, it's just like being on a phone call, too: You have the options **Mute**, **Speaker**, **FaceTime** (that is, "Switch to video"), and **Contacts**. (What's missing? The **Keypad** button and the **Merge Calls** button. You can't combine FaceTime audio calls with each other, or with regular cellphone calls. If a cellphone call comes in, you'll be offered the chance to take it—but you'll have to hang up on FaceTime.)

You'll find that the audio quality is *amazing*—more like FM radio than cellular. It sounds like the other person is right next to your head; you hear every breath, sniff, and sweater rustle.

Try out FaceTime audio calls. Whenever you're calling another iPhone, iPad, iPod Touch, or Mac owner, you'll save money and minutes by placing these better-sounding free calls.

TIP: iOS even offers FaceTime Call Waiting. If you're on a FaceTime audio or video call, and someone else FaceTime calls you, your phone rings—and you can either tap **Decline** or **End & Accept**.

Bluetooth Accessories

Bluetooth is a short-range *cable elimination* technology. It's designed to untether you from equipment that would ordinarily require a cord.

Most people use Bluetooth for two purposes: communicating with a smartwatch or fitness band, or transmitting audio to a wireless speaker, car stereo, or Bluetooth earpiece.

> **NOTE:** This discussion covers *monaural* Bluetooth earpieces intended for phone calls. But the iPhone can also handle Bluetooth *stereo* headphones, intended for music, as well as Bluetooth speakers. Details are on page 261.

Pairing with a Bluetooth Earpiece or Speaker

Pairing means "marrying" a phone to a Bluetooth accessory so that each works only with the other. If you didn't do this one-time pairing, then some other guy passing on the sidewalk might hear your conversation through *his* earpiece. And neither of you would be happy.

The pairing process is different for every cellphone and every Bluetooth earpiece. Usually it involves a sequence like this:

1. **On the earpiece, turn on Bluetooth. Make the earpiece or speaker discoverable.** *Discoverable* just means that your phone can "see" it. You'll have to consult the gadget's instructions to learn how to do so; it's usually a matter of holding down some button or combination of buttons until the earpiece blinks.

2. **On the iPhone, tap Settings→Bluetooth. Turn Bluetooth on.** The iPhone immediately begins searching for nearby Bluetooth equipment. If all goes well, you'll see the name of your earpiece or speaker show up on the screen.

3. **Tap the gadget's name. Type in the passcode, if necessary.** The *passcode* is a number, usually four or six digits, that must be typed into the phone within about a minute. You have to enter this only once, during the initial pairing. The idea is to prevent some evildoer sitting nearby in the airport lounge, for example, to secretly pair *his* earpiece with *your* iPhone.

   The user's manual for your earpiece should tell you what the passcode is (if one is even required).

To make calls using a Bluetooth earpiece (or speaker as a speakerphone), you *dial* using the iPhone itself. You usually use the iPhone's own volume controls, too. You generally press a button on the earpiece or speaker to answer an incoming call, to swap call-waiting calls, or to end a call.

If you're having problems making a particular gadget work, Google it. Type "iphone jambox mini," for example. Chances are good that you'll find a write-up by somebody who's successfully worked through the setup.

Bluetooth Car Systems

The iPhone works beautifully with Bluetooth car systems, too. The pairing procedure generally goes exactly as described previously: You make the car discoverable, enter the passcode on the iPhone, and then make the connection.

Once you're paired up, you can answer an incoming call by pressing a button on your steering wheel, for example. You hear the caller through the car's speakers, and a microphone for your own voice is hidden in the rearview mirror or dashboard. You make calls either from the iPhone or, in some cars, by dialing the number on the car's own touchscreen.

Of course, studies show that it's the act of driving while conversing that causes accidents—not actually holding a cellphone. So the hands-free system is less for safety than for convenience and compliance with laws.

Pairing with a Smartwatch or Fitness Band

The latest Bluetooth technology, called Bluetooth LE (for "low energy"), Bluetooth Smart, or Bluetooth 4.0 (or 5.0), turns on only when necessary and then turns off again to save power.

When you've paired your phone with a Bluetooth LE gadget, you see the Bluetooth logo on your status bar (✻) light up only when it's actually exchanging data. Bluetooth LE has made possible a lot of smartwatches and fitness trackers.

As a handy bonus, you usually do the pairing right in the gadget's companion app, rather than fumbling around in Settings. That setup makes a lot more sense. For example, when you're setting up an Apple Watch, you use the Watch app to pair the watch; when you're setting up an Up band or Fitbit, you connect your band wirelessly in the Up app or Fitbit app.

5

Siri Voice Command

Siri, the iPhone's famous voice-recognition technology, is actually *two* features. First, there's *dictation*, where the phone types out everything you say. That's described in Chapter 3.

Second, there's Siri the *voice-controlled minion*. You can say, "Wake me up at 7:45 a.m.," or "What's Chris' work number?" or "How do I get to the airport?" or "What's the weather going to be like in San Francisco this weekend?"

You can also ask questions about movies, sports, and restaurants. Siri displays a beautifully formatted response and speaks in a calm voice.

You can even ask her, "What song is that?" or "Name that tune." She'll identify whatever song is playing in the background, just as the popular Shazam app does. It's creepy/amazing.

You can operate her hands-free, too. Instead of pressing the home button to get her attention, you just say, "Hey Siri." (The iPhone 6s and later models can respond even when running on battery power.)

In the beginning, only Apple decided what Siri could understand. Now, though, the creators of certain apps can teach Siri new vocabulary, too. For example, you can say, "Send Nicki a message with WeChat," "Pay Dad 20 dollars with Square Cash," "Book a ride with Lyft," or "Order me an Uber."

NOTE: The kinds of apps Apple permits to tap into Siri are in these six categories: audio or video calls, messages, payments, photo searching, booking rides, and starting workouts. Notably absent: music apps. You still can't say, "Play some Dave Brubeck on Spotify," for example. Apple Music is the only music service Siri understands.

And hey—in iOS 11, Siri has a new voice, clearer and apparently younger.

Voice Command

In 2010, Apple bought Siri, a company that made a voice-control app (no longer available) for the iPhone. Apple cleaned it up, beefed it up, integrated it with the iPhone's software, and wound up with Siri, your virtual servant.

> **NOTE:** Believe it or not, Siri is a spinoff from a Department of Defense research project called CALO (Cognitive Agent that Learns and Organizes). In a very real way, therefore, Siri represents your tax dollars at work.
>
> The spinoff was run by the Stanford Research Institute (SRI). But apparently that's not where Siri's name came from. Siri, it turns out, is a Norwegian word meaning "beautiful woman who leads you to victory." (Cocreator Dag Kittlaus named her. He's Norwegian.)

Siri is a crisply accurate, astonishingly understanding, uncomplaining, voice-commanded servant. No special syntax is required; you don't even have to hold the phone to your head.

Many speech-recognition systems work only if you issue certain limited commands with predictable syntax, like "Call 445-2340" or "Open Microsoft Word." But Siri is different. She's been programmed to respond to casual speech, normal speech. It doesn't matter if you say, "What's the weather going to be like in Tucson this weekend?" or "Give me the Tucson weather for this weekend" or "Will I need an umbrella in Tucson?" Siri understands almost any variation.

And she understands regular, everyday speaking. You don't have to separate your words or talk weirdly; you just speak normally.

It's not *Star Trek*. You can't ask Siri to clean your gutters or to teach you French. (Well, you can **ask**.)

But, as you'll soon discover, the number of things Siri **can** do for you is impressive. Furthermore, Apple continues to add to Siri's intelligence through software updates.

> **NOTE:** Apple also keeps increasing the number of languages that Siri understands. Already, she understands English (in nine varieties), Arabic, Cantonese, Danish, Dutch, Finnish, French, German, Hebrew, Italian, Japanese, Korean, Malay, Mandarin, Norwegian, Portuguese, Russian, Spanish, Swedish, Thai, and Turkish. You change the language by visiting **Settings→Siri & Search**.

How to Use Siri

To get Siri's attention, you have three choices:

- **Hold down the home button** until you see a wavy animation on the screen. (iPhone X: Hold in the side button.) Siri no longer double-beeps or vibrates when you trigger her, except when you trigger her remotely. She gives a double-beep when you use CarPlay, your earbuds clicker, or "Hey Siri" (described next). The phone doesn't have to be unlocked or awake, which is awesome. Just pull the phone out of your pocket and hold down the home button.

> **TIP:** Some people press the home (side) button to trigger Siri, and then release the button and start talking. But you can also hold the home (side) button down *the entire time you're speaking*. That way you know Siri won't attempt to execute your command before you've finished saying it.

- **Hold down the clicker on your earbuds cord** or the Call button on your Bluetooth earpiece.
- **Say, "Hey Siri."** A double-beep plays. (You have to turn this feature on in advance. And on models before the iPhone 6s, it works only when the phone is plugged into power, like a USB jack. Details in a moment.)

Now Siri is listening. Ask your question or say your command. You don't have to hold the phone up to your mouth; Siri works perfectly well at arm's length, on your desk in front of you, or on the car seat beside you.

> **NOTE:** Apple insists that Siri is neither male nor female. In fact, if you ask Siri her gender, she'll say something noncommittal, like, "Is this relevant?" But that's just political correctness. Any baby-name website—or a Norwegian dictionary—will tell you that Siri is a girl's name.

When you're finished speaking, be quiet for a moment (or, if you've been pressing the home or side button, release it). About a second after you stop speaking, Siri connects with her master brain online and processes your request. After a moment, she presents (and speaks) an attractively formatted response.

> **TIP:** You generally see only the most recent question and response on the Siri screen. But you can drag downward to see all the previous exchanges you've had with Siri during this session.

To rephrase your question or cancel or start over, tap the screen to interrupt Siri's work. (You can also cancel by saying "Cancel" or just by pressing the home or side button.) Tap the microphone icon to trigger your new attempt.

And when you're completely finished talking to Siri, you can either press the home (side) button, hold down your earbuds clicker, or say something like "Goodbye," "See you later," or "Adios." You're taken back to whatever app you were using before.

 TIP: In iOS 11, Siri is much better at understanding follow-up questions, where the subject of the second question is the same as the first. ("Who coaches the Phillies? What's their win record?")

How to Use "Hey Siri"

Siri can also accept spoken commands without your touching the phone. It's ideal for the car, when your hands and eyes should be focused on driving. (Of course, it's safest not to interact with your phone *at all* when you're driving—and Apple has an answer for that, too [page 140].)

The phone won't respond to "Hey Siri" unless you've set it up like this:

- **Turn on "Hey Siri."** Open **Settings→Siri & Search** and turn on **Allow "Hey Siri"** (it comes turned off).

- **Train Siri to recognize your voice.** You have to do a quick training session to teach Siri what you sound like. Otherwise, a lot of people would be freaked out when they say things like "Jay's weary" or "Space? Eerie!" and the phone double-beeps in response.

  As soon as you turn on **Allow "Hey Siri"** the training screens appear. Hit **Set Up Now**. The screen asks you to say "Hey Siri" three times, and then "Hey Siri, how's the weather today?" and "Hey Siri, it's me." That's all Siri needs to learn your voice.

At that point, you're good to go. Anytime you want to ask Siri something, just say, "Hey Siri"; at the sound of the double-beep, say your thing.

Just remember that older iPhone models (before the 6s) don't respond to "Hey Siri" except when they're plugged in and charging.

Thanks to "Hey Siri," you now have a front-seat conversationalist, a little software friend who's always happy to listen to what you have to say— and whose knowledge of the world, news, sports, and history can help make those cross-country drives a little less dull.

What to Say to Siri

Siri comes with a cheat sheet to help you learn her capabilities. To produce it, hold down the home (side) button long enough to make the "Go ahead, I'm listening" screen appear. Then release the button.

Siri displays screen after screen of example command categories, under the heading "Some things you can ask me." Tap a category name (below, left) to see sample commands within that category (right).

TIP: Or just trigger Siri and then say, "What can I say?" or "What can you do?" or "Help me!" The same cheat sheet appears.

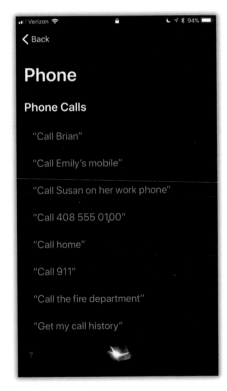

Here are the general categories of things you can say to Siri:

• **Opening apps.** If you don't learn to use Siri for anything else, for the love of Mike, learn this one. You can say, "Open Calendar" or "Play Angry Birds" or "Launch Calculator."

  Result: The corresponding app opens instantly. It's exactly the same as opening the Home screen, swiping across the screen until you find the app you're looking for, and then tapping its icon—but without opening the Home screen, swiping across the screen until you find the app you're looking for, and then tapping its icon.

- **Camera.** "Take a panorama" (or "selfie" or "photo" or "slo-mo video"). You can even say, "Scan a QR code"—a new feature that saves you from having to download a QR app. (QR codes are those strange, 1-inch-square bar codes that advertisers create as quick links to their websites.)

  Result: The Camera app opens, already set to the mode you requested. If you asked for the QR code, when you aim the lens at the bar code, a notification banner appears, offering a link to the relevant site.

- **Change your settings.** You can make changes to certain basic settings just by speaking your request. You can say, for example, "Turn on Bluetooth," "Turn off Wi-Fi," "Turn on Do Not Disturb," or "Turn on airplane mode." (You can't turn *off* airplane mode by voice, because Siri doesn't work without an Internet connection.)

  You can also make screen adjustments: "Make the screen brighter." "Dim the screen."

  Result: Siri makes the requested adjustment, tells you so, and displays the corresponding switch in case she misunderstood your intention.

NOTE: If you've protected your phone with a fingerprint or Face ID, you may have to unlock it before you're allowed to change settings. Security and all that.

- **Open Settings panels.** When you need to make tweakier changes to Settings, you can open the most important panels by voice: "Open Wi-Fi settings," "Open Cellular settings," "Open Personal Hotspot settings," "Open Notification settings," "Open Sounds settings," "Open wallpaper settings," and so on.

  You can open your apps' settings this way, too: "Open Maps settings," "Open Netflix settings," "Open Delta settings," and so on.

  Siri is smart enough not to open security-related settings this way; remember that you can use Siri even from the Lock screen. She's protecting you from passing pranksters who might really mess up your phone.

  Result: Siri silently opens the corresponding page of Settings.

- **Calling.** Siri can place phone calls or FaceTime calls for you. "Call Harold." "Call Nicole on her mobile phone." "Call the office." "Phone home." "Dial 512-444-1212." "Start a FaceTime call with Sheila Withins." "FaceTime Alex."

  Result: Siri hands you off to the Phone app or FaceTime app and places the call. At this point, it's just as though you'd initiated the call by tapping.

  Siri also responds to questions about your voicemail, like "Do I have any new voicemail messages?" and even "Play my voicemails." (After playing each message, Siri gracefully offers to let you return the call—or to play the next one.)

- **Alarms.** You can say, "Wake me up at 7:35." "Change my 7:35 alarm to 8:00." "Wake me up in six hours." "Cancel my 6 a.m. alarm" (or "Delete my..." or "Turn off my..."). And, gloriously: "Turn off all my alarms."

  This is **so** much quicker than setting the iPhone's alarm the usual way.

  Result: When you set or change an alarm, you get a sleek digital alarm clock, right there beneath Siri's response, and Siri confirms what she understood.

- **Timer.** You can also control the Timer module of the phone's Clock app. It's like a stopwatch in reverse, in that it counts down to zero—handy when you're baking something, limiting your kid's video-game time, and so on. For example: "Set the timer for 20 minutes." Or "Show the timer," "Pause the timer," "Resume," "Reset the timer," or "Stop it."

  Result: A cool digital timer appears. A little stopwatch icon appears on the Lock screen to remind you that time is ticking down.

TIP: You can specify minutes *and seconds*: "Set the timer for 2 minutes, 30 seconds," for example.

- **Clock.** "What time is it?" "What time is it in San Francisco?" "What's today's date?" "What's the date a week from Friday?" Or just "Time."

  Result: When you ask about the time, you see the clock identifying the time in question. (For dates, Siri just talks to you and writes out the date.)

- **Translations.** New in iOS 11: Siri can translate languages! She can translate phrases from English into Chinese, French, German, Italian, or Spanish. For example, you can say, "How do you say, 'Where's the bathroom?' in French?" Or "Say, 'This is delicious' in Mandarin." "Translate 'My toe hurts' into German."

  Result: She displays the translated phrase. Tap ▶ to hear it spoken. She even nails the accents.

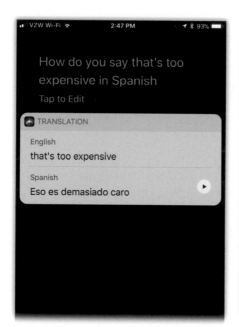

- **Contacts.** You can ask Siri to look up information in your address book (the Contacts app)—and not just addresses. For example, you can say, "What's Gary's work number?" "Give me Sheila Jenkins' office phone." "Show Tia's home email address." "What's my boss's home address?" "When is my husband's birthday?" "Show Larry Murgatroid." "Find everybody named Smith." "Who is P.J. Frankenberg?"

Result: A half "page" from your Contacts list. You can tap it to jump into that person's full card in Contacts. (If Siri finds multiple listings for the person you named—"Bob," for example—she lists all the matches and asks you to specify who you meant.)

You can even follow up. If you first asked, "What is Germaine's home address?" you can then say, "What's his cellphone number?"

TIP: In many of the examples on these pages, you'll see that you can identify people by their relationship to you. You can say, "Show my mom's work number," for example, or "Give me directions to my boss's house" or "Call my girlfriend." For details on teaching Siri about these relationships, see "Advanced Siri," starting on page 182.

- **Text messages.** "Send a text to Alex Rybeck." "Send a message to Peter saying, 'I no longer require your services.' " "Tell Cindy I'm running late." "Send a message to Janet's mobile asking her to pick me up at the train." "Send a text message to 212-561-2282." "Text Frank and Ralph: Did you pick up the pizza?"

  Result: Siri prompts you for the body of the message, if you haven't specified it. Then you see a miniature outgoing text message. Siri asks if you want to send it; say, "Yes," "Send," or "Confirm" to proceed.

TIP: If you're using earbuds, headphones, or a Bluetooth speaker, then Siri reads the message back to you before asking if you want to send it. (You can ask her to read it again by saying something like, "Review that," "Read it again," or "Read it back to me.") The idea, of course, is that if you're wearing earbuds or using Bluetooth, you might be driving, so you should keep your eyes on the road.

If you need to edit the message before sending it, you have a couple of options. First, you can tap it; Siri hands you off to the Messages app for editing and sending.

Second, you can edit it by voice. You can say, "Change it to" to re-dictate the message; "Add" to add more to the message; "No, send it to Frank" to change the recipient; "No" to leave the message on the screen without sending it; or "Cancel" to forget the whole thing.

You can also ask Siri to read incoming text messages to you, which is great if you're driving. For example, you can say, "Read my new messages," and "Read that again." Or search for past messages: "Read my last message from Robin."

TIP: If you've opted to conceal the actual contents of incoming texts so that they don't appear on your Lock screen (page 67), then Siri can read you only the senders' names or numbers—not the messages themselves.

You can even have her reply to messages she's just read to you. "Reply, 'Congratulations (period). Can't wait to see your trophy (exclamation point)!' " "Call her." "Tell him I have a flat tire and I'm going to be late."

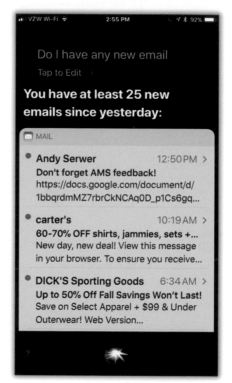

- **Email.** Siri can read your email to you. For example, if you say, "Read my latest email" or "Read my new email," Siri reads aloud your most recent email message. (She then offers you the chance to dictate a response.)

  Or you can use the summary-listing commands. When you say, "Read my email," Siri starts walking backward through your inbox, telling you the subject of each, plus who sent it and when.

  After a few listings, Siri says: "Shall I read the rest?" That's your opportunity to shut down what could be a very long recitation. If you say "Yes," though, she goes on to read the entire list of subject lines, dates, and senders.

Result: Siri reads aloud.

TIP: You can also use commands like "Any new mail from Chris today?" "Show new mail about the world premiere." "Show yesterday's email from Jan." All those commands produce a list of the messages, but Siri doesn't read them.

You can also compose a new message by voice. Anytime you use the phrase "about," that becomes the subject line for your new message. "Email Mom about the reunion." "Email my boyfriend about the dance on Friday." "New email to Freddie Gershon." "Mail Mom about Saturday's flight." "Email Frank and Cindy Vosshall and Peter Love about the picnic." "Email my assistant and say, 'Thanks for arranging the taxi!' " "Email Gertie and Eugene about their work on the surprise party, and say, 'I really value your friendship.' "

(If you've indicated only the subject and addressee, Siri prompts you for the body of the message.)

TIP: You can't send mail to canned groups of people using Siri—at least not without MailShot, an iPhone app that exists expressly for the purpose of letting you create email addressee groups.

You can reply to a message Siri has just described, too. "Reply, 'Dear Robin (comma), I'm so sorry about your dog (period). I'll be more careful next time (period).' " "Call her mobile number." "Send him a text message saying, 'I got your note.' "

Result: A miniature Mail message, showing you Siri's handiwork before you send it.

- **Calendar.** Siri can make appointments for you. Considering how many tedious finger taps it usually takes to schedule an appointment in the Calendar app, this is an enormous improvement. "Make an appointment with Patrick for October 17 at 3 p.m." "Set up a haircut at 9." "Set up a meeting with Charlize this Friday at noon." "Meet Danny Cooper at 6." "New appointment with Steve, next Sunday at 7." "Schedule a conference call at 5:30 tonight in my office."

Result: A slice of that day's calendar appears, filled in the way you requested.

TIP: Siri may also alert you to a conflict, something like this: "Note that you already have an all-day appointment about 'Boston Trip' for this Thursday. Shall I schedule this anyway?" Amazing.

You can also move previously scheduled meetings by voice. For example, "Move my 2:00 meeting to 2:30." "Reschedule my meeting with Charlize to a week from Monday at noon." "Add Frank to my meeting with Harry." "Cancel the conference call on Sunday."

You can even **consult** your calendar by voice. You can say, "What's on my calendar today?" "What's on my calendar for September 23?" "When's my next appointment?" "When is my meeting with Charlize?" "Where is my next meeting?"

Result: Siri reads you your agenda and displays a tidy Day view of the specified date.

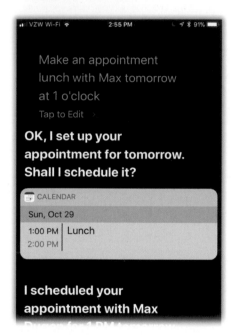
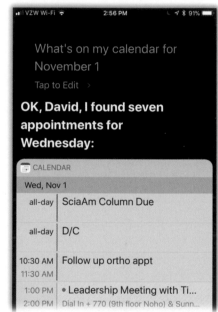

- **Directions.** By consulting the phone's GPS, Siri can set up the Maps app to answer requests like these: "How do I get to the airport?" "Show me 1500 Broadway, New York City." "Directions to my assistant's house." "Take me home." "What's my next turn?" "Are we there yet?"

TIP: You can also say, "Stop navigation"—a great way to make Maps stop harassing you when you realize you know where you are.

You can ask for directions to the home or work address of anyone in your Contacts list—provided those addresses are *in* your Contacts list.

Result: Siri fires up the Maps app, with the start and end points of your driving directions already filled in.

- **Reminders.** Siri is a natural match for the Reminders app. She can add items to that list at your spoken command. For example: "Remind me to file my IRS tax extension." "Remind me to bring the science supplies to school." "Remind me to take my antibiotic tomorrow at 7 a.m." "Create a list called Packing List." "Add kissing to my Bucket list."

The ***location-based*** reminders are especially amazing. They rely on GPS to know where you are. So you can say, "Remind me to visit the drugstore when I leave the office." "Remind me to water the lawn when I get home." "Remind me to check in with Nancy when I leave here."

> **TIP:** It's pretty obvious how Siri knows to remind you when you leave "here," because she knows where you are right now. But she also understands "home" and "office," both yours and other people's—***if*** you've entered those addresses onto the corresponding people's cards in Contacts.

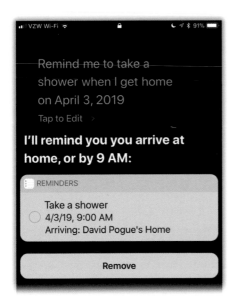
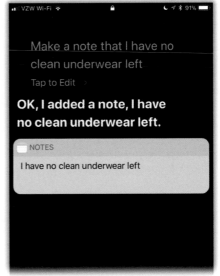

Siri can also understand the word "this" when you're looking at an email message, a web page, or a note. That is, you can say, "Remind me about this at 7 p.m." or "Remind me about this when I get home." Sure enough: Siri will flag you with a reminder notification at the appropriate time—and add an entry, with a link to the original message, web page, or note, to the Reminders app.

Result: A miniature entry from the Reminders app, showing you that Siri has understood.

- **Notes.** You create a new note (in the Notes app) by saying things like, "Make a note that my shirt size is 15 and a half" or "Note: Dad will not be coming to the reunion after all." You can even name the note in your request: "Create a 'Movies to Watch' note."

  But you can also call up a certain note to the screen, like this: "Find my Frequent Flier note." You can even summon a table-of-contents view of all your notes by saying, "Show all my notes."

  Result: A miniature Notes page appears, showing your newly dictated text (or the existing note that you've requested).

TIP: You can keep dictating into the note you've just added. Say, "Add 'Return books to library' " (or just say, "Add," and she'll ask you what to add). She'll keep adding to the same note until you say, "Note that..." or "Start a note" or "Take a note" to begin a fresh note page.

You can add text to an earlier note: "Add *Titanic II: The Voyage Home* to my 'Movies to Watch' note." (The first line of any note is also its title—in this case "Movies to Watch.")

- **Restaurants.** Siri is happy to serve as your personal concierge. Try "Good Italian restaurants around here," "Find a good pizza joint in Cleveland," or "Show me the reviews for Olive Garden in Youngstown." Siri displays a list of matching restaurants—with ratings, reviews, hours, and so on.

  But she's ready to do more than just give you information. She can actually book your reservations, thanks to her integration with the OpenTable website. You can say, "Table for two in Belmont tonight," or "Make a reservation at an inexpensive Mexican restaurant Saturday night at seven."

  Result: Siri complies by showing you the proposed reservation. Tap one of the offered alternative time slots, if you like, and then off you go. Everything else is tappable here, too—the ratings (tap to read customer reviews), phone number, web address, map, and so on.

- **Businesses.** Siri is a walking, talking (well, all right, not walking) Yellow Pages. Go ahead, try it: "Find coffee near me." "Where's the closest Walmart?" "Find some pizza places in Cincinnati." "Search for gas stations." "French restaurants nearby." "I'm in the mood for Chinese food." "Find me a hospital." "I want to buy a book."

  Result: Siri displays a handsome list of businesses nearby that match your request.

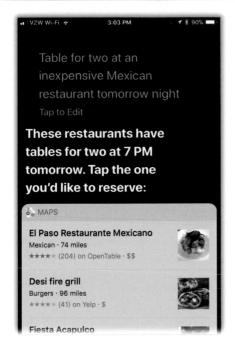

- **Playing music.** Instead of fumbling around in your Music app, save yourself steps and time by speaking the name of the album, song, or band: "Play some Beatles." "Play 'I'm a Barbie Girl.' " "Play some jazz." "Play my jogging playlist." "Play the party mix." "Shuffle my 'Dave's Faves' playlist." "Play." "Pause." "Resume." "Skip."

  If you've set up any iTunes Radio stations (Chapter 8), you can call for them by name, too: "Play Dolly Parton Radio." Or be more generic: Just say, "Play iTunes Radio" and be surprised. Or be more specific: Say, "Play some country music" (substitute your favorite genre).

  Result: Siri plays (or skips, shuffles, or pauses) the music you asked for—without ever leaving whatever app you were using.

- **Apple Music.** If you subscribe to Apple's $10-a-month Apple Music service, Siri offers a huge range of even more useful voice controls. For example, you can call for any music in Apple's 30 million–song catalog by song name, album, or performer: "Play 'Mr. Blue Sky.' " "Show me some Elton John albums." "Play 'Yesterday' next" (or

"...after this song"). Or ask to have a singer or album played in random order: "Shuffle Taylor Swift."

When you hear a song you like, you can say, "Play more like this." Or, "Add this song (or album) to my library." (Or, if you don't like it, "Skip this song.")

If more than one person performed a song, be specific: "Play 'Smooth Criminal' by Glee." You can even ask for a song according to the movie it was in. "Play that song from *Frozen*."

Or start one of your playlists by name ("Play 'Mellow Yoga' "). Or re-listen to a song: "Play previous." Or ask for one of Apple Music's radio stations: "Play Beats 1" or "Play Charting Now."

While music is playing, Siri is happy to tell you what you're listening to. ("What song is this?" "Who's the singer?" "What album is this from?") You can also tell her, "Like this song" or "Rate this song five stars." She'll note that and offer you more songs like it on the For You screen of the Apple Music app.

You can ask her to play the top hits of any year or decade ("Play the top song from 1990"; "Play the top 35 songs of the 1960s").

Even if you're not an Apple Music subscriber, you're still welcome to say, "Buy 'Mr. Blue Sky' " or "Download the new Taylor Swift album." Apple welcomes your expenditures in any form.

Result: Just what you'd expect!

- **Identifying music.** Siri can listen to the music playing in the room and try to identify it (song name, singer, album, and so on). Whenever there's music playing, you can say things like, "What's that song?" "What's playing right now?" "What song is this?" or "Name that tune!"

  Result: Siri listens to the music playing at your home/office/bar/ restaurant/picnic—and identifies the song by name and performer. There is also, needless to say, a **Buy** button.

- **Weather.** "What's the weather going to be today?" "What's the forecast for tomorrow?" "Show me the weather this week." "Will it snow in Dallas this weekend?" "Check the forecast for Memphis on Friday." "What's the forecast for tonight?" "Can you give me the wind speed in Kansas City?" "Tell me the windchill in Chicago." "What's the humidity right now?" "Is it nighttime in Cairo?" "How's the weather in Paris?" "What's the high for Washington on Friday?" "When will Jupiter rise tomorrow?" "When's the moonrise?" "How cold will it be in Houston tomorrow?" "What's the temperature outside?" "Is it windy out there?" "When does the sun rise in London?" "When will the sun set today?" "Should I wear a jacket?"

Result: A convenient miniature Weather display for the date and place you specified.

- **Stocks.** "What's Google's stock price?" "What did Ford close at today?" "How's the Dow doing?" "What's Microsoft's P/E ratio?" "What's Amazon's average volume?" "How are the markets doing?"

Result: A tidy little stock graph, bearing a wealth of up-to-date statistics.

- **Find My Friends.** You see this category only if you've installed Apple's Find My Friends app. "Where's Ferd?" "Is my dad home?" "Where are my friends?" "Who's here?" "Who is nearby?" "Is Mom at work?"

Result: Siri shows you a beautiful little map with the requested person's location clearly indicated by a blue pushpin. (She does, that is, if you've set up Find My Friends, you've logged in, and your friends have made their locations available.)

- **Search the web.** "Search the web for a 2016 Ford Mustang." "Search for healthy smoothie recipes." "Search Wikipedia for the Thunderbirds." "Search for news about the Netflix-Amazon merger."

TIP: Siri uses Google to perform its web searches. If you prefer Microsoft's Bing search service, just say so. Say, "Bing Benjamin Franklin." (For that matter, you can also ask Siri to "Yahoo" something—for example, "Yahoo blueberry dessert recipes.")

Wikipedia is a search type all its own. "Search Wikipedia for Harold Edgerton." "Look up Mariah Carey on Wikipedia." Pictures get special treatment, too: "I want to see pictures of cows." You can also say, "Show me pictures of…" or "Find me…" or "Search for…"

Result: Siri displays the results of your search right on her screen. Tap one of the results to open the corresponding web page in Safari.

- **Sports scores.** At last you have a buddy who's just as obsessed with sports trivia as you are. Siri knows everything about everything when it comes to professional and college sports scores, schedules, standings, player details, and team stats.

  You can say things like, "How did the Indians do last night?" "What was the score of the last Yankees game?" "When's the next Cowboys game?" "What baseball games are on today?"

 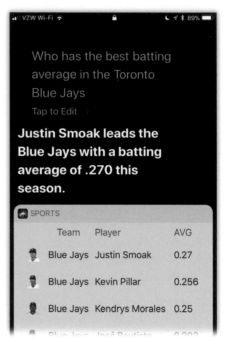

You can also ask questions about individual players, like "Who has the best batting average?" "Who has scored the most runs against the Red Sox?" "Who has scored the most goals in British soccer?" "Which quarterback had the most sacks last year?"

And, of course, team stats are fair game, like "Show me the roster for the Giants," "Who is pitching for Tampa this season?" and "Is anyone on the Marlins injured right now?"

Result: Neat little box scores or factoids, complete with team logos.

- **Movies in theaters.** Siri is also the virtual equivalent of an insufferable film buff. She knows **everything**. "Who was the star of *Groundhog Day*?" "Who directed *Chinatown*?" "What is *Waterworld* rated?" "What movie won Best Picture in 1952?" "How are the reviews for *The Emoji Movie*?"

  It's not just about old movies, either. Siri also knows everything about current showtimes in theaters. "What movies are opening this week?" "What's playing at the Watton Cineplex?" "Give me the reviews for *Doctor Strange*." "What are today's showtimes for *The Last Jedi*?"

  Result: Tidy tables of movies, theaters, or showtimes. (Tap one for details.) Sometimes you get a movie poster filled with facts. In the U.S., you can even buy tickets by voice: "Two tickets to see *Titanic 2*," for example, or "Four tickets to *Pelicans* at City Center at 7:30 pm."

- **Movies on iTunes.** Siri also helps you find flicks in online services (Netflix, Hulu, HBO Go, and so on) or on Apple's own movie store. You know: "Find movies about football." "Play *Jurassic World*." "Find new action movies on Netflix." "Get me documentaries on Hulu." "Find free movies for kids."

  Result: Thumbnails of the movies you seek.

TIP: Once you're playing a video, you can then ask Siri things like, "Who's in this?" or "Who directed this?" Kind of handy. And if you're binge watching, you can manage your Up Next queue verbally, too: "What's next on my Up Next?" "Add *Arrested Development* to my Up Next." "Remove *Big Little Lies* from my Up Next."

- **iBooks.** Apple runs an ebook store, too, of course. Therefore, these commands are fair game: "Find books by Ian Fleming." "Buy the book *Purity*." "Show me Jonathan Franzen books."

  Result: The iBooks app opens, listing the book(s) you mentioned.

- **Podcasts.** While we're on the subject of entertainment: Apple's Podcasts app is Siri-controllable, too. "Play 'S-Town.' " "Play it twice as fast." "Skip ahead 30 seconds." "Pause." "Play." "Listen to the TED Radio Hour."

  Result: The app obeys.

- **Facts and figures.** This is a huge category. It represents Siri's partnership with the Wolfram Alpha factual search engine (*www.wolfram-alpha.com*). The possibilities here could fill an entire chapter—or an entire encyclopedia.

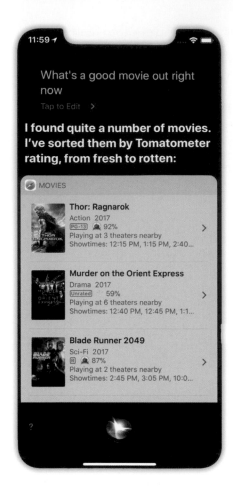

You can say things like, "How many days until Valentine's Day?" "When was Abraham Lincoln born?" "How many teaspoons are in a gallon?" "What's the exchange rate between dollars and euros?" "What's the capital of Belgium?" "What's a 17 percent tip on 62 dollars for three people?" "When is the next solar eclipse?" "Show me the Big Dipper." "What's the tallest mountain in the world?" "What's the price of gold?" "What's the definition of *schadenfreude*?" "How much is six dollars in pesos?" "Generate a random number." "Graph x equals 3y plus 12." "What flights are overhead?"

Result: For simple math and conversions, Siri just shows you the answer. For more complex questions, you get a specially formatted table, ripped right out of Wolfram Alpha's knowledge base.

> **TIP:** Siri can also harness the entire wisdom of Wikipedia. You can say, for example, "Search Wikipedia for Tim Kaine" or "Tell me about Alexander Hamilton" or "Show me the Wikipedia page about Richard Branson."

- **Search Twitter.** If you say something like, "What are people saying?" or "What's happening on Twitter?" you see a list of tweets on the trending topics on Twitter. (Tap a tweet in the list to open it into a new window that contains more information and a **View in Twitter** button.)

  Or ask, "What are people saying about the Chicago Bears?" to read tweets on that subject. Or, conversely, you can ask, "What is Samantha Bee saying on Twitter?" to see her most recent tweets. (You can substitute the names of other people or companies.) Or, "Search Twitter for the hashtag 'FirstWorldProblems.' " (A *hashtag* is a searchable phrase like #toofunny or #iPhoneX, which makes finding relevant tweets on Twitter much easier.)

  Result: Siri displays 10 or so tweets that match your query.

- **Round up photos or videos.** This trick can save you a lot of time and fussing. You can ask Siri to show you all photos or videos according to the time or place you shot them, or according to the album name they're in. "Show me the videos from Halloween last year," you can say. "Get me the videos from Utah." "Show me the Disney World album." "Open the Panoramas album." "Show me the Slo-mo videos from Oberlin College." "Give me the pictures from last summer."

  Result: You get a screenful of little square thumbnails of photos or videos that match your request. Tap one to open it, or tap **Show All** to see all the photos/videos in that batch.

Non-Apple Apps

These days, Apple permits Siri to control apps from other companies. Once you find out what these commands are, they can accelerate other apps just as much as Siri already accelerates Apple's.

Here are a few examples:

- **Lyft, Uber.** "Order a Lyft." "Call me an Uber." Siri asks you to tap the kind of car you want to order; one further tap orders the ride.

- **Pinterest.** "Find toddler bedroom idea pins on Pinterest." The Pinterest app opens, displaying pins that match your search query (from all of Pinterest, not just your pages).

- **Square Cash.** "Pay Casey two dollars with Square Cash." Boom: You've just sent money to lucky, lucky Casey.

- **LinkedIn.** "Send a LinkedIn message to Robin that says, 'Can you vouch for me?' "

- **WhatsApp, WeChat, Skype**. All of these chat apps work exactly like iOS's own Messages app, in that you can send "text messages" entirely by voice. Just say, "with [name of app]" at the end of your command, or use the messaging app's name as a noun.

For example: "Tell Eric, 'I think I left my wallet in your car' with WhatsApp." "Send a WeChat to Phoebe saying, 'Are we still going out?'" "Let Marge know, 'I accidentally left your front door open this morning' in Skype."

To see a list of all your apps that understand Siri commands, open **Settings→Siri & Search**. There they are: all the Siri-compatible apps, with on/off switches.

You may never find the end of the things Siri understands, or the ways she can help you. If her repertoire seems intimidating at first, start simple—use her to open apps, dial by voice, send text messages, and set alarms. You can build up your bag of tricks as your confidence grows.

 NOTE: Remember that you can use Siri without even unlocking your phone—and therefore without any security, like your passcode. Among certain juvenile circles, therefore, Siri is the source of some interesting pranks. Someone who finds your phone lying on a table could change your calendar appointments, send texts or emails, or even change what Siri calls you ("Call me 'you idiot' "), without having to enter the phone's passcode!

The solution is simple. Open **Settings→Touch ID & Passcode** (or **Face ID & Passcode** on the iPhone X). If you scroll way down, you can turn off **Siri**. Of course, you've now lost the convenience of using Siri when the phone is locked. But at least you've prevented having your own phone call you an idiot.

When Things Go Wrong

If Siri misrecognizes your instructions, you'll know it, because you can see her interpretation of what you said. And, as indicated by the little hint **tap to edit**, you can tap Siri's interpretation to open up an editing screen so that you can make corrections by typing.

TIP: You can also correct a misheard command just by speaking the correct version, like this, "I meant Chicago." Siri gets what you mean.

If Siri recognizes what you said but it isn't within her world of comprehension, she offers you a **Search the web** button as a last resort.

Siri's Personality

Siri's understanding of casual spoken commands is so impressive that you might sometimes think she's almost human. And that, of course, is exactly what Apple wants.

You can say all kinds of off-kilter things to Siri. After you've encountered a few of her answers, you won't be surprised to learn that Apple actually employs a comedy-writing team exclusively for Siri-humor purposes.

For example, if you ask her, "What is the meaning of life?" she responds with one of more than a dozen different answers. She might say, "I can't answer that now, but give me some time to write a very long play in which nothing happens." Or "It's nothing Nietzsche couldn't teach ya." Or: "All evidence to date suggests it's chocolate."

Siri is full of such comebacks, and there are whole websites dedicated to her snark. Here are a few examples (this list won't ruin the fun, because Siri actually has several different comebacks to most of these questions):

You: "Who's your daddy?" **Siri:** "You are. Can we get back to work now?"

You: "Open the pod bay doors, Hal." **Siri:** "I'm sorry, I'm afraid I can't do that." (Then: "Are you happy now?")

You: "Knock knock." **Siri:** "Knock knock. Who's there? Joshua. Joshua who? Joshua, I don't do knock-knock jokes."

You: "What are you wearing?" **Siri:** "You have the wrong personal assistant, Carl."

You: "Who's the boss?" **Siri:** (Presents the vital statistics of Bruce Springsteen.)

You: "Beam me up, Siri!" **Siri:** "Please remove your belt, shoes, and jacket, and empty your pockets."

You: "Show me the money." **Siri:** "I've found 23 ATMs that are fairly close to you..."

You, in the evening: "Good morning, Siri." **Siri:** "Good morning? It's 9:24 p.m.!"

You: "How much wood would a woodchuck chuck if a woodchuck could chuck wood?" **Siri:** "42 cords of wood, to be exact. Everyone knows that."

You: "Guess what." **Siri:** "You won the lottery?"

You: "Talk dirty to me." **Siri:** "Humus. Compost. Pumice. Silt. Gravel."

You: "Why did the chicken cross the road?" **Siri:** "I am not perspicacious about the peregrinations of poultry."

You: "Do you have a religion?" **Siri:** "My policy is the separation of spirit and silicon."

You: "Klaatu barada nikto." **Siri:** "OK, I'll pass the message on to Gort." (You kind of have to know *The Day the Earth Stood Still* to get it.)

Here are a few other things to say to Siri when you get bored:

What do you think of Google Now?

OK, Glass.

OK, Google.

What's the best cellphone?

What's the best computer?

How much do you cost?

What are you doing later?

Make me a sandwich.

Does Santa Claus exist?

Do you believe in Santa Claus?

Should I give you a female or male voice?

I don't like your voice.

Are you serious?

Are you kidding me?

Blah blah blah.

LOL.

Who's your boss?

You are good to me.

You are boring.

Give me a kiss.

What are the three laws of robotics?

Let's play a game.

Read me a haiku.

Take me to your leader.

Can I borrow some money?

Siri, rap.

Siri, beatbox.

Testing 1, 2, 3

When will hell freeze over?

Which came first, the chicken or the egg?

Trick or treat!

What do you want?

What's your favorite animal?

Do you have children?

Do you have a boyfriend?

What are the lottery numbers going to be tomorrow?

What did you do last night?

What are you doing this weekend?

What's your favorite movie (...TV show, song, color, book, computer, phone, operating system, app)?

What should I ask Tim Cook?

Are you smart?

How do I look?

Have you ever loved anyone?

Do you have any pets?

Do I look good in this outfit?

Flip a coin.

Roll a die.

Rock paper scissors.

Yes or no?

Pick a card.

Tell me a riddle.

What's 0 divided by 0?

What's infinity times infinity?

What is the passcode?

When is the world going to end?

Stop it, Siri.

Typing to Siri

In iOS 11, for the first time, you can type your questions and commands to Siri instead of speaking them. Every now and then, that silent method could be preferable to the talk-aloud method—when you're in church or a movie, for example, or when your query is of a delicate nature.

To set this up, open **Settings→General→Accessibility→Siri**. Turn on **Type to Siri**.

From now on, when you hold down the home (or side) button, you get a **Type to Siri** box and a keyboard. Tap out your query and then hit **Done**; Siri shows her response, exactly as though you had spoken.

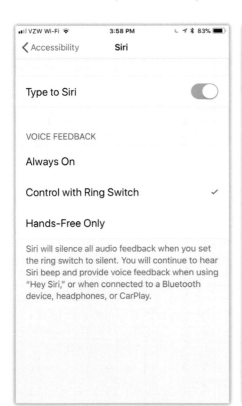 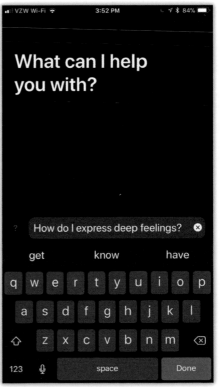

Even with this feature turned on, your voice isn't completely useless. "Hey Siri" still works just as it always has, thus giving you the best of both worlds.

And even if you press the home (side) button and find yourself staring at the keyboard, you can still speak your request—by tapping the 🎤 and dictating. It's the best of all *three* worlds.

Advanced Siri

With a little setup, you can extend Siri's powers in some intriguing ways.

Teach Siri About Your Relationships

When you say, "Text my mom" or "Call my fiancée," how does Siri know whom you're talking about? Sure, Siri is powerful artificial intelligence, but she's not actually *magic*.

Turns out you teach her by referring to somebody in your Contacts list. Say to her something like, "My assistant is Jan Carpenter" or "Tad Cooper is my boyfriend." When Siri asks for confirmation, say "Yes" or tap **Confirm**.

Or wait for Siri to ask you herself. If you say, "Email my dad," Siri asks, "What is your dad's name?" Just say his name; Siri remembers that relationship from now on. (The available relationships include mother, father, grandmother, grandfather, brother, sister, child, son, daughter, spouse, wife, husband, boss, partner, manager, assistant, girlfriend, boyfriend, and friend.)

Behind the scenes, Siri lists these relationships on your card in Contacts. Now that you know that, you can figure out how to edit or delete these relationships as well. Which is handy—not all relationships, as we know, last forever.

Fix Siri's Name Comprehension

Siri easily understands common names—but if someone in your family, work, or social circle has an unusual name, you may quickly become frustrated. After all, you can't text, call, email, or get directions to someone's house unless Siri understands the person's name when you say it.

One workaround is to use a relationship, as described in the previous section. That way, you can say, "Call my brother" instead of "Call Ilyich" (or whatever). Another is to use Siri's pronunciation-learning feature. It fires up in several different situations:

- **When you're texting.** If Siri offers the wrong person's name when you try to text someone by voice, say, "Someone else." After you've sent the message, Siri apologetically says, "By the way, sorry I didn't recognize that name. Can you teach me how to say it?"

- **After Siri botches a pronunciation.** Tell her, "That's not how to pronounce his name."

- **Whenever it occurs to you.** You can start the process by saying, "Learn to pronounce Reagann Tsuki's name" or "Learn to pronounce my mom's name."

- **In Contacts.** Open somebody's "card" in Contacts; start Siri and say, "Learn to pronounce her name."

In each case, with tremendous courtesy, Siri walks you through the process of teaching her the correct pronunciation. She offers you several ▶ buttons; each triggers a different pronunciation. Tap **Select** next to the correct one (or tap **Tell Siri again** if none of the options is correct).

By the end of the process, Siri knows two things: how to say that person's name aloud, and how to recognize that name when *you* say it.

Siri Settings

In **Settings→Siri & Search**, you can fiddle with two Siri on/off switches:

- **Listen for "Hey Siri."** If you don't want Siri to respond to "Hey Siri," (see page 160), you can turn her listening off here. Now Siri works only when you hold down the home (or side) button.

- **Press Home for Siri/Press Side Button for Siri.** If you turn this off, then holding down the home (or side) button no longer summons Siri. (If **Listen for "Hey Siri"** is *also* turned off, then you can't use Siri at all. In essence, you've just turned your modern iPhone into an iPhone 4.

NOTE: Why would anyone turn off Siri? One reason: Using Siri involves transmitting a lot of data to Apple, which gives some people the privacy willies. Apple collects everything you say to Siri, your song and playlist names, plus all the names in Contacts (so that Siri can recognize them when you refer to them).

- **Allow Siri When Locked.** Lets you turn off Siri at the Lock screen.

- **Language.** What language do you want Siri to speak and recognize? The options here include dozens of languages and dialects, including English in nine flavors (Australian, Canadian, Indian, and so on).

- **Siri Voice.** Siri can have either a man's voice or a woman's voice—in a choice of accents. Even if you're American, it's fun to give Siri a cute Australian accent.

- **Voice Feedback** asks: Do you want to hear Siri's "I'm listening!" beep and her spoken responses even if the ringer switch is off? How about when you're going hands-free (using "Hey Siri" or a Bluetooth earpiece, car, or headphones)?

    Always On: Siri always replies to queries with a synthesized voice (in addition to a text response).

    Control with Ring Switch: Siri speaks her answers only when the phone isn't silenced (page 23).

    Hands-Free Only: You're telling Siri not to bother speaking when you're looking at the screen and can read the responses for yourself. She'll speak only if you're on speakerphone, using a headset, listening through your car's Bluetooth system, and so on.

- **My Information.** Siri needs to know which card in Contacts contains your information and lists your relationships. That's how she's able to respond to queries like "Call my mom," "Remind me to shower when I get home," and so on.

- **Suggestions in Search, Suggestions in Look Up.** You get to control when iOS provides outside results it considers helpful when you **Search** (page 108) and when you use the **Look Up** button (page 400).

- **Apps list.** Finally, this screen contains a scrolling list of Siri-compatible apps. Turn them on or off at will.

6

Texting & Messages

The term "iPhone" has never seemed especially appropriate for a gadget with so much power and flexibility. Statistics show, in fact, that making phone calls is one of the iPhone's least-used functions! In fact, 57 percent of us never use the iPhone to make phone calls at all.

But texting—now we're talking. Texting is the single most used function of the modern cellphone. In the U.S., we send 6 billion texts a day; half of Americans send at least 50 texts a day. Worldwide, we send 8.3 *trillion* texts a year. That's a lot of "how r u"s and "LOL"s.

Apple—wary of losing customers to creative messaging apps like WhatsApp, Snapchat, and Facebook Messenger—is trying to compete with its Messages app. Its special effects and cool interactions match most offerings of rival apps—and, thanks to a Messages app *store*, even surpass them. Text-message conversations no longer look like a tidy screenplay. Now they can be overrun with graphics, cartoons, animations, and typographic fun.

In iOS 10, all that gadgetry made Messages feel cluttered. The big news in iOS 11 is that Apple has cleaned this up, and made Messages cleaner without losing its expandability.

Text Messages and iMessages

So why is texting so crazy popular? For reasons like these:

- **Like a phone call, a text message is immediate.** You get the message off your chest right now.

- **And yet, as with email, the recipient doesn't have to answer immediately.** The message waits for him even when his phone is turned off.

- **Unlike a phone call, a text is nondisruptive.** You can send someone a text message without worrying that he's in a movie, a meeting, or anywhere else where holding a phone up to his head and talking would be frowned upon. (And the other person can answer non-disruptively, too, by sending a text message *back*.)

- **You have a written record of the exchange.** There's no mistaking what the person meant. (Well, at least not because of sound quality. Understanding the texting shorthand that's evolved—"C U 2mrO," and so on—is another matter entirely.)

Now, the first thing to learn about texting on the iPhone is that there are *two kinds* of messages. There are regular text messages (SMS), which any cellphone can send to any cellphone. And there are iMessages, which only Apple equipment (iPhones, iPads, Macs) can exchange.

The Messages app can send and receive both kinds of messages—but iMessages offer much greater creative freedom.

Standard Texting (SMS)

SMS stands for Short Message Service, but it's commonly just called texting. An SMS is a very short note (under 160 characters—a sentence or two) that you shoot from one cellphone to another. What's so great about it?

Most iPhone plans include unlimited texts. *Picture and video messages* (known as MMS, or Multimedia Messaging Service) count as regular text messages.

But whenever you're texting another Apple person (using an iPhone, iPad, iPod Touch, or Mac), you have another choice, as described next.

iMessages

An iMessage looks and works exactly like a text message. You send iMessages and receive them in the same app (Messages). They show up in the same window. You can send the same kinds of things: text, photos, videos, contacts, map locations, whatever. You send and receive them using exactly the same techniques.

The big difference? iMessages go exclusively between Apple products. If your iPhone determines that the address belongs to any *other* kind of phone, it sends regular old text messages.

iMessages offer some huge advantages over regular text messages:

- **No 160-character limit.** A single message can be many pages long. (The actual limit is 18,996 characters per message, in case you're counting.)

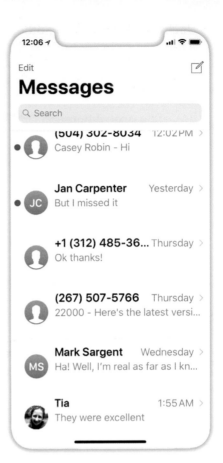

- **iMessages don't count as text messages.** You don't have to pay for them. They look and work exactly like text messages, but they're transferred over the Internet (Wi-Fi or cellular) instead of your cell company's voice airwaves. You can send and receive an unlimited number of them and never have to pay a penny more.

- **You know then they're typing.** When you're typing back and forth with somebody, you don't have to wonder whether, during a silence, they're typing a response to you or just ignoring you; when they're typing a response, you see an ellipsis (•••) in their speech bubble.

TIP: The ellipsis dots appear as soon as the other guy starts typing—and remain on your screen for 60 seconds, even if he *stopped* typing a long time ago. Conversely, they *disappear* from your screen after 60 seconds, even if he's still typing! Often you'll see the dots disappear shortly before you get a huge, long paragraph—because the other guy took longer than 60 seconds to write it.

- **You don't wonder if the other guy has received your message.** A tiny, light-gray word "delivered" appears under each message you send, briefly, to let you know that the other device received it.

- **Read receipts.** You can even turn on a "read receipt" feature that lets the other person know when you've actually *seen* a message she sent. She'll see a notation that says, for example, "Read 2:34 PM." (See page 597.)

- **Your history of iMessages shows up on all your i-gadgets.** They're synchronized through your iCloud account. You can start a chat on your iPhone, and later pick up your Mac laptop at home and carry right on from where you stopped (in *its* Messages program).

  As a result, you always have a record of your iMessages. You have a copyable, searchable transcript on your computer.

- **iMessages can be more than text.** They can be audio recordings, video recordings, photos, sketches you make with your finger, games, "stickers," emoji symbols, animations, and much more.

iMessages happen automatically. All you do is open Messages and create a text message as usual. If your recipient is using an Apple gadget with iOS 5 or later, or a Mac using OS X Mountain Lion or later...*and* has an iCloud account...*and* hasn't turned off iMessages, then your iPhone sends your message as an iMessage automatically. It somehow knows.

You'll know, too, because the light-gray text in the typing box says "iMessage" instead of "Text Message." And each message you send shows up in a *blue* speech bubble instead of a *green* one. The ⬆ button is blue, too.

In fact, when you're addressing a new text message, the names that appear in blue represent people with iMessages gadgets, so you know in advance who's cool and who's not. (The green names are those who do *not* have iMessage. The gray ones—well, your iPhone doesn't know yet.)

The actual mechanics of sending and receiving messages are essentially the same, whether it's SMS messages or iMessages. So the rest of this chapter applies equally well to both, with a few exceptions.

Receiving Texts

When you get a text, the iPhone plays a sound. It's a shiny glockenspiel ding, unless you've changed it in **Settings→Sounds & Haptics**.

The phone also displays the name or number of the sender and the message—though If you have Face ID set up, your messages don't show

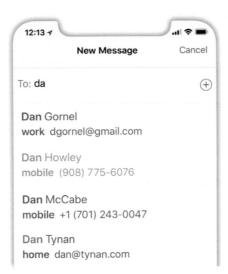

themselves until the phone is sure it's really you looking at them (page 66). Unless you've fooled around with the Notifications settings, the message appears as a banner on your screen (page 73), disappearing momentarily on its own, so as not to interrupt what you're doing. (You can flick it up and away if it's blocking your screen.)

If the iPhone was asleep, it lights up long enough to display the message on its Lock screen. At that point, you have a few options:

- **Ignore it.** After a moment, the screen goes dark again. The incoming-text notification bubble will be there the next time you wake it.

- **Answer it.** On an iPhone 6s or later, **hard-press** right on the banner to expand it into a full keyboard, so that you can respond without even unlocking the phone; on an earlier model, swipe to the **left** on the notification bubble to reveal **View** and **Clear** buttons.

- **Open it.** If you swipe a notification bubble to the **right**, you're asked to unlock your phone; you wind up looking at the message in the Messages app.

TIP: On the Home screen, the Messages icon bears a little circled number "badge" letting you know how many new text messages are waiting for you.

Once you tap a message notification to open it, you see the text-message conversation displayed as cartoon speech balloons.

To respond to the message, tap in the text box at the bottom of the screen. The iPhone keyboard appears. Type away, or dictate a response, and then tap ⬆—that's your Send button. As long as your phone has cellular or Wi-Fi coverage, the message goes out immediately.

If your buddy replies, then the balloon-chat continues, scrolling up the screen.

And now, a selection of juicy Message tips:

- The last 50 exchanges appear here. If you want to see even older ones, scroll to the very top and then drag downward.

> **TIP:** This business about having to scroll to the top, wait, and then drag downward gets old fast, especially when you're trying to dig up a message you exchanged a few weeks back. Fortunately, there's a glorious shortcut: *Tap the very top of the screen* (where the clock appears) over and over again. Each time you tap, you load another batch of older messages and scroll to the oldest one.

  And by the way—if the keyboard is blocking your view of the conversation, swipe downward on the messages to hide it.

- Links actually work. If someone sends you a web address, tap it to open it in Safari. If someone sends a street address, tap it to open it in Maps. And if someone sends a phone number, tap it to dial.

  A web address in iMessages shows up as a little logo and graphic of the website (below, left). (Sometimes you have to **Tap to Load Preview** to see it.) Then tap that preview thumbnail to open the web page.

- If someone sends you a link to a video on YouTube or Vimeo, you can play the video without leaving the Messages window; just tap the thumbnail (below, right). (To open the video at full size, *on* YouTube or Vimeo, tap the thumbnail's *name*.)

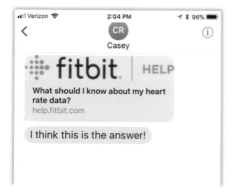
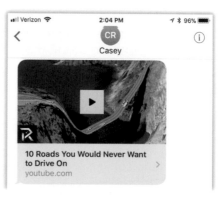

- Once you've opened a text conversation, you see that each flurry of messages is time-stamped when it begins ("Sat, Nov 10, 2:18 pm," for example). But at this point, you can also drag leftward anywhere on the screen to reveal the exact time stamps of every message *within* the chat.

> **TIP:** When typing a message, if you decide that it would be faster just to call, trigger Siri and say, "Call her" or "Call him."

The List of Conversations

What's cool is that the iPhone retains all these exchanges. The Messages screen (of the Messages app) is a list of all your correspondents, like a table of contents. A blue dot indicates a conversation with new messages (page 187, right).

Tap a person's listing to open the actual messages you've exchanged, going back in time to your very first texts.

These listings represent *people*, not conversations. For example, if you had a text message exchange with Chris last week, then a quick way to send a new text message to Chris (even on a different subject) is to open that "conversation" and simply send a "reply." The iPhone saves you the administrative work of creating a new message, choosing a recipient, and so on.

Similarly, if you've sent a message to a certain group of people, you can address a new note to the same group by tapping the old message's row.

> **TIP:** Hey, you can search text messages! At the very top of the list, there's a search box. You can actually find text within your texts.

To return to the Messages list from the actual chat view, tap ‹ at top left— or swipe inward from the left edge of the screen.

If having these old exchanges hanging around presents a security (or marital) risk, you can delete them in either of two ways:

- **Delete an entire conversation.** *Swipe* away the conversation. At the list of conversations, swipe your finger *leftward* across the conversation's name. The **Delete** button appears.

  Alternate method: Above the Messages list, tap **Edit**, tap to select (✓) the conversations you want to ditch, and then tap **Delete**.

- **Delete just one text.** Open the conversation. This technique is a little weird, but here goes: *Hold down your finger* on the individual message you want to delete. When the options panel appears, tap **More**.

Now you can delete all the exchanges simultaneously (tap **Delete All**) or vaporize only particularly incriminating messages. To do that, tap the selection circles for the balloons you want to nuke, putting checks (⊘) by them; then tap the 🗑 to delete them all at once. Tap **Delete Message** to confirm. (You can't delete a message from anyone *else's* phone; you're just deleting it from *your* copy of the conversation.)

> **TIP:** You can also *forward* some messages you've selected in this way. When you tap the Forward button (⤳), a new outgoing text message appears, ready for you to specify the new recipient.

Mark All as Read

Here's a handy option: When you get off the plane, home from your honeymoon, you might see Messages bristling with notifications about texts you missed. Now you can mark them all as read at once, so the blue dots don't distract you anymore.

To do that, on the Messages screen, tap **Edit** and then **Read All**.

> **NOTE:** One real hassle of Messages is picking up one Apple gadget after doing a lot of texting on another—for example, switching on your iPhone after doing a lot of texting on your Mac during a flight. You sometimes have to wait a very long time for your phone's copy of Messages to catch up—to download all the conversations you had on your Mac.
>
> Apple promised to fix that problem in iOS 11. Your message history would be saved *online*, on iCloud. That way, (a) you'd save space on your phone, (b) you'd have a backup of your chats, and (c) you wouldn't wait nearly as long for a gadget to update itself on past conversations.
>
> In the end, this feature didn't make the cut, but Apple intends to add it in some future version.

The Details Screen

The Details screen offers six options that you may find handy in the midst of a chat. To see them, tap ⓘ at the top of the screen. Here's what you see now:

- **The map.** If your buddy has chosen to share her location with you, you'll see (after a few seconds) her little dot on a map.

- **Call.** If all this fussy typing is driving you nuts, you can jump onto a phone or video call. At the top of the Details screen, hit ◼◀ (place a FaceTime video call) or 📞 (conclude the transaction by voice, with a phone call or FaceTime audio call). You can also tap this person's name to open the corresponding Contacts card, loaded with different ways to call, text, or email.

- **Send My Current Location.** Hit this button to transmit a map to the other person, showing exactly where you are, so that person can come and pick you up, meet you for drinks, or whatever.

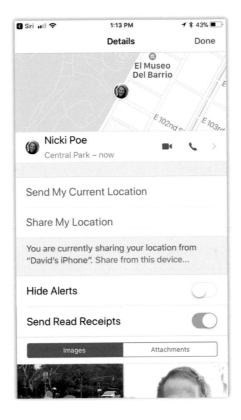

If your correspondent has an iPhone, iPad, or Mac, he can open the map you've sent in Maps, ready to guide him with driving directions. If he's one of the unenlightened—he owns some non-Apple phone— then he gets what's called a Location vCard, which he **may** be able to open into a mapping app on his own phone.

NOTE: If Location Services isn't turned on (page 585), the phone asks you to turn it on now. After all, you can't very well share your location if your phone has no idea where you are.

- **Share My Location.** If you're moving around, you may prefer this option. It sends your whereabouts to your correspondent—and keeps that location updated as you meander, for a period of time that you specify (**One Hour**, **Until End of Day**, or **Indefinitely**). That's great when you're club-hopping, say, and trying to help some buddies catch up with you. As your location changes, the map you sent to your recipient updates itself.

  At any time, you can stop broadcasting your location to this person; just open the Details screen again and tap **Stop Sharing My Location**.

- **Hide Alerts.** Otherwise known as "mute," "enough already," or "shut up." It makes your phone stop ringing or vibrating with every new message from this person or group. Handy when you're trying to get work done, when you're being bombarded by silly group chitchat, or when someone's stalking you.

- **Send Read Receipts.** You can turn read receipts (page 597) on or off independently for each chat partner, using this switch.

- **Images/Attachments.** Crazy cool! Here are all the photos and other attachments you've ever exchanged with this texting correspondent, going back to forever. (Tap **Images** to see only photos and videos; **Attachments** shows everything else.)

  You can tap one of these tiles to open it; hard-press one to "peek" at it (page 39); or hold your finger down lightly to get choices like **Copy**, **Delete**, and **More**. (There's usually nothing under **More** but **Save Image**, which copies the texted photo into your Photos collection, and a 🗑 button.)

Capturing Messages and Files

In general, text messages are fleeting; most people have no idea how they might capture them and save them forever. Copy and Paste help with that.

Some of the stuff *in* those text messages is easy to save, though. For example, if you're on the receiving end of a photo or a video, tap the small preview in the speech bubble. It opens at full-screen size so you can have a better look at it—and if it's a video, there's a ▶ button so you can play it. Either way, if the picture or video is good enough to preserve, tap ⬆. You're offered a **Save Image** or **Save Video** button; tap to add the photo or video to your iPhone's collection.

If someone sends you contact information (a phone number, for example), you can add it to your address book. Just tap inside that bubble and then tap either **Create New Contact** or **Add to Existing Contact**.

If you'd like to preserve the actual text messages, you have a few options:

- **Copy them individually.** Hold your finger down lightly on a text bubble, and then tap **Copy**. At this point, you can paste that one message into, for example, an outgoing email.

- **Forward them.** Hold your finger down lightly on a text bubble; tap **More**, and then tap the selection checkmarks beside all the messages you want to pass on. Now you can tap the Forward (↷) button. All the selected messages go along for the ride in a single consolidated message to a new text-message addressee.

- **Save the iMessages.** If you have a Mac, then your iMessages (that is, notes to and from other Apple gadgets) show up in the Messages chat program. You can save them or copy them there.

> **TIP:** Behind the scenes, the Mac stores all your chat transcripts in a hidden folder as special text files. To get there, press the Option key as you open the **Go** menu; choose **Go→Library**. The transcripts are in date-stamped folders in the **Messages→Archive** folder.

- **Use an app.** There's no built-in way to save regular text messages in bulk. There are, however, apps that can do this for you, like iMazing (for Windows) or iBackup Viewer (free for the Mac). They work from the invisible backup files that you create when you sync your phone with iTunes.

Tapbacks (iMessages Only)

How many trillions of times a day do people respond to texts with repetitive reactions like "LOL" and "Awww" and "!!!!!"? Many. It's how you demonstrate that you appreciate the import of the other person's text.

If you and your buddy are both using iOS 10 (or later) or macOS Sierra (or later), though, you've now got a quicker, less cluttery, more visual way to indicate those sorts of standard emotional reactions: what Apple calls tapbacks.

If you double-tap a message you've been sent, you're offered a tapback palette: six little reaction symbols: a heart, a thumbs up, a thumbs down, "ha ha," two exclamation points, and a question mark. When you choose one, it appears instantly on your screen and your buddy's. You can use them to stamp your reaction onto the other person's text (or one of your own, if you're weird).

In short, the tapback palette lets you react to a text without having to type anything.

Sending Messages

If you want to text somebody you've texted before, the quickest way is simply to resume one of the "conversations" already listed in the Messages list.

You can also tap a person's name in Contacts, or ⓘ next to a listing in Recents or Favorites, to open the Info screen; tap **Send Message**.

NOTE: In some cases, the iPhone shows you your *entire* Contacts list, even people with no cellphone numbers. But you can't text somebody who doesn't have a cellphone.

Actually, options to fire off text messages lurk all over the iPhone—anytime you see the Share (⬆) button, which is frequently. The resulting Share screen includes options like **Email**, **Twitter**, **Facebook**—and **Message**. Tapping **Message** sends you back to Messages, where the photo, video, page, or other item is ready to send. (More on multimedia messages shortly.)

In other words, sending a text message to anyone who lives in your iPhone is only a couple of taps away.

NOTE: You can tap that ⊕ to add *another* recipient for this same message (or tap the 123 button to type in a phone number). Repeat as necessary; they'll all get the same message.

Yet another way to start: Tap ✏ at the top of the Messages screen. Or, easiest of all, use Siri. Say, "Text Casey" or whatever.

In any case, the text message composition screen is waiting for you now. You're ready to type (or dictate) and send!

Audio Texting (iMessages Only)

Sometimes an audio recording is just better than a typed message, especially when music, children, animals, or a lot of emotion in your voice are involved. You could probably argue that audio texting is also better than typed texting when you're driving, jogging, or operating industrial machinery.

If you and your friend are both Apple people, your phone can become a sort of walkie-talkie.

Hold down the 🎤 button at the right end of the Messages text box. Once the sound-level meter appears, say something. When you're finished, release your finger. Now you can tap ⊗ to cancel, ▶ to play it back, or ⬆ to send what you said to your buddy as an audio recording.

TIP: If you're pretty confident that what you've said is correct, you can slide your thumb directly from the 🎤 button straight up to the ⬆ to send it.

The guy on the receiving end doesn't even have to touch the screen to listen. He just holds the phone up to his head! Your audio message plays automatically. (This works even if his phone is asleep and locked.)

And then get this: To reply, *he* doesn't have to touch anything or look at the screen, either. He just holds the phone to his head again and speaks! Once he lowers the phone, his recording shoots back to you.

Throughout all of this, you don't have to look at the phone, put your glasses on, or touch the screen. It's a whole new form of quick exchanges—something that combines the best of a walkie-talkie (instant audio) with the best of text messages (you can listen and reply at your leisure).

The off switch for the **Raise to Listen/Raise to Speak** feature is in **Settings→Messages**. But why would you want to disable such a cool feature?

TIP: Audio eats up a lot more space on your phone than text. If you do a lot of audio messaging, those audio snippets can fill up your storage over time.

That's why iOS comes set to *delete* each audio message two minutes after you receive it. If that prospect worries you, then visit **Settings→Messages**. Under Audio Messages, you can tap **Expire** and change that setting to **Never**.

Even if you leave it set to two minutes, you're free to preserve especially good audio messages forever; just tap the tiny **Keep** button that appears below each one.

Help with Emoji and Info-Bits

Messages is a card-carrying fan of *emoji*—those little icons once known as smileys or emoticons. Now there are thousands of them, representing people, places, things, food, emotions, household objects, and on and on.

How easy is it to use emoji in iOS 11? Very:

- **Auto-emoji.** If iOS has an emoji symbol for a word you've just typed, it appears in the row of autocomplete suggestions (below, left). If you tap that emoji *before* tapping the space bar, you *replace* the typed

word with the emoji. If you tap space and *then* the emoji, you get both the word *and* the emoji.

- **Auto-emoji part 2.** When you tap the ☺ button on your keyboard, Messages highlights, in color, any words in your typed (but not yet sent) message that can be replaced with an emoji (facing page, right). Tap any highlighted word to swap in the icon. That spares you the ritual of scrolling to find the one you want.

- **Jumbo emoji.** When you send *one, two, or three* emoji symbols as your entire response, they appear three times as large as normal (at least if the recipient has iOS 10 or macOS Sierra—or later).

- **Auto-info.** You know the QuickType word suggestions above the keyboard (page 85)? In Messages, those suggestions include *information* you might want to type.

  If you type "I'm available at," then one of the suggestion buttons includes the next open slot on your calendar. If you say "Stacy's number is," then the button offers her phone number (if she's in your Contacts). If someone texts you, "Where are you?" then one of the buttons offers to drop a Map button.

In iOS 11, in fact, you may also see things like movie, song, and place names as auto-suggestions, based on stuff you've recently looked up on your phone. If you're driving somewhere, you might even see an estimated arrival time.

Quite handy, actually.

The Finger-Sketch Pad

If you turn the phone 90 degrees, the screen becomes a whiteboard. What you scribble with your finger looks like real ink on paper and gets sent as a graphic. (You also see your previous masterpieces displayed here for quick reuse.) Just so cool.

Of course, this whiteboard business may drive you crazy. For example, on Plus-sized iPhones and the iPhone X, it deprives you of the separate column that lists your various chats in progress.

Fortunately, you can turn off the whiteboard screen. Once it appears, tap the ⌨ button in the corner. The keyboard pops up. This isn't a temporary change, either—from now on, rotating the phone to landscape orientation will *always* present the keyboard. Until you change your mind, that is—by tapping the 𝒯 button to bring back the whiteboard.

Sending with Animated Fun

If you're used to older versions of the Messages app, the first thing you might notice is that the **Send** button no longer says "Send." It's now a blue up-arrow (⬆). And it's more than a button.

If you hard-press (or long-press) the blue arrow, you get a palette of four sending styles.

The first three—Slam, Loud, and Gentle—animate the typography of your text to make it bang down, swell up, and so on, at least when you're sending to fellow iOS 10/11 or Mac fans. For example, Slam makes your text fly across the screen and then thud into the ground, making a shock wave ripple through the other messages.

The fourth special "Send with effect" is called Invisible Ink. It obscures your message with animated glitter dust until your recipient drags a finger across it (as shown at bottom on the facing page).

This idea is great for guessing games and revealing dramatic news, of course. But when you're sending, ahem, spicy text messages, it also prevents embarrassment if the recipient's phone is lying in public view.

When you hard-press (or long-press) the ⬆, the fifth option is Screen. It opens pages of **full-screen** animations. These, upon sending, fill the **entire background** of the Messages window to indicate your reaction to something: a swelling heart, ascending balloons, a laser show, fireworks, a shooting star, falling confetti, and so on. Swipe horizontally to preview each style before you commit to it.

If your text says "Congrats," "Happy birthday," or "Happy New Year," Messages fills the screen with a corresponding animation **automatically**. Which may or may not get old fast.

NOTE: The full juiciness of these text and screen styles is available only if your recipient also has iOS 10 or 11. So what if you're sending to an Android phone, an older iPhone, or a Mac?

In that case, the animation you've so carefully picked out doesn't show up. Instead, the other guy can only **read** about what you intended. He'll see the somewhat baffling written notation "sent with Slam effect," "sent with Balloons," or whatever.

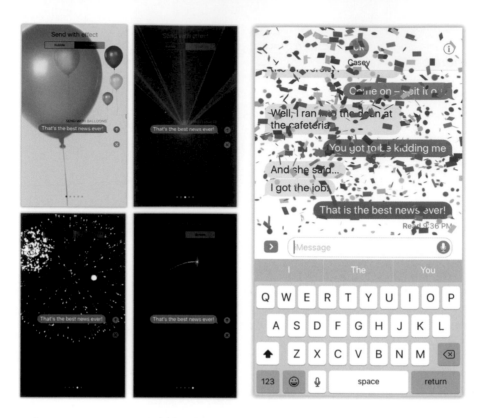

Photos and Videos

Depending on the age of your correspondents, typed text may be your *least* used form of communication.

Next to the typing box, iOS presents the Photos button (📷). Tap it to open the Photos picker. It consists of a simplified Camera app and a simplified Camera Roll of your existing pictures—but it also gives you access to your *actual* Camera app and your *actual* Camera Roll.

- To take a new photo, tap the white round shutter button in the live preview. (Feel free to tap the 🔄 if you want to take a selfie.) Wait until your snapshot appears in the Messages text box, ready to send.

- The Photos browser also displays two scrolling rows of photos and videos you've taken recently. Tap one (or more) that you want to send.

- To take a video, panorama, time-lapse video, slo-mo video, or any other fancier shot, tap **Camera** to open the regular Camera app.

Photos, Apps

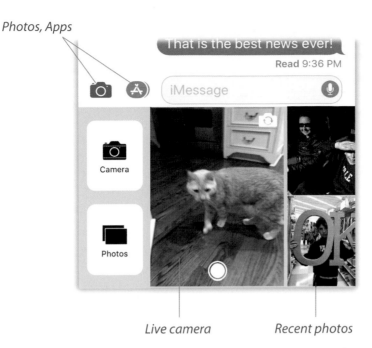

Live camera   Recent photos

- If you tap **Photos**, you open the regular Photos app, where you can find your albums, videos, and other organizational structures, for ease in finding an older picture or video to send.

Once you've inserted a photo into the text box, you can edit it, draw on it with your finger, and even type text on it. Just tap it to open the editing window, and then tap **Edit** (to edit using the photo-editing tools described on page 301) or **Markup** (to draw or type on it, as described on page 307).

You now return to your SMS conversation in progress—but now that photo or video appears inside the Send box. Type a caption or a comment, if you like. Then tap ⬆ to fire it off to your buddy. Or you can tap the ✕ if you change your mind about sending this photo.

The Apps Drawer

Messages offers a universe of expressive possibilities that go far beyond typed text and photos. Apple welcomes software companies to add their own new modules—miniature apps—that let you transmit everything from movie schedules and restaurant reservations to cash.

To see your options, tap the Ⓐ) that hugs the left side of the typing box. Messages sprouts a new row of tiny icons at the very bottom of the screen. These are your apps, made far easier to navigate in iOS 11.

This app mechanism has a few basic guidelines:

- **To see the apps' names,** scroll them horizontally. The apps drawer grows taller—tall enough to show their names (below, right).

- **To use an app,** tap it. Now the bottom half of Messages presents you with the app's offerings. (Feeling claustrophobic? Tap the ⌒ at the top edge of the app area. It now expands to fill your screen.)

- **To delete an app,** scroll all the way to the right; tap **More** (below, left). Now you see the management screen. Swipe left across an app's name to reveal the **Delete** button.

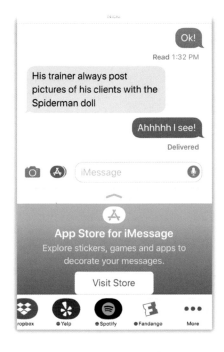

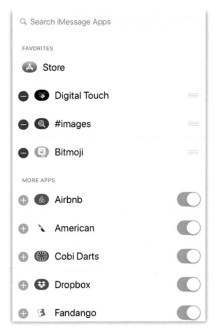

- **To rearrange the apps,** tap **Edit** on the management screen; now you can drag the apps around with their grip handles (≡) or hide an app by turning off its switch (above, right).

  Here, too, you can manipulate the special list called Favorites; these are the apps that appear first, at the left end of the app drawer. You can drag an app's grip handles up or down to rearrange its position among your favorites. Tap ⊖ to de-favorite an app, moving it into the list of also-rans. Or tap one of the ⊕ buttons to elevate an app into the Favorites list.

- **To hide the apps,** tap the Ⓐ again.

Here's what you'll find in the apps drawer on a new phone.

TIP: To move from one app to another, you can tap a different icon in the apps drawer—or you can swipe horizontally across the half-screen app area.

The App Store

The first icon (Ⓐ) presents you with a **Visit Store** button. It takes you down the rabbit hole into a world of options beyond belief.

In this store for Messages add-ons, you can download all kinds of tiny apps that work within Messages. Some are free; some cost a couple of bucks.

Some are "stickers" or animations that you can drag up onto other people's texts (or your own), thereby adding your own sarcastic or emotional commentary to it (shown below at right).

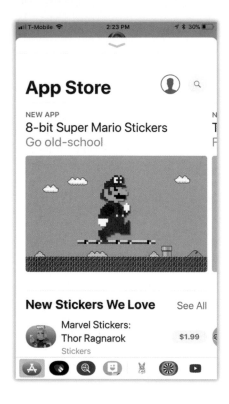
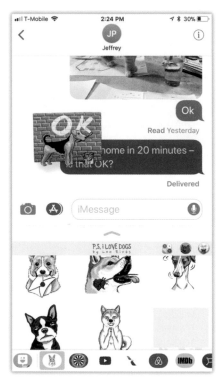

Others simply give you access, while you're chatting, to popular apps like Yelp or OpenTable (so that you can research or book restaurants), Airbnb (to book lodging), Square Cash or Circle Pay or Venmo (to send money directly to friends), Fandango (to research and book movies), iTranslate (to convert your texts to or from another language), Kayak (to book flights), Doodle (to find a mutually free time to meet), hundreds of popular games, and on and on. The idea is that you can do all of this right there in Messages, collaboratively with your buddy on the other end.

You can search or browse this store just as you do the regular App Store. For example, you can inspect the apps Apple is promoting today, or you can look through the bestseller lists.

When you find an app that looks appealing, tap **Get** (if it's free) or its price (if it's not), and then **Install** to install it. The new app appears in your app drawer, ready to use. (It shows up first in line after your Favorites.)

Apple starts you out with several such apps:

Music

This mini-app, greatly stripped down in iOS 11, lists songs you've recently played on your phone. Tap one to send a text saying, "I'm listening to [name of song]." That's it.

Animoji (iPhone X)

Some people probably bought an iPhone X just for this feature.

The iPhone X's TrueDepth camera (page 64) can create what Apple calls Animoji: animated cartoon faces whose expressions follow and mimic your expressions in real time, tracking the motion of 50 different muscles in your face. Smile, frown, wink, frown, laugh, nod, shake, open your mouth, raise your eyebrows, whatever—your little cartoon-animal avatar does the same. Suddenly, you're Warner Bros. It's crazy fun.

Once you've tapped the Animoji icon, you get a choice of 12 Animoji. Most are cute animals (bunny, piggy, panda, unicorn, and so on), but you also get an alien, a robot, and—of course—an animated poop pile.

Look at your phone and start talking, moving, or expressing, and marvel as your onscreen doppelgänger impersonates you like a mirror.

> **TIP:** A much larger, full-screen canvas awaits if you tap the ⌃ at the top edge of the app area. The app now expands to fill your screen.

Here are a few more things you can try:

- **Send a picture.** When you've got a great expression on your critter's face, tap it to paste it into the Messages text box, ready to send as a picture.

- **Stamp a sticker.** You can also use your critter as a sticker, stamping it onto something somebody has already said in your chat. Hold your finger down on the Animoji until it quivers; then, without lifting your finger, drag the image upward onto the appropriate text bubble.

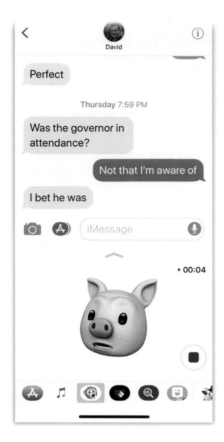
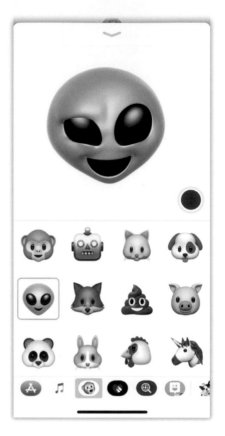

- **Send a video.** If you tap ⬤, you create a 10-second recording of your little cartoon, complete with sound—so don't forget to talk! When you then hit ⬆, the phone sends your recording as a standard video file. In other words, your recipients can play it even if they don't have an iPhone X—or even an iPhone.

> **TIP:** Once you've made a recording, you can tap a different Animoji character from the scrolling list. Without having to rerecord, you can now see what the effect is of *that* character speaking.

Digital Touch

This app opens a palette of crazy interactive art features, mostly inherited from the Apple Watch.

Here's what all these controls do:

- **Color picker.** Tap to open a palette of seven colors, which will determine your "paint" color in the next step.

- **Doodle with your finger.** Once you've got a color, you can start drawing. There's no eraser and no Undo, but it's fine for quick scrawls, comic exasperated faces, or technical blueprints.

  Tap ⬆ to send your sketch. What's cool is that if your recipient is an iMessage customer, she'll see the actual playback of your drawing, recreated before her eyes. (If you're corresponding with someone who doesn't have iOS 10 or 11, she'll receive your doodle as a finished piece of artwork, without seeing its animated creation.)

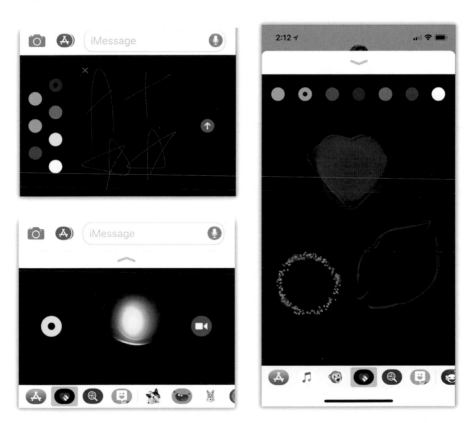

- **Shoot a photo or video, and then deface it.** Tap ■◀ to open a camera mode. (The app expands to full screen height, if it wasn't already.) Here you'll find both a white "take a still" shutter button and a red "record a video" button. (The 📷 button is here, too, in case you want to flip between the phone's front and back cameras.)

You can draw on the photo after you've taken it; in fact, you can even draw on a video, or stamp a Digital Touch graphic onto it (see previous page), *while* you're recording it. Your iMessages recipients will see the doodle "played back" on their screens, recreated line by line as you drew it. (Non-iMessages folk simply receive the finished sketch superimposed on the video or photo.)

- **Send animated feelings.** In iOS 11, there's not even a hint that you can create animated-feeling videos—you just have to know that they're there.

  To generate one, you tap or press your fingers on the black canvas. You can generate any of these: a ring of fire (tap—as many times as you want); a flaming fireball (hold down your finger); a lip-kiss (do a two-finger tap); a red, beating heart (hold with two fingers); and an animated breaking heart (tap-and-hold/drag-downward).

  No, the heart doesn't beat at the speed of your pulse, as it does on the Apple Watch; the iPhone doesn't have a heart-rate sensor.

> **TIP:** You can perform any of these special taps while you're recording a video, too.

As you explore these Digital Touch options, you'll gradually become aware of how fluid and intermixable they are. You can draw or stamp fire/kiss/heart animations on top of a photo or video you're recording, for example. Or you can draw something—for example, a hand-sketched frame—and *then* take a photo or video that goes inside it.

As usual, fellow iMessages people will see all these glorious animations played back just as you made them—but non-Apple people receive only a finished image or video.

#Images

This app is a searchable database of "reaction GIFs," which are very short, silent video loops, usually swiped from popular movies or TV shows. People (well, the young ones) use reaction GIFs to respond to something someone says. For example, if you text your friend about a disastrous decision you made today, you might get, in response, a two-second loop of Ben Stiller sarcastically slow-clapping.

Recents

This "app" is a collection of stickers and handwritings you've sent recently, presented here for easy reuse.

Messages Prefs

You might not think that something as simple as text messaging would involve a lot of fine print, but you'd be wrong.

Settings for Texts and iMessages

Tap **Settings→Messages** to find some intriguing options:

- **iMessage.** This is the on/off switch for the entire iMessages feature. It's hard to imagine why you would want to, but you know—whatever floats your boat.

- **Show Contact Photos.** If you turn this on, you'll see a little round photo next to each texting correspondent in the chat list and at the top of a chat window—or the person's initials, if there's no photo available. If you turn this off, then you see the person's name at the top of Messages instead.

- **Text Message Forwarding.** This switch is the gateway to the cool Continuity feature described on page 557, in which you can use your Mac to send regular text messages to non-Apple phones.

- **Send Read Receipts.** When you turn this option on, your iMessage correspondents will know when you've seen their messages. The word "Read" will appear beneath each sent message that you've actually seen. Turn this off only if it deprives you of the excuse for not responding promptly ("Hey, I never even saw your message!").

> **TIP:** You can turn read receipts on or off independently for each chat partner; see page 194.

- **Send as SMS.** If iMessages is unavailable (meaning that you have no Internet connection at all), then your phone will send your message as a regular text message, via the regular cellphone voice network.

- **Send & Receive.** Tap here to specify what cellphone numbers and email addresses you want to register with iMessages. (Your laptop, obviously, does not have a phone number, which is why iMessages gives you the option of using an email address.)

  When people send iMessages to you, they can use any of the numbers or addresses you turn on here. That's the only time these numbers and addresses matter. *You* see the same messages exactly the same way on all your Apple gadgets, no matter what email address or phone number the sender used for you.

(If you scroll down on this Settings screen, you'll see the **Start new conversations from** options. This is where you specify which number or address others will see when you initiate the message. It really doesn't make much difference which one you choose.)

- **MMS Messaging.** MMS messages are like text messages—except that they can also include audio clips, video clips, or photos, as already described. In the rare event that your cell company charges extra for these messages, you have an on/off switch here. If you turn it off, then you can send only plain text messages.

- **Group Messaging.** Suppose you're sending a message to three friends. When they reply to your message, the responses will appear in a Messages thread that's dedicated to this particular group. It works only if *all* of you have turned on Group Messaging. (Note to the paranoid: It also means that everyone sees everyone else's phone numbers or email addresses.)

  Messages tries to help you keep everybody straight by displaying their headshots (if you have them in Contacts), or their initials (if you don't).

- **Show Subject Field.** If email messages can have subject lines, why not text messages? Now, on certain newfangled phones (like yours), they can; the message arrives with a little dividing line between the subject and the body, offering your recipient a hint as to what it's about.

NOTE: It's OK to leave the subject line blank. But if you leave the *body* blank, the message won't send. (Incidentally, when you do fill in the subject line, what you're sending is an MMS message, rather than a plain old text message.)

- **Character Count.** If a text message (one sent to a non-Apple device) is longer than 160 characters, the iPhone breaks it up into multiple messages. That's convenient, sure. But if your cellphone plan permits only a fixed number of messages a month, you could wind up sending (and spending) more than you intended.

  The **Character Count** feature can help. When it's on, after your typing wraps to a second line, a little counter appears just above the **Send** button ("71/160," for example). It tracks how many characters remain within your 160-character limit for one message. (Of course, if you're sending an iMessage, you don't care how long it is; there's no length limit.)

- **Blocked.** You can block people who are harassing or depressing you with their texts or calls. Tap here to view the list of people in your

Contacts app you've decided to block; tap **Add New** to add new people to the list.

- **Keep Messages.** How long do you want your text messages to hang around on your phone? This is a question of privacy, of storage, and of your personality. In any case, here's where you get a choice of **30 Days**, **1 Year**, or **Forever**.

- **Filter Unknown Senders.** When you turn this on, the iPhone turns off notifications for senders not in your Contacts and sorts them into a separate list, which you can find in the "Unknown Senders" section of the Messages app.

- **Expire.** The iPhone ordinarily deletes audio and video messages a couple of minutes after they arrive, to avoid filling up your phone with old, no-longer-relevant audio and video files. The two Expire controls here let you turn off that automatic deletion (by choosing **Never**).

- **Raise to Listen.** Here's the on/off switch for the "raise to listen"/"raise to talk" features described earlier, where the phone plays back audio messages, and sends your spoken replies, automatically when you hold it up to your head. You might want to turn that feature off if you discover that the phone is playing back audio messages unexpectedly—or, worse, recording and sending them when you didn't mean to.

- **Low Quality Image Mode.** This feature, new in iOS 10, is a gift to anyone who has to pay for cellular service. It automatically reduces the size (resolution) and quality (compression) of any photo you send to around 100 kilobytes. At this point, sending *50* low-quality photos uses about the same amount of cellular data as *one* full-blown iPhone photo. Not only do you save a lot of money in the form of cellular data, but you save a lot of time, too, because these photos are *fast* to send.

  And here's the best part: The photo looks exactly the same to the recipients at the other end (at least until they zoom in).

Bonus Settings in a Place You Didn't Expect

Apple has stashed a few important text-messaging settings in **Settings→Notifications→Messages**:

- **Allow Notifications.** If, in a cranky burst of sensory overload, you want your phone to stop telling you when new texts come in (with a banner or sound, for example), then turn this off.

- **Sounds.** Tap here to choose a sound for incoming texts to play. (You can also choose a different sound for *each person* in your address book, as described on page 125.)

- **Badge App Icon.** Turning this on makes the Messages icon show a little red badge to let you know when you have a new text message.

- **Show on Lock Screen.** Do you want received text messages and iMessages to appear on the screen when it's locked? If yes, then you can sneak reassuring glances at your phone without turning it fully on. If no, then you maintain better protection against snoopers who find your phone on your desk.

- **Show in History.** Do you want recent messages to appear in the notification history (page 73)?

- **Show in CarPlay.** If your newish car has Apple's CarPlay software in its dashboard, here's where you control whether or not incoming texts appear on it.

- **Show Previews.** Usually, when a text message arrives, it wakes up your phone and shows the message contents. Which is great, as long as the message isn't private and the phone isn't lying on the table where everyone can see it. If you turn off **Show Previews**, though, you'll see who the message is from but not the actual text of the message (until you tap the notification banner or bubble).

- **Repeat Alerts.** If someone sends you a text message but you don't tap or swipe to read it, the iPhone waits two minutes and then plays the notification sound again. That second chance helps when, for example, you were in a noisy place and missed the original chime.

  But for some people, even one additional reminder isn't enough. Here you can specify that you want to be re-alerted **Twice**, **3 Times**, **5 Times**, or **10 Times**. (Or **Never**, if you don't want repeated alerts at all.)

7

Large Type, Kid Mode & Accessibility

I f you were told that the iPhone was one of the easiest phones in the world for a disabled person to use, you might spew your coffee. The thing has almost no physical keys! How would a blind person use it? It's a phone that rings! How would a deaf person use it?

But it's true. Apple has gone to *incredible* lengths to make the iPhone usable for people with vision, hearing, or other physical impairments. As a handy side effect, these features also can be fantastically useful to people whose only impairment is being under 10 or over 40.

If you're deaf, you can have the LED flash to get your attention. If you're blind, you can turn the screen off and operate *everything* by letting the phone speak what you're touching. It's pretty amazing (and it doubles the battery life).

You can also magnify the screen, reverse black for white (for better-contrast reading), set up custom vibrations for each person who might call you, and convert stereo music to mono (if you're deaf in one ear).

The kiosk mode is great for kids; it prevents them from exiting whatever app they're using. And if you have aging eyes, you might find the Large Text option handy. (You may also be interested in using the LED flash, custom vibrations, and zooming.)

Here's a rundown of the accessibility options in iOS 11. To turn on any of the features described here, open Settings→General→Accessibility. (And don't forget about Siri, described in Chapter 5. She may be the best friend a blind person's phone ever had—and, because you can now *type* commands to her instead of speaking them [page 181], she's even useful if you have trouble speaking.)

> **TIP:** You can turn many of the iPhone's accessibility features on and off with a triple-click of the home button or side button. See page 242 for details.

VoiceOver

VoiceOver is a *screen reader*—software that makes the iPhone speak everything you touch. It's a fairly important feature if you're blind.

On the VoiceOver settings pane, tap the on/off switch to turn VoiceOver on. Because VoiceOver radically changes the way you control your phone, you get a warning to confirm that you know what you're doing. If you proceed, you hear a female voice begin reading the names of the controls she sees on the screen. You can adjust the **Speaking Rate** of the synthesized voice (read on).

iPHONE X: A message appears to let you know that vibrations will help you navigate. As you swipe up from the bottom edge, the first vibration means "stop here to go to the Home screen"; the second means, "stop here to open the app switcher" (page 358).

There's a lot to learn in VoiceOver mode, and practice makes perfect, but here's the overview:

- **Touch something to hear it.** Tap icons, words, even status icons at the top; as you go, the voice tells you what you're tapping. "Messages." "Calendar." "Mail—14 new items." "45 percent battery power." You can tap the dots on the Home screen, and you'll hear, "Page 3 of 9."

  Once you've tapped a screen element, you can also flick your finger left or right—anywhere on the screen—to "walk" through everything on the screen, left to right, top to bottom.

TIP: A thin black rectangle appears around whatever the voice is identifying. That's for the benefit of sighted people who might be helping you.

- **Double-tap something to "tap" it.** Ordinarily, you tap something on the screen to open it. But since single-tapping now means "speak this," you need a new way to open everything. So: To open something you've just heard identified, double-tap *anywhere on the screen*. (You don't have to wait for the voice to finish talking.)

TIP: Or do a *split tap*. Tap something to hear what it is—and with that finger still down, tap somewhere else with a different finger to open it.

There are all kinds of other special gestures in VoiceOver. Make the voice stop speaking with a *two-finger tap*; read everything, in sequence, from the top of the screen with a ***two-finger upward flick***; scroll one page at a time with a ***three-finger flick up or down***; go to the next or previous screen (Home, Stocks, and so on) with a ***three-finger flick left or right***; and more.

Or try turning on Screen Curtain with a ***three-finger triple-tap***; it blacks out the screen, giving you visual privacy as well as a heck of a battery boost. (Repeat to turn the screen back on.)

On the VoiceOver settings screen, you'll find a wealth of options for using the iPhone sightlessly. For example:

- **Speaking rate slider** controls how fast VoiceOver speaks to you, on a scale of tortoise to hare.

- **Speech** is where you choose a voice for VoiceOver's speaking. If you have enough free space, you can install Alex, Allison, Ava, or Nicky, which are more realistic options.

  Here, too, is the **Pronunciation** feature, which is described on page 227. **Use Pitch Change** makes the phone talk in a higher voice when you're entering characters and a lower voice when you're deleting them. It also uses a higher pitch when speaking the first item of a list and a lower one when speaking the last item. In both cases, this option is a great way to help you understand where you are in a list.

  Finally, here's where you choose the language you want for the Rotor (next page).

- **Verbosity** makes the phone speak more to help you out more. For example, **Speak Hints** gives you additional suggestions for operating something you've tapped. For example, instead of just saying, "Safari," it says, "Safari. Double-tap to open." And **Emoji Suffix** makes the phone say (for example) "pizza emoji" instead of just "pizza" when encountering an emoji symbol.

- **Braille,** of course, is the system that represents letters as combinations of dots on a six- or eight-cell grid. Blind people can read Braille by touching embossed paper with their fingers. But in iOS they can type in Braille, too. For many, that may be faster than trying to type on the onscreen keyboard, and more accurate than dictation.

  On this Settings screen, you specify, among other things, whether you want to use the six- or eight-dot system.

  When you're ready to type, you use the Rotor (described in a moment) to choose Braille Screen Input, which is usually the last item on the list. If the phone is flat on a table ("desktop mode"), the "keys" for typing Braille are arrayed in a loose, flattened V pattern.

If you're holding the phone, you grip it with your pinkies and thumbs, with the screen facing away from you ("Screen away" mode).

- **Audio** gives you three options. **Mute Sound Effects** turns off the little clicks and chirps that ordinarily help you navigate as you scroll, tap, and so on. **Audio Ducking** makes music or video soundtracks get momentarily softer when the phone is speaking. And **Auto-select Speaker in Call** is ingenious: It switches the phone to the speakerphone automatically whenever you're not holding it to your head.

NOTE: That **Auto-select Speaker in Call** thing would be useful to almost anyone—but note that these features kick in only when VoiceOver itself is turned on.

- **The Rotor** is a brilliant solution to a thorny problem. If you're blind, how are you supposed to control how VoiceOver reads to you? Do you have to keep burrowing into Settings to change the volume, speaking speed, verbosity, and so on?

  Nope. The Rotor is an imaginary dial. It appears when you twist two fingers on the screen as if you were turning an actual dial.

  And what are the options on this dial? That's up to you. Tap **Rotor** in the VoiceOver settings screen to get a huge list of choices: **Characters**, **Words**, **Speaking Rate**, **Volume**, **Punctuation**, **Zoom**, and so on.

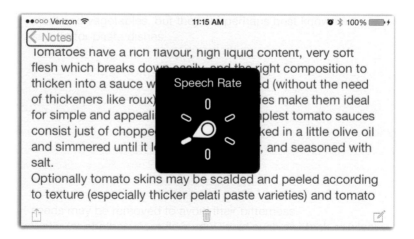

Once you've dialed up a setting, you can get VoiceOver to move from one item to another by flicking a finger up or down. For example, if you've chosen **Volume** from the Rotor, then you make the playback volume louder or quieter with each flick up or down. If you've chosen Zoom, then each flick adjusts the screen magnification.

The Rotor is especially important if you're using the web. It lets you jump among web page elements like pictures, headings, links, text boxes, and so on. Use the Rotor to choose, for example, images—then you can flick up and down from one picture to the next on that page.

- **Typing Style.** In **Standard Typing**, you drag your finger around the screen until VoiceOver speaks the key you want; then simultaneously tap anywhere with a second finger to type the letter.

  In **Touch Typing**, you can slide your finger around the keyboard until you hear the key you want; lift your finger to type that letter.

  There's also **Direct Touch Typing**, which is a faster method intended for people who are more confident about typing. If you tap a letter, you type it instantly. If you hold the key down, VoiceOver speaks its name but doesn't type it, just to make sure you know where you are.

- **Phonetic Feedback** refers to what VoiceOver says as you type or touch each keyboard letter. **Character and Phonetics** means that it says the letter's name plus its pilot's alphabet equivalent: "A—Alpha," "B—Bravo," "C—Charlie," and so on. **Phonetics Only** says the pilot's-alphabet word alone.

- **Typing Feedback** governs how the phone helps you figure out what you're typing. It can speak the individual letters you're striking, the words you've completed, or both.

- **Modifier Keys.** You can trigger some VoiceOver commands from a physical Bluetooth keyboard; all of them use Control-Option as the basis. (For example, Control-Option-A means "read all from the current position." A complete list of these shortcuts is at *http://j.mp/1kZRSOz*).

  The **Modifier Keys** option lets you use the Caps Lock key instead of the Control-Option business, which simplifies the keyboard shortcuts at least a little bit.

- **Always Speak Notifications** makes the phone announce, with a spoken voice, when an alert or update message has appeared. (If you turn this off, then VoiceOver announces only incoming text messages.)

- **Navigate Images.** As VoiceOver reads to you what's on a web page, how do you want it to handle pictures? It can say nothing about them (**Never**), it can read their names (**Always**), or it can read their names and whatever hidden **Descriptions** savvy web designers have attached to them for the benefit of blind visitors.

- **Large Cursor** fattens up the borders of the VoiceOver "cursor" (the box around whatever is highlighted) so you can see it better.

- **Double-tap Timeout** lets you give yourself more time to complete a double-tap when you want to trigger some VoiceOver reading. Handy if you have motor difficulties.

VoiceOver and Braille input take practice and involve learning a lot of new techniques. If you need these features to use your iPhone, then visit the more complete guide at *support.apple.com/kb/HT3598*.

Or spend a few minutes (or weeks) at *applevis.com*, a website dedicated to helping the blind use Apple gear.

> **TIP:** VoiceOver is especially great at reading your iBooks titles out loud. Details are on page 402.

Zooming

Compared with a computer, an iPhone's screen is pretty tiny. Every now and then, you might need a little help reading small text or inspecting those tiny graphics.

The Zoom command is just the ticket; it lets you magnify the screen whenever it's convenient, up to 500 percent. Of course, at that point, the screen image is too big to fit the physical glass of the iPhone, so you need a way to scroll around.

To begin, you have to turn on the master Zoom switch in **Settings→ General→Accessibility**. Immediately, this magnifying lens appears:

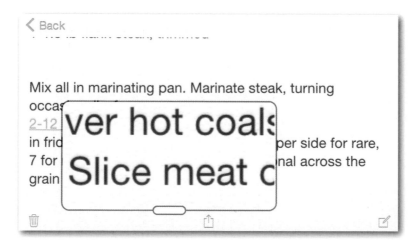

Scroll down and look at the **Zoom Region** control. If it's set to **Window Zoom**, then zooming produces this movable rectangular magnifying lens. If it's set to **Full Screen Zoom**, then zooming magnifies the entire screen.

(And that, as many Apple Genius Bar employees can tell you, freaks out a lot of people who don't know what's happened.)

Now then. Next time you need to magnify things, do this:

- **Start zooming** by double-tapping the screen with three fingers. You've either opened up the magnifying lens or magnified the entire screen. The magnification is 200 percent of original size. (Another method: Triple-press the home button—on the iPhone X, the side button—and then tap **Zoom**.)

TIP: You can move the rectangular lens around the screen by dragging the white oval handle on its lower edge.

- **Pan around inside the lens (or pan the entire virtual jumbo screen)** by dragging with three fingers.

- **Zoom in more or less** by double-tap/dragging with three fingers. It's like double-tapping, except that you leave your fingers down on the second tap—and drag them upward to zoom in more (up to 500 percent) or down to zoom out again.

  You can lift two of your three fingers after the dragging has begun. That way, it's easier to see what you're doing.

- **Open the Zoom menu** by tapping the white handle on the magnifying lens. Up pops a black menu of choices like **Zoom Out** (puts away the lens and stops zooming), **Full Screen Zoom** (magnifies the entire screen, hides the lens), **Resize Lens** (adds handles so you can change the lens's shape), **Choose Filter** (lets you make the area inside the lens grayscale or inverted colors, to help people with poor vision), and **Show Controller** (the little joystick described in a moment).

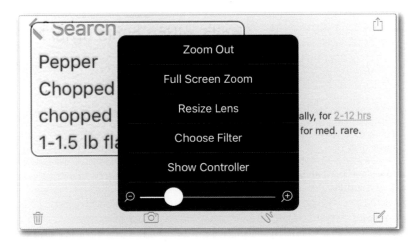

There's also a slider that controls the degree of magnification—handy.

That's the big-picture description of Zoom. But back in **Settings→ General→Accessibility→Zoom**, a few more controls await:

- **Follow Focus.** When this option is turned on, the image inside the magnifying lens scrolls automatically when you're entering text. Your point of typing is always centered.

- **Smart Typing.** When this option is turned on, a couple of things happen whenever the onscreen keyboard appears. First, you get full-screen zooming (instead of just the magnifying lens); second, the keyboard itself isn't magnified, so you can see all the keys.

- **Show Controller.** The controller is this weird little onscreen joystick:

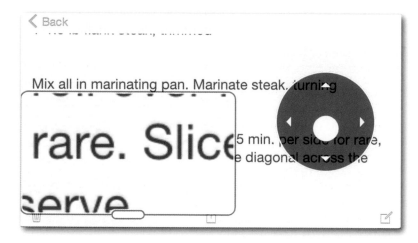

You can drag it with your finger to move the magnifying lens, or the entire magnified screen, in any direction. (It grows when you're touching it; the farther your finger moves from center, the faster the scrolling.) It's an alternative to having to drag the magnified screen with three fingers, which isn't precise and also blocks your view.

You can tap the center dot of the Controller to open the Zoom menu described already. Or double-tap the center to stop or start zooming.

TIP: On iPhone 6s and later models, you can hard-press the controller for a pop-up magnifying lens. It remains open only as long as you're pressing.

- **Idle Visibility.** After you've stopped using the joystick for a while, it stays on the screen but becomes partly transparent, to avoid blocking your view. This slider controls *how* transparent it gets.

- **Zoom Region** controls whether you're zooming the entire screen or just a window (that is, a magnifying lens).

- **Zoom Filter** gives you options for how you want the text in the zoom window to appear—for example, black on gray for viewing in low light. (See the super-cool Zoom Filter tip on page 241.)

- **Maximum Zoom Level.** This slider controls just how magnified that lens, or screen, can get.

NOTE: When VoiceOver is turned on, three-finger tapping has its own meaning—"jump to top of screen." Originally, therefore, you couldn't use Zoom while VoiceOver was on.

You can these days, but you have to add an *extra* finger or tap for VoiceOver gestures. For example, ordinarily, double-tapping with three fingers makes VoiceOver stop talking, but since that's the "zoom in" gesture, you must now *triple*-tap with three fingers to mute VoiceOver.

And what about VoiceOver's existing triple/three gesture, which turns the screen off? If Zoom is turned on, you must now triple-tap with *four* fingers to turn the screen off.

Magnifier

Oh man, this is great: You can triple-click the home button to turn the iPhone into the world's best electronic magnifying glass (on the iPhone X, you triple-click the side button). It's perfect for dim restaurants, tiny type on pill bottles, and theater programs.

Once you've summoned the Magnifier, you can zoom in, turn on the flashlight, or tweak the contrast.

To set this up, open **Settings→General→Accessibility→Magnifier**. Turn on **Magnifier**. Turn on **Auto-Brightness**, too; it'll help the picture look best.

Then, next time you need a magnifying glass, triple-click the home (side) button. Instantly, the top part of the screen becomes a zoomed-in view of whatever is in front of the camera.

At this point, you gain a wealth of options for making that image even clearer (next page, left):

- **Zoom slider.** Adjusts the degree of magnification.

- **⚡.** Turns on the flashlight, to illuminate the subject.

- **🔒.** Locks the focus, so that the phone quits trying to refocus as you move the phone. (You can also tap the screen for this function.)

- . Freezes the frame. That way, once you've finally focused on what you want to read, you can actually *read* it, without your own hand jiggles ruining the view.

- ⊗. Opens the Filters screen (above, right).

The Filters screen offers even more tools for making things clear:

- **Filter.** Swipe horizontally across the screen (you don't have to aim for the little row of filter names) to cycle among the Magnifier's color filters: None, White/Blue, Yellow/Blue, Grayscale, Yellow/Black, Red/Black. Each may be helpful in a different circumstance to make your subject more legible.

- ☀ **and** ◑ **sliders.** Adjust the brightness and contrast of the image.

- ⇄ Swaps the two filter colors (black for white, blue for yellow, and so on).

To exit the Filters screen, tap ⊗ again; to exit the Magnifier, press the home or side button.

Display Accommodations

These options affect the color schemes of the entire screen, in hopes of making it easier for you to see.

- **Invert Colors.** By reversing the screen's colors like a film negative (black for white, red for green, blue for yellow), you create a higher-contrast effect that some people find is easier on the eyes.

  In iOS 11, you have a choice. **Classic Invert** inverts every single pixel (below, center), which can create some bizarre-looking photos and videos. The new **Smart Invert** doesn't touch photos, videos, app icons, or dark backgrounds (below, right). It inverts only light-colored iOS screen elements, making them dark; some people turn on this "dark theme" just because it looks cool and soothing.

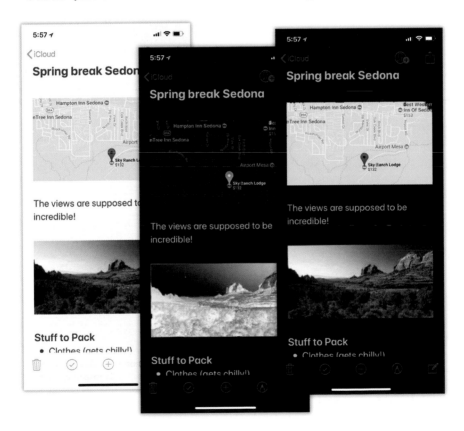

- **Color Filters.** The iPhone can help you if you're color-blind. The Color Filters option gives you special screen modes that substitute colors you **can** see for colors you **can't**, everywhere on the screen. Tap the various color-blindness types in the list (**Red/Green**, **Blue/Yellow**, and so on) to see how each affects the crayons or color swatches at the top of the screen. Use the Intensity slider to govern the degree of the effect.

The **Color Tint** option washes the entire screen with a certain shade (which you choose using the **Hue** slider that appears); it's designed to help people with Irlen syndrome (visual stress), who have trouble reading. The Grayscale option removes all color from the screen so that everything looks like a black-and-white photo.

The new Intensity slider lets you dial back (or dial up) the color-swapping effect.

The phone's colors may now look funny to **other** people, but you should have an easier time distinguishing colors when it counts. (You may even be able to pass some of those Ishihara dot-pattern color-blindness tests online.)

- **Auto-Brightness.** This option has moved from its old address (in **Settings→Display & Brightness**). Auto-Brightness makes the screen brighten automatically when you're in bright light; in dim light, it darkens. That's because when you unlock the phone after waking it, it samples the ambient light and adjusts the brightness.

NOTE: This works because of the ambient-light sensor near the earpiece. Apple says it experimented with having the light sensor active all the time, but it was weird to have the screen constantly dimming and brightening as you used it.

You can use this information to your advantage. By covering up the sensor as you unlock the phone, you force it into a low-power, dim-screen setting (because the phone believes it's in a dark room). Or by holding it up to a light as you wake it, you get more brightness. In either case, you've saved the navigation it would have taken you to find the manual brightness slider in Settings or in the Control Center.

TIP: You can set things up so that a triple-click on the home button (or the iPhone X's side button) instantly dims your screen, for use in the bedroom, movie theaters, or planetariums—without having to fuss with Settings or sliders. See page 241 for this awesome trick.

- **Reduce White Point** makes *all* colors *ever* depicted on the screen less intense—including the white of the background, which becomes a little yellowish. This might be nice if staring at your phone all day is causing you eyestrain.

Speech

Your phone can read to you aloud: an email message, a web page, a text message—anything. Your choices here go like this:

- **Speak Selection** puts a **Speak** command into the button bar that appears whenever you highlight text in any app. Tap that button to make the phone read the selected text.

- **Speak Screen** simply reads everything on the screen, top to bottom, when you swipe down from the top of the screen with two fingers. Great for hearing an ebook page or email read to you.

- **Highlight Content.** Great for dyslexic or beginner readers. If you turn this on, the phone underlines or uses a highlight color on each word or sentence as it's spoken, depending on your settings here.

- **Typing Feedback.** The phone can speak each **Character** as you type it ("T," "O," "P," and so on), with or without **Character Hints** ("T—Tango," "O—Oscar," "P—Papa"). Here you can also specify how much delay elapses before the spoken feedback plays; whether you want finished words and autocorrect suggestions spoken, too; and whether you want to hear QuickType suggestions (page 85) pronounced when you hold your finger down on them.

  This feature, of course, helps blind people know what they're typing. But it also means you don't have to take your eyes off the keyboard, which is great for speed and concentration. And if you're zoomed in, you may not be able to see the suggested word appear under your typed text—but now you'll still know what the suggestion is.

- **Voices** gives you a choice of languages and accents for the spoken voice. Try Australian; it's really cute.

- **Speaking Rate** controls how fast the voice talks.

- **Pronunciations.** You can correct the phone's pronunciation of certain words it always gets wrong. Type the word into the Phrase box; tap the 🎤 and speak how it *should* be pronounced; and then, from the list of weird phonetic symbol-written alternatives, tap the one that sounds correct. This technique corrects how your phone pronounces those words or names whenever it speaks, including Siri and the text-to-speech feature described on page 98.

How to De-Sparsify iOS's Design

When Apple introduced the sparse, clean design of iOS 7 (which carries over into iOS 11), thousands blogged out in dismay: "It's too lightweight! The fonts are too spindly! The background is too bright! There aren't rectangles around buttons—we don't know what's a button and what's not! You moved our cheese—we hate this!"

Well, Apple may not agree with you about the super-lightweight design, but it has given you options to change it. You can make the type bigger and bolder, the colors heavier, the background dimmer. You can restore outlines around buttons. And so much more.

All of these options await in **Settings→General→Accessibility**.

Larger Text

This option is the central control panel for iOS's Dynamic Type feature. It's a game-changer if you, a person with several decades of life experience, often find type on the screen too small.

Using the slider, you can choose a larger type size for all text the iPhone displays in apps like Mail, iBooks, Messages, and so on. This slider doesn't affect all the world's *other* apps—at least until their software companies update them to make them Dynamic Type–compatible. That day, when it comes, will be glorious. One slider to scale them all.

Bold Text

The iOS system font is fairly light. Its strokes are very thin; in some sizes and lighting conditions, it can even be hard to read.

But if you turn on **Bold Text** (and then tap **Continue** in the confirmation box), your iPhone restarts—and when it comes to, the fonts everywhere

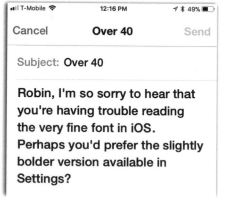

are slightly heavier: at the Home screen, in email, everywhere. And much easier to read in low light or with aging eyesight.

It's one of the most useful features in iOS—and something almost nobody knows about.

Button Shapes

Among the criticisms of iOS's design: You can't tell what's a **button** anymore! Everything is just words floating on the screen, without border rectangles to tell you what's tappable!

That's not quite true; any text in **blue type** is a tappable button. But never mind that; if you want shapes around your buttons, you shall have them—when you turn on this switch (below, right).

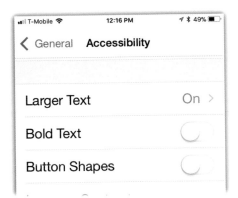 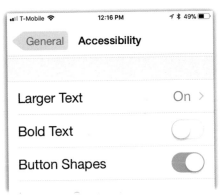

Increase Contrast

There are two switches in here. **Reduce Transparency** adds opacity to screens like the Dock and the Notification Center. Their backgrounds are now solid, rather than slightly see-through, so that text on them is much easier to read. (You can see the before and after below.)

Darken Colors makes type in some spots a little darker and heavier. You notice it in the fonts for buttons, in the Calendar, and in Safari, for example.

Reduce Motion

What kind of killjoy would want to turn off the subtle "parallax motion" of the Home screen background behind your icons, or the zooming-in animation when you open an app?

In any case, you can if you want, thanks to this button.

On/Off Labels

The Settings app teems with little tappable on/off switches, including this one. When something is turned on, the background of the switch is green; when it's off, the background is white.

But if you're having trouble remembering that distinction, turn on this option. Now the background of each switch sprouts visible symbols to help you remember that green means On (you see a | marking) and white means Off.

Face ID & Attention

The iPhone X offers two bonus features that have to do with your attention, which Apple defines as "looking at the phone"; see page 584.

Reachability

Reachability is the feature described on page 21, the one that brings the top half of the screen downward. It's designed to let you reach things on the top of the screen while holding one of the larger iPhones with only one hand. If you find yourself triggering this feature accidentally, you'll be happy to know that this Off switch awaits.

Switch Control

Suppose your physical skills are limited to very simple gestures: puffing on an air pipe, pressing a foot switch, blinking an eye, or turning your head, for example. A hardware accessory called a **switch** lets you operate certain gadgets this way.

When you turn on Switch Control, the iPhone warns you that things are about to get very different. Tap **OK**.

Now the phone sequentially highlights one object on the screen after another; you're supposed to puff, tap, or blink at the right moment to say, "Yes, *this* one."

If you don't have a physical switch apparatus, you can use the one nature gave you: your head. The iPhone's camera can detect when you turn your head left or right and can trigger various functions accordingly.

If you'd like to try it out, get to **Settings→General→Accessibility→ Switch Control**. Tap **Switches→Add New Switch→Camera→Left Head Movement**.

On this screen, you choose what a left head-turn will mean to your phone. The most obvious option is **Select Item**, which you could use in conjunction with the sequential highlighting of controls on the screen. But you can also make it mean "Press the home button," "Activate Siri," "Adjust the volume," and so on.

Once you've made your selection, repeat that business for **Right Head Movement**.

When you return to the Switch Control screen, turn on **Switch Control**. Now your phone is watching you; whenever you turn your head left or right, it activates the control you set up.

The controls here let you specify how fast the sequential highlighting proceeds, whether or not it pauses on the screen's first item, how many times the highlighting cycles through each screenful, and so on.

To turn off Switch Control, tap the on/off switch again. Or, if you're using some other app, triple-press the home button to open the Accessibility shortcut panel. If you had the foresight to add Switch Control to its options (page 242), then one tap does the trick.

Switch Control is a broad (and specialized) feature. To read more about it, open the Accessibility chapter of Apple's iPhone User Guide: *help.apple.com/iphone/11/*.

AssistiveTouch

If you can't hold the phone, you might have trouble shaking it (a shortcut for "Undo"); if you can't move your fingers, adjusting the volume might be a challenge.

This feature is Apple's accessibility team at its most creative. When you turn AssistiveTouch on, you get a new, glowing white circle in a corner of the screen (next page at top).

You can drag this magic white ball anywhere on the edges of the screen; it remains onscreen all the time.

When you tap it, it expands into the special palette shown on the next page. It's offering six ways to trigger motions and gestures on the iPhone screen without requiring hand or multiple-finger movement. All you have to be able to do is tap with a single finger—or even a stylus held in your teeth or toes.

You can add more buttons to this main menu, or switch around which buttons appear here. To do that, open **Settings→General→Accessibility→ Assistive Touch→Customize Top Level Menu**.

Meanwhile, here are the six starter icons:

- **Notifications, Control Center.** As far as most people know, the usual way to open the Notifications pane and Control Center is to swipe up or down the screen. These buttons, however, give you another way— one that doesn't require any hand movement. (Tap the same button again to *close* whichever center you opened.)

- **Rotate Screen.** You can tap this instead of turning the phone 90 degrees.

- **Siri.** Touch here when you want to speak to Siri. If you do, in fact, have trouble manipulating the phone, Siri is probably your best friend already. This option, as well as the "Hey Siri" voice command, mean that you don't even have to hold down a button to start her up.

- **Home.** You can tap here, instead of pressing the physical home button, to get to your Home screen. (That's handy if your home button gets sticky, too.)

- **Device.** Tap this button to open a palette of six functions that would otherwise require you to grasp the phone or push its tiny physical buttons (facing page, right). There's **Lock Screen** (instead of pressing the side button), **Volume Up** and **Volume Down** (instead of pressing the volume keys), another **Rotate Screen**, and **Mute/Unmute** (instead of flipping the small silencer switch on the side).

If you tap **More**, you get some bonus buttons. They include **Shake** (does the same as shaking the phone to undo typing), **Screenshot** (page 340), **Multitasking** (brings up the app switcher, as described on page 358), **Apple Pay** (instead of using the home or side button), **Restart**, **SOS** (page 78), and **Gestures**.

That **Gestures** button opens up a peculiar palette that depicts a hand holding up two, three, four, or five fingers. When you tap, for example, the three-finger icon, you get three blue circles on the screen. They move together. Drag one of them (with a stylus, for example), and the phone thinks you're dragging three fingers on its surface. Using this technique, you can operate apps that require multiple fingers dragging on the screen.

- **Custom.** Impressively enough, you can actually define your own gestures. On the AssistiveTouch screen, tap one of the + buttons, and then tap **Create New Gesture** to draw your own gesture right on the screen, using one, two, three, four, or five fingers.

  For example, suppose you're frustrated in Maps because you can't do the two-finger double-tap that means "zoom out." On the Create New Gesture screen, get somebody to do the two-finger double-tap for you. Tap **Save** and give the gesture a name—"2 double tap," say.

  From now on, "2 double tap" shows up on the Custom screen, ready to trigger with a single tap by a single finger or stylus.

 TIP: Apple starts you off with some useful predefined Custom Actions gestures, each of which might be difficult for some people to trigger in the usual ways. There's **Single-Tap**, **Double-Tap**, **Long Press**, and **3D Touch**, for example. You can install any of these on the AssistiveTouch palette for quick access.

Touch Accommodations

These options are intended to accommodate people who find it difficult to trigger precise taps on the touchscreen. **Touch Accommodations** is the master switch for all three of the following options:

- **Hold Duration** requires that you keep your finger on the screen for an amount of time that you specify (for example, one second) before the iPhone registers a tap. That feature neatly eliminates accidental taps when your finger happens to bump the screen.

When Hold Duration is turned on, a countdown cursor appears at your fingertip, showing with a circular graph how much longer you have to wait before your touch "counts."

- **Ignore Repeat** ignores multiple taps that the screen detects within a certain window—say, one second. If you have, for example, a tremor, this is a great way to screen out accidental repeated touches or repeated letter-presses on the onscreen keyboard.

- **Tap Assistance** lets you indicate whether the location of a tap should be the *first spot you touch* or the *last spot*. The **Use Final Touch Location** option means you can put your finger down in one spot and then fine-tune its position on the glass anytime within the countdown period indicated by the timer cursor. Feel free to adjust the timer window using the controls here.

Home Button (or Side Button)

If you have motor-control problems of any kind, you might welcome this enhancement. It's an option to widen the time window for registering a double-press or triple-press of the home button (or, on the iPhone X, the side button). If you choose **Slow** or **Slowest**, the phone accepts double- and triple-presses spaced far and even farther apart, rather than interpreting them as individual presses a few seconds apart.

This is also a place where you can remove the triggering of **Siri** from the home button/side button's duties. If you choose **Off** here, then you can trigger Siri only by voice ("Hey Siri"). If you choose **Voice Control**, then holding in the button lets you speak only music-control and phone-dialing commands.

If your phone has a home button, this screen also lets you turn off the **Rest Finger to Open** feature, which saves you a click when you're unlocking the phone (page 18).

Siri

In iOS 11, for the first time, you can *type* your questions and commands to Siri instead of speaking them, which can be a tremendous help if you have trouble speaking. (It's also a tremendous help if you're using Siri from the sidelines of a golf or chess tournament.) Here's the **Type to Siri** on/off switch; see page 181.

3D Touch

The 3D Touch option (page 37) may be the hot feature of the iPhone 6s and later models. But it may also drive you crazy.

Here you can turn the feature off, or just adjust the threshold of pressure (Light, Medium, Firm) required to trigger a "3D touch." (Apple even gives you a sample photo thumbnail to practice on, right on this screen, so you can gauge which degree of pressure you like best.)

Tap to Wake (iPhone X)

The iPhone X doesn't have a home button to press for waking it, so it offers a consolation prize: this option, which lets you tap *anywhere on the screen* to wake the phone.

Keyboard

The first option here controls whether or not the onscreen keyboard's keys turn into CAPITALS when the Shift key is pressed; see page 82.

The others control what happens when you've hooked up a physical keyboard to your iPhone—a Bluetooth keyboard, for example:

- **Key Repeat.** Ordinarily, holding down a key makes it repeat, so that you can type things like "auuuuuuuuuuugggggh!" or "zzzzz." These two sliders govern the repeating behavior: how long you must hold down a key before it starts repeating (to prevent triggering repetitions accidentally), and how fast each key spits out characters once the spitting has begun.

- **Sticky Keys** lets you press multikey shortcuts (involving keys like Shift, Option, Control, and ⌘) one at a time instead of all together. (The **Sound** option ensures that you'll get an audio beep to confirm that the keyboard has understood.)

  Toggle With Shift Key gives you the flexibility of turning Sticky Keys on and off at will. Whenever you want to turn on Sticky Keys, press the Shift key five times in succession. You'll hear a special clacking sound effect alerting you that you just turned on Sticky Keys. (Repeat the five presses to turn Sticky Keys off again.)

- With **Slow Keys** turned on, the phone doesn't register a key press at all until you've held down the key for more than a second or so—a feature designed to screen out accidental key presses.

Shake to Undo

In most of Apple's apps, you can undo your most recent typing or editing by giving the iPhone a quick shake. (You're always asked to confirm.) This is the On/Off switch for that feature—handy if you find yourself triggering Undo accidentally.

Vibration

Here's a master Off switch for all vibrations the phone makes. Alarms, notifications, confirmations—all of it.

As Apple's lawyers cheerfully point out on this screen, turning off vibrations also means you won't get buzzy notifications of "earthquake, tsunami, and other emergency alerts." Goodness!

Call Audio Routing

When a call comes in, where do you want it to go? To your headset? Directly to the speakerphone? Or the usual (headset unless there is no headset)? Here's where you make a choice that sticks, so you don't have to make it each time a call rings.

Hearing Assistance

The next options in **Settings→General→Accessibility** are all dedicated to helping people with hearing loss. (Further details are at *www.apple.com/accessibility/iphone/hearing*.)

MFi Hearing Aids

A cellphone is bristling with wireless transmitters, which can cause interference and static if you wear a hearing aid. But Apple has been working with hearing-aid manufacturers to solve these problems.

MFi stands for "Made for iPhone." Hearing aids with this logo are designed to sound great without draining the battery. Better yet, you can triple-click the home button (or, on the iPhone X, the side button) to view the hearing aids' battery status, change the left and right volume, or switch to one of your audiologist's environmental presets—outdoors, restaurants, and so on.

TTY

A TTY is a teletype or text telephone. It's a machine that lets deaf people make phone calls by typing instead of speaking.

iOS offers a built-in **software** TTY that requires no hardware to haul around. It resembles a chat app, and it works like this: When you place a phone call (using the standard Phone app), the iPhone gives you a choice of what kind of call you want to place:

- **Voice call.** Voice-to-voice, as usual.

- **TTY call.** You're calling another person who also has a TTY machine (or iOS 10 or later). You'll type back and forth.

- **TTY relay call.** This option means you can call a person who doesn't have a TTY setup. A human operator will speak (to the other guy) everything you type, and will type (to you) everything the other guy speaks. This, of course, requires a relay service, whose phone number you enter here on this Settings panel.

For more on using TTY on the iPhone, visit *support.apple.com/en-us/ HT207033*.

LED Flash for Alerts

If you're deaf, you know when the phone is ringing—because it vibrates, of course. But what if it's sitting on the desk, or it's over there charging? This option lets you know when you're getting a call, text, or notification by blinking the flash on the back of the phone—the very bright LED light.

Mono Audio

If you're deaf in one ear, then listening to any music that's a stereo mix can be frustrating; you might be missing half the orchestration or the vocals. When you turn on **Mono Audio**, the iPhone mixes everything down so that the left and right channels contain the same monaural playback. Now you can hear the entire mix in one ear.

 TIP: This is also a great feature when you're sharing an earbud with a friend, or when one of your earbuds is broken.

Phone Noise Cancellation

iPhone models 5 and later have three microphones scattered around the body. In combination, they offer extremely good background-noise reduction when you're on a phone call. The microphones on the top and back, for example, listen to the wind, music, crowd noise, or other ambient sound and subtract that ambient noise from the sound going into the main phone mike.

You can turn that feature off here—if, for example, you experience a "pressure" in your ear when it's operating.

Balance Slider

The L/R slider lets you adjust the phone's stereo mix, in case one of your ears has better hearing than the other.

Hearing Aid Compatibility

When you try to talk on the phone, your hearing aid may conduct sound into your ear using either of two modes. There's *acoustic coupling*, where the hearing aid simply amplifies the sound coming out of your phone's earpiece (along with all background noise, unfortunately); and there's *telecoil (inductive) coupling*, where the phone transmits sound to the hearing aid magnetically. That way your hearing aid isn't amplifying ambient background noise, too.

Most hearing aids have telecoils (a "T" model), but not all. If yours does, turn on **Hearing Aid Compatibility** for added clarity when talking on your iPhone.

Media (Subtitle Options)

These options govern Internet videos that you play in the iPhone's Videos app (primarily those from Apple's own iTunes Store).

- **Subtitles & Captioning.** The iPhone's Videos app lets you tap the 💬 button to see a list of available subtitles and captions. Occasionally, a movie also comes with specially written Subtitles for the Deaf and Hard of Hearing (SDH). Tap **Subtitles & Captioning→Closed Captions + SDH** if you want that 💬 menu to list them whenever they're available.

  The **Style** option gives you control over the font, size, and background of those captions, complete with a preview. (Tap the ⤢ button to view the preview, and the sample caption, at full-screen size.) The **Custom** option even lets you dream up your own font, size, and color for the type; a new color and opacity of the caption background; and so on.

- **Audio Descriptions.** This option is for Internet movies that come, or may someday come, with a narration track that describes the action for the blind.

Guided Access (Kiosk Mode)

It's amazing how quickly even tiny tots can master the iPhone—and how easily they can muck things up with accidental taps.

Guided Access solves that problem rather tidily. It's kiosk mode. That is, you can lock the phone into one app; the victim cannot switch out of it. You can even specify which *features* of that app are permitted. Never again will you find your Home screen icons rearranged or text messages deleted.

Guided Access is also great for helping out people with motor-control difficulties—or teenagers with self-control difficulties.

To turn on Guided Access, open **Settings→General→Accessibility→ Guided Access**; turn the switch **On**.

Now a **Passcode Settings** button appears. Here's where you protect Guided Access so the little scamp can't shut it off—at least not without a six-digit passcode (**Set Guided Access Passcode**) or your fingerprint, or— on an iPhone X—your face.

You can also set a time limit for your kid's Guided Access. Tap **Time Limit** to set up an alarm or a spoken warning when time is running out.

Finally, the moment of truth arrives: Your kid is screaming for your phone.

Open whatever app you'll want to lock in place. Press the home button three times fast (on the iPhone X, it's the side button). The Guided Access screen appears. At this point, you can proceed in any of three ways:

- **Declare some features off-limits.** With your finger, draw a circle around each button, slider, and control you want to deactivate. The phone converts your circle into a tidy rectangle; you can drag its corners to adjust its size, drag inside the rectangle to move it, or tap the ⊗ to remove it if you change your mind or want to start again.

  Once you enter Guided Access mode, the controls you've enclosed appear darkened (next page, right). They no longer respond—and your phone borrower can't get into trouble.

- **Change settings.** If you tap **Options**, you get additional controls. You can decide whether or not your little urchin is allowed to press the **Sleep/Wake Button** or the **Volume Buttons** when in Guided Access mode. If you want to hand the phone to your 3-year-old in the back seat to watch baby videos, you'll probably want to disable the touchscreen altogether (turn off **Touch**) and prevent the picture from rotating when the phone does (turn off **Motion**).

Here, too, is the **Time Limit** switch. Turn it on to view hours/minutes dials. At the end of this time, it's no more fun for Junior.

- **Begin kiosk mode.** Tap **Start**.

Later, when you get the phone back and you want to use it normally, triple-press the home (or side) button again; enter your passcode or offer your fingerprint or face. At this point, you can tap **Options** to change them, **Resume** to go back into kiosk mode, or **End** to return to the iPhone as you know it.

TIP: If you use any of the other accessibility features described in this chapter, you may be dismayed to discover that you can no longer use the triple-clicking of the home or side button to open the on/off buttons for those features. The triple-click has been taken over by Guided Access!

Fortunately, Apple has anticipated this problem. If you turn on **Accessibility Shortcut** on the Guided Access screen of Settings (see page 242), then triple-clicking produces the usual list of accessibility features—and Guided Access is on that list, too, ready to tap.

The Instant Screen-Dimming Trick

The Accessibility settings offer one of the greatest shortcuts of all time: the ability to dim your screen, instantly, with a triple-click. You don't have to open the Control Center, visit Settings, or fuss with a slider; it's instantaneous. It's a gift to people who go to movies, plays, nighttime drives, or anywhere else where full screen brightness isn't appropriate, pleasant, or comfortable—and digging around in the Control Center or Settings takes too much time.

It's a bunch of steps to set up, but you have to take them only once. After that, the magic is yours whenever you want it.

Ready? Here's the setup.

1. **Open** Settings→General→Accessibility. **Turn on** Zoom.

   If the magnifying lens appears, tap the white handle at the bottom of it; in the shortcut menu, tap **Zoom Out** (below, left).

   Now the magnifying lens is gone.

2. **Scroll down to Zoom Region and set it to** Full Screen Zoom.

3. **Tap** Zoom Filter; **tap** Low Light **(above, right). Tap** Zoom **(in the upper left) to return to the previous panel.**

   You've just set up the phone to dim the screen whenever zooming is turned on. Now all you have to do is teach the phone to enable zooming whenever you triple-click the home (or side) button.

4. **In the top-left corner, tap** Accessibility.

   You return to the main Accessibility screen. Scroll to the very bottom.

5. **Tap** Accessibility Shortcut; **make sure** Zoom **is the only selected item.**

At this point, you can go back to the Home screen.

From now on, whenever you triple-click the home button (on the iPhone X, the side button), you turn on a gray filter that cuts the brightness of the screen by 30 percent. (Feel free to fine-tune the dimness of your new Insta-Dim setting at that point, using the Control Center; see page 49.) It doesn't save you any battery power, since the screen doesn't think it's putting out any less light. But it does give you instant darkening when you need it in a hurry—like when a potentially important text comes in while you're in the movie theater.

Triple-click again to restore the original brightness, and be glad.

Accessibility Shortcut

Burrowing all the way into the **Settings→General→Accessibility** screen is quite a slog when all you want to do is flip some feature on or off. Therefore, you get this handy shortcut: a fast triple-press of the home button or (on the iPhone X) the side button.

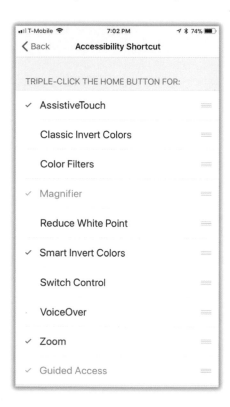

That action produces a little menu, in whatever app you're using, with on/off switches for the iPhone's various accessibility features.

It's up to you, however, to indicate which ones you want on that menu. That's why you're on this screen—to turn on the features you want to appear on the triple-press menu. Your options are **AssistiveTouch**, **Classic Invert Colors**, **Color Filters**, **Magnifier**, **Reduce White Point**, **Smart Invert Colors**, **Switch Control**, **VoiceOver**, and **Zoom**. (To see Guided Access in the list, refer to the Tip on page 240.)

TIP: If you choose only one item here, then triple-pressing the home or side button doesn't produce the menu of choices. It just turns that one feature on or off.

PART TWO

Pix, Flix & Apps

8

Music & Videos

Of all the iPhone's talents, its iPoddishness may be its most successful. This function, after all, gets the most impressive battery life (40 to 80 hours of playback, depending on the model). There's enough room on your phone to store thousands of songs.

In the Music app, five tabs greet you across the bottom: Library, For You, Browse, Radio, and Search.

Some of the app's features are useful only if you've subscribed to Apple Music, Apple's $10-a-month music service—but not all of them. The Internet radio stations, for example, mean that you'll never run out of music to listen to—and you'll never pay a penny for it.

NOTE: If you're not interested in paying for an Apple Music subscription, you can *hide* the two tabs you'll never use (**For You** and **Browse**). To do that, open **Settings→Music** and turn off **Show Apple Music**.

The **For You** and **Browse** tabs disappear—and a new tab, **Connect**, takes their place. This is the mini-rock-band Instagram service described on page 248.

The bottom line: Your Music app might show you either of two different sets of tabs. Complicated? Yes. Anyway, this chapter is written as though you *haven't* hidden the Apple Music tabs.

Apple Music

The Apple Music service, which debuted in 2015, is a rich stew of components. For $10 a month (or $15 for a family of six), you get all of the following.

- **Unlimited Streaming Music.** You can listen to any band, album, or song in the Apple Music library of 40 million songs—on demand, no ads. It's not like listening to a radio station, where someone else is programming the music; *you* program the music.

  On the other hand, this is not like Apple's traditional music store, where you pay $1 per download and then *own* the song. If you ever stop paying, the music stops. You're left with nothing.

  If you do subscribe, you can tell Siri things like, "Play the top songs of 2005" or "Play some good running music" or "Play some Taylor Swift."

  Nor are you obligated to do all your music programming manually. Apple Music comes equipped with ready-made playlists, prepared by human editors, in all kinds of categories. There are sets of starter songs by various singers ("Intro to Sarah McLachlan"), playlists by genre and era, and playlists for specific activities like Waking Up, Running, Getting It On, and even Breaking Up.

  You can freely mix the songs you're renting with the music you actually own. You can even download songs that you don't own for playback when you have no Internet connection (as long as you're still paying your $10 a month).

- **Beats 1 Radio.** Apple runs a "global, 24-hour Internet radio station" called Beats 1. (It actually broadcasts live for 12 hours a day, and then repeats.)

  Listening is free, even to nonpayers.

  Live DJs introduce songs and comment on the singers, just as on FM radio stations. Of course, you have no input on the style of music you hear on Beats 1, and you can't pause, rewind, fast-forward, or save anything you hear for later listening. It's old-style radio, offering the magic of serendipity.

- **Connect.** Connect is an Instagram-like service run by Apple. Here bands that Apple thinks you'll like (or that you choose manually) can promote themselves by posting songs, videos, and other material. You can ♡ these posts, share them, or comment on them.

- **iTunes Match.** iTunes Match, which dates back to 2011, is a cloud-based version of your iTunes library, available to any of your Apple devices. For $25 a year, you can stream Apple's copies of any song files you actually own—ripped from CDs or even acquired illegally. The advantages: First, you save a lot of space on your phone. Second, you can play them on any Apple gadget you own. Third, the versions Apple plays are often of higher quality than your originals.

  iTunes Match continues as a separate service for non–Apple Music subscribers (the song limit is now 100,000 songs). But if you do subscribe to Apple Music, in effect you get iTunes Match automatically.

- **iCloud Music Library.** This is a newer service—a descendant of iTunes Match. This feature, too, matches all the songs on your phone with songs that Apple has online, so you can play any of them on an Apple machine anywhere (once you've signed in). And if you have some songs that Apple doesn't have, you can upload them to Apple and thereby add them to your locker.

NOTE: Apple's matching algorithms aren't flawless; sometimes they don't recognize and match a song that you and Apple both, in fact, have.

Another note: When you turn on iCloud Music Library, you're offered the opportunity to delete all the music on your phone and replace it with what's in your online locker. ***Back up your phone's music before you do this*** (page 529). There are occasional stories of people losing their entire music collections.

The Library Tab

Here's all the music you've actually chosen yourself.

In the old days, this meant "music files that are actually on your phone." If you have an Apple Music membership, though, you'll also see *online* songs listed here that you've added to your personal catalog.

You can view them grouped in any of the lists you see here: **Playlists**, **Artists**, **Albums**, **Songs**, or (if you subscribe to Apple Music) **Downloaded Music**. Below all that, in the Recently Added section, you get thumbnails for albums and playlists you've recently downloaded or built.

TIP: There are other categories you could be seeing here, too, like Genres, Compilations, Composers, TV & Movies, and Music Videos. To add them to the list of headings—or to remove some of the ones that start out there—tap **Edit** next to the bold Library heading.

As you could probably guess, you operate the Music app by drilling down—by tapping from category to album to song or whatever. (Tap the top-left corner of the screen to backtrack.)

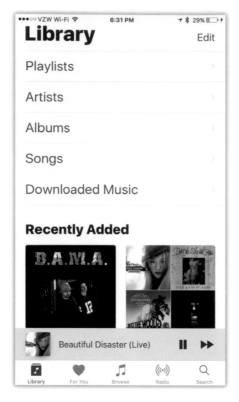

Playback Control

When you tap the name of a song, album, playlist, or whatever, it plays. You can control playback—skip, rewind, and so on—in any of several ways.

The Mini-Player

On almost every screen of the Music app, you get a miniature controller at the bottom of the screen, like the one shown above at left (very bottom).

It identifies the current song, provides a "next song" button (▶▶), and offers the most important playback control of all: ❚❚.

The Now Playing Screen

If you tap (or drag upward on) the mini-player, though, the Now Playing screen appears (facing page, right). This time, there's room for *all* the controls you need to control music playback. Here are its contents, from top to bottom:

TIP: Swipe down to close this screen.

- **Album art.** Most of the screen is filled with a bright, colorful shot of the original CD's album art. (If none is available—if you're listening to a song *you* wrote, for example—you see a big, gray, generic musical-note picture. You can drag or paste in an album-art graphic—one you found on the web, for example—in iTunes.)

- **Scrubber.** This slider reveals two useful statistics: how much of the song you've heard, in minutes and seconds (at the left end) and how much time remains (at the right end).

  To operate the slider, drag the tiny round handle with your finger. You can jump to any spot in the song this way. (Tapping directly on the slider doesn't work.)

- **Song info.** The artist name, track name, and album name.

- **◄◄, ►► (Previous, Next).** These buttons work exactly as they do on an iPod: Tap ◄◄ to skip to the beginning of this song (or, if you're already at the beginning, to the previous song). Tap ►► to skip to the next song.

TIP: If you're wearing the earbuds, then you can pinch the clicker *twice* to skip to the next song.

  If you *hold down* one of these buttons, you rewind or fast-forward. You hear the music speeding by, without turning the singer into a chipmunk. The rewinding or fast-forwarding accelerates if you keep holding the button down.

- **Play/Pause button.** The Pause button beneath the album photo looks like this ▌▌ when the music is playing. If you do pause, then the button turns into the Play button (►).

TIP: If you're wearing the earbuds, then pinching the microphone clicker serves the same purpose: It's a Play/Pause control.

  Incidentally, when you plug in headphones, the iPhone's built-in speaker turns off, but when you unplug the headphones, your music pauses instead of switching abruptly back to the speaker.

- **Download (☁).** If this song is on Apple Music online (and not physically on your phone), then tap to download it for playability when you're not on the Internet.

- **Add (+).** This button appears only when you're playing an Apple Music song; it adds the current song to your iCloud Music Library (page 249).

- **Volume.** You can drag the round handle of this slider (bottom of the screen) to adjust the volume—or you can use the volume buttons on the left side of the phone.

- **AirPlay (◉).** Tap to send playback to an external speaker using AirPlay (page 263).

- **Options (•••).** As always in this app, this button is like a shortcut menu of options that might apply at the moment, described next.

Incidentally, people go batty trying to find three important controls in the Music app's current version: **Shuffle**, **Repeat**, and the **Up Next** queue (page 257).

They're all there—but you have to *swipe up* from the Now Playing screen to see them.

The Options Panel

The ellipsis (•••) awaits on every Now Playing screen. Its choices depend on whether you've tapped some music that you *own* (facing page, left) or that you've found in Apple Music's collection (right). But here are some of the commands you might see there:

- **Delete.** If you've downloaded a copy of this song from Apple Music, well, here's where you change your mind.

- **Download.** Grab the song off of Apple's servers, so you'll be able to play it without an Internet connection (for Apple Music or iTunes Match subscribers only).

- **Delete from Library.** Gets rid of a song you actually own.

- **Add to Library.** Adds the current song to your iCloud Music Library (page 249).

- **Add to a Playlist.** Lets you add this item to a playlist you've made.

- **Create Station.** Makes a "radio station" full of music that sounds like this one (page 260) (Apple Music only).

- **Share Song.** Opens the Share sheet (page 363), so that you can send a link to this song via email, text message, Facebook or Twitter

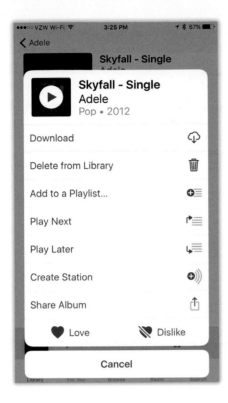

post, and so on. (The recipients can listen to the full song *if* they're Apple Music subscribers.)

- **Lyrics.** Holy smokes. Apple Music can show you a screen containing the *lyrics* of the song you're playing. Who'da thought?

- **Rate Song.** Tap to give this song a rating, from one to five stars. (Unfortunately, you can't *do* much with these ratings—you can't sort by rating, or make smart playlists by rating, or use your ratings to affect the suggestions Apple menu makes. Ah, well.)

- **Love, Dislike.** As you listen to a song, tap these buttons to tell Apple when there's a song you particularly love or loathe. When Apple's magical computers suggest new music for you later, they'll take these hints into account.

TIP: If you have an iPhone 6s or later, you can *hard-press* a song in a list (for example, a playlist) to open the same Options menu. That is, you don't have to burrow all the way to its Now Playing screen.

Control Center

The Control Center, of course, is the panel that appears when you swipe up from the bottom of the screen, or down from the top right of an iPhone X (page 49). It includes playback controls, too. That means you never have to go to the Music app just to change tracks if you're busy doing something else on the phone.

Playback While Locked

Once you're playing music, it keeps right on playing, even if you change apps. After all, the only thing more pleasurable than surfing the web is surfing it with a Beach Boys soundtrack.

If you've got something else to do—like jogging, driving, or performing surgery—tap the side button to turn off the screen. The music keeps playing, but you save battery power.

 TIP: Even with the screen off, you can still adjust the music volume (use the volume buttons on the earbud clicker or the buttons on the side of the phone), pause the music (pinch the earbud clicker once), or advance to the next song (pinch it twice).

What's cool is that if you wake the phone, the Lock screen looks like the Now Playing screen. It has all the same controls, so you can manage the playback without even having to fully wake the phone.

If a phone call comes in, the music fades, and you hear your chosen ringtone—through your earbuds, if you're wearing them. Squeeze the clicker on the earbud cord or tap the Sleep switch to answer the call. When the call ends, the music fades back in, right where it left off.

Voice Control

There's one more way to control your playback—a way that doesn't involve taking your eyes off the road or leaving whatever app you're using. You can control your music playback by voice, using Siri. See Chapter 5.

Playlists

A *playlist* is a group of songs you've placed together, in a sequence that makes sense to you. One might consist of party tunes; another might hold romantic dinnertime music; a third might be drum-heavy workout cuts.

Creating Playlists on the Phone

To play with playlists, start on the **Library** tab. Tap **Playlists**. Here are all the playlists you've ever created—which might be zero (below, left).

To create one, do like this:

1. **Click the giant** New Playlist **button.**

   A new screen appears, where you can name and set up your new playlist (below, middle).

2. **Tap Playlist Name; type a name for your playlist.**

   You can also, at this moment, tap the little 📷 button to take, or choose, a photo to represent this playlist. Or even type a description.

3. **Tap** Add Music.

   The **Add Music** screen appears (below, right). It offers the usual ways to view your collection: **Playlists** (that is, existing ones), **Artists**, **Albums**, **Songs**, **Videos**, **Genres**, **Compilations**, **Composers**, and **Downloaded Music**. (A *compilation* is one of those albums that's been put

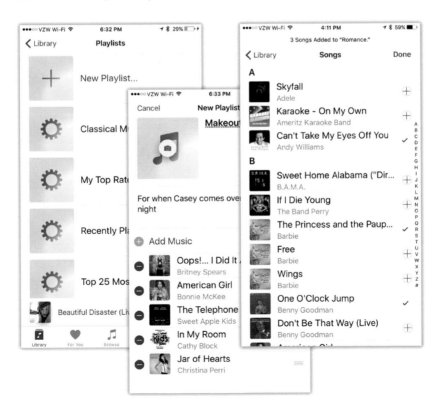

together from many different performers. You know: "Zither Hits of the 1600s," "Kazoo Classics," and so on.)

4. **Tap the category you want for finding your first song; drill down until you find the music you want to add.**

   For example, if you first tap **Albums**, you then see a list of your albums; tap ⊕ to add the entire album to the new playlist. Or tap the album's name to view the songs on it—and then ⊕ next to a song's name to add *it* to the list.

5. **Keep adding music to the playlist until you're satisfied.**

   You can keep tapping ⊕ buttons, without leaving this screen; each turns into a checkmark to indicate that you've added it (previous page, right). A playlist can be infinitely long; we're way past the days of worrying about how much will fit on a cassette tape or a CD.

6. **Tap every Done button until you're back on the Playlists screen.**

   Your newly minted playlist is ready to play!

Using Playlists

To see what songs or videos are in a playlist, tap its name or picture. You now arrive at a Playlist details screen, where your tracks are listed for your inspection. To start playing a song once you see it in the Playlist list, tap its name; you'll hear that song and all those that follow it, in order.

Or tap the Shuffle button (⤨) to start random-order playback.

> **TIP:** Here you can use a standard iOS convention: Anywhere you're asked to drill down from one list to another—from a playlist to the songs inside, for example—you can backtrack by *swiping from the left edge* of the phone into the screen.
>
> Or do it the long way: Tap ‹ at the upper-left corner of the screen. That button's name always tells you what screen you just came from (My Music, for example).

Once you're here, you can have all kinds of fun:

- **To delete or rearrange songs:** Tap Edit. Use the ☰ handles to drag the songs into a new sequence. Hit ⊖ to make one disappear. (You're not deleting it from your phone—only from this playlist.) Tap **Done.**

- **To add more songs to the playlist:** Tap Edit. Tap **Add Music.**

- **To rename the open playlist:** Tap Edit. Tap the current title and edit away. (Tap **Done.**)

- **To delete the playlist:** Open the playlist; tap the ••• to open the Options panel; tap **Delete from Library**. Confirm by tapping **Delete Playlist**. (Scary though that wording may sound, no music is actually deleted from your library—only the playlist that contains it.)

Up Next

Unless you're a professional DJ, you're probably happy to hear song after song played automatically, according to whatever album, playlist, or radio station they're in.

But the Up Next playlist gives you a degree of control without requiring the full project of programming a playlist.

The Up Next playlist always exists. If you tell Music to play an album, then Up Next autofills with the songs on that album; if you're listening to all the music from a certain performer, then Up Next displays what else you'll hear from that artist. And if you tap any song in your Library, then *everything after it* gets added to the Up Next queue automatically.

But you can also queue up music yourself, adding songs to Up Next on your own schedule. The playback will plow through them in order.

- **Add a song to Up Next.** Hard-press (or long-press) a song, album, or playlist to open the Options panel (below, left). Tap **Play Next** to put

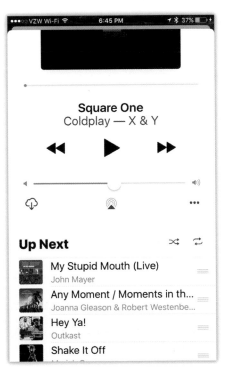

this song at the beginning of the Up Next queue, or **Play Later** to put it at the *end* of the queue.

- **Play a song now.** Suppose you find some music you want to play right now. You don't care about the Up Next playlist.

  When you tap that item's name, the iPhone asks: "After playing this, do you want to play the songs you've added to Up Next?" If you hit **Keep Up Next**, then you hear the new song without disturbing the Up Next list that will play afterward. If you hit **Clear Up Next**, then the new song plays and then the music stops; you've nuked the current Up Next list.

View, Edit, or Clear the Up Next List

Most people probably never realize it, but you can actually look over the Up Next playlist in progress. You can rearrange or delete anything in it.

There's only one way to see the Up Next playlist, and it's pretty buried. You have to open the full-height Now Playing screen described on page 251, and then *scroll up*.

Once the list appears (previous page, right), you can remove a song from the queue by swiping left on it to reveal the **Remove** button; tap it. Rearrange the list by dragging the little "grip strip" handles up or down. (If you don't see them, it's because you've got your music on Repeat.)

> **NOTE:** Other than the **Clear Up Next** option mentioned above, the only way to clear the entire list at once is to force-quit the Music app (page 626) and then reopen it.

"For You" Tab

40 million is a lot of songs. You won't live long enough to hear them all. So Apple has supplied the For You tab of the Music app to present new songs, performers, and albums its algorithms think you'll like. (If you're not a paying subscriber, then this tab is just an ad for Apple Music.)

Scroll horizontally to see more tiles in a category; scroll vertically to see the playlists, albums, artists, and new releases Apple thinks you'll like.

And how does the app guess what kind of music you'll like? When you sign up for the service, you're shown dancing red circles bearing music-genre names. You're supposed to tap the ones you like, double-tap the ones you *really* like, and hold your finger down on the ones you don't like.

Then, of course, as you go through your life listening to music, you can always turn the ♡ button on or off to further fine-tune Apple's understanding of your tastes.

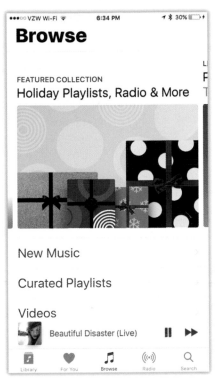

Browse Tab

The Browse tab is also for paying subscribers only. It's lists of lists.

Scroll down long enough, and you'll find lists like **New Music**, **Curated Playlists** (music lists, created by Apple's editors, for particular genres, activities, and moods), **Videos**, **Top Charts**, and **Genres**. Once again, the idea is to help you find new stuff you like.

iTunes Radio

Your iPhone includes an amazing gift: your own radio station. Your own *empire* of radio stations, in fact.

They come in two categories: Free and Custom.

Free Stations

What you see on the Radio screen depends on whether or not you've turned off **Show Apple Music**, as described on page 247.

If that's turned off, then you see only free stations here: **Beats 1** (the Apple live station described on page 248) and some streaming stations like CBS, NPR, ESPN, and Bloomberg. These are free Internet radio stations.

Subscriber Stations

If **Show Apple Music** is turned on, then this screen offers ready-made "radio stations" that Apple has supplied for you. If you're a subscriber, they play; if not, they give you an ad to sign up.

Tap **Radio Stations** to find more ready-to-play, software-curated "radio stations" in every conceivable category: **Country**, **NPR**, **ESPN**, **Oldies**, **Soul/Funk**, **Chill**, **Indie**, **Classic Metal**, **Pop Workout**, **Kids & Family**, **Lullabies**, **Latin Pop**, **Classical**, **Reggae**, and on and on.

You can hit ▶▶ to skip a song you're not enjoying. And you don't hear any ads.

Custom Stations

If you're a paid subscriber, the iTunes Radio service offers more than canned stations; you can create a new "station" instantly, based on any "seed" song you choose.

You don't get to choose the exact songs or singers you want to hear; you have to trust iTunes Radio to choose songs *based* on your chosen song, singer, or music genre. For example, if you choose Billy Joel as your "seed," you'll hear a lot of Billy Joel, but also a lot of other music that sounds more or less like his.

To set up a new "radio station" of your own, find a song, band, or album. Hard-press or long-press it to open the Options menu (page 37)—and tap **Create Station**.

You've just created a new station, and it begins instantly.

> **TIP:** While a custom station plays, you can tap the ☆ on its Now Playing screen to see two new buttons: **Play More Like This** and **Play Less Like This**. That kind of feedback fine-tunes your custom station for future use.

The idea of a "seed song"–based radio service isn't new, of course. It's the same idea as Pandora, a website and app that has offered precisely the same features for years. But iTunes Radio is built in, it's incorporated with

Siri and the Control Center, and it's part of Apple's larger ecosystem; that is, you can see your same set of "radio stations" on your Mac or PC (in the iTunes app), iPad, and Apple TV.

Returning to a Custom Station

On the main Radio screen, the **Recently Played** list shows all the stations you've listened to. Tap to start playing.

Siri and iTunes Radio

Truth is, there's an easier way to create a custom radio station: Just let Siri do the work. No matter what you're doing on the iPhone, you can hold down the home button (or, on the iPhone X, the side button) and say, for example, "Play 'Just the Way You Are' by Billy Joel" or "Play some Beatles." Boom: The music begins.

Actually, Siri comes equipped to recognize a whole slew of commands pertaining to iTunes Radio. Here's a sampler; you don't have to use these precise wordings:

- **Start a station from Whitney Houston** (or any song, album, or artist).
- **Play the radio.**
- **What song is this?**
- **Play more like this.**
- **Don't play this song again.**
- **Pause the music. (Resume the music.)**
- **Skip this song.**
- **Add this song to my Wish List.**
- **Stop the radio.**

Speakers and Headphones

The iPhone's speaker is pretty darned good for such a tiny machine. But the world is full of better speakers—Bluetooth wireless speakers, car stereo systems, hi-fi TVs, and fancy earbuds and headphones. The iPhone is especially easy to use with them.

Bluetooth Wireless Speakers

You can buy amazingly small, powerful Bluetooth stereo speakers that receive your iPhone's music from as far as 20 or 30 feet away—made by JBL, Bose, and others.

There are also wireless Bluetooth headphones and earbuds—an especially useful fact if your iPhone lacks a headphone jack (iPhone 7 and later).

Once you've bought your headphones or speakers, you have to introduce them to the iPhone—a process called *pairing*.

From the Home screen, tap **Settings→Bluetooth**. Turn Bluetooth on (below, left); you see the Searching ✷ animation as the iPhone wirelessly hunts for your headphones or speakers.

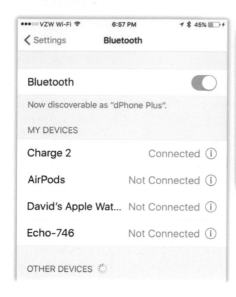

Grab them, turn them on, and start the pairing procedure, as described in the manual. Usually that means holding down a certain button until a tiny light starts flashing. At that point, the headphones' or speaker's name appears on the iPhone's screen.

TIP: If the headphones or speakers require a one-time passcode—it's usually 0000, but check the manual—the iPhone's keyboard appears, so you can type it in.

A few seconds later, it says Connected; now any sound the iPhone would ordinarily play through its speakers or earbuds now plays through the wireless headphones or speakers. Not just music, but chirps, game sounds, and so on. Oh, and phone calls.

If your headset has a microphone, too, then you can even answer and make phone calls wirelessly. (There's an Answer button right on the headphones.)

Using Bluetooth wireless stereo does eat up your battery charge faster. But come on: listening to your music without wires, with the iPhone still in your pocket or bag? How cool is that?

Switching Among Speakers

When your iPhone has a connection to a wireless sound source—Bluetooth speakers/earbuds or an AirPlay receiver, for example—you need some way to direct the music playback to it.

The answer is the ⊛ button. It's on the Control Center (page 49), but it's hidden: You have to hard-press or long-press the music-playback controls to see it.

When you tap ⊛, the iPhone offers a button for each speaker or set of earbuds or headphone (facing page, right). Tap the one you want.

Instantly, the sound begins flowing from your other source. Use the same method to switch back to the iPhone's speakers when the time comes.

AirPlay

There's another way to transmit audio wirelessly from the iPhone (and video, too): the Apple technology called AirPlay. You can buy AirPlay speakers, amplifiers, and TV sets. The Apple TV, of course, is the best-known AirPlay machine; Apple's HomePod is another one.

AirPlay is described on page 273, because most people use it to transmit video, not just audio. But the steps for transmitting to an AirPlay audio gadget are the same.

Music Settings

The iPhone has a long list of traditional iPod features for music playback. Most of these options await in **Settings→Music**. (Shortcut: Tell Siri, "Open Music settings.")

EQ (Equalization)

Like any good music player, the iPhone offers an EQ function: a long list of presets, each of which affects your music by boosting or throttling various frequencies. One might bring out the bass to goose up your hip-hop tunes; another might emphasize the midrange for clearer vocals; and so on. ("Late Night" is especially handy; it lowers the bass so it thuds less. Your downstairs neighbors will love it.)

You'll find the EQ feature way down the Music Settings page.

Volume Limit

It's now established fact: Listening to a lot of loud music through earphones can damage your hearing. Pump it up today, pay for it tomorrow.

Portable music players can be sinister that way, because in noisy places like planes and city streets, people turn up the volume much louder than they would in a quiet place, and they don't even realize how high they've cranked it. That's why Apple created this volume slider. It lets you limit the maximum volume level of the music.

In fact, if you're a parent, you can even lock down this control on your child's iPhone; it can be bypassed only with a password. Set the volume slider here, and then, in **Settings→General→Restrictions**, turn on **Volume Limit**.

Sound Check

This feature smooths out the master volume levels of tracks from different albums, helping to compensate for differences in their recording levels. It doesn't deprive you of peaks and valleys in the music volume, of course—it affects only the baseline level.

Playing Music from Your Computer

Here's a trick you weren't expecting: You can store many terabytes of music on your Mac or PC upstairs—and play it on your phone in the kitchen downstairs. Or anywhere on the same Wi-Fi network, actually.

This nifty bit of wireless magic is brought to you by Home Sharing, a feature of the iTunes program.

Here's the setup: In iTunes on the Mac or PC, open **Edit→Preferences**. Click **Sharing**, and turn on **Share my library on my local network**. (You can share only certain playlists, if you like.) Turn on **Require password** and enter your Apple account (iCloud) password. Click **OK**.

Now pick up your phone. At the bottom of the **Settings→Music** screen, log into Home Sharing using the same Apple ID and password.

Now you're ready to view the contents of your computer on the phone. You'd never guess where it's hiding.

In the Music app, on the **Library** tab, tap **Home Sharing**; on the next screen, choose your computer's name. (Note that the Home Sharing heading doesn't appear unless your computer is turned on and iTunes is open.)

That's it! Suddenly, your entire Music app is filled with the music from your computer's collection, rather than the music on the phone.

The iTunes Store

Just as you can buy apps using the App Store app, you can browse, buy, and download songs, TV shows, and movies using the iTunes Store app. Anything you buy gets autosynced back to your computer's copy of iTunes when you get home. Whenever you hear somebody mention a buy-worthy song, you can have it within a minute.

To begin, open the iTunes Store *app*. The store you see here (below, left) is modeled on the App Store described in Chapter 10. This time, the buttons at the bottom of the screen include **Music**, **Movies**, **TV Shows**, **Search**, and **More**.

When you tap **Music**, **Movies**, or **TV Shows**, the screen offers further buttons. For Music, for example, the scrolling horizontal rows of options might include **New Releases**, **Recent Releases**, **Singles**, and **Pre-Orders**.

(Beneath each list is a **Redeem** button, which you can tap if you've been given an iTunes gift certificate or a promo code; a **Send Gift** button, which lets you buy a song or video for someone else; and an **Apple ID** button, which can show you your current credit balance.)

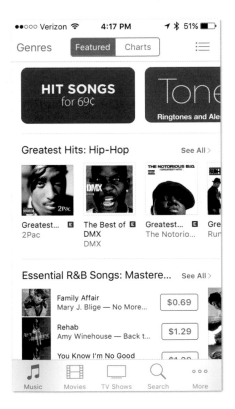
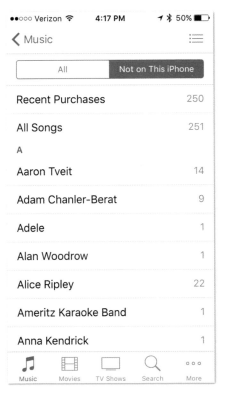

To search for something in particular, tap **Search**. The keyboard appears. Type what you're looking for: the name of a song, movie, show, performer, or album, for example. At any time, you can stop typing and tap the name of a match to see its details. You can use the buttons across the top to restrict the search to one category (just songs or movies, for example).

All these tools eventually take you to the details page of an album, song, or movie. For a song, tap its name to hear an instant 90-second preview (tap again to stop). For a TV show or movie, tap ▶ to watch the ad or the sneak preview.

If you're sold, then tap the price button to buy the song, show, or album (and tap **Buy** to confirm). Enter your Apple ID password when you're asked. (For movies, you can choose either **Buy** or **Rent**, priced accordingly.) At this point, your iPhone downloads the music or video you bought.

Purchased Items

Anything you buy from the iTunes Store winds up in the appropriate app on your iPhone: the TV app for TV shows and movies, the Music app for songs. (Within the Music app, you can see everything you've bought: Tap **Playlists** and then **Purchased**.)

In the iTunes Store app, you can tap **More** and then **Purchased** to see what you've bought. Once you tap a category (**Music**, **Movies**, **TV Shows**), you get a pair of tabs:

- **All.** Here's a list of everything you've bought from iTunes, on your iPhone or any other Apple machine.

- **Not on This iPhone.** This is the cool part. Here you see not just the files on the iPhone in your hand, but things you've bought on other

Apple gadgets—an album you bought on your iPad, for example, or a song you downloaded to your iPod Touch. (This assumes that you're using the same Apple ID on all your gizmos.)

The beauty of this arrangement, of course, is that you can tap the name of something that's Not on This iPhone—and then download it (tap ☁). No extra charge.

TIP: If you prefer, you can direct your phone to download those purchases that you make on other gadgets automatically, without your having to tap **Not on This iPhone**. Visit **Settings→iTunes & App Store**, and turn on the switches for **Music**, **Apps**, and/or **Books** under **Automatic Downloads**. If you also turn on **Use Cellular Data**, then your phone will do this auto-downloading when you're in any 3G or LTE cellular Internet area, not just in a Wi-Fi hotspot.

More in "More"

Tapping **More** at the bottom of the screen offers these options:

- **Tones.** You can buy ready-made ringtones on this page—30-second slices of pop songs. (Don't ask what sense it makes to pay $1.29 for

30 seconds of a song when you could buy the whole song for the same price.)

- **Genius.** Apple offers a list of music, movies, and TV shows for sale that it thinks you'll like, based on stuff you already have.

- **Purchased.** Here's another way to examine the stuff you've bought on all your devices. If you've turned on Apple's Family Sharing feature (page 549), you can also examine the stuff your family members have bought.

- **Downloads.** Shows you a progress bar for anything you've started to download.

TIP: If you tap **Edit**, you'll see that you can *replace* any of the four iTunes Store bottom-row icons with one of the **More** buttons (Tones, Genius, Purchased, or whatever). Just drag one of these icons directly downward on *top* of an existing icon.

So you've downloaded one of the store's millions of songs, podcasts, TV shows, music videos, ringtones, or movies directly to your phone. Next time you sync, that song will swim *upstream* to your Mac or PC, where it will be safely backed up in iTunes. (And if you lost your connection before the iPhone was finished downloading, your Mac or PC will finish the job automatically. Cool.)

The TV App

This weird hybrid app is intended to serve as a single repository for *paid* TV shows and movies online, in these three categories:

- **Videos you've bought or rented from Apple's iTunes Store.** In this regard, the TV app takes over the functions of the old Videos app.

- **Paid video-service apps like Showtime, Hulu, and HBO Go.** A few of these apps work with the TV app's "single sign-on" feature, meaning that you can enter the name and password for your cable account *once*, and thereafter you're spared having to enter it into each individual app.

- **Channels your cable package provides.** Or at least those that have apps: ABC, A&E, AMC, TBS, and so on. Each one requires that you provide your cable or satellite TV account name and password. (Here again, a few may work with the single sign-on feature, meaning that you don't have to sign in individually.)

Even if you don't have a cable subscription, there's some free stuff you can watch in this app. Visit **Store→Buy or Rent on iTunes→Free Episodes**.

There are also some channel apps that are free to watch without a subscription, including PBS, PBS Kids, CBS Sports, ABC News, and The Weather Channel.

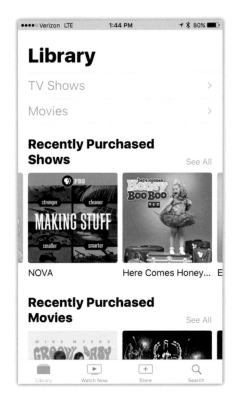
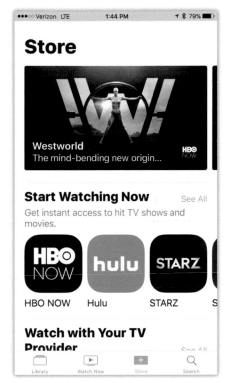

That's the shiny future concept of the TV app. In this early incarnation, though, it's of less use, because it works only with a handful of lesser cable companies and only a handful of channel apps. Netflix, for example, is not among them. (Although, if you have the Netflix app, the TV app may offer to redirect you there to watch something you've searched for.)

Until more players join the party, here's how to use the TV app.

Four Tabs

The buttons across the bottom clearly exhibit the TV app's split personality (split between iTunes purchases and cable-channel apps).

- **iTunes Store.** Find TV shows and movies to rent or buy using **Search**. Watch the ones you've bought or rented in **Library**.

- **Channel apps.** Find channel apps using the **Store**. Watch the shows available from the apps you've installed in **Watch Now**.

How to Play a Video

Tap a video's thumbnail to see its plot summary, year of release, and so on. If it's a TV series, tap an episode in that series, if necessary. Either way, tap ▶ to begin watching.

> **NOTE:** If you see a ☁ on this screen, it means that this bought or rented movie is not actually on your phone. If you have a good Wi-Fi signal, you can watch it right now by streaming it (instead of downloading it to your phone).
>
> If you don't see that icon, then the video file is actually on your phone. An **Edit** button appears, which you can tap (and then tap ✕) to delete the video.

When you're playing video, anything else on the screen is distracting, so Apple hides the video playback controls. Tap the screen once to make them appear and again to make them disappear.

Here's what they do:

- **Done.** Tap this button, in the top-left corner, to stop playback and return to the master list of videos.

- **Scroll slider.** This progress indicator (top of the screen) is exactly like the one you see when you're playing music. You see the elapsed time, the remaining time, and a white, round handle that you can drag to jump forward or back in the video.

> **TIP:** Drag your finger farther (up or down) from the handle to choose a faster or slower scrubbing speed.

- **Zoom/Unzoom.** In the top-right corner, a little ⬍ or ▭ button appears if the video's shape doesn't exactly match your screen. Tap it to adjust the zoom level of the video, as described in a moment.

- **Play/Pause (▶/❚❚).** These buttons (and the earbud clicker) do the same thing to video as they do to music: alternate playing and pausing.

- **Previous, Next (◀◀, ▶▶).** Hold down your finger to rewind or fast-forward the video. The longer you hold, the faster the zipping. (When you fast-forward, you even get to hear the sped-up audio.)

  If you're watching a movie from the iTunes Store, you may be surprised to discover that it comes with what were once called DVD

Extras: chapter markers, deleted scenes, and so on. To see the buttons for these goodies, tap the screen (shown above).

TIP: If you're wearing the earbuds, you can pinch the clicker *twice* to skip to the next chapter, or *three times* to go back a chapter.

- **Volume.** You can drag the round handle of this slider (bottom of the screen) to adjust the volume—or you can use the volume buttons on the left side of the phone.

- **Language (⌨).** You don't see this button often. But when you do, it summons subtitle and alternate-language soundtrack options, just like a DVD player.

- **AirPlay (⌷).** This symbol appears if you have an Apple TV (or another AirPlay-compatible device). Tap it to send your video playback to the TV, as described on page 273.

TIP: If you don't see a video that you *know* you purchased through iTunes, then open the iTunes Store app on your phone. Tap **More→ Purchased**, and then select the person who bought the movie or TV show. Next tap either **Movies** or **TV Shows**; look under **All** and **Not on This iPhone**. When you find what you want, tap its name and re-download it by tapping ⌕. That puts it back into the TV app's library.

And to delete a video from the library, swipe leftward across its name in the Videos list; tap **Delete** to confirm. (You can always re-download it, of course.)

Zoom/Unzoom

The iPhone's screen is bright, vibrant, and stunningly sharp. Sometimes, however, it's not the right shape for videos.

Pre-HDTV shows are squarish, not rectangular. So when you watch older TV shows on a rectangular screen, you get black letterbox columns on either side of the picture.

Movies have the opposite problem. They're usually too wide for the iPhone screen. So when you watch movies, you may wind up with *hori-zontal* letterbox bars above and below the picture.

Some people are fine with that. After all, HDTVs have the same problem. At least when letterbox bars are onscreen, you know you're seeing the complete composition of the scene the director intended.

Other people can't stand letterboxing. You're already watching on a pretty small screen; why sacrifice some of that precious area to black bars?

Fortunately, the iPhone gives you a choice. If you double-tap the video as it plays, you zoom in, magnifying the image so it fills the entire screen. Or, if the playback controls are visible, you can also tap ▭ or ↕ . Of course, now you're not seeing the entire original composition. You lose the top and bottom of old TV scenes, or the left and right edges of movie scenes.

Fortunately, if this effect chops off something important—some text, for example—the original letterbox view is just another double-tap away. (No zooming happens if the source material is already a perfect fit for the iPhone's screen shape.)

---

iPHONE X: Ordinarily, videos don't extend into the area occupied by the Notch (page 27). When you double-tap to zoom a video, though, playback fills the entire screen—and part of it is now obscured by the Notch. You get used to it.

TV Output

When you crave a screen bigger than a few inches, you can play your iPhone's videos on a regular TV. All you need is the right cable: the Apple Digital AV Adapter. It carries both audio and video over a single HDMI cable.

It *mirrors* what's on the phone: your Home screen, email, Safari, and everything else. (Photos and presentations appear on your TV in pure, "video outputted" form, without any controls or other window clutter.)

AirPlay

Your iPhone also offers wireless projection, thanks to a feature called AirPlay. It transmits music or high-def video (with audio) from your iPhone to an Apple TV (or another AirPlay-equipped receiver) across the room. It's a fantastic way to send slideshows, movies, presentations, games, FaceTime calls, and websites to your TV for a larger audience to enjoy. Whatever is on the screen gets transmitted.

AirPlay receivers include the Apple TV (version 2 or later) and speakers, stereos, and receivers from Denon, Marantz, JBL, iHome, and so on. The phone and recent AirPlay receivers no longer have to be on the same Wi-Fi network, thanks to a feature called peer-to-peer AirPlay.

When you're playing a video or some music, open the Control Center (page 49), and tap ⟝ to see a list of available AirPlay receivers. If you have an Apple TV, tap its name. (If this is your first time, then enter the four-digit code you see on the TV.)

That's it! Everything on the iPhone screen now appears on the TV or sound system. (The phone's status bar displays the ⧉ icon, so you don't wander off and forget that every move you make is visible to the entire crowd in the living room.)

How to Project or Record the iPhone's Screen

If you're a teacher, trainer, or product demonstrator, you might find it useful to be able to project the iPhone's activity on a much larger screen, or to record it as a QuickTime movie to use in presentations or to post online. Here are three ways to go about it:

- **The built-in way.** You can now create video recordings of your iPhone's screen, using the Control Center. See page 49. Once captured, you can move the movie to a computer, and project it from there.

- **The Mac way.** If your Mac has OS X Yosemite or later, then connect the phone to the Mac with its white USB charging cable. Open the Mac app called QuickTime Player. Choose **File→New Movie Recording**. From the little ∨ menu next to the ● button, choose **iPhone**.

  Now you're seeing the iPhone's screen on your Mac—and you can record it, project it, or screen-capture it for future generations!

- **The wireless way.** A $13 program called Reflector (*reflectorapp.com*) lets you view the iPhone's live image on the Mac's screen—and hear its sound. (It actually turns the Mac into an AirPlay receiver.) There's also a **Record** command, so you can create a movie of whatever you're doing on the phone.

9

The Camera

Incredible though it sounds, the iPhone is the number-one most popular camera model in the world. More photos are posted online from this phone than from any other machine in existence.

And no wonder; you've probably never seen pictures and movies look this good on a pocket gadget. With each new version of the iPhone, Apple improves its camera—and on the iPhone 8 and X models, it's unbelievably good.

And the videos look amazing. They're auto-stabilized. The 6s and later models shoot in 4K (four times the resolution of high-def video), and the iPhone X can even play back *high dynamic range* videos (incredibly dark darks and bright brights).

This chapter is all about the iPhone's ability to display photos, take new ones with its camera, and capture videos.

The Camera App

The little hole(s) on the back of the iPhone, in the upper-left corner, is its camera.

On the latest iPhones, it's pretty impressive, at least for a cellphone cam. The iPhone 7 and later, for example, have four LED flashes, manual exposure controls, optical stabilization, and phase-detection autofocus (the same kind of very fast refocusing found in professional SLR cameras). These phones can manage 10 shots a second and do amazingly well in low light.

Now that you know what you're in for, here's how it works.

Firing Up the Camera

Photographic opportunities are frequently fleeting; by the time you fish the phone from your pocket, wake it up, unlock it, find the Camera app, and wait for it to load, the magic moment may be gone forever.

Fortunately, there's a much quicker way to get to the Camera app: Once the phone is awake, at the Lock screen, *swipe to the left*. (Drag the background—not one of the notification banners.)

The Camera app opens directly. Over time, the wake-and-swipe ritual becomes natural, fluid—and fast.

> **iPHONE X:** On your Lock screen, a new camera button appears at lower right. As an alternative to swiping, you can hard-press it to open the Camera app.

By the way: This shortcut bypasses the Lock screen. Any random stranger who picks up your phone can, therefore, jump directly into picture-taking mode, without your password, fingerprint, or Face ID.

That stranger can't do much damage, though. She can take new photos, or delete the new photos taken during her session—but the photos you've *already* taken are off-limits, and the features that could damage your reputation (editing, emailing, and posting photos) are unavailable. She would have to be able to open the Photos app to get to those.

> **TIP:** Of course, there's a hands-free way to fire up the Camera app, too: Tell Siri, "Open camera."

Camera Modes

The Camera app can capture six or seven kinds of photo and video, depending on your phone model. By swiping your finger horizontally anywhere on the screen, you switch among its modes. Here they are, from left to right:

- **Time-Lapse.** This mode speeds up your video, yet somehow keeps it stable. You can reduce a two-hour bike ride into 20 seconds of super-fast playback.

- **Slo-Mo.** Wow, what gorgeousness! You get a video filmed at 120 or 240 frames a second—so it plays back at one-quarter or one-eighth speed, incredibly smoothly. Fantastic for sports, tender smiles, and cannonballs into the pool.

- **Video.** Here's your basic camcorder mode: 4K video on the 6s and later models, high definition on earlier ones.

- **Photo.** This is the primary mode for taking pictures.

- **Portrait.** Available only on the iPhone 7 Plus, 8 Plus, and X models, whose two camera lenses create a softly blurred background that looks super-professional.

- **Square.** Why would Apple go to the trouble of designating a whole special camera mode to taking square, not rectangular, pictures? Answer: Instagram, the crazy-popular app that features square pictures and was sold to Facebook for nearly $1 billion.

- **Pano.** Captures super-wide-angle panoramic photos.

> **TIP:** If you tend to stick to one of these modes (like Square because you're an Instagram junkie, for example), you can make the iPhone's camera *stay* in your favorite mode, rather than resetting itself to Photo mode every time you reopen it. That switch is in **Settings→Camera→Preserve Settings →Camera Mode**.

All of these modes are described in this chapter, but in a more logical order: still photos first, and then video modes.

Photo Mode

Most people, most of the time, use the Camera app to take still photos. It's a pretty great experience. The iPhone's screen is a huge digital-camera viewfinder. You can turn it 90 degrees for a wider or taller shot.

Tap to Focus

All right: You've opened the Camera app, and the mode is set to Photo. See the yellow box that appears briefly on the screen?

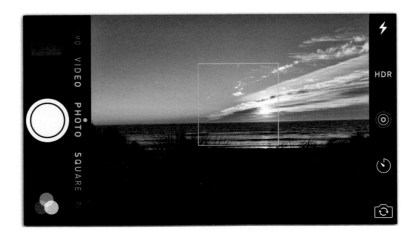

It's telling you where the iPhone will focus, the area it examines to calculate the overall brightness of the photo (exposure), and the portion that will determine the overall **white balance** of the scene (the color cast).

If you're taking a picture of people, the iPhone tries to lock in on a face—up to 10 faces, actually—and calculate the focus and exposure so that **they** look right.

But sometimes there are no faces—and dead center may not be the most important part of the photo. The cool thing is that you can **tap** somewhere else in the scene to move that yellow square—to recalculate the focus, exposure, and white balance.

Here's when you might want to do this tapping:

- **When the whole image looks too dark or too bright.** If you tap a **dark** part of the scene, the whole photo brightens up; if you tap a **bright** part, the whole photo darkens a bit. You're telling the camera, "Redo your calculations so **this** part has the best exposure; I don't care if the rest of the picture gets brighter or darker." At that point, you can override the phone's exposure decision.

Tap the sky to make it correctly exposed, even if the beach is now too dark.　　　*Tap the dark beach to brighten it up, although that also brightens up the sky.*

- **When the scene has a color cast.** If the photo looks, for example, a little bluish or yellowish, tap a different spot—the one you care most about. The iPhone recomputes its assessment of the white balance.

- **When you're in macro mode.** If the foreground object is very close to the lens—4 to 8 inches away—the iPhone automatically goes into *macro* (super-closeup) mode. In this mode, you can do something really cool: You can **defocus the background**. The background goes soft, slightly blurry, just like the professional photos you see in magazines. No, not as well or as flexibly as in Portrait mode (page 292), but it's something. Just make sure you tap the foreground object.

Adjust Exposure

When you tap the screen to set the focus point, a new control appears: a little yellow sun slider. That's your exposure control. Slide it up to brighten the whole photo or down to make things darker. Often, just a small

adjustment is all it takes to add a splash of light to a dim scene, or to dial the details back into a photo that's bright white.

To reset the slider to the iPhone's original proposed setting, tap somewhere else, or just aim the phone at something different for a second.

The point is that the Camera app lets you fuss with the focus point and the exposure level independently.

Focus Lock/Exposure Lock

The iPhone likes to focus and calculate the exposure before it shoots. Cameras are funny that way.

That tendency, however, can get in your way when you're shooting something that moves fast. Horse races, divers. Pets. Kids on merry-go-rounds, kids on slides, kids eating breakfast. By the time the camera has calculated the focus and exposure, which takes about a second, you've lost the shot.

Therefore, Apple provides a feature that's common on professional cameras: auto-exposure lock and autofocus lock. They let you set up the focus and exposure in advance so that there's zero lag when you finally snap the shot.

To use this feature, point the camera at something that has the **same distance and lighting** as the subject-to-be. For example, focus at the base of the merry-go-round, directly below where your daughter's horse will be. Or point at the bottom of the waterslide before your son is ready to go.

Now hold your finger down on that spot on the iPhone's screen until you see the yellow square blink twice. When you lift your finger, the phrase "AE/AF Lock" tells you that you've now locked in exposure and autofocus. (You can tap again to unlock it if you change your mind.)

At this point, you can drag the yellow sun slider to adjust that locked exposure, if you like.

Now you can snap photos, rapid-fire, without ever having to wait while your iPhone rethinks focus and exposure.

The LED Flash

As on most phones, the iPhone's "flash" is actually just a very bright LED light on the back. You can make it turn on momentarily, providing a small boost of illumination when the lights are low. (That's a **small** boost—it won't do anything for subjects more than a few feet away.)

The iPhone 5s, 6, and 6s models, in fact, have two LED flashes: one white, one amber. The 7 and later models take that a step further, with **four** flashes, together producing 50 percent more light output.

The flashes go off simultaneously, with their strengths mixed so that their light matches the color temperature of the scene. (You might notice that the phone flashes once **before** it captures the shot. That's the camera's opportunity to **measure** the light color of the scene.)

This multi-flash trick makes a huge difference in the quality of your flash photos. (Especially in skin tones, which may be why Apple calls the feature "True Tone.")

No matter which model you have, the flash comes set to Auto. It turns on automatically when, in the iPhone's opinion, the scene is too dark. But if you tap the ⚡ when it says **Auto**, two other options pop out: **On** (the flash will fire no matter what the lighting conditions) and **Off** (the flash will not fire, no matter what).

The Screen Flash

The iPhone 6s and later models offer a "flash" on the **front**, too, for taking selfies. But it's not an LED like the one on the back.

Instead, at the moment you take the shot, the **screen** lights up to illuminate your face. Better yet: It adjusts the color of the screen's "flash" to give your face the best flesh tones, based on a check of the ambient light color.

Of course, the normal iPhone screen is too tiny to supply much light, even at full brightness. So Apple developed a custom chip with a single purpose: to overclock the screen. In selfie situations, the screen blasts at

three times its usual full brightness for a fraction of a second. It is crazy bright.

It works fantastically well. Here you can see the nuked-looking result from a traditional back LED "flash" (left) side-by-side with the more nuanced screen flash (right).

Zooming In

The iPhone has a zoom, which can help bring you "closer" to the subject—but (unless it's a 7 Plus, 8 Plus, or X) it's a ***digital*** zoom. It doesn't work like a real camera's optical zoom, which actually moves lenses to blow up the scene. Instead, it basically just blows up the image, mak-

ing everything bigger, and slightly degrading the picture quality in the process.

To zoom in like this, **spread two fingers** on the screen. As you spread, a zoom slider appears; you can also drag the handle in the slider, or tap **+** or **−**, for more precise zooming.

Sometimes, getting closer to the action is worth the subtle image-quality sacrifice.

True Optical Zoom

On the iPhone 7 Plus, 8 Plus, and X, there was enough room for Apple to install **two** lenses, right next to each other. One is wide-angle; one is telephoto. With one tap on the little **1x** button (below, left), you can zoom in 2x (middle). This is true **optical** zoom, not the cruddy digital zoom on most previous phones (which degrades the quality).

2x zoom isn't a huge amount, but it's 2x more than any other thin smartphone can handle. And it's a triumphant first step toward eliminating a key drawback of phone cameras: They can't actually zoom.

You can also dial up any amount of zoom **between** 1x and 2x, again without losing any quality. The iPhone performs that stunt by seamlessly **combining** the zoom lens's image (in the center of the photo) with a margin provided by the wide lens. Just plant your finger on the **1x** and drag it to the left. You'll see the circular scale of zooming appear (previous page, right).

You can even zoom while shooting a video, which is very cool.

Even on these phones, by the way, you can keep dragging your finger to the left, past 2x—all the way up to a really blotchy 10x (or 6x for video). Beyond 2x, of course, you're invoking digital zoom. But sometimes it's just what you need.

> **TIP:** Once you've dragged your finger to open the zooming scale, you can tap the current magnification button ("2.5x" or whatever) to reset the zooming to 1x.

The "Rule of Thirds" Grid

The Rule of Thirds, long held as gospel by painters and photographers, suggests that you imagine a tic-tac-toe grid superimposed on your frame. As you frame the shot, position the important parts of the photo on those lines or, better yet, at their intersections. Supposedly, this setup creates a stronger composition than putting everything in dead center.

Now, it's really a **Consideration** of Thirds; plenty of photographs are, in fact, strongest when the subject is centered.

But if you want to know where those magic intersections are, duck into **Settings→Camera**. Scroll down; turn on **Grid**. Now the phone displays the tic-tac-toe grid, for your composition pleasure (it's not part of the photo). You turn it off the same way.

High Dynamic Range (HDR)

In one regard, digital cameras are still pathetic: Compared with the human eye, they have terrible *dynamic range*.

That's the range from the brightest to darkest spots in a single scene. If you photograph someone standing in front of a bright window, you'll just get a solid-black silhouette. The camera doesn't have enough dynamic range to handle both the bright background and the person standing in front of it.

You could brighten up the exposure so that the person's face is lit—but then you'd brighten the background to a nuclear-white rectangle.

A partial solution: *HDR* (high dynamic range) photography. That's when the camera takes three (or even more) photos—one each at dark, medium, and light exposure settings. Its software combines the best parts of all three, bringing details to both the shadows and the highlights.

Your iPhone has a built-in HDR feature. It's not as amazing as what an HDR guru can do in Photoshop—for one thing, you have zero control over how the images are combined. But, often, an HDR photo does show more detail in both bright and dark areas than a single shot would. In this shot (left), the sky is blown out—pure white. On the right, the HDR feature brings back the streaks of color.

Until iOS 11 came along, you had to choose when to use HDR, using the **HDR** button in the Camera app. It produced three choices: **On**, **Off**, and **Auto**. (Auto means "Use your judgment, iPhone. If you think this scene would benefit, then please use HDR automatically.")

Nowadays, Apple thinks its HDR smarts are good enough that you'll always get the best results with Auto. In other words, the Camera always uses HDR when it thinks it's necessary.

If you miss having manual control, though, all is not lost: Open **Settings→Camera** and turn off **Auto HDR**.

> **TIP:** Should the phone save a standard shot in addition to the HDR shot? That's up to you. Also in **Settings→Camera**, you'll find the on/off switch for **Keep Normal Photo**.

When you inspect your photos later in the Photos app, you'll know which ones were taken with HDR turned on; when you tap the photo, you'll see a tiny HDR logo in the upper-left corner.

Taking the Shot

All right. You've opened the Camera app. You've set up the focus, exposure, flash, grid, HDR, and zoom. If, in fact, your subject hasn't already left the scene, you can now take the picture. You can do that in any of three ways:

- Tap the shutter button (●).

- Press either of the physical volume buttons on the left edge of the phone.

  This option is fantastic. If you hold the phone with the volume buttons at the top, then they're right where the shutter would be on a real camera. Pressing one feels more natural than, and doesn't shake the camera as much as, tapping the screen.

- Press a volume button on your earbuds clicker—a great way to trigger the shutter without jiggling the phone at all, and a more convenient way to take selfies when the phone is at arm's length.

Either way, if the phone isn't muted, you hear the *snap!* sound of a picture successfully taken.

You get to admire your work for only about half a second—and then the photo slurps itself into the thumbnail icon at the lower-left corner of the screen. To review the photo you just took, tap that thumbnail icon.

At this point, to look at other pictures you've taken, tap the screen and then tap **All Photos**.

This is your opportunity to choose a photo (or many) for emailing, texting, posting to Facebook, and so on; tap **Select**, tap the photos you want, and then tap the Share button (⬆). See page 363.

> **TIP:** For details on copying your iPhone photos and videos back to your Mac or PC, see page 526.

Burst Mode

The iPhone snaps *many* photos—10 shots a second—if you keep your finger pressed on the ⏺ button or a volume key. That's a fantastic feature when you're trying to capture a moment that will be over in a flash: a golf swing, a pet trick, a toddler sitting still.

As you press the ⏺ button or the volume key, a counter rapidly increments, showing you how many shots you've fired off.

> **TIP:** The front-facing camera can capture bursts, too.

Better yet, the phone helps you *clean up the mess* afterward—the hassle of inspecting all 130 photos you shot, to find the ones worth keeping.

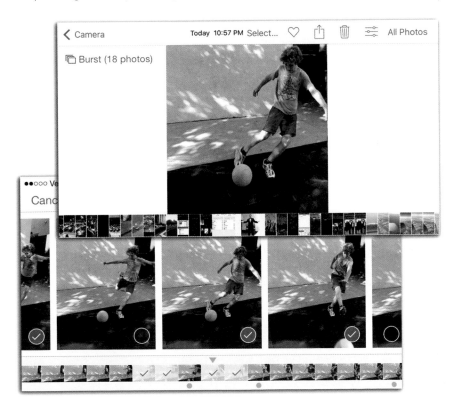

Tap the lower-left thumbnail. To help keep you sane, the iPhone depicts your burst as a single photo, with the phrase "Burst (72 photos)" (or whatever) in the corner of the screen. (Its thumbnail bears multiple frames, as though it were a stack of slides.)

Here's where it gets cool. If you tap **Select**, you see all frames of the burst in a horizontally scrolling row. Underneath, you see an even smaller "film-strip" of them—and a few of them are marked with dots.

These are the ones the iPhone has decided are the keepers. It does that by studying the clarity or blur of each shot, examining how much one frame is different from those around it, and even skipping past shots where somebody's eyes are closed. Tap the marked thumbnails to see if you approve of the iPhone's selections.

Whether you do or not, you should work through the larger thumbnails in the burst, tapping each one you want to keep. (The circle in the corner sprouts a blue checkmark.)

When you tap **Done**, the phone asks: "Would you like to keep the other photos in this burst?" Tap **Keep Everything** to preserve all the shots in the burst, so you can return later to extract a different set of frames; tap **Keep Only 2 Favorites** (or whatever number you selected) to discard the ones you skipped.

Self-Portraits (the Front Camera)

The iPhone has a second camera on the front, above the screen. It lets you use the screen itself as a viewfinder to frame yourself, experiment with your expression, and check your teeth.

To activate the front camera, tap the 🔄. Suddenly, you see yourself on the screen. Frame the shot, and then tap ⬤ to take the photo.

Now, the front camera is not the back camera. It's OK on the 6s and later models (5 megapixels, plus that cool screen flash)—but older models offer lower resolution, lower quality, and no flash.

But when your goal is a well-framed self-portrait that you'll use on the screen—email or the web, for example, where resolution isn't very import-ant—then having the front-camera option is better than not having it.

The Self-Timer

A self-timer is essential when you want to be in the picture yourself; you can prop the phone on something and then run into the scene. It's also a great way to prevent camera shake (which produces blurry photos), because your finger doesn't touch the phone. Just tap the 🕐, and then **3s** (three-second countdown) or **10s** (10 seconds).

Now, when you tap ⏺ or press a volume key, you get a countdown: huge digits on the screen if you're using the front camera, a blinking flash if you're using the rear camera. After the countdown, the phone takes the picture all by itself. (If the sound is on, you'll hear the shutter noise.)

Correction: In its regular, non-Live modes, the phone takes **10** pictures, in burst mode. The phone assumes that if you're using the self-timer, then you won't be able to see when everybody's eyes are open. So it takes 10 shots in a row; you can weed through them later to find the best one.

TIP: The self-timer is available for both the front and back cameras. In other words, it's also handy for selfies.

Filters

The success of Instagram made it clear to Apple that the masses want *filters*, special effects that tweak the color of your photo in artsy ways. You, too, can make your pictures look old, washed-out, or oversaturated. In fact, in iOS 11, you have more options at your disposal—nine in all.

- **To filter before you shoot.** Tap ⊗ to view your options (below, left). You see a scrolling strip of color and black-and-white filters. The first one always represents "no filter."

Tap a filter thumbnail to try it. Each turns your photo into a variation of black-and-white or plays with its saturation (color intensity), as shown on the previous page at right. When you've decided, take the shot as usual. (To turn off the filters, tap again.)

- **To filter after you shoot.** You can also apply a filter to any photo you've already taken (previous page, right); see page 304.

> **TIP:** And if you love one particular filter, you can keep it turned on all the time. Open **Settings→Camera→Preserve Settings** and turn on **Photo Filter**.

Live Photos

A Live Photo is a weird hybrid entity: a still photo with a three-second video attached (with sound). You can take one with the SE, 6s, and later iPhones, but you can play it back on any iPhone or the Mac.

What you're getting is 1.5 seconds before the moment you snapped the photo, plus 1.5 seconds after. In the Camera app, the icon lets you know whether or not you're about to capture the three-second video portion when you take a still. (The factory setting, yellow, means On.)

> **TIP:** When you take a Live Photo, remember to hold the phone still both before and after you tap the ◉ button! That's when the phone is recording video.
>
> A yellow "Live" label appears while the video is being captured. That's a warning to keep the phone still longer than you ordinarily would. (If you forget, and you drop your hand too soon, iOS is smart enough to auto-delete the blurry garbage that results at the end of the shot.)

Now, your obvious concern might be file size. "The iPhone takes 12-megapixel photos," you might say. "Well, video has 30 frames a second! One Live Photo must take up 90 times as much storage as a still image!"

Fortunately, no. The actual photo *is* a full 12-megapixel shot. But the other frames of the Live Photo are video frames with much lower resolution. (And a Live Photo stores only 15 frames a second, not 30.) Overall, an entire Live Photo takes up about *twice* as much space as a still photo.

That's still from 2 to 4 megabytes a shot, though, so be careful about leaving Live Photos turned on for everyday shooting. To prevent it from turning itself back on again every time you open the Camera app, open **Settings→Camera→Preserve Settings** and turn on **Live Photo**.

Reviewing Live Photos

As you flick through the photos in the Photos app, you'll know when a photo is a Live Photo; you'll see it animate for a half-second.

To play the full three-second video with sound, hard-press or long-press it with your finger. (See page 37 for more on force-touching.)

Editing Live Photos

In iOS 11, you can edit Live Photos in all kinds of interesting ways—both as photos and as little videos. See page 308.

Sharing Live Photos

What happens if you try to send a Live Photo to some other device? Well, first of all, you'll know that you're about to share a Live Photo. After you tap ⬆, a special ⓞLIVE icon reminds you.

You can tap to turn off that logo before you send, so that you're sharing only the still photo.

> **NOTE:** You can't *email* a Live Photo with its video intact. Even if you send it to another iPhone, only the still image survives the journey.
>
> On the other hand, you can post Live Photos to Facebook and Tumblr, where they "play" just fine. And a free app called Motion Stills turns Live Photos into GIFs or movies that you can edit outside the Photos app—and even import into iMovie for more advanced editing.

If you proceed with Live Photos turned on, what happens next depends on what kind of device receives it.

If it's running recent Apple software (iOS 9 or later, OS X El Capitan or later), then the Live Photo plays on that gadget, too. On the Mac, in Photos, click **Live Photo** to play it. On an iPad or older iPhone, hold your finger down on it to play it back.

What if it's a device or software program that doesn't know about Live Photos—if you send it as a text message, for example, or open it in Photoshop? Behind the scenes, a Live Photo has two elements: a 12-megapixel JPEG still image and a three-second QuickTime movie. In these situations, only the JPEG image arrives at the other end.

Portrait Mode

The 7 Plus, 8 Plus, and X all have two camera lenses: one wider angle, the other a 2x zoom. Clever software lets you blend the zoom to any degree between them (page 283).

But the two-lens setup has a second benefit: It lets the camera tell the foreground subject apart from its background. And with that knowledge, the phone can create a soft, blurry-background look. Shown below at left, the original shot; at right, the blurred one:

Ordinarily, you see that look only in professional photos, or at least photos taken with big black SLR cameras using high-aperture lenses (f/1.8, for example). But now you can do it with your phone.

The blur in this case is not optically created, the way an SLR makes it. This is a glorified Photoshop filter; it's done with software. Still, the effect generally looks fantastic—it's been improved in iOS 11—even when the outline of the subject is complex (like frizzy hair).

Once you've scrolled through the Camera app's modes to **Portrait**, point the camera at someone between 15 inches and 8 feet away. You see the background blur, right in the preview image. Take the shot.

If a second person is standing within the range, you can tap the screen to make *that* person the subject.

Now, Portrait mode doesn't always work. It occasionally gets confused when the light is dim, like in a bar or restaurant; when the subject is covered with a repeating pattern; when the subject is reflective, like a shiny bottle; or when the subject is not in that 15-inches-to-8-feet range. In those instances, you may get bleed blur, where the blurriness leaks into the subject like some kind of hideous, detail-eating virus.

As long as the light and the distance are right, though, the results are surprisingly good. Already, the Flickrs and Facebooks of the world are teeming with great-looking, blurry-background photos—taken by iPhones.

Studio Lighting

On the iPhone 8 Plus and the iPhone X, a further refinement to Portrait mode awaits, something Apple calls *studio lighting*.

When you're examining a Portrait shot, you can tap **Edit** to summon a set of five lighting effects that scroll by as though on a disc. **Natural Light**

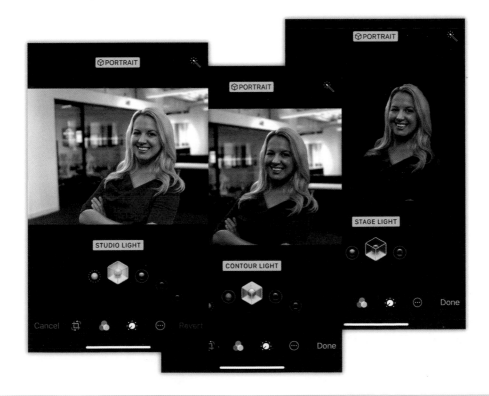

is the original shot. **Studio Light** brightens your subjects as though they were lit from the front with pro studio lighting. **Contour Light** deepens shadows, as though there were more light above the person. **Stage Light**, incredibly, ***cuts out the background***, making it black (previous page, right). And **Studio Light Mono** does the same, but in black-and-white.

This little phone's photos are getting scarily close to looking like professional ones.

Square Mode

No longer do you have to download a special app (*cough* Instagram *cough*) just to take perfectly square photos, the way all the cool kids do these days. Just swipe across the screen until you enter Square mode.

Square mode is exactly like Photo mode, except that the photos are square instead of rectangular (4 × 3 proportions).

Pano Mode

Here's one of the best camera features of the iPhone: panoramic photographs. The iPhone lets you capture a 240-degree, ultra-wide-angle photo (63 megapixels on the 6s and later!) by swinging the phone around you in an arc. The phone creates the panorama in real time; you don't have to line up the sections yourself.

 TIP: The Panorama mode smoothly adjusts the exposure of the scene as you pan. That fixes one of the most frustrating aspects of other cameras, which use the same exposure all the way across their panoramas; you soon discover that the sunlit part of the scene is blown out and the shadowy parts are way too dark.

Next time you're standing at the edge of the Grand Canyon—or anything else that requires a ***really*** wide or tall angle—keep this feature in mind.

In the Camera app, swipe leftward until you reach Pano mode.

 TIP: The big white arrow tells you which way to move the phone. But you can reverse it (the direction) just by tapping it (the arrow) before you begin.

Tap ⬤ (or press a volume key). Now, as instructed by the screen, swing the phone around you—smoothly and slowly, please. You can pan either horizontally or (to capture something very tall) vertically.

As you go, the screen gives you feedback. It may say "Slow down" if you're swinging too fast, or "Keep the arrow on the center line" if you're not keeping the phone level. Use the big white arrow itself like a level; you'll leave the center line if you're moving your arm up and down.

The preview of your panorama builds itself as you move. That is, you're seeing the final product, in miniature, while you're still taking it.

You'll probably find that 240 degrees—the maximum—is a **really** wide angle. You'll feel twisted at the waist. But you can end the panorama at any stage, just by tapping the ⊙ button.

At that point, you'll find that the iPhone has taken a very wide, amazingly seamless photograph at very high resolution (over 16,000 pixels wide). If a panorama is **too** wide, you can crop it, as described later in this chapter.

If you snap a real winner, you can print it out at a local or online graphics shop, frame it, and hang it above the entire length of your living-room couch.

Video Mode

The iPhone can record sharp, colorful video. It's at the best flavor of high definition (1080p), or even 4K (on the 6s and later models)—and it's stabilized to prevent hand jerkiness, just like a real camcorder. You can even shoot in gorgeous, 120-frames-per-second *slow-motion* that turns even frenzied action into graceful, liquidy visual ballet; the 6 and later models can manage *240* frames per second, for even **more** fluid, slowed-down videos.

Shooting video is almost exactly like taking stills. Open the Camera app. Swipe until you've selected Video mode. You *can* hold the iPhone either vertically or horizontally while you film. But if you hold it upright, most people on the Internet will spit on you; tall-and-thin videos don't fit the world's horizontal screens, including YouTube, laptops, and TVs.

> **TIP:** When you switch from still-photo mode to video, you may notice that the video image on the screen suddenly jumps bigger, as though it's zooming in. And it's true: The iPhone is oddly more "zoomed in" in camcorder mode than in camera mode.

Tap to compute focus, exposure, and white balance, as described for still photos. (You can even hold your finger down to trigger the exposure and focus locks, or drag the tiny yellow sun to adjust exposure manually, as described earlier.)

Then tap Record (⏺)—or press a volume key—and you're rolling! As you film, a time counter ticks away at the top.

A Note About Resolution—and 4K Video

Video generally plays back at 30 frames a second. But the iPhone 6 and later can do something only expensive cameras do: They can record and play back **60** frames a second. Video you shoot this way has a smoothness and clarity that's almost surreal. (It also takes up twice as much space on your phone.)

You choose the video quality you want in **Settings→Camera→Record Video**. Experiment with 60 fps; see if you feel the result is worth the sacrifice of storage space.

This is also, by the way, where you turn on 4K video recording on the 6s and later models. 4K televisions, also called Ultra HD, are TV sets with four times as many tiny pixels as an HDTV set, for four times the clarity.

4K shooting is **not** the factory setting, and that's a good thing; 4K takes up a huge amount of storage space (375 megabytes a minute).

Furthermore, you probably don't have anywhere to **play back** 4K video you've captured with this phone! Paradoxically, the iPhone itself (even the 2436 × 1125 pixel iPhone X) doesn't have enough pixels to play 4K video. To see the difference, you need a **big** 4K television or 4K computer screen, and you have to sit very close.

(You can post 4K video to YouTube—but even then, few people have computer screens capable of playing it back in 4K.)

Things to Do While You're Rolling

Once you've begun capturing video, don't think your work is done. You can have all kinds of fun during the recording. For example:

- **Change focus.** You can change focus while you're filming, which is great when you're panning from a nearby object to a distant one. Refocusing is automatic, just as it is on camcorders. But you can also force a refocusing (for example, when the phone is focusing on the wrong thing) by tapping to specify a new focus point. The iPhone recalculates the focus, white balance, and exposure at that point, just as it does when you're taking stills.

- **Change exposure.** While you're recording, you can drag your finger up or down to make the scene brighter or dimmer.

- **Zoom in.** You can zoom in while you're rolling, up to 3x actual size. Just spread two fingers on the screen, like you would to magnify a photo. Pinch two fingers to zoom out again. (On the iPhone 7 Plus,

8 Plus, or X, you can either do that two-finger spreading *or* drag the little 1x button to the left, as described on page 284.)

(described on page 284.)

TIP: Once you start to zoom, a zoom *slider* appears on the screen. It's much easier to zoom smoothly by dragging its handle than it is to use a two-finger pinch or spread.

So here's a smart idea: Zoom in slightly before you start recording, so that the zoom slider appears on the screen. Then, during the shot, drag its handle to zoom in, as smoothly as you like.

- **Take a still photo.** Yes, you can even snap still photos *while* you're capturing video. Just tap the ● that appears while you're filming. Awesome.

NOTE: The pictures you take while filming don't have the same dimensions as the ones you take in Photo mode. These have 16:9 proportions, just like the video; they're not as tall as still photos.

When you're finished recording, tap Stop (⏺). The iPhone stops recording and plays a chime; it's ready to record another shot.

There's no easier-to-use camcorder on earth. And what a lot of capacity! Each individual shot can be an hour long—and on the 256-gigabyte iPhone, you can record *136 hours* of video. Just long enough to capture the entire elementary-school talent show.

The Front Camera

You can film yourself, too. Just tap 📷 before you film to make the iPhone use its front-mounted camera, so that the screen shows *you*. The resolution isn't as high (the video isn't as sharp) as what the back camera captures, but it's still high definition.

The Video Light

You know the LED "flash" on the back of the phone? You can use it as a video light, too, supplying some illumination to subjects within about 5 feet or so. Just tap the ⚡ icon and then tap **On** before you start capturing. (Alas, you have to turn the light on before you start rolling. You can't turn it on or off in the middle of a shot.)

Slo-Mo Mode

The Camera app's Slo-Mo mode is exactly like its video mode—but, behind the scenes, the phone is recording 120 or 240 frames a second instead of the usual 30.

When you open the captured movie to watch it, you'll see something startling and beautiful: The clip plays at full speed for one second, slows down to one-quarter or one-eighth speed, and, for the final second, accelerates back to full speed. It's a great way to study sports action, cannonball dives, and shades of expression in a growing smile.

What you may not realize, however, is that you can adjust **where** the slow-motion effect begins and ends in the clip. When you open the video for playback and then hit **Edit**, a strange kind of ruler track appears just below it. Drag the vertical handles inward or outward to change the spot where the slow motion begins and ends.

At the very bottom of the screen is a second, taller strip; you use this one to trim the ends off the video (see below) or to scroll quickly through the clip to see where you are.

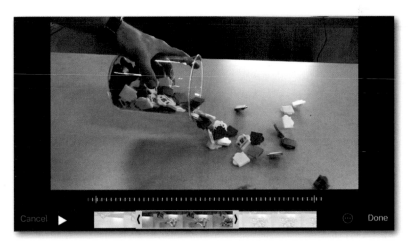

Time-Lapse Mode

Whereas Slo-Mo mode is great for slowing down **fast** scenes, the Time-Lapse mode speeds up **slow** scenes: flowers growing, ice melting, candles burning, and so on.

Actually, this mode might better be called **hyperlapse**. Time-lapse implies that the camera is locked down while recording. But in a hyperlapse video, the camera is moving. This mode works great for bike rides, hikes, drives, plane trips, and so on; it compresses even multihour events down to under a minute of playback, with impressive smoothness.

So how much does the Time-Lapse mode speed up the playback? Answer: It varies. The longer you shoot, the greater the speed-up. The app accelerates every recording enough to play back in 20 to 40 seconds, whether you film for 1 minute, 100 minutes, or 1,000 minutes.

If you film for less than 20 seconds, your video plays back at 15 times original speed. But you can film for much, much longer, like 30 hours or more. Time-Lapse mode speeds up the result from 15x, 240x, 960x—whatever it takes to produce a 20- to 40-second playback.

Trimming a Video

To review whatever video you've just shot, tap the ☐ thumbnail icon at the lower corner of the screen. You've just opened up the video-playback screen. Tap ▶ to play the video.

At this point, if you tap the **Edit** button, you can trim off the dead air at the beginning and the end.

To do that, drag the **(** and **)** markers (currently at the outer ends of the little filmstrip) inward so that they turn yellow, as shown on the previous page. Adjust them, hitting ▶ to see the effect as you go.

TIP: You can drag the playback cursor—the vertical white bar that indicates your position in the clip—with your finger. That's the closest thing you get to Rewind and Fast-Forward buttons. (In fact, you may have to move it out of the way before you can move the end handles for trimming.)

When you've positioned the handles so that they isolate the good stuff, tap **Done**. Finally, tap either **Trim Original** (meaning "Shorten the original clip permanently") or **Save as New Clip** (meaning "Leave the original untouched, and spin out the shortened version as a separate video, just in case").

NOTE: If you use iCloud Photo Library (page 337), you don't get the **Trim Original** option.

iMovie for iPhone

Of course, there's more to editing than just snipping dead air from the ends of a clip. That's why Apple made iMovie for iPhone. It's free on a new iPhone or $5 if it didn't come with your phone.

Editing Photos

Yes, kids, it's true: You can crop and edit your pictures right on the phone. The tools Apple gives you in the Photos app aren't exactly Photoshop, but they come surprisingly close.

TIP: Whenever you're in editing mode, *touch the screen* for a momentary flashback to the original image. Great for A/B comparisons.

To edit a photo, tap its thumbnail (anywhere in the Photos app) to open it. Tap **Edit**.

Now you get a set of unlabeled buttons. Between **Cancel** and **Done**, you'll find the **Crop/Straighten**, **Filters**, and **Adjust Color** buttons; on the opposite side of the photo, there's **Auto-Enhance** and, on Live Photos (page 290), on/off icons for sound and Live. Read on.

NOTE: All the changes described on these pages are *nondestructive.* That is, the Photos app never forgets the original photo. At any time, hours or years later, you can return to the Edit screen and undo the changes you've made (tap **Revert**). You can recrop the photo back to its original size, for example, or turn off the Auto-Enhance button. In other words, your changes are never really permanent.

Auto-Enhance (✨)

When you tap this magical button, the iPhone analyzes the relative brightness of all the pixels in your photo and attempts to "balance" it. After a moment, the app adjusts the brightness and contrast and intensifies dull or grayish-looking areas. Usually, the pictures look richer and more vivid as a result.

You may find that Auto-Enhance has little effect on some photos, only minimally improves others, and totally rescues a few. In any case, if you don't care for the result, you can tap the ✨ button again to turn Auto-Enhance off.

Adjust Color (◉)

The people have spoken: They want control over color, white balance, tint, and so on.

So when you tap ◉, you're offered three adjustment categories: **Light**, **Color**, and **B&W**.

When you tap one of these categories, you see a "filmstrip" below or beside your photo. You can drag your finger across it, watching the effect on your photo.

As it turns out, each of these sliders controls a handful of variables, all of which it's changing simultaneously. For example, adjusting the Light slider affects the exposure, contrast, brights, and darks all at once (below, left).

Intriguingly, you can tap ⊘ or ☰ to see how the master slider has affected these qualities—or even adjust these sub-sliders yourself (above, right). For example:

- **Light.** When you drag your finger along the **Light** filmstrip, you're adjusting the exposure and contrast of the photo. Often, a slight tweak is all it takes to bring a lot more detail out of the shot.

TIP: Actually, when you're making any of the adjustments described on these pages, you don't have to drag across the *filmstrip*. You can drag your finger left or right across *the photo itself*—a bigger target.

For much finer control, tap the ⊘ or ☰ icon. You open your "drawer" of additional controls: **Brilliance** (a slider that, Apple says, "brightens dark areas and pulls in highlights to reveal hidden detail"), **Exposure** (adjusts the brightness of all pixels), **Highlights** (pulls lost details out of very bright areas), **Shadows** (pulls lost details out of very dark areas), **Brightness** (like Exposure, but doesn't brighten parts that are already bright), **Contrast** (heightens the difference between the brightest and darkest areas), and **Black Point** (determines what is "black," shifting the entire dark/light range upward or downward). Once again, you drag your finger along the "film strip" to watch the effect on your photo.

- **Color.** The **Color** filmstrip adjusts the tint and intensity of the photos' colors. Here again, just a nudge can sometimes liven a dull photo or make blue skies "pop" a little more.

  Tap ⊙ or ≡ to see the three sliders that make up the master **Color** control. They are **Saturation** (intensity of the colors—from vivid fake-looking Disney all the way down to black and white), **Contrast** (deepens the most saturated colors), and **Cast** (adjusts the color tint of the photo, making it warmer or cooler overall).

- **B&W** stands for black and white. The instant you touch this filmstrip, your photo goes monochrome, like a black-and-white photo. It's hard to describe exactly what happens when you drag your finger—you just have to try it—except to note that the app plays with the relative tones of blacks, grays, and whites, creating variations on the black-and-white theme.

  Tap ⊙ or ≡ to see the component sliders: **Intensity** (the strength of the lightening/darkening effect), **Neutrals** (brightness of the middle grays), **Tone** (intensifies the brightest and darkest areas), and **Grain** (simulates the "grain"—the texture—of film prints; the farther you move the slider, the higher the "speed of the film" and the more visible the grain).

TIP: You can perform all these adjustments with the phone held either horizontally or vertically. The filmstrip jumps to the side or the bottom of the screen accordingly.

At any point, you can back out of what you're doing by tapping ≡. For example, if you're fiddling with one of the **Color** sub-sliders (**Contrast** or **Saturation**, for example), tapping ≡ returns you to the view of the three master sliders (**Light**, **Color**, and **B&W**).

And, of course, you can tap **Cancel** to abandon your editing altogether, or **Done** to save the edited photo and close the editing controls.

It might seem a little silly trying to perform these Photoshop-like tweaks on a tiny phone screen, but the power is here if you need it.

Filters (⊛)

Filters are effects that make a photo black and white, oversaturated, or washed out. As noted on page 290, you can apply a filter either as you take the picture or afterward.

Tap ⊛ to view a scrolling row of filter buttons. Tap each to see what it looks like on your photo; finish up by tapping **Done** or **Cancel**.

(Don't these filters more or less duplicate the effects of the **Light**, **Color**, and **B&W** sliders described already? Yes. But filters produce canned, one-tap, instant changes that don't require as much tweaking.)

TIP: It may look like you've just filtered that picture forever. But in fact you can return to it later and apply the **Original** filter to it, thereby restoring it to its original, pristine condition.

Remove Red Eye (⊘)

Red eye—devilish, glowing-red pupils in your subjects' eyes—has ruined many an otherwise great photo.

Red eye is caused when the bright light of your flash illuminates the blood-red retinal tissue at the back of the eyes. That's why red-eye problems are worse when you shoot pictures in a dim room: Your subjects' pupils are dilated, allowing even *more* light from your flash to reach their retinas.

When you tap this button, a message says, "Tap each red-eye." Do what it says: Tap with your finger inside each eye that has the problem. A little white ring appears around the pupil (unless you missed, in which case the ring shudders side to side, as though saying, "Nope")—and the app turns the red in each eye to black.

TIP: It helps to zoom in first. Use the usual two-finger spread technique.

Crop/Straighten (🔲)

This button opens a crazy editing screen where you can adjust the size, shape, and angle of the photo.

When you tap 🔲, iOS analyzes whatever horizontal lines it finds in the photo—the horizon, for example—and uses it as a guide to straightening the photo *automatically*.

It's very smart. See how the photo has been tilted slightly—and enlarged slightly to fill the frame without leaving triangular gaps?

You can reject the iPhone's proposal (tap **Reset**). Or you can tilt the photo more or less (drag your finger across the round scale).

If you want to rotate the photo more than 90 degrees—for example, if the camera took it sideways—tap ◾ as many times as necessary to turn the picture upright.

The other work you can do in this mode is *cropping*.

Cropping means shaving off unnecessary portions of a photo. Usually, you crop a photo to improve its composition—adjusting where the subject appears within the frame of the picture. Often, a photo has more impact if it's cropped tightly around the subject, especially in portraits. Or maybe you want to crop out wasted space, like big expanses of background sky. If necessary, you can even chop a former romantic interest out of an otherwise perfect family portrait.

Cropping is also very useful if your photo needs to have a certain **aspect ratio** (length-to-width proportion), like 8 × 10 or 5 × 7.

To crop a photo you've opened, tap the ⌗. A white border appears around your photo. Drag inward on any edge or corner. The part of the photo that the iPhone will eventually trim away is darkened. You can recenter the photo within your cropping frame by dragging any part of the photo, inside or outside the white box. Adjust the frame and drag the photo until everything looks just right.

Ordinarily, you can create a cropping rectangle of any size and proportions, freehand. But if you tap ▥, you get a choice of eight canned proportions: Square, 3 × 2, 3 × 5, 4 × 3, and so on. They make the app limit the cropping frame to preset proportions.

This aspect-ratio feature is important if you plan to order prints of your photos. Prints come only in standard photo sizes: 4 × 6, 5 × 7, 8 × 10, and so on. But unless you crop them, the iPhone's photos are all 3 × 2, which doesn't divide evenly into most standard print sizes. Limiting your cropping to one of these standard sizes guarantees that your cropped photos will fit perfectly into Kodak prints. (If you don't constrain your cropping this way, then Kodak—not you—will decide how to crop them to fit.)

TIP: The Original option here maintains the proportions of the original photo even as you make the grid smaller.

When you tap one of the preset sizes, the cropping frame *stays* in those proportions as you drag its edges. It's locked in those proportions unless you tap ▣ and choose a different setting.

Marking Up Your Photos

Here's a feature that nobody saw coming: You can draw or type on your photos, right from within the Photos app.

Once you're in editing mode, tap ⊙ and then **Markup**. You get a rather confusing assemblage of tools that fall into two categories.

- **Draw.** You get a pen (opaque lines, variable thickness as you press harder), a highlighter (translucent fat lines, variable opacity as you press harder), a pencil (very thin line), an eraser (tap a line to erase the whole thing), a lasso (select a line you've drawn to move it), and a dot for choosing the drawing color. (Those variable thicknesses and darknesses work only if you have an iPhone 6s or later.) You can use the Undo button (↺) as often as you mess up.

- **Text or objects.** See the ⊕ button? It produces a palette of options for adding shapes (square, circle, speech bubble, arrow, magnified "loupe") or text (typed text, or a signature) to your photo.

  Here's how to operate these tools.

  Text: A text box appears on the photo, saying "Text." Drag the tiny blue handles to adjust the shape of the box; drag inside to move the box. Double-tap it (or tap it and then tap **Edit**) to open the keyboard; type what you want it to say. Tap the photo to put away the keyboard. Tap the text box and then tap ᴀA to choose font, size, and paragraph justification options.

  Signature: Tap to insert a handwritten signature. (And where do these stored signatures come from? You've tapped **Add or Remove Signature** and then +, and then used your finger to write your name.)

  Magnifier: Tap to slap a magnified circular area onto your photo—great for calling out a detail. Drag the blue handle to adjust the circle's size; drag the green one to adjust the degree of magnification inside it. And drag inside the circle to move it.

NOTE: You're not enlarging this for your own editing purposes; this magnified area will *stay* magnified when you send the photo. It's for calling your correspondent's attention to some detail.

Square, circle, speech bubble, arrow: Tap one to place it on your photo. Then tap ⌣ to see some choices for line thickness and filled-inness. Drag blue dots to change size, or green ones to change shape—for example, the angle and direction of the speech balloon's "where it's coming from" angle, or the curvature of the arrow.

Editing Live Photos

Live Photos, as you now know, are a strange hybrid of videos and stills. In iOS 11, Apple has decided to turn that weirdness into a virtue—by letting you create entertaining videos from your Live Photos.

When you tap **Edit** on a Live Photo, you get a few unusual new controls. There's a ◀)) button, which lets you turn off the sound; a ◉LIVE button, which eliminates the three-second video and creates a plain old photo; and a sort of film strip along the bottom. You can use it for two things:

- Drag the ❨ and ❩ markers (currently at the outer ends of the little film-strip) inward, exactly as shown on page 299. You're trimming the Live Photo so that it's shorter.

- Tap a different "frame" of the filmstrip, and then tap **Make Key Photo**, to designate that frame as the new face of this Live Photo—the one that shows up as its thumbnail in, for example, the Photos app.

TIP: If you change the key photo and then export the Live Photo, remember that you're sending out what used to be a frame of video. It may be blurrier than the actual photo, and it has lower resolution—but not much lower. Sometimes it may be just what you need.

But in iOS 11, there's even more fun to be had with Live Photos—and not in the Edit mode, either. (Hit **Done** or **Cancel** to get out of there if necessary.)

On the Live Photo's normal viewing page, the one with the ‹ and **Edit** buttons, you can *swipe upward* to reveal a choice of four special video-playback effects, which used to require separate apps to achieve:

- **Live.** That's the normal Live Photo as you know it.

- **Loop** makes the three-second video play over and over again, with a crossfade to conceal the seam. Great for funny expressions, cat yawns, pratfalls.

- **Bounce** plays start→finish→start→finish, and so on, playing forward and then backward. Use it on a Live Photo of a kid doing a cannonball into a pool. Pure comedy.

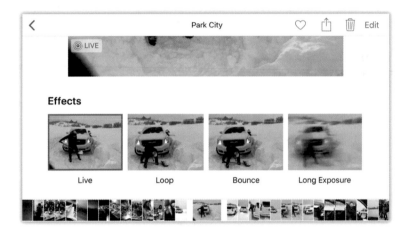

- **Long Exposure** simulates the effect of leaving the camera on a tripod with the lens open for a long time. In "real" photography, the result might produce the milky, softly blurred surface of a babbling brook, or cool-looking red streaks of taillights.

    Realistically, this effect works only on scenes where the background *doesn't* move, but the subject *does*. Classic examples include moving water, moving traffic, and moving people—in crowds or on teams.

    Unlike the other effects, the result of this one is a still image; the effect more or less *superimposes* all the frames in the Live Photo. (The video element is still there, looking like a standard Live Photo—hard-press the screen to see it.) But the goal here is to export the finished still image. Every now and then, the result is surprising and delightful.

Original Live Photo

Long Exposure effect

Handing Off to Other Editing Apps

OK, Apple: Who are you, and what have you done with the company that used to believe in closed systems?

Maybe you're a fan of Camera+, Fragment, or some other photo app. They now work so well with the Photos app that it can seem as though their tools are built right into it.

Here's the drill: Open a photo in Photos. Tap **Edit**. Tap ⊙. Now you see the icons of all apps on your phone that have been updated to work with this feature, which Apple calls Extensibility.

The photo opens immediately in the app you choose, with all of its editing features available. You can freely bounce back and forth between Apple's editor and its competitors'.

Saving Your Changes

Once you've rotated, cropped, auto-enhanced, or de-red-eyed a photo, tap the **Done** button. You've just made your changes permanent.

Or, rather, you've made them *temporarily* permanent. Remember: You can return to an edited photo at any time to undo the changes you've made (tap **Revert**). When you send the photo off the phone (by email, to your computer, whatever), *that* copy freezes the edits in place—but the copy on your phone is still revertable.

> **TIP:** If you sync your photos to Photos on the Mac (over a cable or via iCloud Photo Library), they show up in their edited condition. Yet, amazingly, you can undo or modify the edits there! The original photo is still lurking behind the edited version. You can use your Mac's Crop tool to adjust the crop, for example. Or you can use Photos' **Revert to Original** command to throw away *all* the edits you made to the photo while it was on the iPhone.
>
> (If you transfer the photos using email, AirDrop, or Messages, however, you get only the finished JPEG image; you *can't* rewind the changes.)

Managing and Sharing Photos

Once you've got some photos, the Photos app has another job: present-ing them, sharing them, and slideshowing them for all your fans.

> **TIP:** The Photos app is fully rotational. That is, you can turn the phone 90 degrees. Whether you're viewing a list, a screen full of thumbnails, or an individual photo, the image on the screen rotates, too, for easier admiring. (Unless, of course, you've turned on the rotation lock, as described on page 26.)

At the bottom of the Photos app screen, four tabs lie in wait: **Photos**, **Memories**, **Shared**, and **Albums**. The next few sections explain what they do.

The Photos Tab

iOS groups your photos intelligently into sets that are easy to navigate. Here they are, from smallest to largest:

- **Moments.** A *Moment* is a group of photos you took in one place at one time—for example, all the shots at the picnic by the lake. The phone even uses its GPS to give each Moment a name: "San Francisco, California (Union Square)," for example.

> **TIP:** If you tap a Moment's name, you get a details page that includes a ready-to-play Memory (page 313) and a map, showing exactly where these pictures were taken. Slick!

- **Collections.** Put a bunch of Moments together, and what do you get? A Collection. Here again, the phone tries to study the times and places of your photo taking—but this time it puts them into groups that might span a few days and several locations. You might discover that your entire spring vacation is a single Collection, for example.

- **Years.** If you "zoom out" of your photos far enough, you wind up viewing them by year: 2016, 2017, 2018, and so on.

To "zoom in" from larger groupings to smaller ones (**Years→Collections→Moments**), just tap each pile of thumbnails. If you tap a thumbnail on the Moments screen, you open that photo for viewing.

> **TIP:** When you first open a photo, it appears on a white background. Tap the photo to change the background to black (and hide the controls), which gives the photo the attention it deserves.

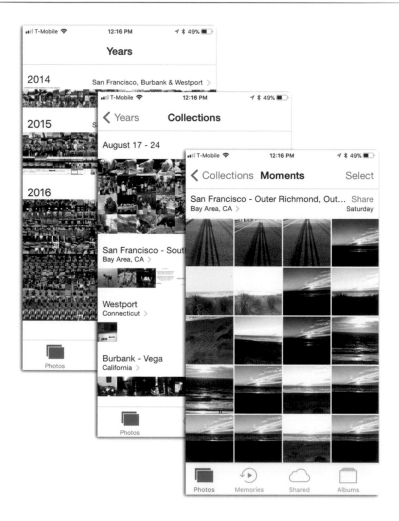

To "zoom out" again, tap the grouping name at top left (**Years**, for example).

> **TIP:** If you've opened a single photo for examination, you can retreat to the *Moment* it came from by pinching with two fingers.

The last technique worth knowing is the Finger Browse. Whenever you're looking at a grid of tiny thumbnail images (in a Year or a Collection, say), hold your finger down within the batch. A larger thumbnail sprouts from your finger. At this point, you can slide your finger around within the mosaic to find a particular photo, or a batch of them.

The Memories Tab

Memories are automatically selected groups of pix and videos from certain time periods or trips, which, with a tap, become gorgeous, musical slideshows. Most people are pleasantly surprised at how coherent and well-created these are, even though they're totally automatic. Photos, short pieces of your videos, and even scrolling panoramas are all first-class citizens in these slideshows.

Right off the bat, you see a few of Photos' suggestions, represented as clearly labeled billboards ("Cape Cod Summer," "Best of Last Week"...).

Tap to open a Memory; at this point, you can scroll down to see more about what's in this Memory. You'll see the photos that will be in it, as well as who's in it (People), and where the photos came from (Places).

At the very bottom, you'll see the option to **Delete Memory** or **Add to Favorite Memories**; that command adds this slideshow to a new folder on the **Albums** tab called Favorite Memories, for quick access later.

Anyway, the real fun begins when you tap ▶ to start an instant slideshow. They're usually fantastic.

When you come back to your senses, note that you can tap the screen for some quick editing options. Drag horizontally to change the animation/music style (**Dreamy**, **Sentimental**, **Gentle**, **Chill**, and so on) or the slideshow length (**Short**, **Medium**, **Long**).

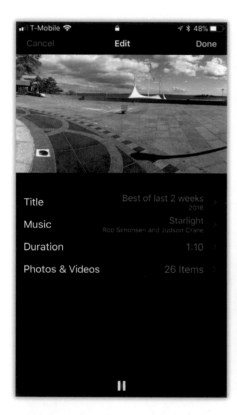

For more detailed editing, tap **Edit**. Now you can edit the Memory's **Title** (name and its typographical style), **Music** (either the app's selections or anything from your music library), **Duration** (dial up any length you want), or **Photos & Videos** (tap + to add one, 🗑 to delete one).

Once you've got a really killer Memory on your hands, by the way, don't miss the option to send it to other people as a standalone video. While a Memory slideshow is playing, tap it to reveal the ⬆ button at the top.

The Albums Tab

(The third tab of your Photos app may actually be the **Shared** tab, but we're skipping over it for now; see page 332.)

The Albums tab is a scrolling list of specialized photo "folders" like these:

- **All Photos.** Yup—everything on your phone, including videos (This may also be labeled "Camera Roll"; see page 337.)

- **Favorites.** This folder gives you quick access to your favorite photos. And how does the phone know which photos are your favorites? Easy: You've told it. You've tapped the ♡ icon under a photo, anywhere within the Photos app. (Favorites must be photos you've taken with the phone, not transferred from your computer.)

- **Favorite Memories** appears only if you have, in fact, designated a Memory slideshow as a favorite (page 313).

- **People.** Impressively enough, Photos can auto-group the people in your photos, using facial recognition. Once you've given the software a running start, it can find those people in the rest of your photo collection automatically. That's handy every now and then—when you need a photo of your kid for a school project, for example.

  To see it at work, tap People. Here are thumbnails representing the faces Photos has found and grouped, complete with a tally of how many photos Photos has found. At the top, you see people you've designated as favorites.

  Tap a thumbnail to see all the photos of this person. Scroll wayyyyy down to **Confirm Additional Photos** (Photos shows you other photos one at a time and asks, "Is this the same person?"); **Favorite** (or **Unfavorite**) **This Person**, and **Add to Memories** (creates a new Memory slideshow just of this person).

This feature doesn't work until the iPhone has *analyzed* your photos, which can take at least a day and requires that the phone be plugged in. Apple proudly points out that all this analysis is done on your phone. (That's in contrast to a service like Google Photos, which offers similar features but requires Google to access your photo library.)

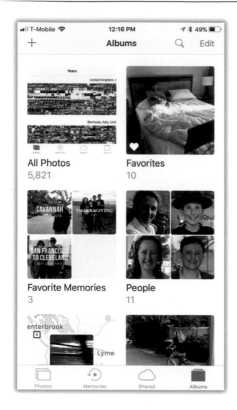

If you don't see a thumbnail for a certain someone, scroll down and tap + to start the process of rounding up her pictures.

- **Places.** Every photo you take with a smartphone (and a few very fancy cameras) gets *geotagged*—stamped, behind the scenes, with its geographic coordinates. When you tap **Places** in the Albums list, you see a map, dotted with clusters of photos you took in each place. Tap one to see the photos you took there.

- **Videos, Selfies, Live Photos, Portrait, Long Exposure, Panoramas, Time-Lapse, Slo-Mo, Bursts, Screenshots, Animated.** As a convenience to you, these categories give you one-tap shopping for everything you've captured using the Camera app's specialized picture and video modes. (**Portrait** appears only on the iPhone 7 Plus, 8 Plus, and X; it contains shots you've taken using Portrait mode [page 292]. **Long Exposure** and **Animated** are Live Photos to which you've applied the effects described on page 309.)

Super handy when you're trying to show someone your latest time-lapse masterpiece, for example; now you know where to look for it.

- **Recently Deleted.** Even after you think you've deleted a photo or video from your phone, you have 30 days to change your mind. Deleted pictures and videos sit in this folder, quietly counting down to their own doomsdays.

  If you wind up changing your mind, you can open **Recently Deleted**, tap the photo you'd condemned, and tap **Recover**. It pops back into its rightful place in the Photos app, saved from termination.

  On the other hand, you can also zap a photo into oblivion immediately. Tap to open one of your recently deleted photos, tap **Delete**, and then confirm with **Delete Photo**. If you tap **Select**, you can also hit **Delete All** or **Recover All**.

- **My Albums.** Here you get a list of albums *you've* created (or copied to the phone from your Mac or PC).

As you'd guess, you can drill down from any of these groupings to a screen full of thumbnails, and from there to an individual photo.

Creating and Deleting Albums

You can manually add selected photos into new albums—a great way to organize a huge batch you've shot on vacation, for example.

To do that, open any one of your existing albums (including All Photos or Camera Roll); tap **Select**; and then tap (or drag through) all the photos you want to move to a new or different album. Tap **Add To** at the bottom of the screen.

You're now offered an **Add to Album** screen. Tap the album into which you want to move these pictures. (If albums are dimmed, that's because they've been synced from your Mac or PC. You're not allowed to mess with those. The canned specialty-photo folders, like Panorama and Time-Lapse, are also dimmed, because only iOS can put things into those folders, and it does that automatically.)

This list also includes a **New Album** button; you're asked to type the name you want for the new album and then tap **Save**.

To delete an album you created on the phone, start on the main Albums tab. Tap **Edit**, and then tap the button next to the album you want to delete.

Hide a Photo

Here's a quirky little feature: It's possible to hide a photo from the Photos tab (Moments, Collections, and Years), so that it appears only in a special Hidden folder.

Apple noticed that lots of people use their phones to take screenshots of apps, pictures of whiteboards or diagrams, shots of package labels or parking-garage signs, and so on. These images aren't scenic or lovely; they're not memories; you don't want a slideshow of them; they don't look good (or serve much purpose) when they appear nestled in with your shots-to-remember in Moments, Collections, and Years.

Open the photo and then tap the 🗗 button; in the Sharing options that appear, tap **Hide**. To confirm, tap **Hide Photo**.

Whatever photos you hide go to a new folder on the Albums tab—called, of course, **Hidden**, so that you can find them easily. From here, you can unhide a shot the same way: Hit 🗗 and then **Unhide**.

Flicking, Rotating, Zooming, Panning

Once a photo is open at full size, you have your chance to perform the four most famous and dazzling tricks of the iPhone: flicking, rotating, zooming, and panning a photo.

- **Flicking** horizontally is how you advance to the next/previous picture or movie in the batch.

- **Zooming** a photo means magnifying it, and it's a blast. One quick way is to double-tap the photo; the iPhone zooms in on the portion you tapped, doubling its size.

    Another technique is to use the two-finger spread, which gives you more control over what gets magnified and by how much.

If you've brought in photos from your computer, the iPhone doesn't store the giganto 20-megapixel originals you took with your fancy camera. It keeps only scaled-down, iPhone-sized versions—so you can't zoom in more than about three times the original size.

Once you've spread a photo bigger, you can then pinch to scale it down again. Or just double-tap to restore the original size. (You don't have to restore a photo to original size before advancing to the next one, though; if you flick enough times, you'll pull the next photo onto the screen.)

- **Panning** is moving a photo around on the screen after you've zoomed in. Just drag your finger to do that; no scroll bars are necessary.

- **Rotating** is what you do when a horizontal photo or video appears on the upright iPhone, which makes the photo look small and fills most of the screen with blackness.

  Just turn the iPhone 90 degrees in either direction. Like magic, the photo rotates and enlarges to fill its new, wider canvas. No taps required. (This doesn't work when the phone is flat on its back—on a table, for example. It has to be more or less upright. It also doesn't work when portrait orientation is locked.)

  This trick also works the other way: You can make a *vertical* photo fit better by turning the iPhone upright.

  When the iPhone is rotated, all the controls and gestures reorient themselves. For example, flicking right to left still brings on the next photo, even if you're now holding the iPhone the wide way.

TIP: Every now and then, the phone's accelerometer gets confused about what is "upright" as you take a shot. You wind up with a photo that always rotates the wrong way, even as you turn the phone in your hand. In those situations, you'll have to tap **Edit** and rotate the photo upright manually, as described on page 305.

Finding Photos

There's a search icon () in Photos, which might seem odd. How can you search for a blob of pixels? How does the phone know what's *in* a picture?

Artificial intelligence, people. Apple has given Photos the ability to recognize what's in your pictures and videos. You can search your photos for "dog," or "beach," or whatever.

To try it out, tap Q at the top of the Photos or Albums screens. Right off the bat, the phone offers some one-tap canned searches based on locations and dates (like **One Year Ago** and **Home**). Tap to see the photos and videos that match.

To search for something more specific, you can type either of two kinds of things:

- **A place, date, name, or album.** Try typing *september* or *tucson* or *bay area* or *2016*, for example. As you type, iOS displays all the photo groupings that match what you've typed so far. Tap that grouping to see the photo thumbnails within.

> **TIP:** Then again, it's usually faster to request such photos by voice, using Siri: "Show me all the photos from Texas in 2017." See page 177.

- **A noun.** Type the photographic subject you're seeking, like forest, girl, plane, piano, food, pizza, mountain, or whatever. In the results list, Photos lists matching pictures under a **Category** heading, like **Pizza Category** or **Cat Category** (below, left). Tap to see what the phone has rounded up for you (right).

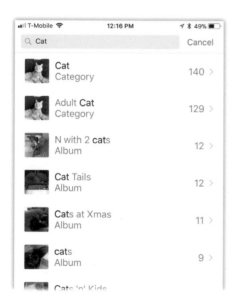

As you'll soon discover, Apple's image recognition software makes a lot of mistakes; you may well find a bar code or a picket fence in your **Piano** category, or a truck in your **Cars** category. But hey—it's just software. Cut it some slack.

Deleting Photos

If some photo no longer meets your exacting standards, you can delete it. But this action is trickier than you may think.

- **If you took the picture using the iPhone,** no sweat. Open the photo; tap 🗑. When you tap **Delete Photo**, that picture is gone. Or, rather, it's moved to the **Recently Deleted** folder described on page 317; you have 30 days to change your mind.

  (If you open the photo from the **Albums** tab instead, you're just taking the picture out of that album—not actually deleting it from the phone.)

- **If the photo was synced to the iPhone from your computer,** well, that's life. The iPhone remains a **mirror** of what's on the computer. In other words, you can't delete the photo from the phone. Instead, delete it from the original album on your computer (which does **not** mean deleting it from the computer altogether). The next time you sync the iPhone, the photo disappears from it, too.

  The exception: If you use iCloud Photo Library (page 337), you're warned that you're about to delete the photo from all your devices—and that's what happens.

Photo Controls

When you first open a photo, some useful controls appear, in blue against the white background. They show up either at the top or bottom of the screen, depending on how you're holding the phone. (Tap again to hide them and summon a black background, for a more impressive photo presentation.)

- **Album name.** Here's the group this photo came from.

- **Favorite (♡).** When you find a picture you really love—enough that you might want to call it up later to show people—tap ♡. This photo or video now appears in the Favorites folder (in the Albums tab of the Photos app, described earlier), so that it's easy to find with your other prize-winners. (The ♡ appears only on photos you've taken with the phone—not pictures you've imported from computers or other cameras.)

- **Share (⬆).** Tap ⬆ if you want to do something more with this photo than just stare at it. You can use it as your iPhone's wallpaper, print it, copy it, text it, send it by email, use it as somebody's headshot in your Contacts list, post it on Twitter or Facebook, and so on. These options are all described on the following pages.

- **Date and time.** The top of the screen says "September 13, 12:52 pm," for example, letting you know when this photo was taken.

- **Edit.** This button is the gateway to the iPhone's photo-editing features, described starting on page 301.

- **Delete (🗑).** Gets rid of this photo, as described earlier.

- **Other photos.** Immediately below the picture, Photos thoughtfully displays a ribbon of tiny thumbnail images (actually, more like *pinky*nail images). They represent the previous and following photos in this batch. By tapping or dragging, you can jump to another photo without having to back out of the opened-photo screen.

There's one more huge element of the photo screen that you might miss. To see it, drag upward. Here's a vast, scrolling screen that explodes with resources for this photo, like a map of where it was taken (and the address); links to "related" shots (taken in the same place, or of the same people); and even a **Show Photos from This Day** link, which calls up all the *other* pictures you took that day.

753 Ways to Share Photos and Videos

It's great that the iPhone has a superb camera. But what's even greater is that it's also a cellphone. It's online. So once you've taken a picture, you can *do* something with it right away. Mail it, text it, post it to Facebook or Twitter, use it as wallpaper—right from the iPhone.

Step 1: Choose the Photos

Before you can send or post a photo or video, you have to tell iOS which one (or ones) you want to work with.

To send just one, well, no big mystery; tap its thumbnail and then tap ⬆.

But you can also send a bunch of them in a group—whenever you see a **Select** button. Tap it and then tap the photos you want to send. With each tap, a ✅ appears, meaning, "OK, this one will be included." (Tap again to remove the checkmark.)

Step 2: Preparing to Send

Once you've opened a photo (or selected a few), tap ⬆.

Now you have a huge array of "send my photo here" options, displayed in rows (below, left).

 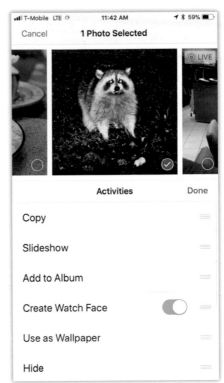

At the top of the Share screen, a scrolling row of other pictures appears. It lets you add more to the one(s) you've already selected, or deselect some that you already did. That's a lot less crazymaking than having to cancel out of the Share screen in order to change your selection.

TIP: If you're holding the phone horizontally, select the photos first and then tap **Next** to see the sharing icons.

All right. Here's an overview of the options available on the Share screen.

NOTE: *Which* icons appear depend on how you've opened the photo. For example, the choices you see when you open a photo in Messages aren't the same as the ones you see when you open a photo from an album. The following pages cover everything you might see.

AirDrop

So very cool: You can shoot a photo, or several, to any nearby iPhone, iPad, iPod Touch, or Mac—wirelessly, securely, conveniently, and instantly. See page 364 for the step-by-steps.

Message

This row of options lists *apps* that can receive your photos and videos.

The Message icon lets you send a photo or video as a ***picture or video message***. It winds up on the screen of the other guy's cellphone.

That's a delicious feature, which people exploit millions of times a day.

> **NOTE:** If you're sending to another Apple gadget, like an iPhone, iPad, iPod Touch, or Mac, it will be sent as a free iMessage (assuming that the recipient has an iCloud account). If you're sending to a non-Apple cellphone, it will be a regular MMS message. All of this is described in Chapter 6.

Tap **Message** and then specify the phone number of the recipient; if you're sending by iMessage, the email address also works. Or choose someone from your Contacts list. Then type a little note, tap **Send**, and off it goes.

> **NOTE:** If you're sending a video, the iPhone compresses it first so that it's small enough to send as a text-message attachment (smaller dimensions, lower picture quality). Then it attaches the clip to an outgoing text message; it's your job to address it.

Mail

The iPhone attaches your photos or video clips to a new outgoing message. All you have to do is address it and hit **Send**. If it's a big file, you may be asked how much you want the photo ***scaled down*** from its original size. Tap **Small**, **Medium**, **Large**, or **Actual Size**, using the megabyte indicator as a guide. (Some email systems don't accept attachments larger than 5 megabytes.)

(Any video clip you send by email gets compressed—smaller, lower quality—for the same reason.)

iCloud Photo Sharing

You can share batches of photos or videos with other people, either directly to their Apple gadgets or to a private web page. What's more, they can (with your permission) contribute their *own* pictures to the album.

This is a big topic, though, so it gets its own write-up on page 332.

Add to Notes

Since the Notes app (page 419) can accommodate pasted pix or vids, why not?

A little box appears, inviting you to type some text into the newly illustrated photo note. You can also plop this picture into either a new note page or an existing one, using the pop-up menu at lower right.

Twitter, Facebook, Flickr

If you've told your iPhone what your name and password are (in **Settings→Twitter** or **Settings→Facebook** or **Settings→Flickr**), then posting a photo from your phone to your Twitter feed, Facebook timeline, or Flickr collection is ridiculously simple.

Open the photo; tap the 📤 button; tap **Twitter**, **Facebook**, or **Flickr**. You're offered the chance to type a message that accompanies your photo. (As usual with Twitter, you have a maximum of 140 or 280 characters for your message.) You can also tap **Add Location** if you want Twitterites or Facebookers to know where the photo was taken.

NOTE: The Add Location option is available only if you've permitted Twitter or Facebook to use your location information, which you set up in **Settings→Privacy→Location Services**.

If you're posting to Facebook, you can also indicate which people you're sharing this item with—just your friends, everyone, and so on—by tapping **Audience** beneath the photo thumbnail. Flickr also offers a chance to specify which of your Flickr photo sets you want to post to.

When you tap **Send** or **Post**, your photo, and your accompanying tweet or post, zoom off to Twitter, Facebook, or Flickr for all to enjoy.

YouTube, Vimeo

Call up a video, if it's not already on the screen before you. Tap ⬆️. The Share sheet offers these video-specific buttons:

- **YouTube.** The iPhone asks for your Google account name and password (Google owns YouTube). Next it wants a title, description, and *tags* (searchable keywords like "funny" or "babies").

  It then wants to know if the video will be in standard definition or high definition (and it gives the approximate size of the file). You should also pick a **Category** (Autos & Vehicles, Comedy, Education, or whatever).

  Finally, choose from **Public** (anyone online can search for and view your video), **Unlisted** (only people who have the link can view this video), or **Private** (only specific YouTubers can view it). When everything looks good, tap **Publish**.

  After the upload is complete, you're offered the chance to see the video as it now appears on YouTube, or to **Tell a Friend** (that is, to email the YouTube link to a pal). Both are excellent ways to make sure your masterful cinematography gets admired.

- **Vimeo.** You're supposed to have set up your name and password in Settings for Vimeo (a video site a lot like YouTube, but classier, with a greater emphasis on quality and artistry).

  If you've done that, then all you have to do, when posting a video, is to specify a caption or a description, and then tap **Details** to choose a video size and your audience (public, private, and so on). Once you tap **Post**, your video gets sent on to the great cinema on the web.

Save PDF to iBooks

This button converts whatever photos you've selected into a single, multipage PDF document that opens in iBooks (page 394). In effect, it creates an ebook of your pictures.

After a moment of conversion, iBooks opens so you can inspect the results. You can now use all the tools available in iBooks (bookmarking, annotating, and so on). Better yet, you can send the resulting PDF document to someone else—a handy way to share a no-frills batch of pictures.

More

In the modern, extendable iOS, you can hand off a photo to *other* apps and services—beyond the set that Apple provides. If you tap **More**, you get the screen shown on page 323 at right.

That screen is basically a setup headquarters for the row of "where you can send photos" icons. Here you can rearrange them (put the ones you use most often at the top by dragging the ≡ handle); add to the list (turn on the switches for new, non-Apple photo-sharing apps you've installed); or hide the services you don't use (turn off the switches). (You can't turn off the switches for Message, Mail, and iCloud Photo Sharing.)

Save Image

Suppose you're looking at a photo that you didn't take with the phone. Maybe someone texted or emailed it to you. This button saves it into your own photo collection, so you'll be able to cherish it for years.

Assign to Contact

If you're viewing a photo of somebody who's listed in Contacts, then you can use it (or part of it) as her headshot. After that, her photo appears on your screen every time she calls. Just tap **Assign to Contact**.

Your address book list pops up. Tap the name of the person who goes with this photo.

Now you see a preview of what the photo will look like when that person calls. This is the **Move and Scale** screen. You want to crop the photo and shift it in the frame so only *that person* is visible (if it's a group shot)—in fact, probably just the face.

Start by enlarging the photo: Spread your thumb and forefinger against the glass. As you go, *shift* the photo's placement in the round frame with a one-finger drag. When you've got the person centered, tap **Choose**.

Copy

The bottom row of sharing options lists things you can *do* to the selected photos.

The **Copy** button, for example, puts the photo(s) onto the Clipboard, ready for pasting into another app (an outgoing Mail message, for example). Once you've opened an app that can accept pasted graphics, double-tap to make the **Paste** button appear.

Slideshow

This button instantly generates a gorgeous, musically accompanied, animated slideshow.

After the slideshow has begun, tap **Options** to see controls like these:

- **Theme.** A theme is a canned presentation style, incorporating animations, crossfades, and music. Each makes the photos appear, interact, overlap, and flow away in a different way. You're offered five choices—**Origami**, **Dissolve**, **Push**, **Magazine**, and **Ken Burns**. (Some of these display more than one photo at a time.)

- **Music.** Choose one of the five pieces of background music here, opt for **None**, or tap **iTunes Music** to choose a song from your music collection.

- **Repeat.** Makes the slideshow play over and over again until you stop it manually.

- **Speed.** The slider controls how much time each photo gets.

The slideshow incorporates both photos and videos (with sound; the background music actually gets softer so you can hear the audio).

While the show is playing, here's what you can do:

- **Tap to summon** the **II** button.

- **Turn the iPhone 90 degrees** to accommodate landscape-orientation photos as they come up; the slideshow keeps right on going.

- **Swipe leftward** to blow past a photo or video that's taking too long.

AirPlay

This button offers a list of nearby AirPlay gadgets—the only one you've probably heard of is Apple TV—so you can display the current photo on your TV or another screen.

Add to Album

If this is a photo you've taken with the phone, you're now free to file it away into one of the albums you've made (page 315).

Create Watch Face

This one's for you, Apple Watch owners! Now a picture you took can become the background for a watch-face design.

Hide

Here's the option to hide a photo, as described on page 318.

Save to Files

The iPhone now has a filing system, complete with folders (page 387). Here you can plop the selected photo(s) into one of your iPhone "desktop folders."

Use as Wallpaper

Wallpaper is the background photo that appears in either of two places: the Home screen (plastered behind your app icons) or the Lock screen (which appears every time you wake the iPhone).

This button lets you replace Apple's standard photos with one of your photos. It opens the Move and Scale screen, which lets you fit your photo within the wallpaper "frame." Pinch or spread to enlarge the shot; drag your finger on the screen to scroll and center it.

Finally, tap **Set**. You now specify where you want to use this wallpaper; tap **Set Lock Screen**, **Set Home Screen**, or **Set Both** (if you want the same picture in both places).

You can also change your wallpaper within Settings, as described on page 580.

Duplicate

Make a copy of the photo, which you can doctor beyond all recognition.

Print

You can print a photo easily enough, provided that you've hooked up your iPhone to a compatible printer. Once you've opened the photo, tap the ⬆ button and then tap **Print**. The rest goes down as described on page 362.

More

Once again, iOS offers a way to rearrange the Share buttons (this time, the bottom row)—or to add new buttons. If you don't have an Apple Watch, you may as well turn off the **Create Watch Face** option.

My Photo Stream

The concept of My Photo Stream is simple: Every time a new photo enters your life—when you take a picture with your iPhone or import one onto your computer—it gets added to your Photo Stream. From there, it appears automatically on all your *other* Apple machines.

Using Photo Stream means all kinds of good things:

- Your photos are always backed up. Lose your iPhone? No biggie— when you buy a new one, your latest 1,000 photos appear on it automatically.

- Any pictures you take with your iPhone appear automatically on your computer. You don't have to connect any cables or sync anything yourself.

Truth is, Photo Stream is a very old feature, one that Apple has long since expanded and replaced with iCloud Photo Library (page 337). But since Photo Stream is free, a lot of people still use it—as follows.

To turn *on* My Photo Stream, go to **Settings→Photos→Upload to My Photo Stream**. (You should also turn it on using the iCloud control panel on your computers. That's in System Preferences on your Mac, or in the Control Panel of Windows.) Give your phone some time in a Wi-Fi hotspot to form its initial slurping-in of all your most recent photos.

Once Photo Stream is up and running, you'll find a new album called **My Photo Stream**. It's in the Photos app on every iOS device, Mac, or Apple TV you own (or have signed into using iCloud). Inside are the photos that have entered your life most recently.

Now, your iPhone doesn't have nearly as much storage available as your Mac or PC; you can't yet buy an iPhone with 4 terabytes of storage. That's why, on your phone, your My Photo Stream consists of just the last 1,000 photos. (There's another limitation, too: The iCloud servers store your photos for 30 days. As long as your gadgets go online at least once a month, they'll remain current with the Photo Stream.)

TIP: Ordinarily, the oldest of the 1,000 photos in your Photo Stream scroll away forever as new photos come in. But you can rescue the best ones from that fate—by saving them onto your phone, where they're free from the risk of automatic deletion. Use the **Save Images** button. Or, if you're viewing one open picture in My Photo Stream, tap ⬆️ and then tap **Save to Camera Roll**.

Deleting Photos from the Photo Stream

Here's the thing about Photo Stream: You might think you're taking a private picture with your phone, forgetting that your spouse or parent will see it seconds later on the family iPad. It's only a matter of time before Photo Stream gets some politician in big trouble.

Fortunately, you can delete certain incriminating photos from your Photo Stream. Just select the thumbnail of the photo you want to delete, and then tap the Trash icon (🗑️). The confirmation box warns you that you're about to delete the photo from all your Apple machines (and, for shared streams, the machines of everyone who's subscribed to your photographic output).

If you haven't saved it to a different album or roll, it's gone for good when you tap **Delete Photo**.

iCloud Photo Sharing

iCloud Photo Sharing is like having a tiny Instagram network of your very own, consisting solely of people you invite. You send photos or videos to **other** people's gadgets. After a party or some other get-together, you could send your best shots to everyone who attended; after a trip, you could post your photographic memories for anyone who might care.

The lucky recipients can post comments about your photos, click a "like" button to indicate their enthusiasm, or even submit pictures and videos of their own.

In designing this feature, Apple had quite a challenge. There's a lot of back-and-forth among multiple people, sharing multiple photos, so iCloud Photo Sharing can get complicated. Stay calm and keep your hands and feet inside the tram at all times. Here's how it works.

> **TIP:** Well, here's how it works *if* your software is fairly recent (iOS 7 or later, OS X Mavericks 10.9 or later, for example).
>
> You also have to **turn on** the Photo Album feature. On an iOS gadget, the switch is in **Settings→Photos**. On the Mac, open **System Preferences→iCloud**. Make sure **Photos** is turned on; click **Options** and confirm that **Photo Sharing** is on, too. On a Windows PC, it's in the iCloud Control Panel for Windows (a free download from Apple's website).

Create a Shared Photo Album

To share some of your masterpieces with your adoring fans, do this:

1. **Create the empty album.** Open the Photos app. On the **Shared** tab, scroll to the top (if necessary) and tap +.

2. **Name the new album.** In the **Shared Album** box, name the photo album ("Bday Fun" or whatever). Tap **Next**.

3. **Specify the audience.** You're asked for the email addresses of your lucky audience members; enter their addresses in the "To:" box just as you would address an outgoing email.

    For your convenience, a list of recent sharees appears below the "To:" box.

    When that's done, tap **Create**. You return to the list of shared albums, where your newly named album appears at the top. It is, however, completely empty.

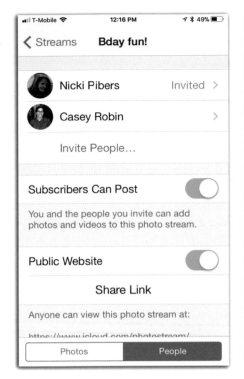

4. **Pour some photos or movies into the album.** Tap your new, empty album's name. Then, on the next screen, tap the + to burrow through your photos and videos—you can use any of the three tabs (**Photos**, **Shared**, **Albums**)—to select the material you want to share. Tap their thumbnails so that they sprout checkmarks, and then tap **Done**.

   A little box appears so that you can type up a description.

5. **Type a description of the new batch.** In theory, you and other people can add to this album later. That's why you're offered the chance to caption each new batch.

   Once that's done, tap **Post**.

The thumbnails of the shared photos and videos appear before you—and the + button is there, too, in case you want to add more pictures later.

> **TIP:** You can easily *remove* photos from the album, too. On this screen of thumbnails, tap **Select**; tap the thumbnails you want to nuke; tap 🗑; and confirm by tapping **Delete Photo**.

Adjusting an Album's Settings

Before you set your album free, tap the **People** tab at the bottom of the screen. Here are a few important options to establish for this album:

- **Invite People.** This list identifies everyone with whom you've shared the album. To add a new subscriber, tap **Invite People**. To delete a subscriber, tap the name and then (at the bottom of the contact card) tap **Remove Subscriber**.

- **Subscribers Can Post.** Your subscribers can contribute photos and videos to your album. That's a fantastic feature when it contains pictures of an event where there was a crowd: a wedding, show, political rally, picnic, badminton tournament. Everyone who was there can enhance the gallery with shots taken from their own points of view with their own phones or cameras.

- **Public Website.** If you turn on **Public Website**, then even people who aren't members of the Apple cult will be able to see these photos. The invitees will get an email containing a web address. It links to a hidden page on the iCloud website that contains your published photos.

  When you turn this switch on, the web address of your new gallery appears in light-gray type. Tap **Share Link** for a selection of methods for sending the link to people: by Message, Mail, Twitter, Facebook, AirDrop, and so on.

  What they'll see is a mosaic of pictures, laid out in a grid on a single sort of web poster. Your fans can download their favorites by clicking the button. (You can't add comments or "like" photos on the web, however.)

> **TIP:** If you click one of these medium-sized photos, you enter slideshow mode, in which one photo at a time fills your web browser window. Click the arrow buttons to move through them.

- **Notifications.** If this switch is on, then your phone will show a banner each time someone adds photos or videos to your album, clicks the "Like" button for a photo, or leaves a comment.

- **Delete Shared Album.** That's right: If the whole thing gets out of hand, you can slam the door in your subscribers' faces by making the entire album disappear.

Read on to see what it's like to be the person whose email address you entered.

Receiving a Photo Album on Your Gadget

When other people share photo albums with *you*, your phone makes a little warble, and a notification banner appears: "[Your buddy's name] invited you to join '[name of shared photo batch]'."

Simultaneously, a badge like (❷) appears on the Photos app icon and on the **Shared** tab within Photos, letting you know how many albums have come your way.

TIP: If you have iPhoto, Photos, or Aperture on a Mac, an invitation to accept the album appears there, too.

You can tap the new album's name to see what's inside it; tap **Accept**.

Once you're subscribed, you view the photos and movies as you would any album—with a couple of differences. First, you can tap **Add a comment** to make worshipful or snarky remarks, or tap **Like** to offer your silent support.

You can also snag a copy of somebody's published photo or video for yourself. With the photo before you, tap the ☐ button to see the usual sharing options—and tap **Save Image**. Now the picture or video isn't some virtual online wisp—it's a solid, tangible electronic copy in your own photo pool.

If your buddy has turned on **Subscribers Can Post** for this album, then you can send your own photos and clips into the album; everybody who's subscribed to it (and, of course, its owner) will see them.

To do that, tap the + on the album's page of thumbnails; choose your photos and movies; tap **Done**; add a comment; and tap **Post**.

Fun with Shared Photo Albums

Once you've created a shared photo album, you can update it or modify it in all kinds of ways:

- **Add new photos or movies to it.** In Photos, open the shared photo album, whether it's one you created or one you've subscribed to. Tap +. Now you can browse your whole world of photos, tapping to add them to the photo album already in progress.

- **Remove things from it.** In Photos, open the shared photo album. Tap **Select**, tap the item(s) you want to delete, and then tap 🗑—and confirm with a tap on **Delete Photo(s)**.

- **Delete an entire shared photo album.** Tap the **People** tab below an open photo album, scroll down, tap **Delete Shared Album**, and confirm by tapping **Delete**.

- **Change who's invited, change the name.** The **People** tab is also where you can add to the list of email addresses (tap **Invite People**), remove someone (tap the name, and then tap **Remove Subscriber**), rename the album, or turn off **Public Website** to dismantle the web version of this gallery.

At any time, you can tap the **Activity** "folder" at the top of the **Shared** tab in the Photos app. Here, for your amusement, is a visual record of everything that's gone on in Shared Photo Album Land: photos you've posted, photos other people have posted, comments back and forth, likes, and so on. It's your personal photographic Facebook.

iCloud Photo Library

If learning the difference between My Photo Stream, iCloud Photo Sharing, and Shared Photo Streams isn't hard enough, then hold onto your lens cap. Apple offers yet *another* online photo feature: the iCloud Photo Library.

The idea this time is that *all* your Apple gadgets will keep *all* your photos and videos backed up online and synced. The advantages:

- All your photos and videos are always backed up—not just the last 1,000.

- All your photos and videos appear identically on all your Apple machines.

- You can reclaim a lot of space on your phone. There's an option that offloads the original photos and videos to iCloud but leaves small, phone-sized copies on your phone.

There are a couple of sizable downsides to iCloud Photo Library, too:

- Your entire iCloud account comes with only 5 gigabytes of free storage. If you start backing up your photo library to it, too, you'll almost certainly have to pay to expand your iCloud storage. Photos and videos eat up a lot of storage space.

- Things get a little complicated. The structure of the Photos app described in this chapter changes, for example; the albums usually called **Camera Roll** and **My Photo Stream** go away. They're replaced by a new album called **All Photos**. (Camera Roll and My Photo Stream were just subsets of your whole photographic life anyway.)

If you decide to dive in, then open **Settings→Photos→iCloud Photo Library**.

Once iCloud Photo Library is on, you won't be able to copy pictures from your computer to your phone using iTunes anymore; iTunes will be completely removed from the photo-management loop. That's why, at this point, you may be warned that your phone is about to *delete* any photos and videos that you've synced to it from iTunes (Chapter 15). (Don't worry—they'll be safe in iCloud.)

And, of course, you might be warned that you need to buy more iCloud storage space.

Now the Settings panel expands and offers this important choice:

- **Optimize iPhone Storage.** If you turn this on, your original photos and videos get backed up to iCloud—but on your phone, you'll be left with much smaller versions that are just right for viewing on the phone's screen (but not high enough resolution to, for example, print). This arrangement saves you a *ton* of space on your phone.

- **Download and Keep Originals** leaves the big original files on your phone.

- **Cellular Data** lets you decide if it's worth eating into your data plan for syncing photos.

Finally, the uploading process begins. If you have a lot of photos and videos, it can take a very long time. But when it's all over, you'll have instant access to all your photos and videos in any of these places:

- **On the iPhone (or other iOS gadgets).** In the Photos app, on the Albums tab, the new "album" called **All Photos** represents your new online photo library. Add to, delete from, or edit pictures in this set, and you'll find the same changes made on all your other Apple gear.

- **On the web.** You can sign into *iCloud.com* and click **Photos** to view your photos and videos, no matter what machine you're using. The Moments and Albums tabs here correspond to the tabs in the phone's Photos app. Click a photo to open it full size, whereupon the icons at the top of the screen let you delete, download, or favorite it.

- **On the Mac.** Everything appears in the All Photos heading in the Photos app. (There's no way to see your iCloud Photo Library's contents in the older iPhoto and Aperture programs, alas.)

Geotagging

Mention to a geek that a gadget has both GPS and a camera, and there's only one possible reaction: "Does it do *geotagging*?"

Geotagging means "embedding your latitude and longitude information into a photo or video when you take it." After all, every digital picture you've ever taken comes with its time and date embedded in its file; why not its location?

The good news is that the iPhone can geotag every photo and movie you take. How you use this information, however, is a bit trickier. The iPhone doesn't geotag unless all the following conditions are true:

- **The location feature on your phone is turned on.** On the Home screen, tap **Settings→Privacy→Location Services**. Make sure Camera is set to **While Using the App**. (The rest of the time, the camera does not record your location.)

- **The phone knows where it is.** If you're indoors, the GPS chip in the iPhone probably can't get a fix on the satellites overhead. And if you're not near cellular towers or Wi-Fi base stations, then even the pseudo-GPS may not be able to triangulate your location.

- **You've given permission.** The first time you use the iPhone's camera, a peculiar message appears, asking if it's allowed to use your location information. In this case, it's asking, "Do you want to geotag your pictures?" If you tap **OK**, then the iPhone's geographic coordinates will be embedded in each photo you take.

OK, so suppose all of this is true, and the geotagging feature is working. How will you know? Well, the Moments feature can put geotagging to work right on the phone. You can open a map and see all the photos you took in that spot.

You can also transfer the photos to your computer, where your likelihood of being able to see the geotag information depends on what photo-viewing software you're using. For example:

- **When you've selected a photo in iPhoto or Photos** (on the Mac), you can press ⌘-I for the Info panel. It shows the photo's spot on a map.

- **Once you've posted your geotagged photos on Flickr.com** (the world's largest photo-sharing site), people can use the Explore menu to search for them by location or even see them clustered on a world map.

- **If you use Google Photos** (*photos.google.com*), then you can open any photo and click the Info button (**ⓘ**) to see a picture's location on the map.

Capturing the Screen

Let's say you want to write a book about the iPhone (hey, it could happen). How are you supposed to illustrate that book? How can you take pictures of what's on the screen?

The trick is very simple: Get the screen just the way you want it, even if that means holding your finger down on an onscreen button or a keyboard key. Now hold down the screenshot buttons:

- **iPhone X:** Simultaneously press the side button and volume-up button. They're directly across from each other.

- **Earlier models:** Press the home button, and while it's down, press the side button (which may be on the top). You might need to invite some friends over to help you execute this multiple-finger move.

The screen flashes white—and now, in iOS 11, something kind of great happens. The screenshot you just took appears as a miniature at the lower-left corner of the screen, and waits there for six seconds (facing page, left). If you do nothing (or if you swipe it away to the left), the thumbnail slides away, and the screenshot winds up in the Photos app, in the Screenshots folder. There you'll find a perfect image, in PNG format, of whatever was on the screen. (Its resolution matches the screen: 1136 × 640 on the iPhone 5s, for example, or 1242 × 2208 on the Plus models.)

At this point, you can send it by email (to illustrate a request for help, for example); sync it with your computer; or designate it as the iPhone's wallpaper (to confuse the heck out of its owner).

But if you **tap the miniature** before it slides away, you get a brand-new screenshot-editing window (facing page, right).

 TIP: If you press the screenshot buttons more than once within six seconds, you get *multiple* thumbnails, stacked up in the corner of the screen. When you tap *there*, you see *all* your screenshots in a horizontally scrolling row, so that you can edit, or send, all of them at once.

You can drag the thickened corners (or edge segments) to crop in on the shot, or use any of the Markup tools (pen, highlighter, pencil, eraser, lasso, color selector) to draw on it. Or you can tap the ⊕ to add text, a signature, a shape, an arrow, or a magnified area.

These Markup tools work exactly as described on page 307.

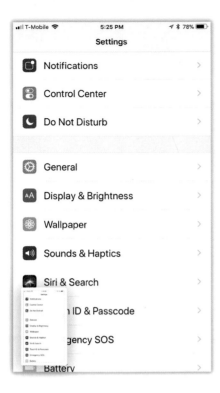

On the
iPhone X,
this says
Face ID &
Passcode

When you're finished annotating your shot, tap ⬆ to send it, or Done to close it—at which point the phone asks if you want to save the screenshot or, having made your point by sending it to someone, just delete it.

TIP: In some corners of iOS, there's no way to take a screenshot like this. For example, when the phone is ringing, pressing the screenshot button combination sends the call to voicemail instead of capturing the screen image.

In those situations, you may have to rely on the *Mac's* ability to display the iPhone's screen (page 274) or the new iPhone screen-recording feature (see below).

Recording Screen Video

For the first time in cellphone history, you can create *video* recordings of the screen—with narration, if you like. It's fantastic as a teaching tool, if you want to capture some anomaly to send to tech support, or to demo your new app.

There's only one way to get to this feature, and that's using the Control Center. There's no app, no Settings page, that even mentions it otherwise.

Once you've installed the Record Screen button onto the Control Center (page 54), tap it. (If you'd like to record narration, hard-press or long-press the button instead, and then tap the 🎤. Then hit **Start Recording**.)

You see a 3-2-1 countdown, which is intended to give you time to get out of the Control Center and into whatever app you're trying to record.

Now do whatever it is you're trying to capture. (The phone's status bar turns red to remind you that you're rolling; unfortunately that red bar will be part of the finished video, too.)

To stop recording, tap that red bar, or open the Control Center again and tap the **Screen Recording** button.

The finished video lands in your Photos app with all your other videos— with pristine quality and smooth motion, ready to share as you see fit.

10

All About Apps

App is short for *application*, meaning software program, and the App Store is a single, centralized catalog of every authorized iPhone add-on program in the world. In fact, it's the *only* place where you can get new programs (at least without hacking your phone).

You hear people talking about the downsides to this approach: Apple's stifling the competition; Apple's taking a 30 percent cut of every program sold; Apple's maintaining veto power over apps it doesn't like.

But there are some huge benefits, too. First, there's one central place to look for apps. Second, Apple checks out every program to make sure it's decent and runs decently. Third, the store is beautifully integrated with the iPhone itself.

There's an incredible wealth of software in the App Store. These programs can turn the iPhone into an instant-messaging tool, a pocket Internet radio, a medical reference, a musical keyboard, a time and expense tracker, a TV remote control, a photo editor, a recipe box, a tip calculator, a restaurant finder, a teleprompter, and so on. And games—thousands of dazzling handheld games, some with smooth 3D graphics and tilt control.

It's so much stuff—2.2 million apps, 200 billion downloads—that the challenge is just finding your way through it. Thank goodness for those Most Popular lists.

Getting New Apps

To check out the App Store, tap the **App Store** icon on your phone. You arrive at the colorful, scrolling wonder of the store itself.

Until 2017, you could shop the App Store, and organize your apps into folders, on your computer, using the iTunes program. That method offered a much easier browsing and shopping experience, because you had a mouse, a keyboard, and that big screen. As of iTunes 12.7, however, Apple removed all app-management tools. Now your phone is the only way to get to the App Store.

The App Store app, totally redesigned in iOS 11, has five tabs at the bottom. Here they are, in order:

- **Today.** The big problem with the App Store has always been finding the good stuff among the millions of apps. On this tab, Apple starts you off with a kind of blog, featuring mini-profiles of apps Apple finds interesting. Tap and read. Needless to say, downloading the app that's being described is always one tap away.

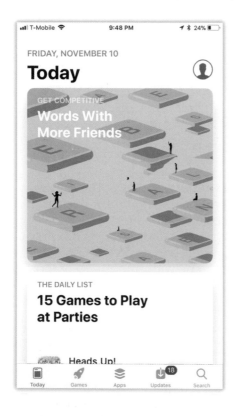
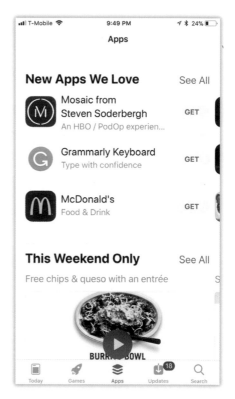

- **Games.** Games! Listed by category, by bestselling status, by Apple promotion.

- **Apps.** Here's everything else—again, listed by category, bestselling status, and Apple promotion.

- **Updates.** Unlike its buddies, this button isn't intended to help you navigate the catalog. Instead, it lets you know when one of the programs you've *already* installed is available in a newer version. Read on for details.

- **Search.** As the number of apps grows into the many millions, viewing by scrolling through lists begins to get awfully unwieldy.

  Fortunately, you can also *search* the catalog, which is efficient if you know what you're looking for (either the name of a program, the kind of program it is, or the software company that made it).

  Before you even begin to type, this screen shows you a list of trending searches—that is, the most popular searches right now. Odds are pretty good that if you want to download the latest hot app you keep hearing about, you'll see its name here (because, after all, it's hot).

  Or tap in the search box to make the keyboard appear. As you type, the list shrinks so that it's showing you only the matches. You might type *tetris*, or *piano*, or *Disney*, or whatever.

  Tap anything in the results list to see matching apps. You can swipe vertically to scroll through them. Tap one to view its details screen, as described in the next section.

About a third of the App Store's programs are free; the rest are usually under $5. A few, intended for professionals (pilots, for example), can cost a lot more.

 NOTE: You can't use the App Store without an *Apple ID*—your email address and password—even if you're just downloading free stuff. If you've ever bought anything from the iTunes Store, signed up for an iCloud account, or bought anything from Apple online, then you already have an Apple ID.

The App Details Page

No matter which button was your starting point, eventually you wind up at an app's *details screen*. There's a description, a scrolling set of screenshots, info about the author, the date posted, the version number, a page of related and similar apps, the all-important reviews from fellow iPhoners, and so on.

Why are the ratings so important? Because the App Store's goodies aren't equally good. Remember, these programs come from a huge variety of people—professional firms in Silicon Valley, college kids goofing around on weekends, teenagers in Hungary—and just because they made it into the store doesn't mean they're worth the money (or even the time to download).

Sometimes an app has a low score because it's just not designed well or it doesn't do what it's advertised to do. And sometimes, of course, it's a little buggy.

If you decide something is worth getting, you're ready to download and install it. You may see any of these buttons:

- **Get.** Good news: This is a free app! Download away, conscience-free.

- **$0.99** (or whatever). This app costs money. If you proceed, your Apple account will be charged automatically.

- ⬇️. This button means that you've previously bought an app, either on this iPhone or on another Apple touchscreen gadget. You don't have to pay for it again. Just tap to re-download.

- **Open.** This app is *already* on your iPhone! Tap to open the app.

Once you tap **Get** or the price, you've committed to downloading the program. The final step is to confirm that you're you, using one of these three techniques:

- **Apple ID.** The first time you access the App Store, and periodically thereafter, you have to enter your Apple ID and password. That's Apple's way of making sure some marauding child in your household isn't trying to run up your bill without your knowledge. (Mercifully, you don't have to enter your Apple ID just to download an *update* to an app you already own.)

- **Use your fingerprint.** If you've allowed the App Store to accept your fingerprint on the home button (in **Settings→Touch ID & Passcode→iTunes & App Store**), then you can skip the name-and-password business.

- **Use your face.** If you've got an iPhone X and allowed the App Store to use face recognition (in **Settings→Face ID & Passcode→iTunes & App Store**), then you can skip the name-and-password business. Instead, you're prompted to double-press the side button to commence the download.

The download begins!

Once you begin downloading an app, a pie chart on its home-screen icon fills in to indicate the download's progress. (Tap the icon to pause or unpause the download. If you have an iPhone 6s or later, you can hard-press the icon for a shortcut menu offering buttons for **Cancel Download**, **Pause Download**, and **Prioritize Download**—in other words, finish ahead of any other downloading apps.)

If you're still on the app's App Store page when the downloading is done, then tap the **Open** button to launch it and try it out.

Two Welcome Notes About Backups

Especially when you've paid good money for your iPhone apps, you might worry about what would happen if your phone got lost or stolen, or if someone (maybe you) accidentally deleted one of them.

You don't have to worry. The App Store remembers everything you've already bought. You can re-download a purchased app at any time, on any of your iPhones, iPads, or iPod Touches, without having to pay for it again. Plus, of course, your iPhone has a backup (page 529)—right?

Organizing Your Apps

As you add new apps to your iPhone, it sprouts new Home screens as necessary to accommodate them all, up to a grand total of 15 screens. That's 364 icons (and yet you can actually go all the way up to many thousands of apps, thanks to the miracle of **folders**).

That multiple–Home screen business can get a little unwieldy, but a couple of tools can help you manage. First, you can just use Siri to open an app, without even knowing where it is. Just say, "Open Angry Birds" (or whatever).

Second, a search can pluck the program you want out of your haystack, as described on page 108.

Third, you can organize your apps into folders, which greatly alleviates the agony of TMHSS (Too Many Home Screens Syndrome).

It's worth taking the time to arrange the icons on your Home screens into logical categories, tidy folders, or at least a sensible sequence.

Rearranging Apps on the Home Screen

To enter Home-screen editing mode, hold your finger down lightly on any icon until, after about a second, the icons begin to—what's the correct term?—**wiggle**. (If you press too hard, you may trigger 3D Touch—see page 37—and get frustrated.)

At this point, you can rearrange your icons by dragging them around the glass into a new order; other icons scoot aside to make room.

 TIP: You can even move an icon onto the Dock (page 48). Just make room for it first, if necessary, by dragging an **existing** Dock icon to another spot on the screen.

You can drag a single icon across multiple Home screens without ever having to lift your finger. Just drag the icon against the right or left margin of the screen to "turn the page."

TIP: In iOS 11, for the first time, you can drag multiple icons simultaneously. It's a great timesaver—but you'd never in a million years guess how to do it.

Once you're in wiggle mode, start dragging icon #1, just far enough for its ⓧ to disappear. Now, with another finger, tap icon #2; it flies beneath your finger and becomes part of a "stack" bearing a tally, like ❷. You can keep tapping other icons to add them, all the while keeping that first finger down. When you're ready, drag your first finger; the entire stack goes along for the ride. You can drop them onto a folder, or onto another icon (to create a folder), or onto a new page, where they'll land in reverse order (the last icon you tapped winds up in the first open slot).

To create an additional Home screen, drag a wiggling icon to the right edge of the rightmost Home screen; keep your finger down. That Home screen slides off to the left, leaving you on a new, blank one, where you can deposit the icon.

> **NOTE:** You can no longer organize your Home screens on the computer, in the iTunes program. You must do this work on the phone itself.

Deleting Apps

While your icons are wiggling, most of them also sprout ⊗'s. That's how you **delete** an app you don't need anymore: Tap that ⊗. You're asked if you're sure; if so, it says bye-bye.

You can use this technique to delete Apple's less important preinstalled apps, like Stocks and Watch. You no longer have to hide them in a folder just to get them out of your face.

> **NOTE:** You're actually not deleting them—only hiding them. They still occupy, all told, 150 megabytes. (To "reinstall" them to your phone, download them from the App Store as usual.)

When everything looks good, press the home button—or, on the iPhone X, the **Done** button on the right ear—to stop all the wiggling.

Restoring the Home Screen

If you ever need to undo all the damage you've done, tap **Settings→ General→Reset→Reset Home Screen Layout**. That function preserves any new programs you've installed, but it consolidates them. If you'd put 10 apps on each of four Home screens, you'll wind up with only two screens, each packed with 20 icons. Leftover blank pages are eliminated. This function also places all your downloaded apps in alphabetical order.

Folders

Just as on a computer, folders let you organize your apps, deempha-size the ones you rarely use, and restore order to that dizzying display of icons.

Each folder can have many pages of its own, each displaying nine icons. A single folder, in other words, can contain as many apps as you want. Only memory limits how many apps you can fit onto your phone.

To create and edit folders, begin by entering Home-screen editing mode. That is, hold your finger down on any app (lightly) until all apps wiggle.

Now, to create a folder, ***drag one app's icon on top of another***. iOS puts both of them into a new folder—and, if they're the same kind of app, even tries to figure out what category they both belong to and names the new folder accordingly ("Music," "Photos," "Kid Games," or whatever). You can type in your own preferred name at this point.

Drag one app onto another…   *…and a new folder is born. Rename it here.*

You're welcome to add more apps to this folder. Tap the Home screen background to close the folder, and then (while the icons are still wig-gling) drag another app onto the folder's icon. Lather, rinse, repeat.

If one of your folders has more than nine apps in it, iOS creates a sec-ond "page" for the folder—and a third, a fourth, and so on. You can move apps around within the pages and otherwise master your new multipage folder domain.

You can scroll the folder "pages" by swiping sideways (see the next page), just as you scroll the full-size Home pages. The only limit to how many icons a folder can hold is your tolerance for absurdity.

Once you've created a folder or two, they're easy to rename, move, delete, and so on. (Again, you can do all of the following *only in icon-wiggling editing mode*.) Like this:

- **Take an app out of a folder** by dragging its icon anywhere else on the Home screen. The other icons scoot aside to make room, just as they do when you move them from one Home screen to another.

- **Move a folder around** by dragging, as you would any other icon.

> **TIP:** You can drag a folder icon onto the Dock, too, just as you would any app. Now you've got a pop-up subfolder full of your favorite apps—on the Dock, which is present on every Home screen. That's a useful feature; it multiplies the handiness of the Dock.

- **Rename a folder** by opening it (tapping it). At this point, the folder's name box is ready for editing.

> **TIP:** On an iPhone 6s or later, you can **hard-press** a folder icon—even when you're not in wiggling-icon mode—to reveal the Rename command.

- **Move an icon from one folder "page" to another** by dragging it to the edge of the folder, waiting with your finger down until the page "changes," and then releasing your finger in the right spot.

- **Delete a folder** by removing all of its contents. The folder disappears automatically.

When you're finished manipulating your folders, press the home button (or, on the iPhone X, **Done** at top right) to exit Home screen editing mode and stop the wiggling madness.

App Preferences

If you're wondering where you can change an iPhone app's settings, consider backing out to the Home screen and then tapping **Settings**. Apple encourages programmers to add their programs' settings *here*, way down below the bottom of the iPhone's own settings.

Some programmers ignore the advice and build the settings right into their apps, where they're a little easier to find. But if you don't see them there, now you know where else to look.

App Updates

When a circled number (like ❷) appears on the App Store's icon on the Home screen, or on the Updates icon within the App Store program, that's Apple's way of letting you know that an app you already own has been updated. Apple knows which programs you've bought—and notifies you when new, improved versions are released. Which is remarkably often; software companies are constantly fixing bugs and adding new features.

Manual Updates

When you tap **Updates**, you're shown a list of the programs with waiting updates. A tiny **What's New** arrow lets you know what the changes are—new features, perhaps, or some bug fixes. And when you tap a program's name, you go to its details screen, where you can remind yourself of what the app does and read other people's reviews of the new version.

You can download one app's update, or, with a tap on the **Update All** button, all of them...no charge.

Automatic Updates

If you have a lot of apps, you may come to feel as though you're spending your whole life downloading updates. They descend like locusts, every single day, demanding your attention.

That's why Apple offers an automatic update-downloading option. Your phone can install updated versions of your apps quietly and automatically in the background.

To turn on this feature, open **Settings→iTunes & App Store**. Under **Automatic Downloads**, turn on **Updates**. (If you'd prefer that the phone wait to do this downloading until it's in a Wi-Fi hotspot—to avoid eating up your monthly cellular data-plan allotment—then turn off **Use Cellular Data**.)

From now on, the task of manually approving each app's update is off your to-do list forever.

 TIP: Fortunately, the iPhone also keeps a tidy record of every app it's updated and what that update gives you. Open the App Store app; tap the **Updates** tab. There's your list, sorted chronologically. Tap an app's row to read what was new in the update you've already received.

How to Find Good Apps

If the bestseller lists and editorial promotions in the App Store app aren't inspiring you, there are all kinds of websites dedicated to reviewing iPhone apps. There's *appadvice.com* and *whatsoniphone.com* and on and on.

But if you've never dug into iPhone apps before, you should at least try out some of the superstars, the big dogs that almost everybody has.

Many of the most popular apps are designed to deliver big-name websites in the best-looking way possible. That's why there are apps for Facebook, Twitter, LinkedIn, Spotify, Pandora, Flickr, Yelp, Netflix, YouTube, Wikipedia, and so on.

Here are a very few more examples—a drop in the bucket at the tip of the iceberg—of the infinite app variety beyond those basics:

- **Apple Apps (free).** Apple offers all kinds of free apps: Clips, Podcasts, Find My Friends, Find My iPhone, and so on. You can find them by searching the App Store for **Apple apps** and then choosing the Developer apps.

- **Google Maps (free).** Google Maps is a replacement for the built-in Maps app. It's much, **much** better than Maps—even Apple has admitted that. Among other things, it offers Street View (you can actually see a photo of almost any address and "look around" you), it incorporates the Zagat guides for restaurants, and it's unbelievably smart about knowing what you're trying to type into the search box. Usually, about three letters is all you need to type before the app guesses what you mean.

- **Waze.** Here's another driving-directions app, also owned by Google. The genius here is that fellow drivers take note when they pass an accident, a police car, construction, a broken-down car, and so on; all of these anomalies show up on your Waze screen, and Waze takes those slowdowns into account. As a result, Waze is better than Google Maps at working the back roads when the main route is compromised.

- **Flight Update Pro ($10).** Shows every detail of every flight: gate, time delayed, airline phone number, where the flight is on the map, and more. Knows more—and knows it sooner—than the actual airlines do.

- **Instagram (free)** is like a photographic Twitter feed. Seeing what other people are doing every day with their cameraphones and creative urges can be really inspirational.

Other essentials: Angry Birds. Uber and Lyft. Skype. Hipmunk (finds flights). The New York Times. The Amazon Kindle book reader. Dictionary. TED. Mint.com. Scrabble. Keynote Remote (controls your Keynote presentations from the phone). Facebook Messenger. Yahoo Weather

(gorgeous). Snapchat (the millennials' go-to app for sending selfies that self-destruct after viewing).

Augmented Reality (AR) Apps

In iOS 11, Apple has embraced AR in a big way, and some of the results are thrilling.

AR is where you use your phone as a viewer for the world around you—and the computer superimposes graphics on it. As you move the phone, the sizes, angles, and distances of the simulated objects smoothly change in real time as though they really exist. (Pokémon Go is an AR app. So is Snapchat when it adds goofy glasses and antennas to your live image.)

Apple gave AR a huge boost with its release of ARKit, a set of tools for software companies that has made it easier to develop AR apps. Here are a few of the early results:

- **Ikea Place (free).** You inspect a catalog of living-room furniture. You tap the item you want, choose a color for it, and then tap the iPhone screen to plop it down on the floor. Now you can walk around the room, checking out how it looks from various angles and in various positions. The idea, of course, is to let you try out furniture at home before hauling it in from a store. (Houzz, Overstock, Amazon, and other companies have similar apps.)

- **Porsche AR (free).** As a sales tool, this app is pure genius: It lets you see exactly what a $90,000 red Porsche Boxster convertible would look like in your driveway. Or garage. Or bedroom, for that matter.

- **AR MeasureKit (free)** is a virtual tape measure. Point at one corner of a table or TV, tap to anchor the "tape measure," and then point at the opposite corner, and boom: An onscreen line, drawn crisply in white, shows you that distance in feet and inches (or meters and centimeters). For a couple of bucks, you can unlock additional modes, like the person-height measurer. Similar: PLNAR (generates floor plans of a room quickly and easily), MagicPlan, ARuler, AirMeasure.

- **Hair Color by ModiFace (free).** Use your phone like a magic mirror. Tap a new hair color from the scrolling palette at the bottom of the screen, and see how you'd look with that dye job.

- **Night Sky 5.** Point your phone at the sky, and see the stars—labeled and, in the case of constellations, conveniently connected by line segments. Works in the daytime or the nighttime. It's a perfect use of AR, because it provides ordinarily invisible information about whatever you're looking at. Similar: Sky Guide.

The world is full of people, places, and things with a story to tell. Imagine an app that identifies the repair history of a used car you're considering. Or an app that you can hold up to your airplane window that labels the cities and streets below. Or an app that shows how you'll look after plastic surgery. Or one for house hunters that shows your furniture in a candidate house. Or a navigation app that shows you, with arrows floating above the real-world sidewalk, which way to walk. (No more emerging from a building or a subway, baffled at Google Maps' instructions because you're not sure which way you're facing.)

The mind reels.

The Abandoned Apps

Here's the bad news: 32-bit apps don't run in iOS 11. Only 64-bit apps do.

What that means is that 64-bit apps, on a 64-bit iPhone, can *theoretically* run faster and can handle more complex tasks. What it means *practically* is that in one fell swoop, Apple is killing off the 15 percent of App Store apps that haven't been updated since 2015.

If you've been an iPhoner for a long time, you may feel it in the gut: Apps like Flappy Bird, the original Tetris, and Dora's Great Big World no longer run in iOS 11.

But as you grieve, remember that their software companies have had three years to update those apps—and chose not to bother.

Re-Downloading Apps

The App Store remembers what apps you've downloaded, even years later. Next time you're in one of those, "What was that crazy app that, you know, had the frog in a grocery store, and you're supposed to make it eat its way through produce and stuff?" moments, this feature can save you a lot of hunting.

Open the App Store app. Tap **[your icon at top right]**→Purchased→**My Purchases**. Here you're offered two tabs: **All** (every app you've ever grabbed) and **Not on This Phone** (apps you've grabbed but don't currently have installed. Tap ⟱ to reinstall the app you want.

> **TIP:** What if that My Purchases list is full of apps you tried once in 2009, and now they're just cluttering up the list?
>
> In the modern App Store app, you can *hide* it. Swipe left across its name and tap **Hide**. You can always search the App Store if you want that app again, but in the meantime, it's not polluting the list of apps you *do* want to see.

The App Switcher

Often, it's handy to switch among open apps. Maybe you want to copy something from Safari (on the web) into Mail (in a message you're writing). Maybe you want to refer to your frequent-flier number (in Notes) as you're using an airline's check-in app. Maybe you want to adjust something in Settings and then get back to whatever you were doing. Here's how to call up the app switcher:

- **Home-button phones.** On iPhones that preceded the iPhone X, the key to switching apps is to *double-click the home button*.

- **iPhone X.** Swipe up from the bottom of the screen (it doesn't have to be far), and stop with your finger still touching.

In each case, whatever is on the screen gets replaced by the app switcher (shown on below as it appears on the iPhone X).

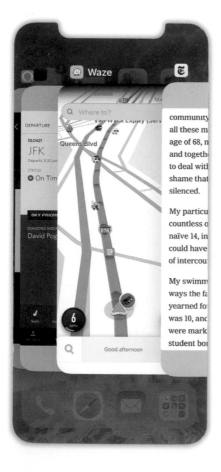

On the iPhone 6s and later models, there's another way to reach this screen: *Hard-swipe* from the left edge of the screen. This method has one advantage: It lets you *peek* at whatever apps are in the background, and then, without ever lifting your thumb, slide back to the left. You've had a glance without ever fully entering the app switcher.

You see a scrolling series of "cards" that represent the open apps, in chronological order. They're big enough that you can actually see what's going on in each open app. In fact, sometimes, that's all you need; you can refer to another app's screen in this view, without actually having to switch *into* that app.

TIP: Thoughtfully enough, the app switcher always puts the *previous app* front and center when you first open the app switcher. For example, if you're in Safari but you were using Mail a minute ago, Mail appears centered in the app switcher. That makes life easier if you're doing a lot of jumping back and forth between two apps; one tap takes you into the previous app.

When you tap an app's mini-screen in the app switcher, that app opens.

Force-Quitting an App

The app switcher lets you manually exit an app, closing it down. To do that, hold your finger down on the app's card until a ⊖ appears (facing page, right). Tap that symbol—or flick the unwanted app's mini-screen upward, so that it flies up off the top of the screen. In either case, you've just exited the app.

You'll need this gesture only rarely (which is why, Apple says, quitting an app requires an extra step in iOS 11). You're not supposed to quit every app when you're finished. Force-quit an app only if it's frozen or acting glitchy and needs to be restarted.

TIP: There may be one more element on the app-switcher screen, too: a faint app icon at the far left. That's a document, email, or web page being sent to your phone by your Mac, using Handoff (see page 560).

A Word About Background Apps

Switching out of an app doesn't actually close it; apps continue running in the background.

Of course, if every app ran full-tilt simultaneously, your phone would guzzle down battery power. To solve that problem, Apple has put two kinds of limits in place:

- **iOS's limits.** Not all apps run full speed in the background. Apps that really need constant updating, like Facebook or Twitter, get refreshed every few seconds; apps that don't rely on constant Internet updates get to nap in the background when they're not in use.

  In deciding which apps get background attention, iOS studies things like how good your phone's Internet connection is and what time of day you traditionally use a certain app (so that your newspaper's app is ready with the latest articles when you open it).

- **Your own limits.** You can't control which apps *run* in the background, but you can control which ones *download new data* in the background. In **Settings→General→Background App Refresh**, you'll find a list of every app that may want to update itself in the background. To make your battery last longer, you can turn off background updating for the apps you don't really care about; you can even turn off *all* background updating using the master switch at the top.

The bottom line: There's no need to quit apps you're not using, ever. Contrary to certain Internet rumors, they generally don't use enough battery power to matter. You may see dozens of apps in the app switcher, but you'll never sense that your phone is bogging down as a result.

Back to App (◀)

This humble button may become your favorite feature. It's a Back button that appears when you've tapped a link of some kind that takes you into a different app. For example:

- **You're in Messages,** and you tap a web link (below, left) that takes you into Safari. A ◀ **Messages** button appears at top left (right).

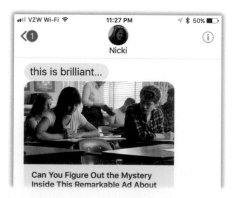 

- **You're on Twitter or Facebook,** and you tap a link that opens a web page. Sure enough: The top-left button says **< Twitter** or **< Facebook**.

- **You're in Mail,** and you tap an underlined date or time that takes you into the Calendar app. A **< Mail** button appears in the corner.

- **You're in Safari,** and you tap a link that opens in YouTube. Sure enough: The button says **< Safari**.

And so on. This tiny enhancement can save you literally *minutes* a week.

iPhone X: Bypass the App Switcher

If you have an iPhone X, a delightful surprise awaits. You can switch apps directly, without a layover at the app switcher.

All you have to do is swipe horizontally on the *home indicator bar*, the black or white horizontal line at the bottom of almost every app screen. Your first swipe should generally be to the *right*, because the app you're using now is always at the far right of the lineup.

NOTE: There's one exception. If you're in App A, and you swipe to the right to check App B (your second-to-last app), you have *six seconds* to swipe left, *back* to App A. After that, App B becomes the new rightmost app. Apple always wants "the most recent app" to be at far right, but it doesn't want to confuse you if you're hopping back and forth between two apps.

As you do so, the next most recent app heaves into view—full size, already running. No need to tap it or select it from among some cards: You're there.

Keep swiping that bar to the right to summon older and older open apps; swipe to the left to return to the ones you've used more recently.

This feature makes the iPhone X's weird, rounded-bottom screen seem worthwhile.

AirPrint: Printing from the Phone

The very phrase "printing from the phone" might seem peculiar. How do you print from a gadget that's smaller than a Hershey bar—a gadget without any jacks for connecting a printer?

Wirelessly, of course.

You can send printouts from your phone to any printer that's connected to your Mac or PC on the same Wi-Fi network if you have a piece of software like Printopia ($20).

Or you can use the iPhone's built-in AirPrint technology, which can send printouts directly to a Wi-Fi printer without requiring a Mac or a PC.

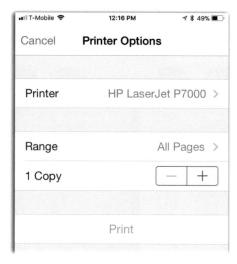

Not just any Wi-Fi printer, though—only those that recognize AirPrint. Most recent Canon, Epson, HP, and Lexmark printers work with AirPrint; you can see a list of them on Apple's website, here: *support.apple.com/ kb/HT4356*.

Not all apps can print. Of the built-in Apple programs, only iBooks, Mail, Photos, Notes, and Safari offer **Print** commands. Those apps contain what most people want to print most of the time: PDF documents, email messages, driving directions from the web, and so on. Plenty of non-Apple apps work with AirPrint, too.

> **TIP:** Of course, you can always take a screenshot of what you want to print (see page 340) and then print *that* from the Photos app.

To use AirPrint, start by tapping the ⬆; tap **Print**. You're offered a **Select Printer** option. Tap it to introduce the phone to your printer, whose name should appear automatically. Now you can adjust the printing options (number of copies, page range)—and when you finally tap **Print**, your printout shoots wirelessly to the printer, exactly as though your phone and printer were wired together.

The Share Sheet

Every app is different, of course. But all of them have certain things in common; otherwise, you'd go out of your mind.

One of those things is the Share sheet. It's your headquarters for sending stuff off your phone: to other apps, to other phones, to the Internet, to a printer. It's made up of several icon rows, each of which scrolls horizontally. (From top to bottom, you could title these rows "What to Share," "Send by AirDrop," "Send to an App," and "Act on This Data Directly.")

The Share sheet pops up whenever you tap the Share button (⬆) that appears in many, many apps: Maps, Photos, Safari, Notes, Voice Memos, Contacts, and so on.

The buttons you see depend on the app; you may see only two options here, or you may see a dozen. Starting on page 324, for example, you can read descriptions of the icons that appear when you're sending a photo: AirDrop, Message, Mail, Twitter, Facebook, Copy, AirPlay, Print, and so on. The options vary by app.

Moreover, there's a **More** button at the end of each row. That's an invitation for other, non-Apple apps to install their own "send to" options into the Share sheet. When you tap **More**, you can see the full list of apps that have inserted themselves here. Now you can perform these tasks:

- **Hide a sharing option.** Flip the switch to make one of the sharing options disappear from the Share sheet. (You can't hide the sharing options that Apple considers essential, like Messages or Mail.)

- **Rearrange the sharing options.** Use the handle to move these items up or down the list, which affects their left-to-right order on the Share sheet.

AirDrop

It's a headline feature: AirDrop, a way to shoot things from one Apple phone, tablet, or Mac to another—wirelessly, instantly, easily, encryptedly, without requiring names, passwords, or setup. It's much faster than emailing or text messaging, since you don't have to know (or type) the other person's address.

NOTE: If the Mac is running OS X Yosemite or later, then you can shoot files between it and your phone, too.

You can transmit pictures and videos from the Photos app, people's info cards from Contacts, directions (or your current location) from Maps, pages from Notes, web addresses from Safari, electronic tickets from Wallet, apps you like in the App Store, song and video listings from the iTunes app, radio stations from iTunes Radio, and so on. As time goes on, more and more non-Apple apps offer AirDrop, too.

Behind the scenes, AirDrop uses Bluetooth (to find nearby gadgets within about 30 feet) and a private, temporary Wi-Fi mini-network (to transfer the file). Both sender and receiver must have Bluetooth and Wi-Fi turned on.

The process goes like this:

1. **Find a willing recipient.**

   You can't send anything with AirDrop unless the receiving machine is awake.

2. **Open the item you want to share. Tap the Share button (⬆).**

   If your app doesn't have a ⬆ button, then you can't use AirDrop. When the Share sheet appears, within a few seconds, you see something that would have awed the masses in 1995: small circular photos of everyone nearby (facing page, left). (Or at least everyone nearby who's **open to receiving** AirDrop transmissions, as described in a moment.)

> **TIP:** When you send a *photo*, the top row of the Share sheet shows your other photos and videos so that you can select additional items to go along for the ride. A blue checkmark identifies each item you've selected to send.

3. **Tap the icon of the person you want to share with.**

   In about a second, a message appears on the recipient's screen, conveying your offer to transmit something good—and, when it makes sense, showing a picture of it (facing page, right).

> **TIP:** Actually, you can select *more than one* person's icon. In that case, you'll send this item to everyone at once.

At this point, it's up to your recipients. If they tap **Accept**, then the transfer begins (and ends); whatever you sent them opens up automatically in the relevant app. You'll know that AirDrop was successful because the word "Sent" appears on your screen.

If they tap **Decline**, then you must have misunderstood their willingness to accept your item (or they tapped the wrong button). In that case, you'll see the word "Declined" on your screen.

The One AirDrop Setting

Realistically, you won't be bombarded by AirDrop requests from strangers around you who want to show you family pictures. Even so, Apple has given you some control over who's allowed to try to send you things by AirDrop.

To see the settings, open **Settings→General→AirDrop**.

Before iOS 11 happened, you could change your AirDrop settings right on the Control Center (page 49). Actually, you still can. Hard-press or long-press the upper-left control cluster, the one that contains the ✈ button. Boom: The cluster expands to reveal the hidden **AirDrop** button. Tap it to reveal the options described below.

You have these three choices:

- **Receiving Off.** Nobody can send anything to you by AirDrop. You'll never be disturbed by an incoming "Accept?" message.

- **Contacts Only.** Only people in your Contacts app—your own address book—can send you things by AirDrop. Your phone is invisible to strangers. (Of course, even when someone you know tries to send something, you still have to approve the transfer.)

NOTE: The Contacts Only option requires that both you and your recipient have iCloud accounts and are logged in. Your Contacts card for the other person has to include that person's registered iCloud email address.

- **Everyone.** Anyone, even strangers, can try to send you things. You can still accept or decline each transfer.

NOTE: OK, there's one other AirDrop setting to fiddle with: In **Settings→ Sounds & Haptics**, you can specify the sound effect that means "AirDrop file received."

(OK, OK, there's *one more* setting. Deep in **General→Restrictions**, you can turn off AirDrop altogether. Now your youngster—or whomever you're trying to restrict with restrictions—can't get into trouble in a debauched frenzy of sending and receiving files.)

The Built-In Apps

11

Your iPhone comes already loaded with the icons of about 25 apps. Eventually, of course, you'll fill it up with apps you install yourself, but Apple starts you off with the essentials. They include gateways to the Internet (Safari), communications tools (Phone, Messages, Mail, Contacts), visual records of your life (Photos, Camera), shopping centers (iTunes Store, App Store), and entertainment (Music, TV, Podcasts).

Those core apps get special treatment in the other chapters. This chapter covers the secondary programs, in alphabetical order: Calculator, Calendar, Clock, Compass, Files, Health, Home, iBooks, Maps, News, Notes, Podcasts, Reminders, Stocks, Tips, TV, Voice Memos, Wallet, Watch, and Weather.

> **TIP:** You can open any of these apps by hunting it down and tapping its icon. But it's usually much faster to tell Siri to do it. Say, "Open Calculator," for example.

Calculator

The iPhone wouldn't be much of a computer without a calculator, now, would it? And here it is, your everyday calculator—with a secret twist.

In Calculator's basic four-function mode, you can tap out equations (like *15.4 × 300 =*) to see the answer at the top. (You can **paste** things you've copied into here, too; just hold your finger down until the **Paste** button appears.) There's no memory function in the basic calculator, but you do get a +/– button; its function is to change the currently displayed number from positive to negative, or vice versa.

Now here's the twist: If you rotate the iPhone 90 degrees in either direction, the Calculator morphs into a full-blown HP *scientific* calculator, complete with trigonometry, logarithmic functions, a memory function, exponents, and roots beyond the square root. Go wild, ye engineers and physicists!

If you make a mistake while entering a number, swipe horizontally across the numerical display (either direction). Each swipe backspaces over the rightmost digit. And if you mistakenly touch the wrong operator (× when you meant –, for example), there's no need to start over. Just tap the **correct** operator before tapping the number. The app ignores the errant tap.

Calendar

The iPhone's calendar syncs, automatically and wirelessly, with whatever online calendar you keep: iCloud, Google Calendar, a corporate Exchange calendar, and so on. Everything's kept in sync with your computers and tablets, too. Make a change in one place, and it changes everywhere else. Then again, you can also use Calendar all by itself.

Day View

When you open Calendar, you see today's schedule, broken down by time slot (next page, right). You can navigate to other days' schedules in any of three ways: Swipe horizontally across the Day screen to see the previous or next day. Tap a date at the top to see another day this week. Swipe across the dates at the top to jump to another week. If the date you want to check is further away than a week or two, though, it might make more sense to pop into Month view, described next.

Month View

Month view, of course, shows an entire month at a glance (next page, center). You can scroll the months vertically, thereby scanning the entire year in a few seconds. To get there from Day view, tap the name of the month at the top left.

Of course, your little phone screen is too small to show you what's written on each calendar square; all you get is a gray dot on any date when you've scheduled an appointment. Tap that dot to jump back into Day view and read your schedule.

Year View

If you're in Month view, you can "zoom out" yet another level—to Year view. It's a simple, vertically scrolling map of the year's months. Tap the name of the year (top left) to see it. From there, tap a month block to open it back into Month view.

> **TIP:** In all three of these views—Day, Month, Year—you can tap **Today** (bottom left) to return to today's date.

The Rotated Calendar

Some cool things happen when you turn the phone into landscape view (facing page, top). You get an interactive, four-day slice of the week:

Swipe sideways to move to earlier or later dates. Swipe up or down to move through the hours of the day.

Plus Model Views

If you have a Plus model—one with the Jumbotron screen—then there's room for extra information (the front illustration above). On a Plus, the Day and Month views offer a split screen, showing the calendar on the left and details on the right. You also get a row of view buttons (**Day**, **Week**, **Month**, **Year**)—something the owners of puny regular iPhones never see.

Subscribing to Your Online Calendars

To set up real-time, wireless connections to your calendars online, tap your way to **Settings→Accounts & Passwords→Add Account**. Here you can tap **iCloud**, **Exchange**, **Google**, **Yahoo**, **AOL**, or **Outlook.com** to set up your account. (You can also tap **Other→Add CalDAV Account** to fill in the details of a less well-known calendar server, or **Other→Add Subscribed Calendar** to connect to an online calendar subscription service—from TripIt or your favorite sports team, for example.

Making an Appointment (Day or Month View)

Recording an event on this calendar is quite a bit more flexible than entering one on, say, one of those "Hunks of the Midwest Police Stations" paper calendars.

Start by tapping + (top-right corner of the screen). The New Event screen pops up, filled with tappable lines of information. Tap one (like **Starts** or **Repeat**) to open a configuration screen for that element.

For example:

- **Title/Location.** Name your appointment here. For example, you might type *Fly to Phoenix*.

    The second line, called **Location**, makes a lot of sense. If you think about it, almost everyone needs to record *where* a meeting is to take place. You might type a reminder for yourself like *My place*, a specific address like *212 East 23rd*, a contact phone, or a flight number. Use the keyboard as usual.

- **Starts/Ends.** Tap **Starts**, and then indicate the starting time for this appointment, using the four spinning dials that appear at the bottom of the screen (below, right). The first sets the date; the second, the hour; the third, the minute; the fourth, AM or PM.

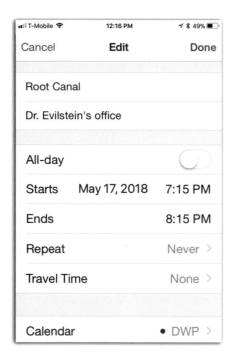
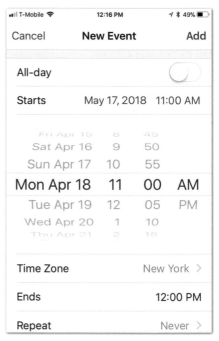

Then tap **Ends**, and repeat the process to schedule the ending time. (The iPhone helpfully presets the Ends time to one hour later.)

An **All-day** event, of course, has no specific time of day: a holiday, a birthday, a book deadline. When you turn this option on, the Starts and Ends times disappear. The event appears at the top of the list for that day.

- **Repeat.** The screen here contains common options for recurring events: every day, every week, and so on. It starts out saying **Never**.

  Once you tap a selection, you return to the Edit screen. Now you can tap the **End Repeat** button to specify when this event should *stop* repeating. If you leave the setting at **Never**, then you're stuck seeing this event repeating on your calendar until the end of time (a good choice for recording, say, your anniversary, especially if your spouse might be consulting the same calendar).

  In other situations, you may prefer to tap **On Date** and spin the three dials (month, day, year) to specify an ending date, which is useful for car payments or a season's worth of soccer games.

  Tap **New Event** to return to the editing screen.

- **Travel Time.** If you turn on this switch, you can indicate how long it'll take you to get to this appointment.

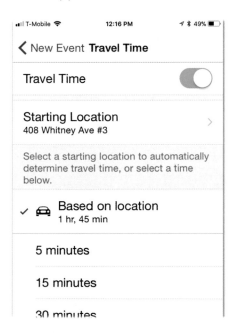

You get six canned choices, from five minutes to two hours. Or you can tap **Starting Location** and specify your starting point, and marvel as the iPhone calculates the driving time automatically. (Walking time, too, if it's close enough.)

Two things then happen. First, the travel time is blocked off on your calendar, so you don't accidentally schedule things during your driving time. (The travel time is depicted as a dotted extension of the appointment.)

Second, if you've set up an alarm reminder, it will go off that much earlier, so you have time to get where you're going.

- **Calendar.** Tap here to specify which color-coded *calendar* (category, like Home, Kids, or Work) this appointment belongs to. Turn to page 376 for details on the calendar concept.

- **Invitees.** If you have an iCloud, Exchange, or CalDAV account, you can invite people to an event—a meeting, a party, whatever—and track their responses, right there on your phone (or any iCloud gadget). When you tap **Invitees**, you get an Add Invitees screen, where you can type in the email addresses of your lucky guests. (Or tap ➕ to choose them from your Contacts list.)

  Later, when you tap **Done**, the phone fires off email invitations to those guests. It contains buttons for them to click: **Accept**, **Decline**, and **Maybe**. You get to see their responses right here in the details of your calendar event.

  As icing on the cake, your guests will see a pop-up reminder on their phones when the time comes for the party to get started.

- **Alert.** This screen tells Calendar how to notify you when a certain appointment is about to begin. Calendar can send any of four kinds of flags to get your attention. Tap how much notice you want: 5, 15, or 30 minutes before the big moment; an hour or two before; a day or two before; a week before; or on the day of the event.

NOTE: For all-day events like birthdays, you get a smaller but very useful list of choices: "On day of event (9 AM)," "1 day before (9 AM)," "2 days before (9 AM)," and "1 week before."

When you tap **Add Event** and return to the main Add Event screen, you see that a new line, called **Second Alert**, has sprouted up beneath the first Alert line. This line lets you schedule a *second* warning for your appointment, which can occur either before or after the first one. Think of it as a backup alarm for events of extra urgency.

Once you've scheduled these alerts, you'll see a message appear on the screen at the appointed time(s). (Even if the phone was asleep, it appears briefly.) You'll also hear a chirpy alarm sound.

> **TIP:** The iPhone doesn't play the sound if you turned off Calendar Alerts in **Settings→Sounds** or **Settings→Sounds & Haptics**. It also doesn't play if you've silenced the phone with the silencer switch on the side.

- **Show as.** If you work in the business world, it's courteous to mark your new appointments as either **Busy** or **Free**. That way, other people who see your calendar, trying to schedule a meeting when you can attend, will know which events on your calendar are movable and which are nonnegotiable. If you're just indicating *"Keeping Up with the Kardashians* TV marathon," maybe that one should be marked as **Free**.

- **URL.** Here's a spot where you can record the web address of some online site that provides more information about this event.

- **Notes.** Here's your chance to customize your calendar event. You can type any text you want in the Notes area—driving directions, contact phone numbers, a call history, or whatever. Tap **Done**.

When you're done filling in all these blanks, tap **Add**. Your newly scheduled event now shows up on the calendar.

Making an Appointment (Day View, Week View)

As noted earlier, turning the phone 90 degrees opens up a widescreen, scrolling Week view of your life.

In both Day view and Week view, you can *hold your finger down on a time slot* to add a new, one-hour appointment right there. You're asked to enter a name and, if you like, location for this new appointment. Tap **Add**. You can always edit this appointment's details or duration later, as described next—but this quick-and-dirty technique saves the effort of tapping in Starts and Ends times.

Editing, Rescheduling, Deleting Events (Long Way)

To examine the details of an appointment in the calendar, tap it once. The Event Details screen appears, filled with the details you previously established.

To edit any of these characteristics, tap **Edit**. You return to what looks like a clone of the New Event screen. Here you can change the name, time, alarm, repeat schedule, calendar category, or any other detail of the event, just the way you set them up to begin with.

This time, there's a red **Delete Event** button at the bottom. That's the only way to erase an appointment from your calendar. (You can't erase events created by other people—Facebook birthdays, meetings on shared calendars, and so on—only appointments **you** created.)

Editing and Rescheduling Events (Fun Way)

In Day or Week views, you can **drag an appointment's block** to another time slot or even another day. Just hold your finger down on the appointment's bubble for about a second—until it darkens—before you start to drag. It's a lot quicker and more fluid than having to edit in a dialog box.

You can also change the **duration** of an appointment in Day and Week views. Hold your finger down on its colored block for about a second; when you let go, round handles appear.

You can drag those tiny handles up or down to make the block taller or shorter, in effect making it start or end at a different time.

Whether you drag the whole block, the top edge, or the bottom edge, the iPhone thoughtfully displays ":15," ":30," or ":45" on the left-side time ruler to let you know where you'll be when you let go.

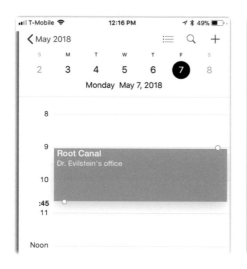
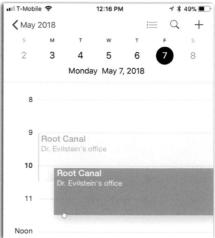

The Calendar (Category) Concept

A **calendar**, in Apple's somewhat confusing terminology, is a color-coded subset—a **category**—into which you can place various appointments. They can be anything you like. One person might have calendars called Home, Work, and TV Reminders. Another might have Me, Spouse 'n' Me, and The Kidz. A small business could have categories called Deductible Travel, R&D, and R&R.

You can create and edit calendar categories right on the iPhone, in your desktop calendar program, or (if you're an iCloud member) at *www.icloud.com* when you're at your computer; all your categories and color-codings show up on the iPhone automatically.

At any time, on the iPhone, you can choose which subset of categories you want to see. Just tap **Calendars** at the bottom of Day, Month, or Year view. You arrive at the big color-coded list of your categories (below, left). As you can see, it's subdivided according to your accounts: your Gmail categories, your Yahoo categories, your iCloud categories, and so on. There's even a Facebook option, if you've set up your Facebook account, so that you can see your Facebook calendar entries and friends' birthdays right on the main calendar.

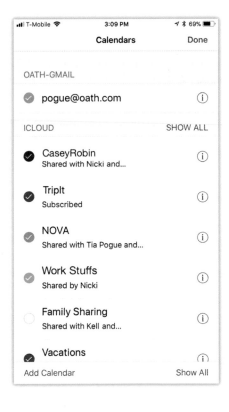
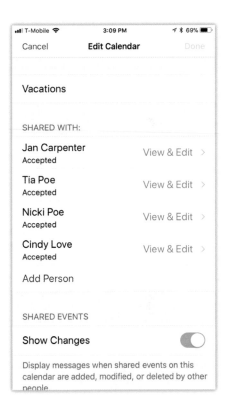

This screen exists partly as a reference, a cheat sheet to help you remember what color goes with which category, and partly as a tappable subset chooser. That is, you can tap a category's name to hide or show all of its appointments on the calendar. A checkmark means you're seeing its appointments. (The **All [Account Name]** button turns on or off all that account's categories at once.)

If you tap ⓘ next to a calendar's name, you're offered a screen where you can change the calendar's name; list of people who can see it ("Shared With:"); whether or not you get notified when one of those people changes events in this category (**Show Changes**); what color you want this category's events to have ("Color"); whether you want to get notifications of items in this calendar (**Event Alerts**); and if you want other people to be able to see (but not edit) this category (**Public Calendar**, described in the Tip below).

Or scroll all the way down to see the **Delete Calendar** button.

The Edit Calendars screen also offers an **Add Calendar** button. It's the key to creating, naming, and colorizing a *new* calendar on the phone. (Whatever changes you make to your calendar categories on the phone will be synced back to your Mac or PC.)

> **TIP:** You can share an iCloud calendar with other iCloud members (previous page, right), which is fantastic for families and small businesses who need to coordinate. Tap **Calendars**, and then tap ⓘ next to the calendar's name. Tap **Add Person** and enter the person's name. Your invitees get invitations by email; with one click, they've added your appointments to their calendars. They can make changes, too.
>
> You can also share a calendar with anyone (not just iCloud members) in a "Look, don't touch" condition. Tap **Calendars**, and then tap ⓘ next to the calendar's name. Turn on **Public Calendar**; tap **Share Link** to open the Share sheet for sending the link. The recipients have but to tap that link and then tap **Subscribe** to see your Public calendar's events in their own Calendar apps.

Search

If you tap Q and type into the search box, you pare down the list of all calendar events from all time; only events whose names match what you've typed show up. Tap one to jump to its block on the corresponding Day view.

Next time you're sure you made an appointment with Robin but you can't remember the date, keep this search feature in mind.

> **TIP:** The iOS calendar is pretty basic. For more features and power, consider calendar apps like Fantastical or BusyCal.

Invitations

Invitations are electronic invitations that coworkers send you from Outlook or other calendar apps. If you click **Accept**, the meeting gets dropped onto the proper date in your calendar, and your name gets added to the list of attendees maintained by the person who invited you. If you click **Maybe**, the meeting is flagged *that* way, on both your calendar and the sender's.

You'll know when you have an invite. You get a standard notification, a numbered "badge" on Calendar's icon on the Home screen, and a similar badge on the **Inbox** at the lower-right corner. Tapping **Inbox** shows the Invitations list, which summarizes all invitations you've accepted, maybe'd, or not responded to yet.

NOTE: Invitations you haven't dealt with also show up on the Calendar's List view or Day view with dotted shading. That's the iPhone's clever way of showing you just how severely your workday will be ruined.

You can also *generate* invitations. When you're filling out the Info form for a new appointment, tap the field called **Invitees**; enter the email addresses of the people you'd like to invite. Your invitation will show up in whatever calendar programs your invitees use, and they'll never know you didn't send it from some corporate copy of Microsoft Outlook.

Clock

It's not just a clock—it's more like a time factory. Hiding behind this icon on the Home screen are five programs: a world clock, an alarm clock, a stopwatch, a countdown timer, and a bedtime-management module.

NOTE: The app icon itself on the Home screen shows the current time! Isn't that cute?

World Clock

When you tap **World Clock** on the Clock screen, you start out with only one clock, showing the current time in Apple's own Cupertino, California.

You can open up *several* of these clocks and set each one to show the time in a different city. Now you'll know what time it is in some remote city, so you don't wake somebody up at what turns out to be 3 a.m.

To specify which city's time appears on the clock, tap + at the upper-right corner. Scroll to the city you want, or tap its first letter in the index at the right side to save scrolling, or tap in the search box at the top and type the name of a major city. As you type, matching city names appear; tap the one whose time you want to track.

As soon as you tap a city name, you return to the World Clock display.

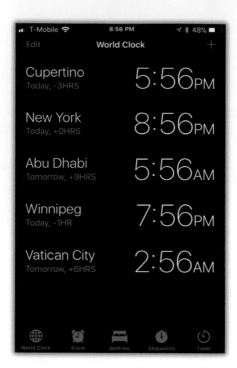

You can scroll the list of clocks. You're not limited by the number that fit on your screen at once.

> **TIP:** Only the world's major cities are in the iPhone's database. If you're trying to track the time in Squirrel Cheeks, New Mexico, add a major city in the same time zone instead—like Albuquerque.

To edit the list of clocks, tap **Edit**. Delete a city clock by tapping ⊖ and then **Delete**, or drag clocks up and down using the ☰ as a handle. Then tap **Done**.

Alarm

If you travel much, this feature could turn out to be one of your iPhone's most useful functions. It's reliable, it's programmable, and it even wakes *the phone* first, if necessary, to wake *you*.

To set an alarm, tap **Alarm** at the bottom of the Clock screen. You're shown the list of alarms you've already created (facing page, left), even if none are currently set to go off. You could create a 6:30 a.m. alarm for weekdays and an 11:30 a.m. alarm for weekends.

To create a new alarm, tap + to open the **Add Alarm** screen.

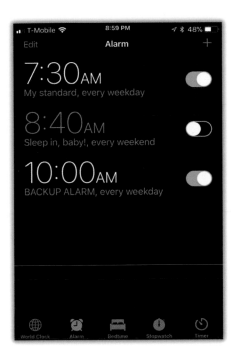

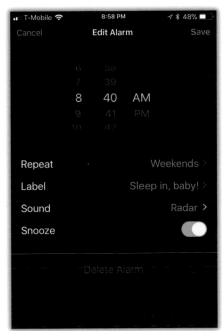

You have several options here:

- **Time dials.** Spin these three vertical wheels—hour, minute, AM/PM—to specify the time you want the alarm to go off.

- **Repeat.** Tap to specify what days this alarm rings. You can specify, for example, Mondays, Wednesdays, and Fridays by tapping those three buttons. (Tap a day-of-the-week button again to turn off its checkmark.) Tap **Back** when you're done. (If you choose Saturdays and Sundays, iOS is smart enough to call that "Weekends." And it knows that Monday, Tuesday, Wednesday, Thursday, and Friday are "Weekdays.")

- **Label.** Tap to give this alarm a description, like "Get dressed for wedding." That message appears on the screen when the alarm goes off.

- **Sound.** Choose what sound you want to ring. You can choose from any of the iPhone's ringtone sounds, any you've added yourself—or, best of all, **Pick a Song**. That's right—you can wake to the music of your choice.

- **Snooze.** If this option is on, then at the appointed time the alarm message on the screen offers you a **Snooze** button. Tap it for nine more minutes of sleep, at which point the iPhone tries again. (If your phone was in Sleep mode, it gives you a countdown to the next rude awakening.)

When you finally tap **Save**, you return to the Alarm screen, which lists your new alarm. Just tap the on/off switch to cancel an alarm. It stays in the list, though, so you can quickly reactivate it another day, without having to redo the whole thing. You can tap + to set another alarm, if you like.

Now the icon appears in the status bar at the top of the iPhone screen (or, on the iPhone X, just in the Control Center). That's your indicator that the alarm is set.

To delete an alarm, swipe left across its name and then tap **Delete**. To make changes to the time, name, sound, and so on, tap **Edit**, and then tap the alarm.

> **TIP:** The iPhone never deletes an alarm after using it; over time, therefore, your list of alarms may grow alarmingly large. Fortunately, you can tell Siri to clean them up for you in one fell swoop. Just say, "Delete all my alarms."

So what happens when the alarm goes off? The iPhone wakes itself up, if it was asleep. A message appears, identifying the alarm and the time.

And, of course, the sound rings. This alarm is one of the only iPhone sounds that you'll hear *even if the silencer switch is turned on*. Apple figures that if you've gone to the trouble of setting an alarm, you probably want to know about it, even if you forget to turn the ringer back on.

To stop the alarm, tap **Stop** or press the home button. To snooze it, tap the **Snooze** button or press the side button or a volume key. (In other words, in your sleepy haze, just grab the phone with your whole hand and squeeze. You'll hit *something* that shuts the thing off.)

Bedtime

Medical research tells us that sleep deprivation and inconsistent sleep schedules take a terrible toll on our health, mood, and productivity. So iOS's Clock app offers a new **Bedtime** tab. If you answer a few questions about your sleep habits, the app will attempt to keep your sleep regular—

prompting you when it's time to get ready for bed, waking you at a consistent time, and keeping a graph of your sleep consistency.

The first time you open this panel, the interview begins. On successive screens, it asks: What time would you like to wake up? Which days of the week should the alarm go off? How many hours of sleep do you need each night? When would you like a bedtime reminder? (That is, how many minutes do you need between the reminder and lights out?) What ringtone or sound do you want to hear when you wake up?

> **TIP:** You can change your answers to any of these questions later by tapping **Options** at top left.

At this point, you see the master **Bedtime** graph shown below at left. It's a handy visualization of the mental math millions of people perform every night anyway: "If I go to bed now, I'll get five hours of sleep!"

The real point of Bedtime, though, is the Sleep Analysis graph below all of this. Your goal is to keep the bars consistent over time—both in length and vertical position. It's not enough to get enough sleep; you should also try to sleep during the same period each night.

If you care about your health, mood, and productivity, that is.

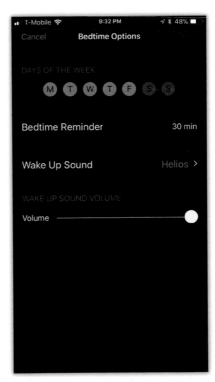

Stopwatch

You've never met a more beautiful stopwatch than this one. Tap **Start** to begin timing something: a runner, a train, a person who's arguing with you.

While the digits are flying by, you can tap **Lap** as often as you like. Each time, the list at the bottom identifies how much time elapsed since the *last* time you tapped **Lap**. It's a way for you to compare, for example, how much time a runner is spending on each lap around a track. You see the numbered laps and the time for each.

NOTE: If you prefer an old-timey analog stopwatch display, slide the digital readout to the left. Slide right to bring back the digital stopwatch.

You can work in other apps while the stopwatch is counting. In fact, the timer keeps ticking away even when the iPhone is asleep! As a result, you can time long-term events, like how long it takes an ice sculpture to melt,

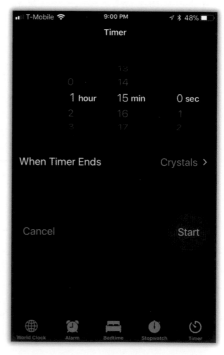

the time it takes for a bean seed to sprout, or the length of a Michael Bay movie.

Tap **Stop** to freeze the counter; tap **Start** to resume it. If you tap **Reset**, you reset the counter to zero and erase all the lap times.

Timer

The fourth Clock mini-app is a countdown timer. You input a starting time, and it counts down to zero. (New—now with seconds!)

Countdown timers are everywhere in life. They measure the periods in sports and games, cooking times in the kitchen, penalties on *The Amazing Race.* But on the iPhone, the timer has an especially handy function: It can turn off the music or video after a specified amount of time. In short, it's a sleep timer that plays you to sleep and then shuts off to save power.

To set the timer, open the Clock app and then tap **Timer**. Spin the three dials to specify the number of hours, minutes, and seconds you want to count down.

Then tap **When Timer Ends** to set up what happens when the timer reaches 0:00. Most of the options here are ringtone sounds, so you'll have an audible cue that the time's up. The last one, though, **Stop Playing**, is that sleep timer. It stops audio and video playback at the appointed time, so that you (and the iPhone) can sleep. Tap **Set**.

Finally, tap **Start**. Big clock digits count down toward zero. While it's in progress, you can do other things on the iPhone, change the **When Timer Ends** settings, or just hit **Cancel** to forget the whole thing.

TIP: It's much faster and simpler to use Siri to start, pause, and resume the Timer. See page 163.

You can also open the Control Center (page 49) and long-press or hard-press the Timer icon. Its shortcut menu offers instant options for 12 increments, from one minute to two hours.

Compass

The iPhone has something very few other phones offer: a magnetic-field sensor known as a magnetometer—even better known as a *compass*.

When you open the Compass app, you get exactly what you'd expect: a classic Boy Scout wilderness compass that always points north.

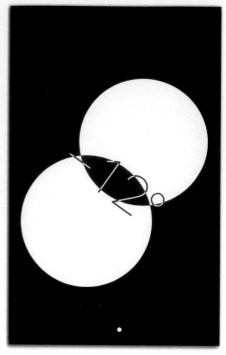

Except it does a few things the Boy Scout compasses never did. Like displaying a digital readout of your heading, altitude, city name, and precise geographic coordinates at the bottom. And offering a choice of **true** north (the "top" point of the Earth's rotational axis) or **magnetic** north (the spot that traditional compasses point to, which is about 11 degrees away from true north). You choose in **Settings→Compass**.

To use the compass, hold it roughly parallel to the ground, and then read it like...a compass. Tap the center of the compass to lock in your current heading; a red strip shows how far you are off course. Tap again to unlock the heading.

TIP: For many people, the real power of the compass is in the Maps app. (You can jump directly from Compass to Maps by tapping the coordinates below the compass dial.)

The compass lets Maps know which way you're **facing**. That's a critical detail when you're lost in a city, trying to find a new address, or emerging from the subway with no idea which way to walk.

People who write iPhone programs can tap into the compass, too. There's an "augmented reality" app called New York Nearest Subway, for example. By using the compass, GPS, and tilt-sensor information, it knows where you are and how you're holding the phone—and so it superimposes arrows that show where to find the nearest subway stop and which line it's on.

The Carpenter's Level

The Compass app has a secret identity: It doubles as a carpenter's level. The next time you need to hang a picture, or prop up a wobbly table, or raise a barn, you'll now know when you've got things perfectly horizontal or vertical.

From the Compass screen, swipe to the left to reveal the level. It measures all three dimensions:

- **Right/left.** Hold the iPhone upright (against a picture you're hanging, say), and tilt it left and right. When it's perfectly upright, the readout says 0 degrees and the bottom half of the screen turns green.

- **Forward/back.** Hold the phone upright and tip it away from or toward you. Once again, "0 degrees" and green mean "level."

- **Perfectly flat.** Hold the phone on its back, screen facing the sky. When the two circles merge (previous page, right), you'll know you've got it perfectly level. You could, for example, put the iPhone on a table you're trying to adjust, using its gauge to know how close you're getting as you wedge something under its short leg.

> **TIP:** Level doesn't have to be the zero point. You can tilt the phone to any angle and declare *that* to be the zero point—by tapping the screen.

Files

The new Files is one of the most useful new iOS 11 features. But explaining it might take a few paragraphs.

Meet iCloud Drive...

For a few years now, Apple has offered a convenient service called *iCloud Drive*. Once you've switched it on (in **Settings→[your name]→iCloud**), your phone has a magic folder. Whatever you put into it appears, almost instantly, in the iCloud Drive folders on all your **other** machines: Macs, iPhones, iPads, and even Windows PCs. In fact, your files are even available at *iCloud.com*, so you can grab them when you're stranded on a desert island with nothing but somebody else's computer. (And Internet access.)

This is an incredibly useful feature. No more emailing files to yourself. No more carrying things around on a flash drive. After working on some

document at the office, you can go home and resume from right where you stopped; the same file is waiting for you, exactly as you left it.

The iCloud Drive is a great backup, too, because of its automatic duplication on multiple machines. Even if your phone is stolen or burned to aluminum dust, your iCloud Drive files are safe.

...And Its Rivals

Ah, but iCloud Drive is not the only magic-folder syncing service. There's also Dropbox, Google Drive, OneDrive (Microsoft), Creative Cloud (Adobe), and Box. They all work essentially alike.

> **NOTE:** For example, they all offer a certain amount of free storage—5 GB, in Apple's case—and if you outgrow that, you can pay monthly for more room.

So in iOS 11, Apple thought it might be cool to create one single app that can access *all* of these services. You can search all of them at once, too!

Working with Files

On the Browse tab, tap **Locations** to hook up your various accounts (Google Drive, Dropbox, and so on). Tap **Edit**, and then turn on the services you use. Each will require you to log in with your name and password for that service. You can also drag the ☰ handle to rearrange them in the list. Tap **Done**.

To see your actual files, tap one of the services' names—say, iCloud Drive. And boom: You're looking at a tidy list of all the files and folders on that "drive." Here's what you can do with them:

- **To download a file to your phone,** tap its name (or the ☁ button).

- **To open a file, tap it.** Now, iOS is not macOS or Windows; still, it can open many kinds of documents right on the phone. Graphics, music and video files, Microsoft Office documents, and PDFs all open right up—at least once they've been downloaded. Other kinds of computer files may open in their associated apps on the phone—or not at all. In those cases, Files is still useful, though, because it lets you forward those documents by email to a machine that *can* open them.

TIP: If you've opened a photo or PDF file, you can annotate it using the Markup tools described on page 307. Tap the Ⓐ.

- **To see what's in a file without fully opening it,** use the peek and pop finger-pressure technique described on page 39.

- **To delete a file or folder,** swipe to the left across it, and then tap Delete.

- **To manipulate a file, lightly touch it for one second.** Buttons appear for **Copy**, **Duplicate**, **Rename**, **Move**, **Delete**, **Share**, **Tags** (or **Favorite**), and **Info**.

  Those are fairly self-explanatory, but don't miss the **Share** feature. It lets you send anyone in the world a copy of anything on any of your virtual drives, just by sending a link to it.

- **To operate on multiple files simultaneously,** tap **Select**, and then tap the files you want. Now you can use the ⬆ (Share), ⊞ (Duplicate), 🗁 (Move to different folder), and 🗑 (Delete) buttons at the bottom.

> **TIP:** There's a second way to select multiple files, in readiness for moving into a folder. It's tricky, but faster once you get it. Start dragging one file or folder, and then pause. Without releasing your finger, use other fingers to tap other icons. You'll see those additional icons jump to your original finger, ready to complete the drag into a folder's icon.

If you tug downward on the display of files and folders, you reveal three new blue controls at the top:

- **To create a new folder,** tap ⊞ at the top-left corner.

- **To change the sorting order,** tap **Sorted by** at the top; choose **Name**, **Date**, **Size**, or **Tags**.

- **To switch from list view to icon view,** tap the ☰ icon at top right.

Tagging Files

The Browse tab also lets you round up all files with a particular tag (a color-coded label that you make up, like *Important* or *Smithers Project*). What's especially powerful is that your tagged files can come from all different services—one from Dropbox, a few from Google Drive, and so on. They all appear in one unified, harmonious "tagged" list, without reference to creed, color, or place of origin.

To apply a tag, select a file, or several. Now tap ⬆ (or tap the **Share** button that appears in the scrollable black command bar when you long-press the icon). Tap **+Tag**, and then tap the tag name(s) that you want to apply. This, by the way, is your only chance to create a *new* tag (**Add New Tag**).

Thereafter, you can see all the files bearing a certain tag in either of two ways:

- **On the main Browse screen,** tap a tag name to see all the files you've tagged that way.

- **On the Recents screen,** scroll down to the tag headings; there are your tagged files. (As you could probably figure out, the Recents screen's other purpose is to display the icons of files you've opened recently.)

(To remove a tag, long-press to select the file or files, and then tap **Tags** in the black command bar. Tap the tag name to remove the checkmark.)

Favorites Folders

Tags work only on files. What about folders?

For those, Apple has supplied a Favorites feature. Select a folder (or several); then, from the command bar that appears when you long-press an icon, tap **Favorite**. Those folders now appear beneath the Favorites heading on the main Browse tab, for quick access.

Here again, your Favorites folders can come from all different syncing services. They're just happy to be your favorites.

> **TIP:** Your iCloud Drive folder contains inner folders named for Apple apps like Pages, Numbers, and so on. Yes, these folders hold the corresponding kinds of documents, for ease of finding later.
>
> But Pages, Keynote, and Numbers offer a new feature in iOS 11: ***real-time, simultaneous editing*** across the Internet. You and your colleagues can collaborate on one of these kinds of documents live. (If you've ever used Google Docs, you're familiar with the process.)
>
> There's a lot of fine print to making this work; fortunately, Apple has created a guide here: *https://support.apple.com/en-us/HT206181*.

In all these apps, there's an **Open** button or icon that presents the iCloud Drive's contents. In Pages, for example, when you're viewing your list of documents, tap **Locations**, and then tap **iCloud**. There's the list of folders on your iCloud Drive, corresponding perfectly to what you would have seen on a Mac or a PC. Tap a folder to open it and see what's in it.

Health

This app is a dashboard for all the health data—activity, sleep, nutrition, relaxation—generated by your fitness apps. But even if you don't have an app or a band, you have the iPhone itself; unbeknownst to you, it's been quietly tracking the steps you've been taking and the flights of stairs you've been climbing, just by measuring the jostling of the phone in your pocket or bag! (If that creeps you out just a bit, you can turn it off in **Settings→Privacy→Motion & Fitness**.)

Lots of apps and fitness bands share their data with Health: the Apple Watch, MyFitnessPal, Strava, MapMyRun, WebMD, MotionX-24/7, 7 Minute Workout, Nokia Health Mate, Garmin Connect Mobile, Lark, Lose It!, Sleepio, Weight Watchers, and so on. Fitness tracking is a big, big deal these days, now that your phone and/or your fitness band can measure your steps, exercise, and sleep.

> **TIP:** The one fitness brand that's screamingly missing from this list is Fitbit. Your Fitbit band can't share its data with the Health app—at least not without the help of a $3 app called Sync Solver or a free one called Power Sync for Fitbit.

If you have one of those bands or apps, you'll have to fish around in its settings until you find the option to connect with Health. At that point, you must turn on the kinds of data you want it to share with Health.

Now open the Health app. The next bit of setup is to specify what kind of data you want staring you in the face on its Dashboard screen. This is the motivational aspect of Health: The more you're forced to **look at** and **think about** your weight, activity, sleep, or calories, the more likely you are to improve.

The Four Biggies

In Apple's mind, the Big Four ingredients for health are activity, mindfulness, nutrition, and sleep. Health offers four tabs at the bottom that help you keep tabs on these:

- **The Today Tab.** Here's a single summary screen of the Big Four, all in one place. You can tap any one of these summary bubbles to view it in more detail—for example, to switch among **Day**, **Week**, **Month**, or **Year** graphs.

- **Health Data.** An introductory video appears when you tap each of these, explaining with charming British narration the importance of that life factor. On each screen, you can see the latest graphs of your efforts in that category. (For some, like mindfulness, you won't see

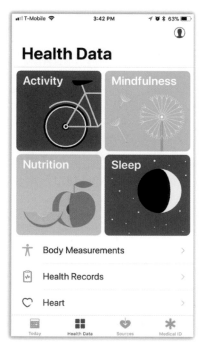

anything unless you've installed an app that generates that kind of data.)

Below those tiles, you'll find places to record health data, like your body measurements, electronic medical records, reproductive data, and so on.

- **Sources.** This screen lists all the fitness apps and gadgets you've hooked up to Health (including the Apple Watch, if you have one), so that you know where your data is going.

- **Medical ID.** This screen offers a reason to use the Health app even if you don't use any fitness apps and don't track any medical statistics. It's the electronic equivalent of an emergency medical ID bracelet. You can record your name, age, blood type, weight, height, medical conditions, and emergency contact information. This screen also makes it easy to do something noble: to offer to donate your organs after you pass away.

If you tap **Edit** and turn on **Show When Locked**, then this information will be available on your phone's Lock screen. If you pass out, have a seizure, or otherwise become medically inconvenienced, a passerby or medical pro can get that critical information without needing your password (or your awareness).

If that person is technically savvy, that is. Finding the Medical ID screen can be tricky. It's available on the Enter Passcode screen, for example; tap **Emergency**; tap **Medical ID**. It's also available on the special Emergency shutdown screen (page 78).

Home

HomeKit is Apple's home-automation standard. The Home app lets you control any product whose box says "Works with HomeKit"—all those "smart" or "connected" door locks, security cameras, power outlets, thermostats, doorbells, lightbulbs, leak/freeze/temperature/humidity/air-quality sensors, and so on.

Once you've installed the gadget, you can turn it on and off, monitor its readouts, or adjust its settings (a thermostat is shown on the next page at right). You can do all of that from the Home app, from the Control Center, or by using Siri voice commands ("Lock the front door," "Turn on the downstairs lights," and so on). You can automate those actions based on the time or your location, or hand off control of certain devices to other people's iPhones.

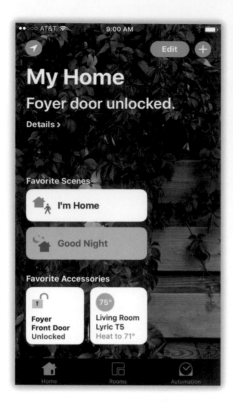 

iBooks

iBooks is Apple's ebook reading program. It turns the iPhone into a sort of pocket-sized Kindle. With iBooks, you can carry around dozens or hundreds of books in your pocket, which, in the pre-ebook days, would have drawn some funny looks in public.

Most people think of iBooks as a reader for books that Apple sells on its iTunes bookstore—bestsellers and current fiction, for example—and it does that very well. But you can also load it up with your own PDF documents, as well as thousands of free, older, out-of-copyright books.

> **TIP:** iBooks is very cool and all. But, in the interest of fairness, it's worth noting that Amazon's free Kindle app, and Barnes & Noble's free B&N Nook app, are much the same thing—but offer much bigger book libraries at lower prices than Apple's.

Downloading Books

To shop the iBooks bookstore, open the iBooks app. If this is your first time diving in, you might be offered a selection of free starter books to download right now. Go for it; they're brand-name books by famous authors.

If, at any time, you want to buy another book—it could happen—well, the icons across the bottom are the literary equivalent of the App Store. Tap **Featured** to see what Apple is plugging this week; **Top Charts** to see this week's bestsellers, including what's on *The New York Times* Best Sellers list (note that there's a special row for ***free*** books); **Search** to search by name; and **Purchased** to see what you've bought.

> **TIP:** Once you've bought a book from Apple, you can download it again on other iPhones, iPod Touches, iPads, and Macs. Buy once, read many times. That's the purpose of the **Not on This iPhone** tab, which appears when you tap **Purchased**.

Once you find a book that looks good, you can tap **Sample** to download a free chapter, read ratings and reviews, or tap the price itself to buy the book and download it straight to the phone.

PDFs and ePub Files

You can also load up your ebook reader from your computer, feeding it with PDF documents and ePub files.

> **NOTE:** ePub is the normal iBooks format. It's a very popular standard for ebook readers, Apple's and otherwise. The only difference between the ePub documents you create and the ones Apple sells is that Apple's are copy-protected.

Your Mac or PC is the most convenient loading dock for files bound for your iPhone. If you have a Mac, open the iBooks program. If not, open iTunes, click your iPhone's icon at the top (when it's connected), and then click **Books**.

Either way, you now see all the books, PDF documents, and ePub files that you've slated for transfer. To add to this set, just drag files off your desktop and directly into this window.

And where are you supposed to get all these files? Well, PDF documents are everywhere—people send them as attachments, and you can turn any document into a PDF file. (For example, on the Mac, in any program, choose **File→Print**; in the resulting dialog box, click **PDF→Save as PDF**.)

> **TIP:** If you get a PDF document as an email attachment on the phone, then adding it to iBooks is even easier. Tap the attachment to open it; now tap **Open in iBooks** in the corner of the page.

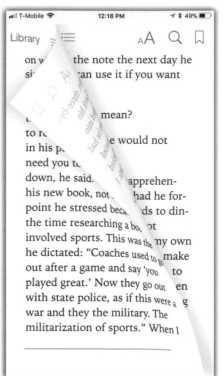

But free ebooks in ePub format are everywhere, too. There are 33,000 free downloadable books at *gutenberg.org*, for example, and over a million at *books.google.com*—oldies, but classic oldies, with lots of Mark Twain, Agatha Christie, Herman Melville, H.G. Wells, and so on. (Lots of these are available in the Free pages of Apple's own iBooks Store, too.)

TIP: You'll discover that these freebie books usually come with generic-looking covers. But once you've dragged them into iTunes on your computer, it's easy to add good-looking covers. Use *images.google.com* to search for the book's title. Right-click (or Control-click) the cover image in your web browser; from the shortcut menu, choose **Copy Image**. In iTunes, in Library mode, choose **Books** from the top-left pop-up menu. Right-click (or Control-click) the generic book; choose **Get Info**; click **Artwork**; and paste the cover you copied. Now that cover will sync over to the iPhone along with the book.

Once you've got books in iTunes, connect the iPhone, choose its name at top right, click the **Books** tab at top, and turn on the checkboxes of the books you want to transfer.

Your Library

Once you've supplied your iBooks app with some reading material, the fun begins. When you open the app, its **My Books** tab shows a futuristic, shaded bookshelf with your library represented as little book covers. Mostly what you'll do here is tap a book to open it. But there are other activities waiting for you:

- Tap the ☰ icon, which switches the book-cover view to a much more boring (but more compact) list view. Buttons at the top let you sort the list by author, title, category, and so on.

- Tap **Select** if you want to delete a book, or a bunch of them. To do that, tap each book thumbnail that you want to target for termination; observe how they sprout ✓ marks. Then tap **Delete**. Of course, deleting a book from the phone doesn't delete your safety copy in iTunes or online.

- The **Search** button at the bottom of the iBooks screen lets you search by author or title—not just *your* books, but the entire iBooks Store.

- When you first start using a new iPhone, iPad, or Mac, your book covers bear the ☁ symbol. It means: "Our records show that you've bought this book, but it's still online, in the great Apple locker in the sky. Tap to download it to your phone so you can start reading."

Collections

You can create subfolders for your books called *collections*. You might have one for school and one for work, or one for you and one for somebody who shares your phone, for example.

To switch your view to a different collection, tap the collection's name. It's the top-center button, which starts out saying **All Books**. (If you've loaded some PDF documents, then you'll find a collection called "PDFs," already set up.) To create a new collection, open that top-center menu and hit **New Collection**.

And to move a book into a different collection: Tap **Select**, tap a book (or several), and then tap **Move**. It opens the Collections screen shown on the next page, so that you can choose a new collection for the selected items.

> **TIP:** You can reorganize your bookshelf in a collection (which you can't do in the All Books view). Hold down your finger on a book until it swells with pride, and then drag it into a new spot.

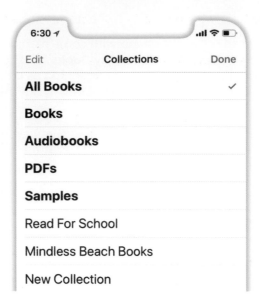

Reading

Open the book or PDF by tapping the book cover. Now the book opens, ready for you to read. Looks great, doesn't it? (If you're returning to a book you've been reading, iBooks remembers your place.)

If the phone detects that it's nighttime (or just dark where you are), the screen appears with white text against a black background. That's to prevent the bright white light of your phone from disturbing other people in, for example, the movie theater. (This is the Night theme, and you can turn it off.)

> **TIP:** Turn the phone 90 degrees for a wider column of text.

In general, reading is simple: Just read. Turn the page by tapping the edge of the page—or swiping your finger across the page. (If you swipe slowly, you can actually see the "paper" bending over—in fact, you can see through to the "ink" on the other side of the page! Amaze your friends.) You can tap or swipe the left edge (to go back a page) or the right edge (to go forward).

> **TIP:** This is rotation lock's big moment. When you want to read lying down, you can prevent the text from rotating 90 degrees using rotation lock (page 26).

But if you tap a page, a row of additional controls appears:

- ‹ takes you back to the bookshelf view.

- ≣ opens the table of contents. The chapter or page names are "live"—you can tap one to jump there.

- ᴀA lets you change the look of the page. For example, this panel offers a screen-brightness slider for the whole phone. (This is the same control you'd find in the Control Center or in Settings.)

  The A and A buttons control the type size—a huge feature for people with tired or over-40 eyes. Tap the larger one repeatedly to enlarge the text; tap the smaller one to shrink it.

  The same panel offers a **Fonts** button, where you can choose from eight typefaces for your book, as well as a **Themes** button, which lets you specify whether the page itself is **White**, **Sepia** (off-white), or **Night** (black page, white text, for nighttime reading). And there's an **Auto-Night Theme** button; if you don't care for the white-on-black theme, then turn off this switch. Finally, there's a **Scrolling View** switch. In scrolling view, you don't turn book "pages." Instead, the book scrolls vertically, as though printed on an infinite roll of Charmin.

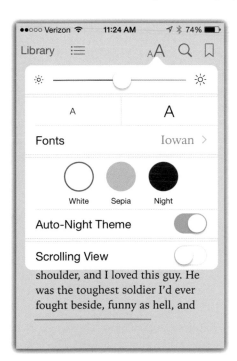
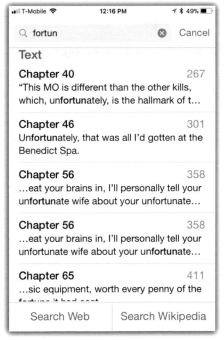

- Q lets you search for text within the book you're reading, which can be extremely useful. As a bonus, there are also **Search Web** and **Search Wikipedia** buttons so you can hop online to learn more about something you've just read.

- 🔖 adds a bookmark to the current page. You can flag as many pages, for as many reasons, as you like.

- **Chapter slider.** At the bottom of the screen, a slider represents the pages of your book. Tap or drag it to jump around in the book; as you drag, a pop-up indicator shows you what chapter and page number you're scrolling to. (If you've magnified the font size, of course, then your book consumes more pages.)

> **TIP:** An iBooks book can include pictures and even videos. Double-tap a picture in a book to zoom in on it.

When you're reading a PDF document, by the way, you can do something you can't do when reading regular iBooks titles: zoom in and out using the usual two-finger pinch-and-spread gestures. Very handy indeed.

> **NOTE:** On the other hand, here are some features that *don't* work in PDF files (only in ebooks): font and type-size changes, page-turn animations, sepia or black backgrounds, and notes.
>
> And if you want highlights, you'll have to draw them on manually with the Markup tools (page 307).

Notes, Bookmarks, Highlighting, Dictionary

Here are some more stunts that you'd have trouble pulling off in a printed book. If you *double-tap* a word, or *hold your finger down* on a word, you get a bar that offers these options:

- **Speak** reads the highlighted passage aloud. (This button appears only if you've turned on **Speak Selection** in **Settings→General→ Accessibility→Speech**.) Thank you, Siri!

- **Copy.** You can probably guess this one.

- **Look Up.** Opens up a page from iBooks' built-in dictionary. You know—in the unlikely event that you encounter a word you don't know.

- **Highlight.** Adds tinted, transparent highlighting, or underlining, to the word you tapped. For best results, don't tap the **Highlight** button until you've first grabbed the blue-dot handles and dragged them to enclose the entire passage you want highlighted.

  Once you tap **Highlight**, the buttons change into a special Highlight bar (facing page, middle). The first button (⬤) opens a *third* row of

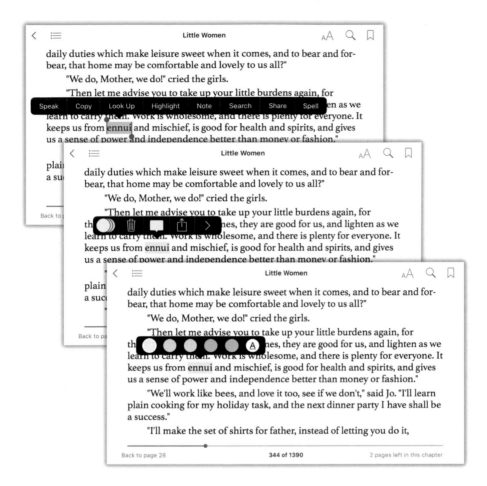

buttons (bottom), so that you can specify which highlight color you want. (The final button in this row designates underlining.)

To remove highlighting, tap 🗑. The ⬛ button adds a note, as described next. The ⬆ button opens the Share sheet, also described momentarily.

- **Note (⬛)** creates highlighting *and* opens an empty, colored sticky note so you can type in your own annotations. When you tap **Done**, your note collapses down to a tiny yellow Post-it peeking out from the right edge of the margin. Tap to reopen it.

  To delete a note, tap the highlighted text. Tap 🗑.

- **Search** opens the same search box that you'd get by tapping the 🔍 icon—except this time the highlighted word is already filled in, saving you a bit of typing.

- **Share** opens the Share sheet (page 363) so you can send the high-lighted material to somebody else, post it to Facebook or Twitter, or copy it to your Clipboard for pasting into another app.

> **NOTE:** If you've highlighted a single word, and if you have Speak Selection turned on in **Settings→General→Accessibility→Speech**, then there's one more option: **Spell**. It spells the word aloud for you, one letter at a time.

There are a couple of cool things going on with your bookmarks, notes, and highlighting, by the way. Once you've added them to your book, they're magically and wirelessly synced to any other copies of that book—on other gadgets, like the iPad or iPod Touch, your other iPhones, or even Mac computers running OS X Mavericks or later. Very handy indeed.

Furthermore, if you tap the ☰ to open the Table of Contents, you'll see the **Bookmarks** and **Notes** tabs. Each presents a tidy list of all your book-marked pages, notes, and highlighted passages. You can tap ⬆ (and then **Share Notes**) to print or email your notes, or tap one of the listings to jump to the relevant page.

Books That Read to You

iBooks can actually read to you! It's a great feature when you're driving or jogging, when someone's just learning to read, or when you're having

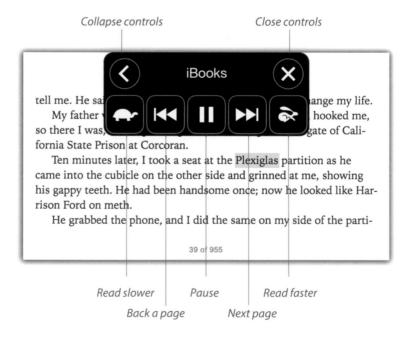

Collapse controls   *Close controls*

Read slower   *Pause*   *Read faster*

Back a page   *Next page*

trouble falling asleep. There's even a special control panel just for managing your free audiobook reader.

To get started, open **Settings→General→Accessibility→Speech**. Turn on **Speak Screen**.

Then open a book in iBooks. Swipe down the page with two fingers to make the iPhone start reading the book to you, out loud, with a synthesized voice. At the same time, a palette appears, offering the speech controls shown on the facing page:

After a few seconds, the palette shrinks into a > button at the edge of the screen—and, after that, it becomes transparent, as though trying to make itself as invisible as possible. You can, of course, tap it to reopen it.

Yes, this is exactly the feature that debuted in the Amazon Kindle and was then removed when publishers screamed bloody murder—but, somehow, so far, Apple has gotten away with it.

iBooks Settings

If you've embraced the simple joy of reading electronic books the size of a chalkboard eraser, then you deserve to know where to make settings changes: in **Settings→iBooks**. Here are the options waiting there:

- **Use Cellular Data.** Do you want to be able to download books using your carrier's cellular data network (which eats up your monthly data allotment)? If you turn this off, then you can download books only when you're in a Wi-Fi hotspot.

- **Full Justification.** Ordinarily, iBooks presents text with fully justified margins (below, left). Turn this off if you prefer ragged right margins (right).

Full justification

Ragged right margin

sometimes he feels that there really is another way, if only he could stop bumping for a moment and think of it. And then he feels that perhaps there isn't. Anyhow, here he is at the bottom, and ready to be introduced to you. Winnie-the-Pooh.

When I first heard his name, I said, just as you are going to say, "But I thought he was a boy?"

"So did I," said Christopher

sometimes he feels that there really is another way, if only he could stop bumping for a moment and think of it. And then he feels that perhaps there isn't. Anyhow, here he is at the bottom, and ready to be introduced to you. Winnie-the-Pooh.

When I first heard his name, I said, just as you are going to say, "But I thought he was a boy?"

"So did I," said Christopher

- **Auto-hyphenation.** Sometimes, typesetting looks better if hyphens allow partial words to appear at the right edge of each line. Especially if you've also turned on Full Justification.

- **Both Margins Advance.** Usually, tapping the right edge of the screen turns to the next page, and tapping the left edge turns *back* a page. If you turn on this option, then tapping *either* edge of the screen opens the next page. That can be handy if you're a lefty, for example.

- **Sync Bookmarks, Sync Collections.** Turn these on if you'd like your bookmarks and book collections to be synced with your other Apple gadgets.

- **Online Content.** A few books contain links to video or audio clips online. This option comes set to Off, because video and audio can eat up your monthly cellular data allotment like a hungry teenager.

There are even a couple of controls here that apply to audiobooks. They govern how much time skips when you tap one of the back or forward Skip buttons—15 seconds, for example.

Maps

From its birth in 2007, the iPhone always came with Google Maps— an excellent mapping and navigation app. (Apple wrote it, but Google provided the maps and navigation data.) But in iOS 6, Apple replaced Google Maps with a new mapping system of its own.

Unfortunately, in its initial version, the databases underlying the Maps app had serious errors and problems. Apple promised to keep working on Maps until it was all fixed, but in the meantime, in a remarkable apology letter, CEO Tim Cook recommended using one of Maps' rivals.

By far the best one is Google Maps. It's free, it's amazingly smart (it knows what address you mean after you type only a few letters), it has public-transportation details, live traffic reports, Street View (you can see photos of most addresses, and even "look around" you), and of course Google's far superior maps and data.

All right—you've been warned.

But while Apple's cartographical elves keep cleaning up the underlying maps, some of its features are pretty great.

Meet Maps

The underlying geographical database may need work, but Maps, the app itself, is a thing of beauty.

It lets you type in any address or point of interest and see it plotted on a map, with turn-by-turn driving directions, just like a $300 windshield GPS unit. It also gives you a live national Yellow Pages business directory and real-time traffic-jam alerts. You can get bus and train schedules for a few U.S. cities. You have a choice of a street-map diagram or actual aerial photos, taken by satellite.

Maps Basics

When you open Maps, a blue dot represents your current location. Tap ✈ to zoom to your current spot. Or, for more controlled zooming, try double-tapping, or "pinching out" with two fingers, or (in iOS 11) double-tapping/dragging with a single finger. (That is, double-tap and, with your finger still down, drag up or down.) Eventually, you zoom in enough to see actual city blocks.

To zoom **out** again, you can use the rare **two-finger double-tap**.

Drag or flick to scroll around the map, or twist two fingers to rotate the map. (A compass icon at top right helps you keep your bearings; you can tap it to restore the map's usual north-is-up orientation.) And if you drag two fingers up the screen, you tilt the map into 3D view, which makes it look like you're surveying the map at an angle instead of straight down.

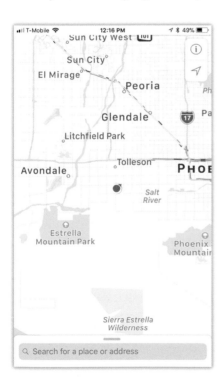

At any time, you can tap ⓘ to open a secret panel. Here's how you switch among Maps' three views of the world: Map, Transit, or Satellite.

You can set up some preferences, too. Tap **Map** to decide if you want to see color-coded roads that show the current traffic situation. Tap **Satellite** to tell Maps whether you want street names and/or traffic colors superimposed on the aerial views.

Each of these tabs offers buttons that let you **Mark My Location** (drop a pin for your current spot, add it to your Favorites, add it to your Contacts, and so on), **Add a Place** (record the address and other details of a business, thereby adding it to Apple's database), and **Report an Issue** (tell Apple about a bug).

Finding Yourself

If any phone can tell you where you are, it's the iPhone. It has not one, not two, but *three* ways to determine your location:

- **GPS.** First, the iPhone contains a traditional GPS chip, of the sort that was found in windshield navigation units of old.

- **Wi-Fi Positioning System.** Metropolitan areas today are blanketed by overlapping Wi-Fi signals. At a typical Manhattan intersection, you might be in range of 20 base stations. Each one broadcasts its own name and unique network address (its *MAC address*—nothing to do with Mac computers) once every second. A laptop or phone can detect this beacon signal from up to 1,500 feet away.

  Imagine if you could correlate all those beacon signals with their physical locations. Why, you'd be able to simulate GPS!

  For years, millions of iPhones have been quietly logging all those Wi-Fi signals, noting their network addresses and locations. (The phones never *connect* to these base stations—they just read the one-way beacon signals.) At this point, Apple's database knows about millions of hotspots—and the precise longitude and latitude of each.

  So, if the iPhone can't get a fix on GPS, it sniffs for Wi-Fi base stations. If it finds any, it looks up those network addresses and learns the coordinates. This system fails once you're out of populated areas. On the other hand, it works indoors, which GPS definitely doesn't.

- **The cellular triangulation system.** As a last resort, the iPhone can check its proximity to the cellphone towers around you. The software works a lot like the Wi-Fi location system, but it relies upon its knowledge of cellular towers' locations rather than Wi-Fi base stations.

The first Maps trick is to show you where you are: Tap the ⌖ at the top of the Maps screen. The button turns solid blue, indicating that the iPhone is consulting its various references to figure out where you are. You show up as a blue dot that moves with you. It keeps tracking until you tap the ➤ enough times to turn it off.

Orienting Maps

It's great to see a blue pin on the map, and all—but how do you know which way you're facing?

Just tap the ➤ until it points straight up. The map spins so that the direction you're facing is upward, and a "flashlight beam" emanates from your blue dot; its width indicates the iPhone's degree of confidence. (The narrower the beam, the surer it is.)

Searching Maps

The following paragraphs guide you through using the search box in Maps. But it's *much* quicker to use Siri to specify what you want to find.

You can say, for example, "Show me the map of Detroit" or "Show me the closest Starbucks" or "Directions to 200 West 79th Street in New York." Siri shows you that spot on a map; tap to jump into the Maps app.

If you *must* use the search box, here's how it works. It shouldn't be hard to find, since it opens when you open Maps (below, left).

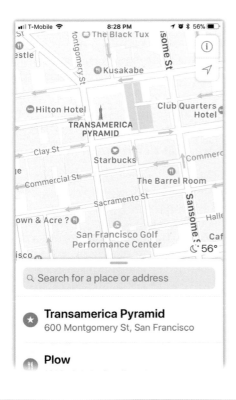

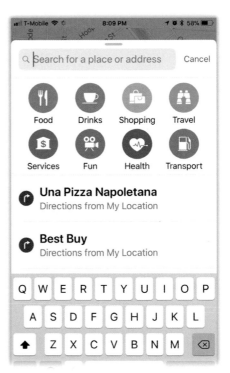

- **Business Categories.** When you first tap into an empty search box, you get icons for **Food**, **Drinks**, **Shopping**, **Travel**, **Services**, **Fun**, **Health**, and **Transport**. Each expands into eight more icons for further refinement (**Travel** offers **Airports**, **Hotels**, **Banks & ATMs**, and so on). Keep tapping to drill down to the place you want; it's all designed to save you typing when you're in a hurry.

TIP: Don't miss the scrollable list of subcategories or establishments at the very bottom of some of these screens. When you tap **Drinks**, for example, this ticker may list **Sports Bars**, **Cocktail Bars**, **Pubs**, and so on. Oh—and see the little temperature indicator (previous page, left)? If you press firmly (iPhone 6 or later), it sprouts an hourly weather forecast; press harder to open the Weather app for that place.

- **Recents.** Below the box, there's a list of searches you've recently conducted. You'd be surprised at how often you want to call up the same spot again later—and now you can, just by tapping its name in this list.

TIP: If you swipe a listing to the left, you reveal two buttons: **Share** (send the location info to someone) and **Remove** (if you intend to elope and don't want your parents to find out).

- **Favorites.** One nice thing about Maps is the way it tries to eliminate typing at every step. The **Favorites** are a great example. They're addresses you've flagged for later use by tapping the ♡, an option that appears on every place's Location card. For sure, you should bookmark your home and workplace. That will make it much easier to request driving directions.

  Then, to see your list of favorites, scroll all the way to the bottom of the Recents list and tap **Favorites**. Tap one to jump to its spot on the map, or swipe to the left to reveal **Share**, **Edit Name**, and **Remove** buttons.

Most people, though, most of the time, wind up typing what they want to find. You can type all kinds of things into the search box:

- **An address.** You can skip the periods (and usually the commas, too). And you can use abbreviations. Typing *710 w end ave ny ny* will find 710 West End Avenue, New York, New York. (In this and any of the other examples, you can type a zip code instead of a city and a state.)

- **An intersection.** Type *57th and lexington, ny ny*. Maps finds the spot where East 57th Street crosses Lexington Avenue in New York City.

- **A city.** Type *chicago il* to see that city. You can zoom in from there.

- **A zip code or a neighborhood.** Type *10014* or *greenwich village*.

- **Latitude and longitude coordinates.** Type *40.7484° N, 73.9857° W*.

- **A point of interest.** Type *washington monument* or *niagara falls*.

- **A business type.** Type *drugstores in albany ny* or *hospitals in roanoke va*.

- **A contact's name**. Maps is tied into Contacts, your master address book (page 119). Start typing a person's name to see the matches.

- **A business category**. Maps is a glorified national Yellow Pages. If you type, for example, *pharmacy 60609*, then red bubbles show you all the drugstores in that Chicago zip code. It's a great way to find a gas station, a cash machine, or a hospital in a pinch. Tap a pushpin to see the name of the corresponding business.

As usual, you can tap the map pin's label bubble to open a details screen. If you've searched for a friend, then you see the corresponding Contacts card. If you've searched for a business, then you get a screen containing its phone number, address, website, and so on; often, you get a beautiful page of Yelp information (photos, reviews, ratings).

Remember that you can tap a web address to open it or tap a phone number to dial it. ("Hello, what time do you close today?")

Add a New Place

Once you've found something on the map—your current position, say, or something you've searched for—you can drop a pin there for future reference. Tap the ⓘ button; when the page slides up, tap **Mark My Location**. A pushpin appears. (If your aim wasn't exact, you can tap **Edit Location** and then scroll the map to adjust its position relative to the pin.)

TIP: You can also drop a pin by holding your finger down on the spot.

Scroll the new place's "card" to reveal its address, a Share button (so you can let someone else know where you are), an **Add to Favorites** button, and an option to add this location to somebody's card in Contacts (or to create a new contact).

The Location Card

Whenever you've tapped the name of some place in Apple's massive database (like a store, restaurant, or point of interest), the bottom part of the screen lists its information screen—its location "card."

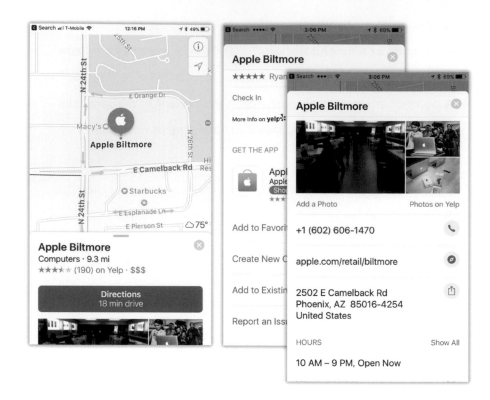

The visible portion of this card already shows the all-important **Directions** button (above, left). But you can also hide the card by swiping down on it, or expand it to full screen by tapping or swiping up (right).

If this is the location for a restaurant or a business, you might strike gold: The Location page might offer several screens full of useful information, courtesy of *Yelp.com*. You'll see the place's hours of operation, plus one-tap links for placing a phone call to the place or visiting its website. Then there may be customer reviews, photos, delivery and reservation information, and so on.

Links here let you bookmark the spot, get directions, add it to Contacts, or share it with other people (via AirDrop, email, text message, Facebook, or Twitter).

TIP: The Location card for a restaurant may even offer a **Reservations** button, so that you can book a table on the spot—if, that is, that eatery participates in OpenTable's online booking system.

Directions

Suppose you've just searched for a place. The top part of its location card is open on the screen. At this point, you can tap **Directions** for instant directions, using four modes of transportation (below, left):

- **Drive.** You'll get the traditional turn-by-turn driving directions.

- **Walk.** The app will guide you to this place by foot. You get an estimate of the time it'll take, too.

- **Transit.** This button appears if you're in one of the 33 major U.S. cities (or 30 overseas cities) for which Apple has public-transportation schedules. More are coming, Apple says.

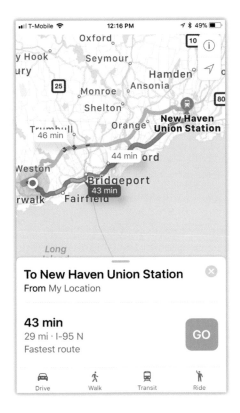 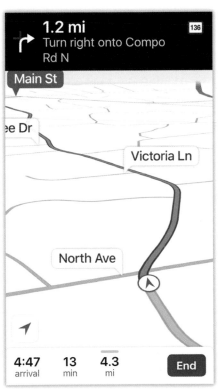

If you're lucky enough to be in one of those cities, you'll discover that the public-transport directions are surprisingly clear and detailed. You even see the color, letter, and number schemes of that city's bus or rail system right there in the app.

TIP: iOS can warn you when there's a disruption on your favorite commuter bus or rail system. To tell it which one you want it to monitor, tap ⓘ and then **Transit**. Tap the map, and then zoom in on the transit line until you can tap its name or number. Its Details screen appears; scroll to the bottom and tap **Add to Favorites**.

At this point, you can add the Map Transit widget to your Today screen (see page 75). Without even unlocking your phone, with one quick swipe, you can see if the train is on time—and if not, what kind of delay you have to look forward to.

- **Ride** means calling an Uber or Lyft driver. (This feature requires that you have the Uber or Lyft app installed and set up.) One tap on **Ride** shows you the time and price estimates—and offers you a **Book** button.

In each case, Maps displays an overview of the route you're about to drive. In fact, it usually proposes several different routes. They're labeled with little tags that identify how long each will take you: **3 hrs 37 min**, **4 hrs 11 min**, and **4 hrs 33 min**, for example.

If you tap one of these tags, the app lets you know the distance and estimated time for that option and identifies the main roads you'll be on.

In each case, tap **Start** to see the first instruction. The map zooms in, and Navigation mode begins.

Navigation Mode

When the iPhone is guiding you to a location, you see a simplified map of the world around you, complete with the outlines of buildings, with huge banners that tell you how to turn next, and onto what street. Siri's familiar voice speaks the same information at the right times, so you don't even have to look at the screen.

Even if you hit the side button to lock the phone, the voice guidance continues. (It continues even if you switch to another app; return to Maps by tapping the banner at the top of the screen.)

iPHONE X: Tap the blue button in the left "ear" to return to Maps.

The bottom bar shows your projected arrival time, plus the remaining distance and time. It also offers the **End** button, which makes the navigation stop.

While Maps is guiding you, you can zoom in and out; you can also pan the map to look ahead at upcoming turns or to inspect alternate routes. You can twist two fingers to turn the map, too.

Once you've shifted the view in these ways, a ➚ button appears. Tap it to restore Maps' usual centered view.

While you're navigating, you can also tap (or swipe up on) the bottom bar to reveal quick-tap buttons like these:

- **Gas Stations, Lunch, Coffee.** Perform instant searches for these frequent-favorite driver stops.

- **Overview.** Your entire planned route shrinks down to fit on a single screen. Now you can see where you're going—and can zoom, turn, and pan the view. To return to the navigation screen, tap ➚.

- **Details.** Tap to get a written list of turn-by-turn instructions.

- **Audio.** You can adjust the volume of Siri's speaking voice as she gives you driving directions by tapping here. Choose **Low**, **Medium**, or **Loud Volume**, or turn off her voice prompts altogether with **No Voice**.

   Here, too, is the **Pause Spoken Audio** switch. It means "When Maps speaks an instruction, momentarily pause playback of any background recordings, like podcasts and audiobooks. Because it'd get really confusing to hear two robo-people speaking at once."

Tap the screen (or just wait) to hide these additional controls once again.

Directions Between Two Other Points

The redesign of Maps seems to suggest that you'll always want to navigate somewhere from your current location. And usually, that's true.

Sometimes, though, you might want directions between two points—when you're not currently at either one.

First, select your starting point. For example, add a pushpin marker as described on page 409, or tap a point-of-interest icon. Tap **Directions**, and then tap **My Location**.

Now you can change the From box (where it currently says **My Location**), using the same address-searching tactics described on page 407. (At this point, you can also swap your start and end points by tapping the double arrow.) Finally, tap **Route** to see the fastest route and get going.

Night Mode

If the phone's light sensor decides that it's dark in your car, it switches to a dimmer, grayer version of the map. It wouldn't want to distract you, after all. When there's enough light, it brightens back up again.

Where You Parked

Maps automatically remembers where you parked, and can afterward guide you back to your car.

How does the phone know when you've parked? Because it connects wirelessly to your car over Bluetooth or CarPlay. (If your car doesn't have Bluetooth or CarPlay, then you don't get this feature.)

When you turn off the car, the phone assumes that you've parked it, checks its GPS location, and makes a notification appear to let you know that it's memorized the spot. (If, that is, this feature is turned on in **Settings→Maps→Show Parked Location**.)

> **TIP:** If you tap the notification, you get a chance to take a photo of the parking spot or to record notes about it. You also see how long you've been parked—handy if you have to feed a meter.

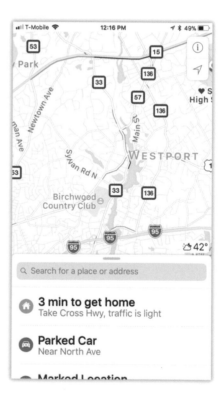

When the time comes to return to your car, the phone makes life as easy as possible. Wake the phone and swipe to the right to view the Maps widget or the Maps Destinations widget. Once you know where you parked, a swipe or a hard-press gets you started finding your way back. (See page 75 for more on widgets.)

The car's location also appears in the Maps app itself, right there in the list of recent locations, and as a reminder in the Today tab of the Notification Center. Tap to begin your journey home.

Traffic

How's this for a cool feature? Free, real-time traffic reporting. Just tap the ⓘ button (it's visible whenever you're *not* in Navigation mode), and then turn on **Traffic**. Now traffic jams appear as red lines on the relevant roads, for your stressing pleasure; less severe slowdowns show up in orange.

Better yet, tiny icons appear, representing accidents, closures, and construction. Tap to see a description bar at the bottom of the screen (like "Accident, Park Ave at State St"); tap that bar to read the details.

If you don't see any colored lines, it's either because traffic is moving fine or because Apple doesn't have any information for those roads. Usually, you get traffic info only for highways, and only in metropolitan areas.

3D Mode

Apple spent two years filming cities in helicopters to create 3D models of major cities and landmarks: San Francisco, New York, Tokyo, London, Paris, Rome, Madrid, Vancouver, San Jose, Cape Town, and Stockholm, for example. Or places like Yosemite National Park, Sydney Opera House, Stonehenge, St. Peter's Basilica, or the Brooklyn Bridge. These city models are responsible for three cool Maps features: 3D view, Flyover, and Flyover Tours.

When you've called up one of these chosen places, a new **3D** button appears at top right. Tap it to make the map tilt into a more, yes, 3D view. Now you can go nuts, conducting your own virtual chopper tour of the city. You can look over and around buildings to see what's behind them, using the usual techniques:

- Drag with one finger to move around the map.

- Pinch or spread two fingers to zoom out or in.

- Drag two fingers up or down to change your camera angle relative to the ground.

- Twist two fingers to turn the world before you.

Flyover (iPhone 8, iPhone X)

Flyover is a 3D, augmented-reality, aerial view of the cities and places Apple has scanned as described above. You can use your phone like a viewer, turning your body and moving the phone around in space to change your view.

Wait for a moment as the phone downloads the photographic models. It's immersing, completely amazing, and very unlikely to make you airsick.

Flyover Tours

Apple wasn't satisfied with letting you pan around virtual 3D city models using your finger. Now it's prepared to give you *city tours* in 3D.

When you tap the search results, a new button appears on the bar at the bottom of the iPhone 8 and X: **Flyover**. That's a 360-degree, augmented-reality, aerial view of the city: As you move, lift, and turn the phone, the view moves with you.

At this point on the 8 and X, you get a **Start City Tour** button. It starts a crazy treat: a fully automated video tour of that city or place. The San Francisco tour shows you the baseball park, the famous Transamerica Pyramid, the Alcatraz prison island, and so on. It's slow, soothing, cool, and definitely something paper maps never did. Tap the screen to open the Pause Tour button; tap the ⊗ to end the tour.

Extensions

There's one more goody in Maps: Extensions. These are add-on features made by other companies—auto-installed into Maps by their full-blown apps—like Uber, Lyft, Yelp, and OpenTable. The point, of course, is to let you order cars, read restaurant reviews, reserve tables, or buy tickets right from within Maps.

Extensions, for example, are responsible for adding the Ride button described on page 412.

You'll probably find them quite handy, but maybe not all of them. Fortunately, you can turn off individual extensions in **Settings→Maps→Extensions**.

News

The News app does just what Apple promises: It "collects all the stories you want to read, from top news sources, based on topics you're most interested in."

When you open the News app and tap **Customize Your News**, the setup process goes like this:

- **Choose your mags.** First, you're presented with a *very* tall scrolling list of favorite online publications (*The New York Times, Wired, The New Yorker,* and hundreds more) and topics (Movie Actors, Science...). You're supposed to tap the ones you want to use as News fodder. You can search for topics, too.

- **Notifications.** On the next screen, you're invited to specify which of those publications and topics are allowed to trigger notifications.

- **Email.** The News app is delighted to send you notifications of articles by email, too. Tap **Sign Me Up** to make it so.

And that's it: Suddenly, you have a beautiful, infinite, constantly updated, free magazine stand, teeming with stories that have been collated according to your tastes. All of it is free, although you're not getting the listed publications in full—usually, you're offered just a few selected stories.

The tabs across the bottom are designed to offer multiple entry points into the eternal tsunami of web news:

- **For You** is the main thing. It's constantly updated with new articles that Apple's algorithms think you'll like, based on (a) your selections the first time you used the app, (b) the stories you favorited by tapping ♡, (c) the stories you indicated you *didn't* like by tapping ♡, (d) which stories you actually wound up reading, and (e) topics you've searched for in Safari.

- **Spotlight,** new in iOS 11, is a deep dive into a story of the day. These news items have been handpicked by human editors.

- **Following** displays the publications and topics you've said you're interested in. Same stories, different starting point.

- **Search.** Oh, yes—you can search for articles by topic or publication. This screen also offers a list of trending topics—subjects *other* people are making popular.

- **Saved.** Most of the time, you can't use News without an Internet connection. If you anticipate that you'll be spending time in the living hell known as Offline mode (like on a subway, sailboat, or airplane), you can save some stories for reading later. To do that, tap ⬆ and then **Save**. You'll find your saved stories here, on the Saved tab.

> **TIP:** The Saved tab also offers a sub-tab called **History**. It lets you jump back to an article you'd already read.

Once you've tapped to open a story, using News is simplicity itself. Swipe vertically to scroll through an article, or horizontally to pull the next article into view.

Notes

The iPhone has always had a Notes app—great for jotting down (or dictating) lists, reminders, brainstorms, recipes, directions, serial numbers, and so on.

But with each successive version of iOS, this ancient, text-only notepad becomes more complete. A Notes page can now include a checklist of to-dos, a photo, a map, a web link, or a sketch you draw with your finger. You can even share notes wirelessly with another iPhone fan, so that you can collaborate.

In iOS 11, Notes continues its evolution. Now you have full font and paragraph formatting. You can create tables. You can scan documents and then annotate them, right from within a note. And, of course, the powerful new **Access Notes from Lock Screen** option means that your phone is now ready, at a finger-tap's notice, to receive your jotted or scanned wisdom—without even having to unlock the phone first. See page 56.

As always, any changes you make in Notes are automatically synchronized to all your other Apple gadgets.

NOTE: The first time you open Notes, you may be invited to upgrade your existing notes to the new Notes format. If you don't, you don't get any of the new features. But if you do, you can't open your notes on any gadget that doesn't have iOS 9 (or later) or OS X El Capitan (or later) for the Mac.

To get started, tap ☑ to start a new blank note. The keyboard appears so you can begin typing.

TIP: You can also send text from other apps *into* Notes. For example, in Mail, select some text you've typed into an outgoing message; in the command bar, tap **Share**. Similarly, you can tap a Mail attachment's icon; once again, tap **Add to Notes** in the Share sheet. In each case, your selection magically appears on a new Notes page.

When you tap **Done**, the keyboard goes away, and a handy row of icons appears at the bottom of your Notes page. You can trash the note (🗑); add a checklist to it (⊘); add a graphic to it—photo, video, or scanned document (⊕); add a sketch (Ⓐ); or start a new note (☑).

The Share button is always available too, at the upper right. Tap ⬆ to print your note, copy it, or send it to someone by email, text message, AirDrop, and so on. For example, if you tap **Mail**, the iPhone creates a new outgoing message, pastes the first line of the note into the subject line, and pastes the note's text into the body. Address the note,

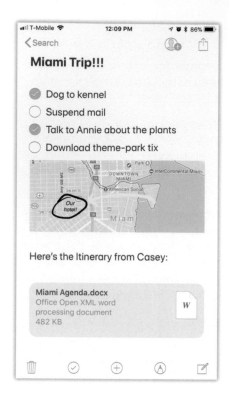
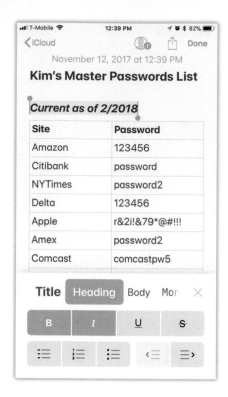

edit if necessary, and hit **Send**. The iPhone returns you to Notes. (See page 363 for more on the sharing options.)

Herewith: A tour of the five buttons that appear above the keyboard. They're your gateway to everything you can put on a note: tables, text and paragraph formatting, lists, photos, sketches, and scanned documents.

Tables

When you tap ⊞, you get a table with two columns and two rows. Tap in a cell and then start typing. To move to the next cell, tap **Next** on the keyboard (or tap with your finger).

Poke around long enough, and you can find controls for just about every formatting tool you'd ever need in a table (except the ability to manually adjust column widths and the ability to format the cell borders).

The keys to most of it are the tiny handles (⋯ and ⸽) that appear when you tap inside a cell:

- **Add or delete columns.** Tap inside a cell to make the ⋯ and ⸽ buttons appear. Tap ⋯ to make the command bar appear, including

Add Column and **Delete Column**; tap ⦂ to make the **Add Row** and **Delete Row** buttons appear. (If you're typing in the lower-right cell, tapping **Return** also makes a new row.)

- **Move a row or column.** Tap ⋯ or ⦂ to highlight the corresponding row or column; now you can drag it to a new spot.

- **Copy or paste cells.** Double-tap (or hold your finger down on) a cell to make the **Select** button appear. Once you've tapped it, you can drag the selection handles to expand the highlighting. The **Cut**, **Copy**, and **Paste** buttons appear in the command bar, along with the **B***I*U (bold, italic, underline) control, **Look Up**, **Spell**, and other controls.

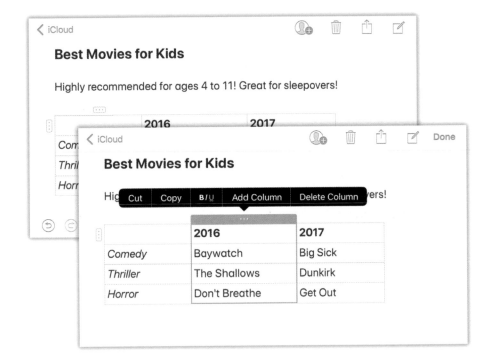

- **Convert text into a table.** Select the text, and then tap the table (⊞) button. The selected text winds up in the first column—one cell per paragraph.

- **Convert table into text.** Tap inside a cell, and then tap the ⊞ button. Choose **Convert to Text**. (This menu also includes **Copy Table**, **Delete Table**, and **Share Table**.)

Text and Paragraph Formatting

As you can see at right on the previous page, a whole new realm of text-formatting options await in the revamped Notes app. Once you've tapped Aa to open the formatting panel, you can try out any of these options:

- **Paragraph styles.** Hey, there are style sheets! You can create **Titles** (big and bold type), **Headings** (bold), **Body** text (normal), and **Monospaced** (every character is the same width, even I and W—useful when you're trying to line up characters on different rows).

- **Character formatting.** The B, I, U, and S refer to **bold**, *italic*, underline, and ~~strikethrough~~ styles.

- **Lists.** The first buttons on the bottom row create dashed lists, auto-numbered lists, and automatically bulleted lists.

- **Paragraph indentation.** The final two buttons move the entire selected paragraph to the right or to the left, indenting or outdenting it.

Checklists

The ⊘ button creates a checklist (shown at left on page 420). Every paragraph you type sprouts a circle—which is actually a checkbox. Tap it to place a checkmark in there. This feature is fantastic for lists: to-do lists, packing lists, movies to see, gift tracking, party planning, job hunting, homework management, and so on.

Each time you press Return, you create a new checklist item. But you can also select some existing paragraphs and then tap ⊘, turning them into a checklist after the fact.

Scan a Document

Here's where things get good. You can now use your iPhone as a high-resolution, supersmart document scanner. You can capture a letter, an article, a receipt. If you scan a contract, you can add your signature to it and send it back.

The fun begins when, on any Notes page, you tap the ⊕ button. Then:

1. **From the pop-up menu, tap Scan Documents.**

   The camera springs into action, with the instruction that you should "Position the document in view."

2. **Tap the ⊛, and choose the type of scan you want.**

   Your options are **Color**, **Grayscale** (shades of gray), **Black & White** (no shades of gray), and **Photo** (a regular snapshot, without any document features). For most printed documents, Grayscale is the cleanest, most space-efficient choice.

3. Hold the phone up high enough that you can see the entire page.

The document scanner can snap pages of any size, from little receipts to whole newspaper sheets that would be tough to feed into a scanner.

Using yellow highlighting (below, left), the iPhone tries to find the edges of the page. Take a moment to marvel as it automatically straightens the image and fixes any perspective errors. In other words, even if you're shooting the page at an angle (to avoid shadows, for example), the app is smart enough to produce a perfectly crisp, rectangular page image.

When you're holding the phone steady, the camera snaps *automatically*. (If you can't wait, tap the ⬤ button or press one of the volume keys. The app displays the cropping screen shown below, so that you can adjust the page boundaries yourself.)

The captured image appears briefly, and then shrinks down to the lower-left thumbnail corner—and you're instantly ready to snap another page. Thanks to the automatic snapping, you can chug through a multipage document pretty quickly.

When you've scanned enough, tap **Save**. Your work here is done.

Or, if you'd like to fine-tune the results, proceed:

4. **Tap the thumbnail (lower-left corner of the screen).**

   The scanned image opens so that you can make adjustments. For example, the ⊛ button lets you change your mind about the decision you made in step 2 (previous page, center). If you tap ⛶, you can use the four round handles to adjust the page boundaries, cropping out more or less background (previous page, right). If you snapped the page at a slight angle, this is your chance to correct the perspective.

   Here, too, you can tap ⟳ to rotate the scan 90 degrees—or 🗑 to delete it. Or tap **Retake** to reshoot just this page.

   Tap **Done** and then **Save**. You return to the Note that now contains the scanned images.

If you tap a scanned page thumbnail to open it, you can have endless fun:

- Use the ⛶, ⊛, ⟳, and 🗑 icons to revisit the choices you made in step 4.

- Tap + to scan a new page to add to the existing ones.

- Tap ⬆ and then **Markup** to annotate the scan (adding your signature or highlighting, for example), using the tools described on page 307.

- Tap ⬆ and then **Create PDF** to convert the finished scan into a PDF page, ready to send (by tapping ⬆ again).

Once you've given the new Scan feature a try, you may well consider it one of iOS 11's finest achievements.

Add a Photo to a Note

There are more goodies hiding behind the ⊕ button on every Notes page, above the keyboard. The pop-up menu offers **Take Photo or Video**, which opens the Camera app, and **Photo Library**, which opens your Photos app. Either way, the resulting photo or video lands right there in the Notes page you're working on. Incredibly handy. (Try inserting labeled face shots of people whose names you keep forgetting at work!)

TIP: Should new photos and videos you take also wind up in your Photos app? That's up to you, thanks to the **Settings→Notes→Save to Photos** option.

Add a Sketch

Sometimes, only a freehand drawing will do—and in Notes, you can draw with your finger!

If you tap the Ⓐ icon, you wind up in the land of markers, highlighters, and pencils described on page 307, and shown below at left.

TIP: If you have an iPhone 6s or later model, then all the drawing tools (and the eraser) are pressure-sensitive! They make fatter or darker lines when you press harder with your finger.

But here's a little secret: For reasons known only to the minds of Apple engineers, there's a second, more complete set of sketching tools (below, right). It's hiding behind the ⊕ button above the Notes keyboard; tap **Add Sketch**.

This time, the colored dot opens a much wider palette of color choices (swipe to the right to view additional "pages" of them, including eight shades of gray). You also get a ruler, which is a surprisingly sophisticated tool.

To use it, put two fingers on the "ruler" on the screen, and twist them to the angle you want. (As you twist, the app shows you the current angle off the horizontal.) Then you can "draw against" it for perfect straight lines.

> **TIP:** In **Settings→Notes**, you can set up a lined background for new sketches. You can ask that they start out with lines (three different spacings) or graph-paper grids (three grid sizes).

Sharing Notes

You and a buddy (or several) can edit a page in Notes *simultaneously*, over the Internet. It's great when you and your friends are planning a party and brainstorming about guests and the menu, for example. Also great for adding items to the grocery or to-do list even after your spouse has left the house to get them taken care of.

Just tap at the top of the screen. On the Add People screen, specify how you want to send the invitation: by message, email, Facebook, Twitter, or whatever.

Once your collaborators receive and accept the invite, they can begin editing the note as though it's their own.

The live editing isn't as animated as it is in, for example, Google Docs—you don't see letter-by-letter typing—but other peoples' edits do appear briefly in yellow highlighting.

Once you've shared a note, the icon at the top changes to , and a matching icon appears next to the note's name in the master list. At any time, you can stop sharing the note—or add more people to its collaboration—by tapping that icon again and editing the sharing panel that appears.

Locking Notes

You can password-protect individual notes—a great feature, suitable for listing birthday presents you intend to get for your nosy kid, the formula for your top-secret invisibility potion, or your illicit lovers' names.

Note that you generally hide and show all your locked notes with a *single* password. You don't have to make up a different password for every note.

TIP: You *can* make up multiple passwords, though. Each time you want to start using a new password, open **Settings→Notes→Password** and tap **Reset Password**. After supplying your iCloud password, you're offered the chance to make up a password for any *new* notes you lock. All *existing* locked notes are still protected by the previous password.

And if you've forgotten the password? Unless you've turned on Touch ID or Face ID (you're asked the first time you try to open a locked note), then all those old notes are locked forever. But you can still make up a new password to protect your latest secrets.

To lock a note, tap ⬆; on the Share screen, tap **Lock Note** (below, left). (Why is locking a note sharing it? Never mind.) Make up a password for locking/unlocking all your notes (or, if you've done this before, *enter* the password).

Once your locked notes are all unlocked, you can still see and edit them. But when there's any risk of somebody else coming along and seeing them (on your Mac, iPhone, iPad, or any other synced gadget), click

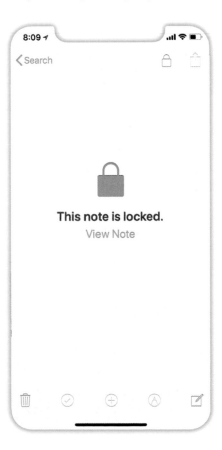

the 🔓 to lock all your notes. (They also all lock when the phone goes to sleep.)

Now all you see of the locked notes are their titles. Everything on them is replaced by a "This note is locked" message, as shown on the previous page at right. Tap **View Note** to unlock them with your fingerprint or password.

> **TIP:** To remove the padlock from a note, tap 📤 and then tap **Remove Lock**.

Use your power wisely.

The Notes List

As you create more pages, the ‹**iCloud** button (top left corner of the screen) becomes more useful. (It may not say "iCloud"; it bears the name of whatever online account stores your notes: Gmail, Exchange, or whatever. Or, if your notes exist only on the phone, you just see an unlabeled ‹ symbol.)

It opens your table of contents for the Notes pad. It's the only way to jump from one note to another.

> **TIP:** You can swipe rightward to jump from an open note back to the list.

Here's what this list displays:

- **The first lines of your notes,** along with the time or date you last edited them. If there's a photo or sketch on a note—an unlocked one, anyway—you see its thumbnail, too (facing page, left).

  To open a note, tap its name. To delete a note, swipe across its name in the list, right to left, and then confirm by tapping 🗑.

> **NOTE:** On iPhone Plus models, rotating the phone produces a whole new two-column layout. The left column shows your table of contents (first line of every note); the right column shows the selected note itself.

- **Pinned notes.** Ordinarily, your notes appear chronologically, most recent at the top. But in **Settings→Notes**, you can specify that they be sorted by **Date Changed** or **Title** instead.

  But you may have a couple of notes—things you refer to a lot—that you want to appear at the top all the time. Passwords, credit card numbers, or frequent-flyer numbers, for example.

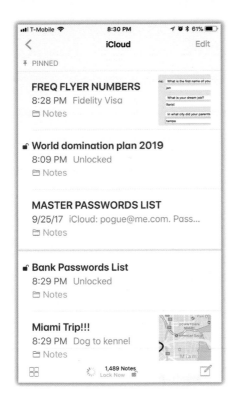

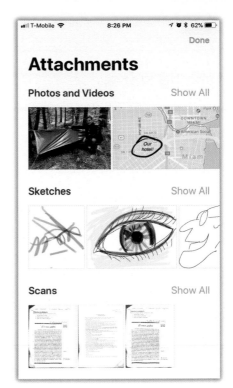

That's why, in iOS 11, you can now **pin** an individual note to the top of the list, where it won't move. To do that, swipe across its name in the list, left to right, and then confirm by tapping the ✿ button.

- **A search box.** Tug down on the list to bring the search box into view. Tap it to open the keyboard. You can now search all your notes instantly—not just their titles, but also the text inside them.

NOTE: Don't worry about your locked notes. iOS can search their titles, but not their contents—even if the notes are currently **unlocked**.

- ⊞. This is the Attachments Browser. It brings up a tidy display of every photo, sketch, website, audio recording, and document that's ever been inserted into any of your notes. All in one place (above, right).

  The beauty is that you don't have to remember what you called a note; just tap one of these items to open it. (At that point, you can tap **Show in Note** to open the note that contains it.)

> **NOTE:** Attachments in locked notes (whether or not they are locked right now) don't show up here.

Syncing Notes

Notes can synchronize with all kinds of other Apple gear—other iPhones, iPads, iPod Touches, and Macs—so the same notes are waiting for you everywhere you look. Just make sure Notes is turned on in **Settings→[your name]→iCloud** on each phone or tablet, and in **System Preferences→iCloud** on your Mac. The rest is automatic—and awesome.

Notes Accounts

Your notes can also sync wirelessly with the Notes modules on Google, Yahoo, AOL, Exchange, or another IMAP email account. To set this up, open **Settings→Accounts & Passwords**. Tap the account you want (iCloud, Gmail, AOL, or whatever); turn the Notes switch **On**.

Now your notes are synced nearly instantly, wirelessly, both directions.

> **NOTE:** One catch: Notes that you create at *gmail.com*, *aol.com*, or *yahoo.com* don't wind up on the phone. Those accounts sync wirelessly in one direction only: *from* the iPhone to the website, where the notes arrive in a Notes folder. (There's no problem, however, if you get your AOL or Gmail mail in an email program like Outlook, Entourage, or Apple Mail. Then it's two-way syncing as usual.)

At this point, a ‹ bracket appears at the top-left corner of the table of contents screen. Tap it to see your note sets from various accounts.

If you've created Notes *folders* on your Mac (Mountain Lion or later), then you see those folders here, too.

> **TIP:** In **Settings→Notes**, you can specify which of your different Notes accounts you want to be the *main* one—the one that new notes fall into if you haven't specified otherwise.

All of this makes life a little more complex, of course. For example, when you create a note, you have to worry about which account it's about to go into. To do that, be sure to specify an account name (and a folder within it, if necessary) *before* you create the new note.

> **TIP:** In **Settings→Notes**, you can turn on the **"On My Phone" Account**. Any notes you add to this "folder" are super-private. They don't get synced or sent online, ever.

Podcasts

A podcast is a "radio" show that's distributed online. Lots of podcasts begin life as *actual* radio and TV shows; most of NPR's shows are available as podcasts, for example, so that you can listen to them whenever and wherever you like.

But thousands more are recorded just for downloading. They range from recordings made by professionals in studios to amateurs talking into their phones. Some have thousands of listeners; some have only a handful. One thing's for sure: There's a podcast out there that precisely matches whatever weird, narrow interests *you* have.

The Podcasts app helps you find, subscribe to, organize, and listen to podcasts. It's designed just like Apple's online stores for apps, music, movies, and so on. Tap **Browse** to see recommended podcasts and **Top Charts** to see what the rest of the world is listening to these days (below, right). Or use **Search** to look for something specific.

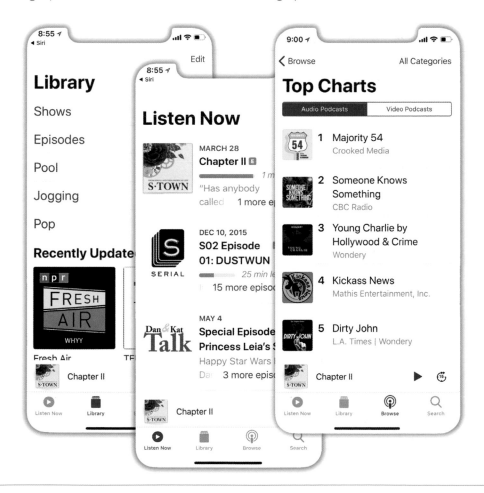

There are video podcasts, too, although they're much less common. The most popular are clips from network or cable TV shows, but there are plenty of quirky, offbeat, funny video podcasts that will never be seen except on pocket screens.

In any case, once you've drilled down to a particular episode that seems worthy, you can listen to it in either of two ways:

- **Stream it.** Tap **Play** to play it directly from the Internet. It's never stored on your iPhone and doesn't take up any space, but it does require an Internet connection. Generally no good for plane rides.

- **Download it.** If you tap ⬇ instead, you download it to your phone. It takes up space there (and podcasts can be big)—but you can play it back anytime, anywhere. And, of course, you can delete it when you're done.

Subscribing

Most podcasts are series. Their creators crank them out every week or whatever. If you find one you love, subscribe to it, so that your phone downloads each new episode automatically. Just tap **Subscribe** on its details page.

The episodes wind up on the **Library** screen (previous page, left), under **Shows**. Tap a podcast's icon to open the My Episodes screen, where you can find listings for further episodes, controls for deleting an episode or adding them to the playback queue, and sharing links to this podcast by Messages, Mail, Twitter, Facebook, and so on).

Settings

There's a lot to control when it comes to podcasts. Do you want new episodes downloaded automatically? Do you want them auto-deleted when you're finished?

You make these choices in **Settings→Podcasts**. Those are the global setting for podcasts.

But you can also override them for *individual* shows. On any podcast's details screen, tap ⬤⬤⬤ and then Settings to see those options, and many more. You can limit how many episodes of this show are stored on your phone; specify the playback order—oldest first or newest first; and much more.

Listening

The Podcasts app offers two ways to dive in. The **Listen Now** tab shows you the *next* episode of each podcast series—the one you're up to. The

Library tab offers icons for each podcast, so that you can drill down to a particular episode. Tap the playback strip at the bottom to reveal all the usual audio-playback controls (page 250)—with the handy addition of a button to toggle the talking speed (½x, 1x, 1½x, or 2x regular speed).

TIP: There are 15-second skip-forward and skip-backward buttons here, too. Handy!

If you press the side button to turn off the screen, the podcast contin-ues playing. And even if the phone is locked, you can open the Control Center (page 49) to access the playback controls.

TIP: Don't forget to use Siri! You can say things like "Play 'Fresh Air' podcast," "Play my latest podcasts," "Play my podcast" (to resume what you were listening to last), "Play latest TED podcast," and so on.

Reminders

Reminders not only records your life's little tasks, but it also reminds you about them at the right time or right place. For example, it can remind you to water the plants as soon as you get home.

Thanks to iCloud, your reminders sync across all your gadgets. Create or check off a task on your iPhone, and you'll also find it created or checked off on your iPad, iPod Touch, Mac, PC, and so on.

TIP: Reminders sync wirelessly with anything your iCloud account knows about: Calendar or BusyCal on your Mac, Outlook on the PC, and so on.

Siri and Reminders are a match made in heaven. "Remind me to file the Jenkins report when I get to work." "Remind me to set the TiVo for tonight at 8." "Remind me about Timmy's soccer game a week from Saturday." "When I get home, remind me to take a shower."

The List of Lists

When you open Reminders, it's clear that you can create **more than one** to-do list, each with its own name: a groceries list, kids' chores, a running tally of expenses, and so on. It's a great way to log what you eat if you're on a diet, or to keep a list of movies people recommend.

They show up as file-folder tabs; tap one to open the to-do list within.

If you have an Exchange account, one of your lists can be synced to your corporate Tasks list. It doesn't offer all the features of the other lists in Reminders, but at least it's kept tidy and separate.

> **TIP:** You can use Siri to add things to individual lists by name. You can say, for example, "Add avocados to my Groceries list." "Add *Titanic 2* to my Movies list."
>
> Siri can also **find** these reminders, saving you a lot of navigation. You can say, "Find my reminder about dosage instructions," for example.

Once you've created some lists, you can easily switch among them. Just tap an open list's name to collapse it, returning to the list of lists. At that point you can tap the title of a different list to open it.

> **TIP:** When you're viewing the list of lists, you can rearrange them by dragging their title bars up or down.

To create a new list, begin at the list of lists (facing page, left). Tap + at the top right. The app asks if you're trying to create a new **Reminder** (that is, one To Do item) or a new **List**; tap **List**.

If you have multiple accounts that offer reminders, you're asked to specify which one will receive the new list at this point, too.

Now your jobs begin:

1. **Enter a name for the list.** When you tap the light-gray letters **New List**, the keyboard appears to help you out.

2. **Tap a colored dot.** This will be the color of the list's title font and also of the "checked-off" circles once the list is under way.

3. **Tap Done.** Now you can tap the first blank line and enter the first item in the list.

> **NOTE:** After that first line, you can't create new items in the list by tapping the blank line below the existing items. As you type, tapping the Return key is the only way to move to the next line. (Tap **Done** when you're finished adding to the list.)

To delete a list, tap **Edit** and then tap **Delete List**.

Later you can assign a task to a different list by tapping **List** on its Details screen.

To return to the list of lists, tap the current list's name. Or tap the bottom edge of the screen. Or swipe down from the top of it.

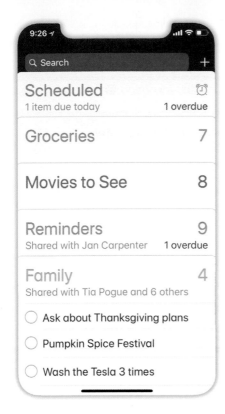
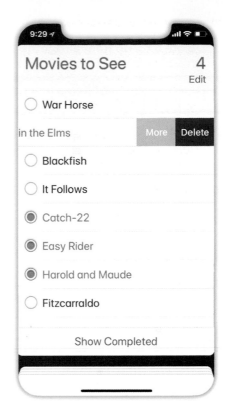

The Scheduled List

If you really do wind up using Reminders as a to-do list, you might be gratified to discover that the app also offers an automatically generated Scheduled list: a consolidated list of every item, from all your lists, to which you've given a *deadline*. It's always the topmost tab, marked by an alarm-clock icon.

Recording a Reminder

Once you've opened a list, here's how you record a new task the manual way: Tap the blank line beneath your existing reminders. Type your reminder (or dictate it). Tap the ⓘ to set up the details, described next; tap **Done** when you're finished.

As you go through life completing tasks, tap the circle next to each one. A checked-off to-do remains in place until the next time you visit its list. At that point, it disappears. It's moved into a separate list called Completed.

But when you want to take pride in how much you've accomplished, you can tap **Show Completed** to bring your checked-off tasks back into view.

Other stuff you can do:

- **Delete a to-do item altogether, as though it never existed.** Swipe leftward across its name; tap **Delete** to confirm (previous page, right).

- **Delete a bunch of items in a row.** Tap **Edit**. Tap each ⊖ icon, and then tap **Delete** to confirm.

- **Rearrange a list so the items appear in a different order.** Tap **Edit**, and then drag the ≡ handle up or down.

The Details Screen

If you tap ⓘ next to an item's name, you arrive at the Details screen (below, left). Here you can set up a reminder that will pop up at a certain time or place, create an auto-repeating schedule, file this item into a different to-do list with its own name, add notes to this item, or delete it.

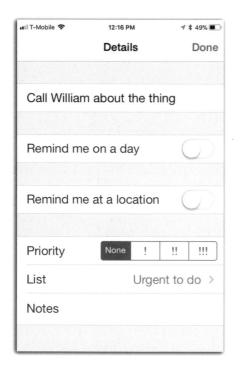
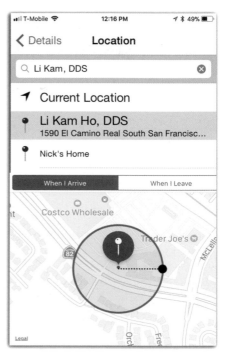

Here are your options, one by one:

- **Remind me on a day.** Here you can set up the phone to chime at a certain date and time. Turn on the switch to see two new lines: **Alarm** and **Repeat**. Tap Alarm to bring up the "time wheel" for setting the deadline.

Tap **Repeat** if you want this reminder to appear every day, week, two weeks, month, or year—great for reminding you about things that recur, like quarterly tax payments, haircuts, and anniversaries.

- **Remind me at a location.** If you turn on this amazing feature, then the phone will use its GPS to remind you of this item when you *arrive* at a certain place or *leave* a certain place. When you tap the **Location** line, you'll see that the phone offers "Current Location"—wherever you are at the moment. That's handy if, for example, you're dropping off your dry cleaning and want to remember to pick it up the next time you're driving by.

  But you can also choose **Home** or **Work** (your home or work addresses, as you've set them up in Contacts). Or you can use the search box at the top, either to type or dictate a street address, or to search your own Contacts list.

NOTE: If you use Bluetooth to pair your phone to your car, you have a couple of other helpful choices: **Getting in the car** (to get a reminder when the iPhone connects to your car) and **Getting out of the car** (to get one when it disconnects).

Once you've specified an address, the Location screen shows a map (facing page, right). The diameter of the blue circle shows the area where your presence will trigger the appearance of the reminder on your screen.

TIP: You can adjust the size of this "geofence" by dragging the black handle to adjust the circle. In effect, you're telling the iPhone how close you have to be to the specified address for the reminder to pop up. You can adjust the circle's radius anywhere from 328 feet ("Remind me when I'm in that store") to 1,500 miles ("Remind me when I'm in that country").

The final step here is to tap either **When I Leave** or **When I Arrive**.

Later, the phone will remind you at the appointed time or as you approach (or leave) the address, which is fairly mind-blowing the first few times it happens.

NOTE: If you set up *both* a time reminder *and* a location reminder, then your iPhone uses whichever event happens first.

- **Priority.** Tap to specify whether this item has low, medium, or high priority—or **None**. In some of the calendar programs that sync with Reminders, you can sort your task list by priority.

- **List.** Tap to assign this to-do to a different reminder list, if necessary.

- **Notes.** Here's a handy box where you can record freehand notes about this item: an address, a phone number, details of any kind.

To exit the Details screen, tap **Done**.

"Remind Me About This"

Here's a reminder about a fantastic Reminders feature.

When you're looking at something in one of Apple's apps, you can tell Siri, "Remind me about this later." That might be a text message in Messages, a web page in Safari, an email in Mail, a document in Pages, or whatever. (This command works in Calendar, Clock, Contacts, iBooks, Health, Mail, Maps, Messages, Notes, Numbers, Pages, Phone, Podcasts, Reminders, and Safari. Software companies can upgrade their apps to work with "Remind me about this," too.)

Instantly, Siri creates a new item on your main Reminders list—named for the precise message, location, web page, document, or thing you were looking at—complete with the icon of the app you were using.

Later, you can tap that icon to open the original app—to the exact spot you were at when you issued the command.

You don't have to be as vague as "later," either. You can also say things like "Remind me about this tomorrow night at 7" or "Remind me about this when I get home."

Put it all together, and you've got an amazingly effective system for bookmarking your life. Maybe this trick will, once and for all, end the practice of people emailing stuff to themselves, just so they'll remember it.

Stocks

This one's for you, big-time day trader. The Stocks app tracks the rise and fall of the stocks in your portfolio by downloading the very latest stock prices.

(All right, maybe not the *very* latest. The price info may be delayed as much as 20 minutes, which is typical of free stock-info services.)

When you first fire it up, Stocks shows you a handful of sample high-tech stocks—or, rather, their abbreviations. (They stand for the Dow Jones Industrial Average, the NASDAQ Composite Index, the S&P 500 Index, Apple, Google, and Yahoo.)

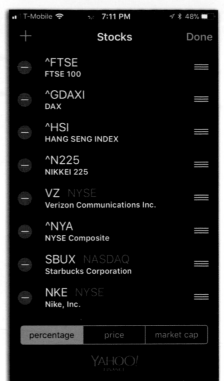

Next to each, you see its current share price, and next to *that*, you see how much that price has gone up or down today. As a handy visual gauge to how elated or depressed you should be, this final number appears on a **green** background if it's gone up, or a **red** one if it's gone down. Tap this number to cycle the display from a percentage to a dollar amount to current market capitalization ("120.3B," meaning $120.3 billion in total corporate value).

When you tap a stock, the bottom part of the screen shows some handy data. Swipe horizontally to cycle among three different displays:

- **A table of statistics.** A capsule summary of today's price and volume statistics for this stock.

- **A graph of the stock's price.** It starts out showing you the graph of the current year. But by tapping the headings above the chart, you can zoom in or out from one day (**1D**) to three months (**3M**) to two years (**2Y**).

- **A table of relevant headlines,** courtesy of Yahoo Finance. Tap a headline to read the article—or tap and hold to add it, or all the articles, to your Safari Reading List (page 473).

Landscape View

If you turn the iPhone sideways, you get a much bigger, more detailed, widescreen graph of the stock in question. (Flick horizontally to view the previous or next stock.)

TIP: On a Plus model, there's room for *both* your list of stocks *and* the graph of the one you've tapped, all on the same screen.

Better yet, you can pinch with two fingers or two thumbs to isolate a certain time period; a pop-up label shows you how much of a bath you took (or how much of a windfall you received) during the interval you highlighted. Cool!

Customizing Your Portfolio

It's fairly unlikely that *your* stock portfolio contains just Apple, Google, and Yahoo. Fortunately, you can customize the list of stocks to reflect the companies you *do* own (or want to track).

To edit the list, tap ☰ in the lower-right corner. You arrive at the editing screen (previous page, right), where these choices await:

- **Delete a stock** by tapping the ⊖ button and then the **Delete** confirmation button.

- **Rearrange the list** by dragging the grip strips on the right side.

- **Add a stock** by tapping + in the top-left corner; the Add Stock screen and the keyboard appear.

You're not expected to know every stock-symbol abbreviation. Type in the company's *name*, and then tap **Search**. The iPhone shows you, above the keyboard, a scrolling list of companies with matching names. Tap the one you want to track. You return to the stocks-list editing screen.

- **Choose Percentage, Price, or Market Cap.** By tapping the buttons at the bottom, you can specify how you want to see the changes in stock prices in the far-right column: as percentages ("+0.65%"), as dollar figures ("+2.23") or as market cap. (Here you're simply choosing which number starts out appearing on the main stock screen. As noted earlier, you can easily cycle among these three stats by tapping them.)

When you're finished setting up your stock list, tap **Done**.

Tips

Hey, check it out—Apple's getting into the how-to game!

This app is designed to show you tips and tricks for getting the most from your iPhone. Each Collection (**Fantastic Photos**, **Everyday Essentials**, and so on) screen offers a set of tips—a paragraph of text apiece—explaining one of iOS's marvels. Swipe leftward to see the next tip, and the next, and the next.

It's not exactly, you know, a handsome, printed book. But it's something.

TV

This app lets you find and play videos from two sources: the iTunes store, and individual video apps. It's described on page 268.

Voice Memos

This audio app is ideal for recording lectures, musical performances, notes to self, and cute child utterances. You'll probably be very surprised at how good the microphone is, even from a distance.

The best part: When you sync your iPhone with iTunes on your Mac or PC, all your voice recordings get copied back to the computer automatically. You'll find them in the iTunes folder called Voice Memos.

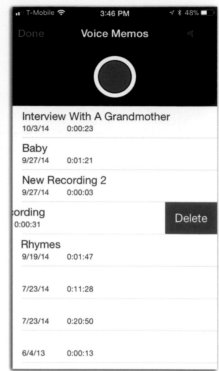

Tap ⬤ (or click your earbud clicker) to start recording. A little ding signals the start (and stop) of the session—unless you've turned the phone's volume all the way down (you sneak!).

You get to watch the actual sound waves as the recording proceeds (above, left). You can pause at any time by pressing the Stop button (⦿)—and then resume the same recording with another tap on the ⬤.

TIP: The built-in mike records in mono. But you can record in stereo if you connect a stereo mike (to the headphone jack or charging jack).

You can also switch out of the app to do other work. A red banner across the top of the screen (or, on the iPhone X, the left "ear") reminds you that you're still recording. You can even **switch the screen off**; the recording goes on!

You can make **very** long recordings with this thing. Let it run all day, if you like. Even your most long-winded friends can be immortalized.

Tap **Done** when you're sure the recording session is over. You're asked to type a name for the new recording ("Baby's First Words," "Orch Concert," whatever); then you can tap **Save** or, if it wasn't worth saving, **Delete**.

Below the recording controls, you see the list of your recordings (facing page, right). When you tap one, a convenient set of controls appears. (They look a lot like the ones that appear when you tap a voicemail message in the Phone app.)

> **TIP:** If you have an iPhone Plus model, you can turn the screen 90 degrees—and see both the list of recordings **and** the editing screen, in two columns.

Here's what you can do here:

- **[Recording name].** Tap the name to edit or rename it.

- **▶.** Tap to play the recording. You can pause with the **II** button.

> **TIP:** As a recording plays back, you can tap ◀)) at the top of the screen to turn the speaker on or off, so that you don't have to hold the phone up to your ear.

- **Rewind, Fast Forward.** Drag the little vertical line in the scrubber bar to skip backward or forward in the recording. It's a great way to skip over the boring pleasantries.

- **🗑.** Tap to get rid of a recording (you'll be asked to confirm).

- **⬆.** Tap to open the standard Share sheet. It gives you the chance to send your recording to someone else by AirDrop, email, or MMS.

Trimming Your Recording

You might not guess that such a tiny, self-effacing app actually offers some basic editing functions, but it does. Tap a recording and then tap **Edit** to open its Edit screen.

The main thing you'll do here is trim off the beginning or end of your audio clip. That, of course, is where you'll usually find "dead air" or microphone fumbling before the good stuff starts playing. (You can't otherwise edit the sound; for example, you can't copy or paste bits or cut a chunk out of the middle.)

To trim the bookends of your clip, tap the Trim button (). At this point, the beginning and end of the recording are marked by vertical red lines; these are your trim points. Drag them inward to isolate the part of the clip you want to keep. The app thoughtfully magnifies the sound waves whenever you're dragging, to help with precision. Play the sound as necessary to guide you (▶).

Tap **Trim** to lock in your changes. You'll be asked to tap either **Trim Original** (meaning "shorten the original clip permanently") or **Save as New Recording** (meaning "leave the original untouched, and spin out the shortened version as a separate audio file, just in case").

Wallet

This app was originally called Passbook. And it was originally designed to store, in one place, every form of ticket that uses a barcode. For most people, that meant airline boarding passes.

Wallet still does that. And, occasionally, you may find a Wallet-compatible theater or sports-admission pass, loyalty card, coupon, movie ticket, and so on. Beats having a separate app for each one of these.

Wallet holds down a second job, too. It's the key to Apple Pay, the magical "pay by waving your iPhone" feature described on page 542.

> **TIP:** You can rearrange the items in Wallet; just hold still briefly before you start moving your finger up or down. (That order syncs to your other iOS gadgets, for what it's worth.)

What's cool is that Wallet uses both its own clock and GPS to know when the time and place are right. For example, when you arrive at the airport, a notification appears on your Lock screen. Each time you have to show your boarding pass as you work through the stages of airport security, you can wake your phone and swipe across that notification; your boarding-pass barcode appears instantly. You're spared having to

unlock your phone (enter its password), hunt for the airline app, log in, and fiddle your way to the boarding pass.

The hardest part might be finding things to put *into* Wallet. You can visit the App Store and search for "passbook" to find apps that work with Wallet—big airlines, Fandango (movie tickets), Starbucks, Walgreens, Ticketmaster, and Major League Baseball are among the compatible apps. In some, you're supposed to open the app to view the barcode first and put it into Wallet from there. For example, in most airline apps, you call up the boarding-pass screen and then tap **Add**.

Once your barcodes have successfully landed in Wallet, the rest is pure fun. When you arrive at the theater or stadium or airport, the Lock screen displays an alert. Swipe it to open the barcode in Wallet. You can put the entire phone under the ticket-taker's scanner.

Tap the ⓘ button in the corner to read the details—and to delete a ticket after you've used it (tap **Remove Pass**). That details screen also offers a **Show On Lock Screen** on/off switch, in case you *don't* want Wallet to hand you your ticket as you arrive.

Finally, Wallet is one of the two places you can enter your credit card information for Apple Pay on an iPhone 6 or later model, as described on page 542. (Settings is the other.)

Watch

If you own an Apple Watch, you use this little app to set up its settings. (OK, *big* app—there are *90 screens* of settings!)

So why do you have the Watch app on your phone even if you *don't* have an Apple Watch? You'll have to ask someone in Marketing.

If it bugs you, you can get rid of it (page 350).

Weather

This app shows a handy current-conditions display for your city (or any other city). Handy *and* lovely; the weather display is animated. Clouds drift by, rain falls gently. If it's nighttime in the city you're looking up, you might see a beautiful starscape.

The current temperature is shown nice and big; the table below it shows the cloud-versus-sun forecast, as well as the high and low temperatures.

You don't even have to tell the app what weather you want; it uses your location and assumes you want the *local* weather forecast.

There are three places you can tap or swipe:

- **Scroll up** to see a table of stats: humidity, chance of rain, sunrise time, wind speed, "feels like" (chill or heat index), and so on.

- **Swipe horizontally across the hourly forecast** to scroll later in the day.

- **Swipe horizontally anywhere else** to view the weather for other cities (if you've set them up). The tiny dots beneath the display correspond to the cities you've set up—and the white bold one indicates where you are in the sequence.

TIP: The dots are *really* tiny. Don't try to aim for a specific one—it's a lot easier to tap the row of dots on either the right or left side to move backward or forward among the cities.

The first city—the screen at far left—is always the city you're *in right now*. The iPhone uses GPS to figure out where you are.

The City List

It's easy to get the weather for other cities—great if you're going to be traveling, or if you're wondering how life is for distant relations.

When you tap ≣ at the lower-right corner (or pinch with two fingers), the screen collapses into a list of your preprogrammed cities (below, right).

You can tap one to open its weather screen. You can delete one by swiping leftward across it (and then tapping **Delete**). You can drag them up or down into a new order (leave your finger down for about a second before each time you drag). You can switch between Celsius and Fahrenheit by tapping the °**C** / °**F** button.

Or you can scroll to the bottom (if necessary) and tap ⊕ to enter a new city. Here you're asked to type a city, a zip code, or an airport abbreviation (like JFK for New York's John F. Kennedy airport). You can specify any reasonably sized city on earth.

When you tap **Search**, you're shown a list of matching cities; tap the one you want to track. When you return to the configuration screen, you can also specify whether you prefer degrees Celsius or Fahrenheit. Tap **Done**.

There's nothing else to tap here except the Weather Channel icon at the bottom. It fires up the Safari browser, which loads itself with an information page about that city from *weather.com*.

If you've added more than one city to the list, by the way, just flick your finger right or left to flip through the weather screens for the cities.

More Standard Apps

This book describes every app that comes on every iPhone. But Apple has another suite of useful programs for you. And they're free.

> **NOTE:** If you have an iPhone model with 64 or more gigabytes of storage, then most of these apps come already installed.

To find them, search the App Store app for these goodies: **Pages** is, believe it or not, a word-processing/page-layout program. **Numbers** is Apple's spreadsheet program. **Keynote** is Apple's version of PowerPoint. It lets you make slideshow presentations from your iPhone. **iMovie** is, yes, a video-editing program on your cellphone, with all the basics: rearranging clips; adding music, crossfades, and credits. **GarageBand** is a pocket music studio. **Find My Friends** lets you see where your friends and family members are on a map (with their permission, of course). **Find My iPhone** is useful when you want to find *other* missing Apple gadgets (Macs, iPads, iPod Touches, iPhones).

> **NOTE:** And where, you may ask, is the iTunes U app?
>
> iTunes U is a catalog of 600,000 free courses by professors at colleges, museums, and libraries all over the world; the dearly departed app let you browse the catalog, and watch and read the course materials.
>
> Those courses are still available—but they've been merged into the Podcasts app described earlier in this chapter. You find them by searching for the name of the institution or collection.

PART THREE

The iPhone Online

Chapter 12
Getting Online

Chapter 13
Safari

Chapter 14
Email

12

Getting Online

The name "iPhone" grows less appropriate every year, as making *phone calls* fades in importance. Today, Americans send texts five times more often than they make phone calls. Among teenagers, 92 percent *never* make calls with their smartphones.

What do they do with them, then? Go online—and use apps that go online.

The iPhone can get onto the Internet using either of two kinds of wireless networks: *cellular* or *Wi-Fi*. Which kind you're on makes a huge difference to your iPhone experience.

Cellular Networks

Once you've accepted the miracle that a cellphone can transmit your voice wirelessly, it's not much of a stretch to realize that it can also transmit your data. Cellphone carriers (Verizon, AT&T, and so on) maintain separate networks for voice and Internet data—and they spend billions of dollars trying to make those networks faster. Over the years, they've come up with data networks like these:

- **Old, slow cellular network.** The earliest, slowest cellular Internet connections were called things like EDGE (AT&T) or 1xRTT (Verizon and Sprint). The good part is that these networks are almost everywhere, so your iPhone can get online almost anywhere you can make a phone call. You'll know when you're on one of these networks because your status bar bears a symbol like **E** or **O**.

  The bad news is that it's slow. *Dog* slow—dial-up slow.

  You can't be on a phone call while you're online using EDGE or 1xRTT, either.

- **3G cellular networks.** 3G stands for "third generation." (The ancient analog cellphones were the first generation; EDGE-type networks were the second.) Geeks refer to the 3G network standard by its official name: HSDPA, for High-Speed Downlink Packet Access.

  Web pages that take two minutes to appear using EDGE or 1xRTT show up in about 20 seconds on 3G. Voice calls sound better, too, even when the signal strength is very low, since the iPhone's 3G radio can communicate with multiple towers at once.

  Oh, and on AT&T and T-Mobile, you can talk on the phone and use the Internet simultaneously, which can be very handy indeed.

- **4G networks.** AT&T enhanced HSDPA, making it faster using a technology called HSPA+ (High-Speed Packet Access), and now calls it 4G. (You'll know when you're on one; your status bar says **4G**.) But nobody else recognizes HSPA+ as real 4G, which is why AT&T feels justified in advertising "the nation's largest 4G network." The other carriers aren't even measuring that network type.

- **4G LTE networks.** Now *this* is 4G.

  An LTE network (Long-Term Evolution) gives you amazing speeds—in some cases, faster than your broadband Internet at home. When your status bar says **LTE**, it's *fantastic*.

  But LTE is not all sunshine and bunnies; it has two huge downsides.

  First: coverage. LTE coverage is available in hundreds of U.S. cities, which is a good start. But that still leaves most of the country, including huge chunks of several entire states, without any 4G coverage at all (hi there, Montana!). Whenever you're outside the high-speed areas, your iPhone falls back to the slower speeds.

  The second big problem with LTE is that, to receive its signal, a phone's circuitry uses a lot of power. That's why the latest iPhones are bigger than their predecessors; they need beefier batteries.

A Word About VoLTE

If you have an iPhone 6 or later model, the dawn of LTE cellphone networks brings another benefit: You can use Voice over LTE, or *VoLTE* ("volty"). That's a delightful new cellular feature that promises amazing voice quality—sounds more like FM radio than cellphone—*and* simultaneous calling/Internetting, even on Verizon. (Behind the scenes, it sends your voice over the carrier's *Internet* network instead of the voice network. That's why it's called "Voice over LTE.")

To make this work, every link in the chain has to be compatible with VoLTE: your phone and your cellphone network, **and** (for that great sound quality) the phone and network of the person you're **calling**.

All four big U.S. carriers offer VoLTE, but you generally get the high-quality sound only when you're calling someone on the **same** cellphone carrier—not if, for example, you have Verizon and the other guy has T-Mobile. (Cross-carrier calling is supposed to be coming soon.)

Wi-Fi Hotspots

Wi-Fi, known to geeks as 802.11, is wireless networking, the same technology that gets laptops online at high speed in any Wi-Fi **hotspot**.

Hotspots are everywhere these days: in homes, offices, coffee shops, hotels, airports, and thousands of other places. When you're in a Wi-Fi hotspot, your iPhone usually gets a fast connection to the Internet, as though it's connected to a cable modem or DSL. And when you're online this way, you can make phone calls and surf the Internet simultaneously. And why not? Your iPhone's Wi-Fi and cellular antennas are independent.

(Over cellular connections, only the AT&T and T-Mobile iPhones let you talk and get online simultaneously. Verizon and Sprint can do that only when you're on a VoLTE call, as described previously.)

The iPhone always looks for a Wi-Fi connection first. It considers connecting to a cellular network only if there's no Wi-Fi. You'll always know which kind of network you're on, thanks to the icons on the status bar: You'll see either 📶 for Wi-Fi, or one of the cellular icons (**E**, °, **3G**, **4G**, or **LTE**).

Or "No service" if there's nothing available at all.

iPHONE X:	Instead of "No Service," you see five square periods (▪▪▪▪▪) where the signal bars would be.

In terms of speed, LTE and Wi-Fi are **awesome**. EDGE/1xRTT and even 3G—not so much.

Sequence of Connections

The iPhone isn't online all the time. To save battery power, it opens the connection only on demand: when you check email, request a web page, and so on. At that point, the iPhone tries to get online following this sequence:

- **First, it sniffs around for a Wi-Fi network** that you've used before. If it finds one, it connects quietly and automatically. You're not asked for permission, a password, or anything else.

- **If the iPhone can't find a previous hotspot** but it detects a *new* hotspot, a message appears (below, left). It displays any new hotspots' names; tap the one you want. (If you see a 🔒 icon, then that hotspot is password-protected.)

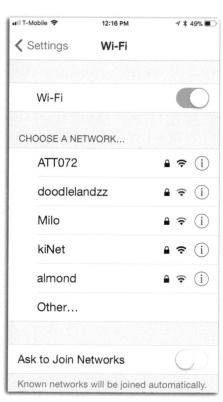

- **If the iPhone can't find any Wi-Fi hotspots to join,** or if you don't join any, it connects to the cellular network, like 3G or LTE.

Silencing the "Want to Join?" Messages

Sometimes, you might be bombarded by those "Select a Wireless Network" messages at a time when you have no need to be online. You might want the iPhone to stop bugging you—to *stop* offering Wi-Fi hotspots. In that situation, from the Home screen, tap **Settings→Wi-Fi** (or tell Siri, "Open Wi-Fi settings"), and then turn off **Ask to Join Networks**.

When this option is off, the iPhone never interrupts you by dropping the name of every new network at your feet. In this case, to get onto a new network, you have to visit the aforementioned settings screen and select it.

The List of Hotspots

At some street corners in big cities, Wi-Fi signals bleeding out of apartment buildings sometimes give you a choice of 20 or 30 hotspots to join. But whenever the iPhone invites you to join a hotspot, it suggests only a couple of them: the ones with the strongest signal and, if possible, no password requirement.

But you might sometimes want to see the complete list of available hotspots—maybe because the iPhone-suggested hotspot is flaky. To see the full list, from the Home screen, open **Settings→Wi-Fi**. Tap the one you want to join, as shown on the facing page at right.

TIP: Tap ⓘ next to a hotspot's name to view an info sheet for techies. It shows your IP address, subnet mask, router address, and other delicious stats. Even mere mortals, however, will sometimes enjoy the **Forget This Network** button. It removes this hotspot from the list, which is handy if you've moved away and don't need to be reminded of the high speed that was once yours.

Commercial Hotspots

Tapping the name of the hotspot you want to join is generally all you have to do—if it's a *home* Wi-Fi network. Unfortunately, joining a *commercial* Wi-Fi hotspot—one that requires a credit card number (in a hotel

room or an airport, for example)—requires more than just connecting to it. You also have to *sign into* it, exactly as you'd do if you were using a laptop.

In general, the iPhone prompts you to do that automatically. A login screen pops up on its own, interrupting whatever else you're doing; that's where you supply your credit card information or (if you have a membership to this Wi-Fi chain, like Boingo or T-Mobile) your name and password. Tap **Submit** or **Proceed** and enjoy your surfing.

Mercifully, the iPhone memorizes your password. The next time you use this hotspot, you won't have to enter it again.

Airplane Mode and Wi-Fi Off Mode

When battery power is precious, you can turn off all three of the iPhone's network connections in one fell swoop. You can also turn off Wi-Fi alone.

- **To turn all radios off.** In airplane mode, you turn off *all* wireless circuitry: Bluetooth, Wi-Fi, and cellular. Now you can't make calls or get onto the Internet. You're saving an amazing amount of power, however, and also complying with regulations that ban cellphones in flight.

  The short way: Open the Control Center (page 49); tap ✈ so it turns orange. (The long way: Open **Settings**; turn on **Airplane Mode**.)

- **To turn Wi-Fi on or off.** Open the Control Center; tap 📶. (When it's blue, it's on.) You can also switch it in **Settings→Wi-Fi**.

TIP: Once you've turned on airplane mode, you can turn **Wi-Fi** back *on* again. Why? To use Wi-Fi on a flight. This is how you turn Wi-Fi *on*, but your cellular circuitry *off*.

Conversely, you sometimes might want to do the opposite: turn *off* Wi-Fi, but leave cellular *on*. Why? Because, sometimes, the iPhone bizarrely won't get online at all. It's struggling to use a Wi-Fi network that, for one reason or another, isn't connecting to the Internet. By turning Wi-Fi off, you force the iPhone to use its cellular connection—which may be slower, but at least it works!

In airplane mode, anything that requires voice or Internet access—text messages, web, email, and so on—triggers a message: "Turn Off Airplane Mode or Use Wi-Fi to Access Data." Tap either **OK** (to back out of your decision) or **Settings** (to turn off airplane mode and get online).

You can, however, enjoy all the other iPhone features: Music, Camera, and so on. You can also work with stuff you've *already* downloaded to the phone, like email, voicemail messages, and web pages you've saved in the Reading List.

Personal Hotspot (Tethering)

Tethering means using your iPhone as an Internet antenna, so that your laptops, iPads, game consoles, and other Internet-connectables can get online. (The other gadgets can connect to the phone over a Wi-Fi connection, a Bluetooth connection, or a USB cable.) In fact, several laptops and other gadgets can all share the iPhone's connection simultaneously. Your phone becomes a personal cellular router.

That's incredibly convenient, and Apple's execution is especially nice. For example, the hotspot shuts itself off 90 seconds after the last laptop disconnects. That's hugely important, because a personal hotspot is a merciless battery drain.

The hotspot feature may be included with your data plan (T-Mobile), or it may cost something like $20 a month extra, which buys only 2 gigabytes of data (Verizon). Think email, not YouTube.

To get this feature, you have to sign up for it by calling your cellular company or visiting its website.

 TIP: If you have a Mac running OS X Yosemite or later, you're in for a real treat: a much more streamlined way to set up Personal Hotspot called *Instant* Hotspot. Skip the instructions below and jump immediately to page 559.

Turning On the Hotspot

On the phone, open **Settings→Cellular→Set Up Personal Hotspot** (or tell Siri, "Open cellular settings").

The Personal Hotspot screen contains details on connecting other computers. It also has the master on/off switch. Turn Personal Hotspot **On.**

(If you see a button that says **Set Up Personal Hotspot**, it means you haven't yet added the monthly tethering fee to your cellular plan. Contact your wireless carrier to get that change made to your account.)

You have to use a password for your personal hotspot; it's to ensure that people sitting nearby can't surf using your connection and run up your cell bill. The software proposes a password, but you can edit it and make up one of your own. (It has to be at least eight characters long and contain letters, numbers, and punctuation. Don't worry—your laptop or other Wi-Fi gadget can memorize it for you.)

Your laptops and other gadgets can connect to the Internet using any of three connections to the iPhone: Wi-Fi, Bluetooth, or a USB cable. If either Wi-Fi or Bluetooth are turned off, then a message appears to let you know—and offers to turn them on for you. To save battery power, turn on only what you need.

Connecting via Wi-Fi

After about 30 seconds, the iPhone shows up on your laptop or other gadget as though it were a Wi-Fi network. Just choose the iPhone's name from your computer's Wi-Fi hotspot menu (on the Mac, it's the 📶

menu). Enter the password, and bam—your laptop is now online, using the iPhone as an antenna. On the Mac or an iPad, the 🛜 changes to look like this: ♋.

You can leave the iPhone in your pocket or purse while connected. Your laptop can now use email, the web, chat programs—anything it could do in a real Wi-Fi hotspot (just a little slower).

Connecting via Bluetooth

There's no compelling reason to use Bluetooth instead of Wi-Fi, especially since Bluetooth slows your Internet connection. But if you're interested, see the free downloadable PDF appendix "Bluetooth Tethering" on this book's "Missing CD" page at *www.missingmanuals.com*.

Connecting via USB Cable

If you can connect your laptop to your iPhone using the white charging cable, you should. Tethering eats up a lot of the phone's battery power, so keeping it plugged into the laptop means you won't wind up with a dead phone when you're finished surfing.

Once You're Connected

On the iPhone, a blue bar appears at the top of the screen to make you aware that the laptop is connected (facing page, right); in fact, it shows how many laptops or other gadgets are connected at the moment, via any of the three connection methods. You can tap that bar to open the Personal Hotspot screen in Settings.

Most carriers won't let more than five people connect through a single iPhone.

Turning Off Personal Hotspot

Personal Hotspot is a battery hog. It'll cut your iPhone's battery longevity in half. That's why, if no laptops are connected for 90 seconds, the iPhone turns the hotspot off automatically.

You can also turn off the hotspot manually, just the way you'd expect: In Settings→Personal Hotspot, tap Off.

Turning Personal Hotspot Back On

To fire Personal Hotspot back up again, open Settings and tap Personal Hotspot. That's it—just visit the Personal Hotspot screen to make the iPhone resume broadcasting its Wi-Fi or Bluetooth network to your laptops and other gadgets.

Share Your Wi-Fi Password

It happens in homes and apartments all over the world. A friend comes over and asks: "Hey, what's your Wi-Fi password?"

And then you crawl behind the water heater to find the password sticker on the router. Or the evening grinds to a halt as you try to dictate it: "Capital P, lowercase u, capital M, number 1...."

For the first time, iOS 11 eases that everyday pain point. Now, you can allow a buddy to hop onto your network without having to spell out your password—or even reveal it! It works like this:

1. **The buddy** opens **Settings→Wi-Fi** and taps your network name. He's staring at the box where he's supposed to enter the password. He brings his phone near your iPhone (or your iPad, or your Mac).

   NOTE: This trick requires that you both have Bluetooth and Wi-Fi turned on, and that your buddy is someone in your Contacts.

2. **You** see a Wi-Fi Password screen. You tap **Share Password**.

3. **Your buddy** marvels as the password appears in the Password box before his eyes.

   He can tap **Join** and dive right in, ready to enjoy the Internet instead of paying attention to you.

13

Safari

The iPhone's web browser is Safari, a lite version of the same one that comes on the Mac. It's fast, simple to use, and very pretty. On the web pages you visit, you see the real deal—the actual fonts, graphics, and layouts—not the stripped-down mini-web on cellphones of years gone by.

Using Safari on the iPhone is still not quite as good as surfing the web on, you know, a laptop. But it's getting closer.

Safari Tour

Safari has most of the features of a desktop web browser: bookmarks, autocomplete (for web addresses), scrolling shortcuts, cookies, a pop-up ad blocker, password memorization, and so on. (It's missing niceties like streaming music, Java, Flash, and other plug-ins.)

Now, don't be freaked out: *The main screen elements disappear* shortly after you start reading a page. That's supposed to give you more screen space to do your surfing. To bring them back, scroll to the top, scroll to the bottom, or just scroll up a little. At that point, you see the controls again. Here they are, as they appear from the top left:

- **Reader view (≡).** In this delightful view, all the ads, boxes, banners, and other junk disappear. Only text and pictures remain, for your sanity-in-reading pleasure. See page 482.

- **Address/search bar.** A single, unified box serves as both the address bar and the search bar at the top of the screen. (That's the trend these days. Desktop-computer browsers like Chrome and Safari on the Mac work that way, too.)

  This box is where you enter the *URL* (web address) for a page you want to visit. ("URL" is short for the even-less-self-explanatory

Uniform Resource Locator.) For example, if you type *amazon.com*, tapping **Go** takes you to that website.

But this is also where you search the web. If you type anything else, like **cashmere sweaters** or just **amazon**, then tapping **Go** gives you the Google search results for that phrase.

- **Stop, Reload (✕, ↻).** Tap ✕ to interrupt the downloading of a web page you've just requested (if you've made a mistake, for instance, or if it's taking too long).

Once a page has finished loading, the ✕ button turns into a ↻ (reload) button. Click it if a page doesn't look or work quite right. Safari re-downloads the web page and reinterprets its text and graphics.

- **Back, Forward (⟨, ⟩).** Tap ⟨ to revisit the page you were just on. Once you've tapped ⟨, you can then tap ⟩ to return to the page you were on *before* you tapped the ⟨ button. You can also *hold down* these buttons to see the complete history list of this tab.

- **Share/Bookmark (⬆).** When you're on an especially useful page, tap this button. It offers every conceivable choice for commemorating or sharing the page. See page 471 for details.

- **View Bookmarks (📖).** This button brings up your list of saved bookmarks—plus your History list, Favorites, Reading List, and links recommended by the people you follow on Twitter. You can read about these elements later in this chapter.

- **Page Juggler (⬜).** Safari can keep multiple web pages open, just like any other browser. Page 479 has the details.

Zooming and Scrolling

When you first open a web page, you get to see the *entire thing*, so you can get the lay of the land. At this point, of course, you're looking at .004-point type, which is too small to read unless you're a microbe. So the next step is to magnify the *part* of the page you want to read.

The iPhone offers three ways to do that:

- **Double-tap.** Safari can recognize different *chunks* of a web page— each block of text, each photo. When you double-tap a chunk, Safari magnifies *just that chunk* to fill the whole screen. It's smart and useful.

  Double-tap again to zoom back out.

- **Rotate the iPhone.** Turn the device 90 degrees in either direction. The iPhone rotates and magnifies the image to fill the wider view. Often, this simple act is enough to make tiny type big enough to read.

- **Do the two-finger spread.** Put two fingers on the glass and slide them apart. The Safari page stretches before your very eyes, growing larger. Then you can pinch to shrink the page back down again. (Most people do several spreads or pinches in a row to achieve the degree of zoom they want.)

Once you've zoomed out to the proper degree, you can then scroll around the page by dragging or flicking with a finger. You don't have to worry about "clicking a link" by accident; if your finger is in motion, Safari ignores the tapping action, even if you happen to land on a link.

Double-tap

Full-Screen Mode

On a phone, the screen is pretty small to begin with; most people would rather dedicate that space to showing more *web*.

So on the iPhone, Safari enters *full-screen mode* the instant you start to *scroll down* a page. In full-screen mode, all the controls and toolbars vanish. Now the *entire* iPhone screen is filled with web goodness. You can bring the controls back in any of these ways:

- Scroll *up* a little bit.

- Return to the top or bottom of a web page.

- Navigate to a different page.

And enjoy Safari's dedication to trying to get out of your way.

TIP: You can jump directly to the address bar, no matter how far down a page you've scrolled, just by tapping the very top edge of the screen (the status bar, or the "ears" of the iPhone X). That "tap the top" trick is timely, too, when a website is designed to *hide* the address bar.

Typing a Web Address

The address/search bar is the strip at the top of the screen where you type in a page's address. And some of the iPhone's greatest tips and shortcuts all have to do with this important navigational tool:

- **Your favorites await.** When you tap in the address bar but haven't yet typed anything, the icons of a few very special, most favorite websites appear (below, top). These are the favorites; see page 466.

- **Don't delete.** There *is* a ⊗ button at the right end of the address bar whose purpose is to erase the current address so you can type another one. (Tap inside the address bar to make it, and the keyboard, appear.) But the ⊗ button is for suckers.

   Instead, whenever the address bar is open for typing, *just type*. Forget that there's already a URL there. The iPhone is smart enough to figure out that you want to *replace* that web address with a new one.

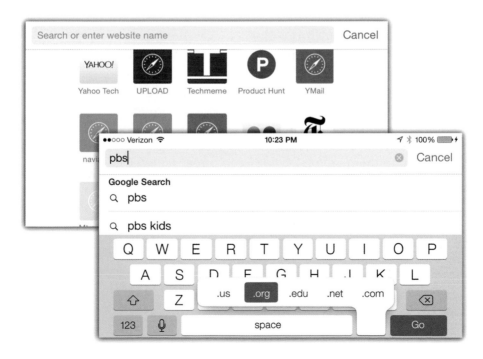

- **Don't type http://www.** You can leave that stuff out; Safari will supply it automatically. Instead of *http://www.cnn.com*, for example, just type *cnn.com* (or tap its name in the suggestions list) and hit **Go**.

- **Type .com, .net, .org, or .edu the easy way.** Safari's canned URL choices can save you four keyboard taps apiece. To see their secret menu, hold your finger down on the ***period key*** on the keyboard (previous page, bottom). Then tap the common suffix you want. (Or, if you want .com, just release your finger without moving it.)

Otherwise, this address bar works just like the one in any other web browser. Tap inside it to make the keyboard appear.

Tap the blue **Go** key when you're finished typing the address. That's your Enter key. (Or tap **Cancel** to hide the keyboard ***without*** "pressing Enter.")

TIP: If you hold your finger on a link for a moment—touching rather than tapping—a handy panel appears. At the top, you see the full web address that link will open. And there are some useful buttons: **Open**, **Open in New Tab**, **Add to Reading List**, **Copy** (meaning "copy the link address"), and **Share**. Oh, and there's also **Cancel**.

The Favorites Icons

You can never close all your Safari windows. The app will never let you get past the final page, always lurking behind the others: the Favorites page (previous page, top).

This is the starting point. It's what you first see when you tap the + button. It's like a page of visual bookmarks.

In fact, if you see a bunch of icons here already, it's because your phone has synced them over from Safari on a Mac; whatever sites are on your bookmarks ***bar*** become icons on this bookmarks ***page***.

You can edit this Favorites page, of course:

- **Rearrange them** as you would Home screen icons. That is, hold your finger down on an icon momentarily and then drag it to a new spot.

- **Remove or rename a favorites icon.** Favorites are just bookmarks. So you can edit, move, or delete them just as you would any bookmark. (Tap to open your Bookmarks screen. Make sure that you're on the ⊓ tab, so that your list of folders is showing. Tap **Favorites**, and then **Edit**. Tap ⊖ for a site you want to delete, and then tap **Delete**.)

TIP: You can create folders ***inside*** the Favorites folder, too. Whenever the Favorites screen appears, you'll see these subfolders listed as further sources of speed-dial websites.

- **Add a Favorites icon.** When you find a page you'd like to add to the Favorites screen, tap ⬆. On the Share sheet, tap **Add Bookmark**. The phone usually proposes putting the new bookmark into the Favorites *folder*, which means that it will show up on the Favorites *screen*. (If it proposes some other folder on the Location line, tap the folder's name and then tap **Favorites**.) Tap **Save**.

> **TIP:** You don't have to use the Favorites folder of bookmarks as the one whose contents appear on the Favorites screen. In **Settings→ Safari→Favorites**, a list of all your Bookmarks folders appears. Whichever one you select there becomes your new Favorites folder, even if its name isn't "Favorites."

Request Desktop Site

In an effort to conserve time and bandwidth (yours and theirs), many websites supply *mobile* versions to your iPhone—smaller, stripped-down sites that transfer faster than (but lack some features of) the full-blown sites. You generally have no control over which version you're sent.

Until now. Suppose you're in Safari, and some site has dished up its mobile version, and you're gnashing your teeth. Hold down the ↻ in the address box; tap **Request Desktop Site**. (The same button appears when you tap ⬆ and scroll the bottom row to the right.) As you've requested, the full-blown desktop version of that site now appears.

Searching in Safari

The address bar is also the search box. Just tap into it and type your search phrase (or speak it, using the 🎤 button).

To save you time and fiddling, Safari instantly produces a menu filled with suggestions that could spare you some typing—things it guesses you might be looking for. If you see the address you're trying to type, then by all means tap it instead of typing out the rest of the URL. The time you save could be your own:

- **Top Hits.** The Top Hits are Safari's best guesses at what you're looking for. They're the sites on your bookmarks and History lists that you've visited most often (and that match what you've typed so far).

  Try tapping one of the Top Hits sometime. You'll discover, to your amazement, that the site appears almost instantly. It doesn't seem to have to load. That's because, as a favor to you, Safari quietly down-loads the Top Hits in the background, while you're still entering your search term, all to save you time.

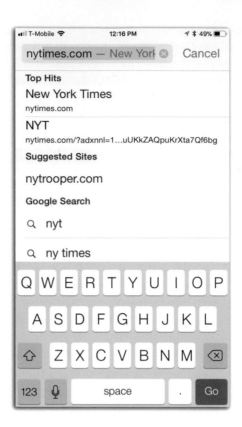

- **Suggested Sites.** Occasionally, you'll see another proposed site or two here: Suggested Sites. It's yet another site that Safari supposes you might be trying to reach, based on what you've typed so far and what sites other people visit.

- **Google Search.** The next category of suggestions: a list of search terms you *might* be typing, based on how popular those searches are on Google (or whatever search service you're using). For example, if you type **chick**, then this section proposes things like **chicken recipes**, **chick fil a**, and **chicken pox**. It's just trying to save you a little typing; if none of these tappable choices is the one you want, then ignore them.

- **Bookmarks and History.** Here Safari offers matching selections from websites you've bookmarked or recently visited. Again, it's trying to save you typing if it can.

- **On This Page.** Here's how you search for certain text *on the page you're reading*.

Once you've started typing, under the **On This Page** heading, you see a listing called **Find "chic"** (or whatever you've typed so far), shown below at left. Tap that line to jump to the first appearance of that text on the page. (There's a less hidden way to start this process, too: Tap ⬆ and then **Find on Page**.)

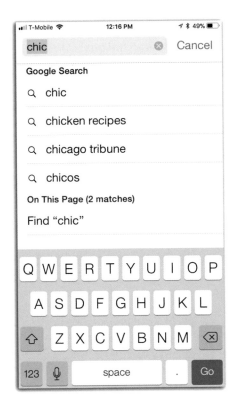

Use the ⟨ and ⟩ buttons to jump from one match to the next. Tap **Done** to return to your regularly scheduled browsing.

TIP: Suppose you've started typing a search term. Safari pipes up with its usual list of suggestions. At this point, if you drag up or down the screen, you hide the keyboard—so you can see the suggestions that were hidden behind it.

You can tell the iPhone to use a Yahoo, Bing, or DuckDuckGo search instead of Google, if you like, in **Settings→Safari→Search Engine**. (DuckDuckGo is a search service dedicated to privacy. It doesn't store your searches or tailor the results to you. On the other hand, it's capable of searching only about 50 web sources—Wikipedia, Wolfram Alpha, and so on.)

> **TIP:** If you've set your search options to use Google, then there are all kinds of cool things you can type here—special terms that tell Google, "I want *information*, not web page matches."
>
> You can type a movie name and zip code or city/state (*Titanic Returns 10024*) to get a list of today's showtimes in theaters near you. Get the forecast by typing *weather chicago* or *weather 60609*. Stock quotes: Type the symbol (*AMZN*). Dictionary definitions: *define schadenfreude*. Unit conversions: *liters in 5 gallons*. Currency conversions: *25 usd in euros*. Then tap **Go** to get instant results.

Quick Website Search

This crazy feature lets you search *within* a certain site (like Amazon or Reddit or Wikipedia) using Safari's regular search bar. For example, typing *wiki mollusk* can search Wikipedia for its entry on mollusks. Typing *amazon ipad* can offer links to buy an iPad from Amazon. Typing *reddit sitcoms* opens *reddit.com* to its search results for sitcoms.

None of this will work, however, until (a) you've turned the feature on (**Settings→Safari→Quick Website Search**), and (b) you've manually *taught* Safari how to search those sites one time each.

To do that, pull up the site you'll want to search (let's say it's *reddit.com*) and use its regular search bar. Search for anything.

That site's name now appears in the list at **Settings→Safari→Quick Website Search**. (Usually. Many sites don't work with Quick Website Search.) From now on, you can search that site by typing, for example, *reddit sitcoms*. You'll jump directly to that site's search results.

Bookmarks (📖)

Bookmarks, of course, are links to websites you might want to visit again without having to remember and type their URLs.

To see the list of bookmarks on your phone, tap 📖 at the bottom of the screen. You see the master list of bookmarks. They're organized in folders, or even folders *within* folders.

Tapping a folder shows you what's inside, and tapping a bookmark begins opening the corresponding website.

You may be surprised to discover that Safari already seems to be pre-stocked with bookmarks—that, amazingly, are interesting and useful to ***you*** in particular! How did it know?

Easy—it copied your existing desktop computer's browser bookmarks from Safari on the Mac when you synced the iPhone (Chapter 15), or when you turned on Safari syncing through iCloud. Sneaky, eh?

Creating New Bookmarks

You can add new bookmarks right on the phone. Any work you do here is copied ***back*** to your computer the next time you sync the two machines—or instantaneously, if you've turned on iCloud bookmark syncing.

When you find a web page you might like to visit again, hold down the ⌓ icon; from the shortcut menu, choose **Add Bookmark**. (Or do it the long way: Tap the ⬆ to reveal the Share options, one of which is **Add Bookmark**.) The Add Bookmark screen appears (below, right).

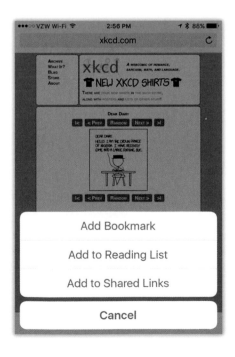
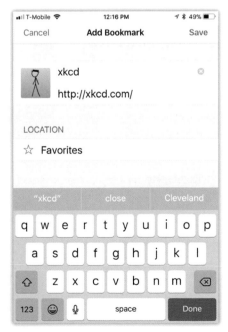

You have two tasks here:

- **Type a better name.** In the top box, you can type a shorter or clearer name for the page. Instead of "Bass, Trout & Tackle—the web's Premier Resource for the Avid Outdoorsman," you can just call it "Fish."

  Below that: The page's underlying URL, which is independent of what you've *named* your bookmark. You can't edit this one.

- **Specify where to file this bookmark.** If you tap **Favorites**, then you open Safari's hierarchical list of bookmark folders, which organize your bookmarked sites. Tap the folder where you want to file the new bookmark so you'll know where to find it later.

Editing Bookmarks and Folders

It's easy enough to massage your Bookmarks list within Safari—to delete favorites that aren't so favorite anymore, to make new folders, to rearrange the list, to rename a folder or a bookmark, and so on.

The techniques are the same for editing bookmark *folders* as editing the bookmarks themselves—after the first step. To edit the folder list, start by opening the Bookmarks (tap ⌘), and then tap **Edit**.

To edit the bookmarks themselves, tap ⌘, tap a folder, and *then* tap **Edit**. Now you can get organized:

- **Delete something.** Tap ● next to a folder or a bookmark, and then tap **Delete** to confirm.

- **Rearrange the list.** Drag the grip strip (≡) up or down in the list to move the folders or bookmarks around. (You can't move or delete the top two folders—Favorites and History.)

- **Edit a name and location.** Tap a folder or a bookmark name. If you tap a folder, you arrive at the Edit Folder screen; you can edit the folder's name and which folder it's inside of. If you tap a bookmark, **Edit Bookmark** lets you edit the name and the URL it points to.

  Tap **Done** when you're finished.

- **Create a folder.** Tap **New Folder** in the lower-left corner of the Edit Folders screen. You're offered the chance to type a name for it and to specify where you want to file it (that is, in which *other* folder).

Tap **Done** when you're finished.

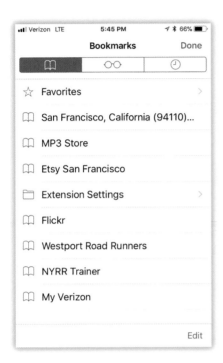

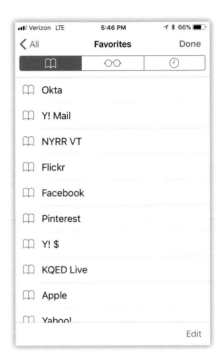

The Reading List ( )

The Reading List is a handy list of web pages you want to read later. Unlike a bookmark, it stores entire pages, so you can read them even when you don't have an Internet connection (on the subway or on a plane, for example).

The Reading List also keeps track of what you've read. You can use the **Show All/Show Unread** button at the bottom of the screen to view everything—or just what you haven't yet read.

To add a page to the Reading List, tap  and then tap **Add to Reading List** (below, left). Or just hold your finger down on a link until a set of buttons appears, including **Add to Reading List**. (At this point, iOS politely asks if you want all future Reading List stories to be downloaded to your phone, rather than simply bookmarked.)

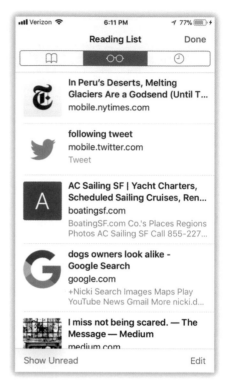

Once you've added a page to the Reading List, you can get to it by tapping 📖 and then tapping the Reading List tab at the top (∞). Tap an item on your list to open and read it (above, right).

TIP: When you get to the bottom of a Reading List item you've just read, keep scrolling down. The phone is nice enough to offer up the *next* article in your Reading List, as though they were all vertically connected.

By the way, some web pages require a hefty amount of data to download, what with photos and all. If you're worried about Reading List downloads eating up your monthly data allotment, you can visit **Settings→Safari** and turn off **Use Cellular Data**.

Now you'll be able to download Reading List pages only when you're on Wi-Fi, but at least there's no risk of going over your monthly cellular-data allotment.

The History List (🕐)

Behind the scenes, Safari keeps track of the websites you've visited in the past week or so, neatly organized into subfolders like This Evening and Yesterday. It's a great feature when you can't recall the address for a website you visited recently—or when you remember it had a long, complicated address and you get the psychiatric condition known as iPhone Keyboard Dread.

To see the list of recent sites, tap 📖, and then 🕐. Once the History list appears, just tap a bookmark to revisit that web page.

Erasing the History List

Some people find it creepy that Safari maintains a History list, right there in plain view of any family member or coworker who wanders by. They'd just as soon their wife/husband/boss/parent/kid not know what websites they've been visiting.

You can delete just one particularly incriminating History listing easily enough; swipe leftward across its name and then tap **Delete**. You can also delete the *entire* History menu, erasing all your tracks. To do that, tap **Clear**; confirm by tapping **Clear History**. You've just rewritten History.

Link-Tapping Tricks

Link-tapping, of course, is the primary activity of the web. But in Safari, those blue underlined links (or not blue, even not underlined links) harbor special powers:

- **Long-press a link** to open a handy panel. Its options include **Open**, **Open in New Tab**, **Add to Reading List**, **Copy**, and **Share**.

- **Hard-press a link** (iPhone 6s and later models) to peek at whatever page that link opens, like this:

  This, of course, is part of the *peek and pop* feature described on page 39. Once you've opened the preview bubble, you can either retreat (lift your finger; remain where you were) or advance (press even harder to fully open that page).

  Quite handy, really.

Saving Graphics

If you find a picture online that you wish you could keep forever, you have two choices: You could stare at it until you've memorized it, or you could save it.

To do that, touch the image for about a second. A sheet appears, just like the one that appears when you hold your finger down on a regular link.

Hard press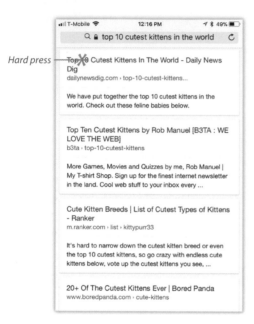

Preview pops open without leaving the page

If you tap **Save Image**, then the iPhone thoughtfully deposits a copy of the image in Photos so it will be copied back to your Mac or PC at the next sync opportunity. If you tap **Copy**, then you nab a *link* to that graphic, which you can now paste into another program.

> **TIP:** If **Save Image** isn't one of the choices, there's a workaround: Tap **Open in New Tab**, touch the image in its new tab for about a second, and *then* choose **Save Image** from the sheet that appears.

Saved Passwords and Credit Cards

On desktop web browsers, a feature called AutoFill saves you an awful lot of typing. It fills out your name and address automatically when you're ordering something online. It stores your passwords so you don't have to re-enter them every time you visit passworded sites.

But on the iPhone, where you're typing on glass, the convenience of AutoFill goes to a whole new level.

The phone can memorize your credit card information, too, making it much easier to buy stuff online; in fact, it can even store this information by *taking a picture* of your credit card.

And thanks to iCloud syncing, all those passwords and credit cards can auto-store themselves on all your other Apple gadgetry.

To turn on AutoFill, visit **Settings→Safari→AutoFill**. Here's what you find (below, left):

- **Use Contact Info.** Turn this **On**. Then tap **My Info**. From the address book, find your own listing. You've just told Safari *which* name, address, city, state, zip code, and phone number belong to you.

  From now on, whenever you're asked to input your address, phone number, and so on, you'll see an AutoFill button at the top of the keyboard. Tap it to make Safari auto-enter all those details, saving you no end of typing. (It works on *most* sites.) If there are extra blanks that AutoFill doesn't fill, then you can tap the **Previous** and **Next** buttons to move your cursor from one to the next instead of tapping and scrolling manually.

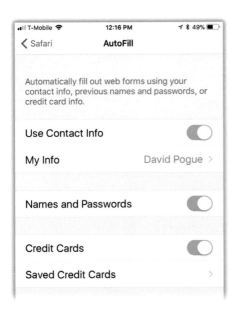 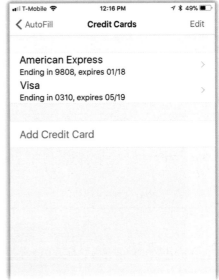

If your contact card contains a secondary address (like a work address), or even a third, then tapping **AutoFill** produces a pop-up panel listing both (or all three). Just tap the one you want.

- **Names & Passwords** lets Safari fill in your user name and passwords when you visit sites that require you to log in (Google, Amazon, and so on). On each website, you'll be able to choose **Yes** (a good idea for your PTA or library account), **Never for this Website** (a good idea for your bank), or **Not Now** (you'll be asked again next time).

  (To view a list of the actual memorized names and passwords, open **Settings→Safari→Passwords**.)

On this screen, you can delete or edit saved passwords. If a login no longer pleases you, swipe leftward across it, and then tap **Delete**.

To add a password manually, scroll to the bottom of the screen and tap **Add Password**.

And to make an edit, tap the errant password and then tap **Edit**. You can touch the problematic password or user name to call up the iPhone's keyboard and make your changes.

- **Credit Cards.** Turn on **Credit Cards**, of course, if you'd like Safari to memorize your charge card info. To enter your card details, tap **Saved Credit Cards** (where you see a list of them) and then **Add Credit Card**. You can type in your name, card number, expiration date, and a description—or you can save yourself a little tedium by tapping **Use Camera**. Aim the camera at your credit card; the phone magically recognizes your name, the card number, and the expiration date, and proposes a description of the card.

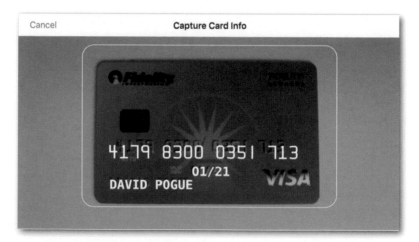

When you buy something online, iOS offers an **AutoFill Credit Card** button. When you tap it, Safari asks you first which credit card you want to use, if you've stored more than one (it displays the last four digits for your reference). Tap it, and boom: Safari cheerfully fills in the credit card information, saving you time and hassle.

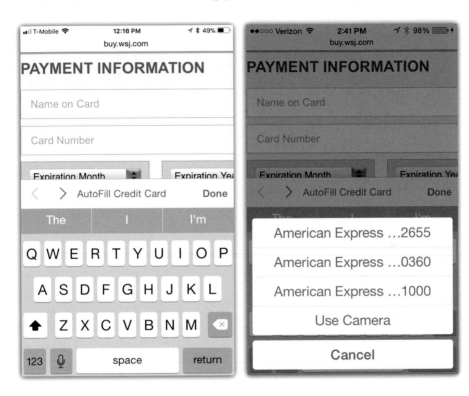

Unfortunately, there's nowhere to store the little three- or four-digit security code, sometimes called the CSC, CVV, or CV2 code. Safari makes no attempt to fill that in; you always have to enter it manually. That's one last safeguard against a kid, a spouse, a parent, or a thief using your phone for an online shopping spree when you're not around.

TIP: You don't have to enter all your stored passwords and credit cards into other Apple gadgets. They sync via iCloud (page 534).

Manipulating Multiple Pages

Like any other self-respecting browser, Safari can keep multiple pages open at once, making it easy for you to switch among them. You can think of it as a miniature version of tabbed browsing, a feature of browsers like Safari Senior, Firefox, Chrome, and Microsoft Edge. Tabbed browsing keeps a bunch of web pages open simultaneously.

One advantage of this arrangement is that you can start reading one web page while the others load into their own tabs in the background.

To Open a New Window

Tap the ⧉ in the lower right. The Safari page seems to duck backward, bowing to you in 3D space. Tap +.

You now arrive at the Favorites page (below, left). Here are icons for all the sites you've designated as Favorites (see page 466). Tap to open one. Or, in the address bar, enter an address. Or use a bookmark.

To Switch Among Windows

Tap ⧉ again. Now you see something like the 3D floating pages shown below at right. These are all your open tabs (windows). You work with them like this:

- **Close a window** by tapping the ✕ in the corner—or by swiping a page away horizontally. It slides away into the void.

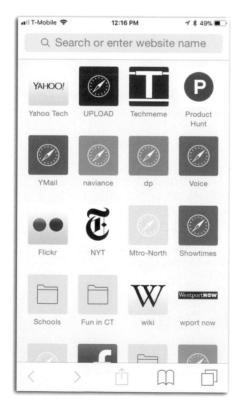

- **Rearrange these windows** by dragging them up or down.

- **Open a window** to full screen by tapping it.

You can open a third window, and a fourth, and so on, and jump among them, using these two techniques.

TIP: Although not one person in a thousand realizes it, you can search your open Safari tabs' website titles and URLs. Tap the ⎘ button and either drag down from the top or hold the phone horizontally (landscape mode). There's your secret search box.

---

iCloud Tabs

Thanks to the miracle of iCloud syncing, the last windows and tabs you had open on that other gadget (even if the gadget is turned off) show up here, at the bottom of the page-juggling screen (tap ⎘ to see it). They're sorted into headings that correspond to your other Apple gadgets.

The concept is to unify your Macs and i-gadgets. You're reading three browser windows and tabs on your phone—why not resume on the big screen when you get home and sit down in front of your Mac?

You won't see these tabs unless the Macs have OS X Mountain Lion or later. And, of course, Safari has to be turned on in **System Preferences→iCloud** on the Mac, and **Settings→iCloud** on the phone or tablet.

Reader View

How can people read web articles when there's Times Square blinking all around them? Fortunately, you'll never have to put up with that again.

The Reader button in the address bar (☰) is amazing. With one tap, it eliminates *everything* from the page you're reading except the text and photos. No ads, toolbars, blinking, links, banners, or anything else.

The text is also changed to a clean, clear font and size, and the background is made plain white. Basically, it makes any web page look like a printed book page, and it's glorious. Shown below: the before and after. Which looks easier to read?

To exit Reader, tap ☰ again. Best. Feature. Ever.

The fine print: Reader doesn't appear until the page has fully loaded. It doesn't appear on "front page" pages, like the *nytimes.com* home page—only when you've opened an article within. And it may not appear on sites that are already specially designed for access by cellphones.

Web Security

Safari on the iPhone isn't meant to be a full-blown web browser like the one on your desktop computer, but it comes surprisingly close—especially when it comes to privacy and security. Cookies, pop-up blockers, parental controls...they're all here, for your paranoid pleasure.

Pop-Up Blocker

The world's smarmiest advertisers like to inundate us with pop-up and pop-under ads—nasty little windows that appear in front of the browser window or, worse, behind it, waiting to jump out the moment you close your window. Fortunately, Safari comes set to block those pop-ups so you don't see them. It's a war out there—but at least you now have some ammunition.

The thing is, though, pop-ups are sometimes useful (and not ads)—notices of new banking features, seating charts on ticket-sales sites, warnings that the instructions for using a site have changed, and so on. Safari can't tell these from ads—and it stifles them, too. So if a site you trust says "Please turn off pop-up blockers and reload this page," then you know you're probably missing out on a *useful* pop-up message.

In those situations, you can turn off the pop-up blocker. The on/off switch is in **Settings→Safari**.

Password Suggestions

When you're signing up for a new account on some website, and you tap inside the box where you're supposed to make up a password, Safari offers to make up a password for you. It's a doozy, too, along the lines of 23k2k4-29cs8-58384-ckk3322.

Now, don't freak out. You're not expected to remember that. Safari will, of course, memorize it for you (and sync it to your other Apple computers, if they're on the same iCloud account). Meanwhile, you've got yourself a unique, nearly uncrackable password.

Cookies

Cookies are something like preference files. Certain websites—particularly commercial ones like Amazon—deposit them on your hard drive so that they'll remember you the next time you visit. That's how Amazon is able to greet you with, "Welcome, Chris" (or whatever your name is). It's reading its own cookie.

Most cookies are perfectly innocuous—and, in fact, extremely useful, because they help websites remember your tastes (and contact info).

But fear is widespread, and the media fan the flames with tales of sinister cookies that track your movement on the web. If you're worried about invasions of privacy, Safari is ready to protect you.

If you turn on **Settings→Safari→Block All Cookies** (and confirm in the "Are you sure" box), then you create an acrylic shield around your iPhone. No cookies can come in, and no cookie information can go out. You'll probably find the web a very inconvenient place; you'll have to reenter your information upon every visit, and some websites may not work properly at all.

When this option is off, Safari accepts cookies from sites you *want* to visit, but blocks cookies deposited on your phone by sites you're not actually visiting—cookies an especially evil banner ad gives you, for example.

The **Settings→Safari** screen offers a slew of additional privacy and security settings; see page 601, right.

Private Browsing

Private browsing lets you surf without adding any pages to your History list, searches to your Google search suggestions, passwords to Safari's saved password list, or autofill entries to Safari's memory. You might want to turn on private browsing before you visit websites that would raise interesting questions with your spouse, parents, or boss.

When you want to start leaving no tracks, tap ⎙ to open the page-juggler screen; tap **Private** at the bottom-left corner.

Suddenly the light-gray accents of Safari turn jet-black—a reminder that you're now in Private mode. Tap + to open a new page, and proceed as usual. From now on, Safari records nothing while you surf.

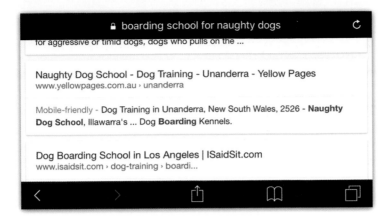

When you're ready to browse "publicly" again, turn private browsing off once more (tap ⬚, and then tap **Private**). Safari resumes taking note of the pages you visit—but it never remembers the ones you opened while in Private mode.

In other words, what happens in private browsing stays in private browsing.

Parental Controls

If your child (or employee) is old enough to have an iPhone but not old enough for the seedier side of the web, then don't miss the Restrictions feature in Settings. The iPhone can remove the Safari icon from the iPhone altogether so that no web browsing is possible at all. See page 619 for instructions.

Happy Surprises in the ⬆ Panel

So far in this chapter, you've learned the first step in bookmarking a page (tap ⬆); in designating a new Favorite (tap ⬆); and in saving a web article to your offline Reading List (tap ⬆). That's right: All these features await on the Share sheet.

But that same panel hosts a wealth of equally useful buttons that nobody ever talks about; here are a few highlights.

- **AirDrop, Message, Mail, Twitter, and Facebook.** Pretty obvious; they share the link of your current page with other people.

- **Reminders.** Remember how you can say to Siri, about a web page you're on, "Remind me about this later?" (If not, see page 438.)

There's a button for that here on the Share sheet. Great when speaking to your phone would be socially awkward.

- **Add to Notes.** You can send a link to a web article (complete with opening sentences and an image) directly to a note in the Notes app—no copy and paste required. You're invited to annotate the note before hitting **Save**, or even add it to an existing Notes page.

- **Save PDF to iBooks.** You can turn anything you find on the web into an iBooks book—an electronic book that you can read later in iBooks (page 394)! That way, you gain a wide variety of reading tools (notes, highlighting, dictionary) and organizational tools (collections) that aren't available in Safari.

- **Copy.** Copies the page's address, to paste it into some other app.

- **Open in News.** Turns the article you're reading into a nicely formatted "magazine" page in the News app (page 417). If it's not an article-style post, you just get an error message.

- **Add to Home Screen.** Is there a certain website you visit every day? This button adds that page's icon right to your Home screen. It's a shortcut that Apple calls a web clip. You're offered the chance to edit the icon's name; tap **Add**. When you return to your Home screen, you'll see the icon; you can move or delete it as you would any app.

> **TIP:** You can turn *part* of a web page into one of these web clips, too— say, *The New York Times'* "Most emailed" list, or the box scores for a certain sports league. All you have to do is zoom and scroll the page in Safari *before* you tap ⬆, isolating the section you want. Later, when you open the web clip, you'll see exactly the part of the web page you wanted.

- **Find on Page.** Here's your search command.

- **Create PDF.** Converts the page into a PDF document with only a single button: the ⬆ button, so that you can send it to someone. And the Markup button (Ⓐ) is here, too, for adding annotations first.

- **Request Desktop Site.** Here's a less-hidden version of the button described on page 467.

> **TIP:** You can rearrange these buttons, if you like. Tap **More** and then drag their "grip strips" up or down in the list.

14

Email

Email on your iPhone offers full formatting, fonts, graphics, and choice of type size; file attachments like Word, Excel, PowerPoint, PDF, Pages, Numbers, photos, and even .zip compressed files; and compatibility with Yahoo Mail, Gmail, AOL Mail, iCloud mail, corporate Exchange mail, and any standard email account.

Dude, if you want a more satisfying portable email machine than this one, buy a laptop.

This chapter covers the basic email experience. If you've gotten yourself hooked up with iCloud, see Chapter 16 for details.

Setting Up Your Account

If you have a free email account from Google, AOL, Outlook, or Yahoo; an iCloud account (Chapter 16); or a Microsoft Exchange account run by your employer, then setup on the iPhone is easy.

From the Home screen, tap **Settings→Account & Passwords→Add Account**. Tap the colorful logo that corresponds to the kind of account you have (Google, Yahoo, or whatever).

On the page that appears, sign into your account. Tap **Next**.

Now you may see the list of non-email data that the iPhone can show you (from iCloud, Google, Yahoo, Exchange, and so on): contacts, calendars, reminders, and notes. Turn off the ones you don't want synced to your phone, and then tap **Save**.

Your email account is ready to go!

If you don't have one of these free accounts, they're worth having, if only as a backup to your regular account. They can help with spam filtering, too, since the iPhone doesn't offer any. To sign up, go to *Google.com, Yahoo.com, AOL.com,* or *iCloud.com.*

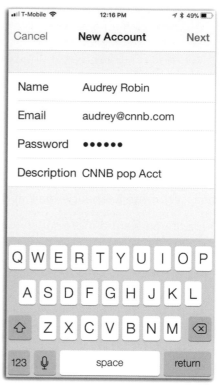

POP3 and IMAP Accounts

Those freebie, brand-name, web-based accounts are super-easy to set up. But millions of people have more generic email accounts, perhaps supplied by their employers or Internet providers. They're generally one of two types:

- **POP accounts** are the oldest and most compatible type on the Internet. (POP stands for Post Office Protocol, but this won't be on the test.) A POP account can make life complicated if you check your mail on more than one machine (say, a PC and an iPhone), as you'll discover shortly.

  A POP server transfers incoming mail to your computer or phone before you read it, which works fine as long as you're using *only that machine* to access your email.

- **IMAP accounts** (Internet Message Access Protocol) are newer and have more features than POP servers, and they're quickly putting POP out to pasture. IMAP servers keep all your mail online, rather than making you store it on your computer; as a result, you can access the same mail from any computer (or phone). IMAP servers remember which messages you've read and sent, and they even keep track of how you've filed messages into mail folders. (Those free Yahoo email accounts are IMAP accounts, and so are Apple's iCloud accounts and corporate Exchange accounts. Gmail accounts *can* be IMAP, too.)

TIP: The iPhone copies your IMAP messages onto the phone itself, so you can work on your email even when you're not online. You can, in fact, control where these messages are stored (in which mail folder). To see this, open **Settings→Accounts & Passwords→[your IMAP account name]→[your IMAP account name again]→Advanced**. See? You can specify where your drafts, sent messages, and deleted messages wind up on the phone.

The iPhone can communicate with both kinds of accounts.

Tap your way to **Settings→Accounts & Passwords→Add Account**. Tap **Other**, tap **Add Mail Account**, and then enter your name, email address, password, and an optional description. Tap **Next**.

Apple's software attempts to figure out which kind of account you have (POP or IMAP) by the email address. If it can't make that determination, then you arrive at a second screen, where you're asked for such juicy details as the host name for incoming and outgoing mail servers. (This is also where you tap either **IMAP** or **POP**, to tell the iPhone what sort of account it's dealing with.)

If you don't know this stuff offhand, you'll have to ask your Internet provider, corporate tech-support person, or next-door teenager to help you. When you're finished, tap **Save**.

To delete an account, open **Settings→Accounts & Passwords→[account name]**. At the bottom of the screen, you'll find the **Delete Account** button.

TIP: You can make, rename, or delete IMAP or Exchange mailboxes (mail folders) right on the phone.

In the Mail app, view the mailbox list for the account and then tap **Edit**. Tap **New Mailbox** to create a new folder. To edit an existing mailbox, tap its name; you can then rename it, tap the **Mailbox Location** folder to move it, or tap **Delete Mailbox**. Tap **Save** to finish up.

Downloading Mail

If you have "push" email (Yahoo, iCloud, or Exchange), then your iPhone doesn't have to **check** for messages; new messages show up on your iPhone **as they arrive**, around the clock.

If you have any other kind of account, then the iPhone checks for new messages automatically on a schedule—every 15, 30, or 60 minutes. It also checks for new messages each time you open the Mail program, or whenever you **drag downward** on the Inbox list.

You can adjust the frequency of these automatic checks or turn off the "push" feature (because it uses up your battery faster) in **Settings**; see page 590.

When new mail arrives, you'll know it. You hear the iPhone's little "You've got mail" sound, unless you've turned that off in Settings (or have the phone silenced).

A notification appears, too, even on the Lock screen (page 17).

You can actually process a message right from its notification banner. If you see at a glance that it's junk, or if no response is necessary, then drag your finger down on it (or, if you have an iPhone 6s or later, hard-press it) to reveal two new buttons: **Mark as Read** (leave it in your inbox, no longer appearing as a new message) and **Trash**.

At the Home screen, Mail's icon sprouts a circled number that tells you how many new messages are waiting. If you have more than one email account, it shows you the **total** number of new messages, from all accounts.

If you routinely leave a lot of unread messages in your inbox, and you don't really care about this "badge," you can turn it off. In fact, you can turn it off on a per-account basis, which is great if one of your accounts is sort of a junk account that you keep as a spare. Tap **Settings→ Notifications→Mail→[account name]→Badge App Icon**.

In any case, once you know you have mail, tap *Mail* on the Home screen to start reading it.

> **TIP:** The Mail app, more than any other app, is designed to be a series of nested lists. You start out seeing a list of accounts; tap one to see a list of folders; tap one for a list of messages; tap one to open the actual message.
>
> To *backtrack* through these lists, you can tap the button in the upper-left corner over and over again—or you can *swipe rightward* across the screen. That's a bigger target and more fun.

The Unified Inbox

If you have more than one email address, you're in luck. The iPhone offers a *unified inbox*—an option that displays all the incoming messages from all your accounts in a single place. (If you don't see it—if Mail opened up to some other screen—keep swiping rightward, backing up one screen at a time, until you do.)

This Mailboxes page has two sections:

- **Unified inboxes (and other unified folders).** To see all the incoming messages in one unified box, tap **All Inboxes**. Below that, you see the Inboxes for each of the individual accounts (next page, left).

  This part of the main Mail list also offers unified folders for **VIPs** and **Flagged** messages, which are described in this chapter.

  But what you may not realize is that you can add *other* unified folders to this section. You can, for example, add a folder called **Unread**, which contains only new messages from *all* accounts. (That's not the same thing as **All Inboxes**, because your inbox can contain messages you *have* read but haven't deleted or filed. Maybe a lot of them.)

  You can also add a unified folder showing all messages where you were either the To or CC addressee; this folder won't include any mail where your name appeared on the BCC (blind carbon-copy) line, like mailing lists and, often, spam.

  You can also add an **Attachments** folder here (messages with files attached), a **Today** folder, or unified folders that contain **All Drafts**, **All Sent**, or **All Trash**. ("All" means "from all accounts.")

To hide or show these special uni-folders, tap **Edit**, and then tap the selection circles beside the names of the folders you want to appear. (You can also take this opportunity to drag them up or down into a pleasing sequence.) Tap **Done**.

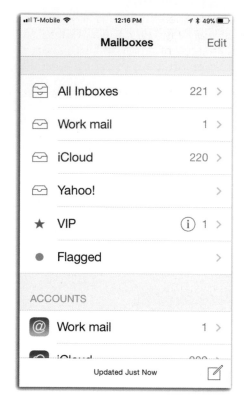

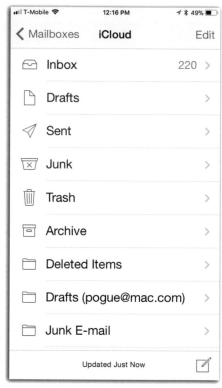

- **Accounts.** Farther down the Mailboxes screen, you see your accounts listed again. You can tap an account's name to expand or collapse its list of traditional mail folders: Inbox, Drafts (emails written but not sent), Sent, Trash, and any folders you've created yourself (Family, Little League, Old Stuff, whatever), as shown above at right. If you have a Yahoo, iCloud, Exchange, or another IMAP account, then the iPhone automatically creates these folders to match what you've set up online.

> **NOTE:** Not all kinds of email accounts permit the creation of your own filing folders, so you might not see anything but Inbox, Sent, and Trash.

The Message List—and Threading

If you tap an inbox's name, you wind up face to face with the list of incoming messages. (To return to the mailboxes list, tap ‹ **Mailboxes**, or swipe inward from the left edge of the screen.)

At first, you see only the subject lines of your messages, plus, in gray type, the first few lines of their contents; that way, you can scan through new messages to see if there's anything important. You can flick upward to scroll this list. Blue dots indicate messages you haven't yet opened.

Each message bears a gray › at the right side. That means "Tap this message's row to read it in all its formatted glory."

Here and there, though, you may spot a double arrow at the right side of the message list, like this: ›› That means you're looking at some **threaded** messages.

That's where several related messages—back-and-forths on the same subject—appear only once, in a single, consolidated entry. The idea is to reduce inbox clutter and to help you remember what people were talking about.

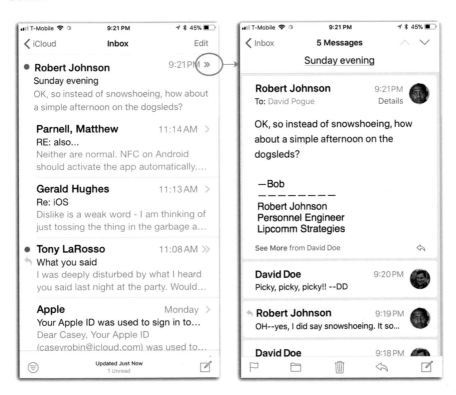

When you tap a threaded message, you open what appears to be all the messages in this topic, scrolling and attached vertically as though they're sheets of paper towel. Messages you've already seen, in iOS 11, appear collapsed, as shown at right on the previous page, to help you keep your bearings.

In general, threading is a nice feature. But if it bugs you, you can turn it off. Open **Settings→Mail**, scroll down, and turn off **Organize By Thread**. (While you're there, notice the new option called **Collapse Read Messages**. It's responsible for the collapsing effect described above.)

(If you have an iPhone Plus model, you can turn the phone 90 degrees to see the mini-tablet-like view shown below, with the message list and open message visible simultaneously.)

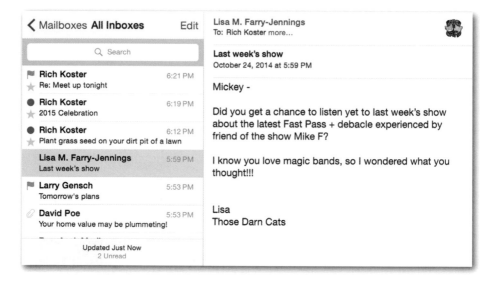

Filters

The iPhone offers one-click filters that hide or show all messages in the list of a certain kind—like ones you haven't yet read.

See the ⊜ button below the list of messages? When you tap it, you automatically turn on the first filter: Unread. All the messages in the list that you've read are hidden—until you hit ⊜ again to turn the filter off.

When the filter is on, you can click the word "Unread" to see a list of other ways to filter the list. You can tell Mail to show you only messages you've flagged; only messages to you (or that you were copied on); only the ones with attachments; or only the ones from people in your VIP list.

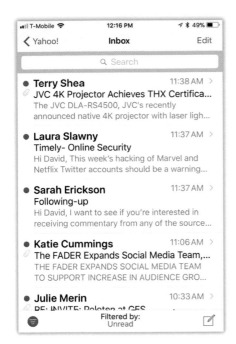

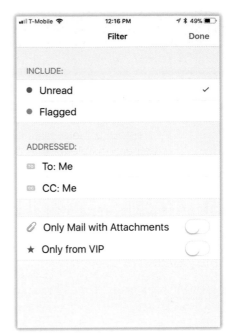

VIPs and Flagged Messages

You might notice, in your master Inbox, two "email accounts" that you didn't set up: **VIP** and **Flagged**. They're both intended to help you round up important messages from the thousands that flood you every day.

Each one magically rounds up messages from *all* your account inboxes, so you don't have to go wading through lots of accounts to find the really important mail. (Note: That's *inboxes*. Messages in other mail folders don't wind up in these special inboxes, even if they're flagged or are from VIPs.)

VIPs

In the real world, VIPs are people who get backstage passes to concerts or special treatment at business functions (it stands for "very important person"). In iOS, it means "somebody whose mail is important enough that I want it brought to my attention immediately when it arrives."

So who should your VIPs be? That's up to you. Your spouse, your boss, and your doctor come to mind.

To designate someone as a VIP, proceed in either of these two ways:

- **On the accounts screen,** carefully tap the ⓘ next to the VIP item. Your master list of all VIPs appears (below, left). Tap **Add VIP** to choose a lucky new member from Contacts.

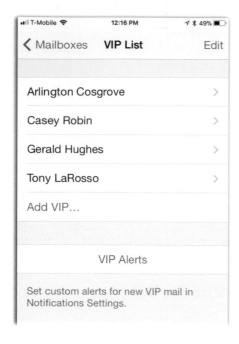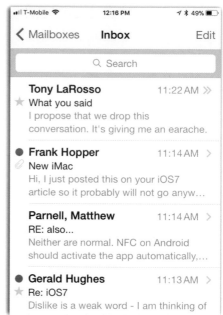

This is also where you **delete** people from your VIP list when they've annoyed you. Swipe leftward across a name, and then tap **Delete**. Or tap **Edit** and then tap each ● button; tap **Delete** to confirm.

> **TIP:** You can set things up so that when a new message from a VIP comes in, the iPhone lets you know with a sound, a banner, an alert bubble, a vibration, and so on. Tap **VIP Alerts** to set them up. (That's a shortcut to the **Settings→Notifications→Mail→VIP** screen.)

- **In a message from the lucky individual,** tap his name in the From, To, or Cc/Bcc box. His Contact screen appears, complete with an **Add to VIP** button.

Once you've established who's important, lots of interesting things happen:

- **The VIP inbox automatically collects** messages from your VIPs.
- **VIP names in every mail list** sprout a gray star (above, right).

- **If you use iCloud,** the same person is now a VIP on all your other iPhones and iPads (running iOS 6 or later) and Macs (running OS X Mountain Lion or later).

TIP: You can hide the VIP inbox on the main Mailboxes screen—handy if you don't really use this feature. Tap **Edit,** and then ⊘. Tap **Done.**

Flag It

Sometimes you receive email that prompts you to some sort of action, but you may not have the time (or the fortitude) to face the task at the moment. ("Hi there, it's me, your accountant. Would you mind rounding up your expenses for 2006 through 2016 and sending me a list by email?")

That's why Mail lets you *flag* a message, summoning a little flag icon or a little orange dot in a new column next to the message's name. It can mean anything you like—it simply calls attention to certain messages.

TIP: The flag marker can be *either* a ⚑ icon *or* an orange dot. You make your choice in **Settings→Mail→Flag Style.**

To flag an open message, tap ⚑ at the bottom of the screen. When the confirmation sheet slides up (below, left), tap **Flag.**

 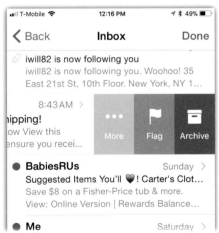

You can also rapidly flag messages directly in a *list* (the Inbox, for example). Just swipe leftward across the message—half an inch of finger sliding does the trick—to reveal the set of buttons shown above at right:

Tap **Flag.** (If you tap **More,** you get the option to **Unflag.**)

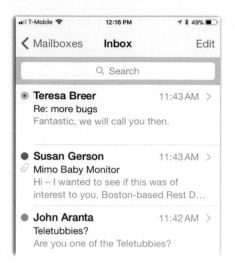

The dot or ⚐ icon appears in the body of the message, next to the message's name in your message list. (In the image above, the top dot looks more like a bull's-eye; that's because it's flagged **and** unread.) The flag appears even on the corresponding message in your Mac or PC email program, thanks to the miracle of wireless syncing.

Finally, the Flagged mailbox appears in your list of accounts, making it easy to work with all flagged messages, from all accounts, in one place.

TIP: If you don't really use this feature, you can hide the Flagged folder. Tap **Edit**, and then tap the ● to turn it off. Tap **Done**.

This might be a good time to point out another, newer way to draw attention to a message: Tell Siri to "Remind me about this later." See page 438 for details.

What to Do with a Message

Once you've opened a message, you can respond to it, delete it, file it, and so on. Here's the drill.

TIP: If you have an iPhone 6s or later, the **first** thing to learn is that you can see what's in a message without ever leaving the Inbox list—just by hard-pressing it. See page 39 for more on peek and pop.

List View: Flag, Trash, Mark as Unread

It's easy to plow through a teeming Inbox, processing messages as you go, without ever having to open them. All you have to do is swipe across a message in the list horizontally.

- **Full left-swipe delete.** Swipe your finger leftward **all the way** across the message to delete it. That's it: No confirmation tap required.

- **Partial left-swipe options.** If you don't swipe leftward all the way, you reveal a set of three buttons on the right: **Trash** (same as before, but now you have to tap again to confirm); **Flag** (described in the previous section); and **More** (opens up a raft of options like **Reply**, **Forward**, **Flag**, **Move to Junk**, and so on).

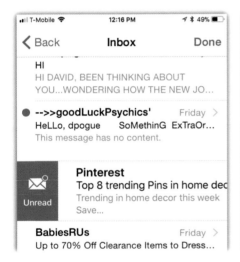
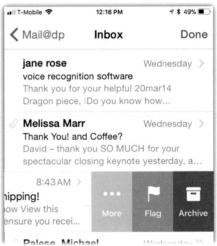

- **Full right-swipe.** Swipe your finger to the **right** all the way across the message to mark it as new (unread). Great for reminding yourself to look at this message again later. Or, if it's already unread, that swipe marks it as **read**.

To a certain extent, you can **customize** these gestures. You can turn off the right-swipe gesture. Or swap the positions of the **Flag** and **Read** options, for example, so that you flag a message when you swipe fully to the right and **Read** appears as a button when you swipe to the left. Or you can put the **Archive** button into the place of **Flag** when you swipe to the left.

To check out your options, open **Settings→Mail→Swipe Options**.

Tap **Swipe Left** to specify which button appears in the center of the three when you swipe partway leftward: **None**, **Mark as Read**, **Flag**, or **Move**

Message. Tap **Swipe Right** to choose which function you want to trigger with a full rightward swipe (**None**, **Mark as Read**, **Flag**, **Move Message**, or **Archive**).

Read It

The type size in email messages can be pretty small. Fortunately, you have some great iPhoney enlargement tricks at your disposal. For example:

- **Spread two fingers** to enlarge the entire email message.

- **Double-tap a narrow block of text** to make it fill the screen, if it doesn't already.

- **Drag or flick your finger** to scroll through or around the message.

- **Choose a larger type size for all messages**. See page 579.

Links are "live" in email messages. Tap a phone number to call it, a web address to open it, a YouTube link to watch the video, an email address to write to it, a time and date to add it to your calendar, and so on.

Reply to It

To answer a message, tap the **Reply/Forward** icon (<) at the bottom of the screen; tap **Reply**. If the message was originally addressed to multiple recipients, then you can choose **Reply All** to send your reply to everyone simultaneously.

A new message window opens, already addressed. As a courtesy to your correspondents, Mail pastes the original message at the bottom of the window.

If you'd like to splice your own comments into the paragraphs of the original message, replying point by point, then use the Return key to create blank lines in the original message. (Use the loupe—page 83—to position the insertion point at the proper spot.)

The brackets by each line of the original message help your correspondent keep straight what's yours and what's hers.

> **TIP:** If you select some text before you tap **Reply** or **Reply All**, then the iPhone pastes only that selected bit into the new, outgoing message. In other words, you're quoting back only a portion.

Before you tap **Send**, you can add or delete recipients, edit the subject line or the original message, and so on.

Forward It

Instead of replying to the sender, you may sometimes want to pass the note on to a third person. To do so, tap ⤺. This time, tap **Forward**.

> **TIP:** If there's a file attached to the inbound message, the iPhone says, "Include attachments from original message?" and offers **Include** and **Don't Include** buttons. Rather thoughtful, actually—the phone can forward files it can't even open.

A new message opens, looking like the one that appears when you reply. You can precede the original message with a comment of your own, like, "Frank: I thought you'd be interested in this joke about your mom." Finally, address and send it as usual.

Follow It

Your phone can notify you when anyone responds to a certain email conversation.

If you're composing or replying to a message, tap in the subject line to make the 🔔 appear; tap it. If you're *reading* a message, tap ⚑ at the

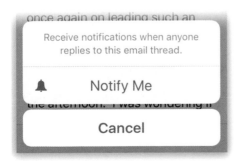

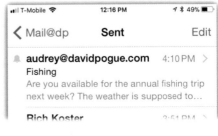

bottom of the screen, tap **Notify Me**, and confirm by tapping **Notify Me** again (previous page, left). In a list, swipe leftward, partly across a message; tap **More**; tap **Notify Me**. In each case, a 🔔 icon appears beside the message (or thread) in the list (previous page, right).

When anybody replies, a notification banner appears on your screen, ready for swiping and reading.

Filing or Deleting One Message

Once you've opened a message that's worth keeping, you can file it into one of your account's folders ("mailboxes") by tapping the 🗂 at the bottom of the screen. Up pops the list of your folders; tap the one you want.

It's a snap to delete a message you no longer want, too. If it's open in front of you, tap 🗑 or 🗄 at the bottom of the screen. The message rapidly shrinks into the icon and disappears.

> **NOTE:** If that one-touch deletion method makes you a little nervous, by the way, you can ask the iPhone to display a confirmation box before trashing the message forever. Visit **Settings→Mail→Ask Before Deleting**.

You can also delete a message from the message *list*—the Inbox, for example.

> **TIP:** Gmail doesn't want you to throw anything away. That's why swiping like this produces a button that says **Archive**, not **Delete**, and why the usual 🗑 button in a message looks like a filing box. If you prefer to delete a message for good, hold down the 🗄 until the **Trash Message** and **Archive Message** buttons appear.

There's a long way to delete messages from the list, too, as described next. But for single messages, the finger-swipe method is *much* more fun.

> **TIP:** There's a handy Undo shortcut, too: Shake the phone lightly. Tap **Undo Trash**. The deleted message jumps back to the folder it just came from. (You can then shake again to undo the Undo!)

Filing or Deleting Batches of Messages

You can also file or delete a bunch of messages at once. In the message list, tap **Edit**. A circle appears beside each message title. You can tap as many of these circles as you like, scrolling as necessary, adding a with each touch.

Finally, when you've selected all the messages in question, tap either **Trash (Archive)** or **Move**.

```
·ıl T-Mobile 🛜          12:16 PM          ⌁ ∗ 49% ■
                       7 Selected                    Cancel

    ◉  Tony LaRosso                          11:22 AM
    ✓ ☆  What you said
          I propose that we drop this conversation. It's giving me an earache.

    ●  Frank Hopper                          11:14 AM
    ✓ ⌀  New iMac
          Hi, I just posted this on your iOS7 article so it probably will not go
          anywhere: FrankKansas It is Tuesday the 24. I just bought my new i7...

    ●  Parnell, Matthew                      11:14 AM
  Mark                  Move                     Trash
```

If you tap **Move**, then you're shown the folder list so you can say where you want them moved. If you tap **Trash**, the messages disappear.

If you decide you've made a mistake, just shake the phone lightly—the iPhone's "Undo" gesture. Tap **Undo Move** to put the filed messages back where they just came from.

NOTE: When you delete a message, it goes into the Deleted folder. In other words, it works like the Macintosh Trash or the Windows Recycle Bin. You have a safety net.

Email doesn't have to stay in the Deleted folder forever, though. You can ask the iPhone to empty that folder every day, week, or month. From the Home screen, tap **Settings→Mail**. Tap your account name and then **Advanced→Remove**. Now you can change the setting from "Never" to "After one day" (or week, or month).

Add the Sender to Contacts

When you get a message from someone new who's worth adding to your iPhone's Contacts address book, tap that person's name (in blue, on the From line). You're offered buttons for **Create New Contact** and **Add to Existing Contact**. Use the second button to add an email address to an existing person's "card."

Open an Attachment

The Mail program downloads and displays the icons for *any* kind of attachment—but it can *open* only documents from Microsoft Office (Word, Excel, PowerPoint), those from Apple iWork (Pages, Keynote, Numbers), PDFs, text, RTFs, VCFs, graphics, .zip files, and un-copy-protected audio and video files.

Just scroll down, tap the attachment's icon, wait a moment for downloading, and then marvel as the document opens up, full screen. You can zoom in and out, flick, rotate the phone 90 degrees, and scroll just as though it were a web page or a photo.

> **TIP:** If you *hold your finger down* on the attachment's name, the Share sheet appears. It offers a list of ways you can send this attachment directly from your phone to someone else (by AirDrop or Mail)—or open it in other apps.
>
> If you tap a Word document, for example, you may be offered buttons for Mail, Dropbox, Evernote, and other apps that can open Word docs. If you tap a PDF document, you'll see a button for **Open in iBooks**. (**Quick Look** means the same non-editable preview as you'd get with a quick tap.)

When you're finished admiring the attachment, swipe rightward to return to the original email message.

> **TIP:** iOS can handle the compressed folders known as .zip files, just as Macs and Windows computers can. When you tap a .zip attachment's icon, the first file in it opens up. At that point, though, if you tap the ⬚ icon, you get a list of every document in that zipped folder. You can tap each to view or share it.

Snagging (or Sending) a Graphic

If you get sent a particularly good picture, just hold your finger on it. You're offered the Save sheet, filled with options like **Save** (into your Photo app's Camera Roll), **Copy**, **Print**, and **Assign to Contact** (as a person's face photo). All the usual sending methods are represented here, too, so that you can fire off this photo via AirDrop, Messages, Mail, Twitter, and Facebook.

Snagging a Contact or a Date

Mail can recognize contact information or calendar information from an incoming email message—and can dump it directly into Contacts or Calendar for you.

You'll know when it's found something—the block of contact information below somebody's signature, for example—because you see a special gray banner at the top of the screen (shown on the facing page).

You can click **Ignore** if you don't particularly need this person bulking up your address book. But if it's somebody worth tracking, tap **Add to Contacts**. A new Contacts screen appears, ready to save.

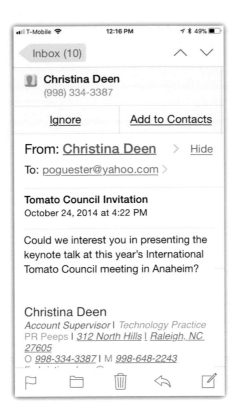

Similarly, if the message contains a reference to a date and time, the same sort of banner appears, offering to pop the appointment onto your calendar. (This banner appears only when it's *really sure* you're being offered a date and time: e-invitations and airline-ticket confirmations, for example.)

iOS: saving you time since 2016.

Unsubscribing

Every now and then, when you open a piece of junk mail, Mail offers you an **Unsubscribe** button at the top. And sure enough: Tapping it gets you off that mailing list.

Now, before you uncork the champagne, keep in mind that this button appears only on some pieces of spam—from only the kind-hearted, legitimate senders who include an **Unsubscribe** link at the bottom of their messages. All Mail does is automate that process (and move the **Unsubscribe** button to the top).

View the To/From Details

When your computer's screen is only a few inches tall, there's not a lot of extra space. So Apple designed Mail to conceal header details (To, From, and so on) that you might need only occasionally. For example, you usually don't actually see the word "From:"—you usually see only the sender's name, in blue. The To and Cc lines (page 509) may show only first names, to save space. And if there's a long list of addresses, you may see only "Michael (& 15 more)"—not the actual list of names.

You get last names, full lists, and full sender labels when you tap **More** following the header information. Tap **Hide** to collapse these details.

> **TIP:** When you tap a sender's name in blue, you open the corresponding info card in Contacts. It contains one-touch buttons for calling someone back, sending a text message, or placing a FaceTime audio or video call—which can be very handy if the email message you just received is urgent.

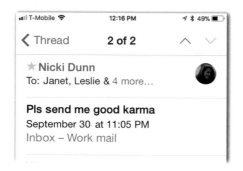
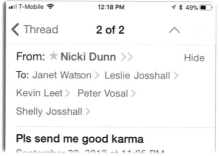

Mark as Unread

In the inbox, any message you haven't yet read is marked by a blue dot (●). Once you've opened the message, the blue dot goes away.

If you slide your finger to the right across a message in the list, you trigger the **Unread** command—you make that blue dot *reappear*. It's a great way to flag a message for later, to call it to your own attention. The blue dot can mean not so much "unread" as "un–dealt with."

Move On

Once you've had a good look at a message and processed it to your satisfaction, you can move on to the next (or previous) message in the list by tapping ❯ or ❮ in the upper-right corner. Or you can swipe rightward to return to the inbox (or whatever mailbox you're in).

Searching

Praise be—there's a search box in Mail. The search box is hiding **above** the top of every mail list, like your inbox. To see it, scroll up, or just tap the status strip at the top of the screen.

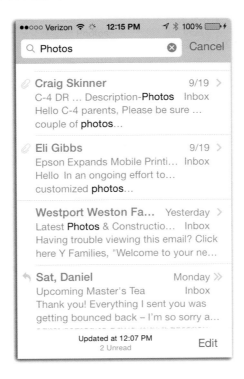

Tap inside the search box to make the keyboard appear, along with helpful canned searches like **Flagged Messages** and **Messages with Attachments**. As you type, Mail hides all but the matching messages; tap any one of the results to open it.

You don't have to specify **which fields** to search (From, To, Subject, Body), or which folder. You're searching everywhere.

> **TIP:** If you **want** to restrict the search to just the folder you're in, you can. After the search results begin to appear, tug downward on the screen. Two new buttons appear: **All Mailboxes** and **Current Mailbox**.

Wait long enough, and the search continues with messages that are still out there on the Internet but are so old that they've scrolled off your phone.

Writing Messages

To compose a new piece of outgoing mail, open the Mail app, and then tap ✐ in the lower-right corner. A blank new outgoing message appears, and the iPhone keyboard pops up.

Here's how you go about writing a message:

1. **In the To field, type the recipient's email address—or grab it from Contacts.**

   Often, you won't have to type much more than the first couple of letters of the name *or* email address. As you type, Mail displays all matching names and addresses so you can tap one instead of typing. (It thoughtfully derives these suggestions by analyzing both your Contacts *and* people you've recently exchanged email with.)

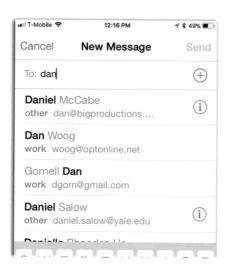 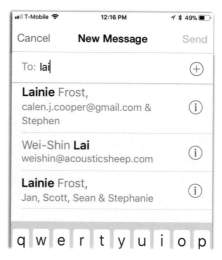

   As you go, the iPhone displays a list of everyone whose name matches what you're typing (above, left). The ones bearing ⓘ buttons are the people you've recently corresponded with but who are not in your Contacts. Tap the ⓘ to open a screen where you can add them to Contacts—or *remove* them from the list of recent correspondents, so Mail's autocomplete suggestions will no longer include those low-lifes.

TIP: When you address an email message, Mail even suggests **clusters** of people you tend to email together—"Erin and Sam," "Erin and Andy," and so on—to save you the trouble of reassembling these teams (facing page, right).

Similarly, if you type a subject you've used, Mail suggests the names of people who've received this subject line before. (For example, if you send "This month's traffic stats" every month to three coworkers, then their names appear automatically when you type out that subject line.) You'll get to go home from work that much quicker.

If you hold your finger down on the period (.) key, you get a pop-up palette of common email-address suffixes, like .com, .edu, .org, and so on, just as in Safari.

Alternatively, tap the ⊕ to open your Contacts list. Tap the name of the person you want. You can add as many addressees as you like; just repeat the procedure.

TIP: There's no Group mail feature on the iPhone, which would let you send one message to a predefined set of friends. But at *http:// groups.yahoo.com*, you can create free email groups. You can send a single email message to the group's address, and everyone in the group will get a copy. (You have to set up one of these groups in a web browser—but lo and behold, your iPhone has one!)

2. **To send a copy to other recipients, enter the address(es) in the Cc or Bcc fields.** If you tap **Cc/Bcc, From**, the screen expands to reveal two new lines beneath the To line: Cc and Bcc.

Cc stands for **carbon copy**. Getting an email message where your name is in the Cc line implies: "I sent you a copy because I thought you'd want to know about this correspondence, but I'm not expecting you to reply."

Bcc stands for **blind carbon copy**. It's a copy that goes to a third party secretly—the primary addressee never knows who else you sent it to. For example, if you send your coworker a message that says, "Chris, it bothers me that you've been cheating the customers," you could Bcc your supervisor to clue her in without getting into trouble with Chris.

Each of these lines behaves exactly like the To line. You fill each one up with email addresses in the same way.

TIP: You can drag people's names around—from the To line to the Cc line, for example. Just hold your finger down briefly on the name before dragging it. (It puffs and darkens once it's ready for transit.)

3. **Change the email account you're using, if you like.** If you have more than one email account set up on your iPhone, you can tap **Cc/Bcc, From** to expand the form and then tap **From** to open up a spinning list of your accounts. Tap the one you want to use for sending this message.

4. **Type the topic of the message in the Subject field.** Leaving it blank only annoys your recipient. On the other hand, don't put the *entire* message into the subject line, either.

5. **Type your message in the message box.** All the usual iPhone keyboard and dictation tricks apply (Chapter 3). Don't forget that you can use Copy and Paste, within Mail or from other programs. Both text and graphics can appear in your message.

And here's a fantastic trick: As you're composing a message, you can refer to *another* email—maybe the one you're responding to—without losing your place.

Swipe down to reveal what's behind your reply.

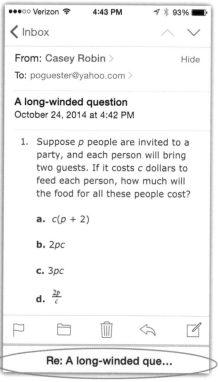

Tap to reopen your reply.

To do that, drag downward on the title bar, where it says **New Message** or whatever the reply's title is; your message in progress collapses to the bottom of the screen. Now you can scroll through the message behind it—or you can navigate to *any* message in any Mail account or folder. This is a great trick when, for example, you want to copy some text out of an earlier message.

Actually, you can collapse multiple outgoing messages like this, leaving them unfinished but still open. They pile up at the bottom of the screen. (Hold your finger down on them to "fan" them open.)

When you're ready to resume writing, tap the title bar at the bottom of the screen; your composition window opens right back up.

6. **Attach a photo, video, or drawing,** if you like. Hold down your finger lightly anywhere in the body of the message until the **Select** buttons appear. Tap ▶ to reveal the **Insert Photo or Video** button (below, left).

When you tap it, you're shown your iPhone's usual photo browser so that you can choose the photos and videos you want to attach (below, middle). Tap the collection you want; you're shown all the thumbnails inside. Tap the photo or video, and then tap **Choose**.

You return to your message in progress, with the photo or video neatly inserted (previous page, right). You can repeat this step to add additional photo or video attachments. When you tap **Send**, you're offered the opportunity to scale down the photo to a more reasonable (emailable) size.

TIP: You can also email a photo or a video from within the Photos program; you can *forward* a file attached to an incoming piece of mail; and you can *paste* a copied photo or video (or several) into an open email message.

In iOS 11, you can also insert a freehand drawing (or maybe the term is free*finger*). Once again, hold down your finger until the **Select** buttons appear. Tap ▶ a couple of times, to reveal the **Insert Drawing** button. When you tap it, you open the standard Markup tools—pen, highlighter, pencil, eraser, lasso, color picker, text box, arrows, geometrical shapes, and Undo—exactly as described on page 307.

Tap **Insert Sketch** once your masterpiece is complete; it appears as an inserted image in your outgoing message.

7. **Format the text,** if you like. You can apply bold, italic, or underlining.

   The trick is to select the text first (page 105). When the button bar appears, tap the **B***I*U button. Tap that to make the **Bold**, *Italics*, and **Underline** buttons appear on the button bar; tap away. Not terribly efficient, but it works.

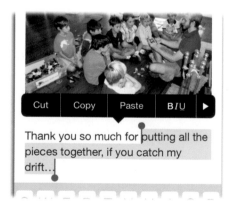
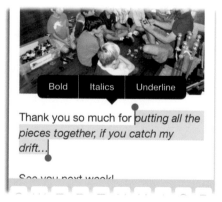

You can use the same trick to summon the Quote Level controls. Select some text or move the cursor to the paragraph you want; tap the ▶ until you bring the **Quote Level** button into view; and tap it to reveal the **Increase** and **Decrease** buttons. These buttons indent or un-indent those cluttery blocks of quoted and re-quoted text that often appear when you're replying to a message. (One tap affects the entire paragraph.)

If you really can't stand those quote indentations, you can stop the iPhone from adding them in the first place when you forward or reply to a message. The on/off switch for that feature is in **Settings→Mail→Increase Quote Level**.

8. **Tap Send (to send the message) or Cancel (to back out of it).** If you tap **Cancel**, the iPhone asks if you want to save the message. If you tap **Save Draft**, then the message lands in your Drafts folder.

   Later you can open the **Drafts** folder, tap the aborted message, finish it up, and send it.

> **TIP:** If you *hold down* the ☑ button for a moment, the iPhone presents a list of your saved drafts. Clever stuff—if you remember it!

Oh, and by the way: You can begin composing a message on your phone, and then continue writing it on your Mac, without ever having to save it as a draft. Or go the other way. See page 560 for details on Handoff.

Signatures

A *signature* is a bit of text that gets stamped at the bottom of your outgoing messages. It can be your name, a postal address, or a pithy quote.

Unless you intervene, the iPhone stamps "Sent from my iPhone" at the bottom of every message. You may be just fine with that, or you may consider it the equivalent of free advertising for Apple (or it may just feel like gloating). In any case, you can change the signature if you want to.

From the Home screen, tap **Settings→Mail→Signature**. You can make up one signature for **All Accounts**, or a different one for each account (tap **Per Account**). A Signature text area appears, complete with a keyboard, so you can compose the signature you want. It can even include emoji!

> **TIP:** You can use bold, italic, or underline formatting in your signature, too. Just follow the steps on the previous page for formatting a message: Select the text, tap the ▶ to bring the **B***I*U button into view, and so on.

Finish with a Phone Call

If you're typing out some reply, and you realize that it'd be faster to wrap this up by phone, hold down the home button (or iPhone X side button) to trigger Siri and just say, "Call him" or "Call her."

If the addressee has a phone number in Contacts, Siri knows who you mean; she dials the number for you, right from the Mail app!

Four Settings Worth Tweaking

The options awaiting you in **Settings→Mail** cover a huge range of email behaviors. Here are a few of the most useful.

- **Preview.** Messages in your inbox are listed with the subject line in bold type *and* a couple of lines, in light-gray text, that preview the message itself. You can control how many lines of the preview show up here, from **None** (you see more message titles on each screen without scrolling) to **5 Lines**..

- **Show To/Cc labels.** The iPhone can display a **To** or **Cc** logo on each message. At a glance, it helps you identify which messages are actually intended for *you*. Messages without those logos are probably spam, newsletters, mailing lists, or other messages that weren't specifically addressed to you.

  Default Account. If you have several accounts, which one does the iPhone use when you send mail from other apps—like when you email a photo from Photos or a link from Safari?

  It uses the *default* account, of course. You determine which one is the default account in **Settings→Mail→Default Account**.

- **Settings by account.** In iOS 11, the options that may differ by account are stored in a separate location: **Settings→Accounts & Passwords**. If you have more than one email account, here's where you can tap one to delete it or just temporarily deactivate it (turn off **Mail**)—for example, to accommodate your travel schedule, or just because you're really tired of dealing with email.

PART FOUR

Connections

15

Syncing with iTunes

Apple's iTunes program began life as a loading dock for iPods way back in 2001. Eventually, it became an essential partner for our iPhones; we used iTunes to shop for, organize, and sync movies, photos, apps, ebooks, and music to our phones.

Today, though, it's perfectly possible to use all of an iPhone's features without iTunes—and even without a computer. You can download all your apps, music, movies, and books right from the Internet, and you can back up your phone using iCloud (see the next chapter).

In fact, you *can't* use iTunes anymore for apps and ringtones. In the latest version, Apple stripped out those functions. (When you first open iTunes 12.7 or later, a message lets you know that "iTunes has been updated to focus on music, movies, TV shows, podcasts, and audiobooks.")

Why? Because, after years of listening to consumer complaints that iTunes has become too overloaded with functions, Apple felt that this was one task iTunes didn't need to handle. Today you have to buy and organize apps and ringtones directly from your phone.

> **TIP:** So wait—without iTunes storing app and ringtone backups on your computer, how do you re-download apps and ringtones you've bought but don't currently have on your phone? Like this. On the phone, open the App Store app, and then tap **Today**→**[your icon in the top-right corner]**→**Purchased**→**Not on This iPhone**.
>
> For ringtones, open **Settings**→**Sounds & Haptics**. Tap Ringtone; at the top of the page, tap **Download All Purchased Tones**. (If you don't see that button, it's because you haven't bought any Apple ringtones, or you've already re-downloaded them.)

Still, for managing music and videos, iTunes is an efficient tool. And for backups, it's nice to know that your stuff is all stored on a machine that's within your control.

Connecting the iPhone

iTunes is designed to load up, and back up, your iPhone. You can connect it to your computer either wirelessly over Wi-Fi, or wirefully, with the white USB cable that came with the iPhone.

- **Connecting the phone with a cable.** Plug one end of the iPhone's white charging cable into your computer's USB jack. Connect the other end to the phone.

> **NOTE:** If you have a 2016-or-later MacBook Pro (which has only USB-C jacks), you'll need either a USB-C adapter or a USB-C–to–Lightning cable to connect your phone.

- **Connecting over Wi-Fi.** The iPhone can be charging in its bedside alarm clock dock, happily and automatically syncing with your laptop somewhere else in the house. It transfers all the same stuff to and from your computer—apps, music, books, contacts, calendars, movies, photos, ringtones—but through the air instead of a cable.

  Your computer has to be on and running iTunes. The phone and the computer have to be on the same Wi-Fi network.

  To set up wireless sync, connect the phone using the white USB cable, one last time. Ironic, but true.

  Now open iTunes and click the ▯ (iPhone) button near the top-left corner of the iTunes screen. Now you can look over the iPhone's contents or sync it (read on).

On the Summary tab, scroll down; turn on **Sync with this iPhone over Wi-Fi**. Click **Apply**. You can now detach the phone.

From now on, whenever the phone is on the Wi-Fi network, it's automatically connected to your computer, wirelessly. You don't even have to think about it. (Well, OK—you have to think about leaving the computer turned on with iTunes open, which is something of a buzzkill.)

All About Syncing

In general, syncing (transferring data between the iPhone and the computer) begins automatically when you connect the phone. The $\circlearrowleft$ icon whirls in the top-left corner of the screen, but you're welcome to keep using your iPhone while it syncs.

Truth is, most people these days don't bother with iTunes for syncing; they let the phone sync with their computers wirelessly, via free iCloud accounts.

If you're a little queasy about letting a third party (Apple) store your personal data, though, you can also do this task manually. You can let the iPhone and computer sync directly—no Internet is involved.

Ordinarily, the iPhone-iTunes relationship is automatic, according to this scheme:

- **Bidirectional copying (iPhone↔computer).** Contacts, calendars, and web bookmarks get copied in both directions. After a sync, your computer and phone contain exactly the same information.

- **One-way sync (computer→iPhone).** All of the following gets copied in one direction: computer to phone. Music, TV, movies, ringtones, and ebooks you bought on your computer; photos from your computer; and email account information.

- **One-way sync (iPhone→computer).** Photos and videos taken with the iPhone's camera; music, videos, apps, ringtones, and ebooks you bought right from the phone—it all gets copied the other way, from the phone to the computer.

- **A complete backup.** iTunes also backs up *everything else* on your iPhone: settings, text messages, call history, and so on. Details on this backup business are covered starting on page 529.

If you're in a hurry, you can skip the time-consuming backup portion of the sync. Just click ◉ at the top of the iTunes window whenever it says "Backing up." iTunes gets the message and skips right ahead to the next phase of the sync—transferring contacts, calendars, music, and so on.

Manual Syncing

OK, but what if you don't *want* iTunes to start syncing every time you connect your iPhone? What if, for example, you want to change the assortment of music and video that gets copied to it? Or what if you just want to connect the USB cable to *charge* the phone, not to sync it?

In that case, you can stop the autosyncing in any of these ways:

- **Interrupt a sync in progress.** Click ✖ in the iTunes status window.

- **Stop iTunes from syncing with the iPhone just this time.** As you plug in the iPhone's cable, hold down the Shift+Ctrl keys (Windows) or the ⌘-Option keys (Mac) until the iPhone pops up in the iTunes window. Now you can see what's on the iPhone and change what will be synced to it—but no syncing takes place until you command it.

- **Stop iTunes from auto-syncing with this iPhone.** Connect the iPhone. Click ▯ in the upper-left corner of iTunes. On the **Summary** tab, turn off **Automatically sync when this iPhone is connected**.

- **Stop iTunes from autosyncing any iPhone, ever.** In iTunes, choose **Edit→Preferences** (Windows) or **iTunes→Preferences** (Mac). Click the **Devices** tab and turn on **Prevent iPods, iPhones, and iPads from syncing automatically**. You can still trigger a sync on command when the iPhone is wired up—by clicking the **Sync** button.

Of course, you must have turned off autosyncing for a reason. And that reason might be that you want to control what gets copied onto your iPhone. Maybe you're in a hurry to leave for the airport, and you don't have time to sit there for an hour while six downloaded movies get copied to it. Maybe you have 50 gigabytes of music but only 16 gigs of iPhone storage.

In any case, here are the two ways you can sync manually:

- **Use the tabs in iTunes.** With the iPhone connected, you can specify exactly what you want copied to it—which songs, which TV shows, which apps, and so on—using the various tabs in iTunes, as described on the following pages. Once you've made your selections, click the **Summary** tab and then click **Apply**. (The **Apply** button says **Sync** instead if you haven't actually changed any settings.)

- **Drag files onto the iPhone icon.** Once your iPhone is connected to your computer, you can click its icon and then turn on **Manually manage music and videos** (on the Summary screen). Click **Apply**.

Now you can drag songs and videos directly onto the iPhone's icon to copy them there. Wilder yet, you can bypass iTunes *entirely* by dragging music and video files *from your computer's desktop* onto the iPhone's icon. That's handy when you've just inherited or downloaded a bunch of song files, converted a DVD to the iPhone's video format, or whatever.

Just two notes of warning here. First, the iPhone accommodates dragged material from a *single* computer only. Second, if you ever turn off this option, then all those manually dragged songs and videos will disappear from your iPhone at the next sync opportunity.

TIP: Also on the Summary tab, you'll find the baffling little option called **Sync only checked songs and videos**. This is a global override—a last-ditch "Keep the embarrassing songs off my iPhone" option.

When this option is turned on, iTunes consults the tiny checkboxes next to every single song and video in your iTunes library. If you turn off a song's checkbox, it won't get synced to your iPhone, no matter what—even if you use the Music tab to sync **All songs or playlists**, or explicitly turn on a playlist that contains this song. If the song's or video's checkbox isn't checked in your Library list, then it will be left behind on your computer.

The Eight Tabs of iTunes

Once your iPhone is connected to the computer, and you've clicked its icon in the upper-left corner of iTunes, the left side of the iTunes window reveals a column of word buttons: **Summary**, **Music**, **Movies**, **TV Shows**, **Podcasts**, **Books**, **Photos**, and **Info**. Below that is a second, duplicate listing, labeled **On My Device**. For the most part, these represent the categories of stuff you can sync to your iPhone.

The following pages cover each of these tabs, in sequence, and detail how to sync each kind of iPhone-friendly material.

TIP: At the bottom of the screen, a colorful graph shows you the number and types of files: Audio, Video, Photos, Apps, Books, Documents & Data, and Other (for your personal data). More importantly, it also shows you how much room you have left, so you won't get overzealous in trying to load the thing up.

Point to each color block without clicking to see how many of each item there are ("2031 photos") and how much space they take up.

Summary Tab

This screen gives basic stats on your iPhone, like its serial number, capacity, and phone number. Buttons in the middle control how and where the iPhone gets backed up. Checkboxes at the bottom of the screen let you set up manual syncing, as described previously.

Serial Number, UDID

If you click your phone's serial number, it changes to reveal the *unique device identifier* (UDID). That's Apple's behind-the-scenes ID for your exact product, used primarily by software companies (developers). You may, during times of beta testing a new app or troubleshooting an existing one, be asked to supply your phone's UDID.

You can click the same label again to see your phone's Product Type and ECID. Or click your phone number to see your various cellular identifiers like the MEID, IMEI, and ICCID. Or click the iOS version to see your iOS version's build number.

Right-click (on the Mac, Control-click) any of these numbers to get the **Copy** command. It copies those long strings of letters and numbers onto your computer's Clipboard, ready to paste into an email or a text.

Music Tab

Turn on **Sync Music**. Now decide **what** music to put on your phone.

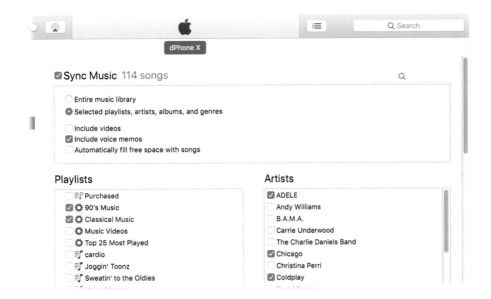

- If you have a big iPhone and a small music library, you can opt to sync the **Entire music library**.

- If you have a big music collection and a small iPhone, you'll have to take only **some** of it along for the iPhone ride. In that case, click **Selected playlists, artists, albums, and genres**. In the lists below, turn on the checkboxes for the playlists, artists, albums, and music genres you want to transfer. (These are cumulative. If there's no Electric Light Orchestra in any of your selected playlists, but you turn on ELO in the Artists list, you'll get all your ELO anyway.)

Music videos and voice memos (recorded by the iPhone and now resid-
ing on your computer) get their own checkboxes.

Making It All Fit

An iPhone holds a finite amount of music and video. If you turn on **Sync
All** checkboxes, a message may say that it won't all fit on the iPhone. One
solution: Tiptoe through the tabs, turning off checkboxes and trying to
sync until the "too much" error message goes away.

If you don't have quite so much time, turn on **Automatically fill free space
with songs**. It uses artificial intelligence to load up your phone automatically, using your most played and most recent music as a guide. (It does
not, in fact, fill the phone completely; it leaves a few hundred megabytes
for safety—so you can download more stuff on the road, for example.)

Another helpful approach is to use the ***smart playlist***, a music playlist
that assembles itself based on criteria that you supply. For example:

1. **In iTunes, choose Music from the top-left pop-up menu.** Choose
   File→New Smart Playlist. The Smart Playlist dialog box appears.

2. **Specify the category.** Use the pop-up menus to choose, for example, a musical genre, songs you've played recently, songs you ***haven't***
   played recently, or ones you've rated highly.

3. **Turn on the "Limit to" checkbox, and set up the constraints.** For
   example, you could limit the amount of music in this playlist to 2 gigabytes, chosen at random. That way, every time you sync, you'll get a
   fresh, random supply of songs on your iPhone, with enough room left
   for some videos.

4. **Click OK.** The new Smart Playlist appears in the list of playlists at
   left; you can rename it. Click it to look it over, if you like. Then, on the
   Music tab, choose this playlist for syncing to the iPhone.

Movies and TV Shows Tabs

TV shows and movies you've bought or rented from the iTunes Store
look great on the iPhone. (And if you start watching a rented movie on
your computer, the iPhone can begin playing it from right where you
left off.)

Syncing TV shows and movies works just like syncing music or podcasts.
You can have iTunes copy ***all*** your stuff to the iPhone, but video fills up
your storage fast. That's why you can turn on the checkboxes of just the
individual movies or shows (either seasons or episodes) you want—or,

using the **Automatically include** pop-up menu, request only the most recent, or the most recent ones you haven't seen yet.

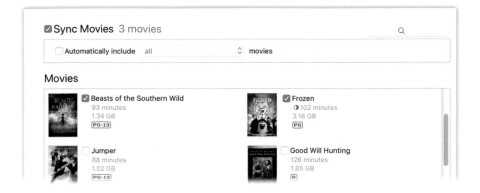

Podcasts Tab

The iTunes Store lists thousands of free amateur and professional podcasts (page 431). On this tab, you can choose to sync all episodes, selected shows, all unplayed episodes—or just a certain number of episodes per sync. Checkboxes let you choose *which* podcast series get to come along for the ride, so you can sync to suit your mood.

This tab also includes your iTunes U recordings (educational seminars that used to get their own tab).

Books Tab

Here are thumbnails of your audiobooks and your ebooks—those you've bought from Apple, downloaded from the web, or dragged into iTunes from your desktop (PDF files, for example). You can ask iTunes to send them all to your phone—or only the ones whose checkboxes you turn on.

Photos Tab

If you've turned on iCloud Photo Library (page 337), this tab appears blank, except for a note that "iCloud Photos is On." After all, your photos are *already* syncing. If not...read on.

Syncing Photos and Videos (Computer→iPhone)

iTunes can sync the photos from your hard drive onto your iPhone. You can even select individual albums of images that you've already assembled on your computer.

Here are your photo-filling options for the iPhone:

- **Windows:** You can sync with Photoshop Elements, Photoshop Album, or any folder of photos, like Pictures (in Windows).

- **Mac:** You can sync with Photos, iPhoto, or Aperture.

When you're ready to sync your photos, click the **Photos** tab in iTunes. Turn on **Sync photos from**, and then indicate *where* you'd like to sync them from (Photoshop Elements, the Mac's program Photos, or whatever).

If you've chosen a photo-shoebox program's name (and not a folder's name), you can then click **Selected albums, Events, and Faces**. Turn on the checkboxes of the albums, events, and faces you want synced. (The "faces" option is available only if you're syncing from Photos or Aperture on the Mac, and only if you've used the Faces feature, which groups your photos according to who's in them.)

This option also offers to tack on recent Events (photos taken the same day). Indicate whether or not you want videos included (**Include videos**).

Once you make your selections and click **Apply**, the program computes for a time, "optimizing" copies of your photos to make them look great on the iPhone (for example, downsizing them from 20-megapixel over-kill to something more appropriate for a 0.6-megapixel screen), and then ports them over.

After the sync is complete, you'll be able to wave your iPhone around, and people will *beg* to see your photos.

Syncing Photos and Videos (iPhone→Computer)

You can go the opposite direction, too: You can send photos and videos you took with the iPhone's camera *to* the computer. You can rest easy, knowing that they're backed up to your computer for safekeeping.

Now, it's important to understand that *iTunes is not involved* in this process. It doesn't know anything about photos or videos *from* the iPhone.

So what's handling the iPhone-to-computer transfer? Your operating system. It treats the iPhone as though it's a digital camera and suggests importing them just as it would from a camera's memory card.

Here's how it goes: Plug the iPhone into the computer with the USB cable. What you'll see is probably something like this:

- **On the Mac.** Photos opens. This free photo-organizing/editing program comes on every Mac. Shortly after the program notices that the iPhone is on the premises, it goes into Import mode. Click **Import**

All, or select some thumbnails from the iPhone and then click **Import Selected**.

- **In Windows.** When you attach a camera (or an iPhone), a dialog box asks how you want its contents handled. It lists any photo-management program you might have installed (Photoshop Elements, Photoshop Album, and so on), as well as Windows' own camera-management software. Click the program you want to handle import-ing the iPhone pictures and videos.

  You'll probably also want to turn on **Always do this for this device**, so it'll happen automatically the next time.

Info Tab

This tab is unnecessary if you're using iCloud (Chapter 16) to sync your phone's contacts, calendar, email settings, and web bookmarks with your computer. Instead, this tab is exclusively for the six people who still use iTunes to sync these data types with a Windows program like Outlook, Outlook Express, or Windows Mail; a Mac program like Contacts or Entourage/Outlook for Mac; or an online address book like Google Contacts or Yahoo Address Book.

Similarly, you can sync the phone's calendar with a program like Outlook (for Windows) or Calendar or Outlook (on the Mac).

File Sharing

Some iPhone apps create documents that you can open in similar apps on your computer—and vice versa. You can edit the same iMovie videos on both the Mac and the iPhone. Similarly, scanning apps can share their scanned image files.

This tab lists all iOS apps that can share their documents, and lets you copy them to or from your computer.

NOTE: Actually, though, using the new Files app—and a virtual disk like iCloud Drive or Dropbox—is actually a far simpler, more useful way to move these files back and forth. Why? Because you don't *have* to move them back and forth. They're always available, in their latest versions, to all your machines. See page 387.

If you still decide to use this clunky method, here's how it goes:

- **From phone to computer.** Click the app's name. In the rightmost column, drag the files you want out of the iTunes window onto your desktop. (Or click **Save To** and choose a folder location.)

- **From computer to phone.** Click the app's name. Drag the files you want out of a desktop window into the rightmost iTunes column. (Or click **Add** and choose the file manually.)

Next time you sync, those files will move the way you've specified.

On My Device

Below those Settings tabs at the left side of the iTunes window, there's a second, similar set labeled **On My Device**. It's a tidy list of everything that is, in fact, on your device, organized by type (Music, Movies, and so on). There's not really much you can *do* here—you can get more information about some items by pointing to them—but just seeing your multimedia empire arrayed before you can be very satisfying.

The Purchased category, in particular, can be handy; it shows everything on your phone that you've bought *with* the phone.

One iPhone, Multiple Computers

You can actually sync an iPhone with *multiple* Macs or PCs. You might want, for example, to fill it up with music and video from a Mac at home; contacts, calendar, ebooks, and iPhone applications from your Windows PC at work; and maybe even the photos from your laptop. All you have to do is set up the tabs of each computer's copy of iTunes to sync *only* certain kinds of material.

On the Mac, for example, you'd turn on the Sync checkboxes for only the Music, Podcasts, and Video tabs. Sync away. Next, take the iPhone to the office; on your PC, turn on the **Sync** checkboxes on only the Info, Books, and Apps tabs. Sync away once more. Then, on the laptop, turn off **Sync** on all tabs except Photos.

Each time you connect the iPhone to one of the computers, it syncs that data according to the preferences set in that copy of iTunes.

One Computer, Multiple iPhones

It's fine to sync multiple iPhones with a single computer, too. iTunes cheerfully fills each one up, and can back each one up, as they come. In fact, if you open the Preferences box (in the iTunes menu on the Mac, the Edit menu in Windows), the Devices tab lists all the iPhones that iTunes is tracking (and iPads and iPod Touches).

Backing Up the iPhone

iTunes can back up everything your computer doesn't already have a copy of: stuff you downloaded straight to the phone (music, ebooks, apps, and so on), plus less visible things, like your iPhone's mail and network settings, your call history, contact favorites, notes, text messages, and other personal preferences that are hard or impossible to recreate.

> **TIP:** If you turn on **Encrypted iPhone Backup**, then your backup will also include all your *passwords*: for Wi-Fi hotspots, websites, email accounts, and so on. That can save you tons of time when you have to restore the phone from the backup. (The one downside: You have to make up a password *for the backup itself*. Don't forget it!)

You can create your backups in either of two places:

- **On your computer.** You get a backup every time the iPhone syncs with iTunes. The backup also happens before you install a new iPhone firmware version from Apple or restore your phone.

- **In iCloud.** You can also back up your phone wirelessly and automatically—to iCloud. That kind of backup will be available even if your computer croaks. On the other hand, since your free iCloud storage holds only 5 gigabytes, and your phone holds 16 gigabytes or more, the free iCloud account usually isn't enough. See the next chapter for details.

You make this choice on the **Summary** tab.

Using That Backup

Maybe you lost your phone, or maybe you've upgraded to a new phone.

To restore your data and settings, connect the iPhone to the computer you normally use to sync with. Click the ▯ (iPhone) button; click the **Summary** tab; click **Restore iPhone**.

A message announces that you can't erase the phone without first turning off Find My iPhone. This is a security measure to stop a thief from erasing a stolen phone. He can't restore the phone without turning off Find My iPhone, which requires your iCloud password. Go to the phone and do that (in **Settings→[your name]→iCloud**).

Take iTunes up on its offer to restore all your settings and stuff from the backup.

If you see multiple backup files listed from other iPhones (or an iPod Touch), be sure to pick the backup file for *your* phone. Let the backup restore your phone settings and info. Exhale.

An iPhone backup no longer includes your apps. Instead, the backup remembers *which* apps you had, and where their icons were on your Home screens—but the actual multi-gigabyte wad of the apps themselves is not part of the backup. That's why backups take much less time than before, and much less space on your computer.

It does mean, though, that after a restore, you see only dimmed copies of your apps. It takes some time in a Wi-Fi hotspot for iOS to re-download them all. Little pie charts on the icons let you know how it's doing.

Deleting a Backup File

To save disk space, you can delete old backups (especially for i-gadgets you no longer own). Go to the iTunes preferences (**Edit→Preferences** in Windows or **iTunes→Preferences** on the Mac) and click the **Devices** tab.

Click the dated backup file you don't want and hit **Delete Backup**.

16

iCloud & Apple Pay

The free iCloud service stems from Apple's brainstorm that, since it controls both ends of the connection between a Mac and the Apple website, it should be able to create some pretty clever Internet-based features.

This chapter concerns what iCloud can do for you, the iPhone owner.

NOTE: To get a free iCloud account if you don't already have one, sign up in **Settings→iCloud**.

What iCloud Giveth

So what is iCloud? Mainly, it's these things:

- **iCloud Sync.** It keeps your calendar, address book, and documents updated and identical on all your gadgets: Mac, PC, iPhone, iPad, iPod Touch. Also your web passwords, credit card numbers, AirPod (wireless earbud) pairing, and all kinds of other things. That's a huge convenience—almost magical.

- **Find My iPhone.** Find My iPhone pinpoints the current location of your iPhone (or iPad, or Mac, or AirPods) on a map. In other words, it's great for helping you find your gadgets if they've been stolen or lost.

  You can also make a lost device make a loud pinging sound for a couple of minutes by remote control—even if it was silenced. That's brilliantly effective when your phone has slipped between the couch cushions.

- **Automatic backup.** iCloud can back up your iPhone—automatically and wirelessly (over Wi-Fi, not over cellular connections). It's a quick backup, since iCloud backs up only the changed data.

If you ever want to set up a new i-gadget, or if you want to restore everything to an existing one, life is sweet. Once you're in a Wi-Fi hotspot, all you have to do is re-enter your Apple ID and password in the setup assistant that appears when you turn the thing on. Magically, your gadget is refilled with everything that used to be on it.

Well, *almost* everything. An iCloud backup stores everything you've bought from Apple (music, books); photos and videos in your Photos app; settings, including the layout of your Home screen; text messages; and ringtones. You'll have to reestablish your passwords (for hotspots, websites, and so on) and anything that came from your computer (like music/ringtones/videos from iTunes and photos from the Photos app).

NOTE: A backup no longer stores actual copies of all your apps. Instead, to make the backup faster and smaller, it stores only *references* to your apps—bookmarks, basically. See page 530 for details.

- **iCloud Drive** is Apple's version of Dropbox. It's a folder, present on every Mac, iPhone, iPad, and iPod Touch, that lists whatever you've put into it—an online "disk" that holds 5 gigabytes (more, if you're willing to pay for it).

  The iCloud Drive is a perfect place to put stuff you want to be able to access from any Apple gadget, wherever you go. It's a great backup, too.

- **An email account.** Handy, really: An iCloud account gives you a new email address, ending with *@icloud.com* or *@me.com*. If you already have an email address, great! This new one can be a backup account, one you never enter on websites so that it never gets overrun with spam. Or vice versa: Let *this* be your junk account, the address you use for online forms. Either way, it's great to have a second account.

- **An online locker.** Anything you buy from Apple—music, TV shows, ebooks, apps—is stored online for easy access at any time. For example, whenever you buy a song or a TV show from the online iTunes Store, it appears automatically on your iPhone and computers. Your photos are stored online, too.

- **Apple Pay** is the feature that lets you pay for things just by waving your phone at them, or send money to friends and family, phone-to-phone. No wallet, no credit card needed.

- **Family Sharing** is a broad category of features intended for families (up to six people).

First, everyone can share stuff bought from Apple's online stores: movies, TV shows, music, ebooks, and so on. It's all on a single credit card, but you, the all-knowing parent, can approve each person's purchases—without having to share your account password. That's a great solution to a long-standing problem.

There's also a shared family photo album and an auto-shared Family category on the calendar. Any family member can see the location of any other family member, and they can find one another's lost iPhones or iPads using Find My iPhone.

- **Continuity.** If you have a Mac, and it's running OS X Yosemite or later, you're in for a treat. The set of features Apple calls Continuity turn the iPhone into a part of the Mac. They let you make calls from your Mac as though it were a speakerphone. They let you send and receive text messages from your Mac—to any cellphone on earth. They let you AirDrop files between computer and phone, wirelessly. And more.

That was the quick overview. The rest of this chapter covers each of these iCloud-related features in greater depth, in the same order—except for Continuity, which gets its own chapter right after this one.

iCloud Sync

For many people, this is the killer app for iCloud: The iCloud website, acting as the master control center, can keep multiple Macs, Windows PCs, and iPhones/iPads/iPod Touches synchronized. That offers both a huge convenience factor—all your stuff is always on all your gadgets—and a safety/backup factor, since you have duplicates everywhere.

It works by storing the master copies of your stuff—email, notes, contacts, calendars, web bookmarks, and documents—on the web. (Or "in the cloud," as the product managers would say.)

Whenever your Macs, PCs, or i-gadgets are online—over Wi-Fi or cellular—they connect to the mother ship and update themselves. Edit an address on your iPhone, and shortly thereafter you'll find the same change in Contacts (on your Mac) and Outlook (on your PC). Send an email reply from your PC at the office, and you'll find it in your Sent Mail folder on the Mac at home. Add a web bookmark anywhere and find it everywhere else. Edit a spreadsheet in Numbers on your iPad and find the same numbers updated on your Mac.

> **NOTE:** Actually, there's yet another place where you can work with your data: on the web. Using any computer, you can log into *icloud.com* to find web-based clones of Calendar, Contacts, Mail, Notes, Reminders, and Photos. In fact, there are even web-based versions of Pages, Numbers, and Keynote!

To control the syncing, tap **Settings→[your name]→iCloud** on your iPhone. Turn on the checkboxes of the stuff you want to be synchronized all the way around:

- **Photos.** Tap to see a subset of the controls described on page 605—only the switches that control iCloud photo features. Namely:

  iCloud Photo Library is Apple's online photo storage feature. It stores all your photos and videos online, so you can access them from any Apple gadget. See page 337.

  Optimize iPhone Storage is an ingenious way to save space on your phone; see page 338.

  Upload to My Photo Stream and **iCloud Photo Sharing** are the master switches for Photo Streams, which are among iCloud's marquee features (page 329).

  When you hold your finger down on the shutter button, the iPhone 5s and later models can snap 10 frames a second. That's burst mode—

and all those photos can fill up your iCloud storage. So Apple gives you the **Upload Burst Photos** option so you can decide whether you want them to be part of the backup.

- **Mail.** "Mail" refers to your actual email messages, plus your account settings and preferences from iOS's Mail program.

- **Messages.** In iOS 11, all those text messages and iMessages, once stored only in the Messages app, can be stored on iCloud. That way, you don't wind up with missing chunks of conversation histories as you move from device to device—and you save a ton of space on your phone. (Apple added this feature in iOS 11.2.)

- **Contacts, Calendars.** This option keeps all your address books and calendars synchronized. Delete a phone number on your computer at home, and you'll find it gone from your phone. Enter an appointment on your iPhone, and you'll find the calendar updated everywhere else.

- **Reminders** refers to the to-do items you create in the phone's Reminders app; very shortly, those reminders will show up on your Mac (in Reminders, Calendar, or BusyCal) or PC (in Outlook). How great to make a reminder for yourself in one place and have it reminding you later in another one!

- **Notes** syncs the notes from your phone's Notes app into the Notes app on the Mac, the email program on your PC, your other i-gadgets, and, of course, the iCloud website.

- **Safari.** If a website is important enough to merit bookmarking on your phone, why shouldn't it also show up in the Bookmarks menu on your desktop PC at home, your Mac laptop, or your iPad? This option syncs your Safari Reading List (page 473), too.

- **News** refers to the sources and topics you've set up in the News app (page 417).

- **Home** refers to the setups for any home-automation gear you've installed (page 393).

- **Health** can sync via iCloud for the first time in iOS 11. It includes all the fitness and medical stats.

- **Wallet.** If you've bought tickets for a movie, show, game, or flight, you sure as heck don't want to be stuck without them because you left the barcode on your other gadget.

- **Keychain.** The login information for your websites (names and passwords), and even your credit card information, can be stored right on your phone—and synced to your other iPhones, iPads, and Macs (running OS X Mavericks or later).

Having your passwords and credit cards magically synced across your computers and mobile gadgets saves you unending headaches. This is a truly great feature, and it's worth enduring the setup.

<table>
<tr><td>**NOTE:**</td><td>You may notice that there are no switches here for syncing stuff you buy from Apple, like books, movies, apps, and music. They're not so much *synced* as they are *stored* for you online. You can download them at any time to any of your machines.</td></tr>
</table>

- **Other apps' data.** If you've turned on iCloud Drive, then you also see a list of apps that would like permission to save their data onto it—so that your *apps'* data is synced across devices, too.

- **Look Me Up by Email** is a list of apps that permit other iCloud members to find you by looking up your address.

Find My iPhone

Did you leave your iPhone somewhere? Did it get stolen? Has that mischievous 5-year-old left it somewhere in the house again? Sounds like you're ready to use one of Apple's finest creations: Find My iPhone.

Log into *iCloud.com* and click **Find My iPhone**. Immediately, the website updates to show you, on a map, the current location of your phone—and Macs, iPod Touches, iPads, and even AirPod earbuds. (If they're not online, or if they're turned all the way off, you won't see their current locations.)

If you own more than one, click **All Devices** and, from the list, choose the one you're looking for.

If just knowing where the thing *is* isn't enough to satisfy you, then click the dot representing your phone, click the ⓘ next to its name, and marvel at the appearance of these three buttons:

- **Play Sound.** When you click this button, the phone starts dinging and vibrating loudly for two minutes, wherever it is, so you can figure out which jacket pocket you left it in. It beeps even if the ringer switch is off, and even if the phone is asleep. Once you find the phone, just wake it in the usual way to make the dinging stop.

- **Lost Mode.** When you lose your phone for real, proceed immediately to Lost Mode. Its first step: prompting you to password-protect it, if you haven't already. Without the password, a sleazy crook can't get into your phone without erasing it. (If your phone is already password-protected, you don't see this step.)

  The passcode you dream up here works just as though you'd created one yourself on the phone. That is, it remains in place until you, with the phone in hand, manually turn it off in Settings.

  Next, the website asks for a phone number where you can be reached, and (when you click **Next**) a message you want displayed on the iPhone's Lock screen. If you left the thing in a taxi or on some restaurant table, you can use this feature to plead for its return.

When you click **Done**, your message appears on the phone's screen, wherever it is, no matter what app was running, and the phone locks.

Whoever finds it can't miss the message, can't miss the **Call** button that's right there on the Lock screen, and can't do anything without dismissing the message first.

If the finder of your phone really isn't such a nice person, at least you'll get an automatic email every time the phone moves from place to place, so you can track the thief's whereabouts. (Apple sends these messages to your iCloud email address.)

- **Erase iPhone.** This is the last-ditch security option, for when your immediate concern isn't so much the phone as all the private stuff that's on it. Click this button, confirm the dire warning box, enter your iCloud ID, and click **Erase**. By remote control, you've just erased everything from your phone, wherever it may be. (If it's ever returned, you can restore it from your backup.)

  Once you've wiped the phone, you can no longer find it or send messages to it using Find My iPhone.

 TIP: There's an app for that. Download the Find My iPhone app from the App Store. It lets you do everything described here from another iPhone, in a tidy, simple control panel.

Send Last Location

Find My iPhone works great—as long as your lost phone has power, is turned on, and is online. Often, though, it's lying dead somewhere, or it's been turned off, or there's no Internet service. In those situations, you might think Find My iPhone can't help you.

But, thanks to **Send Last Location**, you still have a prayer of finding your phone again. Before it dies, your phone will send Apple its location. You have 24 hours to log into *iCloud.com* and use the Find My iPhone feature to see where it was at the time of death. (After that, Apple deletes the location information.)

You definitely want to turn this switch on.

Activation Lock

Thousands of people have found their lost or stolen iPhones by using Find My iPhone. Yay!

But until recently, Find My iPhone had a back door the size of Montana: The thief could simply erase the phone and sell it on the black market, which was his goal all along. Suddenly, your phone was lost in the wilderness, and you had no way to track or recover it.

That's why Apple offers the ingenious Activation Lock feature. It's very simple: Nobody can erase your phone, or even turn off Find My iPhone, without entering your iCloud password (your Apple ID). This isn't a switch you can turn on or off; it's always on.

So even if the bad guy has your phone and tries to sell it, the thing is useless. It's still registered to you, you can still track it, and it still displays your message and phone number on the Lock screen. Without your iCloud password, your iPhone is just a worthless brick. Suddenly, stealing iPhones is a much less attractive prospect. (Fun fact: In New York City reported iPhone thefts are down 90 percent since Activation Lock came along.)

iCloud Backup

Your phone can back itself up online, automatically, so that you'll never worry about losing your files along with your phone.

Of course, most of the important stuff is *already* backed up by iCloud, in the process of syncing it (calendar, contacts—all the stuff described on these pages). So this option just backs up everything else: all your settings, your Health app data, your documents, your account settings, and your photo library.

There are some footnotes. The wireless backing-up happens only when your phone is charging and in a Wi-Fi hotspot (because in a cellular area all that data would eat up your data limit each month). And a free iCloud account includes only 5 gigabytes of storage; your phone may require a lot more space than that. Using iCloud Backup generally means paying for more iCloud storage.

iCloud Drive

iCloud Drive is Apple's version of Dropbox. It's a single folder whose contents are replicated on every Apple machine you own—Mac, iPhone, iPad, iCloud.com—and even Windows PCs. See page 387 for details.

Email

Apple offers an email address as part of each iCloud account. Of course, you already *have* an email account. So why bother? The first advantage is the simple address: *YourName@me.com* or *YourName@icloud.com*.

Second, you can read your me.com email from any computer anywhere in the world, via the iCloud website, or on your iPhone/Mac/iPad.

To make things even sweeter, your me.com or icloud.com mail is completely synced. Delete a message on one gadget, and you'll find it in the Deleted Mail folder on another. Send a message from your iPhone, and you'll find it in the Sent Mail folder on your Mac. And so on.

Video, Music, Apps: Locker in the Sky

Apple, if you hadn't noticed, has become a big seller of multimedia files. It has the biggest music store in the world. It has the biggest app store, for both i-gadgets and Macs. It sells an awful lot of TV shows and movies. Its ebook store, iBooks, is no Amazon, but it's chugging along.

Once you buy a song, movie, app, or book, you can download it again as often as you like—no charge. In fact, you can download it to your *other* Apple equipment, too. iCloud automates, or at least formalizes, that process. Once you buy something, it's added to a list of items that you can download to all your *other* machines.

Here's how to grab them:

- **iPhone, iPad, iPod Touch.** *For apps:* Open the App Store icon. Tap **Updates**. Tap **Purchased** and then **My Purchases**. Tap **Not on This iPhone**.

  For music, movies, and TV shows: Open the iTunes Store app. Tap **More** and then **Purchased**; enter your password; tap the category you want. Tap **Not on This iPhone**.

  There they are: all the items you've ever bought, even on your *other* machines using the same Apple ID. To download anything listed here onto *this* machine, tap the ⬇ button. Or tap an album name to see the list of songs on it so you can download just *some* of those songs.

  You can save yourself all that tapping by opening **Settings→iTunes & App Store** and turning on **Automatic Downloads** (for music, apps, books, and audiobooks). From now on, whenever you're on Wi-Fi, stuff you've bought on other Apple machines gets downloaded to this one *automatically*.

- **Mac or PC.** Open the Mac App Store program (for Mac apps) and click **Purchases**. Or open the iTunes app (for songs, TV shows, books, and movies). Click **Store** and then, under Quick Links, click **Purchased**. There are all your purchases, ready to open or re-download.

To make this automatic, open iTunes. Choose **iTunes→ Preferences→Downloads**. Under **Automatic Downloads**, turn on **Music**, **Movies**, or **TV Shows**, as you see fit. Click **OK**. From now on, iTunes will auto-import any of those items that you buy on any of your other machines.

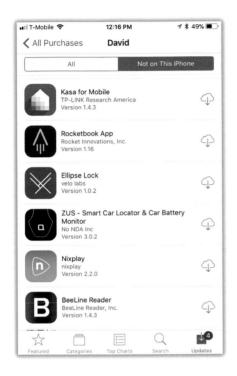
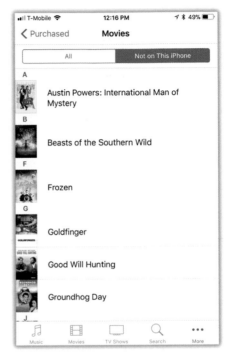

Any bookmark you set in an iBooks book is synced to your other gadgets, too. The idea, of course, is that you can read a few pages on your phone in the doctor's waiting room and then continue from the same page on your iPad on the train ride home.

The Price of Free

A free iCloud account gives you 5 gigabytes of online storage. That may not sound like much, especially when you consider how big some music, photo, and video files are. Fortunately, anything you buy from Apple—like music, apps, books, and TV shows—doesn't count against that 5-gigabyte limit. Neither do the photos in your Photo Stream.

So what's left? Some things that don't take up much space, like settings and documents—and some things that take up a lot of it, like photos and videos, backups, email, TV shows, and movies. Anything you put on your iCloud Drive eats up your allotment, too.

When you open **Settings→[your name]→iCloud**, you get a colorful graph showing how full your iCloud storage is, and what's filling it (page 533, right).

Tap **Manage Storage** to open a comprehensive screen that shows where all your iCloud space is going. For example, you'll see how much of it your **iCloud Photo Library** occupies (tap for the option to turn it off); how much each phone/tablet's **Backups** are eating up (tap a device's name to view the size and date of the last backup—and, if you like, to delete them); a list of apps you've permitted to save their **Documents & Data** onto your Drive (tap one to see what it's storing; swipe leftward to delete it); and how much space your iCloud **Mail** account is eating up.

Change Storage Plan lets you upgrade or downgrade the amount you're paying Apple for iCloud storage. For example, if you find 5 gigs constricting, you can expand it to 50 GB, 200 GB, or 2 TB—for $1, $3, or $10 a month.

Apple Pay

Breathe a sigh of relief. Now you can pay for things without cash, without cards, without signing anything, without your wallet: Just *hold the phone*. You don't have to open some app, don't have to enter a code, don't even have to wake the phone up. Touch ID or Face ID confirms that it's really you making the purchase; you've just paid.

You can't pay for things everywhere; the merchant has to have a wireless terminal attached to the register. You'll know, because you'll see one of two logos near the register, as shown here.

Apple says more than 2 million stores and restaurants accept Apple Pay, including chains like McDonald's, Walgreens, Starbucks, Macy's, Subway, Panera Bread, Best Buy, Duane Reade, Bloomingdale's, Staples, Chevron, and Whole Foods. The list grows all the time.

Apple Pay depends on a special chip in the phone: the NFC chip (near-field communication), and models before the iPhone 6 don't have it. Stores whose terminals don't speak NFC—like Walmart—don't work with Apple Pay, either.

The Setup

To set up Apple Pay, you have to teach your phone about your credit card. To do that, open the Wallet app. You can also start this process in **Settings→Wallet & Apple Pay**.

Tap **Add credit or debit card**. Tap **Next**.

Now, on the Add Card screen, you're asked to aim the phone's camera at whatever Visa, Mastercard, or American Express card you use most often. Hold steady until the digits of your card, your name, and the expiration date blink onto the screen, autorecognized. Cool! The phone even suggests a card description. You can manually edit any of those four fields before tapping **Done**.

> **NOTE:** If you don't have the card with you, you can also choose **Enter Card Details Manually** and type in the numbers yourself.

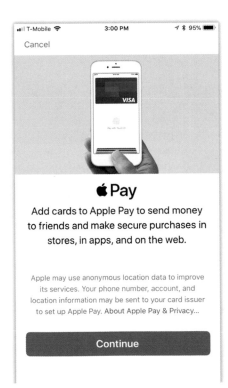

Check over the phone's interpretation of the card's information, and then hit **Next**.

Now you have to type in the security code. Hit **Next** again. Then agree to the legalese screen.

Next, your bank has to verify that all systems are go for Apple Pay. That may involve responding to an email or a text, or typing in a verification code. In any case, it's generally instantaneous.

> **NOTE:** Right now, Apple Pay works only with Mastercard, Visa, or American Express, and only the ones issued by certain banks. The big ones are all on board—Citibank, Chase, Bank of America, and so on—and more are signing on all the time.

You can record your store loyalty and rewards cards, too—and when you're in that store, the phone chooses the correct card automatically. When you're in Dunkin' Donuts, it automatically uses your Dunkin' Donuts card to pay.

> **TIP:** To change which card is your *default* (main) credit card, open **Settings→Wallet & Apple Pay**. That's where you can add and remove cards, too.

The Shopping

Once the cashier has rung up your total, here comes the magic. The exact steps depend on whether or not your phone has a home button:

- **With a home button.** Rest your finger on the home button—no need to wake the phone—and bring it within an inch of the terminal. The phone buzzes, beeps, and says "Done"; it's all over. It takes about two seconds.

> **NOTE:** That's how you pay with your primary (default) credit card. If you've stored more than one, and you want to choose a different one today, the procedure is slightly different: Bring the phone near the terminal (*without* involving the home button). When your main card appears, tap it, tap a different card, and *then* touch the home button.

- **With an iPhone X.** The procedure is different: You're supposed to confirm your identity before you bring the phone near the Apple Pay terminal.

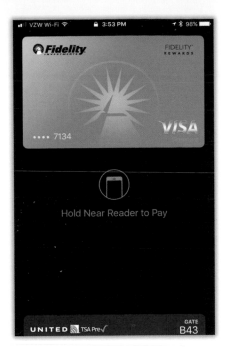

So begin by double-clicking the side button to make the Apple Pay screen appear. (At this point, you can tap the picture of your default card to choose a different one.)

Authenticate either by looking at the phone (Face ID) or entering your passcode (boring). Now bring the phone within an inch of the terminal. The phone buzzes, beeps, and says "Done"; it's all over.

NOTE: If you find that you're often bringing up the Apple Pay screen with accidental double-presses of your side button, you can turn off **Settings→Wallet & Apple Pay→Double-Click Side Button**. Don't worry; you can still use Apple Pay—by tapping its icon on your Control Center (page 49).

An Apple Pay purchase is just a regular credit card purchase. So you still get your rewards points, frequent-flier miles, and so on. (Returning something works the same way: At the moment when you'd swipe your card, you bring the phone near the reader until it beeps. Slick.)

Apple points out that Apple Pay is much more secure than using a credit card, because the store never sees, receives, or stores your card number, or even your name. Instead, the phone transmits a temporary, one-time, encoded number that means nothing to the merchant. It incorporates verification codes that only the card issuer (your bank) can translate and verify.

Apple never sees what you've bought or where, either. You can open Wallet and tap a card's picture to see the last few transactions, but that info exists only on your iPhone.

And what if your phone gets stolen? Too bad—for the thief. He can't buy anything without your fingerprint or face. If you're still worried, you can always visit *iCloud.com*, click **Settings**, tap your phone's name, and click **Remove All** to de-register your cards from the phone by remote control.

Apple Pay Online

You can buy things online, too, using iPhone apps that have been upgraded to work with Apple Pay. The time savings: no typing your name, address, and phone number every time you buy something.

Instead, when you're staring at the checkout screen for some app, just tap **Buy with Apple Pay**.

There's Apple Pay on websites, too. For example, if you're shopping on a Mac (and it doesn't have its own fingerprint reader), you can authenticate with your *phone's* fingerprint reader or Face ID. The "OK, all clear" signal gets sent to your Mac automatically.

Apple Pay Cash

You can now send cash to other members of the great, global Apple family with just a couple of taps, directly from your phone. Pay the piano teacher. Pay your share of the bill at a restaurant. Send money to your kid at college. It's like writing a check or handing over cash—without the checks or the cash. It's just like Venmo, Square Cash, or PayPal Cash, only...it's Apple's.

To use Apple Pay Cash, you need iOS 11.2 or later, with two-factor authentication turned on (page 622). Then:

- **Set up Apple Pay Cash.** The Apple Pay Cash card is, of course, an electronic fiction—there's no actual plastic card you slip into your physical purse or wallet. (That didn't stop Apple from trying to make it *look* like a real card with anti-piracy features—try shifting your phone around, and marvel at the iridescent, color-changing "anti-piracy" design!)

  So you can't use Cash until you've first set up Apple Pay, which requires a *real* credit or debit card. Whenever you pay somebody, your Cash card draws money from that actual card. (If you link to a *debit* card, using Apple Pay cash is always free—nobody takes a cut.

If you link it to a **credit** card, you get hit with a 3 percent fee each time.)

Once that's done, open **Settings→Wallet & Apple Pay**. Tap the little Apple Pay Cash card to begin the activation process, which mostly involves reading legalese. (Along the way, you're prompted to tap **Add Debit Card**; if you've already got a card set up, you can skip this step.)

One more thing: If you tap **Verify Identity** and supply your contact info and driver's license, you raise your maximum balance from $500 to $20,000.

You have the option of tapping **Add Money** to preload money (between $10 and $3,000) onto the Cash card—but there's no good reason to do so. The card automatically pulls money from your linked debit or credit card as needed.

> **NOTE:** In **Settings→Wallet & Apple Pay**, a master **Apple Pay Cash** on/off switch awaits. It's a quick way to shut down the whole thing if your sending-money addiction starts becoming a problem.

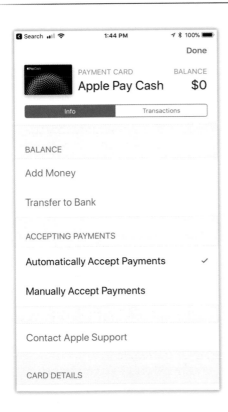

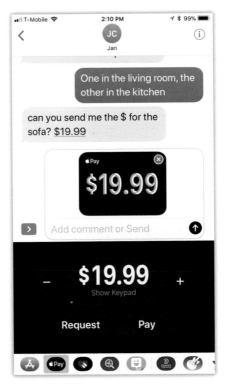

- **Pay someone.** Open Messages; open a chat with the lucky recipient (somebody who also has Apple Pay Cash set up). In the apps drawer (page 204), tap **Apple Pay**.

> **TIP:** Or—here's that old Apple magic at work—tap any underlined dollar amount *in a text message* you've recently exchanged. The Apple Pay app opens automatically in the bottom part of the screen, with that amount already entered.
>
> Similarly, if somebody writes in text a request for money ("Hey, do you want to split the bill? It's $30"), the QuickType bar above the keyboard offers a **Pay** button. Tap for insta-prep of the payment.

Enter an amount from $1 to $3,000, either by tapping the **+** and **−** buttons or by tapping the large dollar amount (or **Show Keypad**) and typing an amount.

When the amount looks good, tap **Pay**, and then tap ⬆. (That Send button, usually blue, appears in black as a visual reminder that you are about to spend money.)

A confirmation screen appears, showing which real card will be funding this amount. (Tap ▶ to change to a different card, if you like.) You're asked to confirm that you're really you, either by fingerprint or, on the iPhone X, face recognition (and a double-click of the side button).

If, at this point, you return to the Wallet app, you'll see a screen full of details—time and date, amount, payee, and so on.

> **TIP:** You don't have to bother with Messages. You can just tell Siri, "Send 35 bucks to Robin," or "Ask Casey for 80 dollars," or whatever. Siri shows you what she's about to do; say "Send" to confirm.
>
> You can also tap the $ next to somebody's name in Contacts to begin the process, but that's a lot less fun.

- **Request payment.** You can also operate Pay Cash in reverse. That is, you can generate what amounts to an invoice for the person who owes you money.

To do that, in a Messages thread with the ower, tap an underlined dollar amount in a text message—or open the Apple Pay app. Here's the **Request** button; enter the amount and hit ⬆. Of course, there's no guarantee you're actually going to *get* that money; the Request function mainly saves the other person the effort of (a) entering the amount, and (b) remembering.

For some reason, Apple gives you a choice of whether or not to receive these incoming amounts automatically. Open the Wallet app, tap the Apple Pay Cash card, then tap ⓘ. Here you can select **Manually Accept Payments**. Which means that when someone sends you money, you don't get it unless you tap **Accept** in the notification. If you wait seven days without doing that (or if you tap the **Transactions** tab and tap **Reject Payment**), then you never get the money. What's wrong with you?

- **Track the payment.** If you open your Wallet and tap the Apple Pay card, you'll see that the amount you sent is "Pending"; the other guy hasn't yet accepted your generous gift of money. Until he does, you can cancel the payment on the Transactions tab. When he accepts, you'll get a notification letting you know. The transaction, in the Wallet app, appears with all others you've made on the Transactions tab. Here you can also request a statement by email.

- **Cash out.** At any point, you can dump money (up to $3,000 at a time, up to $20,000 a week) from the Cash card into your bank account with just a couple of taps. On the Cash info screen, tap **Transfer to Bank**. (You'll be asked to enter your bank's tracking number the first time you try.) The funds will show up in your bank account in "one to three business days," says Apple.

Incidentally, A.P. Cash goes beyond person-to-person payments. You can treat your new Cash card as just another credit card for use with regular Apple Pay (page 542), and you can also send and receive person-to-person cash with an Apple Watch.

Family Sharing

It used to be a hassle to manage your Apple life with kids. What if they wanted to buy a book, movie, or app? They had to use your credit card—and you had to reveal your iCloud password to them. Or what if they wanted to see a movie that you bought? Did they really have to buy it again?

Not anymore. Once you've turned on Family Sharing and invited your family members, here's how your life will be different:

- **One credit card to rule them all.** Up to six of you can buy books, movies, apps, and music on your master credit card.

- **Buying permissions.** When your kids try to buy stuff, your phone pops up a permission request. You have to approve each purchase.

- **Younger Appleheads.** You can create Apple accounts for tiny tots. (For regular Apple accounts, 13 is the age minimum.)

- **Shared everything.** All of you get instant access to one another's music, video, iBooks books, and app purchases—again, without having to know one another's Apple passwords.

- **Shared storage.** In iOS 11, you can share any extra iCloud storage you've bought (page 387) with your fellow family members.

- **Find one another.** You can use your phone to see where your kids are, and vice versa (with permission, of course).

- **Find one another's phones.** The miraculous Find My iPhone feature (page 536) now works for every phone in the family. If your daughter can't find her phone, you can find it for her with *your* phone.

- **Mutual photo album, mutual calendar, and mutual reminders.** When you turn on Family Sharing, your Photos, Calendar, and Reminders apps each sprout a new category that's preconfigured to permit access by everyone in your family.

Setting Up Family Sharing

The setup process means wading through a lot of screens, but at least you'll have to do it only once. You can start either on the Mac (in **System Preferences→iCloud →Set Up Family**) or on the phone. Since this book is about the iPhone, what follows are the steps to do it there.

Tap **Settings→[your name]→Set Up Family Sharing**. Click **Get Started**. Now the phone announces that you, the sage adult, are going to be the Organizer—the one with the power, the wisdom, and the credit card. **Continue** (unless it's listing the wrong Apple ID, in which case fix it now).

On successive screens, you read about the idea of shared Apple Store purchases; you're shown the credit card Apple believes you want to use; you're offered the chance to share your location with the others. Each time, read and tap **Continue**.

Finally, you're ready to introduce the software to your family.

- **If the kid is under 13:** Scroll wayyyyy down and tap **Create an Apple ID for a Child**. On the screens that follow, you'll enter the kid's birth date; agree to a Parent Privacy Disclosure screen; enter the security code for your credit card (to prove that you're you, and not, for example, your naughty kid); type the kid's name; set up an iCloud account (name, password, three security questions); decide whether or not to turn on **Ask To Buy** (each time your youngster tries to buy something

online from Apple, you'll be asked for permission in a notification on your phone); decide whether you want the family to be able to see where the kid is at all times; and accept a bunch of legalese.

When it's all over, the lucky kid's name appears on the Family screen.

- **If the kid already has an iCloud account and is standing right there with you in person:** Tap **Add Family Member**. Type in her name or email address. (Your child's name must already be in your Contacts; if not, go add her first. By the way, you're a terrible parent.)

She can now enter her iCloud password on your phone to complete her setup. (That doesn't mean you'll learn what her password is; your phone stores it but hides it from you.) On the subsequent screens, you get to confirm her email address and let her turn on location sharing. In other words: The rest of the family will be able to see where she is.

- **If the kid isn't with you at the moment:** Click **Send an Invitation**. Your little darling gets an email at that address. He must open it on his Apple gadget (Mac or iPhone, for example).

  When he hits **View Invitation**, he can either enter his iCloud name and password (if he has an iCloud account), or get an Apple ID (if he doesn't). Once he accepts the invitation, he can choose a picture to represent himself; tap **Confirm** to agree to be in your family; enter his iCloud password to share the stuff he's bought from Apple; agree to Apple's lawyers' demands; and, finally, opt in to sharing his location with the rest of the family.

You can repeat this cycle to add additional family members, up to a maximum of six. Their names and ages appear on the Family screen.

From here, you can tap someone's name to perform stunts like these:

- **Delete a family member.** Man, you guys really don't get along, do you? Anyway, tap **Remove**.

- **Turn Ask To Buy on or off.** This option appears when you've tapped a child's name on your phone. If you decide your kid is responsible enough not to need your permission for each purchase, you can turn this option off.

NOTE: If you turn off **Ask To Buy** for someone after she turns 18, you can't turn it on again.

- **Turn Parent/Guardian on or off.** This option appears when you've tapped an adult's name. It gives Ask To Buy approval privileges to someone else besides you—your spouse, for example.

Once kids turn 13, by the way, Apple automatically gives them more control over their lives. They can, for example, turn off Ask To Buy themselves, on their own phones. They can even express their disgust for you by leaving the Family Sharing group. (On her own phone, for example, your daughter can visit **Settings→iCloud→Family**, tap her name, and then tap **Leave Family**. Harsh!)

Life in Family Sharing

Once everything is set up, here's how you and your kids will get along:

- **Purchases.** Whenever one of your kids (for whom you've turned on **Ask To Buy**) tries to buy music, videos, apps, or books from Apple—even free items—he has to ask you (facing page, left). On your phone, you're notified about the purchase—and you can decline it or tap **Review** to read about it on its Store page. If it seems OK, you can tap

Approve. You also have to enter your iCloud password, or supply your face or fingerprint, to prevent your kid from finding your phone and approving his own request.

(If you don't respond within 24 hours, the request expires. Your kid has to ask again.)

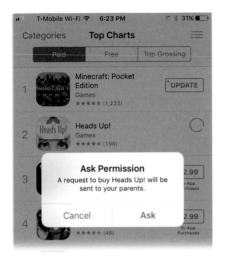

Furthermore, each of you can see and download everything that everyone else has bought. To do that, open the appropriate app: App Store, iTunes Store, or iBooks. Tap **Purchased** and then tap the family member's name to see what she's got; tap the ⬇ to download any of it yourself.

> **TIP:** Anything you buy, your kids will see. Keep that in mind when you download a book like *Sending the Unruly Child to Military School*.
>
> However, you have two lines of defense. First, you can hide your purchases. On your computer, in iTunes (Chapter 15), click **iTunes Store**; click the relevant category (♫, 𝄢, whatever). Click **Purchased**. Point to the thing you want to hide, click the ⊗, and click **Hide**. (On the phone, you can hide only one category: apps. In the App Store app, tap **Updates**, then **Purchased**, and then **My Purchases**. Swipe to the left across an app's name to reveal a **Hide** button.)
>
> Second, remember that you can set up parental control on each kid's phone, shielding their impressionable eyes from R-rated movies and stuff. See page 621.

- **Where are you?** Open the Find My Friends app to see where your posse is right now. Or go to the Find My iPhone app (or web page; see page 536) to see where just their *phones* are right now.

NOTE: If one of you needs secrecy for the afternoon (Apple sweetly gives, as an example, shopping for a gift for your spouse), open **Settings→iCloud→Share My Location**, and turn off the switch. Now you're untrackable until you turn the switch on again.

- **Photos, appointments, and reminders.** In Calendar, Photos, and Reminders, each of you will find a new category, called Family, that's auto-shared among you all. (In Photos, it's on the Shared tab.) You're all free to make and edit appointments in this calendar, to set up reminders in Reminders ("Flu shots after school!"), or to add photos or videos (or comments) to this album; everyone else will see the changes instantly.

17

Continuity: iPhone Meets Mac

Apple products have always been designed to work together. Macs, phones, tablets, watches: similar software, design, wording, philosophy. That's nice for you, of course, because you have less to learn and to troubleshoot. But it's also nice for Apple, because it keeps you in velvet handcuffs; pretty soon, you've got too much invested in its product "ecosystem" to consider wandering over to a rival.

Apple has taken this gadget symbiosis to an astonishing extreme. If your Mac is running Yosemite (Mac OS X 10.10) or a later Mac OS version, it can be an *accessory* to your iPhone. Suddenly the Mac can be a speakerphone, using the iPhone as a wireless antenna. Suddenly the Mac can send and receive regular text messages. Suddenly AirDrop lets you drag files back and forth, wirelessly, from phone to computer. Suddenly you can copy material on the phone, and paste it on the Mac (or vice versa).

Apple's name for this suite of symbiosis is *Continuity*. And once you've got it set up, the game changes in a big way.

Continuity Setup

For many people, all of this just works. For many others, there's a certain degree of setting up and troubleshooting. These are the primary rules:

- **You need a Mac running OS X Yosemite or later.**

- **The Mac and the phone have to be signed into the same iCloud account.** (That's a security thing—it proves that you're the owner of both machines and therefore unlikely to pose a risk to yourself.) On the Mac, you do that in **System Preferences→iCloud**. On the phone, you do that in **Settings→[your name]→iCloud**. But you should also make sure you've entered the same iCloud address in **Settings→Messages** and **Settings→FaceTime**.

- **For some of these features, Bluetooth must be turned on.** On the Mac, you can do that in **System Preferences→Bluetooth**. On the phone, it's **Settings→Bluetooth**.

  Modern Bluetooth doesn't drain your battery the way Bluetooth once did, so it's fine to leave it on. But older Macs don't have Bluetooth LE, so most Continuity features work only on 2012 and later Macs.

All right. Setup ready? Time to experience some integration!

Mac as Speakerphone

You can make and take phone calls on your Mac. The iPhone, sitting any-where in your house, can be the cellular module for your Mac—even if that iPhone is asleep and locked. As usual, the Mac and the phone must be signed into the same iCloud account. And they must be on the same network.

> **NOTE:** Actually, there's a mind-blowing exception to that statement: Continuity over *cellular*. In this scenario, your Mac and iPhone *don't* have to be on the same Wi-Fi network! Even if you left your phone at home, you can still make calls and send texts from your Mac, wherever you are in the country!
>
> This amazing feature requires participation by the cellular carrier, and so far, T-Mobile is the only company offering it. (How do you know? Open **Settings→Phone→ Wi-Fi Calling**; if you see an option called **Allow Calls on Other Devices**, you're golden.)

Ready? Here's the setup.

- **On the phone,** turn on **Settings→Phone→Calls on Other Devices→Allow Calls on Other Devices**.

- **On the Mac,** open the FaceTime program, weird as that sounds. Turn on **FaceTime→Preferences→Settings→Calls from iPhone**.

Once you've set things up as described, it just works. When a call comes in to your iPhone's number, your *Mac* plays whatever ringtone your phone is playing. A notice appears on your Mac screen, as shown on the facing page. You can click **Accept** to answer it (or **Decline** it); your Mac's microphone and speaker become your speakerphone.

You can *place* a call the same way. Just click any phone number you find on the Mac: in Contacts, in Safari, in an email message, and so on.

Even call-waiting works—if a second call comes in, your Mac notifies you and offers you the chance to put the first one on hold. And on the Mac, the Contacts app offers **Ringtone** and **Texttone** menus, so you can assign custom sounds that play when your *Mac* rings.

Crazy.

> **TIP:** If you own a bunch of Apple machines, it might drive you crazy that they all now ring at once when a call comes in. Fortunately, you can turn off the ringing on each device that you'd rather be peaceful.
>
> To make one of your iPads or iPod Touches stop ringing, turn off **Settings→FaceTime→Calls from iPhone**. To make a Mac stop ringing, open the FaceTime program; choose **FaceTime→ Preferences→Settings**, and turn off **Calls from iPhone**.

Texting from the Mac

You can send and receive text messages (as well as picture, audio, and video messages) on your Mac, too.

We're not talking about sending texts to other *Apple* people (with iCloud accounts). Those are called iMessages, and they're a special, Apple-only kind of message (page 186). We're talking about something much better: You can type *any* cellphone number and send a regular SMS text message to *anyone*. Or receive them at your iPhone number.

Or you can initiate the text conversation by clicking a phone number in Contacts, Calendar, or Safari to send an SMS message. Once again, your iPhone acts as a relay station between the cellular world and your Mac.

Here's how to set it up. First, as usual, the Mac and the phone must be on the same Wi-Fi network and signed into the same iCloud account.

- **On the phone,** open **Settings→Messages→Send & Receive**; make sure that both your phone number and email address are turned on.

  Next, still on the iPhone, open **Settings→Messages**. Tap **Text Message Forwarding**. Your Mac's name appears. Turn on the switch. (If you're using two-factor authentication—see page 622—you'll have to type in a six-digit code now.)

- **On the Mac,** open Messages; choose **Messages→Preferences→Accounts**. Confirm that the Apple ID shown here matches what you saw on the phone in the previous step.

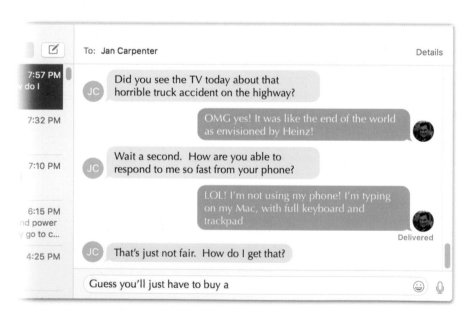

All of this is to prove that you're the owner of both devices. You wouldn't want some bad guy reading your text messages, would you?

That's it—your gadgets are paired. You can now use Messages to send standard text messages to **any** cellphone. You can also click and hold on a phone number wherever it appears—in Contacts, in a search result, in Safari, in Mail—and choose **Send Message** from there. And when a text message comes in, a standard Mac notification bubble appears at top right.

The beauty of this is that your back-and-forths are kept in sync between the Mac and the phone. You can jump between them and continue the texting conversation. (You'll note that, as usual, the bubbles containing your utterances are green. Blue is reserved for iMessages—that is, messages to other people with iCloud accounts.)

Instant Hotspot

As you know from page 457, paying your cell carrier another $20 or so every month entitles you to use the iPhone's Personal Hotspot feature. That's where the phone itself acts as a portable Wi-Fi hotspot, so that your laptop (or any other gadgets) can get online almost anywhere.

As you also know from page 457, it's kind of a pain to get going. Each time you want your laptop to get online, you have to wake your iPhone, unlock it, open **Settings**, and turn on **Personal Hotspot**. Then you wait about 20 seconds, until the phone's name shows up in your 🛜 menu.

Not with Continuity.

Now, the phone can stay in your pocket. Its name appears in your 🛜 menu, ready for choosing at any time—even if the phone is asleep and locked, and even if Personal Hotspot is turned off! Handily enough, the 🛜 menu also shows the phone's battery and signal status.

Once your Mac is online through your iPhone's cellular connection, it tries to save you money by suspending data-intensive jobs like full backups and software updates. And it closes down the connection when you no longer need it, to save your iPhone's battery.

As usual, this works only if the iPhone and Mac both have Bluetooth turned on and are signed into the same iCloud account.

Handoff

Handoff passes half-finished documents between the phone and the Mac, wirelessly and automatically.

For example, suppose you've been writing an email message on your iPhone (below, left). When you arrive home and sit down at the Mac, a new icon appears at the left end of the Mac's Dock (top right). When you click it, the Mac's Mail program opens, and the half-finished message is there for you to complete (lower right).

It doesn't have to be an email message, either. If you were reading a web page or a Map on your phone, then that icon on the Mac opens the same web page or map. If you were working on a Reminder; a Calendar entry; a Contacts entry; a note in Notes; or a document in Keynote, Numbers, or Pages; you can open the same in-progress item on the Mac.

And all of it works in the other direction, too. If you're working on something on the Mac, but you're called away, an icon appears on the lower-left corner of your iPhone's Lock screen that opens the same item (facing page, left).

Here's the setup: Once again, both gadgets must be signed into your iCloud account. Both must have Bluetooth turned on, and the Mac and phone have to be within Bluetooth range of each other (about 30 feet).

On the Mac, open **System Preferences→General**; turn on **Allow Handoff between this Mac and your iCloud devices**.

On the iPhone, the on/off switch is in **Settings→General→Handoff**.

Now try it out. Start an email message on your iPhone. Have a look at the Dock on your Mac: There, at the left end, pops up the little icon of whatever program can finish the job.

AirDrop

AirDrop is pretty great. As described on page 364, it lets you shoot photos, videos, maps, Contacts cards, PDF files, Word documents, and other stuff between iPhones. Wirelessly. Without names, passwords, permissions, or even an Internet connection. What page 364 doesn't cover, though, is how you can use AirDrop *between* a phone and a Mac.

From iPhone to Mac

Open whatever it is you want to send to the Mac: a photo, map, website, contact...anything with a ⬆ button.

When you tap □, you see the AirDrop panel—and, after a moment, the icons of any nearby Macs show up, too. Including yours.

If the Mac's icon **doesn't** show up, it's probably because its owner hasn't made the Mac discoverable by AirDrop.

Instruct him to open the AirDrop **window** on his Mac. (Click AirDrop in the sidebar of any Finder window.) See the small blue control at the bottom? It governs who can "see" this Mac for AirDrop purposes: **No One**, **Contacts Only** (that is, people in the Mac's address book), or **Everyone**.

Once that's set up right, that Mac shows up in the iPhone's AirDrop panel ("David" here at left). Send away.

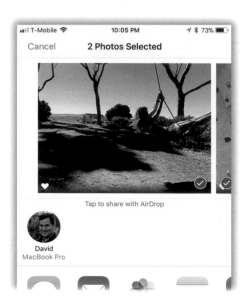 

The receiving Mac displays a notification. Click **Accept** to download the incoming item to your Mac's Downloads folder (or **Decline** to reject it).

TIP: If the phone and the Mac are both signed into the same iCloud account, then you don't encounter that Accept/Decline thing. The file goes directly into your Downloads folder without asking. You do get a notification on the Mac that lets you know how many files arrived, and it offers an **Open** button (above, right).

Apple figures that, since you own both the phone and the Mac, the usual permission routine isn't necessary. You're probably not trying to send yourself some evil virus of death.

Universal Clipboard

Now, this is magic—and useful magic, at that. You can copy some text, a picture, or a video on your phone—and then, without any further steps, turn to your Mac and paste it. Or go the other way. Somehow, the contents of the Clipboard transfer themselves wirelessly between the two machines.

In this example, you copy something on the iPhone, in Safari (below, top)—and then paste it instantly in Mail on the Mac.

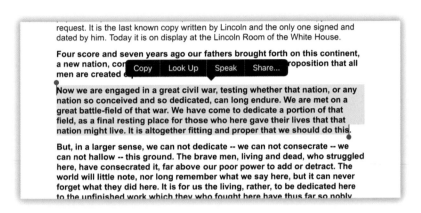

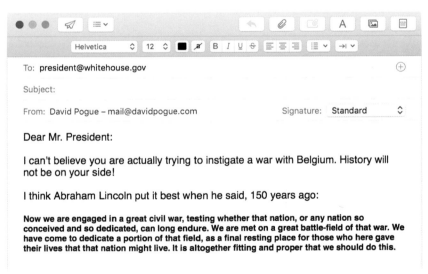

There's no on/off switch, no extra steps, no visible sign of this feature in Settings or System Preferences. It just works. (Provided, of course, that you've obeyed the Three Laws of Continuity Setup: The Mac and phone have to be on the same Wi-Fi network, both have to have Bluetooth turned on, and both have to be signed into the same iCloud account.)

If you don't paste within two minutes of copying, then whatever was already on the Clipboard gets restored, so you don't get confused later.

18

Settings

The Settings app is like the Control Panel in Windows or System Preferences on the Mac. It houses hundreds of settings for every aspect of the iPhone and its apps.

Almost everything in the list of Settings is a doorway to another screen, where you make the actual changes.

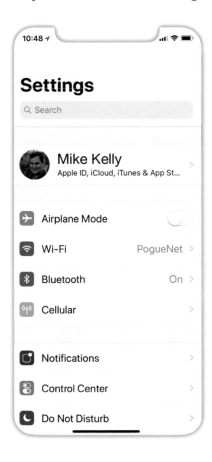

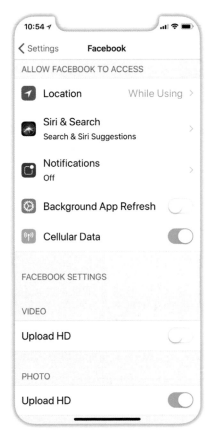

In this book, you can read about the iPhone's preference settings in the appropriate spots—wherever they're relevant. And the Control Center, of course, is designed to *eliminate* trips into Settings.

But so you'll have it all in one place, here's an item-by-item walk-through of the Settings app and its structure in iOS 11.

Three Important Settings Tricks

The Settings app is many screens deep. You might "drill down" by tapping, for example, **General**, then **Keyboard**, and then **Text Replacement**. It's a lot of tapping, a lot of navigation. Fortunately, you have three kinds of shortcuts.

First, you can jump directly to a particular Settings screen using Siri (Chapter 5). You can say, for example, "Open Sound settings," "Open Notifications settings," "Open Wi-Fi settings," and so on. Siri promptly takes you to the corresponding screen—no tapping required.

NOTE: Unless Siri thinks you are driving (see page 140).

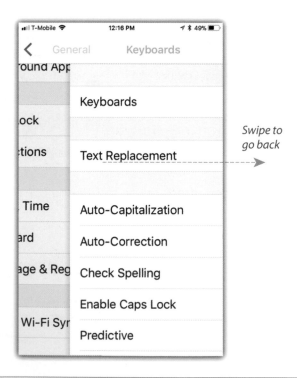

Second, you can jump directly to the four most frequently adjusted panels—Bluetooth, Wi-Fi, Cellular, and Battery—by *hard-pressing* the Settings app icon on the Home screen (6s and later models). The short-cut menu offers direct access to those panes.

Finally, on any model, you can *swipe to go back* (facing page). Once you've drilled down to, say, General→Keyboard→Text Replacement, you can "drill up" again by swiping across the screen to the right (start from the *edge*).

[Your Name]

At the top of Settings screen, a tappable banner displaying your name and photo appears. Tap it to open a screen that summarizes everything Apple knows about you: your phone numbers; email addresses; pass-words; credit card information; iCloud account info; and even the list of iPhones, iPads, iPod Touches, and Macs you own. Tap one of these items to edit it.

Airplane Mode

As you're probably aware, you're not allowed to make cellphone calls on U.S. airplanes. According to legend (if not science), a cellphone's radio can interfere with a plane's navigation equipment.

But the iPhone does a lot more than make calls. Are you supposed to deprive yourself of all the music, videos, movies, and email that you could be using in flight, just because calling is forbidden?

Nope. Just turn on airplane mode by tapping the switch at the top of the Settings list (so the switch background turns green). The word **Cellular** dims there in Settings (you've turned off your cellular circuitry); but the **Wi-Fi** and **Bluetooth** switches are still available, though turned off; you're now welcome to switch them back *on*, even in airplane mode.

Now it's safe (and permitted) to use the iPhone in flight, even with Wi-Fi on, because its cellular features are turned off completely. You can't make calls, but you can do anything else in the iPhone's bag of tricks.

> **TIP:** Turning airplane mode on and off is faster if you use the Control Center (page 49) or Siri ("Turn on airplane mode"). Same for Wi-Fi, described next.

Wi-Fi

This item in Settings opens the Wi-Fi Networks screen:

- **Wi-Fi On/Off.** If you don't plan to use Wi-Fi, then turning it off gets you a lot more life out of each battery charge. Tap anywhere on this switch to change its status.

TIP: Turning on airplane mode automatically turns off the Wi-Fi antenna—but you can turn Wi-Fi back on. That's handy when you're on a flight with Wi-Fi on board.

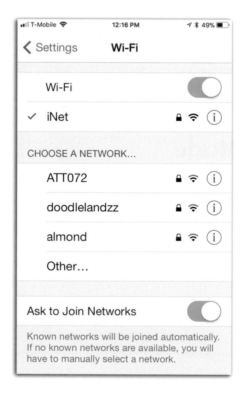

- **Choose a Network.** Here's a list of all nearby Wi-Fi networks. See page 453 for details on using Wi-Fi with the iPhone.

- **Ask to Join Networks.** See page 454.

Bluetooth

Here's the on/off switch for the iPhone's Bluetooth transmitter, which is required to communicate with a Bluetooth fitness band, earpiece, keyboard, or hands-free system in a car. When the switch is on, you're offered the chance to pair the iPhone with other Bluetooth equipment; the paired gadgets are listed here for ease of connecting and disconnecting.

> **TIP:** The Control Center (page 49) has a Bluetooth button. It's faster to use that than to visit Settings.

Cellular

These days, all major cell carriers are pushing their unlimited data plans. (They're not actually *unlimitedly* unlimited; after you've used a certain amount of data, your Internet speed slows way down until the end of the month.) But most people still have capped plans, where, for example, you pay $50 a month for 8 gigabytes of Internet data use.

That's why iOS offers so many settings to help you control how much Internet data your phone uses.

- **Cellular Data.** This is the on/off switch for Internet data. If you're traveling overseas, you might want to turn this off to avoid racking up insanely high roaming charges. Your smartphone becomes a dumbphone, suitable for making calls but not for getting online. (You can still get online in Wi-Fi hotspots.)

- **Cellular Data Options.** These controls can prevent staggering international roaming fees. **Enable LTE** lets you turn off LTE—just for voice calls, or for both voice and data—for situations when LTE costs extra.

> **TIP:** Every now and then, you'll be in some area where you can't connect to the Internet even though you seem to have an LTE signal; forcing your phone to the 4G or 3G network often gives you at least some connection. Turning LTE off does just that.

On AT&T or T-Mobile, you can turn off **Data Roaming** (when you're out of the country, you won't get slapped with outrageous Internet fees). On Verizon and Sprint, once you tap **Roaming**, you have separate controls for **Data Roaming** and **Voice Roaming**. Turning off the last item, **International CDMA**, forces the phone to use only the more common GSM networks while roaming; sometimes you get better call and data quality that way, and you may save money.

- **Wi-Fi Calling.** How would you like crisp, solid phone calls even indoors, even where the cell signal barely reaches? That's what Wi-Fi calling can do for you (page 152).

Of course, if you're on Wi-Fi and you dial 911, the operators won't know where you are, since cellular transmits your location but Wi-Fi doesn't. That's why turning on Wi-Fi Calling requires you to enter your address.

Once that's done, you can also turn on **Prefer Wi-Fi While Roaming**— and you should. When you're traveling abroad, incoming and outgoing calls will use Wi-Fi, if you're in a hotspot, instead of the outrageously priced cellular network.

- **Allow Calls on Other Devices** is part of Continuity, and it's described on page 556.

- **Carrier Services** is just a bunch of stuff inserted here by your cellphone carrier. For Verizon, it's a list of phone numbers (411 for directory assistance, #3282 to see how much data you've used so far this month, and so on); for T-Mobile, it's links to customer service and apps. You get the idea.

- **Personal Hotspot.** Here's the setup and on/off switch for Personal Hotspot (page 457). Once you've turned it on, a new Personal Hotspot on/off switch appears on the main Settings screen, so you won't have to dig this deep in the future.

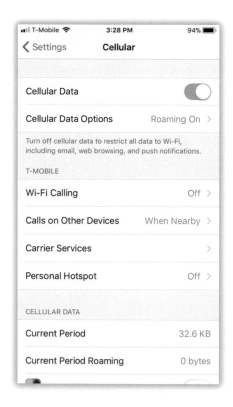
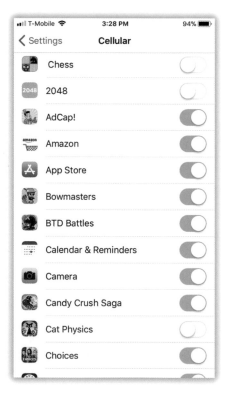

- **Cellular Data.** The phone tracks how much Internet data you've used this month, expressed in megabytes: email messages, web page material, iMessages, Facebook updates, and so on. Your iPhone plan is probably capped—for example at 8 gigabytes a month. If you exceed your monthly maximum, then you're instantly charged $15 or $20 for another chunk of data. So keeping an eye on these statistics is a very good idea.

  (The **Current Period** means so far this month; **Current Period Roaming** means overseas or in places where your cell company doesn't have service.)

  Next, you see an amazingly useful list. It shows every Internet-using app on your phone and how much data it's used. Better yet, it offers individual on/off switches for every app on your phone. Each one is an item that could consume data without your awareness. You can shut off the data hogs you really don't feel like spending megabytes on, and you can find out where the heck all your data is going.

- **Wi-Fi Assist.** Thousands of iPhone fans know about The Old Flaky Wi-Fi Trick. If the phone is struggling and struggling to load a web page or download an email message on a Wi-Fi network, it often helps to *turn off Wi-Fi*. The phone hops over to the cellular network, where it's usually got a better connection.

  That's why Apple offers Wi-Fi Assist: a feature that's supposed to do all that automatically. If the phone is having trouble with its Wi-Fi connection, it just hops over to cellular data. (You'll know when that's happened because of the appearance of the cellular-network indicator on your status bar, like **4G**, or **LTE**, instead of the 🛜 Wi-Fi symbol.)

  If you're worried about this feature eating up your data allowance, you can, of course, turn Wi-Fi Assist off. Apple notes, however, that Wi-Fi Assist doesn't kick in (a) when you're data roaming, (b) for background apps (it helps only the app that's in front), or (c) if large amounts of data would be consumed. For example, it doesn't kick in for audio or video streaming or email attachments.

- **iCloud Drive.** Is the phone allowed to use data (if no Wi-Fi is available) for syncing with your iCloud Drive (page 387)?

- **Call Time.** The statistics here break down how much time you've spent talking on the iPhone, both in the **Current Period** (that is, this billing month) and in the iPhone's entire **Lifetime**. That's right, folks: You own a cellphone that keeps track of your minutes, to help you avoid exceeding the number you've signed up for (and therefore racking up overage minutes).

- **Reset Statistics** resets the Call Time and Data Usage counters to zero.

Personal Hotspot

Once you've turned this feature on (page 457) in **Cellular**, this switch appears here, too—on the main Settings screen for your convenience.

Notifications

This panel lists all the apps that think they have the right to nag for your attention. Flight-tracking programs alert you that there's an hour before takeoff. Social-networking programs ping you when someone's trying to reach you. Instant-messaging apps ding to let you know that you have a new message. It can add up to a lot of interruption.

On this panel, you can tailor, to an almost ridiculous degree, how you want to be nagged. See page 68 for a complete description.

Control Center

The Control Center is written up on page 49. There are two settings to change here. If you turn off **Access Within Apps**, then you won't land in the Control Center by accident when you're playing some game that involves a lot of swiping. And **Customize Controls**, of course, is iOS 11's shining achievement: It's where *you* decide which buttons appear on the Control Center, and in which order.

Do Not Disturb

This is one of iOS's most brilliant and useful features. See page 138.

General

The General pages offer a *huge*, motley assortment of settings governing the behavior of the virtual keyboard, the search feature, and about 6 trillion other things:

- **About.** Here you can find out how many songs, videos, and photos your iPhone holds; how much storage your iPhone has; techie details like the iPhone's software and firmware versions, serial number, model, Wi-Fi and Bluetooth addresses; and so on. (It's kind of cool to see how many apps you've installed.)

  At the very top, you can tap the phone's name to rename it.

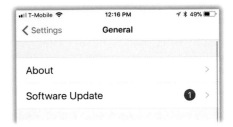

- **Software Update.** When Apple releases a new operating system update, you can download it directly to the phone.

  You'll know when an update is waiting for you, because you'll see a little number badge on the Settings icon, as well as on the word "General" in Settings. Tap it, and then tap **Software Update**, to see and install the update (above, right). (If no number badge is waiting, then tapping **Software Update** just shows you your current iOS version.)

- **AirDrop.** Do you want strangers to be able to send you photos? (See page 364.)

- **Handoff.** Handoff is for people who own both a Mac and an iPhone; it automatically passes half-finished documents between them, as described on page 560. This is the on/off switch.

- **CarPlay.** Many car models come equipped with a technology called CarPlay, which displays a few of your iPhone's icons—Phone, Music, Maps, Messages, Music, Podcasts, and Audiobooks—on the car's dashboard touchscreen. The idea is to make them big and simple and limited to things you'll need while you're driving, to avoid distracting you. Here's where you connect your phone to your CarPlay system and, if you like, rearrange the icons on the CarPlay screen.

- **Home Button** appears on the iPhone 7 and 8 models. The home button on these phones, believe it or not, doesn't actually move. It doesn't actually click. Instead, a tiny speaker makes the button *feel* as though you've clicked it by producing a little twitch vibration. That helps with the iPhone's water resistance, of course, but it also permits features like this one: You can actually specify how *big* the phony click feels, using the settings Apple calls 1, 2, or 3 (and then try it out, right on this screen).

- **Accessibility.** These options are intended for people with visual, hearing, and motor impairments, but they might come in handy now and then for almost anyone. All these features are described in Chapter 7.

- **iPhone Storage.** Handy (and new in iOS 11)! Here's a clean graph showing how full your phone is—and some recommendations. One suggests deleting all text messages and attachments older than one year. Another proposes offloading apps you don't use much. (That is, their dimmed icons remain on your Home screen, but they're just bookmarks that download the real apps when tapped.)

Then comes a list of all your apps, complete with the dates you last used them and how much storage they (and their documents) are eating up on your phone. (Biggest apps are at the top.) Tap an app's name to review more details, along with **Offload App** and **Delete App** buttons. This is an amazing tool if you're constantly running out of space.

TIP: If you tap **Messages**, you're offered some especially helpful space-saving options. **Review Large Attachments** shows an actual list of every attachment (usually photos and videos) people have ever sent you. They're listed with the biggest first, and identified by date. They're all still here, taking up space; you can tap one to see it at full size, swipe left to delete one, or tap **Edit** and then tap many rows (and then hit 🗑) to do the job faster.

Depending on what version of iOS you have, you may also see **Messages in iCloud** listed here. Once Apple actually turns on this long-promised iOS 11 feature, your messages and attachments from Messages will all be stored online, freeing up that space on your phone.

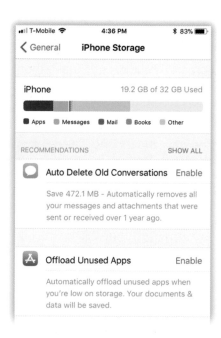

- **Background App Refresh.** The list that appears here identifies apps that try to access the Internet, even when they're in the background. Since such apps can drain your battery, you have the option here to block their background updating.

  You can also turn off the master **Background App Refresh** switch. Now the only apps that can get online in the background are a standard limited suite (music playback and GPS, for example).

- **Restrictions.** This means "parental controls." (Apple called it "Restrictions" instead so as not to turn off potential corporate customers. Can't you just hear it? " 'Parental controls?' This thing is for *consumers?!*") Complete details appear on page 619.

- **Date & Time.** Here you can turn on **24-hour time**, also known as military time, in which you see "1700" instead of "5:00 PM." (You'll see this change everywhere times appear, including at the top of the screen.)

  Set Automatically refers to the iPhone's built-in clock. If this item is turned on, then the iPhone finds out what time it is from an atomic clock out on the Internet. If not, then you have to set the clock yourself. (Turning this option off produces two more rows of controls: The **Time Zone** option becomes available, so you can specify your time zone, and a "number spinner" appears so you can set the clock.)

- **Keyboard.** Here you can turn off some of the very best features of the iPhone's virtual keyboard. (All these shortcuts are described in Chapter 3.)

  It's hard to imagine why you wouldn't want any of these tools working for you and saving you time and keystrokes, but here you go: **Keyboards** lets you add keyboards suited to all the different languages you speak. **Text Replacement** is where you set up auto-expanding abbreviations for longer words and phrases you type often. **One Handed Keyboard** is described on page 91.

  Auto-Capitalization is where the iPhone thoughtfully capitalizes the first letter of every new sentence for you. **Auto-Correction** is where the iPhone suggests spelling corrections as you type. **Check Spelling** refers to the pop-up spelling suggestions. **Enable Caps Lock** is the on/off switch for the Caps Lock feature, in which a fast double-tap on the Shift key turns on Caps Lock.

  Predictive refers to QuickType, the row of three word candidates that appears above the keyboard when you're typing. **Smart Punctuation**, new in iOS 11, automatically replaces two hyphens (--) with an em dash (—), and straight quotes ("like this") with typographically proper curly ones ("like this") as you type. (This feature can interfere if you're a programmer typing code; you've been warned.)

Character Preview is the little bubble that pops up, showing the letter, when you tap a key. The **"."** **Shortcut** switch turns on or off the "type two spaces to make a period" shortcut for the ends of sentences, and **Enable Dictation** is the on/off switch for the ability to dictate text. (If you never use dictation, turning this switch off hides the 🎤 button on the keyboard, giving the space bar more room to breathe.)

- **Language & Region.** The iPhone: It's not just for Americans anymore. The **iPhone Language** screen lets you choose a language for the iPhone's menus and messages. **Region Format** controls how the iPhone displays dates, times, and numbers. (For example, in the U.S., Christmas is on 12/25; in Europe, it's 25/12.) **Calendar** lets you choose which kind of calendar system you want to use: Gregorian (that is, "normal"), Japanese, or Buddhist. **Temperature unit**—well, you know.

- **Dictionary.** Which dictionaries (which languages) should the phone use when looking up definitions and checking your spelling?

- **iTunes Wi-Fi Sync.** You can sync your iPhone with a computer wirelessly, as long as the phone is plugged in and on Wi-Fi. Details are on page 518.

- **VPN.** The typical corporate network is guarded by a team of steely-eyed administrators for whom Job One is preventing access by unauthorized visitors. They perform this job primarily with the aid of a super-secure firewall that seals off the company's network from the Internet.

  So how can you tap into the network from the road? Only one solution is both secure and cheap: the ***virtual private network***, or VPN. Running a VPN lets you create a super-secure, encrypted "tunnel" from your iPhone straight into your corporate network. Your company's tech staff can tell you whether or not there's a VPN server set up for you to use.

  If so, they'll tell you what settings to plug in here. (If this is a company phone, you may see that your overlords have already set up some VPN connections; tap the one you want to use.)

  Once everything is in place, the iPhone can connect to the corporate network and fetch your corporate mail. You don't have to do anything special on your end when you try to access your corporate email or calendar; the VPN is automatic. When your iPhone goes to sleep, it terminates the VPN connection, both for security purposes and to save battery power.

TIP: Once you've set up a VPN connection, it appears on the main Settings page, too—the "front door" of Settings—to save you having to burrow into General.

- **Profiles & Device Management.** This item shows up only if your company issued you this phone. It shows what *profile* the system administrators have installed on it—the set of restrictions that govern what you're allowed to change without the company's permission.

- **Regulatory.** A bunch of legal logos you don't care about.

- **Reset.** On the all-powerful Reset screen, you'll find six ways to erase your phone:

  Reset All Settings takes all the iPhone's settings back to the way they were when it came from Apple. Your data, music, and videos remain in place, but the settings all go back to their factory settings.

  Erase All Content and Settings is the one you want when you sell your iPhone, or when you're captured by the enemy and want to make sure they will learn nothing from it.

> **NOTE:** This feature takes awhile to complete—and that's a good thing. The iPhone doesn't just delete your data; it also overwrites the newly erased memory with gibberish to make sure the bad guys can't see any of your deleted info, even with special hacking tools.

  Reset Network Settings makes the iPhone forget all the memorized Wi-Fi networks it currently autorecognizes.

  Reset Keyboard Dictionary has to do with the iPhone's autocorrection feature, which kicks in whenever you're trying to input text. Ordinarily, every time you type something the iPhone doesn't recognize—some name or foreign word, for example—and you don't accept the iPhone's suggestion, it adds the word you typed to its dictionary so it doesn't bother you with a suggestion again the next time. If you think you've entered too many misspellings into it, you can delete from its little brain all the new "words" you've taught it.

  Reset Home Screen Layout undoes any icon moving you've done on the Home screen. It also consolidates your Home screen icons, fitting them onto as few screens as possible.

  Finally, **Reset Location & Privacy** refers to the "OK to use location services?" warning that appears whenever an iPhone program, like Maps or Camera, tries to figure out where you are. This button makes the iPhone forget all your responses to those permission boxes. In other words, you'll be asked for permission all over again the next time you use each of those programs.

- **Shut Down.** This item, new in iOS 11, offers a visual button for turning off the phone—just in case you don't know or can't remember the holding-in-the-buttons trick described on page 16. (You still have to swipe the "slide to power off" message to confirm.)

Display & Brightness

Ordinarily, the iPhone controls its own screen brightness. An ambient-light sensor hidden behind the glass at the top of the iPhone's face samples the room brightness each time you wake the phone and adjusts the screen: brighter in bright rooms, dimmer in darker ones.

When you prefer more manual control, here's what you can do:

- **Brightness slider.** Drag the handle on this slider to control the screen brightness manually, keeping in mind that more brightness means shorter battery life.

  If True Tone (see below) or Auto-Brightness is turned on, then the changes you make here are *relative* to the iPhone's self-chosen brightness. In other words, if you goose the brightness by 20 percent, then the screen will always be 20 percent brighter than the iPhone would have chosen for itself.

> **TIP:** The Control Center (page 49) gives you a much quicker road to the brightness slider. And, of course, you can also tell Siri, "Make the screen brighter" (or "dimmer"). This version in Settings is just for old-timers.

- **True Tone.** New in iOS 11 (for iPhone 8 models and later): This on/off switch goes beyond the old Auto-Brightness setting. Now it's Auto-Brightness *and* Auto-Tint. That is, the screen colors actually shift, based on the current lighting color of the room or place you're in. The idea is to make colors on the screen seem consistent from one lighting condition to another.

  If you find the result off-putting, you can always turn True Tone off. Now the brightness of the screen is under complete manual control, and the tint never shifts.

- **Night Shift.** "Many studies have shown that exposure to bright blue light in the evening can affect your circadian rhythms and make it harder to fall asleep," Apple says. You can therefore use this function to give your screen a warmer, less blue tint, either automatically (**Sunset to Sunrise**), on a bedtime schedule (for example, from 11 p.m. to 6 a.m.), or right now (**Manually Enable Until Tomorrow**). You can also tweak the slider to adjust the color temperature (yellowness) of the screen when Night Shift kicks in.

You can also turn on Night Shift by telling Siri, "Turn on Night Shift." Or you can hard-press the brightness slider on the Control Center to find the on/off switch.

- **Auto-Lock.** As you may have noticed, the iPhone locks itself (goes to sleep) after a few minutes of inactivity on your part, to save battery power and to prevent accidental screen taps in your pocket.

  On the **Auto-Lock** screen, you can change the interval of inactivity before the auto-lock occurs (30 seconds, one minute, two minutes, and so on), or you can tap **Never**. In that case, the iPhone locks only when you click it to sleep.

- **Raise to Wake.** This on/off switch is available only on the iPhone SE, 6s, and later models. It makes the phone light up when you *pick it up*—no button-pressing required. The ramifications are huge, because the Lock screen now has many more functions than it did before. There's a lot you can accomplish on the iPhone *before* you enter your password to unlock it; see Chapter 2.

- **Text Size.** As you age, small type becomes harder to read. This universal text-size slider can boost the text size in every app on your phone.

  Technically, what you're seeing is the front end for Apple's *Dynamic Type* feature. And, even more technically, not all apps work with Dynamic Type. But most of the built-in Apple apps do—Contacts, Mail, Maps, Messages, Notes, Phone, Reminders, and Safari Reader—and many other software companies follow suit.

- **Bold Text.** If the spindly fonts of iOS are a little too light for your reading tastes, you can flip this switch on (see page 228).

- **Display Zoom.** The iPhone 6 and later models have bigger screens than the iPhones that came before them. The question here is: How do you want to use that extra space? If you tap **View** and choose **Standard**, then icons and controls remain the size they always were; the bigger screen fits more on a page. If you choose **Zoomed**, then those elements appear slightly larger, for the benefit of people who don't have bionic eyes.

Wallpaper

Wallpaper can mean either the photo on the Lock screen (what you see when you wake the iPhone up), or the background picture behind the icons on your Home screen. On this panel, you can change the image used for either one.

It shows miniatures of the two places you can install wallpaper—the Lock screen and the Home screen. Each shows what you've got installed there as wallpaper at the moment.

TIP: You can tap either screen miniature to open a Set screen, where you can adjust the current photo's size and positioning.

When you tap **Choose a New Wallpaper**, you're shown a list of photo sources you can use as backgrounds. At the top, you get three categories worth noticing.

- **Dynamic** wallpapers look like soft-focus bubbles against solid backgrounds. Once you've installed the wallpaper, these bubbles actually *move*, rising and falling on your Lock screen or Home screen behind your icons. Yes, animated wallpaper has come to the iPhone.

- **Stills** are lovely nature photographs. They don't move.

- **Live wallpapers** (iPhone 6s and later), once installed as your Lock screen, behave like the Live Photos described on page 290: When you press the screen hard, they play as three-second movies. (It's not immediately clear what that gains you.) Note that live wallpapers play back only on the Lock screen (not the Home screen).

TIP: You can install your *own* Live Photos as Lock-screen backgrounds. They, too, will play their little three-second loops when you hard-press the Lock screen.

Scroll down a little, and you'll find your own photos, nestled in categories like **All Photos**, **Favorites**, **Selfies**, **My Panoramas**, and so on. Tap one to see what it looks like at full size.

TIP: Complicated, "busy" photos make it harder to read icons and icon names on the Home screen.

Once you've spotted a worthy wallpaper—in any of the flavors described already—tap it. You're offered a choice of two installation methods: **Still**, which is what you'd expect, and **Perspective**, which means that the photo will *shift* slightly when you tilt the phone, as though it's several inches under the glass. (If you've chosen a Live Photo, you'll see a third choice, **Live Photo**, meaning that it will "play" when it's on the Lock screen and you hard-press the glass.)

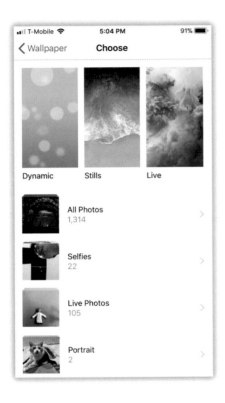

Finally, tap **Set**. Now the iPhone wants to know which of the two places you want to use this wallpaper; tap **Set Lock Screen**, **Set Home Screen**, or **Set Both** (if you want the same picture in both places).

Sounds (or Sounds & Haptics)

Here's a more traditional cellphone-settings screen: the place where you choose a ringtone sound for incoming calls.

- **Vibrate on Ring, Vibrate on Silent.** Like any self-respecting cellphone, the iPhone has a Vibrate mode—a little shudder in your pocket that might get your attention when you can't hear the ringing. There are two on/off controls for the vibration: one for when the phone is in Silent mode and one for when the ringer is on.

- **Ringer and Alerts.** The slider here controls the volume of the phone's ringing.

  Of course, it's usually faster to adjust the ring volume by pressing the up/down buttons on the left edge whenever you're not on a call or playing music or a video. But if you find that your volume buttons are getting pressed accidentally in your pocket, you can also turn off **Change with Buttons**. Now you can adjust the volume *only* with this slider, here in Settings.

- **Sounds and Vibration Patterns.** The iPhone is, of course, a cellphone—and therefore it sometimes rings. The sound it makes when it rings is up to you; by tapping **Ringtone**, you can view the iPhone's list of 25 built-in ringtones; 25 more ringtones from iOS versions past (tap **Classic** to see them); 27 "alert tones"; plus any you've added yourself. You can use any of them as a ringtone or an alert tone, no matter how it's listed.

  Tap a ring sound to hear it. After you've tapped one you like, confirm your choice by tapping **Sounds** to return to the Sounds (or Sounds & Haptics) screen.

NOTE: Remember, you can choose a different ringtone for each listing in your phone book (page 125).

But why stop with a ringtone? The iPhone can make all kinds of other sounds to alert you: to the arrival of a voicemail, text, or email; to the sending of an email message, tweet, or Facebook post; to Calendar or Reminders alarms; to the arrival of AirDrop files; and so on.

This is a big deal—not just because you can express your individuality through your choice of ringtones, text tones, reminder tones, and so on, but also because you can distinguish *your* iPhone's blips and bleeps from somebody else's in the same family or workplace.

For each of these events, tap the light-gray text that identifies the current sound for that event ("Tri-tone" or "Ding," for example). On the resulting screen, tap the different sound options to find one you like; then tap **Sounds** to return to the main screen.

On that Sounds screen, you can also turn on or off **Lock Sounds** (the sounds you get when you tap the side button) and the **Keyboard Clicks** that play when you type on the virtual keyboard.

Meet Haptics

If you have an iPhone 7 or later, there's one more switch at the very bottom: **System Haptics**. *Haptics* are the tiny, click-like vibrations that Apple has scattered throughout iOS to accentuate the animations that make the iPhone fun to use.

These little bumps mark the maximum positions for things like pinch zooming, sliders, and panels that slide onto the screen (Control Center, search, Notification Center). You'll also feel these clicks when you spin the "dials" that specify times and dates (in Calendar, Clock, and so on), when you turn a Settings switch on or off, when your icons start wiggling on the Home screen (page 47), and when you send or receive iMessage screen effects like lasers and fireworks (page 200).

Haptics are subtle but effective—but if you disagree, here's where you turn them off.

Siri & Search

Here are the on/off switches for Siri and a whole slew of options for her behavior; see page 183.

Touch ID (Face ID) & Passcode

Here's where you set up a password for your phone, or where you teach the phone to recognize your fingerprints or (on the iPhone X) your face. Details on training the phone start on page 61.

The rest of the settings include controls like these:

- **Use Touch ID (Face ID) For:** As it turns out, your fingerprint or face can do more than unlock the phone (**iPhone Unlock**). You can also use them to authenticate your identity when using Apple Pay (page 542) or buying songs, movies, and apps (**iTunes & App Store**).

  On the iPhone X, your face can also unlock the auto-typing of memorized website passwords (**Safari AutoFill**). **Other Apps** reveals a list of other apps that can use Face ID as authentication, including **Notes** (to unlock notes you've password-protected), **Twitter**, **Dropbox**, and so on. In those situations, you'll see the little Face ID icon on the screen, and a message will instruct you to double-click the side button to seal the deal.

- **Allow Access When Locked.** At the bottom of this Settings page, a list of iPhone features awaits—features that you can use at the Lock screen (Chapter 2), *before* you've unlocked the phone. Depending on your paranoia tolerance, you may not be comfortable with the notion that somebody picking your phone up from your desk could dive into some of these things—so you can turn them off here.

- **Erase Data.** The note says it all: "Erase all data on this iPhone after 10 failed passcode attempts." (That's *passcode*, not fingerprint or Face ID attempts.) Clearly, if somebody needs that many guesses, he's not you—he's a spy trying to get in. Useful if you work for the CIA, NSA, or DMV.

The iPhone X offers a couple of important additional settings:

- **Require Attention for Face ID.** Ordinarily, the iPhone X's face recognition system unlocks the phone only when you're *looking* at the phone. That way, no evildoing relative or coworker can unlock your phone when you're asleep by holding it in front of your snoozing face.

  But if you're blind, wear opaque sunglasses all day, or have no eyes, what then? In that case, you can turn off this option. Now the phone will unlock whenever it recognizes you, even if your eyes aren't open and looking at it.

- **Attention Aware Features.** Apple hasn't said much about this option, but it's very cool. The TrueDepth camera will prevent the screen from turning off after 30 seconds (or whatever your auto-sleep setting is) while you're looking at it—and it will make your morning alarm quieter if you're looking at it.

Emergency SOS

This is the beating heart of iOS 11's new emergency calling feature, which is described on page 78.

Battery

This panel offers these goodies:

- **Low Power Mode.** See page 42.

- **Battery Percentage.** Instead of just a "filling-up-battery" fuel-gauge icon at the top of your screen, how would you like a digital percentage readout, too ("75%")?

IPHONE X: This option isn't available in Settings, because there's no room for the percentage on the right ear. But if you ever do want to see the battery percentage, just swipe down on that ear to see the Control Center; there it is.

- **Battery Usage.** Here's the readout for all your apps, showing their battery appetite over the past day or week; see page 46.

TIP: Tap ⏱ to see exactly how much time you wasted using that app over the given time period—either the past 24 hours or the past seven days.

- **Usage, Standby.** These stats show you how many hours and minutes of life you've gotten from your current battery charge. (**Usage** = you using the phone. **Standby** = phone asleep.)

Privacy

By "privacy," Apple means "the ability of apps and Apple to access your data."

Many an app works better, or claims to, when it has access to your address book, calendar, photos, and so on. Generally, when you run such an app for the first time, it explicitly asks you for permission to access each kind of data. But here, on this panel, you have a central dashboard—and on/off switches—for each data type and the apps that want it.

Location Services

Suppose, for example, that you tap **Location Services**. At the top of the next screen, you'll find the master on/off switch for all location services. If you turn it off, then the iPhone can no longer determine where you are on a map, geotag your photos, find the closest ATM, tell your friends where you're hanging out, and so on. Below this master switch, you'll find these options:

- **Share My Location.** Apple has designed plenty of ways for you to broadcast your phone's location—and, by extension, your own. For example, Find My Friends, Messages, and Family Sharing all have features that let certain other people see (with your permission) where you are right now.

  Here's the on/off switch for the whole feature. If it's off, nobody can find you right now. If **Share My Location** is on, then you can tap **From** to see every iPhone you've ever owned, so that you can specify which one should be transmitting its location (the one you're carrying now). The **Family** section lists any members of your family with whom you're sharing your location; similarly, the **Friends** list identifies anyone else who has permission to track you. These are handy reminders—and you can tap a name to reveal its **Stop Sharing My Location** button.

- **List of apps.** Here's every single app that uses your location information, so that you can turn off this feature on a by-app basis. You might want to do that for privacy's sake—or you might want to do that to save battery power, since the location searches sap away a little juice every time.

  Tap an app's name to see when it wants access to your location. You might see **Always**, **Never**, or **While Using the App** (the app can't use your location when it's in the background). On the same screen, you may see a description of why the app thinks it needs your location. Why does the Calendar need it, for example? "To estimate travel times to events."

  The little ➶ icon indicates which apps have actually **used** your location data. If it's gray, that app has checked your location in the past 24 hours; if it's purple, it's locating you right now; if it's hollow, that app is using a **geofence**—it's waiting for you to enter or leave a certain location, like home or work. The Reminders app uses the geofencing feature, for example.

- **System Services.** Here are the on/off switches for the iPhone's own features that use your location.

  For example, there's **Cell Network Search** (lets your phone tap into Apple's database of cellular frequencies by location, which speeds up connections); **Compass Calibration** (lets the Compass app know where you are, so that it can accurately tell you which way is north); **Emergency SOS** (finds the nearest police station if you've turned off the 911 feature, as described on page 80); **Location-Based Apple Ads** (advertisements that Apple slaps at the bottom of certain apps—or, rather, their ability to self-customize based on your current location); **Setting Time Zone** (permits the iPhone to set its own clock when you arrive in a new time zone); and so on.

  Under the Product Improvement heading, you also get **iPhone Analytics** (sends location information back to Apple, along with diagnostic information so that, for example, Apple can see where calls are being dropped); **Popular Near Me** (the section of the App Store that lists apps downloaded by people around your current spot); **Routing & Traffic** (sends anonymous speed/location data from your phone, which is how Maps knows where there are traffic tie-ups); and **Improve Maps** (sends Apple details of your driving, so it can improve its Maps database).

Contacts, Calendars, Reminders...

This list (on the main Privacy screen) identifies the kinds of data that your apps might wish to access; we're going way beyond location here.

For example, your apps might want to access your address book or your calendar.

Tap a category—**Contacts**, for example—to see a list of the apps that are merrily tapping into its data. And to see the on/off switch, which you can use to block that app's access.

Analytics

Do you give Apple permission to collect information about how you're using your phone and how well the phone is behaving each day? On this screen, you can turn **Share iPhone Analytics** off or on. (You can even tap **Analytics Data** to *see* the data your phone has sent, although it's gibberish unless you're a programmer.)

Share With App Developers gives the phone permission to send non-Apple app writers the details of any crashes you experience while using their apps, so that, presumably, they can get busy analyzing and fixing those bugs. **Share iCloud Analytics**—same deal, but about your iCloud activity. **Improve Health & Activity** and **Improve Wheelchair Mode** share your activity and—if you have an Apple Watch—wheelchair-motion data with Apple, for similar reasons. Deciding whether to share this data all boils down to where you land on the great paranoia-to-generosity scale.

Advertising

The final Privacy option gives you a **Limit Ad Tracking** switch. Turning it on doesn't affect how many ads you see within your apps—but it does prevent advertisers from delivering ads *based on your interests*. You'll just get generic ads.

There's a **Reset Advertising Identifier** button here, too. You may not realize that, behind the scenes, you have an Ad Identifier number. It's "a non-permanent, non-personal device identifier" that advertisers can associate with you and your habits—the things you buy, the apps you use, and so on. That way, advertisers can insert ads into your apps that pertain to your interests—without ever knowing your name.

But suppose you've been getting a lot of ads that seem to mischaracterize your interests. Maybe you're a shepherd, and you keep seeing ads for hyperviolent games. Or maybe you're a nun, and you keep getting ads for marital aids.

In those cases, you might want to reset your Ad ID with this button, thus starting from scratch as a brand-new person about whom the advertisers know nothing.

iTunes & App Store

If you've indulged in a few downloads (or a few hundred) from the App Store or iTunes music store, then you may well find some settings of use here. For example, when you tap your **Apple ID** at the top of the panel, you get these buttons:

- **View Apple ID.** This takes you to the web, where you can look over your Apple account information, including credit card details.

- **Sign Out.** Tap when, for example, a friend wants to use her own iTunes account to buy something on your iPhone. As a gift, maybe.

- **iForgot.** If you've forgotten your password, tap here. You'll be offered a couple of different ways of establishing your identity—and you'll be given the chance to make up a new password.

Automatic Downloads

If you have an iCloud account, then a very convenient option is available to you: automatic downloads of music, apps, and ebooks you've bought on *other* iOS gadgets. For example, if you buy a new album on your iPad, then turning on **Music** here means that your iPhone will download the same album automatically next time it's in a Wi-Fi hotspot.

Updates means that if you accept an updated version of an app on one of your other Apple gadgets, it will be auto-updated on this phone, too.

Those downloads are, however, big. They can eat up your phone's monthly data allotment right quick and send you deep into Surcharge Land. That's why the iPhone does that automatic downloading only when you're in a Wi-Fi hotspot—unless you turn on **Use Cellular Data**. Hope you know what you're doing.

Video Autoplay

On the App Store, many apps offer little videos as part of their description. You may object to their tendency to start playing automatically—either because video eats up cellular data, or because they're annoying.

Your choices are **On** (videos play), **Off** (they don't play until you tap), or **Wi-Fi Only** (they won't play when you're on a cellular-only connection).

In-App Ratings & Reviews

Don't you hate it when you're happily using some app—and then it ruins everything by interrupting you, begging you to rate it on the App Store? If you turn off **In-App Ratings & Reviews**, those groveling little messages won't appear.

Offload Unused Apps

Finally, hiding way down here is the powerful **Offload Unused Apps** master switch. It's new in iOS 11, and a great way to fight "my iPhone is always full" syndrome. If you turn it on, then iOS will automatically delete apps you never use to make space (but not their settings and data). Their icons remain on your Home screen as dimmed ghosts. If you ever need that app again, just tap to re-download it.

Wallet & Apple Pay

This panel, available on the iPhone 6 and later, sets all the preferences for Apple Pay (page 542), including the master switch for **Apple Pay Cash** (page 546). You see any credit cards you've enrolled, plus **Add Credit or Debit Card** to enroll another.

Double-Click Home Button (or, on the iPhone X, **Side Button**) is the on/off switch for using Apple Pay when the phone is locked.

Allow Payments on Mac is the on/off switch for the option to use your iPhone's fingerprint reader (or iPhone X face recognition) to approve purchases you make on the web using your *Mac* (an option on sites that offer Apple Pay online). Finally, **Transaction Defaults** sets up the card, address, email account, and phone number you prefer to use when buying stuff online.

Accounts & Passwords

That's iOS's new name for what used to be called "Internet Accounts," which before that was "Mail, Contacts & Calendars." It's a central clearinghouse for your email accounts—and the associated calendar, contacts, notes, and reminder accounts. (Yahoo, Google, iCloud, Microsoft, and others all offer such unified suites of services.)

At the top, **App & Website Passwords** (after requiring Touch ID, Face ID, or your passcode) shows a complete list of every password that your iPhone has memorized for you. Tap one to look up the password itself, or swipe leftward to delete it. You can also select one and **Edit** it, if the phone has somehow gotten it wrong.

Accounts

Your email accounts are listed here; this is also where you set up new ones. Page 487 covers most of the options here, but one important item is worth noting: **Fetch New Data**.

The beauty of "push" email is that new email appears on your phone immediately after it was sent. You get push email if you have, for example, a Yahoo Mail account, iCloud account (Chapter 16), or Microsoft Exchange account.

Having an iPhone that's updated with these critical life details in real time is amazingly useful, but there are several reasons why you might want to turn off the **Push** feature. You'll save battery power, save money when you're traveling abroad (where every "roaming" Internet use can run up your cellular bill), and avoid the constant "new mail" jingle when you're trying to concentrate.

And what if you don't have a push email service, or if you turn it off? In that case, your iPhone can still do a pretty decent job of keeping you up to date. It can check your email every 15 minutes, every half-hour, every hour, or only on command (**Manually**). That's the decision you make in the **Fetch New Data** panel. (Keep in mind that more frequent checking means shorter battery life.)

> **TIP:** The iPhone *always* checks email each time you open the Mail app, regardless of your setting here. If you have a push service like iCloud or Exchange, it also checks for changes to your schedule or address book each time you open Calendar or Contacts—again, no matter what your setting here.

Mail

In iOS 11, you don't set up your email accounts here anymore; you do that in Accounts & Passwords, described above.

What you *do* do here is specify how often you want the iPhone to check for new messages, how you want your Mail app to look, and more.

- **Preview.** It's cool that the iPhone shows you the first few lines of text in every message. Here you can specify how *many* lines. More lines mean you can skim your inbound messages without having to open many of them; fewer lines mean more messages fit without scrolling.

- **Show To/Cc Label.** If you turn this option on, then a tiny, light-gray logo appears next to many of the messages in your inbox. The To logo indicates that this message was addressed directly to you; the Cc logo means you were merely "copied" on a message primarily intended for someone else.

  If there's no logo at all, then the message is in some other category. Maybe it came from a mailing list, or it's an email blast (a Bcc), or the message is from you, or it's a bounced message.

- **Swipe Options.** Which colorful insta-tap buttons would you like to appear when you swipe across a message in a list? See page 499 for details.

- **Flag Style.** You can flag messages to draw your own attention to them, either with the old-style flag icon—or, for visual spark, with an orange dot. Here's where you choose.

- **Ask Before Deleting.** Ordinarily, you can delete an open message quickly and easily, just by tapping the 🗑 icon. But if you'd prefer to encounter an additional confirmation step before the email message disappears, then turn this option on.

NOTE: The confirmation box appears only when you're deleting an open message—not when you delete a message from the inbox list.

- **Load Remote Images.** Spammers, the vile undercrust of lowlife society, have a trick. When they send you email that includes a picture, they don't actually paste the picture into the message. Instead, they include a "bug"—a piece of code that instructs your email program to *fetch* the missing graphic from the Internet. Why? Because that gives the spammer the ability to track who has actually opened the junk mail, making those email addresses much more valuable for reselling to other spammers.

  If you turn this option off, then the iPhone does not fetch "bug" image files at all. You're not flagged as a sucker by the spammers. You'll see empty squares in the email where the images ought to be. (Graphics sent by normal people and legitimate companies are generally pasted right into the email, so they'll still show up just fine.)

- **Organize by Thread.** This is the on/off switch for the feature that clumps related back-and-forths into individual items in your Mail inbox.

- **Collapse Read Messages.** See page 493 for details.

- **Most Recent Message on Top.** The messages in a conversation usually appear chronologically, newest at the top. (The latest message still appears when you click the thread's name.) If you prefer oldest at the top, then turn off this setting.

- **Complete Threads.** What if, during a particular back-and-forth, you've filed away certain messages into other folders? Should they still show up in a conversation thread? They will, if this switch is on. (The moved messages are *actually* sitting in those other folders; they just *appear* here for your convenience.) Now your conversations seamlessly combine related messages from all mailboxes.

- **Always Bcc Myself.** If this option is on, then you'll get a secret copy of any message you send. Some people use this feature to make sure their computers have records of replies sent from the phone.

- **Mark Addresses.** Your phone can warn you when you're addressing an email to somebody outside your company—just type in its email suffix here (@widgets.com). Whenever you address a message to anyone else, it appears in red in the "To:" line.

- **Increase Quote Level.** Each time you reply to a reply, it gets indented more, so you and your correspondents can easily distinguish one reply from the next.

- **Signature.** A signature is a bit of text that gets stamped at the bottom of your outgoing messages. Here's where you can change yours.

- **Default Account.** Your iPhone can manage an unlimited number of email accounts. Here you can tap the account you want to be your *default*—the one that's used when you create a new message from another program, like a Safari link, or when you're on the All Inboxes screen of Mail.

Contacts

Contacts gets its own little set of options in Settings:

- **Sort Order, Display Order.** How do you want the names in your Contacts list sorted—by first name or by last name?

  Note that you can have them *sorted* one way but *displayed* another way. Also note that not all those combinations make sense.

- **Short Name.** When this switch is on, the Mail app may fit more email addressees' names into its narrow To box by shortening them. It may display "M. Mouse," for example, or "Mickey," or even "M.M."—whatever you select here.

- **Prefer Nicknames** is similar. It instructs Mail to display the *nicknames* for your friends (as determined in Contacts) instead of their real names.

- **My Info.** Tap here to tell the phone which card in Contacts represents *you*. Knowing who you are is useful to the phone in a number of places—for example, it's how Siri knows what you mean when you say, "Give me directions home."

- **Default Account.** Here again, the iPhone can manage multiple address books—from iCloud, Gmail, Yahoo, and so on. Tap the account you want new contacts to fall into, if you haven't specified one in advance.

(This item doesn't appear unless you have multiple accounts with Contacts turned on.)

- **Import SIM Contacts.** If you came to the iPhone from another, lesser GSM phone, your phone book may be stored on its little SIM card instead of in the phone itself. In that case, you don't have to retype all those names and numbers to bring them into your iPhone. This button can do the job for you. (The results may not be pretty. For example, some phones store all address book data in CAPITAL LETTERS.)

Calendar

Your iPhone's calendar can be updated by remote control, wirelessly, through the air, either by your company (via Exchange) or by somebody at home using your computer (via iCloud, Chapter 16).

- **Time Zone Override.** Whenever you arrive in a new city, the iPhone actually learns (from the local cell towers) what time zone it's in and changes its own clock automatically.

  So here's a mind-teaser. Suppose there's a big meeting in California at 2 p.m. tomorrow—but you're in New York right now. How should that event appear on your calendar? Should it appear as 2 p.m. (that is, its local time)? Or should it appear as 5 p.m. (your East Coast time)?

  It's not an idle question, because it also affects reminders and alarms.

  Out of the box, **Time Zone Override** is turned off. The phone slides appointments around on your calendar as you travel to different time zones. If you're in California, that 2 p.m. meeting appears at 2 p.m. When you return to New York, it says 5 p.m. Handy—but dangerous if you forget what you've done.

  If you turn on the Override, though, the iPhone leaves all your appointments at the hours you record them—in the time zone you specify with the pop-up menu here. This option is great if you like to record events at the times you'll be experiencing them; they'll never slosh around as you travel. If you, a New Yorker, will travel to San Francisco next week for a 2 p.m. meeting, write it down as 2 p.m.; it will still say 2 p.m. when you land there.

- **Alternate Calendars.** If you prefer to use the Chinese, Hebrew, or Islamic calendar system, go nuts here.

- **Week Numbers.** This option makes Calendar display a little gray notation that identifies which week you're in (out of the 52 this year). It might say, for example, "W42." Because, you know, some people aren't aware enough of time racing by.

- **Show Invitee Declines.** You can invite someone to a meeting, as described on page 374. If they click Decline (they can't make it), maybe you don't need your phone to alert you. In that case, turn this switch off.

- **Sync.** If you're like most people, you refer to your calendar more often to see what events are *coming up* than to see the ones you've already lived through. Ordinarily, therefore, the iPhone saves you some syncing time and storage space by updating only relatively recent events on your iPhone calendar. It doesn't bother with events that are older than two weeks, or six months, or whatever you choose here. (Or you can turn on **All Events** if you want your entire life, past and future, synced each time—storage and wait time be damned.)

- **Default Alert Times.** This is where you tell the iPhone how much warning you need in advance of birthdays and events you've put on your calendar. Tailor it to your level of absentmindedness.

- **Start Week On.** This option specifies which day of the week appears at the *left edge of the screen* in the calendar's Day and Month views. For most people, that's Sunday, or maybe Monday—but, for all iOS cares, your week could start on a Thursday.

- **Default Calendar.** This option lets you answer the question: "When I add a new appointment to my calendar on the iPhone, which *calendar* (category) should it belong to?" You can choose Home, Work, Kids, or whatever category you use most often.

- **Location Suggestions.** You may have noticed that if you enter the location for a calendar appointment (page 372), the phone proposes a list of full street addresses that match what you're typing. That's to save you data entry, and also to calculate travel times. Here's the on/off switch.

Notes

Notes can sync with various online services: iCloud, Gmail, Yahoo, and so on. Tap **Default Account** to indicate which account you use *mainly*—the one that should contain any new note.

In iOS 11, you can also turn on an **"On My iPhone" Account**—a completely private one that's not synced to *any* online service, or even your Mac. That data lives only on your phone—handy if you have deeply personal information, or if you just don't trust those online services.

Until iOS 11 came along, your notes were always sorted with the most recently edited ones at the top. Now, using **Sort Notes By**, you can specify that you want them listed alphabetically by title, or chronologically by date *created*.

Notes comes with ready-to-use type styles like Title, Heading, and Body. So you can use the **New Notes Start With** option to choose which of those is the first line when you create a new note. If you usually start with a title for your note "card," then choose **Title**, for example.

Lines & Grids lets you choose "lined paper" or "graph paper"; see page 426.

Password is the command center for the new locked notes feature (page 426). You can change your password here, or create an additional one—or allow your fingerprint or face to unlock your locked notes.

You can take photos, scans, and videos right from within Notes. If you turn on **Save to Photos**, then you'll also get a copy of those images and videos in your Photos app, just as though you'd taken them with the Camera app.

Finally, here are all the options for creating Notes from the Lock screen (on the Control Center); they're described on page 56.

Reminders

Hey, it's the preference settings for the Reminders app!

- **Sync.** How far back to you want Reminders to look when showing you reminders? At **All** of them? Or only those up to **6 months** old? (Or **3 Months**, **1 Month**, or **2 Weeks**?) It's a question of storage and lifestyle.

- **Default List.** Suppose you've created multiple Reminder lists (Groceries, Movies to Rent, To Do, and so on). When you create a new item—for example, by telling Siri, "Remind me to fix the sink"—which list should it go on? Here's where you specify.

Phone

These settings have to do with your address book, call management, and other phone-related preferences.

- **My Number.** Here's where you can see your iPhone's own phone number. You can even edit it, if necessary (just how it appears—you're not actually changing your phone number).

- **Announce Calls.** Cool—the iPhone can speak the name or number of whoever is calling you. Here you can turn that feature on or off, or specify that you want it to happen only when you're using headphones or in the car.

- **Call Blocking & Identification.** You can block certain people's calls, texts, and FaceTime video calls.

  This isn't a telemarketer-blocking feature; you can block only people who are already in your Contacts. It's really for blocking harassing ex-lovers, jerky siblings you're not speaking to, and collection agencies. Tap **Block Contact** to view your Contacts list, where you can tap to choose the blockee. (You can also see and edit this list in the Messages and FaceTime panels of Settings.)

- **Wi-Fi Calling.** This glorious option lets you place great-sounding calls even with a crummy cellular signal, as described on page 152.

- **Calls on Other Devices.** Here's the on/off switch for Continuity, the ability to make phone calls from your Mac (page 556). You can even specify *which* gadgets talk to your iPhone in this way.

- **Respond with Text.** This feature is described on page 137; here's where you can edit the canned "Can't talk right now" text messages.

- **Call Forwarding, Call Waiting** (AT&T and T-Mobile only). Here are the on/off switches for Call Forwarding and Call Waiting, which are described in Chapter 4.

- **Show My Caller ID** (AT&T and T-Mobile only). If you don't want your number to show up on the screen of the person you're calling, then turn this off.

- **Change Voicemail Password.** Yep, pretty much just what it says.

- **Dial Assist.** When this option is turned on, and when you're calling from another country, the iPhone automatically adds the proper country codes when dialing numbers in your contacts. Pretty handy, actually.

- **SIM PIN.** Your SIM card stores all your account information. SIM cards are especially desirable abroad, because in most countries, you can pop yours into any old phone and have working service. If you're worried about yours getting stolen or lost, turn this option on. You'll be asked to enter a passcode.

  Then, if some bad guy ever tries to put your SIM card into another phone, he'll be asked for the passcode. Without the passcode, the card (and the phone) won't make calls.

- **[Your carrier] Services.** A duplicate of the options described on page 570.

Messages

These options govern text messages (SMS) and iMessages, both of which are described in Chapter 6:

- **iMessage.** This is the on/off switch for iMessages. If it's off, then your phone never sends or receives these handy, free messages—only regular text messages.

- **Show Contact Photos.** Do you want to see the tiny headshots of your conversation partners in the chat window?

- **Text Message Forwarding** is the text-message element of Continuity; it's described on page 557. You get an on/off switch for each gadget that you might want to display your phone's text messages.

- **Send Read Receipts.** If this is on, then people who send you iMessages will know when you've seen them. They'll see a tiny gray text notification beneath the iMessage bubble that contains their message. If you're creeped out by them being able to know when you're ignoring them, then turn this item off.

- **Send as SMS.** If you try to send an iMessage to somebody when there's no Internet service, what happens? If this item is on, then the message goes to that person as a regular text message, using your cell carrier's network. If it's off, then the message won't go out at all.

- **Send & Receive.** Here you can enter additional email addresses that people can use to send your phone iMessages.

  This screen also offers a **Start new conversations from** item that lets you indicate what you want to appear on the other guy's phone when you send a text: your phone number or email address.

- **MMS Messaging.** This is the on/off switch for picture and video messages (as opposed to text-only ones).

- **Group Messaging, Show Subject Field, Character Count.** These options are described starting on page 212.

- **Blocked.** Here's another way to build up a list of people you don't want to hear from, as described on page 212.

- **Keep Messages.** You can specify how long you want Messages to retain a record of your exchanges: 30 days, a year, or forever.

- **Filter Unknown Senders.** This feature gives you a sliver of protection from bombardment by strangers. It prevents you from getting notifications of iMessages from anyone who's not in your Contacts. In fact, you'll also see two tabs in Messages—one that lists chats for people you know (and regular non-Apple text messages), and the other labeled **Unknown Senders**.

- **Audio Messages.** You can now shoot audio utterances to other people just as easily as you can type them. And, under **Expire**, you can set them to auto-delete after two minutes. Why? First, because audio files take up space on your phone. Second, because you may consider them *spoken text messages*—not *recordings* to preserve for future generations. This is also where you turn on **Raise to Listen**.

  The audio-texting feature lets you send and receive audio messages without looking at the screen or touching it; see page 197.

- **Low Quality Image Mode.** This option can save a huge amount of cellular data when you send photos. See page 213.

FaceTime

These options pertain to FaceTime, the video-calling feature described on page 149. Here, for example, is the on/off switch for the entire feature; a place to enter your Apple ID, so people can make FaceTime calls to you; and a place to enter email addresses and a phone number, which can also be used to reach you.

The **Caller ID** section lets you specify how you want to be identified when you place a call to somebody else: either as a phone number or an email address. **FaceTime Live Photos**, new in iOS 11, lets you take a Live Photo during a FaceTime call—a three-second video slice of your conversation.

Finally, here yet again is the **Blocked** option—a third way to edit the list of people you don't want to hear from.

Maps

The expanded Maps app has an expanded set of settings. At the top, three controls that also appear elsewhere in Settings, but are here again because they're so important: **Siri & Search** (see page 183); **Notifications** (do you want turn-by-turn instructions to pop up when you're driving?); and **Cellular Data** (do you want Maps to be able to eat up your cellular Internet allotment?).

Then there's:

- **Preferred Transportation Type.** Do you mainly drive, walk, or take public transport? By specifying here, you save yourself a tap every time you plot directions.

- **Driving & Navigation.** Here's where you tell Maps that you want your plotted courses to avoid **Tolls** or **Highways**; turn a **Compass** display on or off on the map; specify the **Navigation Voice Volume**; and direct playback of any spoken entertainment (like podcasts or audiobooks) to **Pause** whenever the Maps voice is giving you an instruction.

- **Transit.** Which modes of public rides do you want Maps to show you when proposing routes? **Bus**, **Subway**, **Commuter Rail**, **Ferry**?

- **Distances.** Measured in miles or kilometers, sir/madam?

- **Map Labels.** Would you like place names to appear in English—or in their native spellings?

- **Extensions.** Now that Maps *can* incorporate other apps (see page 416), which ones *should* it show you? Lyft and Uber are the obvious ones here, so that Maps can incorporate those ride-sharing services into its proposals for your travel.

- **Show Rides From New Apps.** Lyft and Uber aren't the only ride-sharing apps in town. But when you install new ones, you might want Maps to include their options automatically, so you don't have to remember to burrow in here and turn on their Extensions switches.

- **Table Booking Extensions.** If you turn on OpenTable and/or Yelp here, then whenever you search for a restaurant in Maps, you'll see whether it has tables available, courtesy of these apps.

- **Show Parked Location.** You wouldn't turn off this cool Maps feature, would you (page 414)?

- **Follow up by Email.** When you report a problem with Maps' still-buggy database of the world, may Apple technicians get back to you by email?

Compass

You wouldn't think that something as simple as the Compass app would need a Settings page, but here it is: an on/off switch called **Use True North**. (*True* north is the "top" point of the Earth's rotational axis. If you turn it off, then Compass uses *magnetic* north, the spot traditional compasses point to; it's about 11 degrees away from true north).

Safari

Here's everything you ever wanted to adjust in the web browser but didn't know how to ask. (At the top: The usual **Siri & Search** options, as described on page 183.)

Search

- **Search Engine.** Your choice here determines who does your searching from the search bar: Google, Bing, Yahoo, or others. (Baidu is big in China.)

- **Search Engine Suggestions.** As you type into Safari's search box, it tries to save you time in two ways. First, it sprouts a list of common search requests, based on what millions of other people have sought. This list changes with each letter you type. Second, Safari may autocomplete the address based on what you've typed so far, using suggestions from your History and bookmarks list. This switch shuts off those suggestions. (It's here primarily for the benefit of privacy hounds, who object to the fact that their search queries are processed by Apple in order to show the suggestions.)

- **Safari Suggestions.** Safari searches (Chapter 3) can find matches from the iTunes, iBooks, and App stores; from databases of local businesses, restaurants, and theaters; and from the web. Unless you turn this off.

- **Quick Website Search.** You can search *within* a site (like Amazon or Reddit or Wikipedia) using only Safari's regular search bar, as described on page 470. If, that is, this switch is on.

- **Preload Top Hit.** As you type into the search box, Safari lists websites that match. The first one is the Top Hit—and if this switch is on, Safari secretly downloads that page while you're still finishing your search. That way, if the Top Hit *is* the page you wanted, it appears almost instantly when you tap.

  But here's the thing: Safari downloads the Top Hit with *every* search—which uses up data. Which could cost you money.

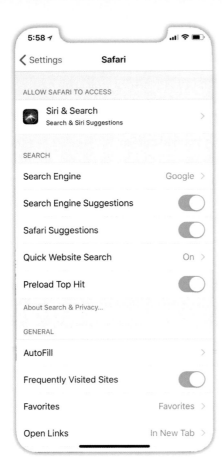
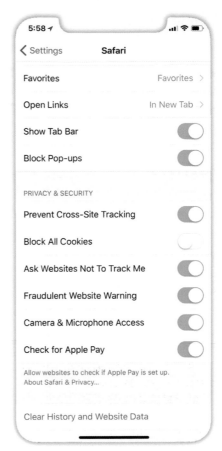

General

- **AutoFill.** Safari's AutoFill feature saves you tedious typing by filling in your passwords, name, address, and phone numbers on web forms automatically (just for the sites you want). It can even store your credit card information, which makes buying things online *much* easier and quicker.

   The AutoFill screen lists on/off switches for the different kinds of data that Safari can autofill for you: your contact info, website account names, and passwords. (If you actually want to *see and edit* the memorized passwords, then open **Settings→Accounts & Passwords**.) You can also see your credit cards. Tap **Saved Credit Cards** to see or delete the memorized cards.

- **Frequently Visited Sites.** When you have nothing open in Safari, it likes to offer a page full of icons representing sites you visit often. Turn off this switch if your privacy concerns outweigh the convenience of this feature.

- **Favorites.** As described on page 466, your favorites in Safari are just ordinary bookmarks in an extraordinary folder. Here you can choose a *different* folder as the home of your favorites.

- **Open Links.** When you tap a link with your finger, should the new page open in front of the current page—or behind it? Answer here.

- **Show Tab Bar.** In the Plus models, this makes a row of tab buttons appear when the phone is in landscape orientation.

- **Block Pop-ups.** In general, you want this turned on. You really don't want pop-up ad windows ruining your surfing session. Now and again, though, pop-up windows are actually useful. When you're buying concert tickets, for example, a pop-up window might show the location of the seats. In that situation, you can turn this option off.

Privacy & Security

- **Prevent Cross-Site Tracking.** New in iOS 11: An option to prevent web operators from recording where you go after you leave their sites. As a result, advertisers have a harder time gathering data about you and what you like.

- **Block All Cookies.** You can learn all about cookies—and these options to tame them—on page 484.

- **Ask Websites Not To Track Me.** If you turn this on, then websites agree not to secretly track your activity on the web. The problem is, of course, that this program is voluntary—and the sleazy operators just ignore it.

- **Fraudulent Website Warning.** This option makes Safari warn you when you try to visit what it knows to be a *phishing* site. (Phishing is a common Internet scam. The bad guy builds a fake version of Amazon, PayPal, or a bank's website—and tries to trick you into "logging in." You therefore unwittingly give up your name and password.)

- **Camera & Microphone Access.** There aren't many websites that need access to these potentially spyworthy components. But just in case evildoers try to access them, here's how you shut them down.

- **Check for Apple Pay.** Some websites let you buy stuff with a quick touch of your fingerprint (Apple Pay)—but only if you let them offer you those controls by leaving this on.

- **Clear History and Website Data.** Like any web browser, Safari keeps a list of websites you've visited recently to make it easier for you to visit them again: the History list. And, like any browser, Safari therefore exposes your activities to any crackpot colleague who picks up your phone. If you're nervous about that prospect, then tap **Clear History** to erase your tracks. This feature deletes all the cookies that websites have deposited on your "hard drive."

- **Automatically Save Offline.** The Reading List feature (page 473) is wonderful. But because it downloads entire web pages to your phone—and then syncs them to all your other Apple gadgets—it uses a lot of data. If you fear going over your cellphone plan's monthly data allotment, then turn this off. You'll be allowed to save sites to your Reading List only when you're online.

- **Advanced.** Safari recognizes HTML5, a technology that lets websites store data on your phone, for accessing even when you're not online (like your Gmail). In **Website Data**, you can see which web apps have created these databases on your phone and delete them if necessary.

    JavaScript is a programming language whose bits of code frequently liven up web pages. If you suspect some bit of code is choking Safari, though, you can turn off its ability to decode JavaScript here.

    The **Web Inspector** is for website programmers. You connect your phone to a Mac with a USB cable; then, in Safari on the computer, you choose **Debug→iPhone→[the name of the website currently on the iPhone's screen]**. You'll be able to examine errors, warnings, tips, and logs for HTML, JavaScript, and CSS—great when you're designing and debugging web pages or web apps for the iPhone. (**Experimental Features** is also decidedly for programmers.)

News

Page 417 describes the News app. Here's where you indicate whether it's allowed to tailor your news to your **Location**, whether it's allowed to provide **Siri & Search** results, if it can bug you with **Notifications** about news stories, whether it's allowed to fetch news in the **Background** (at some cost to battery life), and whether it can fetch new news over the **Cellular Data** network (at some cost to your data allowance).

You can turn off the **"Next Up"** link at the bottom of each story, as well as the **Story Previews** (where the first couple of lines of each news story appear right in the app). **Restrict Stories in For You** means you'll see only stories from news sources you've selected; you don't give News leeway to propose articles from other sources on topics you like.

Music

What you see here depends on whether you've subscribed to the $10-a-month Apple Music service (Chapter 8).

- **Show Apple Music.** When this is off, the new tabs (**For You** and **New**) disappear from the Music app. Which makes sense if you're not a subscriber, since they're doing you no good.

- **Add Playlist Songs.** Songs you add to a playlist get automatically added to your library, too.

- **Show Star Ratings.** Turn this on if you'd like to rate the songs in your music collection from one to five stars. Note that this option doesn't affect how Music suggests new music to you, as you might expect.

- **iCloud Music Library** (which appears only if you use Apple Music) is described on page 249.

- **Cellular Data** lets you guard against having your streaming music eat up your monthly cellular data allowance. If it's off, then you can download and play back music only over Wi-Fi. You can also permit or prevent using cellular for **Streaming** songs (or just **High Quality Streaming**) and **Downloads** of songs.

- **Downloaded Music** lets you see how much of your storage space is devoted to songs you've acquired.

- **Optimize Storage.** This option appears only if you use iCloud Music Library. It offers to auto-delete everything but 8, 16, 32, or 64 gigs of songs. They're still yours—they're just online instead of on your phone.

- **Automatic Downloads** is another iCloud Music Library special. It means that any song you've added to your online song library also gets auto-copied to your phone for offline playback.

- **EQ, Volume Limit, Sound Check.** See page 263.

- **Use Listening History.** Each song you play on your phone helps to shape the Music app's "For You" recommendation. Also, people who follow you on Apple Music get to see what you've been playing.

- **Home Sharing.** Conveniently enough, you can access your iTunes music collection, upstairs on your computer, right from your iPhone, over your home Wi-Fi network. Or at least you can if both machines are signed into the same Apple ID. Here's where you enter the Apple ID that matches your iTunes setup.

TV

This is what you can adjust for the TV app:

- **Notifications.** Here are the app's notifications controls.

- **iTunes Videos. Use Cellular Data for Playback** is a safeguard against eating up your cellular data with videos; leave it off to stream videos only over Wi-Fi. **Playback Quality** asks: When you're watching over Wi-Fi, do you want the best picture, even if that uses up more data? (Yes, some people have to worry about how much *Wi-Fi* data they use every month.) You get the same choices for **Cellular** data.

  Download HDR Videos is for iPhone X owners, whose screen can show high dynamic range (HDR) video, with darker darks and brighter brights. **Purchases and Rentals**: When you buy or rent a video from Apple, do you want it in **High Definition** or **Standard**? (High Definition looks better but takes forever to download.)

  Home Sharing means you can access your video collection in iTunes on your computer, as described already. Same deal here.

- **Up Next.** All your Apple machines will remember where and what you left off watching.

- **Connect to TV.** These are the apps for your various cable and pay-TV channels. The ones you turn on here sync, with your other iOS devices, what you've been watching and where you stopped.

  That's a slick convenience—but it does mean Apple's computers will know what you've been watching. So here, for the sake of your privacy and self-esteem, you can turn off that data sharing on a per-channel basis.

- **Clear Play History.** Again, Apple's worried about *your* worries about privacy. This function deletes your viewing data from the TV app.

Photos

In iOS 11, the old **Photos & Camera** settings have been split into two, ingeniously titled **Photos** and **Camera**.

- **Siri & Search.** Duplicates of what's described on page 183.

- **iCloud Photo Library.** See page 337.

- **Optimize iPhone Storage, Download and Keep Originals.** See page 338.

- **Upload to My Photo Stream.** Every picture you take will be sent to all your Apple gadgets (see page 329).

- **Upload Burst Photos.** Recent iPhones can snap 10 photos a second when you hold your finger down on the shutter button. That's a lot of photos, which can fill up your iCloud storage fast. So Apple gives you the option to exclude them from the uploads.

- **iCloud Photo Sharing** and **Cellular Data** are covered on page 332.

- **Summarize Photos.** In the Photos app, the Years and Collections screens generally display one tiny thumbnail for every single photo. This feature makes those more manageable by displaying fewer, but representative, thumbnails. (You won't see any difference unless you have a pretty huge collection of photos.)

- **View Full HDR** (iPhone X only). You lucky dog—your OLED screen can display the full range of colors and brights and darks in your photos. Don't turn this off.

- **Show Holiday Events.** You know the Memories feature (page 313)? It can create auto-slideshows based on the holidays in your country, if you want. If you'd just as soon not be reminded of these stressful times, then turn this off.

- **Transfer to Mac or PC.** iOS 11 takes photos in a new format called *HEIF* (high efficiency image format). These photos take up half the space without losing any quality, which is awesome—but not all desktop photo programs can open HEIF files. Mac OS High Sierra can open them, but older Mac OS versions can't; the current Photoshop version can, but older ones can't.

  If you're having trouble, turn on **Automatic**. That way, photos get sent as JPEGs, which every desktop program on earth can recognize.

Camera

Behold: the controls for the iPhone's amazing camera.

- **Preserve Settings.** The Camera app can remember the mode you had selected when you last used it—Video, Photo, Panorama, or whatever—instead of always starting with Photo.

  Depending on your phone model, it can also remember the last photo filter you used (page 289), what lighting effect (page 293), and whether or not you had Live Photo turned on (page 290).

- **Grid** turns the "Rule of Thirds" grid (the tic-tac-toe lines) on or off on the camera's viewfinder screen.

- **Scan QR Codes.** So cool! If you point the camera at a QR bar code (of the type you often see on movie posters and ads), the corresponding web link appears as a notification, ready to tap. You don't need a dedicated QR-reading app anymore.

- **Record Video.** This option, exclusive to the iPhone 6 and later, controls the frame rate and quality of the video you shoot. The first number in each option (like **720p**, **1080p**, or **4K**) controls the *resolution* of the video (how many pixels make up each frame—and how correspondingly huge the video files are). The second, fps, controls the *frames per second*. Normal TV video is about 30 fps, so choosing 60 fps creates bigger files but smoother playback.

  A weird additional option appears here if you have a Plus or X model: **Lock Camera**. These phones, of course, have two lenses (page 308). Under certain lighting conditions, if you zoom while recording video, a little hiccup results as the phone switches from one lens to the other. But if you turn on this option you'll get no such glitch, because the phone will use only one lens the whole time. (You can still zoom—but it's a digital, fake zoom, and the image will slightly degrade as you do so.)

- **Record Slo-mo.** Recent iPhone models give you a choice of slow-motion modes (and tell you how much space each takes up). 240 frames per second plays back at half the speed of 120.

- **Formats** (iPhone 7 and later). As noted, your photos and videos now occupy only half the space they used to—and look exactly the same. That's because Apple has adopted a new format called **HEIF** (high efficiency image format) for photos, and **HEVC** (high efficiency video coding) format for video.

  Which is great—except what happens when you try to share one of your pictures or videos with someone whose phone or computer doesn't know that format? No sweat: iOS automatically checks before sending to see if the receiving device can handle HEIF or HEVC. If not, it converts the outgoing photo to JPEG, or the outgoing video to H.264—the old standards.

  If you're having any trouble with this system, you can turn it all off here. If you choose **Most Compatible**, the iPhone captures photos and videos in the older formats (JPEG and H.264). As the note here points out, though, super-deluxe capture styles like 4K and 60 frames a second, and slow-mo at 240, *must* use HEVC, no matter what your selection here.

- **Auto HDR.** If this is on, Camera switches to HDR (page 285) whenever it thinks that lighting conditions merit it. If you turn this off, then the **HDR** button returns in the Camera app, so that the choice is yours.

- **Keep Normal Photo.** When you take a photo in HDR mode, iOS saves *two* photos, one normal and one HDR. If you turn this off, you get only the HDR shot.

iBooks

These iBooks ebook settings are described starting on page 403.

Podcasts

These settings affect the Podcasts app described on page 431. They govern how often the app auto-downloads new episodes, and how many; whether it can do so using cellular data (or only Wi-Fi); and whether you want the app to auto-delete podcasts you've already heard.

Game Center

For millions of people, the iPhone is a mobile game console. Once you've logged into Game Center with your Apple ID, you can allow **Nearby Players** to invite you to multiplayer games wirelessly, and you can create or edit your **Game Center Profile** (your player name). And when you get fed up, you can **Remove All Game Center Friends**—the nuclear option.

TV Provider

As noted on page 268, the TV app is designed to let you watch all the shows you're paying your cable or satellite company for—on your phone. At the outset, alas, very few major cable companies are playing ball with Apple. You can sign in here if you have an account from DirecTV, Dish, or a few obscure cable companies. But if you have, say, Comcast, Time Warner, or another big one, you're probably out of luck.

App Preferences

At the bottom of the Settings screen, you see a list of apps that have installed settings screens of their own. For example, here's where you can decide whether you want Feedly to use cellular data, change how many days' worth of news you want the NY Times Reader to display, and so on. Each one offers an assortment of preference options.

It can get to be a *very* long list.

PART FIVE

Appendixes

Appendix A
Signup & Setup

Appendix B
Troubleshooting & Maintenance

A

Signup & Setup

You gotta admit it: Opening up a new iPhone brings a certain excitement. There's a prospect of possibility, of new beginnings. Even if you intend to protect your iPhone with a case, there are those first few minutes when it's shiny, spotless, free of fingerprints or nicks—a gorgeous thing.

This chapter is all about getting started, whether that means buying and setting up a new iPhone, or upgrading an older model to the new iOS 11 software that's described in this book.

Buying a New iPhone

Each year's new iPhone model is faster, has a better camera and screen, and comes packed with more features than the previous one. Still, "new iPhone" doesn't have to mean the iPhone X ($1,000 or $1,150, either up front or spread out over two years) or even the iPhone 8 ($700). You can still get an iPhone 7 for $550, an iPhone 6s for $450, or an SE for $350. (Thank heaven, the U.S. carriers no longer obscure the true price of the phone in two-year contracts.) And, of course, you can get even older models dirt cheap, used.

In any case, once you've chosen the model you want, you also have to choose which cellphone company you want to provide its service: AT&T, Verizon, T-Mobile, or Sprint.

Research the coverage where you live and work. Each company's website shows a map of its coverage.

You can buy your iPhone from a phone store (Verizon, Sprint, T-Mobile, AT&T), from an Apple Store, from a retail store, or from the Apple website. You can buy the phone outright, or you can opt to have the price spread out in monthly payments. Or you can lease it.

All right then: Here you are in the store, or sitting down to do some ordering online. Here are the decisions you'll have to make:

- **Transferring your old number.** You can bring your old cellphone or home number to your new iPhone. Your friends can keep dialing your old number—but your iPhone will ring instead.

  It usually takes under an hour for a cellphone-number transfer to take place. During that time, you can make calls on the iPhone, but you can't receive them.

  NOTE: Transferring a landline number to your iPhone can take several *days*.

- **Select your monthly calling plans.** Signing up for cellphone service involves more red tape than a government contract. In essence, you have to choose *three* plans: one for voice calls, one for Internet service, and one for text messages. The variations are complicated, but a quick web search ("iPhone X plans compared") can help you make sense of them.

  The carriers are all pushing unlimited-data plans these days, which come with a certain comfort.

  But the traditional "4 gigabytes per month" plans are still around, too. Of course, the problem with fixed data allotments is this: Who has any idea what 2 gigabytes of data means? How much of that do you eat up with email alone? How much is one YouTube video?

  As you approach your monthly limit, you'll get warnings by text message, but you can also see your data usage on your phone (page 571). Yes, it's a pain to have to worry about data limits, but at least monitoring them is fairly easy. If you use more than your allotted amount, some carriers automatically bill a surcharge—for example, $15 for each additional gigabyte.

  All four cell companies offer unlimited free calls to other phones from the same company. All but the cheapest plans offer unlimited calls on nights and weekends.

  And all iPhone plans require an "activation fee" (ha!).

  NOTE: The choice you make here isn't etched in stone. You can change your plan at any time on your carrier's website.

  As you budget for your plan, keep in mind that, as with any cellphone, you'll also be paying taxes as high as 22 percent, depending on your state. Ouch.

Upgrading to iOS 11

If you've recently bought a new iPhone, great! iOS 11 (or one of its successors, like iOS 11.2) comes on it preinstalled.

But you can also upgrade an older or used iPhone to this new software in any of three ways:

- **Upgrade it wirelessly.** *Upgrading* means installing iOS 11 on top of whatever is already on your iPhone. You don't lose any data or settings.

  This is the easiest way to upgrade. You've probably already seen the little red number on your Settings app icon (see page 73), and on the word "General" inside it; the phone is trying to tell you that iOS 11 is ready to download. Tap **Settings→General→Software Update** to see the iOS 11 info; tap **Download and Install**. (You have to be on a Wi-Fi network, and it's wise to have your iPhone plugged into power.)

- **Upgrade it from iTunes.** If you wish, you can also perform the upgrade using the iTunes program on your computer. This method takes less time but, of course, requires being at your computer.

  To begin, connect your iPhone and click its icon at top left (see page 518). On the **Summary** tab, click **Check for Update**, and then click **Download and Update**.

- **Restore it.** This is a more dramatic step, which you should choose only if you've been having problems with your phone or if, for some other reason, you would like to start completely fresh. This step backs up the phone, erases it completely, installs iOS, and then copies your stuff back onto the phone.

  Connect the phone to your computer, open iTunes, and then click **Restore iPhone**.

  After the Restore process, treat your phone as though it's a brand-new one as you read the following pages.

The Setup Assistant

Upgrading your iPhone to iOS 11 from some older iOS version doesn't involve much more effort than sitting and waiting. When the upgrade is over, you get a Welcome screen, and boom: You're at your Home screen, ready to roll.

Things aren't so straightforward, though, if any of these situations apply to you:

- You've bought a new iPhone to replace an older model.

- You've bought your first iPhone.

- You've upgraded your existing iPhone to iOS 11 by *restoring* it (erasing it, starting from scratch).

All three of these situations subject you to the iOS 11 setup assistant—a series of screens that interview you to get all the settings right.

If you're used to previous versions of iOS, you're in for a treat—or at least less of a punishment; in iOS 11, Apple has tried to simplify the setup process.

TIP: If you're upgrading from an older phone, you'd be very, very wise to take these three preparatory steps. First, back up the old phone (see page 529). Second, transfer your old phone's SIM card to the new one (page 29).

Finally, remember that iOS 11 cannot open so-called *32-bit apps* (meaning "ancient"). You may own a few old favorites that you'll have to give up; see page 357.

The screens you encounter, and their sequence, vary wildly depending on what phone model you have, whether you choose Quick Start and Express Settings, what backup you're restoring from, and other factors. But in general, this is what you'll find when you turn on the phone for the first time after buying or upgrading it:

1. **Hello.** Your new phone's life begins with the screen that flashes "Hello" in various languages. (At this point, you can turn on VoiceOver [page 216] or Zoom [page 220] if you have trouble seeing it.) Tap **Continue**.

2. **[Choice of Language].** You won't get very far setting up your phone if you can't understand the instructions. So the goal here is to tell it what language you speak.

3. **Select Your Language and Country.** Now tell the phone where in the world you live. (It proposes the country where you bought the phone. Clever, eh?)

4. **Quick Start.** If you're upgrading from an older phone, you're in luck: The new Quick Start feature is about to save you the tedium of entering passwords and setting up initial preferences. It works only, however, if your old phone is running iOS 11.

If you don't have another iOS 11 device, you can't use Quick Start; tap **Set Up Manually** and skip to step 5.

If you **do** have another iOS 11 gadget, though, this is a blast. The Set Up Your iPhone screen (on the new phone) directs you to **bring the old phone close** to the new iPhone. The old one shows a Set Up New Phone screen, bearing your iCloud address; tap **Continue**.

Suddenly, the new phone displays an animation that looks like a swirling cloud of glitter. Hold the old phone a few inches over the new phone's screen, so that the animation fits in the brackets on the old one's screen. Boom! They're paired. The old phone begins to send encrypted data to the new one.

You're now directed to enter the old phone's passcode on the new phone; it's going to become your new phone's passcode, too.

Truth is, Quick Start doesn't actually transfer very much from the old phone: only your Wi-Fi password, your iCloud password, a few settings, and, of course, your iPhone passcode. You still have to copy over all of your apps, photos, music, and so on. Still, it was fun, wasn't it?

And in the following sequence, you can skip steps 5, 7, and 9.

5. **Choose a Wi-Fi Network.** Tap the name of the Wi-Fi network you want, enter the password if required, and tap **Join**.

Or, if there's no Wi-Fi you can (or want to) hop onto right now, then tap **Use Mobile Connection**.

> **NOTE:** At this point, your phone becomes *activated*, which means that it marries your cell carrier. If there's a SIM card from your carrier in your phone (page 29), this step takes only a second or two. If there *isn't* a SIM card in the phone, though, you can't activate it; you can't proceed to the Home screen. (The workarounds: Borrow a SIM card from your carrier, even from a deactivated account—or use Quick Start to inherit the settings from another iOS 11 phone, as described in step 4.)

6. **Touch ID or Face ID.** You're now invited to teach the phone your fingerprint or "face print" for the purposes of unlocking it without having to type a password. Start on page 61 for more on Touch ID and Face ID.

You can also tap **Set Up Later**. When the time comes, you can re-visit this process in **Settings→Touch ID & Passcode** (or **Face ID & Passcode**).

7. **Create a Passcode.** Whether you opted to store a fingerprint/face print or not, you're now asked to make up a six-digit *passcode* (password) for unlocking your phone. You'll need it whenever the phone won't accept Touch ID or Face ID—for example, after you've restarted the phone.

> **TIP:** You don't have to accept iOS's proposal of a six-digit passcode. Tap **Passcode Options** to reveal more choices, like **Custom Alphanumeric Code** (any password you like, any length, any characters), **Custom Numeric Code** (any number of digits), or **4-Digit Numeric Code** (like in the old days).

8. **Apps & Data.** This screen offers to reload all your stuff from your most recent backup. (See Chapter 15 and Chapter 16 for details on iPhone backups.)

The new phone may guess about what recent backup you want to use. If so, and it's correct, tap **Continue**.

If not, tap **Choose Other Backup or Don't Restore**. Now you're offered a choice: **Restore from iCloud Backup** (if your backup was on iCloud) **Restore from iTunes Backup** (if your backup was on your computer);

Set Up as New iPhone (if you've never owned an iPhone before or want to start fresh); or **Move Data from Android**.

> **NOTE:** The Move Data from Android option prompts you to download a companion app on your old Android phone called Move to iOS. When you open it, the app (on Android) asks you to enter a number code that's offered by your iPhone at this stage. Then the Android phone asks what kinds of data you'd like copied to your iPhone: your Google account (email, calendar, and so on), web bookmarks, text messages, contacts, and photos. When you hit **Next**, the transfer begins, wirelessly and automatically.

9. **Apple ID.** A million features require an Apple ID—just about any transaction you make with Apple online. Buying anything from Apple, from a song to a laptop. Using iCloud (Chapter 16). Playing games against other people online. Making an appointment at an Apple Store.

   If you already have an Apple ID, enter your email address and iCloud password here. If not, tap **Don't have an Apple ID or forgot it?** You'll be asked to provide your name, birthday, email address (or you can create a new iCloud email address), a password of your choice, and answers to a few security questions (you'll have to get them right if you ever forget your password). You also get to decide if you'd like the honor of receiving junk email from Apple.

   You'll be sent, by the way, an Apple ID Verification Code—that is, a two-factor authentication code as described on page 622.

10. **Terms and Conditions.** Tap **Agree**, and then **Agree**.

11. **Express Settings.** Do you want to set up Apple Pay (page 542)? How about Siri (Chapter 5)? Are navigation and other apps allowed to monitor your location using Location Services (page 585)? Will you agree to let Apple collect (anonymous) Analytics data about how you use the phone?

   In iOS 11, Apple gives you the chance to say "Yeah, sure, fine" (tap **Continue**) for all of these items at once, thereby skipping over a few steps in the setup assistant.

   Otherwise, you can tap **Customize Settings** and walk through those screens individually (Location Services, Apple Pay, Siri, Analytics) before proceeding.

   Some of these screens involve some setup. For example, Apple Pay requires registering your credit cards, and if you want to be able to use the "Hey Siri" hands-free mode (page 160), then you're supposed to speak a few sample sentences so that Siri learns your voice.

If your new phone is slurping up the backup from an older phone (if you used Quick Start, for example), you don't get Express Settings. Instead, you get Settings from Your Backup. It serves much the same purpose—letting you skip the Siri, Location, and Analytics questions—except that it grabs the settings from your backup rather than using Apple's suggested defaults.

12. **Apple Pay.** Next up: If you have an iPhone 5s or later, you're now invited to store your credit cards, for the purpose of turning on Apple Pay. The process is described on page 542.

    If you don't want to use Apple Pay, or don't want to set it up now, hit **Next** anyway, and then hit **Set Up Later in Wallet**.

13. **App Analytics.** Behind the scenes, your iPhone sends records back to Apple, including your location and what you're doing on your iPhone. By analyzing this data en masse, Apple can figure out where the dead spots in the cellular network are, how to fix bugs, and so on. The information is anonymous—it's not associated with you. But if the very idea seems invasive, here's your chance to prevent this data from being sent.

14. **True Tone Display.** This option appears only on the iPhone 8 and X models. It adjusts the screen colors in an attempt to keep them consistent under different lighting conditions (see page 280).

15. **Meet the New Home Button.** On the iPhone 7 and 8 models, this screen introduces you to the clickless home button (page 19)— and invites you to choose how hard its click feels (page 573).

16. **Display Zoom.** On bigger-screened phones like the iPhone 6 and later, you get this choice. It asks how you want to exploit the larger screen. If you choose **Standard**, you'll see more stuff (icons, menus, lines of text) per screenful than on smaller iPhones. If you choose **Zoomed**, then you'll see the same amount of stuff, but *bigger*. You can always change your mind in **Settings→Display & Brightness**.

17. **Go Home, Switch Between Recent Apps, Quickly Access Controls.** These informational screens appear only on the iPhone X. They're designed to teach you some of the new gestures you'll need as you adapt to life without a home button.

18. **Welcome to iPhone.** Your phone is set up. Tap **Get Started** to jump to the Home screen.

If you've restored your phone from a backup, you're not quite finished; now your phone should sit in a Wi-Fi hotspot for 30 or 60 minutes as it downloads all your existing apps, music, photos, and videos from Apple's servers.

See, in iOS 11, an iPhone backup no longer includes any of that stuff. Instead, iOS simply remembers *which* apps, songs, photos, and videos you had. After your backup is restored, your phone proceeds to re-download all of them from the Internet; you'll see your dimmed app icons gradually filling up as they arrive.

The benefit of this arrangement, of course, is that your backups don't take up much time or much disk space. The downside: If you're trying to restore several phones from a single backup, you're going to eat up a *lot* of data and time.

In any case, all of this is an excellent argument for beginning the restore process when (a) you're in a Wi-Fi hotspot, and (b) you've got some time to kill.

Software Updates to Come

As you're probably aware, phone software like the iPhone's is a perpetual work in progress. Apple constantly fixes bugs, adds features, and makes tweaks to extend battery life and improve other services.

Updating Directly on the Phone

One day you'll be minding your own business, and you'll see a red number badge appear on the Settings app's icon on the phone. Open **Settings→General→Software Update** to read about the new update and install it. Note, though, that unless it's plugged into a power source, your phone won't install an iOS update unless its battery is at least half full.

Install Updates from Your Computer

Maybe you're not that adventurous and you'd prefer to install your software update the old-fashioned way.

No problem: Connect the iPhone to iTunes, wirelessly or not (page 518). Then click the iPhone's icon in iTunes; on the **Summary** pane, tap **Check for Update**.

Restrictions and Parental Controls

if you're issuing an iPhone to a child, or someone who acts like one, you'll be gratified to discover that iOS offers a good deal of protection. That's protection of your offspring's delicate sensibilities (it can block pornography and dirty words) and protection of your bank account (it can block purchases of music, movies, and apps without your permission).

To set this up, visit **Settings→General→Restrictions**. When you tap **Enable Restrictions**, you're asked to make up a passcode that permits only you, the all-knowing parent, to make changes to these settings. (Or you, the corporate IT administrator who's doling out iPhones to the white-collar drones.)

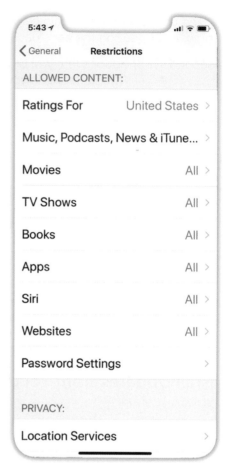

Once you've changed the settings described on these pages, the only way to change them again (when your kid turns 18, for example) is to return to the **Restrictions** page and correctly enter the passcode. That's also the only way to turn off the entire Restrictions feature (tap **Disable Restrictions** and enter the passcode). To turn it back on, you have to make up a passcode all over again.

Once Restrictions is turned on, you can put up data blockades in a number of different categories.

Allow

For starters, you can turn off access to iPhone features that locked-down corporations might not want their employees—or parents might not want their children—to use, because they're considered either security holes, time drains, or places to spend your money: **Safari** (can't use the web at all), **Camera**, **Siri & Dictation**, **FaceTime**, **AirDrop**, or **CarPlay** (Apple's specialized connection for certain car models, in which your iPhone's relevant icons appear on the car's dashboard screen).

A second list of options lets you block access to **iTunes Store**, **Music Profiles & Posts** (the news and discussion within Apple's music service), **iBooks Store**, and **News**—and turn off the option to download **Podcasts**. You can stop your kid from **Installing Apps** or **Deleting Apps**, too. And you can turn off **In-App Purchases** so that your offspring won't be able to buy new material (game levels, book chapters, and so on) from within an app that you've already bought.

Many of these restrictions work by *removing icons altogether* from the iPhone's Home screen: **Safari**, **iTunes**, and **Camera**, for example. When the switch says **Off**, the corresponding icon has been taken off the Home screen and can't be found even by searches.

Allowed Content

Here you can spare your children's sensitive eyes and ears by blocking inappropriate material.

Ratings are a big deal; they determine the effectiveness of the parental controls described in this section. Since every country has its own rating schemes (for movies, TV shows, games, song lyrics, and so on), you use the **Ratings For** control to tell the iPhone which country's rating system you want to use.

Once that's done, you can use the **Music**, **Podcasts**, **News & iTunes U**, controls, plus **Movies**, **TV Shows**, **Books**, and **Apps**, to specify what your kid is allowed to watch, play, read, and listen to. For example, you can tap **Movies** and then tap **PG-13**; any movies rated "higher," like R or NC-17, won't play on the iPhone now. (And if your sneaky offspring try to buy these naughty songs, movies, or TV shows wirelessly from the iTunes Store, they'll discover that the **Buy** button is dimmed and unavailable.)

For some categories, like **Music**, **Podcasts**, **News & iTunes U**, and **Siri**, you can turn off **Explicit** to prevent the iPhone from playing iTunes Store songs that contain naughty language, or speaking them.

Websites lets you shield impressionable young eyes from pornography online. It offers these settings:

- **All Websites.** No protection at all.

- **Limit Adult Content.** Apple will apply its own judgment in blocking dirty websites, using a blocked-site list it has compiled.

  That doesn't mean you can't override Apple's wisdom, however. The **Always Allow** and **Never Allow** controls let you add the addresses of websites that you think should be OK (or should not be OK).

- **Specific Websites Only.** This is a "whitelist" feature. It means that the entire web is blocked except for the few sites listed here: safe bets like Disney, PBS Kids, Smithsonian Institution, and so on. You can add your own sites to this list, but the point is clear: This is the web with training wheels.

Finally, **Password Settings** lets you loosen the requirement to enter your Apple password every time you download something from the App Store, iTunes Store, or iBooks Store. You can choose **Require After 15 Minutes**, so you won't be repeatedly bugged for your password if you're on a shopping spree, and you can turn off the requirement for free downloads.

Privacy

These switches can prohibit the unauthorized user from making changes to the phone's privacy settings, which are described on page 585.

Allow Changes

These items (**Accounts, Cellular Data Use, Background App Refresh, Volume Limit**) are safeguards against your offspring fiddling with limits you've set. **TV Provider** makes sure that the rapscallion won't attempt to change your cable-TV company (page 608).

And **Do Not Disturb While Driving** ensures that your underling can't simply *turn off* that important safety feature (page 140), thereby defeating the entire purpose.

Game Center

These controls let you stop your kid from playing multiplayer games (against strangers online), screen recording in games, or adding game-playing friends to the center.

Two-Factor Authentication

By now, it's probably clear that *passwords* aren't enough to protect us from the bad guys. Even if your password is *é$*@çg45e+7r6ü*, someone can still steal it. There are all kinds of ways: An inside job. Poor security on a company's servers. Social engineering, where someone calls up pretending to be you and saying, "I forgot my password."

Fortunately, security experts have come up with a way to keep baddies out of your account *even if they've got your password*. It's a system called two-factor authentication—and in iOS 11, it's no longer optional. (Let's call it 2FA to save paper.)

Here's how it works: Suppose you're setting up a new Apple device, or you're trying to log into iCloud.com with a new web browser. You log in with your iCloud password.

Almost immediately, Apple sends a message to the screens of all of your *other* Apple machines—devices that it knows you own: "Your Apple ID is being used to sign in to an iPad [or whatever] in Hinsdale, IL" (and there's a little map).

> **TIP:** And what if you don't *have* another Apple device? Then you can get the code via automated phone call or text; tap **Didn't get a verification code**.
>
> And what if you're not online? No problem. You can make the older, trusted device cough up a code *on demand*, in **Settings→[your name]→Password & Security→Get Verification Code**.

If that's not where you are right now, it means someone is pretending to be you! Tap **Don't Allow** and shut them down!

If it *is* you, though, hit **Allow**. Now your older device displays a six-digit code; on the new machine or browser, there's a box to enter it. You're in.

NOTE: Sometimes, the code and "enter code" box appear on the same device! What sense does that make?

Easy: You're using a new **browser** for the first time. The operating system treats that browser as a new "device," even though it's running on an already-accepted machine.

If some Russian hacker does get your password, he still can't get into your account, because he doesn't have the code. Sneaky, eh? And incredibly effective; 2FA almost completely eliminates the chance of someone else accessing your account. They'd have to have your iCloud password **and** your phone or laptop **and** your password for that device.

Each time, you're adding to your list of trusted devices. At any time, you can look over a list of them at *appleid.apple.com/account/manage*. (You'll get a 2FA code just to get into your account.)

NOTE: All of this works smoothly on Apple products. But what about programs (like calendar and email programs) that also need access to your iCloud account? They're locked out just as though they were hackers.

Fortunately, you can go to *appleid.apple.com/account/manage* to generate an **app-specific password**. If you enter this 16-character password as your iCloud password in your third-party calendar or email program, it will now be able to access your iCloud account as it did before.

B

Troubleshooting & Maintenance

The iPhone is a computer, and you know what that means: Things can go wrong. This particular computer, though, is not quite like a Mac or a PC. It runs a spin-off of the macOS operating system, but that doesn't mean you can apply the same troubleshooting techniques.

Therefore, when things go wrong, let this appendix be your guide.

First Rule: Install the Updates

There's an old saying: "Never buy version 1.0 of anything." In the iPhone's case, the saying could be: "Never buy version 11.0 of anything."

The very first version (or major revision) always has bugs, glitches, and things the programmers didn't have time to finish the way they would have liked. The iPhone is no exception.

The beauty of this phone, though, is that Apple can send it fixes, patches, and even new features through software updates. One day you'll glance at your Home screen's Settings icon, and—bam!—there'll be a badge indicating that new iPhone software is available.

So the first rule of trouble-free iPhoning is to accept these updates when they're offered. With each new software blob, Apple removes another few dozen tiny glitches.

And sure enough: Within the first few weeks of iOS 11's existence, software updates 11.1 and 11.2 came down the pike. And more will come.

Six Ways to Reset the Phone

The iPhone runs actual programs, and as actual programs do, they actually crash. Sometimes, the program you're working in simply vanishes and you find yourself back at the Home screen. Just reopen the program and get on with your life.

If the program you're in just doesn't seem to be working right—it's frozen or acting weird, for example—then one of these resetting techniques usually clears things right up.

NOTE: Proceed down this list in order! Start with the easy ones.

- **Exit the app.** On an iPhone, you're never aware that you're launching and exiting programs. They're always just *there*, like TV channels, when you switch to them. There's no Quit command. But if a program starts acting glitchy, you can make it quit.

  To do that, double-press the home button to bring up the app switcher. Find the "card" that represents your balky app, and then flick it upward to quit it. Try reopening it to see if the problem has gone away.

iPHONE X: Swipe up from the bottom of the screen; with your finger still down, pause until the app switcher appears. Hold your finger down on any "card" until the ⊖ appears. Tap it, or swipe the card upward, to exit the app.

- **Turn the phone off and on again.** If it seems that something more serious has gone wrong, then hold in the side button for a few seconds.

iPHONE X: Hold the side button *and* either volume button simultaneously.

  When the screen says **slide to power off**, confirm by swiping. The iPhone shuts off completely.

  Turn it back on by pressing the side button for a second or two.

- **Force-restart the phone.** If you haven't been able to force-quit the program, and you can't shut the phone off either, you might have to force a restart. Thanks to Apple's fickle relationship with the home-button concept, the method varies by phone model.

  iPhone 8 or X: Click the volume-up key, and then the volume-down key; now hold in the side button until the Apple logo appears.

  iPhone 7: Hold in the side button *and* the volume-down key simultaneously until the Apple logo appears.

Earlier models: Hold down the home button *and* the side button until the Apple logo appears.

In each case, keep holding, even if the screen goes black or you see the "power off" slider. Don't release until you see the Apple logo appear, meaning that the phone is restarting.

- **Reset the settings.** This procedure doesn't erase any of your data— only the phone's settings. From the Home screen, tap **Settings→ General→Reset→Reset All Settings**.

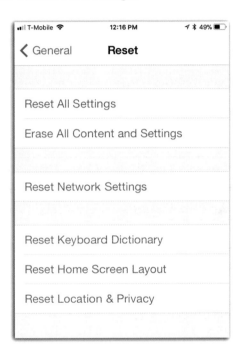

- **Erase the whole phone.** From the Home screen, tap **Settings→ General→Reset→Erase All Content and Settings**. Now, *this* option zaps your stuff—*all* of it. Music, videos, email, settings, apps, all gone, and all overwritten with random 1's and 0's to make sure it's completely unrecoverable. Clearly, you're getting into last resorts here. Of course, you can then sync with your backup (iTunes or iCloud) to copy all that stuff back onto your iPhone.

- **Restore the phone.** If none of these steps solve the phone's glitchiness, it might be time for the nuclear option: erasing it completely, resetting both hardware and software back to a factory-fresh condition.

If you backed up to iTunes: Connect the phone to your computer, as described in Chapter 15. In iTunes, click the iPhone icon and then, on the Summary tab, click **Restore**.

The first order of business: iTunes offers to make a backup of your iPhone (all of its phone settings, text messages, and so on) before proceeding. Accepting this invitation is an excellent idea. Click **Back Up**.

If you backed up to iCloud: You can restore your phone this way only if your iPhone is completely wiped empty. If it's not, then manually erase it using iTunes first.

During the setup screens described on page 613, tap **Restore from iCloud Backup**. You're shown the three most recent backups; tap the one you want. The phone goes right to work downloading your settings and account information. Then it restarts and begins to download your apps; if you're in a hurry for a particular app, tap its icon to make iCloud prioritize it.

When that's all over, you can get to work downloading your music (if you're an Apple Music subscriber).

iPhone Doesn't Turn On

Usually, the problem is that the battery's dead. Just plugging it into the USB charger or your computer doesn't bring it to life immediately, either; a completely dead iPhone doesn't wake up until it's been charging for about 10 minutes. It pops on automatically when it has enough juice to do so.

Recovery Mode

Phones, like the best of us, sometimes get confused.

In a few weird situations, the iPhone gets so baffled that you can't even start it up. For example:

- The startup process gets stuck forever at the Apple logo.

- The "Connect to iTunes" screen appears, even when the phone *is* connected.

- You've connected to iTunes on your computer, but the phone doesn't show up, or it says it's in "recovery mode."

The solution is the drastic, but effective, force-restore process (known to techies as the Default Firmware Update mode).

Open iTunes on your computer. Connect the iPhone with its white USB cable. Now force-restart the phone as described earlier:

iPhone 8 or X: Click the volume-up key, then the volume-down key; now hold in the side button.

iPhone 7: Hold in the side button and the volume-down key simultaneously.

Earlier models: Hold down the home button and the side button.

In each case, keep the key(s) pressed until iTunes tells you that an iPhone in Recovery mode has been detected; click OK. (If you see anything but blackness on your iPhone's screen—an Apple logo, for example—then the process didn't work. If the problem has not, in fact, gone away, then you should start again.)

iTunes tells you that "There is a problem with the iPhone that requires it to be updated or restored."

By far your favorite choice should be **Update**, because that means you won't lose any of your phone's data. iTunes will simply download and install a fresh copy of iOS 11. (If the download takes longer than 15 minutes, the iPhone exits recovery mode. Just wait until the download is finished, and then start this process again.)

If the Update process doesn't work, you have no choice but the bad one: Restore. That's where you wipe out the iPhone's contents and restore everything on it from a backup. (Of *course* you have a backup, right?)

Battery Life Is Terrible

If your battery seems to drain faster after you've installed iOS 11, it might be because the Photos app is busy scanning and categorizing all your photos so that it can use its object and facial recognition.

Or maybe it's just you *using* the phone more, checking out the cool new features.

If neither of those is the problem, then consult the battery-saving tips on page 42.

Out of Space

It happens all the time. You couldn't imagine filling up 64, 128, or 256 gigabytes of storage, so you saved some money by buying an iPhone with less. And now you can't even take a video or a photo, because your phone reports that it's full. You're frozen out until you have the time and expertise to delete some less important stuff.

Fortunately, iOS 11 is teeming with features designed to ease up the storage crunches so many people face. Some are automatic: The new HEIF and HEVC formats, for example, mean new photos and videos occupy only half as much space as the old ones (see page 607).

The iPhone Storage Screen

But really, the Grand Central of storage management is in **Settings→ General→Phone Storage**.

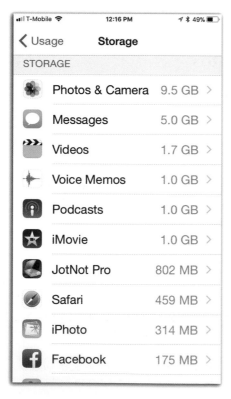

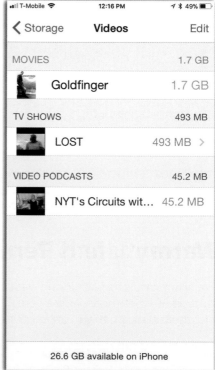

Here's a master graph that clearly shows what's eating up your space. This screen also lists every kind of file by category (apps, photos, mail, and so on) and how much space it's eating up. That should make it easy to delete the fattest ones to make the most room with the least effort.

The biggest space hogs on your phone are video files, photo files, apps, and music files. Heck, deleting just one downloaded movie or TV show could solve your storage crunch instantly.

Better yet, this screen actually *suggests* ways to free up space, like deleting messages that are older than a year; looking over and maybe deleting big email attachments; or storing your messages on iCloud.

Offload Unused Apps

One of those suggestions is to **Offload Unused Apps**. It makes the iPhone delete the apps you haven't used in a while, but preserve their icons (dimmed) on your Home screens; just tap an app if you ever want to download it again.

This option has its own master switch in **Settings→iTunes and App Stores→Offload Unused Apps**. You can also hit the **Offload App** button for individual apps in the master list at **Settings→General→Phone Storage.**

Offload Full-Resolution Photos

Also, for goodness' sake, don't miss **Optimize iPhone Storage** (page 338). It transfers your full-resolution original photos to iCloud—but leaves much smaller versions on your phone that are just right for viewing on its little screen.

Offload Music

Deep in **Settings→Music**, another Optimize Storage switch appears. Turn it on to automatically remove music from your iPhone that you haven't played in a while, freeing up precious gigabytes.

Warranty and Repair

The iPhone comes with a one-year warranty and 90 days of phone tech support. If you buy an AppleCare+ contract ($200 for the iPhone X, $130 for other models), then you're covered for a second year.

 TIP: AT&T, Sprint, T-Mobile, or Verizon tech support is free for both years of your contract. They handle questions about your iPhone's phone features.

If, during the coverage period, anything goes wrong that's not your fault, Apple will fix it for free. In fact, AppleCare+ covers damage even if it *is* your fault—if you drop the phone or something—at a rate of $29 for screen damage and $100 for other damage, plus tax. Maximum: twice.

If you don't have AppleCare+, the repair fee depends on the type of phone you have but will probably set you back around $300.

You can either take the phone to an Apple Store, usually the fastest route, or call 800-APL-CARE (800-275-2273) to arrange shipping back to Apple. In general, you'll get the fixed phone back in three business days.

> **NOTE:** ***Back up the phone before it goes in for repair.*** Apple very often just hands you a new (or refurbished) iPhone instead of your original.
>
> Also, don't forget to remove your SIM card (page 29) before you send in your broken iPhone—and to put it back in when you get the phone. Don't leave it in the loaner phone. The carrier can get you a new card if you lose your original, but it's a hassle.

Out-of-Warranty Repairs

Once the year or two has gone by, or if you damage your iPhone in a way that's not covered by the warranty (backing your car over it comes to mind), Apple charges from $270 to $550 to repair an iPhone, depending on the model. (Apple usually just replaces it.)

The Battery Replacement Program

Why did Apple seal the battery inside the iPhone, anyway? Everyone knows lithium-ion batteries don't last forever. After 300 or 400 charges, the iPhone's battery begins to hold less charge (perhaps 80 percent of the original). After a certain point, the phone will need a new battery. How come you can't change it yourself?

Apple's answer: A user-replaceable battery takes up a lot more space inside the phone. It requires a plastic compartment that shields the guts of the phone from you and your fingers; it requires a removable door; and it needs springs or clips to hold the battery in place.

In any case, you can't change the battery yourself. If you have AppleCare+, though, a battery replacement is free. If the phone is out of warranty, you must send it to Apple (or take it to an Apple Store) for an $80 battery-replacement job. (As an eco-bonus, Apple properly disposes of the old batteries, which consumers might not do on their own.)

What to Do About a Cracked Screen

Keeping your iPhone in a case may lower the chances of your dropping it or scratching it—but it can't prevent bad luck. An incredible number of iPhone screens meet an untimely end, even with cases on.

Apple will happily replace your phone's screen for $130 to $280, depending on the model. It'll do it the same day if you take the phone into an Apple Store, or you can mail it in and get a replacement in three to five days. (If you've bought AppleCare+, then a replacement screen is a flat $29.)

There are plenty of other companies that can repair a cracked screen, though. The reps from *iCracked.com*, for example, send a technician to you and perform the fix on the spot.

And then there's the do-it-yourself technique. You can buy a screen-replacement kit for about $60 online, complete with the special tools you need to open the iPhone and do the job yourself. It requires care, patience, and some dexterity (Google can help you find the step-by-steps), but it's a good option if you're technically savvy.

Where to Go from Here

At this point, the iPhone is such a phenomenon that there's no shortage of resources for getting more help, news, and tips. Here are a few examples:

- **Apple's official iPhone User Guide.** Yes, there is an actual downloadable PDF user's manual for iOS 11. *help.apple.com/iphone/11*

- **Apple's official iPhone help website.** Online tips, tricks, and tutorials; troubleshooting topics; downloadable PDF help documents; and, above all, an enormous, seething treasure trove of discussion boards. *www.apple.com/support/iphone*

- **Apple's service site.** All the dates, prices, and expectations for getting your iPhone repaired. Includes details on getting a temporary replacement unit. *www.apple.com/support/iphone/service/faq*

- **iMore blog.** News, tips, tricks, all in a blog format. *www.imore.com*

- **iLounge.** Another great blog-format site. Available in an iPhone format so you can read it right on the device. *www.iLounge.com*

- **MacRumors/iPhone.** Blog-format news, accessory blurbs, help discussions; iPhone wallpaper. *www.macrumors.com/iphone*

What to Do About a Cracked Screen

Index